SOCIAL DEVIATION

THE MACMILLAN COMPANY
NEW YORK · BOSTON · CHICAGO · DALLAS
ATLANTA · SAN FRANCISCO

MACMILLAN AND CO., LIMITED
LONDON · BOMBAY · CALCUTTA · MADRAS
MELBOURNE

THE MACMILLAN COMPANY
OF CANADA, LIMITED
TORONTO

Social Deviation

By

JAMES FORD

Department of Sociology, Harvard University

New York

THE MACMILLAN COMPANY

1939

Published April, 1939

SET UP AND ELECTROTYPED BY T. MOREY & SON

PRINTED IN THE UNITED STATES OF AMERICA

To my wife
KATHERINE MORROW FORD
*with gratitude for her constant aid
and collaboration*

PREFACE

Social change in recent years has been rapid in the fields covered by Applied Sociology, and especially that of Social Pathology. Many traditional policies of state and local governments have since 1933 been either displaced or dominated by Federal policies, systematic, coördinated, and subject to long-range planning. The entrance of the Federal government into the fields of poor relief in 1933, and social security in 1935, may, in the perspective of history, rank in importance with the inauguration of the Elizabethan poor laws or the English Poor Law of 1834. Scarcely less radical have been the developments in research, in the treatment of many types of handicap, and in economic and social planning.

The student seeks primarily a thorough understanding of existing conditions and policies. Because a course in Social Pathology commonly provides his first systematic study of social deviation and its consequences, emphasis upon current issues and policies and their interrelations may well take prior place. Nevertheless, the reciprocal relations of social data and sociological principles need to be shown in such an introductory course, even though the student may pursue theory at will in later and more advanced courses, after he has illustrative, factual data at his command.

In no branch of sociology is its synthetic function more requisite than it is in the field of social pathology. The initial standards of reference by which deviation is recognized proceed from the group culture by way of medicine, psychiatry, criminology, economics, and a host of other sciences. Current treatment of deviate individuals or groups, and of social "reforms" and policies—legitimate subject matter for objective treatment by sociology—likewise largely proceeds from these other disciplines.

While seeking objectivity in this volume the author has nevertheless undertaken to apply, among other standards of reference, an optimum standard, as outlined in Chapter IV, with which the reader may compare his own value system. The purpose is not dogmatic but solely to stimulate the student to develop his own system of thought (as distinguished from opinion or emotional reaction) among the almost infinite complexities of the subject matter. Here lies the teacher's opportunity in classroom discussion to aid the student to distinguish mental stereotypes and unsupported opinions from views backed by evidence and judgment.

The concept of social deviation has been utilized in the title and throughout the book because of the limitations of the concepts of social disorganization and social pathology, as outlined in Chapter I. The individuals and problem groups with which this volume is concerned are identified by their departure or deviation from accepted standards of reference. Such standards are outlined in Chapters I and IV and elaborated in other chapters. Negatively valued deviations are obviously the field of social pathology. Positively valued deviations, comprised under the rubrics "genius," "leadership," etc., will be treated in a book in the field of Community Organization, which is now in process.

The deviations of the individual are treated ahead of deviations within economic, family, and group relationships, so that the roles of biological, physical, and mental factors may be understood before dealing with human relations in these larger environments. There is fuller treatment of personal deviations (handicaps) and economic inadequacy (poverty) than of other subtopics, because these are the traditional subject matter of courses in social pathology. There is briefer treatment of the pathology of family and group relationships because ordinarily college students will find these subjects covered amply in other courses—e.g., the Family, Social Conflict, Community Organization, and Social Work—where the deviations in question will be seen in their larger bearings.

The purpose of the *Questions for Discussion or Examination* which follow each chapter is primarily to suggest to the student a basis for organizing his information and his thinking. The purpose of the section entitled *Problems for Individual Study* is to facilitate the assignment of original work by the student. The suggestions for supplementary readings are almost exclusively limited to American and English works because these are so much more readily available to students. To save space few references have been made to articles in periodicals and conference proceedings. Particular care has been taken in the footnotes and reference lists to expedite the use of library catalogues by students in their researches.

Acknowledgment is here made to the authors and publishers cited for their generous coöperation in permitting the quotations from their writings (individually acknowledged in footnote references), and to my wife, Katherine Morrow Ford, and The Macmillan Company for their consent to the incorporation, chiefly in Part III and Chapters XXX and XXXI of considerable sections of our earlier collaborative essay entitled "The Abolition of Poverty."

To Ellsworth Faris I am especially grateful for his careful reading of the galley proof and his excellent suggestions and criticisms. From my colleagues Dr. Robert K. Merton and Dr. Edward P. Hutchinson, and my assistants Nicholas J. Demerath and Walter C. McKain I received many penetrating criticisms and recommendations, chiefly with regard to chapters in Parts I, IV, and V, for which I wish to express my appreciation. To Katherine Morrow Ford I am deeply indebted for continuous assistance and invaluable collaboration throughout this study.

JAMES FORD

CAMBRIDGE, MASSACHUSETTS
February 23, 1939

CONTENTS

PART I. FIELD AND METHOD

CONTENTS

Policy—Classification of Moral Objectives—Diversity in Sectarian Objectives—Schools of Ethical Thought—Individual Pleasure as Goal—The Common Good—Happiness as Goal—Self-Realization and Self-Development—Egoistic versus Altruistic Objectives—The Organization of Interests—The Inductive Approach to Objectives—Social Purpose and Optimum Standards—The Goals of Social Work—Social Pathology and Social Control.

PART II. PERSONAL HANDICAPS, PHYSICAL AND MENTAL

Society and the Individual—Social Pathology of the Handicapped—Earlier Terminology of Social Pathology—The Handicapped—Borderline Cases—Tests—Multiple Handicaps—Incapacities versus Handicaps—Personal Inadequacies—Individual Uniqueness—Latent Capacities—Causes of Inadequacy—Ignorance and Undereducation—Miseducation—Prevention of the Marginal Disabilities: Increased Schooling—Training of Judgment and Character—Training for Social Participation—Control of Environment—Necessity of Differential Diagnosis.

Mental and Physical Handicaps—Mental Handicap—How to Recognize Retardation—Definitions—Standards of Reference—Physical Examination—Mental Tests—Tests of Social Inadequacy—The Extent of Feeblemindedness—The Distribution of "Intelligence"—Recent Estimates—Social Statistics of Feebleminded—Types—Relative Importance of Causative Factors—Social Consequences of Feeblemindedness—History of Social Provision for Feebleminded—Treatment—Training—Institutional Provision—Prevention—Registration.

Definitions—Standards of Reference—Extent—Types and Classification of Mental Diseases—Social Consequences of Mental Disorder—The Search for Causes—Heredity—Environmental Factors—Causes and Trends in Organic Psychoses—The Functional Psychoses—History of Treatment—Institutional Provision—Relativity of Social Policy.

CONTENTS

PART IV. SOCIAL PATHOLOGY OF FAMILY
AND GROUP LIFE

PART I
FIELD AND METHOD

CHAPTER I

DEFINITIONS AND CLASSIFICATION

Sociology, Pure and Applied.—Poverty and handicaps are sociological phenomena whether viewed with reference to their incidence, causation, effects, treatment, or prevention. Sociology as a pure or descriptive science is concerned with them as evidences of human interrelationships. For it is the task of sociology to analyze social phenomena in order to discover the principles which underlie them and their relations to each other and to nonsocial factors.

As a science, sociology views man's reactions and the social problems that emerge, as dispassionately as the geologist studies the earth's structure, or the biologist examines through his microscope the reactions of the amoeba. Curiosity and emotions such as the "passion for truth" may and do serve as dynamic elements in scientific research. But the "passion for reform" is likely to interfere with clear thinking, the consideration of all alternatives, and sound judgment. Still more inimical to the scientific spirit is the bias of the advocate who seeks to justify a foregone conclusion or make a "case" for his client or party. The temper of all science—physical, biological, social—is dispassionate.

As a theoretical science, sociology is concerned with the gamut of man's social relations and of group endeavors from the first records of early man to the present day. Applied sociology tends to limit itself to the application of the principles discovered by sociology and other sciences to contemporary conditions, problems, issues, and measures. If, in doing so, it makes fresh syntheses of existing data and independent studies from which new principles are derived or earlier generalizations are subjected to qualification of statement, it invades the field of pure sociology. Because of its closeness to the facts and issues of daily life, this is likely to occur, and useful contributions may be made.

Sociology and the Social Sciences.—The generalizations of sociological theory proceed not only from the researches and speculations of sociology but also from assembling, comparing, and reinterpreting the findings of the correlative social sciences: anthropology,

3

history, political science, economics, law, and the neighboring sciences of biology, psychology, and pedagogy. These generalizations of sociology may be modified in turn by applied sociology because the latter is in more frequent and wider contact with the arts of social work, medicine, politics, and legislative or moral reform, and with the human beings—the units and objects of their service—whose personalities and case problems frequently fail to fit the preëstablished general rules. Individual cases are among the major correctives of crude generalizations. Applied sociology may thus often serve as a quasi-experimental test of some broad sociological theorem.

These statements are not intended as a criticism of sociology. The physical sciences are centuries old and have reached their present degree of exactness through a long process of trial and error, affirmation, challenge, experimentation, followed by discard and reformulation, or by increasing refinements of earlier accepted principles. Sociology, by way of contrast, is often said to be in its infancy. Its antecedents were history and speculative political or moral philosophy on the one hand and forensic diatribes on the other. As a systematized, positive science it is scarcely a century old. So dependent is it upon the discoveries of biology, psychology, anthropology, and a host of other sciences, that it cannot fairly be blamed for its slow progress; for they too are "young" sciences.[1]

Applied Sociology and Social Reform.—Applied sociology is interwoven in its studies with social work, social legislation, and the framing of social policy. This fact is sometimes deplored by "pure" sociologists who recognize that such alliances may lead to the intrusion of emotionalism, and even of bias. Many an applied sociologist has failed to differentiate his reformist interests as citizen from his fact-seeking interests as scientist, with consequent injury to his service in the latter field. Nevertheless, with recognition of such dangers, the applied sociologist who can maintain his intellectual integrity, while advising and aiding in the planning and execution of social policies, can contribute more of value because of such contacts and involvement in the details of constructive social activity.

Analogy may be found in the field of medicine, which is both an applied science and an art. The practitioner, though dependent for

---

[1] It should of course be noted that these other sciences are also at many points influenced by and dependent upon sociology. Scientific progress in the social sciences is reciprocal involving their continuous interrelation and mutual support.

his medical lore upon the laboratory and field studies of the pure sciences of anatomy, physiology, bacteriology, epidemiology, and pathology—to name but a few—is able from his intimate contact with cases (which like the applied sociologist or social worker, he seeks to cure) to contribute valuable observations. He finds that "circumstances modify cases" and that cases (individual make-up and reaction) modify circumstances. Variations in human reaction to infection or medication, discoverable only in the field practice of the physician, lead often to revision of the initial findings of the pure scientist. It is not justifiable to deprive medicine of its prestige as a science merely because it is, at the same time, an art. Its value, both as science and as a field of human service, is enhanced by its synthesis of these dual functions.

Sociology and Poverty.—The branches of sociology, pure and applied, which deal with the problems of poverty and handicap are numerous. The study of Social Origins, deals with conditions and their treatment in the earliest social aggregations and among our more primitive contemporaries. Social History studies origins and developments of the past four millenniums among the ancestors (and collaterals) of our present civilizations. The angle of approach and major subject matter are reasonably self-explanatory in the fields designated as Social Economics, Social Politics, Sociological Jurisprudence, Educational Sociology, Social Psychology, Urban Sociology, or Rural Sociology. Limited but precise methodologies of research or treatment are today suggested by the subjects of Social Research, Experimental Sociology, Social Statistics, Social Diagnosis, Social Case Work, Social Medicine, Social Legislation, Social Administration, and Social Revolution. All of the above deal with poverty and handicaps, yet no one of them, with the possible exception of the highly specialized techniques of Social Diagnosis, Social Case Work, and Social Medicine, narrowly construed, deals with these problems exclusively.[2]

Applied sociology is concerned with all of the contemporary social problems, each of which involves some degree of maladapta-

[2] Among the many recent works on the classification and scope of the social sciences in their relation to sociology, two are particularly useful from the point of view of classification because of both their comprehensiveness and their attention to detail, namely: Barnes, Harry Elmer, editor—*The History and Prospects of the Social Sciences;* Alfred A. Knopf, 1925: and Ogburn, William Fielding, and Goldenweiser, Alexander, editors—*The Social Sciences and Their Interrelations;* Houghton Mifflin Company, 1927.

tion or conflict on the part of individuals or groups. These include problems of international relationships such as war, tariff, and immigration, and of intranational relationships such as assimilation, mobility and migration, industrial strife and labor problems, political malfunctionings, revolutions, religious antagonisms, crime and delinquency, problems of slums and unwholesome housing, of illiteracy and ignorance, of the misuse of leisure time, and a wide range of other situations which may involve opposition of interests, maladjustments, deviations, or inadequacies, and may require social interference and control.

Social Pathology.—From this large mass of contemporary social problems it is customary and proper to select for intensive study those which are concerned with the inadequacies of individuals in their social relationships or with nominal or statistical groups designated as maladjusted, handicapped, or substandard. The angle of approach is the deviation or inadequacy of the individual, its sources, consequences, and correctives. Physical or mental abnormalities, antisocial behavior and delinquency, low standards of living and dependency, and the interrelations of these various maladjustments and of their social treatment and prevention are thus treated together under the caption of social pathology, or the sociology of substandard statistical groups.

Social pathology is that branch of applied sociology which is concerned with the classification (nosology or taxonomy), causation (etiology), structure (anatomy), conditions or manifestations (symptomatology), and treatment (therapeutics) of handicaps, poverty, delinquency, or other forms of individual and social inadequacies or maladjustment.

The Individual as Unit of Study.—Since the individual is, within one classificatory context, the unit of social groups there is justification for the specific treatment of the factors in the individual's make-up, genetic or acquired, which may influence his social relationships. Since it is inconceivable that an individual should from birth to death live apart from social relationships, the unit of our study is not the *individuus* but the personality (*socius*) or the self conceived in terms of its social relationships. All human behavior is social in both its causes and consequences.

Social Pathology and Organismic Sociology.—Pathology derivatively is the science of disease. Hence the term social pathology suggests that the subject matter consists of morbid conditions within a social organism. This connotation is unfortunate in view of the fact that the bio-organismic concept of society has been discarded for more than a generation by inductive sociology. It was characteristic of early social theories, however, to compare society, or more commonly the state, with the individual; to find that the state, like man, was composed of living cells (individuals); that it had its own alimentary system (economic institutions and functions), its circulatory system (transportation and communication), its members and organs, and its brain and nervous system (usually designated as the government, though sometimes as its aristocracy). From this analogy it was argued that society like the individual was a biological organism subject to the biological laws of birth, growth, maturity, old age, decay, and death.

The analogy is of ancient origin, traceable to early religious writings of India, as well as to Greek and Roman philosophers. In one form or another it has been elaborately expounded by many persons conspicuous in the development of sociological thought. Organismic sociology was elaborated among others by Herbert Spencer, A. Schäffle, René Worms, J. Novicow, and Paul de Lilienfeld.[3] Their theories were challenged by their contemporaries and subsequent writers on the grounds that society, if an organism, could represent only the lowest form of organic life, not higher than that of the amoeba. For the organs lack fixity of location, the members are amorphous, and the intelligence or brain is not centralized but diffused among all the individuals or "cells" of the social organism. Furthermore, it was argued that the useful concepts of social unity, growth or evolution, and human interdependence can be maintained without the assumption of the biological analogy.[4]

Argument from analogy always involves the danger that too much weight will be given to the analogy with resulting confusion of thought. Contemporary inductive sociology has therefore abandoned both the bio-organismic theory of society and use of the organic analogy. It now systematizes its data on the structure and

[3] Spencer, Herbert—*The Principles of Sociology*, Vol. I, Part II; D. Appleton and Company, 1901. Schäffle, Albert E.—*Bau und Leben des socialen Körpers*, Vol. I, Books II–IV; H. Laupp'schen Buchhandlung, 1881. Worms, René—*Organisme et société;* V. Giard & E. Brière, 1896. Novicow, J.—*La théorie organique des sociétés, défense de l'organicisme;* V. Giard & E. Brière, 1899. Lilienfeld, Paul de—*La pathologie sociale;* V. Giard & E. Brière, 1896.

[4] For a sketch of the bio-organismic theories, together with detailed references and brief criticisms, see Sorokin, Pitirim—*Contemporary Sociological Theories*, Chapter IV; Harper & Brothers, 1928.

functional interrelations of social groups, not in terms of "the social organism" but rather as social organization.

Social Organization.—If by a process of abstraction social organization or the established positions and modes of interaction of men could be viewed statically, in a moment of time, it would appear as a complex of personal and group interrelationships, including social structures—corporate and institutional as well as noncorporate—and with bases relatively intangible and incommensurable in the consciousness, emotions, attitudes, and thoughts of the individuals of whom social groups are constituted.

Since the life of individuals and of social groups is never static, social organization is viewed as the highly complex process through which social institutions and structures are built up, relationships developed, and relative order and harmony maintained. Through propinquity, social institutions, and community of interests in the fields of economic or cultural life, personalities and groups tend toward increasing social organization. But side by side with the unifying factors in this dynamic social process there are factors divisive in nature tending to split groups, destroy institutions, or shift the directions of social change. Both the unifying and the divisive factors emanate from, and operate through, individuals under influences and motivations of infinite complexity—physical, geographic, biologic, physiological, psychological, economic, and cultural or else as in Durkheim's terminology as *faits sociaux* are made up of beliefs, tendencies, and practices of the group taken collectively.[5]

Social Disorganization.—The subject matter of social pathology, the problems of human inadequacy and maladjustment, may also be dealt with under the rubric of social disorganization. Failures to conform to the rules of the group, whether customs, mores, or statute law, and positive revolt against the forces which make for social unity and stability, as well as evidences of degeneration or decay at

[5] Bushee, Frederick A.—*Social Organization;* Henry Holt and Company, 1930. Cooley, Charles Horton—*Social Organization;* Charles Scribner's Sons, 1909. Elliott, Mabel A., and Merrill, Francis E.—*Social Disorganization;* Harper & Brothers, 1934. Hertzler, Joyce O.—*Social Institutions;* McGraw-Hill Book Company, Inc., 1929. Hiller, E. T.—*Principles of Sociology;* Harper & Brothers, 1933. MacIver, R. M.—*Society: A Textbook of Sociology;* Farrar & Rinehart, Inc., 1937. Queen, Stuart Alfred, Bodenhafer, Walter Blaine, and Harper, Ernest Bouldin—*Social Organization and Disorganization;* Thomas Y. Crowell Company, 1935. Rivers, W. H. R.—*Social Organization;* Alfred A. Knopf, 1924. See also the works of Émile Durkheim, and Gehlke, Charles Elmer—*Émile Durkheim's Contributions to Sociological Theory;* Columbia University Press, 1915.

any point in the social structure, are listed as types of social disorganization. Unless the process of disorganization is stayed the groups in question tend to be weakened or broken.

If social organization is construed as a moving equilibrium (an analogy almost as hazardous as that of the "social organism") social disorganization consists of the factors, social in their origin or manifestation, which threaten that equilibrium. In terms of human interest and aspiration, social disorganization consists of those threats to or changes in social structure, institutions, rules, or even attitudes which thwart man's socialized desires or endanger his health, growth, freedom, or achievement. Utilizing either definition it is clear that social organization may be weakened by relative increase in the number of its handicapped citizens, or by increase in the volume of poverty, because of the reduction in standards of living which such increases entail. Increases in dependency and social parasitism, or in delinquency and antisocial behavior, may menace social organization still more. But social organization is threatened also wherever rapid change in one field of endeavor is not accompanied by the necessary changes in other social relationships, as for example where invention produces technological unemployment without concomitant reabsorption of labor, or where the rapid growth of cities is unaccompanied by adaptation of the city plan and the civic institutions.

Even if poverty or handicap do not increase, social organization is threatened by their very presence. Much that is characteristically called social disorganization would more appropriately be termed *under*organization. For there has never existed a society in which disintegrating and thwarting elements were not present in some degree. Much poverty, such as that associated with technological unemployment, is evidence of transition or social reorganization.

The sociology of substandard groups discovered statistically, or the analysis of individual deviations and social inadequacies, their nature, causes, consequences, and treatment, may at every point be considered in terms of social organization and disorganization, as well as in terms of pathologic functioning.

Sociology versus the Normative Sciences.—A distinction is often drawn between the pure sciences, which by means of inductive methods attempt to determine principles which underlie our world and the forms of life upon it, and the normative sciences, which by methods speculative or inductive attempt to establish criteria of judgment. In the latter group we find logic concerned with norms of truth, and esthetics and ethics which establish norms of beauty and goodness respectively. Wherever these normative sciences proceed exclusively by the inductive method they are pure sciences, even though concerned with norms. Where their methods are metaphysical and speculative they are branches of philosophy.

Dividing lines between the pure sciences and the normative studies are less sharp than the controversial literature pertaining to them would make them appear to be. Any science viewed methodologically establishes and applies criteria of accuracy (truth) which relate it to logic. This is essential since science must perfect its tools. The study of value judgments is not inconsistent with the purposes of science.[6]

When social sciences, however, make evaluative judgments they invade the field of ethics. Concepts of justice, of rights, and of ideal or optimum conditions are not merely incidental in many standard works in economics, government, and law but are prominent under such captions as "distributive justice" or "penal justice," "standards of living," the "rights" of citizens or of labor, "optimum" administration or organization. Ethical considerations tend still more to dominate a considerable fraction of works in applied economics (*e.g.* problems of labor and industry, banking, or public finance), government (especially politics and administration), pedagogy (especially in the framing of curricula, and in problems of discipline, organization, and administration). When a work in social science passes from the *study* of judgments to the *making* of judgments of value, it ceases at that point to be pure science.

Social science studies facts. In social life there are customary modes of behavior. There are also norms—beliefs about what one should do. Both of these are studied as data by social science. Applied social science, however, goes further; it accepts the norms of the group (or of the dominant class, or of some particular coterie) and attempts to show how the knowledge available can be utilized to attain these norms in practice. Hence a first task of the applied social scientist is to know what these norms are that he is going to take for granted, and then develop criteria for measuring the actual achievement or lack of achievement with reference to these norms.

---

[6] Another distinction between the descriptive and the normative sciences is that the former is concerned with judgments of fact (is-judgments) while the latter is concerned with judgments of the ideal or of what should be (ought-judgments).

Standards of Reference.—Social pathology, to establish limits in its own field of study, requires the formulation of a criterion of normality below which will be found the individuals or groups which constitute its subject matter. Social disorganization similarly presupposes a concept of organization as standard of reference. This phase of the literature of both subjects is incomplete, because they are both new as fields of study. The terms which they so freely employ—maladjustment, maladaptation, demoralization, inadequacy, instability, conflict—tend to be vague and inexact.

Some movement in the direction of precision is noted where normality is consistently defined in terms of (1) the arithmetical mean, or (2) the statistical median (or middle point in a series in which items are arranged by the order of their magnitude). Where the term "typical" is used there is danger of vagueness, or of measurement based upon limited observations, unless this term is identified with the statistical modal point, or point of greatest frequency of distribution in the statistical series.[7]

Experience increasingly demonstrates, however, that these convenient statistical dividing points, the mean, median, and mode, do not correspond with the dividing points between health and disease, between organization and disorganization, adequacy and inadequacy, adjustment and maladjustment. The average man, whether the term is used in the sense of mean, median, or mode, may not enjoy good health but suffer minor disabilities of a physical nature, such as defective eyesight or dental caries. His education and his income may fall considerably short of that needed to meet many of life's demands. Thus the average man may on occasion be a social problem or retard one form or another of social organization. Many of the researches upon which social pathology must base its tentative judgments supply only the types of statistical criteria which in themselves are insufficient for its use as standards of reference.

Other standards of reference can, however, be applied. These we may group in four major categories: (1) legal standards; (2) scientific standards, including those of biology, pathology, psychiatry, and on occasion those of endocrinology, somatology, pedagogy, sanitary engineering, city planning, and a wide variety of others;

---

[7] Day, Edmund E.—*Statistical Analysis;* The Macmillan Company, 1925. Chaddock, Robert Emmet—*Principles and Methods of Statistics;* Houghton Mifflin Company, 1925.

(3) empirical standards arrived at by an examination and synthesis
of all of the foregoing types, viewed in terms of their bearing upon
social inadequacy and social disorganization; and (4) optimum
standards arrived at by metaphysical speculation and termed
"absolutes," or by inductive process and termed social objectives.
Sudden shifts from one set of standards to another are characteristic of the existing literature of social pathology and social disorganization and are probably necessary until through extensive
research more specific standards can be agreed upon and widely
utilized. The student should, however, be continuously on his guard
to recognize the standards employed and the implications of each.

Legal Standards.—Legal standards, whether incorporated in the
statute law relating to dependency and vagrancy, health and disease, building and housing, hours and conditions of labor, minimum
wages, commitment to institutions, crime and punishment, marriage and divorce, liquor and drug traffic, or any other problems
with which social pathology is concerned, have their roots in tradition and the common law. Their actual form and content, however,
is largely determined through a compromise attained in legislative
chambers between conflicting interests and viewpoints. Many such
standards, especially those relating to physical and mental disease,
incorporate the findings of science. But legislative standards tend
to lag far behind the outposts of science, and to incorporate the
scientific findings of the preceding generation rather than of contemporary pioneers. Not infrequently, also, laws are obscure at one
point or another, or incorporate the prejudiced judgments of the
putative majority group which effected their passage, or, for varied
reasons, fall short of effective enforcement. Thus, for example, a
law regarding the commitment of the insane may, because of conditions in its wording or enforcement, fail to cover all of the persons
who because of mental disease are a source of danger to themselves
or to others. The minimum standards established by statute law
thus tend to fall below the standards of contemporary scientific
practice, and to designate merely the minimally acceptable types
of social conduct in various spheres. They thus provide a standard
of reference insufficiently high to make possible a proper division of
social groups for the purposes of social pathology, or of social treatment.

Scientific Standards.—Though legal standards determine with a
high degree of finality which individuals in the populace are "crim-

inals," "paupers," or "insane," the findings of many sciences are necessary to ascertain the dividing line between normal mentality on the one hand and subnormal or abnormal mentality on the other. Such scientific criteria are indispensable in the process of differentiating each type of handicap from normality, and for distinguishing subtypes. In many instances a wide variety of sciences must be called upon to effect satisfactory definitions, and to diagnose and correctly place individual cases. The pathologist works jointly with the psychiatrist, endocrinologist, toxicologist, epidemiologist, and eugenist in the analysis of mental diseases, and with somatologists, orthopedists, and others to define and identify physical abnormalities.

Empirical Standards.—Sociology, being unable for its own purposes to use exclusively any one of the foregoing standards, makes its own syntheses and reformulations of these criteria, while supplementing with its own. The primary concern of social pathology is with social conditions, their causes and consequences, and with evidences of defect or abnormality either in social organization or in the social process. If social pathology is defined in terms of adaptation, the evidences of maladaptation must be sought; if in terms of deviation one must define the normality from which a given condition deviates. Always there is involved the discovery and appraisal of the social consequences of the poverty, handicap, marital difficulties, criminality, or other conditions under consideration.

From such analysis of consequences the social pathologist may arrive at a definition of his own criterion or standard in sociological terms, which will incorporate, in so far as may prove wise or necessary, the standards arrived at by statistics, law, medicine, and other sciences. In defining the feebleminded he may make use of the intelligence quotients reached by psychometry, and for subgroups may use on occasion the definitions of the census, of the laws of his state, of the endocrinologists and psychiatrists. Nevertheless, his contribution through definition is made by his judgment as to what constitutes mental subnormality in terms of behavior in the domestic circle, the school, the job, or in terms of adequacy to meet the current requirements of family, industry, citizenship, and general social participation.

The researches of the social pathologist may indicate that the concept of normality may properly be varied with reference to time and place. An intelligence quotient adequate to meet the social demands of backward races may not prove adequate for the requirements of our higher contemporary civilization. A standard of living adequate in the reign of Queen Elizabeth would at many points fail to meet the exigencies of contemporary life. A person able to make adjustments in backward rural areas may be incapable of effective social participation in the New York City, Chicago, or Los Angeles of today.

When the scientist turns from the measurement of social conditions to the examination of social action he finds that moral evaluations have been made by social groups to set goals for action. Distinctions have arisen between standards which are "practical" or expedient in the sense that they are "the best available in the circumstances" to accomplish a given purpose, and standards which are deemed reasonable and desirable—"toward which society should move." Among standards of living, for example, the "subsistence level" has been differentiated from the "decency or comfort level." [8] Among housing standards the existing legal minimum is contrasted with standards which incorporate provisions not merely for shelter, safety, and sanitation, but also for privacy, convenience, wholesome living, and the amenities of life.[9]

Optimum Standards or Value Judgments.—Any of the foregoing criteria may be used either (1) for measurement, to ascertain distribution, which is a function of descriptive science; or (2) to clarify objectives and determine the size of the group to be brought up to a specified level, which is a normative function. The optimum standard, however, connotes the perfect or ultimate, and may be valueless consequently for measurement; since ordinarily entire populations will fall short of the norms which its proponents devise. Nevertheless, the framing of optimal standards has the decided merit of establishing an ultimate goal toward which society may progress, and in its details may provide a check list of the ultimate desiderata with reference to which each contemporary type of social inadequacy and each contemporary legal, scientific, or em-

[8] Eliot, Thomas D.—*American Standards and Planes of Living;* Ginn and Company, 1931.

[9] Ford, James, with the collaboration of Morrow, Katherine, and Thompson, George N.—*Slums and Housing, with Special Reference to New York City: History, Conditions, Policy,* Vol. II, Chapter XXXIII, "Housing Standards"; Harvard University Press, 1936. Gries, John M., and Ford, James, editors—*Housing Objectives and Programs;* The President's Conference on Home Building and Home Ownership, Vol. XI, 1932.

pirical norm can be assayed. Science may study such standards as data and examine their distribution and application. Their formulation is, however, the province of ethics. Optimum standards will be discussed in a later chapter.

QUESTIONS FOR DISCUSSION OR EXAMINATION

1. Define sociology, applied sociology, and social work. Show their inter-relations.
2. What is the relation of sociology to social reform?
3. Define and contrast the fields of social pathology and social disorganization. Can you think of any problem which belongs to one of these two fields but not to the other?
4. Is either (a) society, or (b) the state, an organism? What are the values and the dangers of the bio-organismic analogy?
5. Distinguish normative sciences from pure sciences. Is social ethics a branch of sociology?
6. How would you define normality? Show the values and limitations of each of the major categories of standards.

PROBLEMS FOR INDIVIDUAL STUDY

1. Make a critical comparison of definitions of sociology and of classifications of its subject matter, from standard works on principles of sociology.
2. Compare and contrast both definitions and classifications, in standard works on social pathology and social disorganization.
3. Analyze an issue of the *Proceedings* of the National Conference of Social Work or of the *Social Work Year Book*, or several issues of the *Survey Graphic*, to discover and classify the evidences which they contain of either social pathology or social disorganization.
4. Analyze any text in sociology, social pathology, or social work to discover criteria or standards of reference employed.
5. Make an independent study of the methods of determining "normality."

SUGGESTIONS FOR SUPPLEMENTARY READINGS

Barnes, Harry Elmer, editor—*The History and Prospects of the Social Sciences;* Alfred A. Knopf, 1925.

Bossard, James H. S.—*Social Change and Social Problems;* Harper & Brothers, revised edition, 1938.

Bristol, Lucius Moody—*Social Adaptation;* Harvard University Press, 1915.

Bushee, Frederick A.—*Social Organization;* Henry Holt and Company, 1930.

Cooley, Charles Horton—*Social Organization;* Charles Scribner's Sons, 1909.

Cooley, Charles Horton—*Social Process;* Charles Scribner's Sons, 1922.

Durkheim, Émile—*Division of Labor in Society* (translated by George Simpson); The Macmillan Company, 1933.

Durkheim, Émile—*The Rules of Sociological Method* (translation from the eighth French edition by Sarah A. Solovay and John H. Mueller); University of Chicago Press, 1938.

Elliott, Mabel A., and Merrill, Francis E.—*Social Disorganization;* Harper & Brothers, 1934.

Ellwood, Charles—*Methods in Sociology;* Duke University Press, 1933.

Fairchild, Henry Pratt—*Outline of Applied Sociology;* The Macmillan Company, 1916.

Giddings, Franklin Henry—*Studies in the Theory of Human Society;* The Macmillan Company, 1922.

Gillette, John M., and Reinhardt, James M.—*Current Social Problems;* American Book Company, 1937.

Gillin, John Lewis—*Social Pathology;* The Century Co., 1933.

Gillin, John Lewis, and Blackmar, Frank W.—*Outlines of Sociology,* Part Two, Chapter IX, "Social Organization," and Part Five, "Social Pathology"; The Macmillan Company, third edition, 1930.

Hayes, Edward Cary—*Sociology and Ethics;* D. Appleton and Company, 1921.

Hertzler, Joyce O.—*Social Institutions;* McGraw-Hill Book Company, Inc., 1929.

Hiller, E. T.—*Principles of Sociology;* Harper & Brothers, 1933.

Lamson, Herbert Day—*Social Pathology in China;* The Commercial Press, Limited (Shanghai, China), 1934.

Lilienfeld, Paul de—*La pathologie sociale;* V. Giard & E. Brière (Paris), 1896.

Lundberg, George A.—*Social Research;* Longmans, Green and Co., 1929.

Lundberg, George A., Bain, Read, and Anderson, Nels—*Trends in American Sociology;* Harper & Brothers, 1929.

MacIver, R. M.—*Society: A Textbook of Sociology;* Farrar & Rinehart, Inc., 1937.

Mangold, George B.—*Social Pathology;* The Macmillan Company, 1932.

Odum, Howard W., and Jocher, Katharine—*An Introduction to Social Research;* Henry Holt and Company, 1929.

Ogburn, William Fielding—*Social Change;* B. W. Huebsch, Inc., 1922.

Ogburn, William Fielding, and Goldenweiser, Alexander, editors—*The Social Sciences and Their Interrelations;* Houghton Mifflin Company, 1927.

Park, Robert E., and Burgess, Ernest W.—*Introduction to the Science of Sociology;* University of Chicago Press, 1924.

Queen, Stuart Alfred, Bodenhafer, Walter Blaine, and Harper, Ernest Bouldin—*Social Organization and Disorganization;* Thomas Y. Crowell Company, 1935.

Queen, Stuart Alfred, and Mann, Delbert Martin—*Social Pathology;* Thomas Y. Crowell Company, 1925.

Rice, Stuart A., editor—*Methods in Social Science;* Committee on Scientific Method in the Social Sciences of the Social Science Research Council, University of Chicago Press, 1931.

Rivers, W. H. R.—*Social Organization;* Alfred A. Knopf, 1924.

Ross, Edward Alsworth—*Principles of Sociology;* D. Appleton-Century Company, third edition, revised, 1938.

Shenton, Herbert—*The Practical Application of Sociology;* Columbia University Press, 1927.

Sorokin, Pitirim—*Contemporary Sociological Theories;* Harper & Brothers, 1928.

Southard, E. E., and Jarrett, Mary C.—*The Kingdom of Evils;* The Macmillan Company, 1922.

Stamp, Sir Josiah—*The Science of Social Adjustment;* The Macmillan Company, 1937.

Thomas, William I., and Znaniecki, Florian—*The Polish Peasant in Europe and America*, Vol. II, "Social Disorganization"; Alfred A. Knopf, 1927.

Ward, Lester F.—*Applied Sociology;* Ginn and Company, 1906.

CHAPTER II

HISTORY OF CLASSIC SOCIAL SURVEYS OF EUROPE

Antiquity of Pathologic Conditions.—The problems of poverty, handicaps, delinquency, and other maladjustments have always concerned mankind. It has seldom been easy to wrest a living from nature, especially outside the tropical zone. Even the most primitive families have had to face the problem of support of mutilated or otherwise handicapped members, coping with accident and disease and their consequences. Struggle with outside enemies and the violators of tribal customs and mores have made punishment necessary since before the dawn of history.[1]

Despite millenniums of experience with these problems the scientific approach to their treatment is relatively recent. Although early tribal practices, as well as early statute law, were often based on amassed information and experience, detailed studies of these problems, if made, escaped permanent record. The judgments of political and religious leaders became incorporated in social practice but often grew out of the play of superstition or the expression of arbitrary domination instead of inductive reasoning.

There is evidence of wisdom in early Hebrew practices regarding commerce and property.[2] The social philosophies of Plato and Aristotle represent a notably high degree of speculative thinking on these and related problems, but in the main fail to support their judgments with what this generation would term adequate evidence. The fulminations of the Hebrew prophets or of Cicero reveal much concerning the conditions of their time and interest in social behavior and well-being. The early historians, whether in the Old Testament or the writings of Herodotus or Pliny, elaborate more fully but descriptively concerning the conditions of living in their own times.

---

[1] Hobhouse, L. T.—*Morals in Evolution*, especially Chapters II "Forms of Social Organization," III "Law and Justice," and VIII "Property and Poverty"; Henry Holt and Company, fourth edition, 1923: and Westermarck, Edward—*The Origin and Development of the Moral Ideas;* Macmillan and Co., Limited, 1906–17.

[2] *E.g.* Leviticus, Chapter XIX, 9–11 and 35–36, and Chapter XXV.

Modern science, however, demands the systematization of accurate knowledge, the counting of cases, the discovery of causes, interrelations, and trends. These have been hinted at in earlier writings but such documents display little of social and economic research.

Beginnings of Social Research: The Census.—The first statistical studies were apparently censuses either of man power or fighting strength on the one hand or of taxable properties on the other. Such counts of people or of property are recorded in the Old and New Testaments [3] as well as in ancient Persia, Egypt, and Greece.[4] In Rome both property and population were frequently counted. The *Domesday Book* of William the Conqueror at the middle of the eleventh century in England was a detailed list of taxable property, and contains illuminating data relating to the distribution of wealth in England in its period.[5]

The periodic and systematic collection of detailed population data virtually began a century and a half ago with the inauguration of the Federal decennial census of the United States in 1790, and the 1801 census in England, Scotland, and Wales.[6] Each decade since this period has usually witnessed an increase in the types of social data assembled until within the past half century much systematized information has been made available in the leading countries of the world concerning age, sex, nativity, occupation, and other characteristics of their populations. Today, the amount of pauperism, the volume of many types of defectiveness and handicap, the numbers and types of institution inmates, the amount of illiteracy and of schooling, mortality rates by diseases, and other interests of the social pathologist are widely covered. Estimates are increasingly offered of national and per capita wealth, of wages and income distribution, of natural resources and other data pertinent to this field of interest.[7]

[3] Exodus XII, 37; Numbers I; 2 Samuel XXIV; 1 Chronicles XII, 23–37; XXI, 1–5; XXIII, 3–5; Nehemiah VII, XI.

[4] Herodotus, Book VII, relates the crude methods employed for measuring the size of armies.

[5] *Domesday Book*, or *The Great Survey of England of William the Conqueror*, A.D. MLXXXVI . . . photo-zincographed . . . at the Ordnance Survey Office, Southampton. Colonel Sir H. James . . . director, Southampton, 1861–64, 33 volumes.

[6] Sweden and Norway gathered some useful population data somewhat earlier. See Walter F. Willcox' article on " Census " in *Encyclopaedia Britannica*, eleventh edition, Vol. 5, pp. 662–669.

[7] Thus in the United States there were statistics of slavery from 1790; industrial data from 1810; number of aliens from 1820; of deaf, dumb, and blind from

Early Sources of Social Data.—Prior to the scientific period many revealing documents of contemporaries, whether diaries, letters, travels, accounts, fiction, or drama, reveal conditions of poverty or behavior prevalent in some restricted area or period of time. One can glean much of value with regard to conditions of poverty from Juan-Luis Vivès, *Concerning the Relief of the Poor*, a letter addressed to the Senate of Bruges, January 6, 1526.[8] Information concerning charitable alms, hospitals, and provision for lepers was included in John Stow's *Survey of London*, first published in 1598. Observations upon social conditions can be gathered from Pepys' *Diary* (1660–69), Daniel Defoe's *The Journal of the Plague Year* (1722), and the works of many another interested commentator upon the life of the poor in England before the end of the eighteenth century.[9] Our most useful comparative documents, however, for the earlier periods are those of present day historians who have weighed, sifted, assembled, and generalized upon all available documents of the past.[10]

1830; education, occupations from 1840; pauperism, crime, wages from 1850; with ever increasing subdivision of these and other topics in recent censuses. Willcox, *ibid*. See next chapter.

[8] Translated by Margaret M. Sherwood from the original Latin, as found in Volume IV, pp. 420–494 of the complete works of Vivès, edited by Gregory Majan, and printed at Valencia in the year 1783; Studies in Social Work, No. 11, The New York School of Philanthropy, February, 1917.

[9] Defoe used the statistical method in a broadside entitled *Giving Alms No Charity*, published in 1704. Contemporary reprints of the above mentioned works by John Stow, Samuel Pepys, and Daniel Defoe are accessible in Everyman's Library published by J. M. Dent & Sons, Ltd., London, and E. P. Dutton & Co., New York.

[10] See especially Ashley, W. J.—*An Introduction to English Economic History and Theory*, three volumes; G. P. Putnam's Sons, 1901–03. Cunningham, William—*The Growth of English Industry and Commerce*, three volumes; Cambridge University Press, 1910–19. Hammond, J. L., and Hammond, Barbara—*The Town Labourer, 1760–1832: The New Civilisation;* Longmans, Green and Co., 1920 (first edition, 1917): *The Skilled Labourer, 1760–1832;* Longmans, Green and Co., 1919: *The Rise of Modern Industry;* Harcourt, Brace and Company, Inc., 1926 (fifth edition, revised 1937): *The Age of Charities, 1832–1854: A Study of Discontent;* Longmans, Green and Co., 1930. Leonard, E. M.—*The Early History of English Poor Relief;* Cambridge, at the University Press, 1900. Mackay, Thomas—*A History of the English Poor Law;* P. S. King & Son, Ltd., 1899. Rogers, James E. Thorold—*The Economic Interpretation of History;* G. P. Putnam's Sons, 1888. Usher, Abbott Payson—*An Introduction to the Industrial History of England;* Houghton Mifflin Company, 1920. Webb, Sidney and Beatrice—*English Local Government: English Poor Law History: Part I, The Old Poor Law;* Longmans, Green and Co., 1927: *Part II, The Last Hundred Years*, 2 vols.; published by the authors, 1929. From these one can glean a reasonably accurate picture of the conditions of poverty and the development of social policy with regard to the poor for England prior to the era of social research.

Early English Surveys: Davies and Eden.—Comprehensive research in these problems virtually begins in the last decade of the eighteenth century. In 1795 Reverend David Davies published family budgets and other data which were summarized in *The Case of Labourers in Husbandry, Stated and Considered*. Davies' method was to make records during his visits to parish families, covering their income and expenditures. He began to do this in 1787 and then sent samples to friends in various parts of England asking them to do likewise. These returns comprised budgets of one hundred and thirty-three families, collected from fifteen counties in England, three in Scotland, and two in Wales. Expenditures for each individual item were put down for a full week and multiplied by fifty-two to represent the annual budget for food and miscellanies. To this were added expenditures for rent, fuel, clothing, sickness, and other items. This total was contrasted with the weekly earnings of the members of the household, similarly multiplied by fifty-two. Annual deficits were found, in spite of poor relief, which led Davies to recommend the establishment of a legal minimum wage.[11]

Sir Frederick Morton Eden, in England, published in 1797 a three volume work entitled *The State of the Poor*. Eden, like Davies, gathered information from clergymen and others, but supplemented this method by sending out an investigator with an extensive questionnaire. In addition to wage and budget matters he inquired concerning customary diet and the ages of members of the family. Fifty-four budgets were published in one of the appendices of Volume III, and others appear elsewhere in Volumes II and III. Eden recognized the difficulty of ascertaining annual earnings or of arriving at these by multiplying weekly earnings by fifty-two. He noted also that many families questioned were inaccurate or insincere. He was careful therefore to qualify his generalizations.[12]

Belgian Studies: Ducpétiaux.—On the Continent Ducpétiaux contributed between 1843 and 1855 five useful studies on physical

[11] Davies, Rev. David—*The Case of Labourers in Husbandry, Stated and Considered. With an appendix containing a collection of accounts, shewing the earnings and expenses of labouring families, in different parts of the kingdom;* G. G. and J. Robinson (London), 1795.

[12] Eden, Sir Frederick Morton—*The State of the Poor*, Preface, p. xxvi, Vol. I: originally published in three volumes, recently republished in one abridged volume, edited by A. G. L. Rogers; E. P. Dutton & Co., 1929.

and moral conditions of young workingmen, on pauperism in Belgium, and on workingclass budgets.[13] The latter study, which had been outlined by Quételet, found that approximately one-third of the families examined were dependent at least in part upon relief. The food budget of workingmen was discovered to be inferior to the standard rations of soldiers and even of prisoners.

For more than thirty years Ducpétiaux served as Inspector General of prisons and charitable institutions of Belgium. As an administrator he arranged for improvement of the treatment of the insane, farm colony reform schools for young vagrants, reduction of capital punishment, inauguration of international congresses in the fields of penology and charity and of decennial censuses of charities and corrections.[14]

French Studies: Le Play.—Despite these preliminary researches, the credit for formulating and applying intensive case study methods is quite generally conceded to Frédéric Le Play. During the period from 1823 to 1855 Le Play, who was a teacher of metallurgy in Paris, spent his vacations in the study of workingclass families in many of the countries of Europe. With the help of local teachers and ministers he located families deemed "typical" and then made arrangements to live in the home of each selected family as a paying guest for several weeks. He made records of each item of income and expenditure and continuous observations upon the economic and social life of the family, the attitudes and behavior of its members, and carefully wrote up his findings in a series of fifty-five family monographs, the first thirty-six of which were published in 1855 in three volumes under the title *Les ouvriers européens.* The remainder were published in his revised edition of 1879 which comprised six volumes, one of which was devoted to an outline of his methods of study and analysis.[15]

---

[13] Ducpétiaux, Édouard—*De la condition physique et morale des jeunes ouvriers et des moyens de l'améliorer*, 2 vols., 1843; *Le Paupérisme en Belgique—Causes et remèdes*, 1844; *Enquête sur la condition des classes ouvrières et sur le travail des enfants en Belgique*, 1848; *Mémoire sur le paupérisme dans les Flandres*, 1850; and *Budgets économiques des classes ouvrières en Belgique, subsistances, salaires, population*, 1855.

[14] Ducpétiaux' contributions to penological literature comprise—*De la peine de mort*, 1827; *Du progrès et de l'état actuel de la réforme pénitentiare et des institutions préventives aux États-Unis, en France, en Suisse, en Angleterre et en Belgique*, 3 vols., 1837–38; *Statistique des tribunaux et des prisons de la Belgique*, 1834; and *Des conditions d'application du système de l'emprisonnement séparé ou cellulaire*, 1857.

[15] Le Play, Frédéric—*La méthode d'observation*, which is Vol. I of the six volume edition of *Les ouvriers européens;* Alfred Mame et fils, 1879.

Le Play's method was to induce each family to analyze its annual income by listing all property and its income, receipts both in goods and in money, subventions, wages of each member of the family, and receipts from family industries. Expenditures covered foods, rent, light, heat, and household furnishings, clothing and laundry for each member of the household, and expenses for religion, education, recreation, health, taxes, insurance, debts, and savings. Le Play went beyond mere accounting to describe and evaluate the family's history and mode of living and to comment upon the habits and status of each of its members.

Although it may be maintained credibly that there is no such thing as a typical family, Le Play's monographs upon the study of actual workingclass families set new high standards in social research. His methods may be criticized at a number of points,[16] but he clearly remains the first expositor of scientific methods of analysis of family budgets and standards of living.

In 1856 Le Play founded the *Société internationale des études pratiques d'économie sociale*, which has published since 1881 *La Réforme Sociale*. His associates and followers continued his methods of family study in a serial publication, *Les Ouvriers des Deux Mondes*, of which ten volumes were issued comprising ninety-one additional monographs.[17]

German Studies: Engel.—The most prominent continental figure in the field of statistical research upon standards of living of the working classes in the latter part of the nineteenth century was Ernst Engel. Engel had been a student of Le Play and in his youth had accompanied him in some of his monographic studies. He subsequently directed the statistical department of Saxony and later of Prussia. In addition to his general statistical output, Engel, in 1857, prepared important analytical comparisons of the works of Eden, Le Play, Ducpétiaux, and others.[18]

---

[16] Elaborated in Zimmerman, Carle C., and Frampton, Merle E.—*Family and Society*, pp. 65–69; D. Van Nostrand Company, Inc., 1935.

[17] For analysis of the Le Play method see Cheysson, E., and Toque, A.—"Les budgets comparés des cent monographies de familles" in *Bulletin de l'Institut International de Statistique*, Vol. V, 1890: Sorokin, Pitirim—*Contemporary Sociological Theories*, Chapter II; Harper & Brothers, 1928: also Zimmerman and Frampton, *op. cit.*

[18] Erroneous interpretation popularized in 1875 by Carroll D. Wright as Engel's Laws affirmed that with increase of family income (1) a smaller percentage is expended for food while (2) the percentage expended for clothing remains approximately the same, (3) the percentage for rent, fuel, and light

Engel sought the ratio between expenditures for food and for other essentials—devising a unit of consumption for the purpose of measurement. He noted that living costs vary somewhat with occupation and that expenditures are related to location, urban or rural. He found that as income increases more animal foods are consumed and there are greater expenditures for clothing, especially for children. His primary contribution rested in his analytical interpretation of prior studies and in his methodology.[19]

The Beginning of Comprehensive Local Social Surveys: Booth.—Local studies of poverty of the systematic and comprehensive type virtually begin with the classic research of Charles Booth entitled *Life and Labour of the People in London.*[20] In 1890, General William Booth of the Salvation Army had published a sensational volume entitled *In Darkest England, and the Way Out*, which had depicted East London as a dangerous quarter in which destitution, degeneracy, and criminality were general.[21] Meanwhile it had become apparent to Charles Booth, owner of steamship lines which docked on the Thames in East London, that the dangers of that district had been greatly overstated. In the late eighties he determined to ascertain the actual volume of poverty and criminality. His *Life and Labour of the People* began with the examination of East London but extended to analysis of poverty in each of the other districts of London. Studies on labor conditions and of the religious and social service agencies of London followed. More

remains the same, but (4) the percentage for sundries including health, education, and recreation increases with the increase of income.

Engel's Laws thus interpreted stimulated similar researches in many countries. Frank Hatch Streightoff in 1911, in *The Standard of Living among the Industrial People of America* (Houghton Mifflin Company, 1911), showed from many American studies that the first of these four laws, indicated as (1) above, is true after income reached a certain point; (2) may be untrue as clothing expenditures tend to increase; and (3) though approximately true for most of the country is untrue for New York City where decrease in the percentage for rent is noted; (4) is invariably true. Later studies in Germany and elsewhere noted that the percentages allotted to rent were affected by the social status and ambitions of the groups studied. For detailed critical analysis of this literature see Zimmerman, Carle C.—*Consumption and Standards of Living;* D. Van Nostrand Company, Inc., 1936.

[19] Ably discussed in Zimmerman, Carle C.—*ibid.*, and Zimmerman and Frampton, *op. cit.*, pp. 52–57.

[20] Booth, Charles—*Life and Labour of the People in London;* Macmillan and Co., Limited, 1902. The data which follow are taken chiefly from First Series: *Poverty*, Vol. I, East, Central and South London, pp. 28–72.

[21] Booth, William—*In Darkest England, and the Way Out;* International Headquarters of the Salvation Army, 1890.

than fifteen years were devoted to this research. When completed, in 1902, this investigation comprised seventeen volumes.

Since existing census figures yielded little concerning the incomes and lives of the poor of London, and since it was obviously impractical to obtain direct data from four million people, Booth hit upon an ingenious expedient. Finding that the city's four hundred school attendance officers visited the homes of all families on premises rated at not more than £ 40 per year, he sought and obtained permission from the London School Board to go over their records and recollections with each school visitor for each such family. The data thus obtained were then checked and rechecked by means of interviews with school teachers, sanitary inspectors, case workers of the Charity Organization Society, the police, hospital almoners, officers of friendly societies and trade unions, and even the agents of manufacturers of sewing machines. This was done by investigators employed by Booth. Their data were verified by Booth himself through interviews and visits to each district. Care was exercised to avoid both overstatement and understatement.

The East London district at that time had a population of 909,000. These were divided by Booth into eight classes of which the lowest, Class A, consisted of "some occasional labourers, street-sellers, loafers, criminals, and semi-criminals." This group was estimated at 11,000, or $1\frac{1}{4}$ per cent of the population. Many were homeless outcasts or inmates of common lodging houses. Class B received only casual earnings. There were about 100,000 persons, or $11\frac{1}{4}$ per cent of the whole population in this class, many of them widows or deserted women. Together Classes A and B made up the "very poor" who lived in a state of chronic want.

Class C, with intermittent earnings, numbered 75,000, or about 8 per cent of the population. They were largely seasonal workers whether stevedores, porters, or laborers in building trades. Many received good wages when working but were commonly improvident. The women brought in some income from charing, washing, or needlework. Class D, with small regular earnings, comprised 129,000 people or nearly $14\frac{1}{2}$ per cent of the population. This was a group that had a hard struggle to make ends meet but were steady at work which required little skill, and paid their way. Women and children supplemented the family income. Classes C and D were termed by Booth the "poor." Their incomes at that time ranged from "18s. to 21s. per week for a moderate family." Their

means were barely sufficient for decent independent life, and they
lived under a continuous struggle to obtain the necessaries of life.
This careful study revealed that not more than 35 per cent of the
population of East London were in poverty according to the standards used, and only 1¼ per cent were classified as loafers, criminals,
and semicriminals.

The remaining Classes, E, F, G, and H, comprising 577,000
persons, or 65 per cent of the East London population, were as
follows: Class E, with regular standard earnings from 22s. to 30s. per
week, 42 per cent; Class F, the best paid of the artisans earning from
30s. to 50s. per week, 13½ per cent; Class G, lower middle class, shopkeepers, small employers, clerks, and subordinate professional men, 4
per cent; Class H, upper middle class employing servants, 5 per cent.

In Volume II of the Poverty Series Booth covered the entire
population of London, estimated at over four million people, and
found altogether 30.7 per cent in poverty. He discovered also that
31.5 per cent lived under crowded conditions with two or more
persons per room, or else were resident in common lodging houses.[22]

Booth's study, the findings of which have been so briefly outlined
here, is notable for its comprehensiveness, its pioneering methods
of detailed analysis, and its dispassionate and carefully qualified
statements. The scientific approach requires a determination to
accumulate all pertinent data, to weigh all evidence, to render all
interpretations just and accurate, and to make no generalizations
which are not warranted by the data assembled. By these criteria
Booth's *Life and Labour of the People in London* is commonly conceded
to be the first truly scientific study of urban conditions of poverty.

Rowntree's Survey of York.—Following closely Booth's method
so as to make interurban comparisons possible, B. Seebohm Rowntree, in 1899, conducted an investigation upon social conditions in
the city of York, England. It was first published in 1901 under the
title *Poverty; A Study of Town Life*.[23] This research profited at every
point by the previous experience of Booth, but made sharper distinctions among types and causes of poverty and examined more
deeply into costs of living, housing, recreation, and various other
factors of the urban life of industrial workers.

[22] *Op. cit.*, Vol. II, and also Final Volume, pp. 9–10.
[23] Rowntree, B. Seebohm—*Poverty; A Study of Town Life;* Macmillan and Co.,
Limited, 1901. For methodology see particularly Chapters I, II, III, VIII, and
IX.

York was a provincial city, primarily industrial, which at the time of the investigation had a population of about 76,000 persons. Rowntree's study was more intensive than that conducted by Booth, for his investigators actually visited the homes of 11,560 families comprising 46,754 individuals, or nearly two-thirds of the population. Most of the inhabitants lived in separate houses, as the few tenements were confined to the central portions of the city. A railway company was the largest employer. There was no predominating industry, but between two and three thousand persons were employed in cocoa and confectionary works. The investigation did not include the servant-keeping class, nor did it cover all persons engaged in domestic service. It was, however, virtually complete for the industrial population. The house-to-house canvass secured precise data regarding many particulars of housing and occupation, supplemented by remarks indicating family status or conditions of living. Although often it was possible to obtain direct information regarding wages, the family earnings in general had to be estimated.

Rowntree divided his population into classes in a manner different from that employed by Booth. He found 2.6 per cent of the whole population in his Class A, earning under 18s. per week; in Class B, with family income of from 18s. to (but not including) 21s., 5.9 per cent; in Class C, 21s. and under 30s., 20.7 per cent of the population. By close calculation, the minimum weekly expenditure upon which physical efficiency could be maintained in York at that time for a family of father, mother, and three children, was found to be 21s. 8d., of which 12s. 9d. was allowed for food, 4s. for rent, and 4s. 11d. for clothing, light, fuel, etc. The weekly allowance of 21s. 8d. permitted no expenditure of any kind beyond what was "absolutely necessary for the maintenance of merely physical efficiency." [24]

Distinguishing between primary poverty, where total earnings are insufficient to obtain the minimum necessaries for the maintenance of merely physical efficiency, from secondary poverty in which earnings would be sufficient for maintenance were not some portion of them applied to savings or to wasteful expenditure, Rowntree found 9.91 per cent of the population of York in primary poverty and 17.93 per cent in secondary poverty.

The percentage of the population of York below the poverty line

[24] *Ibid.*, p. 297 of 1908 edition.

corresponded very closely to that discovered by Booth in London. The percentages were 27.84 for York as compared with 30.7 for London.

Surveys of Industrial Cities: Bowley.—Following approximately the same methods of study, but with further statistical refinements, Professor A. L. Bowley and A. R. Burnett-Hurst examined this same problem in five other English industrial cities, Reading, Northampton, Warrington, Bolton, and Stanley, in 1913. Poverty rates were found to be lower than in York.[25] Ten years later Professor Bowley and Margaret H. Hogg, in a volume entitled *Has Poverty Diminished?* repeated the examination of these same industrial cities. In the intervening years the wages of unskilled workers had approximately doubled while there had been only a 70 per cent increase in the cost of the minimum standard of life. The percentage of families in poverty had consequently declined; though they found it still true that one child in every six was below the poverty line at some period of his youth.[26]

London Resurveyed.—The value of comparative studies is made still further apparent by *The New Survey of London Life and Labour*, undertaken by the London School of Economics and Political Science under the direction of Sir Hubert Llewellyn Smith in 1928.[27] Forty years had elapsed since the beginning of the investigation by Charles Booth. Sir H. Llewellyn Smith had been associated with Booth in the earlier study and was thus able closely to approximate the standards and methods utilized so that the new data would be comparable with those of the earlier period. The progress of statistical and social science in the intervening years,

[25] Bowley, A. L., and Burnett-Hurst, A. R.—*Livelihood and Poverty;* G. Bell and Sons, Ltd., 1915.

[26] Bowley, A. L., and Hogg, Margaret H.—*Has Poverty Diminished?* especially pp. 20–25; P. S. King & Son, Ltd., 1925. Other British and Irish social surveys, each of which offers some definite contribution to our knowledge of the conditions, causes, or effects of poverty, will be found in the list of references following this chapter. The most voluminous study of poverty and major reference for its period is the *Report of Royal Commission on the Poor Laws and Relief of Distress* which is accompanied by thirty-three volumes of evidence and appendices including many original studies. It was published in London in 1909–10. See also Great Britain, Board of Trade—*Cost of Living of the Working Classes*—Report of an inquiry into workingclass rents, housing and retail prices, with the standard rates of wages in the principal industrial towns of the United Kingdom; London, 1898 (Cd. 3864).

[27] *The New Survey of London Life and Labour*, nine volumes; P. S. King & Son, Ltd., 1930–35.

however, made possible at some points more complete data and greater precision.

One of the methods employed between 1928 and 1930 in the New Survey was to examine a random sample of workingclass households, covering twelve thousand in all. The study was so organized as to make possible comparisons with the original survey by Charles Booth and with the two surveys by Professor Bowley. A second investigation was a "street survey" following more closely Booth's methods and covering conditions of approximately twenty-six thousand families with school children, using information from school attendance officers supplemented by other sources such as the boards of guardians, employment exchanges, and the police. The street survey and the house sample inquiry revealed that the percentage of the population below the poverty line, by standards approximating those of Booth, was only about one-third that found by Booth forty years before. Overcrowding rates, however, continued high because of the housing shortage. In the Eastern Survey Area twenty-six per cent of the population were still living two or more to a room.[28] In brief, one person in ten in the Eastern Survey Area, which comprised six more boroughs than Booth's East London, and one person in seven of those now living in the latter area, were in poverty in the sense that they suffered from privation "which if long continued would deny them all but the barest necessities, and cut them off from access to many of the material and cultural benefits of modern progress."[29]

Nearly half of these were poor because of unemployment or underemployment. Low wages and old age were responsible for less poverty than in Booth's time. Destitution had been greatly reduced by the development of social legislation and especially social insurance in the intervening years. If, however, the dividing line for poverty had been so drawn as to place among the poor those whose purchasing power is not greater than that of the unskilled worker, three-quarters of the population of Booth's East London would have been placed below the poverty line in his day and one-half would be found there today.[30]

A Regional Social Survey: Merseyside.—Outstanding among the general urban surveys, for its inclusiveness, is the *Survey of Mersey-*

[28] *Ibid.*, Vol. III, p. 20, and p. 228.
[29] *Ibid.*, Vol. III, p. 8.
[30] *Ibid.*, Vol. III, p. 12.

side.[31] This study was undertaken by the University of Liverpool with the assistance of the Rockefeller Foundation of America. Professor A. M. Carr-Saunders served as chairman of the survey committee, and Mr. D. Caradog Jones as its director. Material was gathered between the years 1929 and 1932 not only for the city of Liverpool but for the contiguous area comprising in all four county boroughs and six urban districts. The first volume dealt primarily with the development of the area, the distribution and composition of the population, incomes, and expenditures, and problems of poverty, overcrowding, and municipal housing. The second volume covered conditions of labor and industry. The third included detailed studies of health, education, recreation, and religion, and of infants, school children, adolescents, families, and pensioners. Unlike preceding surveys, it also closely analyzed the problems of each of the subnormal groups, the deafmutes, the blind, feebleminded, crippled, and the destitute together with the related problems of public administration.

Having determined the minimum net income requisite to keep a given family out of poverty, it was found that 16.1 per cent of the total families sampled were below the poverty line and that practically one-half of the families lacking any wage-earner were in poverty. Overcrowding was found in 10.8 per cent of the families sampled. Like the New Survey of London, the Merseyside investigation justified the inference that destitution today is not normally due to lowness of wage rates but to unemployment or underemployment.[32]

Summary.—A close examination of social investigation in England and neighboring countries reveals (1) that scientific study of poverty has existed for less than a century and a half; (2) that methodologies of research have improved; (3) that the more intensive investigations have covered but a limited area—chiefly metropolitan or industrial communities; (4) that special difficulties in the assembling of data have rendered it impossible to make accurate detailed studies of incomes and expenditures over large areas; (5) that the costs of a comprehensive national survey of poverty that would cover all pertinent data would be prohibitive; and (6) that for the present one must rely upon sampling as a chief

[31] Jones, D. Caradog, editor—*The Social Survey of Merseyside*, three volumes; University Press of Liverpool, Hodder & Stoughton Ltd., 1934.
[32] *Ibid.*, Vol. I, pp. 166–167.

source of inferences concerning the nature, incidence, causes, and social consequences of poverty.

QUESTIONS FOR DISCUSSION OR EXAMINATION

1. How do you account for the late beginnings of social research?
2. Trace the development of studies of family budgets from 1795.
3. Trace the development of urban social surveys.
4. How do you account for the apparent reduction of the volume of urban poverty in England since Booth's first study?
5. How and where has the poverty line been drawn? Where should it be drawn?
6. What are the relative merits of the regional survey as compared with the community survey?

PROBLEMS FOR INDIVIDUAL STUDY

1. Analyze available data *re* poverty for a selected country and period (*e.g.* seventeenth century England) with reference to (a) methodology, (b) findings.
2. Compare any two of the studies listed in the book references from the point of view of (a) the methods of study employed, (b) the classification of subject matter employed, (c) the findings concerning poverty.
3. A critical examination of the methodology of Le Play, Rowntree, or of the more recent surveys of London, or Merseyside.
4. Exposition of Engel's law, and of the criticisms and modifications of the law made by subsequent students of family budgets.
5. History of census taking in England or other selected country, with special attention to the collection by governments of data essential to the study of social pathology.

SUGGESTIONS FOR SUPPLEMENTARY READINGS

Bell (Florence), Lady—*At the Works: A Study of a Manufacturing Town* [Middlesborough]; Edward Arnold (London), 1907.

Booth, Charles—*Life and Labour of the People in London*, seventeen volumes; Macmillan and Co., Limited, 1902.

Bowley, A. L.—*The Nature and Purpose of Measurement of Social Phenomena;* P. S. King & Son, Ltd., 1915.

Bowley, A. L., and Burnett-Hurst, A. R.—*Livelihood and Poverty;* G. Bell and Sons, Ltd., 1915.

Bowley, A. L., and Hogg, Margaret H.—*Has Poverty Diminished?;* P. S. King & Son, Ltd., 1925.

Bradford—*The Texture of Welfare: a Survey of Social Service in Bradford;* Bradford Council of Social Service (London), 1923.

Branford, Sybella, and Farquharson, Alexander—*An Introduction to Regional Surveys;* The Le Play House Press, 1924.

Brindley, W. H.—*The Soul of Manchester;* Manchester University Press, 1929.

Butler, C. V.—*Social Conditions in Oxford;* Sidgwick & Jackson (London), 1912.

Cadbury, Edward, Matheson, M. Cécile, and Shann, George—*Women's Work and Wages: a Phase of Life in an Industrial City;* T. Fisher Unwin (London), 1906.

Cathcart, E. P., and Murray, A. M. T.—*Studies in Nutrition: an Inquiry into the Diet of Families in Cardiff and Reading;* H. M. Stationery Office (Medical Research Council, Special Report Series, No. 165), 1932.

Cathcart, E. P., and Murray, A. M. T., assisted by Shanks, M.—*A Study in Nutrition: an Inquiry into the Diet of 154 Families of St. Andrew's;* H. M. Stationery Office (Medical Research Council, Special Report Series, No. 151), 1931.

Crawford, A. F. Sharman—*Cork: A Civic Survey;* Hodder & Stoughton Ltd., 1926.

Curzon, Emmanuel P. de—*Frédéric Le Play, sa méthode, sa doctrine, son oeuvre, son esprit, d'après ses écrits et sa correspondance;* H. Oudin (Poitiers, et Paris), 1899.

Davies, Rev. David—*The Case of Labourers in Husbandry, Stated and Considered;* G. G. and J. Robinson (London), 1795.

Dundee Social Union, Social Inquiry Committee—*Report of Investigation into Social Conditions in Dundee;* J. Leng & Co. (Dundee), 1905.

Eden, Sir Frederick Morton—*The State of the Poor;* E. P. Dutton & Co., 1929.

Edinburgh, City of, Charity Organization Society—*Report on the Physical Condition of Fourteen Hundred School Children in the City; Together with Some Account of Their Homes and Surroundings;* P. S. King & Son, Ltd., 1906.

Engel, Ernst—"Die Lebenskosten belgischer Arbeiter-Familien früher und jetzt"; *Bulletin de l'Institut International de Statistique,* Vol. IX, 1895.

Evans, R.—*Unemployment in Hull. 1923–31;* Hull Community Council, 1933.

Farquharson, Alexander—"Survey of Social Conditions and Problems in Margate"; *Sociological Review,* Vol. XXI, Nos. 1 and 2, 1929.

Ford, P.—*Work and Wealth in a Modern Port: an Economic Survey of Southampton;* George Allen & Unwin Ltd., 1934.

Garbett, Cyril F.—*In the Heart of South London;* Longmans, Green and Co., 1931.

Geddes, Patrick—*Cities in Evolution* (chapters on the "Survey of Cities" and "City Survey for Town Planning Purposes, of Municipalities and Governments"); Williams & Norgate, Ltd., 1915.

Gilchrist, E. J.—*Ipswich: A Survey of the Town;* Ipswich Local Committee of the Conference on Christian Politics, Economics and Citizenship, 1924.

Hanham, F. G.—*Report of Inquiry into Casual Labour in the Merseyside Area;* Henry Young & Sons, Ltd., 1930.

Hankins, Frank H.—*Adolphe Quételet as Statistician;* Columbia University, Longmans, Green and Co., Agents, 1908.

Hawkins, C. B.—*Norwich: A Social Study;* Philip Lee Warner, 1910.

Hornsey Council of Social Welfare—*Hornsey Social Survey;* Hornsey Council of Social Welfare, 1923.

Howarth, Edward G., and Wilson, Mona—*West Ham: A Study in Social and Industrial Problems;* J. M. Dent & Company, 1907.

Hull Community Council—*Social Services in Hull: being Institutions and Charitable Agencies of the City of Hull;* Hull Community Council, 1930.

International Labour Office—*Methods of Conducting Family Budget Inquiries;* International Labour Office Studies and Reports, Series N, No. 9, 1926.

Jebb, Eglantyne—*Cambridge: A Brief Study in Social Questions;* printed for Bowes & Bowes, 1908.

Jennings, Hilda—*Brynmawr: A Study of a Distressed Area;* Allenson & Co., Ltd. (London), 1934.

Jones, D. Caradog, editor—*The Social Survey of Merseyside,* three volumes; University Press of Liverpool, Hodder & Stoughton Ltd., 1934.

Le Play, Frédéric—*Les ouvriers européens,* six volumes; Alfred Mame et fils, second edition, 1879.

Liverpool Economic and Statistical Society—*How the Casual Labourer Lives;* Report of the Liverpool Joint Research Committee on the Domestic Conditions and Expenditure of the Families of Certain Liverpool Labourers, 1909.

Matheson, H. E.—*Social Service in Plymouth;* Civic Guild of Help (Plymouth), 1920.

Mayhew, Henry—*London Labour and the London Poor,* four volumes; Griffin, Bohn, and Company, 1861-62.

Mess, Henry A.—*Industrial Tyneside: A Social Survey made for the Bureau of Social Research for Tyneside;* Ernest Benn Ltd. (London), 1928.

Norwich—*The Destitute of Norwich and How They Live;* Jarrolds (London), 1912.

Orford, E. J.—*The Book of Walworth;* Browning Hall Adult School, 1925-26.

O'Rourke, Horace T.—*The Dublin Civic Survey;* Hodder & Stoughton Ltd., 1925.

Owen, A. D. K.—*Survey of the Standard of Living in Sheffield;* Social Survey Committee, Survey Pamphlet No. 9, June, 1933.

Rackstraw, Marjorie, editor—*A Social Survey of the City of Edinburgh;* Oliver and Boyd (Edinburgh), 1926.

Reeves, Magdalen Stuart—*Round About a Pound a Week;* G. Bell and Sons, Ltd., second edition, 1914.

Rowntree, B. Seebohm—*Poverty; A Study of Town Life;* Macmillan and Co., Limited, 1901.

Rowntree, B. Seebohm, and Lasker, Bruno—*Unemployment: a Social Study;* Macmillan and Co., Limited, 1911.

Sherwell, Arthur—*Life in West London: a Study and a Contrast;* Methuen & Co. (London), second edition, 1897.

Smith, Sir H. Llewellyn (Director)—*The New Survey of London Life and Labour,* nine volumes; P. S. King & Son, Ltd., 1930-35.

Société d'économie sociale—*Les ouvriers des deux mondes;* Au siége de la Société internationale (Paris), 1857-1913.

St. Philip's Settlement Education and Economics Research Society (Sheffield)—*The Equipment of the Workers: an Inquiry into the Adequacy of the Adult Manual Workers for the Discharge of Their Responsibility as Heads of Households, Producers and Citizens;* George Allen & Unwin Ltd., 1919.

Stow, John—*The Survey of London;* E. P. Dutton & Co., 1923.

Streightoff, Frank Hatch—*The Standard of Living among the Industrial People of America;* Houghton Mifflin Company, 1911.

Webb, Sidney and Beatrice—*Methods of Social Study;* Longmans, Green and Co., 1932.

Wells, A. F.—*The Local Social Survey in Great Britain;* published for The Sir Halley Stewart Trust by George Allen & Unwin Ltd., 1935.

Young, Terence—*Becontree and Dagenham: a Report made for the Pilgrim Trust;* Becontree Social Survey Committee, 1934.

Zimmerman, Carle C.—*Consumption and Standards of Living,* Chapter XV; D. Van Nostrand Company, Inc., 1936.

Zimmerman, Carle C., and Frampton, Merle E.—*Family and Society,* Chapters III–VII; D. Van Nostrand Company, Inc., 1935.

CHAPTER III

HISTORY OF SOCIAL SURVEYS IN THE UNITED STATES

Early Sources of Information.—In the American colonies though much legislation was passed relating to the care of the poor and the punishment of criminals, it was apparently framed with very little antecedent study. Information concerning the substandard groups of the seventeenth and eighteenth centuries can be gleaned from city, provincial, and colonial records, church records, diaries, letters, wills, and accounts. Large quantities of these have been assembled and republished in state and town histories. Evidence on the volume of poverty, the typical wages and cost of living of various periods, crime and its treatment, and the development of social legislation may be found in a number of social and economic histories which are readily accessible to the student.[1]

The United States offers no early comprehensive study of poverty like that of Sir Frederick Eden of England in 1797, and no early studies of budgets like those of Davies or Le Play. Textbooks ordinarily state that the history of social investigation in America begins with the Pittsburgh Survey in 1907. Nevertheless much illuminating material comes from the writings of the early foreign visitors, as for example, Brissot de Warville or Chastellux, and from local

---

[1] These include documentary histories by Albert Bushnell Hart and E. Channing; social histories by Arthur M. Schlesinger, Samuel Eliot Morison, and Charles and Mary Beard; economic histories by E. L. Bogart, N. S. B. Gras, Abbott Payson Usher, and Victor S. Clark; provincial, state, and local histories, such as Justin Winsor's *The Memorial History of Boston*, I. N. Phelps Stokes' *Iconography of Manhattan Island*, and William Babcock Weeden's *Economic and Social History of New England;* the documents of New Amsterdam and New Netherland, and similar provincial documents; Benjamin Franklin's *Autobiography*, *Diary of Philip Hone*, S. E. Sewall's *Diary*, and other early biographical writings; Robert W. Kelso's *History of Public Poor Relief in Massachusetts*, Frank Dekker Watson's *The Charity Organization Movement in the United States*, and similar poor relief histories; James Ford's *Slums and Housing*, Part I for the early history of housing conditions and policy; Gustavus Myers' *Ye Olden Blue Laws*, and similar historical treatments of crime and punishment; Arthur W. Calhoun and George Elliott Howard on the history of the American family and matrimonial institutions.

observations and travels such as those of Crèvecœur and Dwight.[2] Somewhat later are the American notes of Harriet Martineau and of Charles Dickens. In addition there are the studies and writings of persons who worked among the poor such as Charles Loring Brace, Mathew Carey, Dorothea Dix, Ezra S. Ely, John H. Griscom, Samuel B. Halliday, James Hardie, Samuel Gridley Howe, Lewis E. Jackson, Josephine Shaw Lowell, Joseph Tuckerman, and other eminent figures.

There are also several useful studies based upon considerable direct observations by private organizations such as the Association for Improving the Condition of the Poor since 1845, the Charity Organization Society of New York City since 1882; and many reports of public commissions such as that on Pestilential Disease which reported to the Common Council of New York City on January 21, 1799; the Boston Committee on the Expediency of Providing Better Tenements for the Poor, June 2, 1846; the Report of the Select Committee appointed to examine into the condition of Tenant Houses in New York and Brooklyn, 1857; the Report of the Council of Hygiene and Public Health of the Citizens Association of New York, 1865; the Report of the Tenement-House Commission of New York of 1884; and that of the Tenement House Committee of New York of 1894.

The Federal Census.—The decennial census has been America's major source of basic social data since its inauguration in 1790. Article I of the Constitution expressly provided for the collecting of statistics of population within three years after the first meeting of the Congress of the United States and within every subsequent term of ten years. The decennial censuses at first were little more than a geographical enumeration of population though they did from the beginning differentiate whites and Negroes, males and females, and the population over sixteen years of age. But by the

---

[2] The observations of travellers include among others the writings of Thomas Auburey; Mark Beaufoy; Bernard, Duke of Saxe-Weimar; James Birket; William N. Blane; Fredrika Bremer; Jacques Pierre Brissot de Warville; François Jean, Marquis de Chastellux; William Cobbett; J. H. St. Jean de Crèvecœur; John Drayton; John M. Duncan; Timothy Dwight; Henry B. Fearon; Mrs. Felton; Francis Hall; Peter Kalm; John Lambert; F. A. F. La Rochefoucault Liancourt; Harriet Martineau; John Melish; E. Montule; Peter Neilson; Josiah Quincy; Robert Sutcliff; Frances M. Trollope; Henry Wansey; Richard Weston; W. Winterbotham; and Charles Wolley. Other references will be found in the works mentioned in footnote 1. See Nevins, Allan, compiler and editor—*American Social History as Recorded by British Travellers;* Henry Holt and Company, 1923.

middle of the last century the recorded data were fairly elaborate and at many points the statistical data collected by the Bureau of the Census, established in 1902, compare most favorably for their comprehensiveness with those of other leading nations of the world.

Special statistical data have been gathered concerning some of the maladjusted groups of the population for more than a century. Enumeration for blind and deaf began in 1830, of the insane and feebleminded in 1840, of paupers and of prisoners in 1850. In this latter year, also, data on births and deaths were recorded and special material was collected concerning religious agencies. Illiteracy and school attendance have been covered by the census since 1840. There was special enumeration of Indians and Chinese from 1860, and of the Japanese from 1870.

Extensions of the Federal function of fact finding, through both the Bureau of the Census and other branches of government, have been greatest within the past half century. Thus morbidity statistics have been published since 1878, first by the Marine Hospital Service, and in more recent years by the United States Public Health Service. There have been data concerning juvenile delinquency since 1880, marriage and divorce since 1889 but going back to 1867, special studies of wages intermittently since 1881, benevolent institutions since 1904, and incomes since 1914. Although the data, whether on wages and incomes or on the paupers, feebleminded, and insane, may be far from complete, they yield much of fundamental importance when utilized in conjunction with the general data on population and occupations, or with intensive local surveys conducted under private or local public auspices.[3]

Settlement Studies.—The social survey began with the settlement movement, in the eighteen nineties. Modelling their purposes and activities upon Toynbee Hall, founded in London in 1884, a number of university trained men and women in America determined to take up residence in the slums of their cities, identify their

[3] The publications of the United States Bureau of the Census include a large number of special studies in addition to the general population census. Their methods of study are usually sketched in the introductions to their various publications. A valuable outline of the work of the various statistical branches of the Federal government will be found in Schmeckebier, Laurence F.—*The Statistical Work of the National Government;* The Institute for Government Research, The Johns Hopkins Press, 1925: also in other publications of the Institute for Government Research.

lives with those of their poorer neighbors, and work coöperatively with them for the improvement of the conditions of life within their districts. The first settlement house in America was the Neighborhood Guild, now known as the University Settlement of New York, founded in 1886 under the direction of Stanton Coit. The second was the College Settlement established in New York by Jean G. Fine (Mrs. Charles B. Spahr) with the help of Vida D. Scudder in 1889. The third was Hull House in Chicago, in 1889, under the direction of Jane Addams and Ellen G. Starr. The fourth was Andover House, now South End House, established in Boston, 1891, by Professor William J. Tucker, with Robert A. Woods as head resident.[4]

It was immediately recognized by settlement workers that they must understand the conditions with which they were surrounded, in order to cope with them. Thus a number of studies were undertaken by university trained people upon problems of poverty, industry, and delinquency during the early eighteen nineties. The more significant of these were often published in the researches of Federal, state, or local governments concerning conditions of labor, health, housing, public recreation, or poverty.[5]

Surveys of Boston.—As examples of the best of urban social studies made by settlement workers one may mention *The City Wilderness* and *Americans in Process*, which dealt respectively with the South End, and the North and West Ends of Boston. Each incorporated the results of many years of field observation, inter-

[4] Woods, Robert A., and Kennedy, Albert J., editors—*Handbook of Settlements;* Charities Publication Committee, Russell Sage Foundation, 1911.

[5] Hull House, for example, took part in the following studies between 1892 and 1910: "In 1892, Investigation of the Sweating System for the State Bureau of Labor Statistics; 1893, The Slums of Great Cities (Chicago) for Department of Labor (Washington); Dietary Investigation for Department of Agriculture (Washington); 1895, Publication of Hull-House Maps and Papers, Studies in Ward and City Conditions; 1896, Investigation of the Saloons of the Nineteenth Ward for Committee of Fifty; 1897, Investigation of the Dietary of the Italian Colony for Department of Agriculture (Washington); General Study of 19th Ward for Ethical Society; 1903, Study of Casual Labor on the Lakes; 1905, An Intensive Study of the Causes of Truancy; Study of Tuberculosis in Chicago; 1907, Investigation into the Selling of Cocaine; 1908, Study of Midwifery (Coöperation with Chicago Medical Society), and Study of the Greeks in Chicago; 1909, Study of Infantile Mortality among Selected Immigrant Groups; 1910, Investigation of the Home Reading of Public School Children."—*Ibid.*, p. 54.

See also *Hull-House Maps and Papers: A Presentation of Nationalities and Wages in a Congested District of Chicago, together with Comments and Essays on Problems Growing out of the Social Conditions,* by Residents of Hull-House; Thomas Y. Crowell & Co., 1895.

views, and analysis of public records.[6] Each discussed the history
of its district, problems of immigration and racial succession, wages
and conditions of labor, health and housing, education and the uses
of leisure, delinquency and problems of citizenship or government,
and the work of local social agencies. Each mapped, street by
street, the nationalities, the industrial character of the population,
and the local institutions for social service.

In the South End fully one-sixth of the families were found to be
in receipt of some form of material aid from charities in the course of
the year, though one-fourth of the people, having family incomes
under $10 per week, were "in the strict sense poor." [7]

Americans in Process reported concerning dependency that "about
twelve per cent. of the population in the North End, and about nine
per cent. in the West End, have received some form of charitable
relief within the past two years. These proportions would include
practically all of those who belong distinctly to the grades of casual
and intermittent workers, together with tramps, loafers, and semi-
criminals. These three lowest types, judging from returns made
by proprietors of cheap lodging-houses for the police records, may
be estimated at three per cent. for the North End and two per cent.
for the West End." [8]

Viewing poverty in the sense of economic insufficiency the authors concluded "about thirty per cent. of West End people, and
about forty per cent. of North End people, are below the line of
poverty as set by Charles Booth in his London studies. The part of
the South End described in *The City Wilderness* stands a few points
higher than the West End. In London there are about thirty districts, each having as many inhabitants as the North End, that
stand lower than it on the scale of poverty, and nearly seventy that
stand lower than the West End." [9]

The Pittsburgh Survey.—Comprehensive and systematic urban
studies, other than those made by settlement workers, were not,
however, made in America until about twenty years after the initiation of Booth's study of *Life and Labour of the People in London*. Then,
with the financial assistance of the Russell Sage Foundation, estab-

[6] Woods, Robert A., editor—*The City Wilderness: A Settlement Study;* Houghton
Mifflin Company, 1899. Woods, Robert A., editor—*Americans in Process: A
Settlement Study;* Houghton Mifflin Company, 1902.
[7] Woods, Robert A., editor—*The City Wilderness,* pp. 249 and 296.
[8] Woods, Robert A., editor—*Americans in Process,* p. 135.
[9] *Ibid.,* p. 137.

lished in 1907, Pittsburgh, Pennsylvania, a city of sharp social contrasts, was closely examined. The investigation was under the direction of Paul U. Kellogg, at that time editor of *Charities and Commons*.[10]
The survey was conducted primarily between the years 1907 and
1909 though its final volume did not appear until 1914.

Unlike Booth's study of London, the initial purpose was not primarily to ascertain the volume of poverty. Instead, the interest centered about the conditions of labor: questions of hours of work,
wages, accidents, and industrial relations. Incidental studies were
made, however, of family budgets, dependent children, housing,
health, and sanitation with emphasis upon the urgent problems of
typhoid fever, crime and the courts, institutional needs, schooling, recreation, city planning, taxation, and civic organization.
Miss Margaret F. Byington's investigation of Homestead, an industrial suburb, is, however, still one of America's best examples of a
well-rounded urban social survey, while graphically portraying the
manner in which the local mills overshadow the home and civic
life of the population as well as their working hours.[11]

When one contrasts the Pittsburgh survey with Booth's study of
London one is impressed with the vivid style of the American study,
its emphasis, at times almost journalistic, upon the most shocking
conditions of life and labor, and its obvious interest in reform.
Nevertheless, care was exercised to secure abundant and accurate
data on all matters covered. The result was a survey selective in its
emphasis, less well rounded than the urban surveys of London or
York, but graphic and effectual.

Its major findings in the field of social pathology were outlined
by Edward T. Devine in the final volume as follows:

"I. An altogether incredible amount of overwork by everybody,
reaching its extreme in the twelve-hour shift for seven days in the week in
the steel mills and the railway switchyards.

"II. Low wages for the great majority of the laborers employed by the

[10] Now known as *The Survey*, a major professional publication for social
workers.

[11] The findings of the Pittsburgh survey were published in six volumes:
Women and the Trades, by Elizabeth Beardsley Butler, 1909; *Work-Accidents and
the Law*, by Crystal Eastman, 1910; *The Steel Workers*, by John A. Fitch, 1910;
Homestead: The Households of a Mill Town, by Margaret F. Byington, 1910;
Wage-earning Pittsburgh and *The Pittsburgh District: Civic Frontage*, both edited by
Edward T. Devine. The first four were published by Charities Publication Com-
mittee, Russell Sage Foundation, the last two by Survey Associates, Russell Sage
Foundation, 1914.

mills, not lower than in other large cities, but low compared with prices, —so low as to be inadequate to the maintenance of a normal American standard of living; wages adjusted to the single man in the lodging house, not to the responsible head of a family.

"III. Still lower wages for women, who receive for example in one of the metal trades, in which the proportion of women is great enough to be menacing, one half as much as unorganized men in the same shops and one third as much as the men in the union.

"IV. An absentee capitalism, with effects strikingly analogous to those of absentee landlordism, of which also Pittsburgh furnishes examples.

"V. A continuous inflow of immigrants with low standards, attracted by a wage which is high by the standards of southeastern Europe, and which yields a net pecuniary advantage because of abnormally low expenditures for food and shelter, and inadequate provision for the contingencies of sickness, accident, and death.

"VI. The destruction of family life, not in any imaginary or mystical sense, but by the demands of the day's work, and by the very demonstrable and material method of typhoid fever and industrial accidents; both preventable, but costing in single years in Pittsburgh considerably more than a thousand lives, and irretrievably shattering nearly as many homes.

"VII. Archaic social institutions, such as the aldermanic court, the ward school district, the family garbage disposal, and the unregenerate charitable institution, still surviving after the conditions to which they were adapted have disappeared.

"VIII. The contrast—which does not become blurred by familiarity with any detail— . . . between the prosperity on the one hand of the most prosperous of all the communities of our western civilization, with its vast natural resources, the generous fostering of government, the human energy, the technical development, the gigantic tonnage of the mines and mills, the enormous capital of which the bank balances afford an indication; and on the other hand the neglect of life, of health, of physical vigor, even of the industrial efficiency of the individual. Certainly no community before in America or Europe has ever had such a surplus, and never before has a great community applied what it had so meagerly to the rational purposes of human life. Not by gifts of libraries, galleries, technical schools, and parks, but by the cessation of toil one day in seven and sixteen hours in the twenty-four, by the increase of wages, by the sparing of lives, by the prevention of accidents, and by raising the standards of domestic life, should the surplus come back to the people of the community in which it is created." [12]

[12] *The Pittsburgh District: Civic Frontage*, pp. 3–4. Subsequent studies and reports on conditions of Pittsburgh have been published by the Interchurch World Federation, Senate Investigation Committees, the University of Pittsburgh Bureau of Economic Research, the Mellon Institute, and the Buhl Foundation. A recent widely inclusive investigation of the community problems and social services of Allegheny County is contained in Klein, Philip—*A Social Study of Pittsburgh;* Columbia University Press, 1938.

Development of Local Surveys.—The value of accurate knowledge of local conditions and problems, and the importance of basing social policies upon full knowledge of conditions, were made apparent by the Pittsburgh survey. In the years following the publication of these volumes the demand for local studies became so great that the Russell Sage Foundation established a Department of Surveys and Exhibits, under the direction of Shelby M. Harrison, who had served on the Pittsburgh survey staff. This Department became an advisory center for such studies throughout the nation and developed survey techniques. Its first investigations were in Scranton, Pennsylvania, Newburgh, New York, and Topeka, Kansas: but its outstanding survey was that of Springfield, Illinois, in 1914.

The Springfield Survey.—Springfield was at that time a capital city of about sixty thousand population. The investigation covered the city's major social problems under nine categories, in each instance examining the extent of the problem and the legislation, agencies, and institutions devised to meet it. It thus covered poverty and the public and private welfare agencies; the care of defectives and the handicapped; delinquency, crime, and the courts and prisons; education and the schools; recreation, housing, industrial conditions; and the administration of the city and county governments. Local records were carefully analyzed; supplementary data were gathered through special investigation; institutions were visited and appraised. Research in each of these fields was followed by interpretation of the data and recommendations for future organization and action.[13]

The findings of the Springfield survey in the field of social pathology displayed inadequate schooling; low wages and incomes, inferior institutional provision for dealing with poverty, defectiveness, physical and mental disease, alcoholism, vice, and criminality; and many defects in public administration.

As the Springfield survey was made upon the request of local citizens and organizations, it was possible to secure the coöperation of over nine hundred citizens as volunteer workers. A feature of exceptional merit from the point of view of social policy was the practice of issuing the nine reports individually. This made it possible for each report to receive its proper emphasis in the minds of the local residents. A committee of citizens and specialists was organ-

[13] Harrison, Shelby M.—*Social Conditions in an American City: A Summary of the Findings of the Springfield Survey;* Russell Sage Foundation, 1920.

ized to follow up the recommendations, whether relating to dependency, crime, defectives, or health, before the next section of the survey was publicized. In other cities it has been found that publication of the findings of a comprehensive investigation as a unit has so overwhelmed the people as to make action difficult. Harrison's method in Springfield has demonstrated its practicality and social utility.

Cleveland Surveys.—Cleveland is one of the best surveyed cities of America. Instead, however, of making a single comprehensive survey of all social problems and institutions at one time, Cleveland has promoted a succession of intensive, specialized investigations.

The first of these was the survey of education conducted under the direction of Dr. Leonard P. Ayres. The problem of education was divided for study into twenty-three subtopics, each treated in a separate monograph. These dealt with school statistics, size of classes, retardation and truancy, school buildings and equipment, organization and administration, the platoon plan, the teaching staff, classes for exceptional children, the school and the immigrant, educational extension, education through recreation, health work in the schools, household arts, school lunches, the public library, the curriculum, vocational training, financing, and measurement of the work of the schools. The monographic volumes were summarized by Dr. Ayres in a volume entitled *The Cleveland School Survey*, and by R. R. Lutz in another entitled *Wage Earning and Education*.[14]

Next followed the Cleveland survey of recreation, which, in seven volumes published between 1916 and 1920, covered the uses made by citizens of their leisure time, the commercialized recreations, and the service rendered by philanthropic and public agencies.[15]

This project was followed by a study of health and hospitals in 1920, under the direction of Dr. Haven Emerson. In a series of eleven monographs the conditions and social resources were closely examined and pertinent recommendations offered.[16]

[14] Ayres, Leonard P.—*The Cleveland School Survey* (summary volume); The Cleveland Foundation, 1916.

[15] Thurston, Henry W.—*Delinquency and Spare Time;* 1918. Bonser, F. G.—*School Work and Spare Time;* 1918. Gillin, John L.—*Wholesome Citizens and Spare Time;* 1918. Haynes, Rowland, and others—*The Sphere of Private Agencies;* 1920. Rumbold, Charlotte, and Moley, Raymond—*Commercial Recreation;* 1920. Haynes, Rowland, and Davies, Stanley P.—*Public Provision for Recreation;* 1920. Haynes, Rowland, and Matson, Carlton K.—*A Community Recreation Program;* 1920. Publisher—The Cleveland Foundation.

[16] *The Cleveland Hospital and Health Survey Report.* List of Parts and Titles—

The Cleveland crime survey was directed by Dean Roscoe Pound and Professor Felix Frankfurter of the Harvard Law School, and was published in 1922 under the title *Criminal Justice in Cleveland*. It contained detailed studies of police administration, prosecution, the courts, penal treatment, and of medical science, psychiatry, legal education, and publicity in their relations to the administration of criminal justice in Cleveland.[17]

A significant feature of the Cleveland studies is that they grew out of manifest need, discovered by discussions in the Cleveland welfare agencies and were, except for the health survey, financed by the Cleveland Foundation, the earliest and one of the best endowed of America's community trusts. The agencies for social service and public welfare in Cleveland are so well organized and experienced that the findings of local studies have been exceptionally well followed up by appropriate planning and action.

In recent years Cleveland, like other American cities, has continued the process of self-investigation, not by elaborate comprehensive series of monographs like the above so much as by individual researches in highly specialized fields. To mention but a single example, the real property inventory made in Cleveland in 1933, by Howard Whipple Green, provided America's first complete local compendium of detailed knowledge of social interest concerning the economic and social aspects of the ownership and use of real estate.[18]

I. Introduction. General Environment. Sanitation. II. Public Health Services. Private Health Agencies. III. A Program for Child Health. IV. Tuberculosis. V. Venereal Disease. VI. Mental Diseases and Mental Deficiency. VII. Industrial Medical Service. Women and Industry. Children and Industry. VIII. Education and Practice in Medicine, Dentistry, Pharmacy. IX. Nursing. X. Hospitals and Dispensaries. XI. Method of Survey. Bibliography of Surveys. Index. Published by The Cleveland Hospital Council.

[17] *Criminal Justice in Cleveland: Reports of the Cleveland Foundation Survey of the Administration of Criminal Justice in Cleveland, Ohio*, Directed and edited by Roscoe Pound and Felix Frankfurter: Part I. Police Administration, by Raymond B. Fosdick; Part II. Prosecution, by Alfred Bettman, assisted by Howard F. Burns; Part III. The Criminal Courts, by Reginald Heber Smith and Herbert B. Ehrmann; Part IV. Correctional and Penal Treatment, by Burdette G. Lewis; Part V. Medical Science and Criminal Justice, by Herman M. Adler, M. D.; Part VI. Legal Education in Cleveland, by Albert M. Kales; Part VII. Newspapers and Criminal Justice, by M. K. Wisehart; Part VIII. Criminal Justice and the American City, by Roscoe Pound; published by The Cleveland Foundation, 1922.

[18] Green, Howard Whipple—*Real Property Inventory of the Cleveland Metropolitan District;* Committee on Real Property Inventory, 1933.

Real Property Inventories.—The value of the Cleveland Real Property Inventory was so significant as to lead the Federal government, through its Department of Commerce in 1934, to conduct similar studies in sixty-four American cities. The findings of real property inventories from the point of view of social pathology may be briefly summarized as follows:

"According to final figures, 34,841 buildings, or 2.3 per cent of the structural units in the 64 cities were in the 'unfit for use' class, and 235,-353, or 15.8 per cent in the class needing structural repairs. The combined group are, therefore, 18.1 per cent of the total. The number of dwelling units in each class would be about 1.4 greater, if the ratio of dwelling units to structures in these classes is average. It is almost certainly higher.

"The summary shows that 16.8 per cent of the occupied dwelling units (not structural units) were crowded or worse, that 13.5 per cent of all dwelling units lacked private indoor toilets, 20.2 per cent had neither bathtubs nor showers, 8.1 per cent lacked modern lighting, and 5.0 per cent were without running water.

"It cannot be demonstrated that these percentages are overlapping and refer to the same houses, but to a large extent they undoubtedly do. The figures vary widely from city to city, but in every city bad housing is present. . . .

"The picture emerging will be of nearly a fifth of our urban population living in dilapidated houses, generally crowded, and typically lacking private indoor toilets and bathtubs. Nearly half of these substandard homes are also without electric lights and about a quarter of them have no running water. More fortunate than this class are a borderline group who live in structurally sound homes, needing paint and other minor repairs, and lacking baths and water closets." [19]

Chicago Studies.—Many cities have experienced intensive study by local universities under the direction of departments of economics, political science, sociology, and social work. As an example, the examination of the social conditions of Chicago made by members of the staff of the University of Chicago and their candidates for higher degrees may be mentioned. In earlier years, stimulated by Professors Albion W. Small and C. R. Henderson, and more particularly in later years, under the guidance of Robert E. Park, Ernest W. Burgess, Sophonisba P. Breckinridge, and Edith Abbott, many of

[19] Wood, Edith Elmer—*Slums and Blighted Areas in the United States*, pp. 84 and 86; Federal Emergency Administration of Public Works, Housing Division Bulletin No. 1, Government Printing Office, 1935.

America's most significant original studies of problems in the field of social pathology have been made.[20]

New York Studies.—New York City has benefited by highly intensive surveys undertaken by universities, foundations, social agencies, and public departments too numerous to outline here.[21]

Professor Giddings of Columbia University in 1901 published his *Inductive Sociology* which became the methodological guide for sociological surveys in New York City and elsewhere by many of his graduate students. Following Giddings' outline rather closely each local study tended to deal with the "social population" under the main headings: situation, aggregation, demotic composition, and demotic unity. The "social mind" was considered under the headings: "like response to stimulus," "mental and practical resemblance," "consciousness of kind," and "concerted volition." These were followed by sections on social organization and the social welfare. Jones in *The Sociology of a New York City Block*, and Woolston in *A Study of the Population of Manhattanville*, each displayed an intimacy with the area under investigation and with its people, their modes of life and attitudes, which brought to their researches some of the specific qualities of the Le Play method, to supplement the inevitable case-counting and psycho-social interpretation. Williams in a hop-growing town near Utica, New York, Sims in an Indiana village, Wilson in a remote New York suburb, and others utilizing the Giddings method succeeded in distinguishing the sociological survey, concerned with the analysis of principles underlying human

[20] In addition to the researches upon tenement house conditions, immigration, and family welfare by Miss Breckinridge and Miss Abbott, these would include scores of original special investigations, as for example: Anderson, Nels—*The Hobo: The Sociology of the Homeless Man;* 1923. Houghteling, Leila—*The Income and Standard of Living of Unskilled Laborers in Chicago;* 1927. Mowrer, Ernest R.—*Family Disorganization: An Introduction to a Sociological Analysis;* 1927. Shaw, Clifford R., with the collaboration of Zorbaugh, Frederick M., McKay, Henry D., and Cottrell, Leonard S.—*Delinquency Areas;* 1929. Thrasher, Frederic M.—*The Gang: A Study of 1,313 Gangs in Chicago;* 1927. Wirth, Louis—*The Ghetto;* 1928. Zorbaugh, Harvey W.—*The Gold Coast and the Slum;* 1929. Published by the University of Chicago Press. A history and summary of these studies to 1929 is submitted in Smith, T. V., and White, Leonard D., editors—*Chicago: An Experiment in Social Science Research;* The University of Chicago Press, 1929.

[21] They can, however, be traced up to 1928 in Eaton, Allen, and Harrison, Shelby M.—*A Bibliography of Social Surveys;* Russell Sage Foundation, 1930: and for the period 1920 to 1930 in Dubois, Florence—*A Guide to Statistics of Social Welfare in New York City;* Welfare Council of New York City, 1930. Later studies can be located by consulting the publications and files of the Welfare Council of New York City and the Russell Sage Foundation library.

relationships, from the social survey of the type employed in Pittsburgh, Springfield, or Cleveland which emphasized social problems and the means to their solution.[22]

Basic to all competent social study is the assembling of essential geographic, ecologic, economic, and engineering data such as are contained in the best of the city plan surveys so far conducted in this country. In 1921 a regional survey of New York was originated by Charles D. Norton and executed, with the financial aid of the Russell Sage Foundation, under the direction of Thomas Adams. Eight volumes of regional survey and two volumes on the regional plan were issued by the committee in the following ten years.[23]

Since excessive density of population, uneconomic distribution of utilities and facilities, dislocation of industry, inadequacies in transit, transportation or sanitary engineering services, insufficient provision for recreation, and unwholesome housing are pathologic conditions, the findings of competent surveys for city or regional planning are fundamental to studies in the field of social pathology.[24]

Middletown.—The Lynds study of Middletown (Muncie, Indiana) like the Giddings studies belongs in the class of sociological urban surveys. Unlike the latter it was not hampered by the peculiar terminology or psycho-sociological concepts of the Giddings school of thought but was at once eclectic and realistic in form and method. No effort was made to prove a thesis. It sought rather to utilize the approach by the cultural anthropologist, formerly ap-

[22] See list of supplementary readings at end of chapter for complete references.

[23] Committee on Regional Plan of New York and Its Environs—*Regional Survey of New York and Its Environs*, Vol. I, *Major Economic Factors in Metropolitan Growth and Arrangement*, by Robert Murray Haig, 1927; Vol. II, *Population, Land Values and Government*, by Thomas Adams, Harold M. Lewis, and Theodore T. McCrosky, 1929; Vol. III, *Highway Traffic*, by Harold M. Lewis, 1927; Vol. IV, *Transit and Transportation*, by Harold M. Lewis, 1928; Vol. V, *Public Recreation*, by Lee F. Hanmer, 1928; Vol. VI, *Buildings: Their Uses and the Spaces about Them*, by Thomas Adams, Wayne D. Heydecker, and Edward M. Bassett, 1931; Vol. VII, *Neighborhood and Community Planning*, by Thomas Adams, Edward M. Bassett, Ernest P. Goodrich, Wayne D. Heydecker, Clarence A. Perry, and Robert Whitten, 1929; Vol. VIII, *Physical Conditions and Public Services*, by Harold M. Lewis, Henry James, and Thomas Adams, 1929. *Regional Plan of New York and Its Environs*, Vol. One, *The Graphic Regional Plan*, by the Staff of the Regional Plan, 1929; Vol. Two, *The Building of the City*, by Thomas Adams, assisted by Harold M. Lewis and Lawrence M. Orton, 1931.

[24] Several bibliographies of city and regional planning have been published by Theodora K. Hubbard, and Katherine McNamara, through which the student may locate the city planning surveys which have been made for any community in which he is interested.

plied only to simpler peoples, and to maintain strict objectiveness in the analyses of local institutions and activities. Trends were plotted from 1890 to 1925, the year of the completion of the survey. These were treated under the six headings: "getting a living; making a home; training the young; using leisure in various forms of play, art, and so on; engaging in religious practices; engaging in community activities." [25] The investigation yielded little of importance directly upon the conditions of poverty and handicaps. Its outstanding contribution was rather on the pathologies of family and sex relationships, the trivialities and tawdriness of daily life whether expressed in work, play, social gatherings, or attitudes on public questions.

Ten years later the Lynds reëxamined this city.[26] Muncie had meanwhile grown from a population of 36,500 to one of nearly 50,000 mostly during the earlier part of the decade under conditions of prosperity. This was followed by prolonged depression with a high volume of unemployment and marked reduction in wages. At one time tax relief aggregated "three times the entire Community Fund budget." [27] Dependent families increased from six per cent of population in 1928 to around twenty-five per cent in 1932. But one is impressed with the massed data revealing mental stereotypes, narrowness of interest, lack of penetration, and slowness to learn as evidence of social inadequacy. Intellectuality and vision from this sample would appear to be deviation from normality, though not from optimum standards.

Trend Toward Specialized Studies.—A decided change has occurred in the types, emphasis, methods, and sponsorship of social investigations in America within the past generation. The comprehensive type of urban social survey which simultaneously studies the many related social problems of the community has been virtually displaced by highly specialized studies of particular problems or factors. In criticism of this trend, it may be noted that the specialized data are sometimes unduly abstracted from their social context. Such intensive researches are too often unrelated to other researches which have been or are being made within the area selected for study.

[25] Lynd, Robert S., and Lynd, Helen Merrell—*Middletown: A Study in Contemporary American Culture;* Harcourt, Brace and Company, Inc., 1929.

[26] Lynd, Robert S., and Lynd, Helen Merrell—*Middletown in Transition: A Study in Cultural Conflicts;* Harcourt, Brace and Company, Inc., 1937.

[27] *Ibid.*, p. 102.

Eaton and Harrison in summarizing the most useful of the fact-finding studies, which had been made as a basis for social action prior to 1928, were able to list 2,775 titles of projects of which only 154 were general surveys. Eighty-two of the latter were surveys of urban conditions and 72 were of rural areas. The remaining 2,621 studies included 625 dealing with schools and education, 469 with health and sanitation, 296 with industrial conditions, 155 with city and regional planning, 152 with delinquency and correction, 112 with housing, 88 with city, county, and state administration, 68 with child welfare, 53 with recreation, 52 with mental hygiene, 48 with religion, 46 with cost of living, 39 with conditions among Negroes, 36 with immigration and Americanization, 35 with taxation, 28 with social agencies, and 26 with vice. New York State led with 392 surveys, Ohio taking second place with 206. Pennsylvania, Illinois, Massachusetts, and California each had over one hundred. Among cities, New York City led with 184, Chicago followed with 109, Cleveland 95, Philadelphia 49, Boston and Pittsburgh with 46 each.[28]

The number of researches listed is only roughly indicative of the volume of studies made, due both to the basis of selection and to the fact that many of the most valuable data for the social scientist and social worker consist in Federal and state census findings, institution reports, special public investigations and hearings, and the reports of a wide variety of municipal, county, state, and Federal officials.

Sponsorship of Social Research.—Sponsorship has undergone equally radical change. No longer are our major social investigations both financed and executed, as in the case of the London and York studies, by men who combine wealth with scientific and civic interest. Instead, the field of social investigation is dominated by governmental research agencies on the one hand, and by philanthropic foundations, international, national, or local, on the other, with occasional coöperative relationships between them. Though some of the best social research still proceeds from universities without aid from either of these major sources, and from private agencies and individuals, the mass of significant studies is endowed.

In America much more than in Europe families of wealth have during their lifetime or through their wills left colossal fortunes to be used for the service of mankind in some specified manner and

[28] Eaton, Allen, and Harrison, Shelby M.—*op. cit.*, pp. xxix–xxxii.

under the control of a self-perpetuating group of trustees. Apparently almost a billion dollars of capital was under the control of the boards of such foundations and community trusts in 1937.[29]

Increasingly the foundations have questioned the desirability of utilizing their funds to subsidize existing agencies or measures and have invested a larger percentage of their incomes in the analysis of conditions, with a view to guidance in future social action. Some, like the Twentieth Century Fund, have conducted researches directly through their own staffs. Others have financed special studies by existing agencies of research. Such is the method employed by the Falk Foundation, which in recent years has fostered studies of income distribution in America and solutions of urgent economic problems with the help of the Brookings Institution of Washington. Similarly, the Rockefeller Foundation has sponsored studies relating to social security and relief administration through the Social Science Research Council of New York and through the social science departments of universities. Others, like the Russell Sage Foundation and the John Simon Guggenheim Memorial Foundation, have primarily promoted individual research.

Coördination of Research Agencies and Techniques.—Virtually all of the foundations display interest in researches which coordinate in a unified program a variety of professional backgrounds and techniques of study. Thus in the field of social pathology the value is recognized of uniting the services of the sociologist, social worker, public administrator, economist, political scientist, psychologist, physician, and also on occasion the city planner, engineer, architect, or others, in researches which will bring together their diverse experience, techniques, interests, and points of view in the solution of a common problem. This method was applied during the presidency of Herbert Hoover in the researches of the White House Conference on Child Health and Protection, the President's Conference on Home Building and Home Ownership, and the President's Research Committee on Social Trends, and by the Russell Sage Foundation in its *Regional Survey of New York and Its Environs*.

Meanwhile techniques of social research have become more specialized and intricate. Prior to the twentieth century the best of studies in the field of social pathology relied exclusively upon careful

[29] Lindeman, Eduard C.—"Foundations in Social Work," *Social Work Year Book 1937*, p. 181; Russell Sage Foundation, 1937. See also Twentieth Century Fund—*American Foundations and Their Fields, 1934;* 1935.

observation, case-counting with the use of standard questionnaires and forms, and careful generalization made from the data thus obtained. The method was scientific where data were gathered systematically and with discrimination and care, and where skill and good judgment were exercised in the tabulation and the interpretation of the findings. Within the present century, however, statistical science has developed and its methods have been elaborated and refined. Promising beginnings have been made by economic and social statisticians with the application of these new techniques to problems in the field of social pathology.

The methods of case analysis have correspondingly developed since the initial studies of Le Play. Beginning with the devices for measurement of intelligence by Binet and Simon, psychometry has originated a wide variety of tests of human capacities. Meanwhile the literature on the methodology of personality and character analysis has been paralleled by equal developments in the fields of vocational analysis, differential medical diagnosis, and somatology. Adding to these the recent contributions of biology and genetics, of physiology and pathology, of neurology, psychopathology, psychoanalysis, and psychiatry, there is now a wealth of procedures to supplement social diagnosis in the analysis of individual variations, conditions, aptitudes, and needs.

Sociology and Social Research.—Sociology, a synthetic science of human relationships and social phenomena, has in the century since Auguste Comte evolved from the mere classification and systematization of available knowledge of social structure and processes, and from a discipline primarily speculative rather than positivistic, to a young science inductive in temper, closely analytical and critical, serious in its determination to discover social processes and the principles underlying them, and keenly critical of its own deficiencies. The field of social pathology, analyzed as it must be by these various techniques and disciplines, coördinating as it does the researches and often the social action of many professional groups, offers a valuable proving ground for social theory.

In spite of the many investigations referred to in this and the preceding chapter, social research is still in its infancy. Most of our human problems and needs have so far eluded analysis. Most apparent progress has been made in researches upon unitary and concrete physical phenomena—as for example, the causes, course, incidence, treatment, consequences, and prevention of typhoid fever or of smallpox—rather than upon phenomena less tangible.

Deficiencies in research may be made more clearly apparent perhaps if we note that America resembles a vast laboratory, reasonably well equipped, in which a mere handful of trained scientists are available to conduct experiments. Our Federal government, forty-eight states, and 3,165 urban communities are continuously passing new laws and inaugurating new practices. The effects of only a tiny percentage of these laws or practices are analyzed. Pressure, influence, self-interest, prejudice, and hunches, in a matrix of politics and compromise, still largely determine what changes shall be made in laws and policies. Yet in an ideal state such changes would be made only as a result of the scientific determination of existing conditions and the consequences of the legislation in question. Progress in research is as essential for the elimination of needless personal pathology and social disorganization as it is for the development of a truly scientific sociology.

QUESTIONS FOR DISCUSSION OR EXAMINATION

1. Outline the trends in social investigation in the United States.
2. Compare European social surveys with those made in America.
3. Discuss the relative merits of the sociological survey, and the social survey in which the primary purpose is reform.
4. What data fundamental to social pathology are contained in real property inventories, and in regional or city plan surveys?
5. Outline (a) the history of the United States Census; (b) sources of data re poverty prior to 1790; from 1790 to 1890; since 1890.

PROBLEMS FOR INDIVIDUAL STUDY

1. A report from each student on the organization, methodology, and content of some one of the surveys mentioned in the text.
2. A report from each student on the city plan, real property inventory, and social surveys of his own city, or some other selected city.
3. History of United States Census reports on (a) dependents; (b) blind and deafmute; (c) feebleminded; (d) insane; (e) prisoners.
4. Critical examination and summary of the observations regarding social conditions by selected early travellers or diarists.

SUGGESTIONS FOR SUPPLEMENTARY READINGS

Ames, Herbert Brown—*"The City below the Hill": A Sociological Study of a Portion of the City of Montreal, Canada;* Bishop Engraving and Printing Company (Montreal), 1897.

Ayres, Leonard P., director—*The Education Survey* (Cleveland), twenty-five volumes; The Cleveland Foundation, 1916.

Chapin, F. Stuart—*Field Work and Social Research;* The Century Co., 1920.

Chapin, Robert Coit—*The Standard of Living among Workingmen's Families in New York City;* Charities Publication Committee, Russell Sage Foundation, 1909.

Committee on Regional Plan of New York and Its Environs—*Regional Survey,* eight volumes, and *Regional Plan,* two volumes; Committee on Regional Plan of New York and Its Environs, 1927–31.

Dubois, Florence—*A Guide to Statistics of Social Welfare in New York City;* Welfare Council of New York City, 1930.

Duffus, R. L.—*Mastering a Metropolis;* Harper & Brothers, 1930.

Eaton, Allen, and Harrison, Shelby M.—*A Bibliography of Social Surveys;* Russell Sage Foundation, 1930.

Eliot, Thomas D.—*American Standards and Planes of Living;* Ginn and Company, 1931.

Elmer, Manuel C.—*A Neighborhood in South Minneapolis;* University of Minnesota, 1922.

Elmer, Manuel C.—*Technique of Social Surveys;* J. R. Miller (Los Angeles), third revised edition, 1927.

Emerson, Haven, director—*The Cleveland Hospital and Health Survey Report,* eleven monographs; The Cleveland Hospital Council, 1920.

Faris, Robert E. L., and Dunham, H. Warren—*Mental Disorders in Urban Areas;* University of Chicago Press, 1939.

Giddings, Franklin Henry—*Inductive Sociology;* The Macmillan Company, 1901.

Goldmark, Pauline, editor—*West-Side Studies;* Russell Sage Foundation, 1914.

Harrison, Shelby M.—*The Springfield Survey,* three volumes; Russell Sage Foundation, 1918–20.

Harrison, Shelby M.—*Social Conditions in an American City: A Summary of the Findings of the Springfield Survey;* Russell Sage Foundation, 1920.

Haynes, Rowland, director—*The Recreation Survey* (Cleveland), seven volumes; The Cleveland Foundation, 1918–20.

Institute of Social and Religious Research—Publications 1921 to date.

Jones, Thomas Jesse—*The Sociology of a New York City Block;* Columbia University Press, 1904.

Kellogg, Paul U., editor—*The Pittsburgh Survey,* six volumes; Russell Sage Foundation, 1910–14.

Kenngott, George F.—*The Record of a City: A Social Survey of Lowell, Massachusetts;* The Macmillan Company, 1912.

Klein, Philip—*A Social Study of Pittsburgh;* Columbia University Press, 1938.

Lynd, Robert S., and Lynd, Helen Merrell—*Middletown;* Harcourt, Brace and Company, Inc., 1929.

Lynd, Robert S., and Lynd, Helen Merrell—*Middletown in Transition;* Harcourt, Brace and Company, Inc., 1937.

McNamara, Katherine—*Bibliography of Planning, 1928–1935;* Harvard University Press, 1935.

Moley, Raymond—*A Review of the Surveys of the Cleveland Foundation;* The Cleveland Foundation, 1923.

More, Louise Bolard—*Wage-Earners' Budgets;* Henry Holt and Company, 1907.

Odum, Howard W., and Jocher, Katharine—*An Introduction to Social Research;* Henry Holt and Company, 1929.

Pettit, Walter W.—*Case Studies in Community Organization;* The Century Co., 1928.

Potter, Zenas L.—*The Newburgh Survey;* Russell Sage Foundation, 1913.

Pound, Roscoe, and Frankfurter, Felix, directors and editors—*Criminal Justice in Cleveland: Reports of the Cleveland Foundation Survey of the Administration of Criminal Justice in Cleveland, Ohio;* The Cleveland Foundation, 1922.

Residents of Hull-House—*Hull-House Maps and Papers: A Presentation of Nationalities and Wages in a Congested District of Chicago, together with Comments and Essays on Problems Growing out of the Social Conditions;* Thomas Y. Crowell & Co., 1895.

Roberts, Peter—*The Anthracite Coal Communities;* The Macmillan Company, 1904.

Schmeckebier, Laurence F.—*The Statistical Work of the National Government;* The Institute for Government Research, The Johns Hopkins Press, 1925.

Shaw, Clifford R., with the collaboration of Zorbaugh, Frederick M., McKay, Henry D., and Cottrell, Leonard S.—*Delinquency Areas;* University of Chicago Press, 1929.

Sims, Newell Leroy—*A Hoosier Village: A Sociological Study with Special Reference to Social Causation;* Columbia University, Longmans, Green and Co., Agents, 1912.

Smith, T. V., and White, Leonard D., editors—*Chicago: An Experiment in Social Science Research;* University of Chicago Press, 1929.

Steiner, Jesse Frederick—*The American Community in Action;* Henry Holt and Company, 1928.

Streightoff, Frances Doan, and Streightoff, Frank Hatch—*Indiana: A Social and Economic Survey;* W. K. Stewart Company (Indianapolis), 1916.

Taylor, Graham Romeyn—*Satellite Cities: A Study of Industrial Suburbs;* D. Appleton and Company, 1915.

Thomas, William I., and Znaniecki, Florian—*The Polish Peasant in Europe and America*, two volumes; Alfred A. Knopf, 1927.

Williams, James M.—*An American Town: A Sociological Study;* The James Kempster Printing Company, 1906.

Wilson, Warren Hugh—*Quaker Hill: A Sociological Study;* Columbia University Press, 1907.

Wirth, Louis—"A Bibliography of the Urban Community," Chapter X of Park, Robert E., Burgess, Ernest W., and McKenzie, Roderick D.—*The City;* University of Chicago Press, 1925.

Wirth, Louis—*The Ghetto;* University of Chicago Press, 1928.

Wood, Arthur Evans—*Some Unsolved Problems of a University Town* (Princeton, New Jersey); University of Pennslyvania, 1920.

Woods, Robert A., editor—*Americans in Process: A Settlement Study;* Houghton Mifflin Company, 1902.

Woods, Robert A., editor—*The City Wilderness: A Settlement Study;* Houghton Mifflin Company, 1899.

Woolston, Howard Brown—*A Study of the Population of Manhattanville;* Columbia University, Longmans, Green and Co., Agents, 1909.

Zimmerman, Carle C., and Frampton, Merle E.—*Family and Society,* Part III; D. Van Nostrand Company, Inc., 1935.

Zorbaugh, Harvey Warren—*The Gold Coast and the Slum;* University of Chicago Press, 1929.

CHAPTER IV

SOCIAL OBJECTIVES AND OPTIMUM STANDARDS

Proximate versus Ultimate Objectives.—The concept of deviation is social. But deviation may be measured in terms of physical or psychological causes of departure from normality (the blind, deaf-mute, and crippled; the mental defectives, epileptics, and insane); or else in terms of violation of group mores or those customs of the group which it enforces either by law (the criminal), or by public opinion expressed in disapproval or ostracism (the divorcee and deserter). Social inadequacy is usually measured by the degree in which an individual, family, or group falls short of a socially acceptable standard of living (the poor or the destitute), or standard of productivity (the inefficient and unemployable). Both deviation and inadequacy may be construed also in terms of development or culture (the crank, the radical, the ignoramus, the uncultivated, the ill-mannered). Less frequent attempts have been made by sociology and its applied sciences and arts of social work, public welfare administration, social legislation, regional planning, or community organization, to formulate ultimate goals conceived for individuals or groups by a process of challenge of existing beliefs and behavior, and thus to define inadequacy in terms of well-considered and comprehensive social objectives.

Perhaps it is not strange that the mass of individuals who make up our social groups should have given little thought to the purpose or goals of personal life, or to the objectives of social organization. The meager training in reasoning which has been afforded them in their schooling or by the exigent demands of daily life, as well as social tradition, lead them largely to accept the ready-made codes of the religious sect to which they happen to be born, of the business world in which they are employed, of the constitutions and laws of their national or local governments, of the etiquette, fashions, customs, and mores of the immediate social class to which they belong—without challenge and usually without recognition of inconsistencies which may exist among these established codes. An individual within their group who does challenge and object to or resist any one of these codes that is taken seriously by the others is likely to be regarded by them as a deviate. To him there may be applied some opprobrious epithet, such as "agnostic," "crank," "radical," or "troublemaker." His deviation is regarded as a threat to social organization, which is commonly construed in terms of the *status quo*.

Nevertheless, progress in so far as it is within man's control is dependent upon a close analysis of conditions, their causes and consequences, of trends and the reasons for the course they take, and of human interests and needs with reference to some concept of life's objectives. The overcoming of pathologic conditions by means of curative treatment is but a half step in the elimination of handicap if the rehabilitated workman cannot find a job, or the cured alcoholic or paretic must return to those very conditions which precipitated his difficulty. A large percentage of social work and social legislation misses its proximate goal, of cure or amelioration, because it fails to see beyond that proximate goal and visualize ultimate objectives in terms of the whole social context.

The Challenge of Social Change.—The application of imagination and intelligence to social reorganization is the province of that type of leadership which can view the immediate goals of the daily routine of social work and social legislation in terms of policies as well as measures, of ultimate· or long-range objectives as well as annual programs. It has been said that the unit of social disorganization is the disorganization or demoralization of the individual. It may with equal accuracy be stated that social reorganization depends upon individual reorganization. But if the reorganization is to be accomplished on a level involving social change that is evolutionary or progressive (whatever the standard of reference) rather than retrogressive, such reorganization must be directed towards the achievement of a well-conceived though probably distant goal comprising some concept of both individual and social development.

Sociology, Social Ethics, and Social Policy.—Sociology, as has been seen, is concerned only with judgments of fact. Individual sociologists in spite of their understanding of the intricacies of human relationships and their conditioning factors may hazard predictions as to the direction that may be taken by social change. Nevertheless, because of the infinite complexities of their data and small mass of adequate evidence at their command the predictions may not agree.[1] Meanwhile man is concerned with his own well-being and seeks to improve the social medium of his daily life. It is natural that he should attempt to apply his reason and imagination to the elimination of deplorable conditions or the improvement of his institutions. The formulation of goals for his endeavor is the province of Social Ethics. The devising of means to overcome the conditions or improve the institutions may be termed Applied Social Ethics wherever objectives are envisaged.[2] Man's efforts to better himself whether crude or wise are, however, but factual data to the sociologist.

It is essential to the comprehension of the field of social pathology that current objectives be understood; for at every point they influence the programs under discussion.

Classification of Moral Objectives.—The nature of goodness, and the goals of human life have preoccupied religion and ethics for thousands of years. Nevertheless there yet remains great diversity of judgment. In brief, moral objectives classified by sources and derivation tend to fall in three major groups: (1) the religious and mystical systems arrived at by revelation or inspiration; (2) the philosophical systems developed largely but not exclusively by speculation; and (3) the scientific and pragmatic systems reached by induction and synthesis.

Diversity in Sectarian Objectives.—Each religion—Christian, Buddhistic, Mohammedan, or other—provides moral codes and objectives, explicit and implicit. Each also leaves some room for divergent interpretations, and sectarian or individual choice. Thus, for example, among Christians some have traditionally relied upon the written Word, others on personal revelation or inspiration. Some have made the ten commandments their major code, while others have modelled their lives on that of Jesus. Some have stressed endeavor for the salvation of their own souls by following the rites

[1] Moreover, it not infrequently occurs that the predictions themselves interfere with the very occurrences predicted. Marx' prediction of the progressive concentration of wealth and increasing misery of the masses, which to some extent prevented these developments, may be taken as a case in point. These predictions of social change may be called, in John Venn's picturesque phrase, "suicidal prophecies." Cf. Merton, Robert K.—"The Unanticipated Consequences of Purposive Social Action"; *American Sociological Review*, Vol. I, No. 6, December, 1936.

[2] Or Social Economics, Social Hygiene, Social Medicine, Social Technology, Social Work, Social Planning, or Social Policy according to the emphasis of the program.

of their church, while others have stressed service to and salvation of their fellow men. Such diversity of emphasis has made historically possible a wide variety of conflicting proximate objectives and behavior in the daily lives of Christians, ranging from the cruelties of the Spanish Inquisition to the gentle ways of the Quakers; from celibacy to monogamy and to plural marriages in some groups; from the prohibition of the use of alcoholic beverages in some sects to their free use by the clergy of others; from communism of property as outlined in the Acts of the Apostles or the cult of poverty to the condonation or encouragement of private wealth; from extreme asceticism and self-mutilation to the cure of disease and church movements for the prevention of social ills. Such varied interpretations have each been ascribed either to scriptural authority, to revelation or inspiration, or to deductive or inductive thought.

Schools of Ethical Thought.—Philosophical speculation has arrived at diverse definitions of "the good," in terms of which is expressed the goal of the individual life. Writers in the field of ethics have arrived at different classifications and nomenclatures for these many systems of thought; but for our purposes it is convenient in simplified terms to distinguish the goal as (1) the pleasure of the individual; (2) the common good, or "the greatest good of the greatest number" expressed commonly in terms of happiness; and (3) self-realization or self-development.

Individual Pleasure as Goal.—Pleasure as the aim of conduct is now generally discarded as a principle, on the grounds both of the practical impossibility of calculating the volume of pleasure which may proceed from a given activity or its anticipation, and of the psychological impossibility of determining in advance whether the choice or act in question will produce any pleasure at all. Hedonism belongs to the naive period of speculative thought which preceded the scientific tabulation of fatigue curves and the analysis of human motivation, wishes, interests, emotions, and behavior. Though many an individual makes the search for pleasure the goal of his personal life, the "pleasure-seeker," after pleasures begin to cloy, is notoriously unhappy and disillusioned.

The Common Good.—The common good as goal has wide currency and often fortunate social implications and consequences. Its practical merit is dependent upon the terms by which it is construed and the methods employed for its achievement. For the common good must inevitably be interpreted in terms of other schools of thought, such as the distribution of pleasure, the increase of general happiness, the removal of pain or thwarting factors, or the provision of opportunities for self-development. If it means the imposition of the proponent's personal ideals upon the reluctant remainder of the population, its value depends upon the nature, quality, and social value of such ideals, and the methods used for their spread.

Happiness as Goal.—Happiness is construed as a "state of being" in which pleasures predominate over pains. As a goal it is psychologically easier of attainment than is the continuous search for pleasure. The promotion of general happiness as purpose of the individual life has many followers among thoughtful people. Nevertheless, it becomes increasingly apparent that happiness is best attained by indirection rather than by direct pursuit. It appears to be essentially a by-product of good health, of reciprocal unselfish affection, of creative activity and achievement, and of the service of others.

Self-Realization and Self-Development.—Self-realization as a goal of conduct connotes the symmetrical development of all the capacities of the self and the fulfilment of all its relations. It is criticized on the grounds that it is incapable of attainment during man's lifetime upon this earth and presupposes the continuation of the developmental process for an infinite stretch of time after this life. Some are not able to make this necessary assumption and substitute the term "self-development" as goal in place of "self-realization." In either case no adequate clue is submitted as to the order of development of man's varied capacities. He requires some basis for choice in determining whether he should next devote his attention, for example, to art, science, philosophy, love, friendship, civic duties, or recreation. Thus idealism, like utilitarianism, would appear to be dependent upon some other system of thought to provide the necessary guide for daily activities and choices.

Egoistic versus Altruistic Objectives.—Reviewing the goals so far considered in terms of the social consequences of the assumption of each, one is immediately impressed with the fact that each falls into one of two main categories, egoism or altruism, according to the outlook or intention of the man who holds it. For each of these aims of life whether the salvation of the soul, pleasure, happiness, or self-realization, may be expressed in selfish terms on the one hand, or humanitarian terms on the other. The crucial issue is: Whose soul is to be saved? Whose pleasure or happiness sought? What self is to be realized or developed? The egoist seeks the salvation of his own soul even at the expense of others, or promotes his own pleasure, happiness, or development without thought of others. In practice egoism often is adopted as a way of life but with results inimical to the public good. Contemporary religion and ethics both tend to believe that the "soul can be saved" only through service; that enduring happiness can be attained only as the by-product of such creative forms of living as contribute to the well-being of others; that the self to be realized or developed is not the *individuus* but the *persona* or the self conceived in terms of all its social relations. The latter is found to be realizable only through the fulfilment of those relations; or in other words, by aiding others in their own process of self-development. Justice, courage, temperance, and wisdom have for two thousand years been recognized as the virtues which sustain the process. Of these wisdom is often construed to be the most fundamental on the grounds that the others inevitably spring from it.

The egoist and the altruist will behave in widely divergent manners when faced with like problems involving moral choice. But all altruists, whether their goals are religious, utilitarian, or perfectionist in type, would react in much the same manner if equally wise. Such, in brief, are the rough generalizations of many ethical specialists when dealing with the objectives in the individual life. This conventional dichotomy into egoism and altruism, however, has been largely abandoned by contemporary psychology and sociology because of the inevitable interpenetration of self-regarding and other-regarding motives in all conduct.

The Organization of Interests.—Returning to the problem of determining how the individual may make his choice at any given moment among divergent modes of behavior, it will be recalled that no one of the systems of thought so far discussed appears to provide a wholly adequate clue. Perry, in his *Moral Economy*, has provided a rational technique, readily applicable under any one of the altruistic systems of ethical thought already described. Perry conceives the good as "the fulfilment of an organization of interests." An interest or "unit of life" is a desire.[3] Goodness, then, consists in the satisfaction of desires. Since, however, there are some desires the fulfilment of which will reduce future potential satisfactions

[3] Perry, Ralph Barton—*The Moral Economy;* Charles Scribner's Sons, 1909.

(such as interest in drunkenness or the perpetration of a crime) the fulfilment of interests becomes *morally* good only when the interests of the self are organized for systematic and congruous fulfilment.

Life's purpose may thus be construed as the fulfilment of a maximum of interests. It is to be accomplished (1) by the search for those interests which are "pregnant"—the fulfilment of which leads to the fulfilment of interests lying beyond, and (2) the organization of life by a systematic ordering of interests so that there will be a maximum of achievement.

The pregnant interests are largely of a social type leading to reciprocal service. Thus, for example, an interest in the promotion of good government or voting for the candidate who best represents it, may lead to the fulfilment of many of the interests of the voter. The tossing of a coin to a beggar on the other hand may fulfil only some narrow interest, such as that of putting a stop to personal discomfort caused by the beggar's whining. This latter is not a pregnant interest since the beggar is not truly helped by the gift. The contribution of that same sum to the family welfare society for the development of a competent diagnosis of ills and their appropriate treatment is, however, a pregnant interest because of the many valuable consequences and reciprocal advantages proceeding from scientific social service. Contribution to the local community chest or service upon its committee, after adequate training, together with intelligent coöperation in wisely planned movements to prevent poverty at its sources, might represent one phase of the systematic ordering of interests. Thus Perry supplies a practical technique which is creative, productive of happiness, and contributory to self-development and the common good.

The Inductive Approach to Objectives.—Realistic empirical procedures appear to lead to altruistic objectives. The individual who carefully checks up the sources and consequences of his motivation and analyzes corresponding behavior in others tends to discover the repercussions of selfishness, the futility of the pursuit of wealth, adulation, or power for their own sakes or for selfish purposes, and the enduring values of service and reciprocity. Biography is replete in instances. To many thinkers history equally appears to record the ultimate destructive consequences of group and national selfishness, whether expressed in wars of aggression, selfish exploitation, or other abuses of power.

By the process of trial and error, and of research into the consequences of individual behavior and of group measures and policies, the conviction appears to grow that social objectives should be expressed as (1) the removal of those elements in life which thwart the physical, mental, moral, or social development of each individual, and (2) the provision of a maximum of opportunity to each individual to make the most of his given capacities in the service of others. The thwarting factors may reside in physical conditions, such as heredity, disease, accident, unwholesome food or drink, or the absence of adequate sanitary control; in economic disorganization and unfair practices; in the mores or moral trends; in inappropriate laws or inadequate schooling. The provision of maximum opportunity for individual development involves a systematic development of institutions for education and culture, work and recreation. The opportunity for the individual to take the next steps in his developmental process should at all times be present if that development is to be an unbroken continuity.

The chief tool in this process appears to be wisdom; involving the application of scientific methods to human problems, research in all pertinent fields, and incorporation in social policy of the findings of research. Human personality and its development thus tend to be recognized as the objective, and social institutions as the means to the fulfilment of that end. Social institutions correspondingly are thus recognized as instrumental values, rather than as ultimates in themselves.

Social Purpose and Optimum Standards.—The instruments of government in democratic countries express this group of altruistic ideals. The preamble to the Constitution of the United States of America phrases the purposes of our democracy: "We the people of the United States, in order to form a more perfect union, establish justice, insure domestic tranquillity, provide for the common defence, promote the general welfare, and secure the blessings of liberty to ourselves and our posterity, do ordain and establish this Constitution for the United States of America."

This in turn is supplemented by the preambles to state constitutions and city charters, by state bills of rights, and preambles to statute law. These latter statements as a rule are not essentially inconsistent with the Federal Constitution but show greater elaboration. The charters or statements of purpose of private corporations and the written codes of business and professional ethics may expand objectives or define in great detail. In so doing, each sets its optimum standards.

The Goals of Social Work.—Since the profession of social work most directly touches the lives of members of the pathologic groups, its present objectives require consideration. Among social workers preoccupation with immediate objectives, such as the relief of poverty or other distress, sometimes precludes the envisioning of ultimates. However, the question "What is the goal of social work?" was made a central topic of discussion by members of the Massachusetts Conference of Social Work in 1925. By allotting sufficient time before the Conference to make reflection possible, a number of thoughtful statements were secured from different branches of the field. Thus, for example, a worker with children defines the aim as "the production of a free personality, who will be able to enter for himself and intelligently into all the relations of life." [4] A probation officer submits that the purpose of his branch of social work is "to open for each child the channels which lead toward a fuller unfolding of his being and to guide his creative impulses so that they may not only not harm him or others, but become an asset to him, to his friends, to his home and to the community"; and he subsequently states that it is "to build toward a socially organized democratic community." [5] The principal of a reform school expresses his goal as the direction of a boy's "*need-to-be-great* into the channel of service." [6] A settlement worker defines social work as "the science of adjusting people to life." [7] A specialist in personnel management submits as objective: "that those engaged in industry will seek and find the fullest possible expression of their fundamental desires in the service of industry." [8]

Dr. Richard Cabot, as Chairman of the Conference, summarized the social worker's goal as "the relief of misery and unhappiness so that people's enfranchised and organized desires can find their expression in the social relationships which are part of their natural outlet." [9] He subsequently expressed the individual and social objective in these terms: "To find and to enlarge the areas of mutual

[4] Baylor, Edith M. H., pp. 3–4 in Cabot, Richard C., editor—*The Goal of Social Work;* Houghton Mifflin Company, 1927.
[5] Weiss, Hans, pp. 29 and 41, *ibid.*
[6] Campbell, George P , p. 74, *ibid.*
[7] Dougherty, Ethel Ward, p. 87, *ibid.*
[8] Smith, Elliott Dunlap, p. 99, *ibid.*
[9] *Ibid.*, pp. 228–229.

interest is the whole duty of man in industry, in international life, or in the closest friendship." [10]

It will be noted that in greater or less degree each of these many compact statements specifies the ultimate objective to be either the removal of thwarting factors, the creation of developmental opportunities, or both, and the development of coöperation to these ends.

Social Pathology and Social Control.—The branch of applied sociology known as social pathology is in no sense a branch of social work but an antecedent discipline. It may nevertheless apply the standards of social work in the measurement of the social phenomena with which it is concerned. Its relations are similar with respect to the more specialized fields of social service administration and public welfare administration. Since human beings look for guidance in their undertakings from the scientific groups concerned, it is natural and proper that social pathology should follow its analysis of human and institutional deficiencies with appraisals of the group's devices for social organization or social control, making use in such appraisal of the standards of reference employed by specialists in social amelioration.

The remaking of the deviate and the overcoming of inadequacy have thus led not only to social work and restrictive legislation but to constructive legislation and broad-gauge planning. Each aspect of social disorganization currently is assumed to be a transition phenomenon. Any plan for rational social progress implies the revamping of social structure and the improving of social relations, institutions, and processes. Where these prove inadequate, it implies social reorganization of a more fundamental type.

QUESTIONS FOR DISCUSSION OR EXAMINATION

1. What do you consider to be the purpose of the individual life? What are your reasons for discarding the other objectives mentioned in this chapter?
2. Comment upon the following as ultimate social objectives: (a) "Nordic supremacy," (b) race improvement, (c) the equal distribution of wealth, (d) increased productivity, (e) the greatest good of the greatest number.
3. How would you express the ultimate social objective? How reconcile it with your answer to question 1? Does it incorporate or exclude the objectives mentioned in question 2? How, and why?
4. What evidences do you see of personal and social drift? Of personal and social mastery?

[10] Cabot, Richard C.—*The Meaning of Right and Wrong*, p. 274; The Macmillan Company, 1933.

5. Apply the technique of "organization of interests" (a) to some personal problem involving choice (*e.g.* selection of field of study for next year), (b) to some national problem (*e.g.* should armaments be increased?).

PROBLEMS FOR INDIVIDUAL STUDY

1. A review, expository and critical, of any book in the following list of references.
2. A study of any one of the schools of ethics with reference to its bearing upon the problem of poverty.
3. Personal ideals, habits, and organization as problems of social control and social reorganization.
4. The social consequences of egoistic objectives.
5. Analysis of the expressed purposes and procedure of selected institutions or legislation in terms of proximate versus ultimate objectives.
6. Comparison of the goals of private agencies (or of social work) and of public agencies (or of social legislation).

SUGGESTIONS FOR SUPPLEMENTARY READINGS

Bossard, James H. S.—*Social Change and Social Problems*, Parts I and VIII; Harper & Brothers, revised edition, 1938.

Bridgman, P. W.—*The Intelligent Individual and Society;* The Macmillan Company, 1938.

Bristol, Lucius Moody—*Social Adaptation;* Harvard University Press, 1915.

Broad, C. D.—*Five Types of Ethical Theory;* Harcourt, Brace and Company, Inc., 1930.

Bruno, Frank J.—*The Theory of Social Work;* D. C. Heath and Company, 1936.

Cabot, Richard C., editor—*The Goal of Social Work;* Houghton Mifflin Company, 1927.

Cabot, Richard C.—*The Meaning of Right and Wrong;* The Macmillan Company, 1933.

Cooley, Charles Horton—*Human Nature and the Social Order;* Charles Scribner's Sons, 1902.

Devine, Edward T., and Brandt, Lilian—*American Social Work in the Twentieth Century;* The Frontier Press, 1921.

Dewey, John, and Tufts, James H.—*Ethics;* Henry Holt and Company, 1908.

Drake, Durant—*The New Morality;* The Macmillan Company, 1928.

Drake, Durant—*Problems of Conduct;* Houghton Mifflin Company, 1921.

Ellwood, Charles A.—*Methods in Sociology;* Duke University Press, 1933.

Ellwood, Charles A.—*The Social Problem: A Reconstructive Analysis;* The Macmillan Company, revised edition, 1919.

Ericksen, Ephraim Edward—*Social Ethics: An Introduction to Moral Problems;* Doubleday, Doran & Company, Inc., 1937.

Fairchild, Henry Pratt—*Outline of Applied Sociology;* The Macmillan Company, 1916.

Faris, Ellsworth, Laune, Ferris, and Todd, Arthur J., editors—*Intelligent Philanthropy;* University of Chicago Press, 1930.

Ford, James—*Social Problems and Social Policy*, Part I; Ginn and Company, 1923.

Giddings, Franklin Henry—*The Scientific Study of Human Society;* University of North Carolina Press, 1924.

Giddings, Franklin Henry—*Studies in the Theory of Human Society;* The Macmillan Company, 1922.

Givler, Robert Chenault—"Ethics," Chapter X of Barnes, Harry Elmer, editor—*The History and Prospects of the Social Sciences;* Alfred A. Knopf, 1925.

Hagerty, James Edward—*The Training of Social Workers;* McGraw-Hill Book Company, Inc., 1931.

Hankins, Frank Hamilton—"Sociology," Chapter VI of Barnes, Harry Elmer, editor—*The History and Prospects of the Social Sciences;* Alfred A. Knopf, 1925.

Hayes, Edward Cary—*Sociology and Ethics;* D. Appleton and Company, 1921.

Hertzler, Joyce O.—*Social Progress;* The Century Co., 1928.

Hetherington, H. J. W., and Muirhead, J. H.—*Social Purpose: A Contribution to a Philosophy of Civic Society;* The Macmillan Company, 1918.

Hobhouse, Leonard T.—*Social Evolution and Political Theory;* Columbia University Press, 1928.

Hobson, J. A.—*Economics and Ethics: A Study in Social Values;* D. C. Heath and Company, 1929.

House, Floyd N.—*The Range of Social Theory;* Henry Holt and Company, 1929.

James, William—*Selected Papers on Philosophy;* E. P. Dutton & Co., 1924.

Janet, Paul—*Histoire de la science politique dans ses rapports avec la morale;* F. Alcan (Paris), fourth edition, 1913.

Karpf, Maurice J.—*The Scientific Basis of Social Work;* Columbia University Press, 1931.

Lippmann, Walter—*A Preface to Morals;* The Macmillan Company, 1929.

Lundberg, George A., Bain, Read, and Anderson, Nels—*Trends in American Sociology;* Harper & Brothers, 1929.

MacIver, R. M.—*The Contribution of Sociology to Social Work;* Columbia University Press, 1931.

Mangold, George B.—*Organization for Social Welfare;* The Macmillan Company, 1934.

Mayo, Elton—*Human Problems of an Industrial Civilization;* The Macmillan Company, 1933.

Mecklin, John M.—*An Introduction to Social Ethics;* Harcourt, Brace and Howe, 1920.

Merton, Robert K.—"Social Structure and Anomie"; *American Sociological Review*, Vol. III, No. 5, October, 1938.

Mill, John Stuart—*Utilitarianism, Liberty, and Representative Government;* E. P. Dutton & Co., 1914.

National Conference of Social Work—*Proceedings.*

North, Cecil Clare—*Social Problems and Social Planning;* McGraw-Hill Book Company, Inc., 1932.

Odum, Howard W., and Willard, D. W.—*Systems of Public Welfare;* University of North Carolina Press, 1925.

Ogburn, William Fielding—*Social Change;* B. W. Huebsch, Inc., 1922.

Perry, Ralph Barton—*The Moral Economy;* Charles Scribner's Sons, 1909.

Pipkin, Charles W.—*The Idea of Social Justice;* The Macmillan Company, 1927.

Queen, Stuart Alfred—*Social Work in the Light of History;* J. B. Lippincott Company, 1922.

Ross, Edward Alsworth—*Social Control. A Survey of the Foundations of Order;* The Macmillan Company, 1901.

Seth, James—*A Study of Ethical Principles;* Charles Scribner's Sons, 1911.

Shenton, Herbert—*The Practical Application of Sociology;* Columbia University Press, 1927.

Sidgwick, Henry—*Outlines of the History of Ethics;* The Macmillan Company, sixth edition (with an additional chapter by A. G. Widgery), 1931.

Sorokin, Pitirim A.—"Sociology and Ethics," Chapter XXV of Ogburn, William Fielding, and Goldenweiser, Alexander, editors—*The Social Sciences and Their Interrelations;* Houghton Mifflin Company, 1927.

Taeusch, Carl F.—*Professional and Business Ethics;* Henry Holt and Company, 1926.

Todd, Arthur James—*The Scientific Spirit and Social Work;* The Macmillan Company, 1919.

Todd, Arthur James—*Theories of Social Progress;* The Macmillan Company, 1918.

Tufts, James Hayden—*America's Social Morality: Dilemmas of the Changing Mores;* Henry Holt and Company, 1933.

Walker, Sydnor H.—*Social Work and the Training of Social Workers;* University of North Carolina Press, 1928.

Wallas, Graham—*The Great Society. A Psychological Analysis;* The Macmillan Company, 1914.

Ward, Lester F.—*Applied Sociology;* Ginn and Company, 1906.

Wright, Henry W.—*Self-Realization: An Outline of Ethics;* Henry Holt and Company, 1913.

Wright, William Kelley—*A General Introduction to Ethics;* The Macmillan Company, 1929.

Young, Kimball, editor—*Social Attitudes;* Henry Holt and Company, 1931.

PART II

PERSONAL HANDICAPS, PHYSICAL AND MENTAL

CHAPTER V

PATHOLOGY OF THE INDIVIDUAL

Society and the Individual.—Since society and the groups of which it is composed, the family, the community, and the workshop are combinations of personalities, it is desirable to seek the sources of pathological relationships in the make-up of individuals as well as in their social milieu. For the type and the level of relationship invariably depend in part upon the multitudinous factors in the composite biologic characteristics of the individuals who effect the given relationship.

Native individual inadequacies result in substandard relationships. Ideal social organization and ideal functioning of social institutions and agencies presuppose the perfection of the individuals who constitute society. If all personalities were sound in body and mind, well integrated, symmetrical in self-organization, with high ideals, dynamic drives, and firm controls, eager and able to perfect their relationships with others, there would be no social disorganization or social pathology.

No such perfected personalities exist. Consequently social perfection has likewise never existed in human history; nor can it exist. Moreover, the dynamics of individual growth require uneven development. Education demands emphasis first upon one factor and then upon another. Such concentration precludes symmetry. It is impossible to develop simultaneously all of the aspects of self, physical, mental, and characterial. Dispersion of effort leads to dilettantism and superficialities.

The life of an individual, as of society, may be expressed as "an ever-flowing becoming," in which progressive personal asymmetry is accompanied by progressive asymmetry in social institutions. The term social disorganization though preferably limited to breaks or declines in social relations and controls is sometimes utilized to include the factors which limit or prevent types of organization deemed desirable. Among these factors or elements are the pathologies or morbid conditions in the physique and mentality of individuals who compose society. Increases in the volume or profundity of individual defects or handicaps involve special adaptations in social structure, diversions of social energy to prevent the harm which defects may cause, utilization of the time and services of more gifted individuals to care for and support those less gifted, the establishment of costly social programs and institutions for the prevention and cure of defects.

Social Pathology of the Handicapped.—The older organismic sociological theories affirmed that individual pathologies collectively produced social pathology in the sense that the social organism was "diseased" by the presence of diseased or defective members. The abandonment by contemporary sociology of the organismic theory has not, however, led to the disuse of the term social pathology. Since it is recognized that in all social relations, functions and activities are affected profoundly by the make-up and tendencies of the individuals who compose the social group, the presence of the handicapped colors all social relations. Attention to their needs is implicit in social policy. They are considered in the councils of state, church, school, industrial corporation, and trade union. They are counted out in determining a nation's man power for war and are excluded from the army. They figure largely in the budget of city, state, and nation. They appear as social liabilities in any type of social accounting or appraisal.

Since the funds and energy available to any group are limited, expenditures for the needs of the handicapped are diverted from uses more constructive or socially advantageous. Social progress may be definitely curbed by the necessity of expending the energies of "whole men" upon the maintenance of "half men." If the handicapped group did not exist or could be eliminated or prevented, the volume of effort now expended upon them could be applied to the perfecting of the social order through special schools for the gifted, the training of wise leadership, the redistribution of wealth, or any other purpose deemed appropriate.

Earlier Terminology of Social Pathology.—When this subject became a field of university study in the latter part of the last century [1] it was dealt with under such headings as "American Charities," or "Dependents, Defectives, and Delinquents." [2] Within

[1] Professor Francis G. Peabody began his teaching of Practical Ethics at Harvard in 1881, dealing with the subjects now termed Social Pathology. At about the same time Professor Graham Taylor at Chicago and Frank B. Sanborn at Cornell covered the same subject matter in university courses.

[2] Amos G. Warner first published his classic textbook under the title *American*

the past generation the terms "charities" and "defectives" have fallen into disfavor. Poverty is seen to be a problem larger than dependency; its prevention vastly greater than a problem of charity. The roots of delinquency are now sought in personality make-up and predelinquent behavior within an intricate social situation. Its conditions, controls, and preventives are intensively examined by modern criminology and the related sciences of government, law, somatology, and psychology.

The term "defectives," because of its popular connotation of mental deficiency, is increasingly deemed opprobrious when applied to the blind, deaf, or crippled. It has been replaced by the terms "maladjusted," "maladapted," and "handicapped." Since the terms maladjusted and unadjusted, misfit and unfit, in many minds suggest characterial defect—misconduct as well as misfortune, and hopelessness—it seems wiser to avoid them as designations for the group about to be considered.

The Handicapped.—The term "handicapped" carries no such unfortunate connotation. It suggests a group recognized as unable to start in life, or at some given point unable to proceed, on even terms with their fellows. It need cause no embarrassment to any self-respecting person of high mentality, culture, and character to have the blindness, deafness, deformity, or chronic illness from which he may suffer, termed a handicap.

There is a wide range in the capacities of individuals. There is usually also a failure to use to the full the capacities with which one is endowed. Individuals with defects, physical or mental, are generally termed the handicapped. Those who do not suffer from defects but still fall far short of their potential performance are termed maladjusted.

Thus a handicap is a physical or mental defect or abnormality, which at some point tends to limit the efficiency of the individual in his economic or social relationships. Nature sets definite limits upon the endowment of all men. It is customary, however, to include in the group designated as "the handicapped" only those who fall clearly below "average," "usual," or "normal" endowment.

Charities in 1894. Charles Richmond Henderson at Chicago first issued his *Introduction to the Study of the Dependent, Defective, and Delinquent Classes* in 1893. Carroll D. Wright's *Outline of Practical Sociology*, in 1899, overlapped this same field, as did also Richmond Mayo-Smith's *Statistics and Sociology*, 1894, and *Statistics and Economics*, 1899. These five books were leading texts at the beginning of the present century.

Among the handicapped are always listed the feebleminded, the insane or mentally diseased, the blind, the deaf, and persons seriously crippled or deformed. With entire propriety there may be added the more profound cases of epilepsy, alcoholism, drug addiction, and chronic invalidism.

Borderline Cases.—On the borderline, with less pronounced departures from normality, are the mentally dull, the emotional deviates, persons with infrequent convulsive seizures, the nearsighted, the hard of hearing, the sufferers from mild chronic ailments, the convalescent, and many who suffer from minor deformities, disfigurements, or other physical peculiarities.

Tests.—The test of the presence of handicap is whether or not the defect, physical or mental, causes the individual's performance in any of life's customary tasks or relations to lag behind the average. If the defect reduces the individual's employability, his social acceptability, his opportunities for marriage and parenthood, his eligibility for service in army or navy, his participation in sports, he is in so far a handicapped person even though by cure or training (or the use of mechanical devices such as artificial limbs for the crippled or powerful lenses for the nearsighted) increased social participation is made possible.

Differentiation of the handicapped from the normal population is easy for the extreme or profound cases. But all persons go through periods in which they are not "up to par." Whether the causative factors lie in infection, excesses or deficiencies in diet, work, or play, in worries or adverse fortunes of business or love, one may find periods of relative dullness, emotional instability, or poorer-than-average performance in any man or woman.

Multiple Handicaps.—The pathologies of the individual thus cover a wide range of types, intensities, and durations. They vary also in their combinations. There are some among the insane who are also inebriate, drug addicts, or cardiac. There are some among the blind who are also deaf [3] or feebleminded. Some epileptic are also feebleminded. Mental deviations are likely to be accompanied by physical deviations.[4] Physical defects affect mental attitudes. Handicaps are often multiple.

[3] See pp. 170–172 for Laura Bridgman and Helen Keller cases.
[4] Hooton, Earnest A.—*The American Criminal*, Vol. I, *The Native White Criminal of Native Parentage;* Harvard University Press, 1939. Hooton, Earnest A.— *Crime and the Man;* Harvard University Press, 1939.

Incapacities versus Handicaps.—There is no sharp dividing line between the personal inadequacy and maladjustments due to deficiencies in the intellectual and moral training, and the handicaps due to morbid physical or mental factors. Individualized clinical study, and even trained observation, can distinguish the extremes— the idiot from the illiterate man of normal intelligence, the pathologic alcoholic or drug addict from the normal man with defective training in self-control, the cripple from the person whose posture or neuromuscular coördinations are poor from lack of physical training. But the marginal statistical groups of morons and mental, physical, or emotional deviates contain many personalities difficult to diagnose. Lack of adequate mental and moral training is fully as common among the non-institutional handicapped as in the general population. Undeveloped capacities complicate the diagnosis, social manifestations, and treatment of handicap. In spite of these difficulties the minor personal incapacities of relatively normal people will be discussed here briefly, to be followed by chapters covering each of the major types of handicap.

Personal Inadequacies.—The term personal incapacity is freely used to explain inferior work but has no generally accepted specific use. When an employer speaks of an employee as incapable he may simply mean that he is untrained for the work to which he is assigned, though properly the term should be used to cover only lack of ability rather than lack of training. So little is known about the native capacities of individuals whose performance is appraised that the term incapacity tends to be used in a strictly objective sense in each specific instance to cover any type of inadequacy in performance. It is probable that most persons, and perhaps all, could as a result of closer analysis and individualized training, improve their performance in time at any given task. Where this is the case the term incapacity means not-yet-developed capacity.

Although an employer may term his employee incapable when the latter does not do satisfactorily the work which has been assigned, there are many possible explanations for the employee's apparent unfitness. The task may never have been properly explained. The methods of performing it may not have been made clear. The employee may be slow-witted but capable, in time, of learning. Or he may suffer from some physical or mental illness or other handicap which puts a definite and possibly permanent limitation upon his ability to understand or do the job assigned. Fatigue or emotional upsets, quite temporary in nature, may have interfered. Yet any one of the above conditions could be partially or wholly overcome by the individualized service of a competent specialist. Clearly much so-called incapacity is merely capacity that is undeveloped or in some way obstructed. The records of case work agencies, and autobiographies as well, frequently show that incapable persons are rendered capable when the sources of difficulty are reached.

Individual Uniqueness.—On the other hand, it is clear from the findings of biological science in the field of human heredity that each person is unique in his combination of traits and capacities. "The number of combinations of genes resulting from the union of any two parents is practically unlimited. This is why no two individuals, even twins, are ever precisely alike in their inheritance unless they spring from the same ovum." [5]

From the above it is reasonable to assume that occasional individuals will be born devoid of certain factors or combinations of factors essential to industrial efficiency, just as some are born blind, deaf, or with mental defect. Presumably weakness of will, feeble inhibitions, high suggestibility, inability to appreciate the moral standards of their time, or inability to conform, may be due in part to inheritance. Only by individualized study can individuals with these latter traits or lacks, who were termed "moral imbeciles" by the earlier researches, be differentiated from others adequately endowed by inheritance, but misbehaving as a result of unfortunate or deficient training. Both groups, however, are at present objectively incapable of meeting certain obligations which society imposes. [6]

Latent Capacities.—The study of human inheritance equally justifies the assumption that each individual being unique in the combination of his genes may have some, and perhaps many, latent capacities which our routine standardized educational system might fail to discover and train. Judged by his performance such an individual may be termed incapable, yet specialized training might reveal many socially useful abilities. Few individuals, for example, have a training in art, music, or the writing of poetry of a type which

[5] Reprinted by permission from *Tomorrow's Children: The Goal of Eugenics,* Huntington, Ellsworth (in conjunction with The Directors of the American Eugenics Society), p. 121; published by John Wiley & Sons, Inc., 1935.

[6] An admirable study of the multiple factors underlying "inability to conform" will be found in Young, Pauline V.—"Defective Social Intelligence as a Factor in Crime"; *American Sociological Review,* Vol. 3, No. 2, April, 1938.

would discover native gifts. The same would be true of mechanical abilities, inventiveness, or leadership. Some persons who could do distinguished work in each of these fields probably go through life unaware of their latent gift.

A crisis occasionally reveals undreamed-of capacities in men and women, which were not elicited in their daily routine. Thus war, by its general conscription and the unusual group of experiences it affords, uncovers many abilities that are not called for in the routine life of a small town or a city slum. A youth, undistinguished in his home town, may return from war wearing a distinguished service medal awarded for some outstanding performance under the peculiar conditions of a military campaign. Courage, ingenuity, persistency, capacity for leadership are but a few of the traits thus discovered.[7]

Causes of Inadequacy.—The causes of personal inadequacy are highly diverse and not always tangible. Upon analysis some seem to be clear cases of undereducation, others of miseducation; some of hereditary defect, others of disease; some of warped mentality, emotional deviations, flabby inhibitions, alcohol or drug addictions, high suggestibility under evil influences or associations, inability properly to consider the future, innate viciousness, and others of mere lack of judgment. A considerable percentage of those termed incapable will be found to suffer from one or more of the minor handicaps—mental dullness or queerness, nearsightedness, difficulty in hearing, chronic uncured illness, or minor deformity.

Ignorance and Undereducation.—Ignorance is responsible for much industrial incapacity and social inadequacy. America, in 1934, had 3,675,000 adult illiterates, 4.89 per cent of the entire population twenty-one years of age or over. Of our present youth only a third of the pupils in the fifth grade of elementary schools graduate from high school, and only one-twentieth graduate from college.[8]

[7] Disasters elicit similar traits. Cases examined by the Carnegie Hero Fund Commission are described by Ernest Poole in an article entitled "Hero Hunters" in *The Reader's Digest* of May, 1937. Johnson O'Connor's laboratory methods of discovering latent capacities are outlined in a popular article by William Seabrook entitled "They Find Out What You're Fit For" in *The Reader's Digest* of August, 1938. See, however, especially O'Connor, Johnson—*Psychometrics: A Study of Psychological Measurements;* Harvard University Press, 1934.

[8] Foster, Emery M.—*Statistical Summary of Education 1933–34* (Being Chapter I of the Biennial Survey of Education in the United States: 1932–34); United States Department of the Interior, Office of Education, Bulletin, 1935, No. 2 (advance pages), p. 13; Government Printing Office, 1937. For elaboration of

Most of this undereducation is accounted for by the still common practice of leaving school to go to work before the high-school age is reached. The Federal Office of Education estimates the schooling of our population twenty-one years of age and over, in 1934, to have been as follows: [9]

EDUCATION	NUMBER	PER CENT
College graduates	2,204,000	2.93
Some college work	3,069,000	4.08
High-school graduates only	5,153,000	6.85
Some high-school work	14,285,000	18.99
Elementary-school graduates only	14,049,000	18.68
Some elementary school	32,781,000	43.58
Illiterates	3,675,000	4.89
Total	75,216,000	100.00

The inadequate education of the sixty-seven per cent of our adult population who have had only elementary-school training or less has undoubtedly reduced the range of their vocational opportunities. Except for the keener and more energetic members of this statistical group, limited schooling means a life of unskilled and semiskilled labor, unstable employment, and correspondingly low income. Raising the age of compulsory school attendance would reduce the number of persons designated as incapable.

Miseducation.—From poorly trained parents or associates many children may learn inferior attitudes and behavior—to whine, to sponge, to indulge in fits of anger or belligerence—which may lead to their early discharge whenever they secure employment, or render them unwelcome in social groups. Workers with warped training are often apt pupils of the "ca' canny" policy—of giving a minimum of effort to work—or of sabotage. Each such prejudiced or destructive attitude or habit when detected may lead to dismissal. Miseducation in conjunction with other factors may equally develop abuse of sedatives and patent medicines, demoralizing sex habits, petty graft or thievery, and parasitism or the frame of mind that the world

these data see *School Life*, September, 1936, and November, 1936. For W. P. A. programs to reduce illiteracy see Aubrey Williams' article in the *New York Times* of January 16, 1938.

[9] *Ibid.*, Table 12—Estimated Education of Population 21 Years of Age and Over, 1934, p 14. "The basic data used in table 12 are the number of college and high-school graduates each year since 1870, life tables compiled by the Bureau of the Census, grade enrollment data reported at various times to the Office of Education, and the number of illiterates and number of persons 21 years of age and over reported by the Bureau of the Census."

"owes" one his living. Thus the teachings of ignorant associates tend to displace the school as agencies of adult education. Bar room conversations, the exhortations of street-corner orators, yellow journalism, and sensational movies may be the only mental pabulum on which such minds are fed outside of the home and shop.

Miseducation of the employer or the professional man may give him a false sense of superiority, render him prejudiced or reactionary and unaware of the sentiments, thoughts, ambitions, qualities, and reactions of persons of a different economic status. The editorials of his conservative newspapers and professional publications, the biased statements issued by his political party, the conversations at his office or club, may never fairly present current issues of labor or politics. As a result he may use the wealth or knowledge at his command to exploit his workers or consumers, or to perpetuate class distinctions, inequalities, and privilege.

Prevention of the Marginal Disabilities: Increased Schooling. —Poverty that grows out of ignorance and miseducation could be considerably reduced if our educational system were so organized that each mind should receive as much education as it could "take." The adoption of a Federal child labor amendment incorporating the requirement of compulsory public school education at least to the age of sixteen years is the essential first step to remove these limitations. Reorganization of the instruction offered in the public schools better to meet the needs of the masses would contribute to the overcoming of prevalent ignorance. More intensive instruction in the later years of school in personal hygiene and the art of living, in economic and governmental organization and function—even if at the expense of some but not all of the contemporary emphasis upon standard subjects—might give better training for life.

Training of Judgment and Character.—Much personal incapacity is, however, traceable to errors in judgment and deficiencies in character training rather than to factual ignorance or lack of schooling. Development of reasoning capacity through courses in arithmetic and science does not necessarily carry over into the affairs of daily life. Judgment has been inadequately trained with regard to the types of problems which future citizens will face in their daily routine.

The case method so highly developed in some of our schools of business and law appears to be the ideal method of providing such training. It is much more effective than precept or command in

developing true morality. For precept grows out of adult experience
in which the child has not yet participated. It is external, based on
authority, and though it may result in objective conformity it often
fails to become incorporated in the inner life and thought-habits
of the child.

By patient, thorough discussion, under wise teachers, of concrete
situations in which a moral choice must be made, moral ideals and
objectives may be arrived at by a process of reasoning. The cases
for discussion can be selected with reference to the characteristic
daily life of the children in the class.[10] By such an experimental approach, rationally viewed in terms of consequences, it may prove
possible to render morality vital to the child, while imparting the
bases of moral judgment.

Training for Social Participation.—In the higher grades broader
questions in civic, economic, and social life can similarly be handled
by the case method. Discussion should be directed by the teacher
in such a way as to bring out all essential arguments for and against
each possible choice. Lying, cheating, whining, fighting, tale-
bearing, self-pity can thus be seen with reference to their effects
upon the individual and his associates. The responsibilities of citizens as individuals, and of nations as well, become apparent. Objectives and ideals become clarified by the pragmatic approach. One
learns to make personal choices, and one's decisions as citizen, by
an analysis of pros and cons and with reference to moral aims which
have emerged as a result of previous case studies. Moral behavior
ceases to be primarily irrational and emotional. A beginning has
been made in the application of reason and judgment to the affairs
of daily life.

Thriftlessness, recklessness, and folly have brought many families
below the poverty line and have made them permanent dependents.

[10] Should John steal coal from the car on the railroad siding when there is no
fuel at home and no money with which to purchase it? If John sells papers and
his father will beat him in case he doesn't bring home forty cents each day, should
he steal or should he beg when he is able to sell only thirty cents' worth of
papers? If a purse has been stolen and Mary knows who took it, should she tell?
If Mary hasn't learned her lesson and a child in the class shows her the answer
while she is reciting, should she use that answer?

A useful guide for teachers is the volume by Cabot, Ella Lyman—*Everyday
Ethics;* Henry Holt and Company, 1907. For adolescents and adults the series
published by *The Inquiry*, New York City, contains many useful suggestions. As
an example consider *And Who Is My Neighbor? An Outline for the Study of Race
Relations in America;* distributed by Association Press, 1924.

Here again ignorance and lack of judgment have played a conspicuous role. The school system has failed to provide training in the organization of life for effective living. More general education in domestic economy, in budget-making, and the art of living would help overcome these difficulties in persons of normal mentality. But the problem is largely one of self-mastery. Most of the drifters among the poor presumably have not been trained to direct their lives, and organize or focus all their activities with reference to the achievement of worthwhile ends.

Although much could be learned in this regard in the courses conducted by the case method just outlined, most persons probably need personal assistance both in determining upon objectives and the means of their attainment. In other words they require individualized social case work. Ideally the public schools should make possible individual conferences with each child to determine his interests and ambitions, to help formulate his objectives and train him to self-guidance, self-control, and self-mastery. Until this essential need can be met within the public school system, society will have to rely upon the provision of this advisory service and character guidance through social case work agencies after their mistakes or inadequacies have already reduced families to dependency. Prevention, however, requires the provision of such service in advance of disaster.

Control of Environment.—Personal incapacity is in large part the product of an environment which elicits or encourages socially undesirable habits and attitudes. In all instances the elimination of such incapacity or the substitution for it of capabilities, efficiency, and desirable behavior involves the provision of clinical opportunities to discover what is wrong in each individual case, and of a social milieu which will educe latent abilities and train them. No individual is wholly bad. Much of what is called badness is the product of ignorance. Most individuals in this group who are social liabilities can be made over into social assets by competent diagnosis and training in an environment which will favor and facilitate the expression and utilization of the discovered qualities. Personal incapacity—so far as it is a product of ignorance, miseducation, or poor moral training—can be progressively overcome, case by case, through individualized treatment and provision for adult education. It can be prevented in future generations by appropriate schooling.

Necessity of Differential Diagnosis.—The study of individual cases quickly dispels the notion of their simplicity. Differential diagnosis may be able to isolate some cases in which relatively normal persons were rendered ineffectual by unfortunate training. It will always find an interplay of factors physical, mental, and social. No two cases will be identical in causation. Even where pronounced physical or mental handicaps are discovered, defects in training will also be apparent. No diagnosis is adequate therefore unless it combines the expert services of physician, psychologist, and sociologist. Treatment and prevention equally involve the coördination of these three fields of knowledge and the related disciplines of biology, endocrinology, somatology, economics, political science, and pedagogy.

QUESTIONS FOR DISCUSSION OR EXAMINATION

1. Explain the need for differential diagnosis and suggest main categories.
2. Define or explain (a) individual uniqueness, (b) latent capacities, (c) borderline cases, (d) a crisis situation.
3. What did the Federal Office of Education in 1934 estimate to be the relative distribution of our population, twenty-one years of age or over, with regard to schooling?
4. Cite examples of miseducation personally known to you.
5. Outline methods for the training (a) of judgment, (b) for social participation, (c) for effective living.

PROBLEMS FOR INDIVIDUAL STUDY

1. A critical analysis of the estimates of schooling made by the United States Office of Education.
2. A critical study of the evidence of biology (including genetics and eugenics) and psychology concerning the uniqueness of each individual.
3. Evaluation of the evidence of works in (a) ethics, or (b) pedagogy concerning the means of developing human character.
4. An outline of the methods employed by social diagnosis and social case work to discover and develop latent capacities.

SUGGESTIONS FOR SUPPLEMENTARY READINGS

Allport, Gordon W.—*Personality: A Psychological Interpretation;* Henry Holt and Company, 1937.

Blacker, C. P., editor—*A Social Problem Group?;* Oxford University Press, 1937.

Bossard, James H. S.—*Social Change and Social Problems;* Harper & Brothers, revised edition, 1938.

Cabot, Richard C.—*Differential Diagnosis,* two volumes; W. B. Saunders Company, fourth edition revised, 1923–24.

Cattell, Raymond B.—*Crooked Personalities in Childhood and After;* D. Appleton-Century Company, 1938.

Dexter, Robert Cloutman—*Social Adjustment;* Alfred A. Knopf, 1927.

Elliott, Mabel A., and Merrill, Francis E.—*Social Disorganization;* Harper & Brothers, 1934.

Gillin, John Lewis—*Social Pathology;* The Century Co., 1933.

Healy, William, Bronner, Augusta F., Baylor, Edith M. H., and Murphy, J. Prentice—*Reconstructing Behavior in Youth: A Study of Problem Children in Foster Families;* Alfred A. Knopf, 1929.

MacCunn, John—*The Making of Character: Some Educational Aspects of Ethics;* The Macmillan Company, revised and rewritten with new chapters, 1920.

Mangold, George B.—*Social Pathology;* The Macmillan Company, 1932.

O'Connor, Johnson—*Psychometrics: A Study of Psychological Measurements;* Harvard University Press, 1934.

Queen, Stuart Alfred, Bodenhafer, Walter Blaine, and Harper, Ernest Bouldin—*Social Organization and Disorganization;* Thomas Y. Crowell Company, 1935.

Queen, Stuart Alfred, and Mann, Delbert Martin—*Social Pathology;* Thomas Y. Crowell Company, 1925.

Richmond, Mary E.—*Social Diagnosis;* Russell Sage Foundation, 1917.

Rogers, Carl R.—*The Clinical Treatment of the Problem Child;* Houghton Mifflin Company, 1939.

United States Office of Education—publications.

Warner, Amos Groswold, Queen, Stuart Alfred, and Harper, Ernest Bouldin—*American Charities and Social Work;* Thomas Y. Crowell Company, fourth edition, 1930.

White House Conference on Child Health and Protection—*The Handicapped Child;* The Century Co., 1933.

CHAPTER VI

MENTAL DEFECTS

Mental and Physical Handicaps.—The handicapped are customarily divided into two groups: those in whom the handicap is mental and those in whom it is physical. This division, though convenient, is not wholly exact since mental handicaps may have a physical basis (biological, physiological, chemical, etc.) or cause physical handicaps (the hysterically paralyzed), and physical handicaps in turn may affect mental attitudes. Nevertheless, there are many points at which methods of social control and treatment for persons mentally subnormal or abnormal must depart from methods utilized in dealing with persons who are mentally normal though physically handicapped. Hence the distinction is convenient and useful.

Mental Handicap.—The mentally handicapped comprise those suffering deficiency in mentality and those who, once normal in their mental development, have become abnormal.[1] The mental defectives are those who in their childhood years give evidence of a pronounced arrest of mental development. The stigmata by which the idiot and low-grade imbecile are recognized may be apparent at birth. Others though born deficient are normal in appearance and may not give unmistakable signs of retardation until of school age or shortly before. Still others, actually normal at birth, suffer arrest of development through accident or illness in infancy or early childhood.

How to Recognize Retardation.—Dr. Potter in a brochure on *Delayed Mental Development in Children* writes:

"The younger the child the more difficult it is to recognize mental retardation, especially retardation of the milder sort. An infant who is unable to hold his head erect at six months, who fails to sit alone at ten

---

[1] Deficiency is, by some, termed amentia as distinguished from dementia or abnormality. The former means arrested mental development. The latter is disordered functioning or deterioration of a mind once normal. As these terms have other uses it has been thought best not to employ them here. See Henderson, D. K., and Gillespie, R. D.—*A Text-Book of Psychiatry for Students and Practitioners*, p. 393; Oxford University Press, 1933.

months, has not walked at eighteen or twenty months, and has not talked at two and one-half or three years of age, should be investigated from the standpoint of his mental development. Unusual docility or unusual fretfulness in the face of good physical health is sometimes an early symptom of mental retardation. Lack of inquisitiveness and failure of the characteristic investigative activities to appear before the age of two and one-half or three years suggest possible mental retardation.

"From the ages of three to five, failure to learn by experience and to acquire reasonable obedience in the face of average good training is likely to indicate faulty intelligence.

"The best indicator during the school period is the child's progress in his classes. Repeated failures in school and inability to keep up with his grade certainly require investigation. The average child of six years does first grade work; seven years, second grade; eight years, third grade; etc. A child two or more years behind in his school work is often, although not always, mentally retarded.

"Mentally retarded children often have difficulty in getting along with playmates of their own age; there is a tendency for them to play with children younger than themselves. They are often teased and "picked" on by other children and are sometimes behavior problems in the home and school. They are apt to display a lack of that characteristic initiative, brightness and alertness of other children, although such traits may not be so noticeably lacking except in outstanding cases of mental retardation." [2]

Definitions.—A generation ago mental deficiency was customarily defined as "a state of mental defect from birth or from an early age, due to incomplete cerebral development, in consequence of which the person affected is unable to perform his duties as a member of society in the position of life to which he was born." [3] It has proved to be impractical as a device for distinguishing the subnormal from the normal because incompleteness of cerebral development can be ascertained only by means of an autopsy. It is probable, also, that there is a large percentage of cases among the high-grade defectives in whom autopsy would fail to demonstrate any structural anomaly in cerebral development. Feeblemindedness as a problem of social pathology necessitates the use of criteria primarily social, supplemented and facilitated, however, by the use of devices for the measurement of mental retardation.

A prevalent definition today is that submitted in the report of the Missouri Code Commission. "The words 'feeble-minded person'

[2] Potter, Howard W.—*Delayed Mental Development in Children*, pp. 1–2; State of New York, Department of Mental Hygiene, Pamphlet No. 8 (no date).

[3] This definition will be found in the Report of the British Royal Commission of 1908: in Goddard, Henry Herbert—*Feeble-mindedness: Its Causes and Consequences;* The Macmillan Company, 1914: and in many other texts of this period.

shall be construed to mean any person afflicted with mental defectiveness from birth or from an early age, so pronounced that he is incapable of managing himself and his affairs and of subsisting by his own efforts, or of being taught to do so, and who requires supervision, control, and care for his own welfare, or for the welfare of others, or for the welfare of the community, and who cannot be classified as an insane person." [4] In essence this definition applies a social criterion in its insistence upon incapacity for self-management and social supervision. It may be questioned, however, whether it should properly exclude those few children in the schools for the feebleminded who are successfully taught self-management. Since also in most jurisdictions the term insanity is a generic legal term, which includes the mentally deficient as well as the mentally abnormal or diseased, it would have been better to have used the more precise term in the definition.

Feeblemindedness is best recognized as a symptom complex covering a wide range of defect, invariably existing at birth or acquired in the earlier years of life before mental development has been completed, and recognized primarily by evidences of mental retardation and social incompetency. It must be shown that the social incompetence is due to incomplete mental development rather than to degeneration from normal states in order to demonstrate clinical feeblemindedness. Social incompetence is recognized by limitations in the child's capacity to learn or plan, by his lack of judgment or foresight, and by his lack of ability to adapt himself to unusual circumstances, or to "make good" by his own efforts.

Standards of Reference.—The differentiation of the mental defective from persons of normal mentality is accomplished by no simple procedure but rather by a careful application of a variety of techniques. These include examination to cover evidence of (1) physical stigmata of degeneracy; (2) mental retardation; and (3) social inadequacy.

Physical Examination.—The physical stigmata or signs of degeneracy include pronounced abnormalities in the shape and size of the head, pronounced asymmetries of face or body, anomalies of the external ear, tongue, palate, etc., as well as external symptoms of the various types of idiocy and imbecility, such as cretinism, mon-

[4] Dr. J. E. Wallace Wallin served as Chairman of the Committee which prepared this definition, which is quoted from Bossard, James H. S.—*Social Change and Social Problems*, pp. 471–472; Harper & Brothers, revised edition, 1938.

golism, microcephaly, hydrocephalus, porencephaly, amaurotic idiocy, and paralytic and epileptic types.

"A general inspection of the individual child being examined may reveal many evidences of mental defect. The general appearance, carriage and bearing of the defective is not that of a well-set-up, confident, attentive, vigorous, normal boy. As a rule, mental defectives are not physically attractive or pleasing in appearance. They usually exhibit a certain degree of inferior motor co-ordination, as shown by awkward, shambling gait, clumsy, uncertain movements, ungraceful and uncouth postures and attitudes, and general lack of grace, alertness and dexterity.

"In addition, the defective usually presents various physical anomalies. His head may be too small, too large, asymmetrical, misshapen, or badly proportioned. The width, breadth and circumference of the cranium should be carefully measured with calipers and tape, and the findings compared with the average measurements. . . . The cephalic index should be ascertained.

"The face is often asymmetrical, badly proportioned and lacks expression. This dull facial expression is partly caused by muscular inertness due to the absence of regular muscular attitudes resulting from the repetition of various intellectual processes. The absence of the fine lines of expression often gives the face a distinctly juvenile or infantile appearance. There may be excessive and meaningless play of the features, such as over-smiling and grinning or scowling. The mouth may be too small or too large, or half-opened when the face is in repose.

"The external ears may show abnormal variation as to size, shape and relative position. They may be too large or too small. They may be very simply formed, with only a rudimentary development of the helix, anti-helix, tragus, anti-tragus, etc., or they may present an almost grotesque over-evolution of some or all of the structural elements. The lobules may be closely adherent. The ears may cling closely to the head or be markedly outstanding. The two ears may be quite dissimilar as to size, shape and position.

"The teeth, jaws and hard palate of the defective often show marked abnormalities. He seldom has a good set of teeth, of proper size, well placed, without discoloration or early decay. The jaws may be badly shaped and proportioned. The hard palate may be excessively vaulted.

"The height and weight of the defective is usually a little less than that of the normal.

"The above evidences of physical inferiority are found quite commonly in cases of mental defect. A defective will usually present one or several of the physical anomalies described. Not all of these abnormalities are found in any one individual, however, nor does every defective exhibit a majority of these defects. A small proportion of defectives do not show any of these characteristic physical signs, but are well-formed and well-developed." [5]

[5] *Regulations for Determining the Number of Children Three Years Retarded in Mental Development* (Chapter 358, Acts of 1931), p. 10; Department of Education and the

Marked stigmata are found chiefly among imbeciles and idiots but not necessarily in the higher grade feebleminded. Stigmata are sometimes, though much less frequently, found also among persons who prove to be of normal or even supernormal intelligence. Hence the diagnosis of mental deficiency cannot rest solely upon such physical signs.

Mental Tests.—Evidence of mental retardation is arrived at by comparing the performance of the feebleminded with that of normal persons of the same physical age at tasks requiring intelligence. It has been possible through the school system to ascertain by periodic tests of children of any given school age what constitutes normal or average performance. A feebleminded child ten years of age may prove, however, to be able to do only the tasks of a normal five-year-old. It is then said to have a mental age of five. By means of such tests the intelligence rating of any child, in terms of mental age, may be ascertained. The processes of distinguishing the feebleminded from the normal, and of subclassifying the feebleminded, are facilitated.

Many forms of tests are used by contemporary psychometry. Psychological testing began with standardized tests of intelligence devised by Binet and Simon, whose first scales for measurement of intelligence in children were published through the years 1905 to 1908.[6] Most schools for the feebleminded and state departments of mental diseases in the United States make use of the Stanford revision of the Binet test by Lewis M. Terman, supplemented by a variety of special tests. The mental age of the child is determined and then divided by the physical age to find the intelligence quotient. In its simpler form, expressing mental and physical age by years rather than months, a child who is five years old and who has a mental age of five would have an intelligence quotient of one. Usually, however, the quotient is multiplied by one hundred for convenience of statement and thus the I.Q. would be expressed as 100. A child of ten who in the tests reveals a mental age of twelve has an I.Q. of 120. A child of ten with a mental age of six has an I.Q. of 60.

The official regulations for determining retardation in Massachusetts state:

Department of Mental Diseases, The Commonwealth of Massachusetts (no date).

[6] Binet, Alfred, and Simon, Th.—*A Method of Measuring the Development of the Intelligence of Young Children* (authorized translation by Clara Harrison Town); Chicago Medical Book Co., 1915.

"The findings in this field must not be used alone any more than the evidence from any one other field, nor must they be allowed to overrule data gathered in other ways. This abstract rating must be corroborative and correlative.

"The examination must not be allowed to fall into the routine mechanical application of any one test. Each individual must be studied as a human being.

"The primary purpose of the psychological examination is the determination of the actual intellectual level of the child examined and his probable scholastic aptitude. To this end a mere statement of mental age should be elaborated by a commentary on the factors influencing academic success: the quality of response, method of approach to new situations, any special abilities or disabilities (language difficulty, specific reading disability, etc.) which are apparent during the examination, power of protracted attention and ease and completeness of comprehension.

"No all-inclusive catalogue of the characteristics of mental defectives can be made, but among the significant findings should be included such factors as a long reaction time, imperfect comprehension of specific directions, inattention and easy distractibility, lack of persistence in the face of a difficult problem, or an unreasonable refusal to abandon a task, absence of critical judgment and an inability to comprehend all the significant factors in a situation. More specifically, the mentally defective individual is apt to succeed on test items dependent on immediate rote memory and comprehension of a simple, concrete problem, and fail those tasks dependent upon foresight, planning and ability to make generalizations from a specific case.

"An adequate examination should include:

"*a.* A mental age rating by a standardized individual test series, preferably the Stanford Revision of the Binet series.

"*b.* Performance tests supplementing these findings to give a more exact clinical picture of its individual." [7]

Although some specialists designate intelligence quotients of 75 or below as feebleminded, the tendency in recent years has been to draw the line at an I.Q. of 70. By means of intelligence quotients the feebleminded are subclassified by the Federal Bureau of the Census as follows:

"A *moron* is a mentally defective person usually having a mental age of 8 years or upwards, or, if a child, an intelligence quotient of 50 or more. As a rule, the upper limit for a diagnosis of mental deficiency should be an intelligence quotient of 69.

[7] *Regulations for Determining the Number of Children Three Years Retarded in Mental Development,* p. 36. The following nonverbal tests are listed as "some of the most useful": Dearborn Form Board No. 3, Healy Form Boards A & B, Healy Picture Completion No. 1 and No. 2, MacQuarrie Test for Mechanical Ability, Porteus Maze Series, and Worcester Series of Form Boards.

"An *imbecile* is a mentally defective person usually having a mental age of 3 years to 7 years, inclusive, or, if a child, an intelligence quotient from 20 to 49, inclusive.

"An *idiot* is a mentally defective person usually having a mental age of less than 3 years, or, if a child, an intelligence quotient of less than 20." [8]

Morgan and some other specialists draw the lines as follows: idiots, I.Q. from 0 to 25; imbeciles, I.Q. from 25 to 50; morons, I.Q. 50 to 70.[9] The American practice is to use the term "feeble-minded" generically to cover all mental defectives; the British practice, however, reserves the term for the moron group and distinguishes the feebleminded from the idiot and imbecile.

Tests of Social Inadequacy.—Mental tests are not sufficient in themselves to prove the presence of feeblemindedness. Social tests are involved in eight of the fields of special study devised by Dr. Walter E. Fernald and known as the "Ten-Point Scale Examination." These explore (1) family history, (2) personal and developmental history, (3) history of school progress, (4) social history, (5) personal characteristics and social conduct, (6) economic efficiency, (7) practical knowledge, (8) school work: in addition to (9) the physical examination, and (10) psychological tests already considered.[10]

By means of such comprehensive examination of habits and behavior, it is usually possible to determine whether the person tested is feebleminded in the sense that he is "incapable from mental defect" of "competing on equal terms with his fellows or of managing himself and his affairs with ordinary prudence." In any large group of persons examined with I.Q.'s in the vicinity of 70 some will be found with I.Q.'s close to, but under, 70 who will not be classified as feebleminded, while others, even with I.Q.'s as high as 80, may, because of abnormal sex suggestibility, for example, require commitment to institutions for the feebleminded.

The Extent of Feeblemindedness.—Since the tests by which mental defectives are ascertained have been applied upon only a small fraction of our population the volume of feeblemindedness

---

[8] Bureau of the Census—*Annual Census of Institutions for Mental Defectives and Epileptics: 1936, Instructions for Filling Out Schedules,* p. 2; Bureau of the Census (no date).

[9] Morgan, John J. B.—*The Psychology of Abnormal People,* p. 338; Longmans, Green and Co., 1937.

[10] Forms for these tests are outlined in *Regulations for Determining the Number of Children Three Years Retarded in Mental Development.*

is not known. The summary of the mental defectives and epileptics in institutions, published by the Federal Bureau of the Census in the year 1937, gives the number of patients on the institution books at the end of the year 1935 as 111,968, of whom 4,414 were in private institutions and 14,529 on parole "or otherwise absent." These figures do not include feebleminded persons in almshouses, prisons, and hospitals for the insane, but are limited to the population in special institutions for mental defectives and epileptics.[11]

Actually the majority of persons who are mentally deficient are either living at home, at large in the community, or are in institutions in which their mental condition is not scientifically ascertained. These include many persons too young to be entered in schools for feebleminded and others who have been trained there and returned to their homes or paroled to jobs in which they have some social supervision. It includes much larger numbers still unrecognized and many who by preference are cared for by their own families.

The Distribution of "Intelligence."—The most comprehensive application of mental tests to our adult population was made upon men drafted for army service in the years 1917 and 1918. After enlistment over one million seven hundred thousand men were given either the Alpha or Beta tests—the former to persons who were literate and the latter to the illiterate and those who lacked adequate command of the English language. Both tests were given to enough persons so that equivalent ratings could be secured. Unlike the Binet-Simon tests administered in our state institutions for the feebleminded, the Alpha and Beta tests were given to groups of from fifty to three hundred men at a time rather than to individuals.[12]

The sample of our population to whom these tests were administered was apparently reasonably typical for males of the age group covered. It excluded, however, at the base all feebleminded persons who were in institutions or who could not meet the tests, both physical and mental, of the draft board. At the other end of the

[11] During the year 1935 there were 8,954 "first admissions of mental defectives to state institutions." Of the first admissions 4,240 were classified as morons, 2,810 imbeciles, 1,645 idiots, and 259 were unclassified. There were 1,603 who were both mentally defective and epileptic. Bureau of the Census—*Mental Defectives and Epileptics in Institutions: 1935;* Bureau of the Census, Release of February 9, 1937.

[12] Yerkes, Robert M., editor—*Psychological Examining in the United States Army;* Memoirs of the National Academy of Science, Vol. XV, Government Printing Office, 1921.

mental scale a large but unknown percentage of the more gifted escaped the draft by serving in executive, subexecutive, or specialized capacities in governmental service or in war industries.

A point scale was used in which a maximum of 212 points might be obtained. The results of the test were at first disconcerting. For the mental ages of these one million seven hundred thousand men as revealed by their performance in the Alpha or Beta tests were distributed as follows:

	Points	Mental Age	Intelligence Distribution, Per Cent
A, Very superior intelligence.	135–212	18 or 19	4.5
B, Superior intelligence	105–134	16 or 17	9.0
C plus, High average intelligence	75–104	15 or 16	16.5
C, Average intelligence	45–74	13 or 14	25.0
C minus, Low average intelligence	25–44	11 or 12	20.0
D, Inferior intelligence	15–24	10 or 11	15.0
D minus and E, Very inferior intelligence	0–14	10 or less	10.0

Contemporary publicists shocked the American public with their naive observation that forty-five per cent of our population, as revealed by these tests, must be "feebleminded," according to the standards of reference then in vogue. For some of the earlier psychometrists had drawn the line between mental deficiency and normality at the mental age, for adults, of twelve years. Yet, under the army tests, twenty-five per cent showed a mental age of eleven years or less, and ten per cent a mental age of ten or less, in spite of the fact that the obviously feebleminded had been debarred by draft boards from enlistment.

These findings have subsequently led to considerable improvements in mental testing, to elaboration of methods of diagnosing feeblemindedness, and to exclusion from the latter category of adults with mental ages of eleven and twelve except where there is evidence of marked social inadequacy. It is now generally agreed that the high percentages of mental ages of ten and eleven in the army tests are to be accounted for in part (though no one knows in how large part) by some or all of the following factors: (1) some men may purposely have done poorly on the tests to escape being sent overseas when it became known that persons of low mentality were to be retained in this country; (2) some of the men took the tests as a joke and purposely did less well than they might have done; (3) some were confused or made self-conscious either by being subjected to tests so unlike any which they had ever faced before, or by the methods of military discipline by which the tests were administered; (4) some of the tests doubtless involved the use of mental processes which had remained inactive in many of the men since they had left public school many years earlier and were thus tests of training and recent experience rather than of intelligence. The latter might be particularly true of word tests. (5) The time allowance may have been inadequate for foreign-born drafted men not yet familiar with the English language.[13]

For these many reasons the army tests cannot be accepted at their face value as an indication of the potential performance of this large sample of our population. It is probable that the performance of many could have been improved had they better understood what was wanted and if they had had recent experience with problems of the types which these tests offered. If this is a correct interpretation, these clearly were not exclusively tests of intelligence and the ratings given therefore may not properly be termed intelligence ratings.

There is a striking parallel revealed by Goddard between the distribution of intelligence as revealed by the army tests and the distribution of ages at which children prior to 1917 left school. Goddard, comparing the army tests with figures of the Federal Office of Education, noted that fourteen per cent of the population left school at the physical age of twelve, which corresponds closely with the twenty per cent of the army group showing a mental age of twelve years. Thirteen per cent left school at eleven years, which is close to the fifteen per cent accorded an eleven-year mental age, and thirteen per cent left school at ten years of age or earlier corresponding to the ten per cent of the mental age of ten or less.[14] These findings (assuming the reliability of the figures of the Office of Education and their applicability to the army draft) suggest the possibility that the Alpha and Beta tests reflected prior schooling. Yet most of the persons had left school presumably from economic necessity rather than because they were incapable of further training. The degree of their educability remains unknown. The extent of feeblemindedness in the United States clearly cannot be gleaned

13 See Brigham, Carl C.—*A Study of American Intelligence;* Princeton University Press, 1923: and Hexter, Maurice B., and Myerson, Abraham—*13.77 versus 12.05; A Study in Probable Error;* The National Committee for Mental Hygiene, Inc., 1924.

14 Goddard, Henry Herbert—*Human Efficiency and Levels of Intelligence,* pp. 113–115; Princeton University Press, 1920.

from these findings. Further research and the application of additional and improved methods of diagnosis will be necessary before the volume of mental deficiency will be known.

Recent Estimates.—The best estimates of the extent of feeblemindedness in America today are revealed in the careful statements of diagnostic specialists residing in states in which there is general testing of all children who are backward in their school work and in which there are also local clinics for the feebleminded to supplement the work of the state schools. Thus in Massachusetts, where travelling psychiatric school clinics have been in existence since 1914 and have covered the state since 1921, findings are expressed as follows:

"It was found that there was a total of 47,616 children in the first grades of those schools in which first examinations of retarded children were held during the year 1935. We may say that this represents the approximate number of new students entering these schools during a single year. We have observed in previous tables that a total of 6,636 children were referred to all clinics because of retardation for *the first time during the year 1935.* Comparing this total of 6,636 with the 47,616 new students entering the schools, we find that new cases of retardation and mental defect discovered during 1935 are 13.9 per cent of the number entering schools during the same year. That is, when we compare the new cases of *retardation* discovered during a single year with the *new children entering school* for the same year, we find that one child in seven is retarded in some degree.

"Dividing the mental defectives from those merely retarded, we note that the *new cases* diagnosed as mentally defective during a single year are 2.8 per cent of the number of children entering school for the first time during a single year. The *new cases* diagnosed as retarded constitute 10.9 per cent of the number of children entering school for the first time. All of this, of course, is for the year 1935. We feel that these percentages of 2.8 for mental defect and 10.9 for retardation give us a much better picture of the relative amounts of these conditions actually present in our school systems." [15]

Popenoe, in 1930, estimated that five per cent of the population of the United States, or six million people, had I.Q.'s under 70. But since only one per cent of these were cared for in institutions "it follows that a large part of the six million must be getting along well enough in the population to be unnoticed unless they are given mental tests." [16] Dr. George S. Stevenson, Director of the Division

[15] *Report of the Division of Mental Deficiency,* pp. 33–34; reprinted from the Annual Report of the Commissioner of Mental Diseases, P. D., 117, 1935, The Commonwealth of Massachusetts.

[16] Popenoe, Paul—*Feeblemindedness Today,* p. 421; reprinted from the *Journal of Heredity,* Vol. XXI, No. 10, October, 1930.

on Community Clinics of the National Committee for Mental Hygiene, states, in 1937, that "the most conservative estimates of the feebleminded put the number in the United States at about 1,000,000." [17] This is the group "unable to compete in our civilization," to which must be added another thirteen per cent of our population suffering from "the more evasive defects of ability to perform complex intellectual activities known as dullness, intellectual subnormality, or retardation." These may, however, "get along" on a simple standard "particularly if temperamentally stable." [18]

The Subcommittee on Problems of Mental Deficiency of the White House Conference on Child Health and Protection estimated that there were in this country eight hundred and fifty thousand handicapped children who were definitely feebleminded and five million six hundred and fifty thousand who were intellectually subnormal. The former group, constituting two per cent of all children, had I.Q.'s of 85 or less "in conjunction with social failure." The latter also had I.Q.'s below 85 and although not feebleminded were "undoubtedly in the mentally handicapped class." [19]

". . . Their low intelligence associated with mental, physical, or social handicaps causes them to be easily confused with the feeble-minded. Such children have sometimes been termed *psuedo-feeble-minded*. The important distinction is that in verbal, social, and educational conditions these children have a much greater potentiality of personal social success at maturity than is the case with the feeble-minded. Some of the groupings in which they may be placed are given.

"*Unadjusted or Maladjusted.* In this group intellectual subnormality is associated with ineffectual behavior, behavior disturbance not sufficiently serious to evoke social judgments of personal-social inadequacy, but in which retardation or intellectual subnormality is association with mental instability, personality defect, psychopathic tendencies, and similar deviations. These children require instruction in special classes in public schools, such as adjustment classes, particular classes, or predelinquent classes, where specialized instruction helps to overcome special disability of behavior in spite of the low intelligence level.

"*Special Mental Disability.* Here retardation or intellectual subnormality is associated with some peculiar mental disability, often basically physical or situational, in attention, memory, perception, or language. Such children require instruction in differential teaching or coaching classes designed to meet their particular needs.

[17] Stevenson, George S.—"Mental Hygiene," *Social Work Year Book 1937*, p. 279; Russell Sage Foundation, 1937.
[18] *Ibid.*
[19] White House Conference on Child Health and Protection—*The Handicapped Child*, pp. 4 and 330–332; The Century Co., 1933.

"Special Educational Disabilities. This group includes those children whose intellectual handicaps are associated with the environmental conditions at home or at school such as illness, pupil-teacher antagonism, bad study habits, as contrasted with the constitutional handicap of the preceding group. Individual instruction (restoration classes) helps such children regain their appropriate educational levels. Mental hygiene may also be of much assistance. Visiting teachers, recreation programs and similar aids should not be overlooked." [20]

It would be futile, until more precise studies are made, to assume that more than two per cent of our population is technically feebleminded. It is, however, important to recognize that the mental retardation of at least ten per cent, and perhaps fifteen per cent or more, is a handicap to the individual in personal, industrial, and social relationships. Such mental inferiority may on occasion cause behavior problems, industrial inefficiency, and waste, and involve a costly expenditure of time, energy, and funds by public and private agencies. If intellectual subnormality were nonexistent such resources could be utilized for purposes far more constructive.

Social Statistics of Feebleminded.—Males predominate among first admissions of mental defectives to state institutions. In 1935, of the patients admitted, 4,957 were male and 3,997 female. Males exceeded females in all categories: moron, imbecile, idiot, and also among the epileptic mental defectives. They may not exceed, however, among the noninstitutional defectives, as specialists generally believe that feebleminded girls are more commonly taken care of in their own homes.

In age distribution the lower age groups presumably predominate among the feebleminded as compared with the general population because feeblemindedness exists from birth or is acquired at an early age, and because mortality rates are higher among the feebleminded. Dayton, in a study of Massachusetts cases, found mortality among idiots approximately five times that of the general population; among imbecile males 2.4 times, and females two times that for their sex; while among morons mortality rates were about the same as that for the general population though slightly higher for females. [21]

Adequate statistics of marriage among the feebleminded are not

[20] *Ibid*, p. 336.

[21] Dayton, Neil A.—*Mortality in Mental Deficiency over a Fourteen Year Period: Analysis of 8,976 Cases and 878 Deaths in Massachusetts,* p. 196; reprinted from the Proceedings of the Fifty-Fifth Annual Session of the American Association for the Study of the Feebleminded, held at New York City, May 25–28, 1931.

available. Since, however, marriage is impossible for idiots and most imbeciles and is prevented for morons during the periods of segregation in institutions, the problem of marriage among the feebleminded is chiefly that of the preponderating group of morons who are not in institutions.

Many of the early studies of fecundity among the feebleminded arrived at the alarming conclusion that they were breeding more rapidly than the general population and much more rapidly than the more gifted elements. It is likely that this is true of the intellectually subnormal not clinically classified as feebleminded, but improbable that it is true of the cases that have had institution care. Dayton, analyzing the families of over twenty thousand retarded children in Massachusetts public schools, after careful correction for sampling errors, concludes that the average number of children for such families is practically the same as that of the general population.[22] Although some, but not all, of the degenerate families which have been closely analyzed, are found to be prolific, the higher mortality rates for the feebleminded, and in some cases sterility produced by venereal disease, tend to correct such tendencies. In terms of inheritance the expectation would be that the greater proportion of defectives would be born to carrier unions (genetic hybrids but somatic normals) rather than to unions of persons themselves defective.[23]

The geographic distribution of the feebleminded requires further study before accurate statements can be made. The White House Conference discussed samplings by the National Committee for Mental Hygiene which revealed a range from one per cent feebleminded in Wyoming to ten per cent each in Kentucky and Texas. Some of this variation, however, is ascribable to the varying criteria used by the research staffs, to undue reliance upon intelligence tests, to differences in racial composition, or the smallness of the sample employed. Until identical criteria are used and the whole population of a state covered, such studies can do little more than indicate the potential gravity of the problem.[24]

[22] Dayton, Neil A.—*Influence of Size of Family upon the Characteristics of the Mentally Deficient;* reprinted from *The American Journal of Psychiatry*, Vol. 91, No. 4, January, 1935. See also Reuter, Edward Byron—*Population Problems*, Chapters XIII, XIV, and XVI; J. B. Lippincott Company, 1923.

[23] *Ibid.*, pp. 800–801.

[24] White House Conference on Child Health and Protection—*op. cit.*, pp. 383–384.

Although there is a preponderance of children from cities in public institutions for the feebleminded, one cannot deduce from this that mental deficiency is more prevalent in cities than in rural communities. A feebleminded child can be looked after by its family more easily in the country than in the city. The social evidences of mental defect are more readily apparent under conditions of urban life, so commitment is more likely. A large number of the degenerate families in which feeblemindedness occurs among some of the offspring in each generation, are rural families, which through social isolation have long escaped discovery and consequent social control. There are still presumably many rural communities in America in which the percentage of mental deficiency is abnormally high.

Types.—Feeblemindedness is not a unitary characteristic. Many types can be isolated and distinguished. In addition to classification by mental age and intelligence quotients already considered, it is customary to distinguish types which reference to behavior and also with reference to causes or predisposing factors. The latter division is differentiated into constitutional or primary cases and reactional or secondary.

Primary feeblemindedness exists in the patient from the time of birth. The condition may be hereditary, or acquired during the foetal period. This group is characterized by biological inferiority usually evidenced by anomalies in height, weight, or physiognomy, by endocrine dysfunction, or by constitutional syphilis.

The secondary or reactional group includes those in whom defect "results from the organic reaction of the normally developing organism to mechanical, chemical or bacterial factors in the environment." It comprises injuries to the brain at or following birth (traumata), from maternal malnutrition or toxic states, from congenital tuberculosis, premature birth, abnormalities in labor or obstetric methods, or bacterial disease. There are, however, some types of feeblemindedness difficult to place in either of these categories and temporarily classified as "degenerative." [25]

Among special types may be mentioned cretinism, caused by congenital deficiency in the secretions of the thyroid glands. Subtypes include true cretins, who are entirely devoid of intellect; semicretins, with some slight ability to speak; and cretinoids, with some capacity for training.

Mongolism is so named because of the slant eyes and other mon-

[25] *Ibid.*, pp. 340–343.

golian features of its victims. It is presumably not hereditary, and may occur in families where the parents are gifted and the other children normal. Mongols usually come within the imbecile group and are good-natured and imitative.

Hydrocephalus is characterized by an excess quantity of cerebrospinal fluid in the brain. The mental range is from idiocy to normality. Microcephaly is characterized by a cone-shaped skull and receding forehead. It is often associated with epilepsy. Amaurotic idiocy is accompanied by forms of paralysis and blindness. There are other paralytic and epileptic types of feeblemindedness, and still others associated with syphilis, encephalitis or other imflammations of the brain, pituitary dysfunction, and other recognized sources.[26]

Relative Importance of Causative Factors.—Parents who have the misfortune to have feebleminded children are inclined to ascribe the condition to a fall upon the head or to childhood diseases. Early books on this subject, such as Barr's *Mental Defectives*, stressed such factors. Intensive studies made in the past thirty years by specialists in eugenics, endocrinology, and psychiatry, have completely changed the emphasis but have not arrived at general agreement.[27]

Heredity is now recognized as the major factor in a considerable percentage of cases. Goddard, in studying three hundred and twenty-seven families of feebleminded children at the Vineland institution in New Jersey, in 1914, concluded that fifty per cent of cases were surely hereditary and that there was possible neuropathic heredity in twenty per cent more.[28] Popenoe estimated that from two-thirds to three-fourths of feeblemindedness is based on the inherited constitution.[29] Others, like Fernald and Myerson, have considered heredity overstressed.[30] There is a presumption, however, that a significant proportion of cases of the types which recur in family charts are hereditary even though the precise mechanism of heredity has not yet been definitely ascertained. There is an equal presumption that certain other primary types which recur in the

---

[26] For detailed discussion of these types see Henderson, D. K., and Gillespie, R. D.—*op. cit.*, pp. 393–402, and Morgan, John J. B.—*op. cit.*, pp. 317–326.

[27] Barr, Martin W.—*Mental Defectives;* P. Blakiston's Son & Co., 1904.

[28] Goddard, Henry Herbert—*Feeble-mindedness: Its Causes and Consequences;* The Macmillan Company, 1914.

[29] Popenoe, Paul—*op. cit.*, p. 428.

[30] Myerson, Abraham—*The Inheritance of Mental Diseases*, pp. 81–85; Williams & Wilkins Company, 1925.

same family, such as cretinism, and syphilitic feeblemindedness, are not hereditary though congenital; though even here some specialists maintain that the diseases in question take this special form because of factors in inheritance. Some of the secondary types of feeble-mindedness might thus have a basis in heredity though produced only under specific environmental conditions. This problem will be treated more fully in a later chapter.

Trauma, taking the form of birth injury or post-natal injury, probably accounts for from five to ten per cent of cases.[31] Endocrine cases, including cretinism and pituitary types, account for five per cent or less.

There is much disagreement among specialists concerning the role of infectious diseases. Syphilis ranks high in some studies, but Goddard failed to find it operative in the three hundred and twenty-seven families which he studied. Solomon finds positive Wassermann reaction, the usual test of the presence of syphilis, in only six per cent of children in schools for the feebleminded as compared with five per cent of children in general hospitals.[32] An arrest of mental development is apparently one of the infrequent sequelae of certain childhood diseases, such as encephalitis, meningitis, and possibly also scarlet fever and tuberculosis.

Goddard ascribed altogether only nineteen per cent of cases to disease, trauma, or toxic factors.[33]   Contemporary researches in endocrinology, the nutritional conditions of the foetal period, the maternal use of drugs or alcohol, and other chemical factors may result in a considerable change of emphasis in future treatments of the etiology of feeblemindedness.

Social Consequences of Feeblemindedness.—In general an appreciation of the social pathology of any handicapped group should involve both an understanding of the reactions of the in-dividual victim to his handicap and an understanding of the effects of the handicap upon his reciprocal relations in his family, educa-tion, work, and his social and civic life. In the case of the feeble-minded their limitations in individual self-expression often make it difficult to ascertain their subjective personal reactions. Like nor-

[31] Doll, Edgar A., Phelps, W. M., and Melcher, Ruth T.—*Mental Deficiency Due to Birth Injuries*, p. 289; The Macmillan Company, 1932.

[32] Solomon, Harry C., and Solomon, Maida Herman—*Syphilis of the Innocent;* United States Interdepartmental Social Hygiene Board, 1922.

[33] Goddard, Henry Herbert—*Feeble-mindedness: Its Causes and Consequences;* The Macmillan Company, 1914

mal persons, however, each is unique, and hence one case may be clinically described as apathetic, another as bewildered, others as resentful, troublesome, or vindictive. Some display happy dispositions and others are unhappy; some are coöperative, others noncoöperative; and so on through the long list of descriptive adjectives. The bias of the investigator as well as the manifold conditions of the personality, training, and environment of the case studied are obviously implicated. The responses to ridicule or to pity, to praise or avoidance, may run through the gamut to be found among persons more normal. Suggestibility and the desire to please persons more gifted than themselves are traits frequently recorded—traits which if exploited by the unscrupulous may involve the adult moron in criminality or prostitution, but which if utilized by parent or school may lead to useful training.

Within a normal family a low-grade feebleminded child is a source of continuous concern and the whole life of the family may be influenced and even dominated by its presence. If the feebleminded person grows up and has a family of his own, which is possible among those of higher grade, the rearing of the next generation suffers from the defective intelligence of the parents, and poverty is almost inevitable. At school the feebleminded child may feel the disgrace of retardation and to the school authorities his presence necessitates the extra cost of special classes or individual instruction. In the workshop the feebleminded boy or man may be the butt of his associates and is more likely than a person more normal to be a source of loss to the employer through unintelligent use of tools or through accidental injury. In social life the lower grade feebleminded are avoided and suffer isolation while those of higher grade, if not unattractive, may associate more freely but may be handicapped by their deficiencies in the scope of their participation.

Feeblemindedness thus tends to mean limited industrial output, limited social contacts, and the diversion of much time, energy, and money for their care. Many alarmists fear the dominance of persons of marginal mentality in the affairs of democracy because of the ease with which their votes may be controlled by political bosses. The recent studies of differential fertility, already quoted, fail to justify the fear that moron voters will soon outnumber the intelligent, yet clearly indicate the importance of appropriate measures for the prevention of inferior births in so far as that may prove practical.

Attempts to estimate the money cost of feeblemindedness to the community would obviously have little value in view of the prevailing uncertainties as to the volume of mental defect. Moreover, most of the harm done by mental deficiency to the victim and his family, and by the victim to the community, is not reducible to economic terms, and is often relatively intangible. Whether the feebleminded person is subjected to ridicule by thoughtless associates or is avoided by them, injury may be done to the handicapped person and his development thwarted. Increased mental activity and proficiency appear to be dependent in large part upon socializing the defective child and upon making possible his participation in group activities.[34]

Prior to 1917 large numbers of sociological studies of inmates of prisons, reformatories, of penal and truant schools for children, and of prostitutes purported to find from a fifth to one-half or more suffering from mental defect. But in this period an adult with a mental age of eleven or twelve under the Binet test was commonly assumed to be feebleminded if his behavior was criminal or delinquent. Following the army tests and subsequent refinements in mental measurement the percentages of inmates in these institutions designated as feebleminded have fallen to less than half their former rate. There is sporadic evidence that the percentage of the feebleminded who are apprehended and sentenced for criminal acts is higher than that in the general population. It is not clear, however, that the volume of delinquent behavior among feebleminded persons is higher than in the general population, for because of their mental deficiency the former may have been more easily apprehended.[35]

Generalizations concerning the social pathology of feeblemindedness must continue to be strictly tentative until the volume of feeblemindedness is accurately known, and until the types are better differentiated and the reactions and limitations of each are better understood. Many attempts at generalization have been inaccurate because of the failure to recognize that among the feebleminded,

[34] See, for example, Beaman, Florence N.—"The Value of Social Factors in the Training of the Defective Child"; *American Journal of Sociology*, Vol. XXXVII, No. 2.

[35] See further Chapter XXIX; also Zeleny, L. D.—"Feebleminded and Criminal Conduct"; *American Journal of Sociology*, Vol. XXXVIII, No. 4: and Young, Pauline V.—"Defective Social Intelligence as a Factor in Crime"; *American Sociological Review*, Vol. 3, No. 2, April, 1938.

as among the normal population, each individual is unique. The diverse findings of specialists to date have made it clear that their observations have been largely subject to the bias of the investigator or to errors as to fact or interpretation. Although mental deficiency is unquestionably a major handicap for its victim and a source of considerable cost to the community, measures for social control remain rough and inexact pending the further elucidation of the social pathology of feeblemindedness through the analysis of this general phenomenon into its component parts for detailed and precise research.

History of Social Provision for Feebleminded.—Until a century ago the feebleminded were among many, but not all, peoples subjected to neglect and even persecution, conditions from which they still sometimes suffer in backward communities. The first notable attempt to educate an idiot was made by Itard in Paris in the first decade of the nineteenth century. His patient, known as the "savage of Aveyron," had been found living like an animal in a forest and unable to speak. Itard succeeded in rendering the boy's senses of taste, touch, and smell more acute, in improving his habits, increasing his wants, and in teaching him to place letters together to spell a few words; but abandoned his experiment after five years.[36]

The effect of Itard's work was to demonstrate that the feebleminded have some capacity for training and to indicate that an important approach is through the training of the senses. This discovery made it possible for Itard's pupil, Edouard Séguin, to devise methods of instruction which, with modifications and improvements, are still in use. In 1837 Séguin founded in Paris the first school for the successful training of lower grade feebleminded. Séguin's method combined the training of senses and muscles, correcting the muscular movements, teaching the child to walk, to grasp, etc. Sense training was begun with the sense of touch, extended to taste, smell, hearing and sight, and then so far as possible coördinated.[37]

As early as 1818 several idiotic children had been received and trained at the American Asylum for the Deaf and Dumb at Hartford. At the instigation of Samuel Gridley Howe, Massachusetts, in 1848, made an appropriation for the establishment of an experimental

[36] Itard, Jean Marc Gaspard—*The Wild Boy of Aveyron* (*Rapports et mémoires sur le sauvage de l'Aveyron*) (translated by George and Muriel Humphrey); The Century Co., 1932.
[37] Séguin, Edward—*Idiocy: And Its Treatment by the Physiological Method;* Teachers College, Columbia University, 1907.

school for idiots—the first state institution in the United States. Howe was in charge of the school and carried it on with the Perkins Institution for the Blind, which he also directed. In 1851 it became the Massachusetts School for Idiotic and Feeble-minded Youth. New York established a school in 1851, Pennsylvania in 1852, Ohio in 1857. Séguin came to America in 1850, and at Howe's invitation spent his first months at the Massachusetts school, going later to the New York, Pennsylvania, Ohio, and Connecticut schools.[38]

Treatment.—Social policy with regard to mental deficiency involves four major groups of measures: first, study to ascertain if there is any means of cure; second, the development of appropriate educational methods; third, social direction of the process of social assimilation and guidance; fourth, study of causes of feeblemindedness with a view to their prevention at the source. Each of these groups of measures has necessitated much preliminary research and is accompanied by continuing research. To date major progress seems to have been made in the field of education though some preliminary work of merit has been done in the direction of prevention.

No hope is held out yet for the cure of feeblemindedness. Nevertheless one type of arrest of mental development, cretinism, has been brought under a degree of control through specific treatments of the thyroid condition from which it originates. Experiments of endocrinologists appear to warrant further research but as yet it is not clear that any type of feeblemindedness other than cretinism will respond to their methods. Attempts to remove the factors which have thwarted mental development by means of brain surgery have so far proved ineffectual. There have been a very few sporadic instances in which the factors retarding mental development in a limited group of types of deficiency have appeared to be removed temporarily by induced fever or other devices, so that some increase resulted in the intelligence quotient. However, the only safe conclusion upon which to build present social policy is that feeblemindedness, except for cretinism, is a permanent and incurable condition of arrested mental development.

Training.—When Dr. Edouard Séguin demonstrated that the condition and performance of the feebleminded could be improved

---

[38] Brief histories of treatment will be found in Davies, Stanley Powell—*Social Control of the Mentally Deficient*, Chapters II and III; Thomas Y. Crowell Company, 1930: and in Ford, James—*Social Problems and Social Policy*, pp. 393–416; Ginn and Company, 1923.

by systematic training adapted to their capacities, the practice of establishing special schools for mental defectives developed. His methods of sense training still serve as one of the bases of instruction of the feebleminded in America.

The condition of all grades of feeblemindedness is to some degree improvable by appropriate measures. For the idiot little can be accomplished save such training in personal cleanliness and in behavior as is given to infants. More of personal cleanliness can be taught to the lower grade imbeciles and they can usually be taught to dress themselves and to follow other instruction appropriate to their mental ages. As one proceeds upward among the mental ages one is impressed with the amount of useful knowledge and training which proves possible. For though a normal child is six years old for only one year of his life, an imbecile who in his adolescent years proves to have a mental age limited at six years, has the rest of his life in which to learn to do the many sorts of things which a normal six-year old can be taught to do. With this degree of capacity he may combine in his later years the strength of an adult.

There are many ways in which feebleminded boys or girls with a mental age of from seven to ten can be rendered socially useful by training. Once they have been taught obedience there are various types of manual labor open to them. Though the response to instruction may be slow each such lesson may be thoroughly learned. Thus the morons and some of the highest grade imbeciles can be useful under supervision, at clearing fields, loading and unloading, and other routine labor of a manual type upon the farm. The moron group according to capacity can be taught a variety of types of work for the home, shop, garden, or farm, and selected industrial arts such as weaving or lacemaking. Where dispositions are good and coöperativeness becomes ingrained, some of the morons in our schools for feebleminded after years of training according to their capacities are capable of self-support and of normal social contacts when they leave the institution.

In the main, however, it is only the high-grade morons who can be so trained as to become self-supporting workers outside of the institution. All others need permanent assistance and supervision either by their families or appropriate institutions, though through their training in the school they will have been taught to be more helpful and very much less of a care to their families or others than they would have been without such training.

In general, the educational policy seeks to overcome unfortunate modes of behavior and vices, to train to read and write where possible, to develop any capacities mental or physical that would make for good behavior and social usefulness, and to train the more competent for one or more types of labor in either the institution, the home, or the community.

Institutional Provision.—Forty-four of our forty-eight states have one or more separate state institutions for the feebleminded. Eleven states have two or more. There are three city or county schools and twenty-seven private institutions.[39] Although only a small percentage of the feebleminded may require such schooling or segregation, the long waiting lists characteristic of these schools and colonies attest the insufficiency of present day accommodations for this group of handicapped. Special classes in public schools for retarded pupils take care of a small portion of the remainder, though largely limited to borderline cases. A few states have travelling clinics with out-patient service and provision for some of the requisite training and social work for feebleminded children in their own homes; but in most states such service is scarcely begun. Thus few have opportunity to develop their limited capacities or to be safeguarded expertly from the adverse environmental conditions to which many of feeble intellect succumb.

Prevention.—A progressive reduction of the volume of feebleminded would be possible only through social control of the causative factors already indicated. How this can be accomplished on the basis of present knowledge is outlined in later chapters dealing with applied eugenics, and the prevention of disease and accident.

Registration.—Indispensable to the programs of both prevention and treatment is accurate detailed knowledge of the volume and incidence of each type of mental retardation and defect. Registration and scientific analysis of all cases within the entire population are thus indicated as necessary for a perfected social policy of care and control. Such registration and research, however, are still in their infancy. In no state are the adult mental defectives known unless they fall into the custody of public institutions. If in colonies for the feebleminded, or under parole from schools for the feebleminded, or in institutions for the insane or epileptic, their mental condition is a matter of record, and research into their condition

---

[39] Grimes, John Maurice—*Institutional Care of Mental Patients in the United States*, pp. 44, 57, and 89; published and distributed by the author, 1934.

is possible. A few additional mental defectives among delinquents and in prisons are subjected to psychiatric investigation and mental tests; but the majority, especially in local jails and county institutions are not. Still less commonly are the essential tests administered to patients in general hospitals, state wards and pensioners, the residents in state and local almshouses or infirmaries, or the recipients of public or private relief. Until this is done and the dimensions of the problem and the forms it takes are known, all programs for social control are necessarily tentative.

Massachusetts has maintained since 1919 a central registry of mental defectives.

". . . Arrangements were made to have all cases of this type reported by mental hospitals, State schools and several other clinics. Each year following, additions have been made to the number of sources reporting mental defectives to the Central Registry. At the present time [1935] we are receiving reports on mental defectives from (1) traveling school clinics; (2) admissions to State hospitals; (3) admissions to State schools; (4) cases placed on the waiting lists of State schools; (5) defective delinquents examined by hospital and Department psychiatrists; (6) outpatient examinations of State hospitals; (7) out-patient examinations of State schools; (8) mental hygiene clinics; (9) habit clinics; (10) child guidance clinics; (11) adjustment clinics; (12) defective delinquents admitted to Bridgewater; (13) mentally defective prisoners examined under the Briggs Law; (14) cases referred to the Division of Mental Deficiency; (15) cases examined by the Division of Mental Hygiene; and (16) children examined by the psychological clinic of the Springfield schools." [40]

For the discovery and study of children who are retarded or who present behavior problems a Massachusetts act, approved May 26, 1931, provides as follows:

". . . The fundamental purposes of the law are: (1) to discover those children of school age who are so retarded in mental development that they can derive but little benefit from the regular academic work of the schools; (2) to provide for these children a practical type of training and supervision which will enable them, so far as possible, to become self-supporting members of society; and (3) to make possible the study of children who show lesser degrees of retardation, but who are no less in need of advice and guidance. . . .

"The State has been divided into fifteen districts, and in each of these districts the school clinic examinations are held under the supervision of one of the State hospitals or State schools. A psychiatrist and a clinic unit has been assigned to each of the fifteen institutions to assist in conducting the examinations in the cities and towns within these districts.

[40] *Report of the Division of Mental Deficiency*, p. 3.

. . . The services of these traveling clinics first became available in 1921 under the direction of the Department of Mental Diseases. . . . Their work has been found to be of especial value in the smaller towns and rural communities of the State. . . .

"It is suggested that all of the following methods be employed by school officials in selecting children to be examined for admission to special classes. These directions apply only to the matter of *examination* and not to *placement* in special class:

"1. By reference to individual school records, select those pupils who have repeated two or more grades.

"2. Select those who have failed to earn promotion for two or more years, yet have been allowed for their best interests to advance with their grades.

"3. Select those who, by an age-grade table, are shown to be retarded in their school work two or more years.

"In communities where it is customary to give group tests, those children who attain an intelligence quotient of .70 or under should be referred for examination. In fact, it is not uncommon to find children in the I.Q. group .70–.79 who are three or more years retarded. In addition, it should be kept in mind that a child may be mentally retarded without being retarded in school work. For example, a child in the first grade with a mental age of 3 or 4 years is obviously retarded mentally and should be referred for examination.

"Care should be taken to exclude from the special classes those low grade mental defectives who would be unable to profit by the instruction given, and who should properly be provided for in the home or in an institution. Psychotic children, epileptics, and bright children who are delinquent do not belong in special classes.

"The new amendment to the law, passed in 1931, broadens the scope of the original law and makes it possible for school superintendents to refer other children to the clinics for examination. Thus, the traveling clinics are now able to assume the prerogatives of adjustment clinics dealing with child problems other than those of retardation alone. These include children presenting lesser degrees of retardation; children with marked behavior problems; or children who in any way seem to be having difficulties in adjusting to the school curriculum." [41]

If such provisions become general throughout the United States the first step will have been taken toward adequate study of the problem. It will greatly facilitate the more precise determination of causes, types, medical care, training, and prevention of feeble-mindedness and mental retardation. The social pathology and public cost of mental deficiency can be gleaned in only a partial and consequently impressionistic manner until records (social, physi-

[41] *Regulations for Determining the Number of Children Three Years Retarded in Mental Development*, pp. 1, 2–3.

cal, mental) are complete. Studies by eugenists, psychiatrists, criminologists, and many other professional groups must await completion of registration and of detailed examination of all cases to bring their research efforts to the requisite degree of precision. At the close of the first century of specialized care of the feebleminded, which began with Itard and Séguin, America is now reaching the threshold of adequate scientific study and of a social policy based upon research both deep and broad.

QUESTIONS FOR DISCUSSION OR EXAMINATION

1. What are the reasons for the disparities in the estimates of the number of mental defectives in the United States?
2. Illustrate how social policy might be affected by accurate knowledge of (a) the volume and percentage of feeblemindedness in our population; (b) the ratios of hereditary and adventitious feeblemindedness; (c) the relative volume of feeblemindedness due to disease and trauma.
3. What arguments would you use to persuade your state legislature to make appropriations for (a) mental testing in public schools; (b) special classes for backward children; (c) travelling clinics; (d) additional schools for feebleminded children; (e) colonies for feebleminded adults.
4. It has been argued that the number of feebleminded should not be reduced as they are necessary to do the menial work of our civilization. What do you think of this? Why?
5. It has been argued that the feebleminded should be put "out of their misery" by gentle, painless death (euthanasia). What do you think of this recommendation? Why?
6. Does feeblemindedness call for Federal measures? For municipal measures? Is it a state problem? Why?

PROBLEMS FOR INDIVIDUAL STUDY

1. Trace the history of public provision for the feebleminded in your state.
2. Compare the social provision for the feebleminded in your state with that of some other selected state.
3. Compare treatises on feeblemindedness of earlier decades—*e.g.* 1900–10—with those written since 1930: (a) *re* definitions; (b) *re* causes; (c) *re* treatment.
4. Prepare an annotated chronology of (a) mental testing; (b) the education of the feebleminded; (c) institutions, schools, and colonies for the feebleminded for England, France, or the United States.
5. Submit a book review (critical appraisal) of some one of the suggested volumes in the following list.

SUGGESTIONS FOR SUPPLEMENTARY READINGS

Anderson, Meta L.—*Education of Defectives in the Public Schools;* World Book Company, 1917.
Binet, Alfred, and Simon, Th.—*A Method of Measuring the Development of the*

Intelligence of Young Children (authorized translation by Clara Harrison Town); Chicago Medical Book Co., 1915.

Bossard, James H. S.—*Social Change and Social Problems*, Chapter XX, "Mental Deficiency: Its Nature and Social Significance," and Chapter XXI, "Mental Deficiency: Its Causes and Social Control"; Harper & Brothers, revised edition, 1938.

Brigham, Carl C.—*A Study of American Intelligence;* Princeton University Press, 1923.

Bronner, Augusta F.—*The Psychology of Special Abilities and Disabilities;* Little, Brown, and Company, 1917.

Burt, Cyril—*The Backward Child;* D. Appleton-Century Company, 1937.

Carlisle, Chester L.—*Preliminary Statistical Report of the Oregon State Survey of Mental Defect, Delinquency, and Dependency;* United States Public Health Service, Bulletin No. 112, Government Printing Office, 1922.

Davies, Stanley Powell—*Social Control of the Mentally Deficient;* Thomas Y. Crowell Company, 1930.

Dearborn, Walter F.—*Intelligence Tests: Their Significance for School and Society;* Houghton Mifflin Company, 1928.

Dearborn, Walter F., Shaw, Edwin A., and Lincoln, Edward A.—*A Series of Form Board and Performance Tests of Intelligence;* Series I, No. 4, Studies in Educational Psychology and Educational Measurement, published by The Graduate School of Education, Harvard University, September, 1923.

Descoeudres, Alice—*The Education of Mentally Defective Children;* D. C. Heath and Company, 1929.

Doll, Edgar A.—*Clinical Studies in Feeble-mindedness;* Richard G. Badger, 1917.

Eaton, Allen, and Harrison, Shelby M.—*A Bibliography of Social Surveys*, References on "Feebleminded," pp. 128–130, and "Mental Hygiene," pp. 219–226; Russell Sage Foundation, 1930.

Elliott, Mabel A., and Merrill, Francis E.—*Social Disorganization*, Chapter XV, "The Mentally Deficient"; Harper & Brothers, 1934.

Fernald, Walter E.—*A State Program for the Care of the Mentally Defective;* The National Committee for Mental Hygiene, Inc., Reprint No. 62, 1919.

Freeman, Frank N.—*Mental Tests: Their History, Principles and Applications;* Houghton Mifflin Company, 1926.

Gesell, Arnold—*The Guidance of Mental Growth in Infant and Child;* The Macmillan Company, 1930.

Gillin, John Lewis—*Social Pathology*, Chapter 7, "Mental Deficiency"; The Century Co., 1933.

Goddard, Henry Herbert—*Feeble-mindedness: Its Causes and Consequences;* The Macmillan Company, 1914.

Goddard, Henry Herbert—*Psychology of the Normal and Subnormal;* Dodd, Mead and Company, 1919.

Great Britain—*Report of the Royal Commission on the Care and Control of the Feeble-minded;* Wyman and Sons, Ltd., 1908.

Hamilton, Samuel Warren, and Haber, Roy—*Summaries of State Laws Relating to the Feebleminded and the Epileptic;* The National Committee for Mental Hygiene, Inc., 1917.

MENTAL DEFECTS 111

Henderson, D. K., and Gillespie, R. D.—*A Text-Book of Psychiatry for Students and Practitioners*, Chapter XIII, "Mental Defect"; Oxford University Press, 1933.

Hollingworth, H. L.—*Abnormal Psychology*, Chapter 8, "The Concept of Feeblemindedness," and Chapter 9, "Characteristics of the Feeble Mind"; The Ronald Press Company, 1930.

Hollingworth, Leta S.—*The Psychology of Subnormal Children;* The Macmillan Company, 1928.

Lapage, C. Paget—*Feeblemindedness in Children of School-Age;* Longmans, Green and Co., second edition, 1920.

Levine, Albert J., and Marks, Louis—*Testing Intelligence and Achievement;* The Macmillan Company, 1928.

Lincoln, Edward A., and Workman, Linwood L.—*Testing and the Uses of Test Results;* The Macmillan Company, 1935.

Lundberg, Emma O.—*A Social Study of Mental Defectives in New Castle County, Delaware;* U. S. Department of Labor, Children's Bureau, Publication No. 24, Government Printing Office, 1917.

Mangold, George B.—*Social Pathology*, Chapter XVI, "Feeble-mindedness"; The Macmillan Company, 1932.

Massachusetts—Annual Reports of the Commissioner of Mental Diseases.

Morgan, John J. B.—*The Psychology of Abnormal People*, Chapter IX, "Abnormalities of Intelligence"; Longmans, Green and Co., 1937.

New York, State of—Annual Reports of the Department of Mental Hygiene.

New York, State of—*A Survey of Methods of Care, Treatment, and Training of the Feebleminded Made at Letchworth Village;* State of New York, Department of Mental Hygiene, 1937.

Newth, A. A. E.—"The Mentally Retarded Child," Chapter I of Blacker, C. P. editor—*A Social Problem Group?;* Oxford University Press, 1937.

Odencrantz, Louise C.—*The Social Worker in Family, Medical and Psychiatric Social Work;* Harper & Brothers, 1929.

Penrose, Lionel S.—*Mental Defect;* Farrar & Rinehart, Inc., 1934.

Phelps, Harold A.—*Contemporary Social Problems*, Chapter X, "Feeblemindedness"; Prentice-Hall, Inc., 1932.

Pintner, Rudolph—*Intelligence Testing: Methods and Results;* Henry Holt and Company, revised edition, 1931.

Porteus, S. D.—*Studies in Mental Deviations;* The Training School (Publication No. 24, Department of Research), Vineland, N. J., 1922.

Queen, Stuart Alfred, and Mann, Delbert Martin—*Social Pathology*, Chapter XXVI, "Mental Deficiency"; Thomas Y. Crowell Company, 1925.

Séguin, Edouard—*Rapport et mémoires sur l'éducation des enfants normaux et anormaux;* F. Alcan (Paris), 1895.

Shuttleworth, G. E., and Potts, W. A.—*Mentally Deficient Children: Their Treatment and Training;* H. K. Lewis & Co., Ltd., fifth edition, 1922.

Terman, Lewis M.—*The Measurement of Intelligence;* Houghton Mifflin Company, 1916.

Thomas, William I., and Thomas, Dorothy Swaine—*The Child in America;* Alfred A. Knopf, 1928.

Thorndike, Edward L., *et al.*—*The Measurement of Intelligence;* Bureau of Publications, Teachers College, Columbia University, 1927.

Treadway, Walter L., and Lundberg, Emma O.—*Mental Defect in a Rural County;* U. S. Department of Labor, Children's Bureau, Publication No. 48, Government Printing Office, 1919.

Tredgold, A. F.—*Mental Deficiency;* Wm. Wood & Co., fifth edition, 1929.

United States Bureau of the Census—*Mental Defectives and Epileptics in Institutions: 1934;* Government Printing Office, 1936.

Wallin, J. E. Wallace—*Clinical and Abnormal Psychology;* Houghton Mifflin Company, 1927.

Wallin, J. E. Wallace—*The Education of Handicapped Children;* Houghton Mifflin Company, 1924.

Wallin, J. E. Wallace—*Problems of Subnormality;* World Book Company, 1921.

White House Conference on Child Health and Protection—*The Handicapped Child*, "Problems of Mental Deficiency," pp. 329–390; The Century Co., 1933.

Yerkes, Robert M., editor—*Psychological Examining in the United States Army;* Memoirs of the National Academy of Science, Vol. XV, Government Printing Office, 1921.

Yerkes, Robert M., Bridges, James W., and Hardwick, Rose S.—*A Point Scale for Measuring Mental Ability;* Warwick & York, Inc., 1915.

Yoakum, Clarence S., and Yerkes, Robert M.—*Army Mental Tests;* Henry Holt and Company, 1927.

CHAPTER VII

MENTAL DISORDERS

Definitions.—Derangement may occur in minds formerly apparently normal. Abnormality, dementia, is thus distinguished from subnormality, amentia. Persons suffering from disorders of mental functioning so serious as to make them appear dangerous to themselves or others, are popularly known as the insane. Insanity, however, is neither a medical nor a psychological concept. It is a legal term. All types of persons who under the laws of a given state are committed to institutions for mental disabilities are covered. Public records and statistics of the insane include many of the feebleminded and epileptic in addition to those suffering from mental disorder. Insanity is thus a generic term which properly should not be utilized exclusively for the mentally diseased or persons once normal in whom mental processes have become disordered.

In criminal law, insanity has been defined as "such unsoundness of mental condition, as, with regard to any matter under action, modifies or does away with individual legal responsibility or capacity." A lawyer, to defend his client on the grounds of insanity, has traditionally been forced to prove that due to disease of the mind his client at the time of the offense was unable "to know the nature and quality of the act he was doing," or "did not know he was doing what was wrong." [1]

Nevertheless a man may be mentally diseased and driven to a criminal act through some obsession, mania, or phobia, and still because of awareness of his act or of its wrongfulness would not be legally insane. It is clear that the medical concept of mental disease and that of insanity as construed before the criminal courts are not identical.

Standards of Reference.—The terms mental disease and mental abnormality presuppose standards of reference in terms of mental

[1] This essentially follows M'Naghten's case (10 Clark and Finnelly, 200 [1843]) which has dominated English and American legal thought and practice in these matters since 1843. For criticism, other tests, and discriminating recommendations, see Glueck, S. Sheldon—*Mental Disorder and the Criminal Law: A Study in Medico-Sociological Jurisprudence;* Little, Brown, and Company, 1925.

113

health and mental normality. The norms utilized in prevailing practice are not however the ideal health or mental functioning, but
rather the average, as ascertained from studies of the general population. Mental disease connotes in physiological terms, a clinically
demonstrable morbid condition of brain or nervous system or of their
functioning. The term mental abnormality implies significant deviation from average or typical mental performance—and in the field
under consideration this means negative deviation as distinguished
from the positive deviation of genius.

Extent.—To determine the extent of mental disorder one is forced
to rely chiefly upon records of the insane in institutions. These records have the limitation that the standard of reference is "certifiabil-
ity," that is to say that the persons covered in these statistics could
be, and were, committed to institutions for mental diseases under the
laws of their respective states. The latest available figures place the
number of patients with mental disease for the United States at the
end of the year 1935 at 466,045.[2] Of these 416,926 were in hospitals
and 49,119 on parole or otherwise absent. Roughly 400,000 suffered
from psychoses and the remainder were chiefly mental defectives,
epileptics, alcoholics, drug addicts, or psychopathic personalities.
There had been over 138,000 admissions in 1935 and nearly 124,000
separations chiefly by discharge, death, or transfer. Of the total,
the vast majority, over 397,000, were in state hospitals, nearly
40,000 in county and city hospitals, over 19,000 in institutions for
United States veterans, and 11,000 in private institutions.[3]

Distribution of patients by sex shows a greater incidence among
males.

"The male patients greatly outnumber the female patients admitted to
State hospitals for mental disease, as shown by the fact that in 1934 there
were 41,283 first admissions of male patients as compared with 28,651
first admissions of female patients. . . .

"Both in 1933 and in 1934, the number of first admissions per 100,000
of the general population of the same sex was considerably higher for
males than for females in the case of patients with cerebral arteriosclerosis, those with general paralysis, those with alcoholic psychoses, and those
in the dementia praecox group; while the ratio of patients to population
was higher for females than for males in the manic-depressive group." [4]

[2] Bureau of the Census—*Patients in All Hospitals for Mental Disease: 1935*, p. 1;
Bureau of the Census, Release of January 28, 1937.

[3] *Ibid.*

[4] Bureau of the Census—*Patients in Hospitals for Mental Disease: 1934*, pp. 10
and 18; Government Printing Office, 1936.

Considered by states, New York led with well over 68,000 cases on the books at the beginning of 1935. Pennsylvania was second with over 35,000. Illinois, Massachusetts, California, and Ohio followed with over 22,000 each. Nevada, the least populous state of the Union, had only 345 patients. New Mexico and Arizona were the only remaining states with fewer than one thousand cases on the hospital books.[5]

"Differences between States in the number of commitments to hospitals for mental disease per 100,000 of the general population, even when commitments to all hospitals are included, cannot be accepted as measuring accurately the existing differences between States in the prevalence of mental disease. Differences between States in the ratio of commitments to population are affected by differences in definition and diagnosis, differences in commitment laws and their administration, and differences in the extent to which hospital facilities are adequate. A low ratio in a State may simply indicate inadequate provision and a high ratio adequate provision for institutional care of mental patients."[6]

Unlike mental deficiency which strikes at birth or in childhood, mental disease is a phenomenon of the mature years of life. Of 63,508 first admissions to state hospitals in 1933 only 319 were under fifteen years of age, and 2,521 from fifteen to nineteen years old. The number doubles for the ages twenty to twenty-four, and increases in the next five-year span. But for each five-year grouping between thirty and forty-nine there are over 6,000 cases. The largest number is at the ages thirty-five to thirty-nine. The average age of first admissions is consistently in the forties.[7]

Excluding feeblemindedness and epilepsy from these figures, it is found that the incidence of all types of insanity appears greater in urban communities than in rural, with the exceptions of certain special types such as Huntington's chorea and the mental abnormalities resulting from pellagra, a malnutrition disease chiefly localized in the rural South.[8] It should be recognized, however, that since the institutions for the insane are largely urban an unknown percentage of the cases ascribed to urban communities may have been rural in

[5] *Patients in All Hospitals for Mental Disease: 1935*, p. 2.
[6] *Patients in Hospitals for Mental Disease: 1934*, p. 10.
[7] *Statistical Abstract of the United States 1936*, p. 73; Government Printing Office, 1936.
[8] Sorokin, Pitirim, and Zimmerman, Carle C.—*Principles of Rural-Urban Sociology*, Chapter XII, "Rural-Urban Mental Disease"; Henry Holt and Company, 1929. Landis, Carney, and Page, James D.—*Modern Society and Mental Disease*, Chapter V; Farrar & Rinehart, Inc., 1938.

origin, though classified as urban because of the temporary city address adopted by the patient or his family pending diagnosis. To some extent, also, certain slowly developing types of mental disease precipitate migratoriness in their victims, so that mental difficulties originating in rural communities may be classified as urban in origin in view of the urban address at the time of commitment. More important is the fact that in rural communities the mildly insane are generally taken care of in their own homes and thus are not covered in the Federal statistics of mental disease.

This disparity in urban-rural incidence, which was pronounced in early censuses, is found by Pollock and Malzberg to be declining in New York State.[9] Massachusetts reports show high rates in some rural counties and lower rates in some of the counties that are largely urban.[10]

Types and Classification of Mental Diseases.—Since the diagnosis and classification of mental and nervous disorder is the province of the branch of medicine known as psychiatry, contemporary differentiations of types must be borrowed from specialists in this field.

Until recently mental diseases were widely classified following, with some modifications, the system of Kraepelin.[11] But owing to the lack of standardization and uniformity accurate statistical summarizations for the country as a whole were not possible. A permanent committee on statistics was formed in the American Psychiatric Association in 1913, which drew up a system of classification adopted in 1917. A new and detailed classification was later drawn up and accepted by the American Psychiatric Association in 1934. Mental hospitals thereupon reclassified their patients.

There are twelve major groupings:

     I. Psychoses Due to or Associated with Infection
    II. Psychoses Due to Intoxication
   III. Psychoses Due to Trauma

---

[9] Pollock, Horatio M., and Malzberg, Benjamin—"Trends in Mental Disease," pp. 463–464; *Mental Hygiene*, Vol. XXI, No. 3, July, 1937.

[10] *Annual Report of the Commissioner of Mental Diseases for the Year Ending November 30, 1935*, pp. 245–246; Public Document No. 117, The Commonwealth of Massachusetts.

[11] Outlined in Hollingworth, H. L.—*Abnormal Psychology*, pp. 55–60; The Ronald Press Company, 1930, and adapted from Diefendorf, A. R.—*Clinical Psychiatry;* The Macmillan Company, 1915, which is "abstracted and adapted from the 7th edition of Kraepelin's, *Lehrbuch der Psychiatrie*."

IV. Psychoses Due to Disturbance of Circulation
V. Psychoses Due to Convulsive Disorders (Epilepsy)
VI. Psychoses Due to Disturbances of Metabolism, Nutrition or Endocrine Function
VII. Psychoses Due to New Growth
VIII. Psychoses Due to Unknown or Hereditary Causes, but Associated with Organic Changes
IX. Disorders of Psychogenic Origin or without Clearly Defined Tangible Cause or Structural Change
X. Undiagnosed Psychoses
XI. Without Psychosis
XII. Primary Behavior Disorders

Of these, XI and XII are dealt with in other chapters. The remaining categories require explanation here.

I. Psychoses Due to or Associated with Infection.—Chief among such infections is syphilis. The Wassermann and other tests determine its presence. The most frequent psychosis associated with syphilis is general paresis, which accounted for 7.3 per cent of first admissions to hospitals for mental disease in 1935. Other forms of neurosyphilis add 1.5 per cent more.[12] Psychoses associated with infection include also encephalitis, meningitis, and other infectious diseases, but together account for less than 1 per cent of all first admissions.

II. Psychoses Due to Intoxication.—Here alcoholic psychoses predominate, accounting for 4.8 per cent of first admissions. In Massachusetts acute hallucinosis is the most frequent alcoholic psychosis dealt with in such hospitals, with delirium tremens (usually treated in other hospitals) second, Korsakow's psychosis third, and less frequent types making up the remainder. Psychoses due to drugs and other exogenous poisons, such as metal and gases, account for only 0.6 per cent of first admissions.

III. Psychoses Due to Trauma.—These include traumatic delirium and post-traumatic personality disorders or mental deterioration. They account for only 0.6 per cent of first admissions.

IV. Psychoses Due to Disturbance of Circulation.—These are responsible for 10.3 per cent of first admissions. Of these cerebral arteriosclerosis is outstanding, accounting for 9.7 per cent of all first admissions.

V. Psychoses Due to Convulsive Disorders (Epilepsy).—This is

[12] The percentages are taken from *Patients in All Hospitals for Mental Disease: 1935*, p. 3.

chiefly "epileptic deterioration" and "epileptic clouded states," together covering 1.9 per cent of first admissions.

VI. Psychoses Due to Disturbances of Metabolism, Nutrition, or Endocrine Function.—These include the senile psychoses, involutional psychoses, such as melancholia, diseases of the endocrine glands, pellagra, and other categories which statistically are relatively unimportant. The senile cases account for 7.6 per cent of first admissions; the involutional cases 2.7 per cent; and the remainder of this category 1.5 per cent, making altogether 11.8 per cent.

VII. Psychoses Due to New Growth.—Chief among these are tumors of the brain. This whole group, however, accounts for only 0.2 per cent of all first admissions.

VIII. Psychoses Due to Unknown or Hereditary Causes, but Associated with Organic Changes.—Although this group covers many types of brain or nervous diseases, they together account for only 0.9 per cent of all first admissions.

IX. Disorders of Psychogenic Origin or without Clearly Defined Tangible Cause or Structural Change.—This is the largest category. It comprises first the psychoneuroses which account for 3.6 per cent of all first admissions. Morgan prefers for this group the term "benign psychoses" and states that they all exhibit "relatively mild symptoms, and they can be treated more easily and with more promise of success than any other mental disorders." [13] The "benign psychoses" include also anxiety hysteria and several forms of conversion hysteria or escape from mental conflict by adopting symptoms characteristic of some disease; psychasthenia, made up of morbid compulsive states, comprising obsessions, tics, spasms, phobias, and indecision; neurasthenia, hypochondriasis, and the various other forms of psychoneurosis.

However, in this same category of disorders of psychogenic origin fall the manic-depressive psychoses, which account for 12.1 per cent of all first admissions; dementia praecox (schizophrenia), 18.9 per cent; paranoia, 1.6 per cent; and psychopathic personality, 1.1 per cent. The psychogenic disorders combined with mental deficiency add 2.9 per cent more. The manic-depressive group oscillate from extreme excitement or exaltation (mania) to extreme depression. The schizophrenic tends to emotional blunting, and to apathy or personal disorganization; the paranoid to delusions of persecution

[13] Morgan, John J. B.—*The Psychology of Abnormal People*, p. 455; Longmans, Green and Co., 1937.

or otherwise and to egocentricity. Each has many varieties, phases, and characteristics essential to diagnosis. Altogether this psychogenic group thus comprises fully 40 per cent, or well over two-fifths of all first admissions.

X. Undiagnosed Psychoses.—This group makes up 3.8 per cent of first admissions.

The categories XI and XII present no psychosis but still account for 15.2 per cent of first admissions to hospitals for mental disease in 1935. Most prominent is alcoholism, 6.4 per cent; second comes mental deficiency, 1.5 per cent; next, drug addiction, 0.9 per cent; psychopathic personality, 0.7 per cent; epilepsy, 0.5 per cent; primary behavior disorders, 0.2 per cent; and personality disorders due to epidemic encephalitis, 0.1 per cent. The remainder of 4.9 per cent is made up of "all other and unknown."

Social Consequences of Mental Disorder.—The recognized symptoms of mental aberration are the major clues in each instance to the pathologic social consequences. Abnormality of mind expresses itself in the personality variously in the forms of irritation, weakness or pain, fantasy, sense of inferiority, frustration, instability, seclusiveness, egocentricity, obsession, delusion, or other symptoms. Personal and social disorganization at all points interpenetrate. Personal disorganization means misunderstanding, fear, trouble, or danger on the part of family and associates. Attempts at accommodation tend to be crude. The handicapped individual may suffer increasing disorientation or unbalance of emotions or will, because of belated recognition of his condition (which may be interpreted as personal idiosyncracy, weakness of character, or "pure cussedness") and the inability of his family, associates, or of public institutions to provide requisite aid. Case histories, recording that which is unique to the individual as well as symptoms shared with other cases similarly diagnosed, often trace lasting pathologic consequences in the lives of children or other members of the family group from the tensions which arise. Where the patient is unemployable there is likely to be poverty. Under some conditions of interaction between the individual and his environment crime is committed. Borderline noninstitutional cases may succeed in precipitating abnormal, morbid, or antisocial behavior in others— whether in the forms of religious mania, sexual abnormalities, or political strife. The social cost of the institutionalization of mental patients and the loss to society of their potential labor is measurable

and large but most of the injury done by their presence in the group
is too intangible to be reducible to appraisal in economic terms.

The Search for Causes.—Attempts have been made by many
authors to name the various factors which produce mental disease
of one type or another and to indicate their relative frequency. Such
classification is almost inevitably influenced by the type of training
and special interest of the author. It is natural that men with medical training should stress disease, that endocrinologists emphasize
glandular malfunctioning, that biologists stress heredity, that psy-
chologists seek sources in the mental and emotional history of the
patient, and the sociologist in his social milieu. By such specialized
approaches knowledge grows.

Heredity.—Early studies of human heredity took insanity, rather
than the subtypes of mental disease, as the unit for which the hereditary tendencies were sought. Even by this crude method some
causal relationship seemed manifest. Later researches excluded traumatic, toxic, and syphilitic cases and other mental disorders associated with physical disease. The forms of mental abnormality which
show an hereditary tendency are beginning to emerge through the
study of the ancestry and siblings of the rest of the hospital patients.

Rosanoff and Orr investigated the families of patients of Kings
Park State Hospital in New York in 1911. They confined their
studies to the pedigrees of families in which the above mentioned
exogenous factors did not appear in the patient. Pedigrees of 72 families were secured, representing 206 different matings and a total of
1,097 offspring. Their findings agreed so closely with the theoretical
expectation under the Mendelian theory, if neuropathic constitution
were regarded as a recessive trait, that they concluded its hereditary
transmission was definitely established.[14]

The Committee on Eugenical Sterilization, between the years
1934 and 1936, examined a large number of studies of the family
histories of the mentally diseased. Some of the authors of these
studies had reached much the same conclusions as Rosanoff; others
had confined themselves to the family histories of schizophrenics or
of manic-depressives. Some had found these latter diseases to be
Mendelian recessives; others were critical. The Committee criti-

---

[14] Rosanoff, A. J., and Orr, Florence I.—*A Study of Heredity in Insanity in the Light
of the Mendelian Theory;* Eugenics Record Office, Cold Spring Harbor, N. Y.,
Bulletin No. 5, October, 1911: reproduced in Ford, James—*Social Problems and
Social Policy,* pp. 428–433; Ginn and Company, 1923.

cized them all in turn for errors in method and on the grounds that proper control studies had not been made. It may be regarded as significant, however, that the Committee concludes "it is probable that there is some hereditary factor operating in the production of dementia praecox" and "it is safe to say that manic-depressive psychosis is inheritable." [15]

Environmental Factors.—The tendency of modern genetics is to recognize the constant interplay of heredity with environment. In the cases of mental disease in which there is recurrence of a specific type of insanity generation after generation, one need not assume the inevitability of recurrence. For on the one hand the trait unless dominant can be eliminated from the stock by outbreeding, and on the other hand if not so eliminated an individual with the unfortunate predisposition may presumably be safeguarded from mental disease if his environment can be properly controlled. In his case, as in that of mentally diseased persons cured through hospital treatment, protection is essential from such precipitating factors as worry, overstrain, irregular living, insomnia, malnutrition, and alcoholism. If the environment of the predisposed can be kept by their families and medical advisers free from disturbing influences, and if the predisposed can live under a wholesome and happy routine as to work, play, meals, and sleep, they need not succumb to the "family taint."

Those forms of mental disease which are not apparently hereditary also involve an interplay of some adventitious factors, whether alcohol, syphilis, or pellagra, with a constitution which has been conditioned both by its unique heredity, and by the individual's experience, training, and environment up to the time of the derangement. Conceivably, if not probably, the types of insanity precipitated by disease or accident, or unfortunate habits of thought or behavior, must be ascribed in part to heredity which makes that particular individual constitutionally susceptible. For only a small fraction of syphilitics eventually succumb to syphilitic insanities, and only a small fraction of alcoholics become victims of the mental disorders of alcoholic origin. Proof is, however, as yet scarcely possible because so little is yet known of the nature of the biological elements

[15] Committee of the American Neurological Association for the Investigation of Eugenical Sterilization (Abraham Myerson, James B. Ayer, Tracy J. Putnam, Clyde E. Keeler, and Leo Alexander)—*Eugenical Sterilization: A Reorientation of the Problem*, pp. 89–112, quotations from pp. 107 and 112; The Macmillan Company, 1936.

or genes which in their combination confer individuality and individual susceptibility.

Relatively little is known also of the basis of selectivity among environing influences, though it is clear that there is a wide variation in responsiveness to an almost infinite variety of factors. Individuals vary greatly in their susceptibility to drugs. Recent studies of allergy seem to indicate the truth of the old statement that one man's meat is another man's poison. Brothers dwelling under what to outward appearances are identical conditions of family and slum life may turn in the case of one to normal constructive activities and in the other to abnormalities or crime.

The sources of abnormal behavior in environmental pressures require careful examination. This may be pursued in terms of human ecology covering adjustments of this statistical group to its physical environment or habitat; in terms of cultural anthropology dealing with the comparative personal adjustments of these cases to the cultures of their own groups; or in terms of psychology dealing with the reactions of individual cases to other individuals. Most notable of sociological studies have been those of Dunham and Faris relating the schizoid personality to cultural isolation and suggesting treatment which will reëstablish social contacts.

". . . General paralysis, and paranoid and hebephrenic schizophrenia, mostly come from the central hobo, rooming-house, and foreign-born and Negro slum areas. Senile psychosis cases come from rooming-house and Negro areas, alcoholic from a broad foreign-born slum area, and catatonic schizophrenia from more restricted foreign-born areas. The manic-depressive rates are much more widely distributed, but show a slight concentration in the better class rooming-house and apartment hotel districts.

". . . Schizophrenia, then (and this is true of several other psychoses as well), comes mainly from hobo, rooming-house, and slum areas, and especially from those sections of the population in each area which are in the minority for that area.

". . . Even a casual inspection suggests that the mobility, confusion, chaos, and personal isolation which are characteristic of these communities could provide only the worst sort of background for mental health, but it is possible to describe the disorganization in more specific detail. . . .

"For the distributions of rates of senile psychosis, psychoneuroses, manic-depressive psychosis, and others, there is no available basis for explanation.

"The distribution of the schizophrenia rates, however, offers a fascinating problem because of the neat distributions, sharp concentrations, and because there is no satisfactory organic explanation of the disorder. Case material furnishes a possible hypothesis that disorganized community factors, in combination with other factors, may be responsible for the abnormality.

"The writer has suggested elsewhere that many, or most, of the typical symptoms of the schizophrenic may be viewed as a result of extreme seclusiveness due to isolation. Given a long, extreme absence of primary contacts with other persons, these various forms of eccentricity which are typical of the schizophrenic will develop. The *basic* cause of schizophrenia, then, will be whatever causes the isolation. The particular form the symptoms take must be explained by the special circumstances of the individual case. . . .

"In those communities, then, in which such conditions as extreme heterogeneity of types, mobility of population, secularization of ideas and individuation of personalities, are most prevalent, and where the person is surrounded by *other* races and nationalities, any person who, from pampering in infancy or any other cause, fails to establish normal social relations, finds it difficult or almost impossible to do so later. Because of the vicious circle effect, the longer the process goes on, the more hopeless the situation of the schizophrenic becomes. This may be the explanation of the apparently unfavorable prognosis in schizophrenia, especially for the older patients. There is no automatic process, either in normal society or in the hospital environment, which will reverse this process once it is well under way." [16]

Causes and Trends in Organic Psychoses.—The classification of mental diseases, already considered, reveals that a large percentage of them are a result of degenerative lesions or of poisoning of the nerve centers by either alcohol, bacterial, or endogenous poisons. Pollock, using statistics of New York State institutions, shows the trends among the organic psychoses as follows:

"It is customary to use the term organic to designate those psychoses which accompany diseases or toxic states of the central nervous system.

[16] Faris, R. E. L.—"Demography of Urban Psychotics with Special Reference to Schizophrenia"; *American Sociological Review*, Vol. 3, No. 2, April, 1938. In the same issue see also Krout, Maurice H.—"A Note on Dunham's Contribution to the Ecology of Functional Psychoses." In addition see Faris, Robert E. L.— "Cultural Isolation and the Schizophrenic Personality"; *American Journal of Sociology*, Vol. XL., No. 2, September, 1934: Dunham, H. W.—"The Ecology of the Functional Psychoses in Chicago"; *American Sociological Review*, Vol. 2, No. 4, August, 1937: Dollard, John—"The Psychotic Person Seen Culturally"; *American Journal of Sociology*, Vol. XXIX, No. 5, March, 1934: and the whole issue of *American Journal of Sociology*, for May, 1937, but especially the articles by Harry Stack Sullivan, Edward Sapir, and Herbert Blumer, Vol. XLII, No. 6, As this book goes to press, new material on this subject has become available in Faris, Robert E. L., and Dunham, H. Warren.—*Mental Disorders in Urban Areas;* University of Chicago Press, 1939.

The whole organic group constitutes between 45 and 50 per cent of new cases. In 1934 among all first admissions to institutions for mental disease in this State, there were 5,604 organic cases, or 47.6 per cent of the total. The group has notably increased in recent years. In 1920, the organic first admissions numbered 2,605 and the percentage of the total was 35.9. In the separate psychoses constituting the organic group the first admissions of the two years were as follows:

Psychoses	1934	1920
Traumatic.	118	17
Senile.	1,038	684
With cerebral arteriosclerosis.	1,975	515
General paresis.	958	882
With cerebral syphilis.	129	58
With Huntington's chorea.	22	15
With brain tumor.	26	18
With other brain or nervous diseases	170	42
Alcoholic.	901	147
Drug or other toxic.	35	20
With pellagra.	...	4
With other somatic diseases	232	203

"The increase in some of the groups is quite striking and the need for preventive action is clearly indicated. . . .

". . . The increase in the traumatic group of first admissions from 17 in 1920 to 118 in 1934 indicates a trend that is likely to become more pronounced as automobiles become more powerful and the use of machinery more extensive. Greater safeguards for the protection of life, limb and brain are clearly indicated.

"Marked increases since 1920 in first admissions in both senile and arteriosclerotic psychoses are noted. In the former group the increase corresponds fairly well with the advancing average age of the population but the increase in the arteriosclerotic first admissions from 515 cases in 1920 to 1,975 in 1934 points to factors other than that of a change in age distribution of the population. Research as to the causes and prevention of arteriosclerosis is greatly needed.

"We come now to the syphilitic psychoses. In 1934 there were 958 general paresis and 129 cerebral syphilis first admissions as compared with 882 and 58 respectively in 1920. Spirochetes were first found in the brains of paretics in 1913 and Ehrlich discovered salvarsan in 1910. Had health departments during these last three decades taken as active measures to prevent the spread of syphilis as they have taken to check typhoid fever and smallpox, the annual number of syphilitic cases among first admissions would have markedly declined. Instead, there were 232 more new syphilitic cases admitted to our hospitals for mental diseases in 1934 than there were in 1913.

"Two lines of action are here indicated; first, exercise of every known means to check the spread of syphilis, secondly, prompt treatment of cases in the initial stage of the disease to prevent the later development of neurosyphilis. A disease as serious as this can never be eradicated by palliative methods.

"The new cases of alcoholic mental disease admitted to the institutions for mental disease in this State in 1934 numbered 901, as compared with 147 in 1920. The low figure of 1920 indicates the possibility of prevention of this group of disorders. The matter presents special difficulties as society is divided as to the best methods of controlling the liquor traffic. In the meantime the trend of alcoholic mental disease is markedly upward.

"Drug psychoses are comparatively few and are not increasing. Psychoses with encephalitis lethargica have come into prominence in recent years. In our civil State hospitals the first admissions with this psychosis increased from 13 in 1920 to 84 in 1934. As the disorder is more prevalent among children than adults and commonly persists for long periods its importance is far greater than the number of first admissions would indicate. Measures are taken to check the spread of the physical disorder but effective means to prevent the psychotic sequela have not been devised.

"Theoretically prevention of a large part of the organic forms of mental disease is possible, but thus far little progress in their elimination has been made." [17]

The Functional Psychoses.—Whether or not the functional disorders are hereditary in nature, heredity cannot serve as the sole explanation. Other predisposing factors may be adolescence, the climateric, or senescence, excessive drinking, worries and strains, while exciting causes may lie in the shock to the emotional system of a death, sudden losses, accident, or battle. Both prevention and recovery are possible. Each has its basis in personality organization.

Dr. Solomon writes:

"From a practical standpoint we may think of the functional disorders under two headings: (1) those in which recovery without defect occurs, and (2) those in which there is a tendency to chronicity or deterioration, or improvement with defect.

"The cases with good prognosis are in a majority of instances cases in which the disorder is chiefly in the emotional field, and receive, as a rule, the medical diagnosis of manic-depressive psychosis or involutional melancholia. While the symptoms may be exceedingly marked and disturbing, the prognosis is, on the whole, good; in fact, complete recovery is the rule in cases of manic-depressive psychosis. Although there is a tendency for a recurrence of the disorder, there is the same good prognosis as to recovery. The duration of an attack varies from a few days to eighteen months, but, on the average, is a matter of five to ten months. The outlook of those suffering from this form of disease is, therefore, often better than that of some patients whose mental symptoms are very much milder,

[17] Pollock, Horatio M.—*What May Be Hoped for in the Prevention of Mental Disease*, pp. 5, 6–7; presented at Quarterly Conference at Albany, March 20, 1930, and revised March 1, 1935.

but whose incapacity may last for a much greater period, and who may, therefore, suffer more and be less efficient as units in the social structure.

"The cases of involutional melancholia are apt to last longer than those of manic-depressive psychosis, and the prognosis is not as satisfactory, as some of these patients do not recover. In the majority of cases, however, the prognosis is good.

"The second large group of functional psychoses are those which have a tendency to deterioration and chronicity, and are usually considered under the medical diagnosis of dementia praecox. These cases are characterized by dissociation or splitting of the psyche, and tend to show disorder of thought (delusions, hallucinations). Beginning, on the average, at the adolescent period and having a bad prognosis, these cases are the saddest and most important of the mental disorders. They likewise represent a high proportion of the cases which enter the State hospitals for mental diseases.

"Finally, mention should be made of paranoia, which is a condition characterized by the development of a delusional system which makes the patient unfit for ordinary social intercourse and which progresses slowly and insidiously. This condition represents the progressive development of a twist of the mind rather than a distinct mental disease.

"As the so-called functional psychoses have no known anatomical basis, they must be considered on a psychological plane. This does not mean that continued search for a physical basis should not be made, but rather that from a practical standpoint they must be studied and treated from a purely mental point of view. While heredity and constitutional factors have a bearing upon the development of these psychoses, they are so intangible that they cannot be considered of any great practical application. Mental factors, life experiences are the elements that must be studied in these cases. Prophylaxis should be directed toward the early development of the individual. Every case should be considered on its own merits and studied from the standpoint of the individual himself, his personal endowments, the past experiences and difficulties he has encountered." [18]

According to Myerson: "Most vulnerable, most poorly adapted to stand the stresses and strains of existence are those whose personality becomes deeply disorganized, whose disturbed somatic and visceral responses become lasting, whose grip on reality disappears and who, therefore, enter upon a period or a life-time of the falsification of reality and the misinterpretation of bodily processes which I here call the *neuropsychoses*." [19]

Preventives and cures alike rest largely in mental hygiene, the

[18] Solomon, Harry C.—"Serious Cases of Mental Disorder or So-called 'Insanity' "; *The Commonhealth*, Vol. IX, No. 2, Massachusetts Department of Public Health.

[19] Myerson, Abraham—*Neuroses and Neuropsychoses: The Relationship of Symptom Groups*, p. 297; reprinted from *American Journal of Psychiatry*, Vol. 93, No. 2, September, 1936.

development of wholesome attitudes, the integration of personality and character on a basis of adequate rest, good physical health, and sound habits. The patient needs help to pull himself together, to learn to accept life, to feel a sense of security. He may need sound sex training to overcome frustration or morbid tendencies. He may require a complete change of environment. He must be helped to a prompt and right decision to overcome a mental conflict. But above all he requires integration, which Myerson defines as "the development of coördinated purpose and the inhibition of the non-relevant drives and trends." [20] The essential technique of both cure and prevention is individualization based upon thorough knowledge of the patient and of his social setting, for without it integration is seldom possible.

History of Treatment.—Society's treatment of the insane has passed through many stages. The early conception that derangement resulted from the possession of the individual by an evil spirit, still survives among many of the contemporary primitive races. It led to treatment by exorcism which might take the form of coaxing, incantation, torture, or other devices to kill or drive out the demon. As the theory of demoniacal possession passed with the advance of civilization the subsequent major type of treatment was restraint, chiefly for the protection of the community. Thus, through many centuries the demented were thrust into dungeons or jails, or were restrained in stocks or by chains. The third stage in this country, that of humanitarian treatment in special institutions, was initiated by Quakers and resulted in the chartering of the Pennsylvania Hospital in 1751. The Eastern State Hospital at Williamsburg, Virginia, was founded in 1768. The former was a private hospital, the latter a public hospice. More significant was the assumption of responsibility by provincial and state governments, beginning with the granting of a royal charter in 1771 to the New York Hospital, now known as Bloomingdale Hospital. Dorothea Lynde Dix found it necessary, beginning in 1843, to go from state to state urging legislators to establish hospitals for the demented, who at that time were still generally confined in cellars, cages, or prisons, under conditions of extreme neglect.

The fourth and present stage of therapeutic treatment, involving medicine, psychology, and social work in the process of discovering the sources of the abnormality of each patient and the means of help-

[20] *Ibid.*, p. 287.

ing him where possible to recovery, virtually begins with the establishment of the first state departments of mental diseases and the
founding of psychopathic hospitals.

New York State was first to appoint a Commissioner on Lunacy,
in 1873. The first state psychopathic hospital was opened at Ann
Arbor, Michigan, in 1906, and that of Boston in 1912. These did,
however, have many precursors, such as the Philadelphia Orthopaedic Hospital and Infirmary for Nervous Disease (1867), and the
Nerve Clinic of the Boston Dispensary (1873).[21] Although humanitarian treatment in America is a full century old, scientific treatment has been a slow development with the roots perhaps in ancient
Greece and Egypt, but its fruition a product of twentieth century
medicine, psychiatry, psychoanalysis, endocrinology, and occupational therapy.

Institutional Provision.—There are in the United States today
well over six hundred hospitals caring for the mentally ill and mentally deficient. Patients in these hospitals are fifty-eight per cent of
all hospital patients of the country.[22] More than half of the hospitals
are owned and controlled by governmental agencies, chiefly by
states, but over one-tenth by counties and cities, and twenty-four by
the Federal government. The remainder are under private ownership, and are usually much smaller and more limited in their scope.[23]

State, as distinguished from local, operation of hospitals has tended
to provide greater efficiency, better classification, and more appropriate treatment. The centralization of responsibility for the care of
the insane under state governments facilitates also provision for differentiation of types and of methods of treatment according to need.
A state may keep its older asylums for its more hopeless cases of involutional or dementia type where the process of deterioration cannot be stayed. Its newer hospitals become research and classification
centers, and in them the cases with a favorable prognosis may remain through their entire institutional treatment. From them they
may be paroled when it is safe to return them to the community under

[21] Sandy, William C.—"Mental Diseases," *Social Work Year Book 1929*, pp. 263–
265; Russell Sage Foundation, 1930.

[22] American Medical Association, Council on Medical Education and Hospitals—"Hospital Service in the United States—Fifteenth Annual Presentation of
Hospital Data"; *Journal of the American Medical Association*, March 7, 1936.

[23] Grimes, John Maurice—*Institutional Care of Mental Patients in the United
States;* published and distributed by the author, 1934. See also Winston, Ellen—
"Indices of Adequacy of State Care of Mental Patients"; *American Sociological
Review*, Vol. 3, No. 2, April, 1938.

aftercare, which involves both medical supervision and psychiatric social work. The term cure is not used, but patients discharged or paroled are referred to as "arrested" or "improved" cases. Some cases, which cannot be paroled to their own families, are boarded out in private homes under the state's supervision.

Within the modern mental hospital attempts are made to enable the patient to live a life that is as nearly natural and as well-rounded as is consistent with his mental condition. Though some patients have to be kept in bed—and even in these circumstances there may be occupational therapy—increasingly regular and appropriate work is found for patients to do. Many patients are found to require colonization in hospital colonies, in which they can engage in outdoor work when weather permits and in indoor workshops.

The many types of therapy range from drugs, baths, massage, heat, and diet, to occupational therapy and suggestion. Each of these is individualized following the medical diagnosis and other analyses. The recreational life of patients ranges from athletic activities through social events, such as dances, musicales, and drama, to the passive recreations of radio, motion pictures, and reading. The function of the hospital is reëducation rather than cure, and covers the whole realm of life instead of being confined to mere surgery or medication.

Psychiatric social work, which had been tried by the Society for the After-Care of the Insane in England around 1880, began in this country in 1905 at the Neurological Clinic of the Massachusetts General Hospital in Boston, under the direction of Dr. James J. Putnam. It is a specialized form of social work which requires knowledge of psychiatry, and provides the assistance of specially trained workers to aid the physician or psychiatrist. More attention can thus be paid to the social needs of each patient both prior and subsequent to discharge. It now covers the social diagnosis of patients, contacts with a wide variety of social service agencies in securing the patient's history or arranging for assistance following parole, the preparation of the home to receive the patient, the selection of boarding homes, and coöperation with clinics for child guidance as well as the out-patient clinics of hospitals.

Relativity of Social Policy.—The social policy of any given year is based upon the generally accepted principles of its period. There is disagreement as to fact and emphasis by partisans of the varied approaches of psychiatry, neurology, endocrinology, psychoanalysis, and experimental psychology. But such disagreement wherever it occurs is of social value in that it precipitates further research to verify or disprove the concepts offered. The statements concerning causes, treatment, and prevention must therefore be looked upon as tentative and not universally acceptable among the many branches of science noted above. They offer suggestions which at this time would generally be considered reasonable, but there will be inevitable changes in emphasis in future years as the process of research and verification goes on.

QUESTIONS FOR DISCUSSION OR EXAMINATION

1. Distinguish the term "insanity" from "mental disease."
2. Compare mental disorder with mental defects.
3. Discuss the social statistics of insanity with reference to age and sex groupings, urban-rural distribution, and geographical distribution.
4. Contrast the twelve major groupings of patients in mental hospitals.
5. Under what conditions, if any, do you consider compulsory sterilization of patients in mental hospitals to be good social policy? Why?
6. Sketch the history of social treatment of the victims of mental abnormality.

PROBLEMS FOR INDIVIDUAL STUDY

1. From the following list of references contrast two works: one representing the psychoanalytical approach and the other that of medicine or psychiatry.
2. Analyze trends of mental deviation in your state over a period of years— as revealed by official statistics.
3. Report on the methods of classification of the insane employed in your state from the beginning of its provision for this group. How are changes in classification to be explained? Seek primary sources.
4. Report upon and evaluate methods of treatment now employed in your state for each of the twelve major groupings of patients.
5. A social audit of some mental hospital from the point of view of (a) economy and efficiency, or (b) adequacy of structure and equipment for health, safety, treatment, and general welfare of patients and staff.

SUGGESTIONS FOR SUPPLEMENTARY READINGS

American Medical Association, Council on Medical Education and Hospitals—"Hospital Service in the United States—Fifteenth Annual Presentation of Hospital Data"; *Journal of the American Medical Association*, March 7, 1936.

American Orthopsychiatric Association—*American Journal of Orthopsychiatry;* published quarterly.

Bassett, Clara—*Mental Hygiene in the Community;* The Macmillan Company, 1934.

Beers, Clifford W.—*A Mind That Found Itself;* Doubleday, Doran & Company, Inc., 1935.

Bentley, Madison, and Cowdry, E. V.—*The Problem of Mental Disorder;* McGraw-Hill Book Company, Inc., 1934.

Bossard, James H. S.—*Social Change and Social Problems,* Chapter XXII, "Mental Diseases and Their Social Significance," Chapter XXIII, "Etiology of Mental Diseases," and Chapter XXIV, "Mental Hygiene"; Harper & Brothers, revised edition, 1938.

Bruno, Frank J.—*The Theory of Social Work,* Chapters XV–XX; D. C. Heath and Company, 1936.

Cannon, Walter B.—*Bodily Changes in Pain, Hunger, Fear, and Rage: An Account of Recent Researches into the Function of Emotional Excitement;* D. Appleton and Company, 1929.

Clark, Mary Augusta, compiler—*Directory of Psychiatric Clinics in the United States;* The National Committee for Mental Hygiene, Inc., 1936.

Committee of the American Neurological Association for the Investigation of Eugenical Sterilization (Abraham Myerson, James B. Ayer, Tracy J. Putnam, Clyde E. Keeler, and Leo Alexander)—*Eugenical Sterilization: A Reorientation of the Problem;* The Macmillan Company, 1936.

Crutcher, Hester B.—*A Guide for Developing Psychiatric Social Work in State Hospitals;* Department of Mental Hygiene, State of New York, 1933.

Deutsch, Albert—*The Mentally Ill in America;* Doubleday, Doran & Company, Inc., 1937.

Eaton, Allen, and Harrison, Shelby M.—*A Bibliography of Social Surveys,* References on "Mental Hygiene," pp. 219–226, and "Psychiatric," p. 252; Russell Sage Foundation, 1930.

Elliott, Mabel A., and Merrill, Francis E.—*Social Disorganization,* Chapter XVI, "The Mentally Deranged"; Harper & Brothers, 1934.

Faris, Robert E. L., and Dunham, H. Warren—*Mental Disorders in Urban Areas;* University of Chicago Press, 1939.

Freud, Sigmund—*Psychopathology of Everyday Life* (authorized English edition with introduction by A. A. Brill); The Macmillan Company (first published 1914), fifteenth impression, 1930.

Gillin, John Lewis—*Social Pathology,* Chapter 8, "Mental Disease"; The Century Co., 1933.

Glueck, S. Sheldon—*Mental Disorder and the Criminal Law: A Study in Medico-Sociological Jurisprudence;* Little, Brown, and Company, 1925.

Grimes, John Maurice—*Institutional Care of Mental Patients in the United States;* published and distributed by the author, 1934.

Groves, Ernest R., and Blanchard, Phyllis—*Introduction to Mental Hygiene;* Henry Holt and Company, 1930.

Hart, Bernard—*The Psychology of Insanity;* Cambridge University Press, 1925.

Healy, William—*Mental Conflicts and Misconduct;* Little, Brown, and Company, 1917.

Healy, William, Bronner, Augusta F., Baylor, Edith M. H., and Murphy, J. Prentice—*Reconstructing Behavior in Youth: A Study of Problem Children in Foster Families;* Alfred A. Knopf, 1929.

Healy, William, Bronner, Augusta, and Bowers, Anna M.—*The Structure and Meaning of Psychoanalysis;* Alfred A. Knopf, 1930.

Henderson, D. K., and Gillespie, R. D.—*A Text-Book of Psychiatry for Students and Practitioners;* Oxford University Press, 1933.

Hillyer, Jane—*Reluctantly Told;* The Macmillan Company, 1926.

Hollingworth, H. L.—*Abnormal Psychology;* The Ronald Press Company, 1930.

Jung, C. G.—*Analytical Psychology* (authorized translation edited by Constance E. Long); Moffat, Yard and Company, 1916.

Jung, C. G.—*The Psychology of Dementia Praecox* (English translation by A. A. Brill); Nervous and Mental Disease Publishing Company, 1909.

Jung, C. G.—*Psychological Types;* Harcourt, Brace and Company, Inc., 1923.

Jung, C. G.—*The Psychology of the Unconscious* (authorized translation, with introduction by Beatrice M. Hinkle); Moffat, Yard and Company, 1916.

Kraepelin, Emil—*Manic-depressive Insanity and Paranoia* (translated by R. Mary Barclay); E. & S. Livingstone (Edinburgh), 1921.

Kraepelin, Emil—*Psychiatrie: Ein Lehrbuch für Studirende und Aerzte;* J. A. Barth, eighth edition (4 vols.), 1909–15.

Landis, Carney, and Page, James D.—*Modern Society and Mental Disease;* Farrar & Rinehart, Inc., 1938.

Lee, Porter Raymond, and Kenworthy, Marion E.—*Mental Hygiene and Social Work;* The Commonwealth Fund, 1929.

Lowrey, Lawson G., and Smith, Geddes—*The Institute for Child Guidance, 1927–1933;* The Commonwealth Fund, 1933.

Mangold, George B.—*Social Pathology*, Chapter XVII, "Mental Disorders," and Chapter XVIII, "Mental Hygiene"; The Macmillan Company, 1932.

May, James V.—*Mental Diseases;* Richard G. Badger, 1922.

McDougall, William—*Outline of Abnormal Psychology;* Charles Scribner's Sons, 1926.

Morgan, John J. B.—*The Psychology of Abnormal People;* Longmans, Green and Co., 1937.

Morgan, John J. B.—*Workbook in Abnormal Psychology;* Longmans, Green and Co., 1936.

Myerson, Abraham—*The Inheritance of Mental Diseases;* Williams & Wilkins Company, 1925.

National Committee for Mental Hygiene—*Mental Hygiene*, published quarterly.

National Research Council, Committee on Psychiatric Investigations—*The Problem of Mental Disorders;* McGraw-Hill Book Company, Inc., 1934.

Pratt, George K.—*Your Mind and You: Mental Health;* Funk & Wagnalls Company, second edition, 1936.

Pressey, Sidney L., and Pressey, Luella Cole—*Mental Abnormality and Deficiency;* The Macmillan Company, 1926.

Rosanoff, Aaron J.—*Manual of Psychiatry;* John Wiley & Sons, Inc., sixth edition, 1927.

Sandy, William C.—"Mental Diseases," *Social Work Year Book 1929;* Russell Sage Foundation, 1930.

Schilder, Paul—*Psychotherapy;* W. W. Norton & Company, Inc., 1938.

Slater, Eliot—"Mental Disorder and the Social Problem Group," Chapter II of Blacker, C. P., editor—*A Social Problem Group?;* Oxford University Press, 1937.

Southard, E. E., and Jarrett, Mary C.—*The Kingdom of Evils;* The Macmillan Company, 1922.

Stevenson, George S., and Smith, Geddes—*Child Guidance Clinics;* Oxford University Press, 1934.

Strecker, Edward A., and Ebaugh, Franklin G.—*Clinical Psychiatry;* P. Blakiston's Son & Co., Inc., fifth edition, 1935.

Thom, D. A.—*Everyday Problems of the Everyday Child;* D. Appleton-Century Company, 1927.

Thomas, Dorothy Swaine, Loomis, Alice M., Arrington, Ruth E., and Isbell, Eleanor C.—*Observational Studies of Social Behavior,* Vol. I: *Social Behavior Problems;* Yale University Press, 1933.

Thomas, William I., and Thomas, Dorothy Swaine—*The Child in America;* Alfred A. Knopf, 1928.

Wallin, J. E. Wallace—*Personality Maladjustments and Mental Hygiene;* McGraw-Hill Book Company, Inc., 1935.

Wechsler, Israel S.—*The Neuroses;* W. B. Saunders Company, 1929.

White, William A.—*Outlines of Psychiatry;* Nervous and Mental Disease Publishing Company, thirteenth edition, 1932.

White House Conference on Child Health and Protection—*The Handicapped Child,* "Problems of Mental Health," pp. 271–326; The Century Co., 1933.

Whitwell, J. R.—*Historical Notes on Psychiatry;* P. Blakiston's Son & Co., Inc., 1937.

Williams, Frankwood E. (addresses by Frankwood E. Williams, C. Macfie Campbell, Abraham Myerson, Arnold Gesell, Walter E. Fernald, and Jessie Taft)—*Social Aspects of Mental Hygiene;* Yale University Press, 1925.

CHAPTER VIII

CONVULSIVE DISORDERS

Definitions.—The term epilepsy, which derivatively means "seizure," has traditionally been applied to a chronic disease characterized objectively by paroxysms or fits in which the patient loses consciousness and in which there is usually a convulsion of the muscles. In certain profound disorders of this category there are recognizable anomalies of disposition and intellectual inferiority. Many persons of otherwise normal mentality and an occasional genius, however, suffer from such attacks. Early textbooks were prone to list Julius Caesar, Napoleon the First, Peter the Great, Richlieu, Lord Byron, Dostoievsky, Flaubert, Handel, Molière, Petrarch, Swift, and even Mohammed, St. Paul, and Swedenborg as epileptics. Specialists today, while recognizing that convulsive attacks probably occurred in these cases, are hesitant to designate them as epileptics.

The contemporary trend is to recognize "epilepsy" as a symptom grouping of diverse disorders, often for convenience termed "the epilepsies," and to differentiate certain types of convulsive disorders as not epileptic in character. This field, like those of mental deficiency and mental derangement already considered, is going through a process of rapid development and reorientation. Many diverse views and classifications are held and ably defended. Since the subject is one obviously undergoing transition few categorical statements can safely be made.

The following definitions and classifications of contemporary scientists are submitted to indicate their respective emphasis. Thus, Morgan states that epilepsy is "the name given to any of several nervous diseases marked primarily by convulsive episodes." [1] Lennox and Cobb define it as "a syndrome characterized by the sudden appearance of paroxysms, of which convulsive movements or loss of consciousness or both, are a principal element." [2] Myerson, in his

[1] Morgan, John J. B.—*The Psychology of Abnormal People*, p. 34; Longmans, Green and Co., 1937.

[2] Lennox, William G., and Cobb, Stanley—*Epilepsy*, p. 4; Medicine Monographs, Vol. XIV, Williams & Wilkins Company, 1928.

more recent writings, notes that the term epilepsy "denotes an entity which no more exists than does 'insanity.' " [3] Henderson and Gillespie state that the term epilepsy has been "used to designate a heterogeneous group of syndromes, of which the most prominent feature is the repeated occurrence of convulsive attacks" and then proceed to reserve the term epilepsy for those cases in which no physical basis for the attack has so far been discovered—cases termed idiopathic. [4]

Types.—The most frequent type of recurrent convulsive disorder is the *grand mal*, in which the individual shortly after some characteristic aura or warning (such as dizziness, or flashes of light) suffers a muscular contraction and drops rigidly to the ground with total loss of consciousness, followed by a convulsion characterized by alternation of relaxation and contraction of muscles and by foaming at the mouth. Each of these is brief in duration but they are followed by coma which may be many minutes or hours in length. The *petit mal* involves momentary or brief loss of consciousness, usually without convulsions. Various other special types are differentiated, even including mental attacks without either convulsions or loss of consciousness, but termed "epileptiform equivalents" and characterized by dream states or automatisms in which sometimes violent or criminal acts are done by the patient with no remembrance on his part.

Extent.—The Bureau of the Census publishes statistics of admissions and discharges of mental defectives and epileptics in state, city, and private institutions. The data which follow cover 153 institutions of which 70 are private, 80 under state jurisdiction, and 3 are city institutions. The total number of first admissions to state institutions in 1934 for epilepsy was 2,664. There were also 925 males and 703 females who were both epileptic and mentally defective. Following the classification of the American Psychiatric Association epileptics were subclassified as "symptomatic" and "idiopathic," the former "signifying cases in which the attacks result from a definite underlying disease" and the latter "signifying attacks resulting from unknown causes." Thus in 1934, 691 of first admissions were classified

[3] Committee of the American Neurological Association for the Investigation of Eugenical Sterilization (Abraham Myerson, James B. Ayer, Tracy J. Putnam, Clyde E. Keeler, and Leo Alexander)—*Eugenical Sterilization: A Reorientation of the Problem*, p. 136; The Macmillan Company, 1936.

[4] Henderson, D. K., and Gillespie, R. D.—*A Text-Book of Psychiatry for Students and Practitioners*, p. 363; Oxford University Press, 1933.

as symptomatic, 1,784 as idiopathic, and the remainder unclassified.[5]

Statistics of first admissions to hospitals for mental disease show that in 1934 there were 1,933 admissions for epileptic psychoses (1,212 male and 781 female) constituting 2.1 per cent of the admissions to mental hospitals. There were also 341 cases of epilepsy without psychoses admitted to these institutions.[6]

In commenting upon their figures, in 1935, the Census Bureau states "It should be clearly recognized, however, that statistics relating to patients in institutions . . . do not furnish even an approximate measure of the total number of such patients, either in the country as a whole or in the several States. The institutions established for the care of mental defectives and epileptics contain only a small part of the total number of such persons. The vast majority of them are not confined in institutions but live at large in the community. Many are inmates of prisons and reformatories, others are in almshouses, and some are in hospitals for mental patients." [7]

The hospital data above cited cover only an insignificant fraction of cases with convulsive disorders, but are a rough indication of the volume of the annual intake of cases in which epilepsy is so profound as to cause danger or pronounced mental deterioration. A larger number of cases would be discovered and recorded, however, if more ample provision were made by the states for this group.

"The only available index of the real incidence of epilepsy was established when over two million men between the ages of eighteen and thirty were given physical examinations during the World War. The results were analyzed and published by the War Department in a volume entitled *Defects in Drafted Men.* It is probable that the diagnoses were partly if not wholly dependent upon histories of childhood and adolescent convulsions. If this history were omitted or denied, many epileptics would have passed the physical test, and hence the defect would have been revealed only when seizure occurred. The experience of the draft officials, however, indicated that these histories were freely volunteered, and when this is considered

[5] In addition there were 122 first admissions of epileptics in city institutions of New York, Missouri, and Louisiana, and 99 both defective and epileptic. In private institutions there were 81 more, plus 46 both defective and epileptic. Bureau of the Census—*Mental Defectives and Epileptics in Institutions: 1934;* Government Printing Office, 1936.

[6] *Statistical Abstract of the United States 1936,* p. 72; Government Printing Office, 1936.

[7] Bureau of the Census—*Mental Defectives and Epileptics in Institutions: 1935,* p. 1; Bureau of the Census, Release of February 9, 1937. The census figures for 1934 have been used in the text rather than those for 1935 because the latter were incomplete at this writing.

in connection with the nature of the disease, it is quite unlikely that many epileptics escaped detection. For this group, therefore, we may consider the results as quite accurate, and may use them to throw light on the probable present incidence of epilepsy among children.

"It was found that 515 in each 100,000 of drafted men were epileptic, the rates varying from a maximum of 1,272 for each 100,000 in Vermont to a minimum of 120 in each 100,000 in South Dakota. These rates may be compared with those for feeble-mindedness—mental deficiency— which is often associated with epilepsy. The average rate among drafted men was 1,206 per 100,000; the maximum was 3,090 in Vermont and the minimum 232 in Arizona. These rates indicate that feeble-mindedness is about two and one-half times as prevalent as epilepsy.

"Generalization from these results for the country as a whole is extremely difficult. The age interval of the drafted men excluded children and all persons beyond thirty-one. As there are relatively few epileptics who live to an advanced age, the rate of epilepsy in the latter group was very low. On the contrary, it is very high in the younger groups. It is difficult if not impossible to know exactly how the latter groups should be weighted in comparison with the drafted men. The two extreme age groups might possibly balance each other, in which case the rate of 515 per 100,000 would be a fair statement of the prevalence of epilepsy in the total population, but it would then be considerably too low for the age groups under twenty years. Probably, a safe estimate for such groups is 800 or 900 for each 100,000 of the total population.

"The indications are that about 150,000 children are affected. Recent studies have shown that those under twenty years of age constitute almost one-fourth of the total number of registered epileptics; that epileptics under twenty years of age constitute nearly 50 per cent of all epileptic admissions to institutions for the mentally ill, and that the percentage increases regularly from the group aged four years and under up to twenty years. Moreover, the rate of first admissions under twenty years of age is higher than that of all epileptics, reaching a maximum in the ages from fourteen to nineteen. Probably if a thoroughgoing effort to detect and report epilepsy in the early years of childhood were made, these rates would change considerably, for many parents still believe that their children will outgrow their epileptic seizures and consequently do not permit institutional commitment or even specialized treatment until the late adolescent age is reached." [8]

Basing their estimate upon the incidence of epilepsy among drafted men, Lennox and Cobb state that "something less than 500,000 persons are subject to 'epilepsy.' " [9] Hollingworth classifies 60 per cent as *grand mal*, 32 per cent as mixed forms, 5 per cent as *petit mal*, and the remaining 3 per cent distributed under relatively

[8] White House Conference on Child Health and Protection—*The Handicapped Child*, pp. 290–292; The Century Co., 1933.
[9] Lennox and Cobb—*op. cit.*, p. 5.

rare types designated as "Jacksonian," "psychic epilepsy," "hystero-
epilepsy," "reflex epilepsy," "affect epilepsy," and "status epilepti-
cus."[10] The above authors and all leading specialists in the field
recognize that estimates of volume and distribution of convulsive
disorders must be tentative until standard definitions and standard
tests can be applied to a wide enough sample of the American population to make the volume and distribution clear. For the present
it is reasonable to assume that the social problem group loosely
called the epileptics comprises three or more cases per thousand
population. There is also a marginal group of unknown dimensions
of persons who have suffered from convulsions, or from lapses of consciousness or automatisms not diagnosed or not classified as epilepsy.

   Social Consequences of the Epilepsies.—Persons who have had
convulsive seizures, like those who have been "cured" of mental
disorder, tend to restrict their subsequent behavior and contacts
either from fear of recurrence or because of specific medical advice.
The restrictions may range from mere avoidance of driving a car or
of the use of alcohol to limitations of diet, and avoidance of crowds
or excitement. Even in mild cases the fact of the possibility of a seizure may dominate behavior and restrict social contacts. Some of
those who have suffered many severe seizures live in perpetual fear
and seek isolation. Family life and group contacts are affected by
whatever symptoms the patient may display, whether sensitiveness,
irritability, emotional explosions, vagueness, vertigoes, or egocentricity. Seizures shock and alarm the bystander, and in some patients the period of automatism may be accompanied by maniacal
excitement and violence or crime. Frequent seizures mean ultimate
deterioration or dementia and a considerable reduction in the life
span. A child with frequent convulsions cannot attend school. An
adult similarly handicapped cannot work in a shop or mill, and may
be incapable of any employment. In extreme cases of convulsive
disorders the patients are a perpetual burden to themselves and to
others, and in most instances become dependents. Healy, in Chicago,
found seven per cent of one thousand juvenile delinquents studied to
be epileptic.[11] Although true epilepsies are fortunately relatively

   [10] Hollingworth, H. L.—*Abnormal Psychology*, p. 484; The Ronald Press Company, 1930.
   [11] Healy, William—*The Individual Delinquent*, p. 416; Little, Brown, and Company, 1915. Healy also found epilepsy sometimes associated with abnormal
sexual development, *ibid.*, pp. 418–419, and with vagrancy, *ibid.*, p. 640. For an
example of the association of epilepsy with crime see case 54 in Southard, E. E.,

rare as compared with feeblemindedness or mental disorder the social cost per case is high.

Heredity.—Earlier studies in this field ascribed a high percentage of cases of epilepsy to inheritance. The Committee of the American Neurological Association for the Investigation of Eugenical Sterilization, in 1936, examined a large number of such studies quoting Oppenheim, Gowers, Spratling, and Binswanger. It criticized their polymorphic theories, for in varying ways each had found a morbid predisposition to epilepsy in offspring of parents largely suffering from mental or physical conditions other than epilepsy.[12] Davenport, in 1911, had concluded that epilepsy was a unit character following the Mendelian law of heredity, though his studies were also of the polymorphic type.[13] His position has been greatly changed in his later writings.

An investigation was made in 1930 by Brown of thirty-six family histories of patients in the Ohio Hospital for Epileptics. Information was secured for 4,792 persons. He concluded:

"The facts elicited by this study of the relatives of epileptics lend weight to the belief that epilepsy is largely a matter of inheritance.

"1. Twenty-three out of thirty-six patients investigated, or 64 per cent, had epileptic relatives.

"2. Twenty-eight out of the thirty-six, or 78 per cent had relatives with a psychosis.

"3. Nine out of the thirty-six, or 25 per cent, had mentally deficient relatives.

"4. Thirty-two out of the thirty-six, or 89 per cent, had relatives who were epileptic, insane, or mentally deficient.

"5. It must be admitted, however, that the exact mechanism of this inheritance has not as yet been definitely established.

"6. The relatives of the patients studied were decidedly below average socially.

"7. A sound sterilization law with proper enforcement would aid considerably in preventing an increase of defective stock." [14]

and Jarrett, Mary C.—*The Kingdom of Evils*, pp. 238–240; The Macmillan Company, 1922.

[12] *Op. cit.*, citing as follows: Binswanger, Otto—*Epilepsy. Nothnagel's System of Medicine*, 12:313, 1918. Gowers, W. R.—*Epilepsy and Other Chronic Convulsive Diseases*, 1901. Oppenheim, H.—*Textbook on Nervous Diseases*, sixth edition, Vol. 2, *Epilepsy;* Schultz and Co., Edinburgh.

[13] Davenport, Charles B.—*Heredity in Relation to Eugenics;* Henry Holt and Company, 1911. Davenport, Charles B., and Weeks, David F.—"Epilepsy"; *Journal of Nervous and Mental Diseases*, 28:64, 1911.

[14] Brown, Ralph R.—*A Study of the Mental and Physical Traits of the Relatives of Epileptics*, p. 636; reprinted from *The Journal of Applied Psychology*, Vol. XIV, No. 6, December, 1930.

Thom, to test out the findings of Echeverria, studied a similar number of married epileptics and a similar number of children, but whereas Echeverria had found 51 per cent of the offspring epileptic Thom found only 1.8 per cent. In brief, Thom found from the records of 1,536 epileptic patients of the Monson State Hospital in Massachusetts that one out of every six was married. There were children from 8 per cent of the marriages, or 138 marriages. The number of offspring was 553, or an average of 4 to each marriage. A history of epilepsy was found in only 10 of these cases, or 1.8 per cent. Of these 6 died in infancy, 2 became confirmed epileptics, and the remaining 2 cases were "arrested." A study of the family histories of 138 epileptics revealed presumptive heredity of epilepsy in 5.8 per cent of the cases.[15]

Studies by Brain in England and Calvert Stein in the United States were quoted to show a higher percentage of epilepsy among the offspring of epileptics than in the general population as represented by control groups, and yet Stein points out that only 3.7 per cent "of the immediate relatives of the institutionalized epileptics themselves give a history of epilepsy." Stein affirms that the results of his study do not justify the conclusion that epilepsy is an inherited condition but recognizes a presumptive germ plasm defect.[16]

In view of contradictory evidence the effect of heredity upon epilepsy is at present uncertain. Nevertheless, on the basis of the studies above quoted, and many others, the Committee of the American Neurological Association for the Investigation of Eugenical Sterilization felt justified in recommending voluntary sterilization in selected cases of epilepsy in which attacks are frequent, with the consent of the patient or those responsible to him.[17]

Other Causes.—New York statistics of first admissions to Craig Colony for 1932, where all but about five per cent of cases have seizures of the *grand mal* type, list etiological factors. For 253 cases these factors

[15] Committee of the American Neurological Association for the Investigation of Eugenical Sterilization—*op. cit.*, p. 138, citing as follows: Echeverria, G.—*On Epilepsy;* William Wood and Co., New York, 1870 (see also *J. Ment. Sci.* 1887, p. 620): Thom, D. A.—"The Frequency of Epilepsy in the Offspring of Epileptics"; *Boston Medical and Surgical Journal*, 175:573–575, April, 1916 and 175:599–600, October, 1916.

[16] *Ibid.*, pp. 139–141, citing as follows: Brain, W. R.—"The Inheritance of Epilepsy"; *Quarterly Journal of Medicine*, 29:299–310, 1925–26. Stein, Calvert—"Hereditary Factors in Epilepsy"; *American Journal of Psychiatry*, 12:989–1027, March, 1933.

[17] *Ibid.*, pp. 179 and 181.

are listed as follows (more than one being present in some cases): 48 head trauma, 38 developmental defects, 48 endocrinopathy, 11 cerebro-vascular sclerosis, and 91 meningo-encephalitis and complicating infections. Fifty-four cases showed family history of convulsions.[18]

Some studies purport to show that migraine, alcoholism, and hereditary syphilis may be found more frequently among epileptics than in the general population and that they may be positive factors. Disturbances of the thymus, thyroid, and parathyroid glands are also suspected as causes. Psychoanalysts explain certain cases in terms of "avoidance of reality" and "wish fulfilment." Present researches into problems of nutrition, oxygen consumption, and physico-chemical processes, and experience in the reduction of seizures by increased oxygen tension, by induced acidosis, and by dehydration may yield data of fundamental importance as to causation.

Treatment.—Important in the cure of epilepsy is the discovery of cases at the onset of the difficulty, and provision for specialized study and care. Reporting and central recording of cases and provision for clinical study in the early stages would make cure or "arrest" possible in many cases which today receive no relief other than that obtained by the use of sedatives. Causes must be sought in each individual case in order to discover what treatment is appropriate. There appears to be abundant evidence that some cases respond to correction of posture or of breathing habits. Others require the application of a diet which will overcome alkalosis, or the discovery and removal of infected teeth or other sources of local infection. Some traumatic cases respond to brain surgery; some conflict cases to psychoanalysis. In glandular cases restoration of normal functioning is indicated.

Unquestionably in this, as in all illnesses, attention should be paid during treatment to both physical and mental hygiene. Response is best where conditions as to sleep, rest, work, and exercise are normal. The patient's discouragement or alarm should be overcome. He must be helped to face life with confidence and zest. Even the cases in which deterioration has set in can have the frequency of their seizures greatly reduced by appropriate diet and medication in addition to the measures above mentioned, though cure may be impossible for them under contemporary conditions.

[18] *Forty-Fourth Annual Report of the Department of Mental Hygiene, July 1, 1931, to June 30, 1932,* p. 337; State of New York, Department of Mental Hygiene, Legislative Document No. 29, 1933.

The Superintendent of Craig Colony in New York State, Dr. Shanahan, outlines the problem of treatment as follows:

". . . The longer the freedom from seizures and the better the adjustment to an ordinary environment, the better the prognosis. Carelessness in mode of life may result in a recurrence of seizures in the most hopeful case. . . . Without potential normality of the organs referred to, cessation of the symptoms of epilepsy cannot be looked for.

"In bringing about readjustment of the mode of life of the epileptic, it is necessary to analyze carefully the symptoms and adapt treatment to the individual. Undue worry, embarrassment and distress tend to provoke symptoms. The patient must be considered as a whole and not solely as a person presenting convulsions or other types of seizures. . . .

"There is no specific treatment for epilepsy. The fundamental principles are therapeutic talks, proper diet, sufficient exercise, congenial occupation, well-balanced by suitable recreation, regular sleep in a well ventilated room, avoidance of undue excitement or worry, a minimum of medication and surgery, and careful attention to elimination.

"Epileptics should have early proper guidance to effect such change in mode of life as may be indicated to prevent the formation of the seizure habit. It is essential that the epileptic patient have normal interests to arouse and sustain mental activity, and all possible opportunities for normal energy outlets." [19]

Grimes reported in 1934 that only ten states had separate institutions for the study and treatment of epileptics. These states had eleven institutions, of which four were hospitals and seven were colonies primarily custodial. The number of patients was slightly over ten thousand. He found these institutions crowded and understaffed. [20]

The Ohio Hospital for Epileptics was the first such separate institution in the United States and was opened in 1893. The best of the state institutions attempt to provide a normal community life for patients in so far as conditions permit. This means schooling and work for the young, regular work for the adults, and recreational advantages for all. A relatively normal type of life can thus be maintained for the epileptic in the state colony while providing properly for his medical care and segregation.

For children of normal mentality in whom convulsions are rare, attendance at public school or college classes has proved possible,

[19] Shanahan, William T.—*Epilepsy and Its Treatment*, pp. 4–5; State of New York, Department of Mental Hygiene, Pamphlet No. 2, Utica State Hospital Press, 1928.

[20] Grimes, John Maurice—*Institutional Care of Mental Patients in the United States*, pp. 49–50; published and distributed by the author, 1934.

especially where the symptoms preceding seizures are recognizable. Others, with more frequent attacks are in some cities provided for in special classes or by home study. Competent medical supervision is necessary. In the absence of such arrangements there will be needless illiteracy in this group and conditions will be aggravated by medical and social neglect.

Prevention.—The dependence of social policy upon the findings of antecedent sciences—in this case upon the findings of medicine and psychology—is nowhere better illustrated than in the case of the handicapped group still officially designated as epileptics. Prevention is dependent upon accurate knowledge of both the volume and distribution of cases on the one hand, and of precise causes upon the other. But since only the more profound cases reach our public institutions leaving the others unrecorded, and since also there is no agreement among specialists as to causes, social policy for prevention can operate only in a manner purely tentative.

It seems a reasonable presumption that devices for social control of heredity, to be considered later, can reduce somewhat the volume of constitutional or idiopathic cases, whether they are applied exclusively to families with hereditary mental defectiveness and mental disease, or are extended to cover families in which there appears to be a specific hereditary epilepsy. Measures for the elimination of alcoholism and syphilis, which are justified on other grounds than their possible relation to epilepsy, may conceivably result in a reduction of the volume of epilepsy. Better practice in obstetrics may reduce the volume of cases of head injuries at birth. Safety campaigns may reduce head injuries to adults. Preventive medicine even though not directed primarily at the reduction of epilepsy may reach some of its obscure sources.

A precise policy for prevention, however, is dependent upon broad and intensive research by specialized branches of medicine and psychology. From such studies more exact data concerning the nature and causes of the conditions under the symptom group known as the epilepsies will, in time, become available to the sociologist, political scientist, legislator, and public executive.

QUESTIONS FOR DISCUSSION OR EXAMINATION

1. Definitions and types of convulsive disorders.
2. Compare the statistics of "epilepsy" with those of "mental disease," and mental defect.

3. Discuss (a) evidence of hereditary epilepsies, (b) other possible causative factors.
4. Outline methods of treatment for the epilepsies.
5. What form should be taken by a preventive social policy for convulsive disorders?

PROBLEMS FOR INDIVIDUAL STUDY

1. Trace the history of studies of inheritance in "epilepsy" and trends in their recommendations with regard to social control.
2. An audit, economic and social, of public provision for epileptics in some selected state.
3. A study of the pathology and contemporary medical and psychological treatment of epilepsy.
4. Critical analysis of the literature purporting to show relations between convulsive disorders and (a) parental alcoholism, (b) alcoholism of the patient.
5. History of (a) the treatment of epilepsies, or (b) public provision for epileptics, tracing the sources of changes in method.

SUGGESTIONS FOR SUPPLEMENTARY READINGS

American Association for the Study of the Feeble-minded and American Association on Mental Deficiency—*Journal of Psycho-Asthenics; Devoted to the Care, Training, and Treatment of the Feebleminded and of the Epileptic;* 1896—

Committee of the American Neurological Association for the Investigation of Eugenical Sterilization (Abraham Myerson, James B. Ayer, Tracy J. Putnam, Clyde E. Keeler, and Leo Alexander)—*Eugenical Sterilization: A Reorientation of the Problem;* The Macmillan Company, 1936.

Davenport, Charles B., and Weeks, David F.—*A First Study of Inheritance in Epilepsy;* Eugenics Record Office, Cold Spring Harbor, N. Y., Bulletin No. 4, 1911.

Dorcus, Roy M., and Shaffer, G. Wilson—*Textbook of Abnormal Psychology,* "The Epilepsies," pp. 287–292; Williams & Wilkins Company, 1934.

Fox, J. Tylor—"Epilepsy and the Social Problem Group," Chapter III of Blacker, C. P., editor—*A Social Problem Group?;* Oxford University Press, 1937.

Henderson, D. K., and Gillespie, R. D.—*A Text-Book of Psychiatry for Students and Practitioners,* Chapter XII, "Epilepsy"; Oxford University Press, 1933.

Hollingworth, H. L.—*Abnormal Psychology,* Chapter 22, "Psychological Correlates of Epilepsy"; The Ronald Press Company, 1930.

Lennox, William G., and Cobb, Stanley—*Epilepsy;* Medicine Monographs, Vol. XIV, Williams & Wilkins Company, 1928.

Morgan, John J. B.—*The Psychology of Abnormal People,* Chapter XVI, "Episodic Disorders"; Longmans, Green and Co., 1937.

Muskens, L. J.—*Epilepsy: Comparative Pathogenesis, Symptoms, Treatment;* Wm. Wood & Co., 1928.

Myerson, Abraham—*The Inheritance of Mental Diseases*, Chapter V, "Epilepsy"; Williams & Wilkins Company, 1925.

New York State Board of Charities—*Nine Family Histories of Epileptics in One Rural County;* Bureau of Analysis and Investigation, State Board of Charities, Albany, 1916.

Rosanoff, Aaron J.—*Manual of Psychiatry;* John Wiley & Sons, Inc., sixth edition, 1927.

Shanahan, William T.—"Epilepsy," *Social Work Year Book 1929;* Russell Sage Foundation, 1930.

Sullivan, Ellen Blythe, and Gahagan, Lawrence—*On Intelligence of Epileptic Children;* Genetic Psychology Monograph, Vol. XVII, No. 5, Clark University, 1935.

Tracy, Edward Aloysius—*The Basis of Epilepsy;* Richard G. Badger, c. 1930.

United States Bureau of the Census—*Mental Defectives and Epileptics in Institutions: 1934;* Government Printing Office, 1936.

White, William A.—*Outlines of Psychiatry;* Nervous and Mental Disease Publishing Company, thirteenth edition, 1932.

CHAPTER IX

VISUAL DISORDERS

Definitions.—The group classified as the blind consists of persons in whom there is complete lack of vision and those in whom vision is so limited as to be of no practical value. In many of our institutions for blind children a majority may have enough of vision to distinguish light from dark or to be aware of large moving objects, but their vision is so limited as to make it impossible for them to make use of it in school work or as a means of earning a living.[1]

Extent.—The Federal Census of 1930 gives the number of blind in the United States as 63,593, or about one to every nineteen hundred persons in our population. The highest ratio, or number per 100,000 population, was found in the state of New Mexico with 143.3, and the lowest in Wyoming with 23.5.[2] Instructions to enumerators have varied from census to census. The instructions in 1930 required them to "Include as *blind* any person who can not see well enough to read, even with the aid of glasses. The test in case of infants must be whether they can apparently distinguish forms and objects; and in the case of older persons who are illiterate whether they presumably can see well enough to read if they knew how to read. Do not include any person who is blind in one eye only." [3] In so technical a field the possibility of error of judgment on the part of enumerators who lack specific training is great. Specialists estimate the number of blind as between 90,000 and 120,000. At most, however, there is probably but one blind person in every thousand of population.

Census statistics of sex distribution among the blind show 36,585, or 57.5 per cent, male, and 27,008, or 42.5 per cent, female; the high rate for males being in part ascribable to the risks of industrial occu-

---

[1] For detailed definitions see Best, Harry—*Blindness and the Blind in the United States*, pp. 126 and 165–168; The Macmillan Company, 1934.

[2] *Statistical Abstract of the United States 1936*, p. 79; Government Printing Office, 1936.

[3] Bureau of the Census—*Fifteenth Census of the United States: 1930, Supplemental Schedule for the Blind and for Deaf-Mutes*, Form 15–103; Government Printing Office, 1930.

pations. Racial distribution reveals 52,924 white, 9,169 Negro, 784 Mexican, 681 Indian, and 35 for other races. The Negro rate is disproportionately high due in part at least to relatively limited medical services. The incidence of blindness among Indians and Mexicans is to some extent due to the ravages of trachoma. Venereal disease may be responsible in part for the high rates of blindness among male whites and the colored races. Marital conditions among the blind do not diverge markedly from the distribution found in the rest of the population. Distribution by age shows only 1,618 less than ten years old, 3,855 from ten to nineteen, 12,043 from twenty to forty-four, 17,855 from forty-five to sixty-four, and 28,152 over sixty-five. Blindness is thus primarily a problem of old age.[4]

Heredity as Cause.—Heredity plays a relatively small part in the production of blindness. There are many indications that its role is much smaller here than in the production of feeblemindedness, mental disease, deafness, and perhaps also epilepsy. The Federal Census of 1910 revealed that 11 per cent of the blind had blind brothers, sisters, parents, or children, but only 3.7 per cent had blind parents, and only 0.7 per cent had blind children. In a large fraction of these cases the cause may have been disease, like trachoma for example, which may spread by contagion from one member of a family to others, rather than heredity.[5]

Although most blindness is not hereditary, Castle is able to list twenty types of eye defect which are hereditary in nature, some of which produce total blindness.[6] In 1909, Dr. Clarence Loeb covered 1,204 selected family records, from reports furnished by institutions for the blind and by oculists. Among the 4,155 children in these families 2,523 were affected, or 60.7 per cent. In all, he found twelve types of blindness to be presumably hereditary. Of these, cataract, retinitis pigmentosa, and atrophy of the optic nerve ac-

---

[4] *Statistical Abstract of the United States 1936*, p. 79. Ages were "unknown" in 70 cases. Publications of the Bureau of the Census have covered the blind in every census beginning with 1830. These can be ascertained readily by consulting Schmeckebier, Laurence F.—*The Statistical Work of the National Government*, pp. 84–85; The Institute for Government Research, The Johns Hopkins Press, 1925.

[5] Bureau of the Census—*The Blind Population in the United States: 1910*; Government Printing Office, 1916, and *The Blind in the United States: 1910*; Government Printing Office, 1917.

[6] Castle, W. E.—*Genetics and Eugenics*, pp. 359–365; Harvard University Press, fourth edition, 1930.

counted for approximately 70 per cent of the cases.[7] It is clear, however, that further research is necessary before the precise role of heredity in the causation of blindness can be determined.

Disease as Cause.—Fully one-half of all blindness is due to disease, most of which is preventable. Of the illnesses which may cause blindness, over one-quarter are general diseases and the remainder are specific diseases of the eye. Of the general diseases which may produce blindness there should be mentioned such common illnesses as measles, scarlet fever, syphilis, and grippe, as well as the less common meningitis, diabetes, smallpox, and typhoid. Most cases of these diseases are wholly curable, but in a very small percentage of each—though a larger percentage in the case of meningitis—there may be permanent impairment of which blindness is one form.

The specific affections of the eye include cataract, which ranks first in frequency; glaucoma, which is second; atrophy of the optic nerve, third; ophthalmia neonatorum, fourth; trachoma, fifth; and many types of pus infections and sympathetic inflammations. Many of the specialists in this field are satisfied that some forms of cataract and glaucoma are hereditary, but research has not progressed far enough to make possible precise statistical differentiation of the hereditary types.

Accident as Cause.—The role of accident is roughly one-third that of disease in the production of blindness, which means that about one-sixth of all blindness is due to accidents or trauma. Blindness is produced either by damage to the eyeball, or by injury to the optic nerve. Foreign substances in the eye, exposure to intense heat or intense light, poisoning, and eye strain all fall in the category of accident or trauma. Thus explosions; metal dust; spattered acids, such as sulphuric or nitric acid; spattered alkalis, including lye, potash, soda, and ammonia; wood alcohol swallowed or inhaled (which may atrophy the optic nerve); excessive use of other drugs, including tobacco; and severe eye strain in mines, schools, or workshops are chiefly responsible for the blindness in this classification.

The following excerpts illustrate types of accidents to children and industrial workers which result in blindness:

". . . In the schools and classes for the blind in the United States there are 500 pupils whose blindness is due to accidents and about 70 are added each year.

[7] Best—*op. cit.*, especially Chapter II, pp. 56–57.

"Findings of a study in which newspaper reports were used as a basis indicate that almost two-thirds of the eye accidents to children are due to weapons (air rifles, slingshots, arrows, etc.), fireworks and explosives." [8]

"In considering the causes of visual loss, corneal opacities, resulting from chemical, mechanical, or ulcerative changes, are by far the most frequent during that part of life of the greatest activity, and in the aged are probably responsible for about eight per cent of the blindness. Corneal opacities interfere with vision by diffusion of light, actual obstruction of the rays, or a severe irregular astigmatism. The size and position of the opacity determine the loss, while the depth of the scar and age of the patient will determine its permanency. The opacity may be slightly influenced by treatment, and in the course of time one is surprised at the rate and extent that clearing has occurred.

"Corneal opacities are, to a great extent, preventable, in that they are usually a result of delayed or improper removal and after-treatment of the simple foreign body in the cornea. This delay may be no fault of the patient; the foreign bodies are often received and no significance attached to the discomfort until several hours later, when the corneal irritation, or beginning ulceration, forces him to seek advice. Too often, however, clumsy attempts at removal by fellow workmen, or unskillful treatment by physicians without proper facilities, produces large abrasions of the cornea; and the failure to apply proper after-treatment results in ulcerations with subsequent scar formation.

"Direct blows from blunt objects with even light or moderate force often result in severe destructive changes to the eye. The globe is filled with fluid and semi-fluid content, and, being incompressible, there is a sudden increase in force, which is transmitted to the other tissues of the eye, resulting in tears or ruptures of one or more of its inner coats and, if severe enough, of the sclera itself. There may be dislocation of the lens and other lacerations of the vital structures. In each case a large amount of blood escapes into the eye, leaving residual changes which markedly affect the usefulness of the eye. After these injuries the vision may be suddenly lost, and, if the trouble is due only to extravasated blood or swelling, the eye may recover its usefulness; on the other hand, minute tears or hemorrhages may escape notice until weeks or months after the injury. With destruction of the retinal elements sight fails.

"Perforating wounds are usually due, in the bottling and engineering industries, to flying glass and broken water gauges, and have become quite common among truck drivers. This type of injury should become less frequent with the introduction of shatter-proof glass. When these wounds involve the cornea only much may often be done with skillful surgery. All injuries involving the lids and eyeball should be treated only by an eye surgeon. . . .

"Due to rigid inspection of workmen's tools, introduction of more labor-

[8] Kerby, C. Edith—*Eye Accidents in Child Play*, p. 13; The National Society for the Prevention of Blindness, Inc., Publication 96, reprinted from *The Sight-Saving Review*, Vol. II, No. 2, June, 1932.

saving methods in manufacturing, and the wearing of goggles by the workmen, together with other protective devices, intraocular foreign bodies have become less frequent. They are still too common, however, and it is seldom that an eye regains useful vision after such an injury. Many cases are reported as recovering normal vision after successful magnet extraction of the object, but in after years most of these eyes suffer other changes, either as a result of entrance or exit of the foreign body, or, as is possible in all eye injuries, because of infection and sequelae. . . .

"The introduction of calcium products into the eye, most commonly lime or carbide, results in opaque deposits, which are extremely difficult to remove and have serious results. Caustic alkalies are most destructive, and acid burns from battery explosions are frequent. Workers often suffer from the effects of exposure to light and heat, and they accuse smoke, chemical fumes, and petroleum gases of causing various ocular conditions. We have seen patients blind, they claim, because they got salt and flour into the eye, and some war veterans still complain of the effects of gas upon the eyes when they attempt to work." [9]

Social Consequences of Blindness.—By severely limiting the range of available occupations and freedom of movement, blindness has usually meant dependency or only partial self-support. Where combined with self-pity and poor training it has led to beggary and parasitism. The pity, repugnance, or avoidance of blind persons by sighted people, wherever it exists, the difficulty with which blind people get about, their inability to see the facial expressions and gestures which qualify the spoken word, all tend to reduce the range of social contacts. Their social isolation has been much reduced in recent years by the increasing availability of books and newspapers in Braille, by the radio, and the introduction of sound in moving pictures. But for most of the child blind there remains the tendency of social life to be limited in large part to persons with similar handicaps, and to their own social organizations.

Yet by the more heroic and gifted among the blind the handicap itself has been turned to account. Helen Keller has written:

". . . Sometimes it seems as if the very substance of my flesh were so many eyes looking out at will upon a world new created every day. The silence and darkness which are said to shut me in, open my door most hospitably to countless sensations that distract, inform, admonish, and amuse. With my three trusty guides, touch, smell, and taste, I make many excursions into the borderland of experience which is in sight of the city of Light. Nature accommodates itself to every man's necessity.

[9] Jones, J. Guy—*The Eye Physician in Industry*, pp. 5–7; The National Society for the Prevention of Blindness, Inc., Publication 107, reprinted from *The Sight-Saving Review*, Vol. II, No. 4, December, 1932.

If the eye is maimed, so that it does not see the beauteous face of day, the touch becomes more poignant and discriminating. Nature proceeds through practice to strengthen and augment the remaining senses. For this reason the blind often hear with greater ease and distinctness than other people. The sense of smell becomes almost a new faculty to penetrate the tangle and vagueness of things. Thus, according to an immutable law, the senses assist and reinforce one another. . . .

"The calamity of the blind is immense, irreparable, but it does not take away our share of the things that count—service, friendship, humor, imagination, wisdom. It is the secret inner will that controls one's fate. We are capable of willing to be good, of loving and being loved, of thinking to the end that we may be wiser. We possess these spirit-born forces equally with all God's children. . . .

"The blind man of spirit faces the unknown and grapples with it, and . what else does the world of seeing men do? He has imagination, sympathy, humanity, and these ineradicable existences compel him to share by a sort of proxy in a sense he has not. When he meets terms of color, light, physiognomy, he guesses, divines, puzzles out their meaning by analogies drawn from the senses he has. I naturally tend to think, reason, draw inferences as if I had five senses instead of three. This tendency is beyond my control; it is involuntary, habitual, instinctive. I cannot compel my mind to say 'I feel' instead of 'I see' or 'I hear.' . . .

". . . Reality, of which visible things are the symbol, shines before my mind. While I walk about my chamber with unsteady steps, my spirit sweeps skyward on eagle wings and looks out with unquenchable vision upon the world of eternal beauty." [10]

Social Provision.—In the United States social provision for the blind takes the form of specialized education; medical treatment; social and industrial training for blind children; vocational rehabilitation for working adults, who have recently lost their sight; placement in appropriate occupations where possible in the outside world, but otherwise in special workshops for the blind or at specialized home work with provision for sale of products; and pensions or institutional care for those who through illness, old age, or other afflictions are unable to work.

Education of Blind Children.—Until recent times a child born blind or acquiring blindness in early years was with rare exceptions restricted to a life of limited social contacts and dependency, and this is still the fate of many. Specialized educational methods are, however, progressively removing these limitations.

The education of the blind in America began somewhat over a century ago, following the first Federal Census of the blind in 1830.

[10] Keller, Helen—*The World I Live In*, pp. 41–42, 85, 86–87 and 133; The Century Co., 1908 edition.

In the preceding year the New England Asylum for the Blind had been incorporated in Boston, and Dr. Samuel Gridley Howe, America's pioneer in the education of the blind, was sent to Europe to study the foreign methods of instruction. His school opened in 1832, the New York institution a year earlier, and that of Pennsylvania in 1833, all of them supported by private funds. By exhibiting their trained pupils before state legislatures public appropriations shortly became available. Kindergarten instruction soon followed, and curricula expanded.

Instruction involves the training of the other senses, particularly hearing and touch, so that their exceptional keenness may be made to compensate for the lack of vision. The child must learn to read by means of its fingers. After experimentation with many methods, a raised type devised by Louis Braille, consisting of groupings of six raised dots, became in 1932 by agreement the system prevalent among all English speaking people.

The child is taught to write on a "braille slate," and in some cases on a specialized braille typewriter. For communication with seeing persons there is instruction in pencil writing in squarehand. Arithmetic, higher mathematics, and geography are taught by the tactual method. The latter has been greatly facilitated by a W.P.A. grant which has made atlases, containing over three hundred embossed maps, available for free distribution to all American schools for the blind. The more gifted pupils can now be trained in all high-school studies, and some upon graduation from schools for the blind attend college and professional schools.

In the absence of special provision for health and physical education, blind children are commonly frail. Hence schools for the blind provide special health training and are now able to give their pupils access to many types of vigorous physical activity.

Instruction in music is general, and in this branch a blind pupil with talent suffers least from lack of sight. Aside from its value as cultural training, music for the gifted blind provides vocational opportunities through the whole gamut from piano tuning to the role of virtuoso.[11]

Blind children generally have aptitude for manual training. Handicrafts, sloyd, and industrial training are an important part of

[11] Reuss, Alexander—*Development and Problems of Musical Notation for the Blind*, translated from the German by Ellen Kerney and Merle E. Frampton; The New York Institute for the Education of the Blind Series, Monogram Number 1, 1935.

the school curriculum. Some may not display aptitude beyond the traditional handicrafts for the blind, weaving, broom, or hammock making, chair caning, mattress making, knitting, and basketry. Others are well trained for vocational opportunities in braille shorthand, typewriting, dictaphone transcription, domestic science, business, and certain branches of agriculture such as poultry raising.

Social training may have to begin with the correction of unfortunate mannerisms and improvement of posture and carriage. It extends, however, to training in the socially approved types of behavior at dances, concerts, and other public gatherings. Through these latter, and through attendance at church social affairs particularly, pupils learn to mingle on a virtual parity with the seeing people present at such gatherings. The development of libraries for the blind, greatly facilitated by the free franking privilege for embossed works established by Congress in 1904, has now made it possible for half of the blind to read. In the past generation the development of the radio has opened to the blind the general cultural life of the nation.

Economic Condition of the Blind.—Once it is realized that only 38.9 per cent of the blind in the United States are between twenty and fifty-nine years of age, it is apparent that the vast majority of blind persons cannot be self-supporting. The 8.6 per cent who are under twenty years of age should for their own good and that of society be continuing their education. The 52.5 per cent that are sixty years of age or over could scarcely be absorbed in American industrial society which provides relatively few opportunities at this time of life even for the sighted. It is scarcely surprising therefore, under contemporary conditions, that only one blind person in twelve is fully self-supporting.[12]

As over nine-tenths of the blind lost their sight after they had become adult, they must have had the advantage of the training which is given to sighted pupils in our public schools, and vocational experience similar to that of their sighted associates. Thus the majority of those between twenty and fifty-nine years of age were probably self-supporting before their loss of vision. Relatively few, however, after such a calamity can return to their previous job. Special occupational training adapted to their capacities is necessary. But vocational rehabilitation was not widely available in America prior to the Congressional act of June 2, 1920, which provided Federal

[12] Percentage distribution given in Best—*op. cit.*, p. 182.

financial assistance to states for the vocational rehabilitation of disabled persons. Section 531 of the Social Security Act, approved August 14, 1935, extended this service. The percentage of the blind who may be rendered self-supporting can now be considerably increased as the education of the child blind and vocational rehabilitation for the adult blind are extended and perfected.

Participation by the blind in the economic life of the community is being promoted also by the establishment of state commissions for the blind or special divisions within state departments of education. In Massachusetts, for example, the Division of the Blind was in touch with 4,075 blind adults in 1936. It maintained six workshops in which 126 were employed. It was able to secure employment in outside occupations for only 38 others. It also conducted sales rooms for articles made by blind men and women, provided home teachers for 638 blind, and granted financial aid to 1,328. The actual number registered between the ages of 21 and 50 was 1,333. The services performed are many and valuable, but success in promoting self-support is still obviously restricted to few.[13]

Pensions for the Blind.—When the Federal Social Security Act was passed in 1935 there were twenty-six states which had some type of pension or monthly allowances for the blind from public funds. The first state to pass such a law was Ohio in the year 1898. The Social Security Act authorized Federal reimbursement to states of one-half of the amount of their pensions to the blind provided the Federal government's share did not exceed $15.00 a month for each person thus assisted. States qualify for Federal funds if the state act is mandatory and covers the entire state, following Federal standard procedure and making required reports. The administration of the plan is left to the state. Connecticut and Massachusetts were the first two states to qualify. Although such assistance amounts to little more than a minimum relief payment, it should serve to remove the vast majority of the blind who are incapable of self-support from dependence upon local charities, and thus dignify their situation within the community. It is not a substitute for vocational rehabilitation for those who can profit by the latter.

Prevention of Blindness.—Since the prevention of blindness is primarily a problem of bringing its causes under social control, the program of prevention must be integrated with the general program

[13] *Annual Report* (reprinted from P.D. 2, Department of Education); Division of the Blind, Department of Education.

of social control of heredity, disease, and accident covered in later chapters. There are, however, certain diseases of the eye which require specific study by pathologists and sociologists in order that their incidence may be rapidly reduced and their effects mitigated.

An excellent example of the result of special research and programs is offered in the case of ophthalmia neonatorum. Thirty years ago more than one child in every four in our schools for the blind had lost its sight as a result of this disease. It is usually acquired in the process of birth by the entrance of gonococci or other bacteria into the eyes of the infant. Within a few days the infected eyes become swollen and inflamed, and unless they are treated quickly sight may be lost within two weeks.

A simple preventive, discovered by Credé, in 1879, consists of placing one or two drops of a one per cent solution of silver nitrate in the corner of each eye of every infant at birth. Through the excellent work of the National Society for the Prevention of Blindness practically all of the American states have now reduced the volume of this disease to a small fraction of its former proportions. State laws in the main provide the prophylactic without charge to physicians and midwives and require reporting of all births and all eye trouble in infants to the Board of Health. This admirably demonstrates how by concentrated effort one of the more serious causes of blindness can be effectively attacked. By this simple, scientific technique, incorporated in law, the number of cases of total blindness in childhood has already been greatly reduced.[14] Steps to perfect enforcement of such legislation can ultimately eliminate blindness from this source.

The National Society for the Prevention of Blindness has promoted the enactment of appropriate laws to cope with this disease and other diseases of the eye, and coöperates with public bodies and private agencies throughout America in educational, curative, and preventive programs. It has initiated many researches and training courses, and provides an admirable example of the type of public service which can be rendered by a private national organization competently staffed. The American Foundation for the Blind,

[14] Report by the Standing Committee on Conservation of Vision—*Prevention of Blindness in Newborn Babies;* Special Reprint Edition issued by The National Society for the Prevention of Blindness, Publication No. D63. In schools for the blind new admissions of children blind from ophthalmia neonatorum were 28.2 per cent of the total admissions in 1907, but only 7.5 per cent in 1932. Best—*op. cit.*, pp. 137–138.

through its researches, statistical organization, experimentation with mechanical appliances, and services to blind individuals and schools, has greatly facilitated the process of prevention though primarily concerned with education and service to the blind.

Sight Conservation.—Another aspect of this problem is the conservation of sight. There is need of providing the type of care for children with partial vision which will prevent progressive impairment of sight. Two children in every thousand need special education in sight-saving classes. The first class in the United States for the education of this group was established in 1913. Today there are about five hundred such classes, available chiefly in the larger cities leaving the children of rural communities and small towns unaided. Periodic examination of the eyes of all school children and immediate treatment of serious defects, though essential to prevention of blindness or serious loss of vision, are still available to only a small percentage of the children of America.

An important part of the program for prevention is the education of parents to recognize eye difficulties, to provide proper lighting for reading or play activities of children, and to secure immediate medical assistance when difficulties in vision or diseases of the eye are noted. The prevention of blindness requires also available clinics in rural counties, as well as in cities, in which examinations, and if necessary treatment, can be provided irrespective of the ability of parents to pay.

QUESTIONS FOR DISCUSSION OR EXAMINATION

1. Definitions, extent, and distribution of blindness by sex, age, and race.
2. What are the causes of blindness and what is their relative importance?
3. By what public measures can the volume of blindness be reduced?
4. Discuss (a) education of the blind, (b) vocational opportunities for the blind.

PROBLEMS FOR INDIVIDUAL STUDY

1. Report on the social pathology of blindness as revealed by autobiographies of the blind.
2. History of social provision for the blind.
3. Analysis of the methods of education for the blind.
4. Social audit of schools and other public facilities for the blind in some selected state.
5. Analysis of the methods of vocational training and placement for the blind in your state.
6. Study of the economic and social problems of persons who have only partial vision.

SUGGESTIONS FOR SUPPLEMENTARY READINGS

American Foundation for the Blind—Reports and publications.

Best, Harry—*Blindness and the Blind in the United States;* The Macmillan Company, 1934.

Eaton, Allen, and Harrison, Shelby M.—*A Bibliography of Social Surveys,* References on "Blindness, Sight Conservation, and Disease of the Eye," pp. 20–22; Russell Sage Foundation, 1930.

Gillin, John Lewis—*Social Pathology,* Chapter 3, "Blindness and Deafness"; The Century Co., 1933.

Howe, Maud, and Hall, Florence Howe—*Laura Bridgman, Dr. Howe's Famous Pupil and What He Taught Her;* Little, Brown, and Company, 1903.

Irwin, Robert B.—"The Blind," *Social Work Year Book 1929;* Russell Sage Foundation, 1930.

Jones, D. Caradog, editor—*The Social Survey of Merseyside,* Vol. Three, Chapter 13, "Sub-Normal Types: The Blind"; University Press of Liverpool, Hodder & Stoughton Ltd., 1934.

Keller, Helen—*Helen Keller's Journal;* Doubleday, Doran & Company, Inc., 1938.

Keller, Helen—*The Story of My Life;* Doubleday, Doran & Company, Inc., 1936.

Keller, Helen—*The World I Live In;* The Century Co., 1920.

Lamson, Mary Swift—*Life and Education of Laura Dewey Bridgman;* Houghton Mifflin Company, 1899.

League of Nations, Health Organisation—*Report on the Welfare of the Blind in Various Countries;* Series of League of Nations Publications (III. Health. 1929. III.8), Official No. C.H. 818, Geneva, 1929.

Lende, Helga, editor—*What of the Blind? A Survey;* American Foundation for the Blind, 1939.

Mangold, George B.—*Social Pathology,* Chapter XI, "The Physically Handicapped," and Chapter XII, "Education, Care and Treatment of Handicapped"; The Macmillan Company, 1932.

National Society for the Prevention of Blindness—Reports and publications.

Parsons, Sir John Herbert—*Diseases of the Eye;* The Macmillan Company, eighth edition, 1936.

Perkins Institution for the Blind—Annual reports.

Queen, Stuart Alfred, and Mann, Delbert Martin—*Social Pathology,* Chapter XXIV, "The Blind and the Deaf"; Thomas Y. Crowell Company, 1925.

Rand, Lotta Stetson, compiler—*Directory of Activities for the Blind in the United States and Canada;* American Foundation for the Blind, second edition, 1932.

Resnick, Louis, and Carris, Lewis H.—*Eye Hazards in Industrial Occupations;* National Society for the Prevention of Blindness, Publication 26, 1924.

United States Bureau of the Census—*The Blind in the United States, 1920;* Government Printing Office, 1923.

United States Bureau of the Census—*The Blind and Deaf-Mutes in the United States, 1930;* Government Printing Office, 1931.

Villey, Pierre—*The World of the Blind* (translated by Alys Hallard); Duckworth, 1930.

White House Conference on Child Health and Protection—*The Handicapped Child*, "The Visually Handicapped," pp. 43–116; The Century Co., 1933.

Wilber, Louise—*Vocations for the Visually Handicapped;* American Foundation for the Blind, 1937.

Works Progress Administration—*Digest of Blind Assistance Laws of the Several States and Territories;* Division of Social Research, Works Progress Administration, Mimeographed, 1936.

World Conference on Work for the Blind—*1931 Proceedings;* 1932.

CHAPTER X

HEARING DISORDERS

Definitions.—It is customary to distinguish persons who are wholly deaf or in whom the sense of hearing is "so slight as to be of no practical value" from those who are hard of hearing. The former, if born deaf or if they acquire deafness within the first years of life, are also mute in the sense that they have not learned to talk as normal children do by hearing others talk. Though still widely termed "deaf and dumb," the deaf regard the words "dumb" and "mute" as opprobrious. They are now no longer necessarily mute, for by means of special methods of instruction they can be taught to speak.

Extent.—The Federal Census of 1930 gives the number of deaf-mutes in the United States as 57,123.[1] For purposes of the census they are defined as "(1) any child under 8 years of age who is totally deaf, and (2) any older person who has been totally deaf from childhood or was born deaf." The instructions further state: "Do not include a person who became deaf after the age of eight either from accident, or from disease, or from old age. A person is to be considered as totally deaf who cannot understand loudly shouted conversation or can understand it only with the aid of an ear trumpet or other mechanical device. In case of infants or young people not old enough to understand conversation, the test should be whether they apparently hear when addressed in a loud tone of voice." [2] Such methods are inadequate to discover and distinguish all deafmutes, especially in the case of infants. No supplementary scientific tests were used. In addition there were 1,942 persons reported as being blind deafmutes.

Of the census deaf 29,267 were male and 27,856 female (a sex disparity much less wide than in the case of the blind). By race 52,193 were white, 4,202 Negro, 410 Mexican, 283 Indian, and 35 of other races. Racial distribution fails to show abnormally high inci-

---

[1] *Statistical Abstract of the United States 1936*, p. 79; Government Printing Office, 1936.

[2] Bureau of the Census—*Fifteenth Census of the United States: 1930, Supplemental Schedule for the Blind and for Deaf-Mutes*, Form 15–103; Government Printing Office, 1930.

dence of this handicap among the colored races of the United States. By age 4,869 were under ten years of age, 11,936 between ten and nineteen, 21,509 between twenty and forty-four, 12,343 between forty-five and sixty-four, and 6,388 sixty-five and over. As compared with the blind, the deaf reveal a more normal age distribution, which means a much larger gross number and higher percentage in the early years of life, with relatively few among the aged.[3]

The highest ratio of the deaf in the population by states was found in Kansas with 62.4 per 100,000 population. New Mexico, Nebraska, and South Dakota with 62.1, 62.0, and 61.3 respectively had high rates. The lowest ratios were for Wyoming with 26.6 and Delaware with 26.8. It is not known in how far these disparities reflect inaccuracies on the part of enumerators. The ratio for the country as a whole is 46.5 deaf for 100,000 population.[4]

Although the deaf have been enumerated in every Federal census beginning with that of 1830, it is impossible to determine whether or not the ratio has increased, because of changes in the definitions or in methods of enumeration.[5] Each census from 1880 to 1920, inclusive, secured supplemental data concerning the blind and deaf on such matters as causes, age at occurrence, degree of education, economic status, occupation, and marital condition. In 1930 such special information was not secured.

Heredity.—Much deafness is apparently hereditary in origin, possibly fully one-third. In America the first of the more notable studies of heredity in this group was made by Alexander Graham Bell, the inventor of the telephone, who devoted a large fraction of his life to scientific research on problems of deafness. Bell had noted the large number of marriages among the deaf in American institutions and the frequency with which many surnames recurred among pupils in such institutions. Compiling data from the 1877 Report of the American Asylum at Hartford, he found that of 2,106 pupils, 693 or nearly 33 per cent were known to have deaf relatives. Many had several, and in a few cases fifteen deaf relatives were recorded. Covering six institutions with 5,823 deaf, 29.5 per cent

---

[3] *Statistical Abstract of the United States 1936*, p. 79. Ages were "unknown" in 78 cases.

[4] *Ibid.*, p. 79.

[5] Schmeckebier, Laurence F.—*The Statistical Work of the National Government*, pp. 84–85; The Institute for Government Research, The Johns Hopkins Press, 1925.

were known to have relatives who were "deaf and dumb." Of 2,262 congenitally deaf pupils, 54 per cent had deaf relatives, while among the noncongenital cases only 13.8 per cent had deaf relatives.[6]

From the same institutions a study of the marriages of the deaf showed that 78.6 per cent of pupils reported mating with deaf persons. The percentage of such marriages had shown a tendency to increase in the decades immediately preceding this study. From analysis of the offspring of such matings it seemed reasonable to conclude that "in a large proportion of cases in which the marriages were productive of deaf offspring both parents had deafmute relatives," and that "non-congenital deafness, if sporadic, seems little likely to be inherited."[7] Family charts and statistical graphs showing the growth of the deaf population, together with elaborate appendices revealing the methods of investigation, completed Bell's pioneer study.

The next important study of this problem was by Edward Allen Fay, entitled *Marriages of the Deaf in America*. When, in 1898, Fay covered records of 4,471 matings in which one or both partners were deaf, it appeared that deafness did not operate like a Mendelian unit character. For among 335 matings in which both parents were congenitally deaf only 25 per cent yielded some deaf offspring, and of 779 offspring only 26 per cent were deaf. Even when the partners belonged to the same deaf strain only 45 per cent of the marriages yielded deaf offspring, and the percentage of children who were deaf was only 30. Nevertheless, if both partners hear but are of deaf strains there is possibility of deafness in the offspring.[8] When these same data were restudied in 1925 by Kraatz, the conclusion was reached that deafness is not a simple recessive, a dominant, or a sex-linked character.[9] There may be more than one type of hereditary deafness, or other explanations may later be found and accepted.

Disease as Cause.—Most deafness is caused by disease. There are many diseases of infancy and early childhood which may result in deafness. Among these scarlet fever tends to take first place, with meningitis a close second. Best ascribed 17.6 per cent of acquired

[6] Bell, Alexander Graham—*Memoir upon the Formation of a Deaf Variety of the Human Race*, pp. 8–9, 11, and 13; National Academy of Sciences, 1883.

[7] *Ibid.*, pp. 16 and 26.

[8] Fay, Edward Allen—*Marriages of the Deaf in America*, pp. 13, 48, 49, and Chapter VII; Volta Bureau, 1898.

[9] Kraatz, J. J.—"Hereditary Deaf-mutism"; *Journal of Heredity*, 1925.

deafness to the former and 17 per cent to the latter disease.[10] Catarrh and colds, brain fever, measles, typhoid, and whooping cough, each on occasion may injure or destroy the sense of hearing. In addition there are many inflammations of the internal ear that produce deafness. Congenital syphilis is also a presumptive cause in certain cases.

Accident as Cause.—Probably not over two per cent of deafness may be ascribed to accidents. Nevertheless, in war times the number of cases of partial or complete loss of hearing among adults as a result of explosions of munitions, whether at the manufacturing plant, in the process of transportation, or at the front, is significantly large.

The Social Consequences of Deafness.—Like the blind, the deaf must endure many personal and social disadvantages in their daily life. These may take the form of unwanted pity, neglect which ranges from inadequate care to the failure of others to include them in conversation or in much of the social life of their families and neighborhoods. The deaf, because of peculiarities of speech or manner, may suffer avoidance by others or even their positive aversion. In the personalities of both the deaf and the hard of hearing there may develop correspondingly self-pity, the suspicion that they are being talked about or that they are looked down upon or are considered a bother, and a sense of inferiority. Social isolation tends to become cumulative. They may be driven to association and marriage only with persons similarly handicapped. They are traditionally less happy than the blind.

Even after they have learned to read lips they usually miss much of general conversation. Intonations do not reach them. The radio and much of the quality of music is lost to them. In the economic world, precluded as they are from conversation, they can seldom secure employment in buying, selling, or types of executive or subordinate work which involve the use of the telephone. They are excluded from many other occupations where lack of hearing means risk of accident. Thus only a limited group of positions are available to them, and at relatively low pay. Though less handicapped industrially than the blind, and much more largely self-supporting, dependency rates are higher among the deaf than in the general population. Dependency or a reduced plane of living is likely also for persons who lose their hearing in adult years.

[10] Best, Harry—"Deaf," *Encyclopaedia of the Social Sciences*, Vol. 5, p. 18; The Macmillan Company, 1931.

The personal and social limitations of deafness in adult years have been expressed by Collingwood, in his *Adventures in Silence:*

"Now and then I meet deaf people who complain bitterly at the treatment which society metes out to them. In most cases I think they are wrong, for we must all admit squarely the foundation fact of our affliction, which is that we may very easily become a trouble and a nuisance socially. We represent perhaps two per cent of the nation's population, and we can hardly expect the other ninety-eight per cent always to understand us. I have had people move away from me as though they expected me to bite them. Some sensitive souls might feel that they were thus associated with mad dogs, but it is better to see the humor of it. For my part, I have come to realize that I am barred from terms of social equality with those who live in the kingdom of sound. I have come to be prepared for a certain amount of impatience and annoyance. I am often myself impatient with those dull souls who depend so entirely upon their ears that they have failed to cultivate the instinct or the intuition which enables us to grasp a situation at a glance. . . .

"Deafness is not even complete silence, for we must frequently listen to head noises, which vary from gentle whispering to wild roars or hideous bellowing. There is little other physical discomfort usually, though some exceptional cases are associated with headache or neuralgia. There is, however, an annoying pressure upon the ears, which is greatly increased by excitement, depression or extreme fatigue. Unseen hands appear to be pressing in at either side of the head. The actual noises are peculiar to the individual in both quantity and quality; there are cases of the 'boilermaker's disease,' where the head is filled with a hammering which keeps time with the pulse. I have known people to be amazed at the 'uncontrolled fury' of the deaf when their anger is fully aroused—perhaps by something which seems trivial enough. They do not realize how a sudden quickening of the heart action may start a greater army of furies to shouting and smashing in the deaf man's brain! . . .

"You have doubtless noticed deaf people who go about with a weary, half-frightened expression, and have wondered why they have failed to 'brace up' and accept their lot with philosophy. You do not realize how these discordant sounds and malignant voices are driving these deaf people through life as a haunted man is lashed along the avenues of eternal doom. Of course his will frequently becomes broken down, and his capacity for consistent and continuous labor is practically destroyed. Do you know that if you were forced to remain for several hours in a roaring factory you would come back to your friends showing the same symptoms of voice and manner which you notice in the deaf? . . .

". . . I fancy that the violent effort to readjust life habits to a new existence bewilders most of us, so that the mind is incapable of working in exactly the old way. Apparently many of the deaf fall into a morbid, hopelessly despondent frame of mind, which does not permit any reasonable and useful research into the habits and landmarks which characterize a strange country." [11]

The liabilities and assets of the deaf in the way of recreation are thus expressed by Calkins:

"On my Index Expurgatorius are:—	*I have left:*—
Conversation in the best sense	Books
The theatre	Pictures, moving and stationary
Lectures	Art—painting, sculpture, archi-
Public dinners, and most pri-	tecture and applied art
vate ones	Natural science
Music	Scenery
Social dancing	Travel, on foot, train, boat, horse,
. . . .	and motor
Being read aloud to.	Exhibition dancing, and all kinds of
	spectacles and pageants
	Games like golf and whist
	Nearly all hobbies.

"I add these two columns and strike a balance. When mitigations and compensations are added, the assets exceed the liabilities, and I am, from a happiness-viewpoint, solvent.

"Nor are all the liabilities total. I have often read a play in advance and derived some entertainment from seeing it without hearing it. And in France and Italy I have done more. There I have an advantage over the visitor who does not understand the language. I get more out of the acting through my long training in observation: the seeing eye, sharpened . . ." [12]

Education.—Institutional care for the deaf had been meagerly provided in several countries prior to 1800. There was however little provision for their education, aside from small private ventures, before the eighteenth century. In the latter part of that century two major pedagogical practices to train the deaf for communication with others were in operation. The sign language is identified with the school founded by Charles Michel, Abbé de l'Épée in France in 1755. Lip reading combined with vocal speech is identified with the schools conducted by Thomas Braidwood in Edinburgh and by Samuel Heinicke near Hamburg and later in Leipzig.

Although there had been a school of the Braidwood type in Virginia in 1812, the first of the permanent schools in the United States was that founded at Hartford, Connecticut, in 1817. It was by

[11] Collingwood, Herbert W.—*Adventures in Silence*, pp. 34, 38–39, 39–40, and 57–58; distributed by The Rural New Yorker, 1923.

[12] Calkins, Earnest Elmo—*"Louder Please!": The Autobiography of a Deaf Man*, p. 255; The Atlantic Monthly Press, 1924.

accident rather than by design that Thomas Hopkins Gallaudet, its founder, adopted the methods of Abbé de l'Épée. For after graduating from Yale College he had gone to Europe to study the Braidwood system. Finding that they regarded their methods as a business monopoly he was forced to go to France to receive his training.[13]

The Connecticut asylum for the education and instruction of "deaf and dumb" persons was incorporated by the state legislature, which gave it an official standing that was shortly reënforced by public grants of financial aid. It was named the American Asylum. In the following year similar schools were opened in New York and Philadelphia. In 1819, the Massachusetts legislature appropriated funds for the education of twenty deaf persons at Hartford. New Hampshire and Vermont made similar appropriations in 1825. New schools quickly followed in Kentucky, Ohio, and Virginia, and in 1857 the Congress of the United States incorporated an institution at Washington, D.C., under the direction of Dr. Edward M. Gallaudet, son of the founder of the Hartford school. By 1864 collegiate instruction was available as one of the departments of the national school in Washington, the first of its kind. It is known as Gallaudet College.[14]

The first instruction in this country was by the sign language, also known as the manual method, expressing ideas and emotions by signs or gestures which do not follow the order of spoken speech. Allen states: "As it is a language of living pictures, such deaf people think in pictures and dream in them." As the manual method is the one most easily learned some schools continue its use though others dispense with it entirely. The manual alphabet or finger spelling is also widely used.

The third form of instruction, known as the oral method, resulted in this country from a report by Horace Mann, who with Dr. Samuel Gridley Howe, in 1843, visited German schools in which this system was employed. It was not until 1864 that a special school, near Boston, was incorporated for its use. In 1867 the Clarke institution opened at Northampton, Massachusetts, as an oral school, and the New York institution was opened during the same year.

In the early history of this movement there was much controversy between the partisans of these three methods. But classes in articu-

[13] Allen, Edward E.—*Education of Defectives;* L. B. Lyon Company, 1899.
[14] *Ibid.* See also Best, Harry—*The Deaf: Their Position in Society and the Provision for Their Education in the United States;* Thomas Y. Crowell Company, 1914.

lation and speech reading gradually became preëminent, especially following notable researches by Dr. Alexander Graham Bell, the formation in 1890 of the American association to promote the teaching of speech to the deaf, and the establishment of the Volta Bureau in Washington by Dr. Bell to collect and diffuse knowledge concerning the deaf.

The tendency has been increasingly away from the segregation of deaf children in institutions during the period of education. Instruction for them is now available in some states in public schools, as for example, the Horace Mann school in Boston. Thus, in Wisconsin, teachers will be provided by state aid for any community in which several deaf children can be brought together within easy access of their homes. Although instruction for the deaf child is inevitably slower than that for normal children—because of the needed emphasis upon language work and the development of means of communication—it is now possible for those so afflicted to secure a well-rounded education including collegiate instruction.

Schools for the Deaf.—There are now in the United States over two hundred schools for deaf children. Of these sixty-four are state residential schools which are either public or enjoying public subsidies and direction; twenty are private or denominational. There are only four states that do not yet have state residential schools, and in some states there are several. The emphasis in recent years has been upon development of public day schools for the deaf. These have already been established in twenty-eight states, and seventy-two of the hundred and twenty-five such schools in 1936 were provided by five states—California, Illinois, Michigan, Ohio, and Wisconsin. Although the education of the deaf is now compulsory in most states the laws are not perfectly enforced. The number of pupils in these schools in 1932 was slightly under twenty thousand. In the city day schools not all of the children are deaf but some are hard of hearing. Since education for deaf children is compulsory there is no stigma of dependency involved in attendance at the state schools or public day schools.[15]

A trend of marked importance has been to discover and make use of any residual hearing which pupils may possess. It has been found that nearly half of the pupils have some power to appreciate sound.

---

[15] *Statistical Abstract of the United States 1936*, pp. 124–125, and Timberlake, Josephine B., and Wright, Betty C.—"The Deaf and the Hard of Hearing," *Social Work Year Book 1937*, pp. 119–122; Russell Sage Foundation, 1937.

The development of electrical hearing aids and experimentation with speech vibration may lead to profound changes in educational methods for this group.

Vocational Training and Placement.—In addition to their formal training the provision of appropriate vocational education is essential for deaf children. The range of occupations for the deaf is considerably larger than that available to the blind. So training for a wide variety of manual arts and vocations is possible. A survey by the United States Office of Education of occupational opportunities for the deaf and the hard of hearing was made in 1934, covering twenty-seven states and the District of Columbia. Altogether 19,580 persons were reached, of whom 67.7 per cent were men and 32.3 per cent women. About one-half the group covered were deaf and the remainder hard of hearing; 33.9 per cent having lost their hearing after the age of eighteen. Only 27.7 per cent of those covered had enough ability to read lips to "understand conversation," and 40.5 per cent had no ability whatever to read lips. Nearly half, 48.9 per cent, had attended only elementary school. Somewhat over half had received some type of occupational training.[16]

An unanticipated discovery of this survey was that men in the hard-of-hearing group appear to be at a disadvantage in holding employment when compared with the profoundly deaf. For of the latter 60.7 per cent of the men and 50.9 per cent of the women were employed, while among those who could hear loud speech without earphones only 51.1 per cent of the men and 48.2 per cent of the women were employed. The percentage of employment was greatest among persons from thirty to fifty years old. The largest proportion of employment was found among men and women of college education, and the smallest among those with little or no school training. There was much greater unemployment among those with no occupational training.[17]

Over two hundred and fifty types of occupation were reported in

[16] Martens, Elise H.—*The Deaf and the Hard-of-Hearing in the Occupational World: Report of a Survey Directed by the United States Office of Education*, pp. 1–22; United States Department of the Interior, Office of Education, Bulletin, 1936, No. 13, Government Printing Office, 1937.

[17] *Ibid.*, pp. 23–38. Further study is necessary to make sure in how far these unexpected findings are due (1) to the abnormal conditions of employment at the time of the survey, (2) the overrepresentation of the deaf in unskilled occupations. Future analysis should differentiate the types of training received and their duration and consider these with reference to the jobs secured, among the deaf, the hard of hearing, and the general population.

the survey. More than one-third of the deaf and hard of hearing were laborers or semiskilled workers in mills or factories. One-fourth of the men were in manufacturing and mechanical trades. Of the employed women 28.1 per cent were operatives or laborers; 19.9 per cent in domestic and personal service, as compared with 5.5 per cent for men; 19.1 per cent in clerical occupations, as compared with 6.3 per cent for men; and 18 per cent in professional or semiprofessional pursuits, in which only 8.4 per cent of the men were employed. Concentration in unskilled or semiskilled fields was found to be much greater for the deaf than for the hard of hearing.[18]

The median weekly earnings of those employed at the time of the survey were approximately $18. There were only 10 per cent who earned $40 or more per week, while 57 per cent received less than $20. Among those trained in schools for the deaf there appeared to be "little relationship between earning power and the extent to which occupational training was followed." Only "16.4 per cent held positions at the time of the survey for which employers said that school trade training was necessary." [19]

In terms of vocational education the implications of this survey would seem to be that the deaf child in vocational courses should acquire a general background in the nature of commerce and industrial organization, as well as skill in handling tools and in operating machinery. A reasonable training in some specific occupation seems desirable even though conditions of the market may lead the graduate to accept employment outside of the trade for which he is trained. Unquestionably there is need for considerable development in vocational analysis and placement, which now are available to only a few.

The Hard of Hearing.—Although less than one person in every thousand is deaf, apparently one person in ten suffers some degree of handicap from defective hearing. The hard of hearing are people "whose hearing is impaired to a degree which interferes seriously with their educational and vocational progress, and with proper social adaptation." [20] Their number is estimated in many official publications at ten million. Since there has been no uniform testing of the hearing of our general population such estimates are

[18] *Ibid.*, pp. 39–58.
[19] *Ibid.*, pp. 59–81.
[20] White House Conference on Child Health and Protection—*The Handicapped Child*, p. 9; The Century Co., 1933.

at best guesses based upon the data available from the testing of special groups such as drafted men, school children, and others. The Committee on the Physically and Mentally Handicapped of the White House Conference on Child Health and Protection estimated that approximately three million children are suffering from impaired hearing and designates two million of these as handicapped.[21] The exact number will not be known, and consequently the special attention needed by the hard-of-hearing child will not be forthcoming in most communities, until standardized testing by means of such devices as acoumeters or audiometers under controlled conditions is made available to every school child.

The child who is hard of hearing, like the deaf child, requires instruction in lip reading, in addition to medical treatment and vocational guidance. In the attempt to treat such cases like normal children, they are taught in public school classes but have supplementary instruction in speech correction and lip reading by special teachers. Increasingly, microphones with individual earphones are being made available in the training of such children, notably in the larger communities of New York and Maryland in the East; Ohio, Minnesota, and Iowa among the Central States; and Utah and California in the West. The hearing of over eight hundred thousand pupils was tested in the year beginning with June, 1935, but only fourteen thousand children are yet being instructed in lip reading in the public schools.[22]

Persons who in their adult years lose their sense of hearing are frequently able to continue at their original occupation. Their education, culture, and vocational experience have already been acquired prior to the onset of their affliction, and their social and institutional contacts may have been well established. But whether or not their condition may prove remediable through mechanical devices, special education in lip reading makes it easier for them to maintain their social contacts and aids them in their occupations. Special classes for such adults, which are increasingly available at public cost, may be made a means to the correction of the tendency to reclusiveness and withdrawal from social life, and may be supplemented by advisory service where necessary in the vocational field.

The American Society for the Hard of Hearing, formed in 1919, to prevent deafness, preserve hearing, and rehabilitate adults with

---

[21] *Ibid.*, pp. 4 and 9.
[22] *Proceedings* of the American Society for the Hard of Hearing, p. 128; 1936.

defective hearing, has local chapters or affiliates throughout the country.   These are performing many essential services to such adults by means of the promotion of voice training and the use of electrical group-hearing aids, by exhibits of devices to aid hearing, by cultural activities and recreational centers, and in some instances by the maintenance of employment bureaus.   The local units are largely operated on a coöperative rather than a philanthropic basis, though some quite properly receive a portion of their funds from local community chests.

Prevention of Deafness and Hearing Defects.—In so far as these handicaps are hereditary or the result of general diseases or of accident, prevention is to be accomplished through programs outlined in later chapters.   Outstanding among the present deficiencies in the prevention of these handicaps is the failure to reach the non-congenital cases in their early stages with proper diagnosis and treatment.   Periodic and skilful testing of all school children is the most practical means of discovering incipient difficulties.   Medical attention by specialists to children and adults alike, irrespective of the capacity to pay, is requisite to prevent needless aggravation of the conditions.   Prevention thus involves discovery and registration of all cases, appropriate medical attention, and special instruction to minimize the disability and make educational, vocational, and social contacts possible.   Much additional research is needed into the causes of these handicaps and the means of prevention.   Better coordination and division of function among existing national organizations for the deaf is indicated.[23]

The Deaf-Blind.—Multiple handicaps are not uncommon.   Any two or three may combine in the same individual and frequently are sequelae of the same disease.   Where blindness and deafness have occurred together the resultant isolation, at first, was deemed insuperable.   With the case of Laura Bridgman, born in 1829, the means of effective training were first devised by Samuel Gridley Howe, to whom she was sent at the age of eight.   She was reached by the sense of touch and taught to identify the names of objects by

[23] The major agencies of research in this field today are the National Research Council, the American Otological Society, the American Medical Association, and the American Standards Association which tests mechanical aids to hearing. The recent establishment of the Coolidge Fund will facilitate research.   Many schools and universities, and organizations of and for the deaf are engaging in special studies.   Important contributions are also being made by the United States Office of Education.

spelling out the words in her hand. She learned to read by means of raised letters, but during her life of sixty years—chiefly spent at the institution—she did not learn to talk except for a few nouns and names.

Helen Keller, born in 1880, was similarly handicapped from the age of two. Her teacher, Miss Anne Sullivan, who took charge of her education five years later, found that Miss Keller was more sensitive than Miss Bridgman to vibrations, and was able to utilize this as well as the sense of touch. Miss Keller was first taught to spell and read raised type and braille. She was then given the vocal instruction for the deaf. By the age of twenty Helen Keller was ready to enter Radcliffe College, to learn to speak French and German, and was able to enjoy travel and several forms of sport.

"I could never have attended the classes at college had it not been for Teacher [Miss Sullivan], who sat beside me during four years and spelled into my hand the lectures word by word. This illustrates impressively what the handicapped may accomplish if normal people coöperate with them in a spirit of comradeship." [24]

With Miss Sullivan as constant companion, guide, interpreter, and secretary, Miss Keller has devoted her life to writing and lecturing, chiefly in the interests of the blind, and has so far overcome the social isolation characteristic of her handicaps, as to become internationally recognized in her profession.

"Lack of hearing has always been a heavier handicap to me than blindness. Sealed ears render more difficult every path to knowledge. The deaf are as hungry for a word as the blind are for a book under their fingers, yet it is harder to find people who will talk with the deaf than people who will supply the sightless with embossed books. That has not been my individual experience, I am glad to say. Sympathy has sweetened my days with society; religion and philosophy have assuaged my sorrows; but I remain unsatisfied, thinking how many deaf persons are immured and lonely through others' neglect or impatience. Regretfully I perceive the impossibility of working for both the blind and the deaf as I have often longed to do. The effort to alleviate either misfortune more than fills a lifetime; and besides, these tasks are redoubled by the endeavor to safeguard human eyes and ears against disease, accident, ignorance. Reluctantly, therefore, I have confined my activities almost exclusively to the dwellers in the Dark Land. . . .

". . . The reason why God permitted me to lose both sight and hear-

[24] Keller, Helen—*Helen Keller's Journal*, p. 71; Doubleday, Doran & Company, Inc., 1938.

ing seems clear now—that through me he might cleave a rock unbroken before and let quickening streams flow through other lives desolate as my own once was. I am content." [25]

QUESTIONS FOR DISCUSSION OR EXAMINATION

1. How are the deaf and hard of hearing identified?
2. Social statistics of the deaf.
3. What is the role of heredity in the causation of deafness?
4. Outline the history of education for the deaf.
5. Compare the deaf and the blind with reference to vocational training and placement.

PROBLEMS FOR INDIVIDUAL STUDY

1. A critical analysis of the literature on the inheritance of deafness.
2. Outline of the work of national organizations for (a) the deaf, or (b) the hard of hearing.
3. A study of the social pathology of hearing defects as revealed in the autobiographies of the deaf or hard of hearing.
4. Social audit of schools or other public institutions for the deaf in some selected state.
5. Analysis (including field study) of methods of teaching speech to the deaf.

SUGGESTIONS FOR SUPPLEMENTARY READINGS

American Association to Promote the Teaching of Speech to the Deaf— *Proceedings*, and *Volta Review*.

American Society for the Hard of Hearing—*Proceedings*, and *Hearing News*.

Bell, Alexander Graham—*Graphical Studies of Marriages of the Deaf;* Volta Bureau, 1917.

Bell, Alexander Graham—*The Mechanism of Speech;* Funk & Wagnalls Company, 1907.

Best, Harry—*The Deaf: Their Position in Society and the Provision for Their Education in the United States;* Thomas Y. Crowell Company, 1914.

Best, Harry—"Deaf," *Encyclopaedia of the Social Sciences*, Vol. 5; The Macmillan Company, 1931.

Calkins, Earnest Elmo—*"Louder Please!": The Autobiography of a Deaf Man;* The Atlantic Monthly Press, 1924.

Collingwood, Herbert W.—*Adventures in Silence;* The Rural New Yorker, 1923.

Conference of Executives of American Schools for the Deaf—*Proceedings*, and *American Annals of the Deaf*.

Convention of American Instructors of the Deaf—*Proceedings*.

Day, Herbert E., Fusfeld, Irving S., and Pintner, Rudolf—*A Survey of American Schools for the Deaf, 1924–1925;* National Research Council, 1928.

Fay, Edward Allen—*Marriages of the Deaf in America;* Volta Bureau, 1898.

Gillin, John Lewis—*Social Pathology*, Chapter 3, "Blindness and Deafness"; The Century Co., 1933.

[25] *Ibid.*, pp. 24–25 and 51.

Jones, D. Caradog, editor—*The Social Survey of Merseyside*, Vol. Three, Chapter 12, "Sub-Normal Types in the Population: The Deaf"; University Press of Liverpool, Hodder & Stoughton Ltd., 1934.

Love, James Kerr—*The Causes and Prevention of Deafness;* Wayne & Son, Ltd., 1913.

Mangold, George B.—*Social Pathology*, Chapter XI, "The Physically Handicapped," and Chapter XII, "Education, Care and Treatment of Handicapped"; The Macmillan Company, 1932.

Martens, Elise H.—*The Deaf and the Hard-of-Hearing in the Occupational World: Report of a Survey Directed by the United States Office of Education;* United States Department of the Interior, Office of Education, Bulletin, 1936, No. 13, Government Printing Office, 1937.

National Research Council—*Research Recommendations of the Second Conference on Problems of the Deaf and Hard of Hearing;* Reprint and Circular Series of the National Research Council, No. 88, 1929.

Peck, Annetta W., Samuelson, Estelle E., and Lehman, Ann—*Ears and the Man: Studies in Social Work for the Deafened;* F. A. Davis Company, 1926.

Queen, Stuart Alfred, and Mann, Delbert Martin—*Social Pathology*, Chapter XXIV, "The Blind and the Deaf"; Thomas Y. Crowell Company, 1925.

Reamer, Jeannette Chase—*Mental and Educational Measurements of the Deaf;* Princeton University Press, 1921.

United States Bureau of the Census—*Deaf Mutes in the United States, Analysis of the Census of 1910, with summary of state laws relative to the deaf as of January 1, 1918;* Government Printing Office, 1918.

United States Bureau of the Census—*Deaf-Mutes in the United States, 1920;* Government Printing Office, 1923.

United States Bureau of the Census—*The Deaf-Mute Population of the United States, 1920;* Government Printing Office, 1928.

United States Office of Education—publications.

Upshall, Charles C.—*Day Schools vs. Institutions for the Deaf;* Teachers College, Contributions to Education No. 389, Columbia University, 1929.

Volta Bureau—publications; Washington, 1899–

White House Conference on Child Health and Protection—*The Handicapped Child*, "The Deaf and the Hard of Hearing," pp. 9–41; The Century Co., 1933.

White House Conference on Child Health and Protection—*Special Education: The Handicapped and the Gifted*, "The Deaf and the Hard of Hearing," pp. 277–346; The Century Co., 1931.

CHAPTER XI

PHYSICAL DEFORMITIES

Definitions.—The physically handicapped comprise, in addition to the blind and deaf already considered, (1) persons crippled or deformed by accident, injury, or amputations; (2) persons congenitally deformed; and (3) persons who have suffered profound impairment of body structure or function as a result of disease.

The White House Conference Committee on Physically and Mentally Handicapped submitted the following definition.

"A crippled child is one, under twenty-one years of age, who by reason of congenital or acquired defects of development, disease or wound, is, or may be reasonably expected to become, deficient in the use of his body or limbs (an orthopedic cripple) including hare lip, cleft palate, and some other handicaps yielding to plastic surgery, and excluding physical difficulties wholly of sight, hearing, or speech, and those affecting the heart primarily, and also excluding serious mental or moral abnormalities unless found in conjunction with orthopedic defects." [1]

In essence, physically disabled adults are those who, in the terms of the Cleveland committee, are "handicapped because they lack the normal use of skeleton or skeletal muscles." [2] Restriction of muscle movements as well as loss of limb or abnormality of appearance may interfere with the individual's capacity for self-support or social participation.

Extent.—Persons suffering from physical handicap are estimated by many to exceed in number those suffering from mental disabilities. The physical handicaps affecting the skeleton and musculature and preventing the use or efficient use of the body or some of its members at industrial work, or limiting the individual's economic and social contacts, bulk large in the records of agencies for relief.

---

[1] White House Conference on Child Health and Protection—*The Handicapped Child*, p. 119; The Century Co., 1933.

[2] Wright, Lucy, and Hamburger, Amy M.—*The Education and Occupations of Cripples, Juvenile and Adult: A Survey of All the Cripples of Cleveland, Ohio, in 1916, under the Auspices of the Welfare Federation of Cleveland;* Publications of the Red Cross Institute for Crippled and Disabled Men, Series 2, No. 3, 1918.

The number of disabled in the United States is not known. Millions have suffered from accidents which have involved temporary disability.[3] In presumably the vast majority of cases the difficulty is either cured or sufficiently remedied so that the individual may make his own adjustment and need not have recourse to any of the agencies of relief or assistance. Even if his handicap does involve application for aid, there is still no central statistical bureau in this country which can satisfactorily advise concerning the volume of such handicaps and differentiate the types of the disabilities incurred. In the absence of standard tests and of a Federal census to record the prevalence of such disabilities one is forced to rely upon estimates of their volume, frequency, and incidence.

A number of state-wide and city-wide counts of cripples have been made in this country, covering the general population, both adults and children. That made in Cleveland in 1916 is still considered the most accurate because it supplemented a complete house-to-house survey with a check-up of the records of schools, hospitals, institutions, and agencies. The enumeration, extending over a period of one year from October, 1915, to October, 1916, discovered 4,186 cripples in a population estimated for 1916 at 674,073. The ratio was thus approximately six cripples to each thousand inhabitants and close to that reached in the Massachusetts census of "lame, maimed, and deformed" in 1905, which was 5.7 per thousand. If this ratio should prove applicable to the entire United States it would mean a disabled population of over seven hundred thousand.[4]

From analysis of all available surveys of crippled children the Committee on Physically and Mentally Handicapped of the White House Conference on Child Health and Protection estimated that there were 2.5 crippled children per thousand general population, or about 300,000 crippled children in the United States.[5]

[3] The National Safety Council, for example, estimates that there were 9,340,000 nonfatal injuries in the United States in 1935. *Accident Facts*—Condensed 1936 Edition; National Safety Council, Inc. Data on the number of crippled children will soon be available through the Children's Bureau of the United States Department of Labor from the registration now in process under the Social Security Act of 1935.

[4] Wright and Hamburger—*op. cit.* Titles of other American surveys will be found in Kessler, Henry H.—*The Crippled and the Disabled;* Columbia University Press, 1935: Eaton, Allen, and Harrison, Shelby M.—*A Bibliography of Social Surveys*, pp. 81–83; Russell Sage Foundation, 1930: White House Conference on Child Health and Protection—*The Handicapped Child:* and in current issues of the *Social Work Year Book.*

[5] White House Conference on Child Health and Protection—*op. cit.*, pp. 4

Social Consequences of Physical Disability.—The consequences of any disability depend in part upon whether it is temporary or permanent, partial or complete. They vary greatly with the nature of the handicap, the personality of the victim, age, economic status, and training. Congenital deformities make necessary a lifetime adjustment. Accommodation is very different and may be easier for persons who are crippled in their adult years. In the absence of special measures the child cripple is likely to suffer from a sense of inferiority; to be introspective or self-centered; to suffer from self-pity; and if avoided or taunted for its defect it may become bitter or vindictive. A person crippled in adult years is likely to suffer severe discouragement, loss of confidence, self-pity, and perhaps fear. The range of employment for each is limited by the deformity —if employment is at all possible—and for the adult cripple a lower plane of living is likely to be necessary. In the absence of thorough-going provision for rehabilitation recourse may be had to begging and parasitism. There are notable exceptions where the crisis has been accepted as a challenge and met with a determination, judgment, and cheerfulness which have overcome all obstacles. Permanent dependency is, however, inevitable for many, and partial or temporary dependency for others. But physical disability, except where associated with mental disability, shows no abnormal correlation with crime or antisocial behavior, aside from begging.[6]

Heredity, and Congenital Causes.—The role of heredity in the production of deformity is less conspicuous than in the case of the other types of handicap considered in previous chapters. Myerson and associate members of the Committee on Eugenical Sterilization mention such crippling affections as chronic progressive chorea (Huntington's Disease), Friedreich's ataxia, spastic spinal paralysis, and various others, eleven in all, under the heading "chronic progressive neurological diseases." There is some evidence that each of

and 132–136. The registers of crippled children in 36 states, Alaska, and Hawaii of June 30, 1937, included the names of 99,722 crippled children. See *Facts about Crippled Children*, p. 1; United States Department of Labor, Children's Bureau, March 1, 1938 (mimeographed).

[6] See, however, possible correlation of low stature and puny physique with certain crimes against property as recorded by Goring, Charles—*The English Convict: A Statistical Study;* H. M. Stationery Office, 1913. There appears to be association between defects and low mental test scores; summarized very briefly with footnote references in Hiller, E. T.—*Principles of Sociology*, pp. 533–535; Harper & Brothers, 1933. Further research is necessary to determine how widely applicable these findings may be.

these may be hereditary.[7] There are several types of physical deformity which appear to be hereditary: *e.g.* scoliosis (dissymmetry of the trunk), achondroplasy (a form of dwarfism), albinism (lack of pigmentation), brachydactylism (two joints in fingers and toes instead of three), polydactylism (excess digits), and syndactylism (union of certain fingers and toes). Though the types of deformity of hereditary nature may be many, the number of actual cases is very small. Only a low and still unknown percentage of the total number of cripples are hereditary cases.

Congenital causes ordinarily account for from 3 to 5 per cent of all cases of disability, but among child cases from 6 to 26 per cent, in the surveys so far made. Congenital cases, however, include in addition to those which are hereditary a group presumably much larger in which the deformity was occasioned by unfavorable conditions of the foetal period, whether accident to the mother while carrying the child, diseases of the mother, malnutrition of the foetus, or abnormalities and injuries in the birth process.

Disease.—The leading cause of disability among children is disease, while accidents and amputations preponderate among adult cases. Infantile paralysis, or poliomyelitis, is the chief disease resulting in disability in most surveys of child cripples in America, though rachitis is the most prominent cause in some German studies, and tuberculosis leads in a survey at Birmingham, England. Syphilis and spastic paralysis are mentioned in very few of the surveys, or are included among the congenital causes.[8]

The White House Conference Committee on Physically and Mentally Handicapped in analyzing twelve local American studies of crippled children found infantile paralysis accounted for from 15.5 (Philadelphia, 1929) to 51 per cent (Chicago, 1924) of crippling; bone tuberculosis from less than 1 per cent to 25 per cent (New York State, 1924–25).[9] Lack of uniformity in definitions and tests largely accounts for the differences, though local epidemics, especially of

[7] Committee of the American Neurological Association for the Investigation of Eugenical Sterilization (Abraham Myerson, James B. Ayer, Tracy J. Putnam, Clyde E. Keeler, and Leo Alexander)—*Eugenical Sterilization: A Reorientation of the Problem*, pp. 145–149; The Macmillan Company, 1936.

[8] A table analyzing the causes of disability, according to fourteen surveys, will be found in Kessler—*op. cit.*, pp. 40–41. Kessler places infantile paralysis first, surgical tuberculosis next in frequency, congenital deformities third, rachitis fourth, and trauma fifth among child cases, pp. 42–43.

[9] White House Conference on Child Health and Protection—*op. cit.*, pp. 137–138.

infantile paralysis, and a variety of population and environmental factors affect distribution.

Posture.—It is not clear how largely crippled conditions are occasioned by unfortunate habits in regard to posture and apparel, but unquestionably there are many cases of needlessly faulty posture and the wearing of unsuitable shoes, for example, which when uncorrected over a period of years cripple their victim or create a large borderline group of reduced efficiency and employability. The Subcommittee on Orthopedics and Body Mechanics of the White House Conference on Child Health and Protection reports as follows:

"Approximate statistics obtained from: the examination of young and middle-aged men during the universal draft of the late World War; postural surveys made of the entering classes of Harvard College by Lee and Brown, by Cook at Yale, and by Thomas and Lindner at Smith; numerous school surveys in different sections of the country have all been consistent with the findings of the Chelsea Survey. This included an intensive and rather complete survey of body mechanics covering a period of two years, among 1,708 children of both sexes varying in age from five to eighteen years, made in 1923 and 1924, under the auspices of the Children's Bureau of the Department of Labor in the Williams Public School of the city of Chelsea, Massachusetts. It was made possible through the coöperation of Frank E. Parlin, Ped.D., then Superintendent of Schools in Chelsea. Over 80 per cent of these children exhibited either C or D grades of body mechanics. There seemed to be a slight tendency for the grade of posture to improve after the middle of the second decade of life, but Lee's and Brown's survey of the entering classes of Harvard placed 80.3 per cent of these young adults in these same C and D groups. Cook's review of 2,200 students at Yale showed only 20 per cent had a normal spinal contour. . . .

". . . In 1928, in a Health Survey made of the school children of Los Angeles, 35,000 children were found to exhibit abnormal postural conditions as compared with 8,000 heart defects. . . .

"We may reasonably believe that perhaps 75 per cent of the male and female youth of the United States exhibit grades of body mechanics which, according to the standards of this Subcommittee, are imperfect.

"A few words may be said in relation to associated static defects, especially those of the spine and feet. Functional scoliosis is a postural defect. By functional scoliosis is meant a lateral curvature of the spine which is attitudinal and shows no structural changes of the vertebrae or ribs. This curvature disappears when good body mechanics is attained. Pronation of the feet, or a tendency toward flattening of the longitudinal arch of the foot and a sagging of the internal malleolus is an extremely common associated static defect. Miss Claire Colestock, Assistant Director of Physical Education of the Pasadena City Schools, reports that of about 200 boys and girls of the fourth, fifth and sixth grades, slightly over

80 per cent exhibited foot defects. About the same percentage was found among the 1,708 school children included in the Chelsea Survey." [10]

Accident.—Whether or not followed by amputations, accident is the major cause of crippled conditions among adults, and is responsible for a needlessly high percentage of such conditions among children. The number of fatal accidents in America each year is approximately one hundred thousand, but Dr. Louis I. Dublin estimates that there are annually "some six million injuries caused by accidents that do not result in death"—a figure much more conservative than that of the National Safety Council. The percentage permanently disabled is small but not accurately known.[11]

The causes of accident have been most closely analyzed in the cases where there were fatalities, and there it was found that 31 per cent of deaths were due to automobile accidents, and roughly 23 per cent each to accidents in the home, in industry, and in public places.[12] Although most of the accidents do not result in permanent handicap and involve only temporary disability, it should be remembered that there is a large borderline group of persons who suffer relatively mild permanent injuries whose occupational efficiency and social contacts are somewhat affected. Since they manage to get along they are not listed in the group termed the "handicapped."

War greatly increases the volume of physical disability. In all the combatant countries over four million persons were disabled by disease, physical or mental, or by injuries received during the World

[10] White House Conference on Child Health and Protection—*Body Mechanics: Education and Practice*, pp. 19–20; The Century Co., 1932. Their references for above quotation as cited by them are: Brown, L. T.—"A Combined Medical and Postural Examination of 746 Young Adults," *Amer. Jour. Orth. Surg.*, Vol. 15, No. 11, November, 1917, p. 774: Cook, R. J.—"Report of the Orthopaedic Examination of 1393 Freshmen at Yale University," *Jour. Bone and Joint Surg.*, Vol. 4, April, 1922; "Results of Exercise for the Correction of Postural Defects," *N. Y. Med. Jour. and Med. Rec.*, Vol. 117, February 7, 1923; and "Postural Defects in College Men," *Amer. Phy. Ed. Review*, Vol. 28, April, 1923: Thomas, Leah C., and Lindner, Amy—"A Few Observations in Body Mechanics," *Research Quarterly of the American Physical Ed. Assn.*, Vol. I, No. 3, October, 1930: Klein, A., and Thomas, L. C.—*Posture and Physical Fitness;* Children's Bureau Publication, No. 205, Government Printing Office, 1931: Los Angeles, *Annual Reports of the Department of Health and Corrective Physical Education*, July, 1926–July, 1929.

[11] Estimate of Dr. Louis I. Dublin, Statistician, Metropolitan Life Insurance Company. White House Conference on Child Health and Protection—*Dependent and Neglected Children*, p. 80; D. Appleton-Century Company, 1933.

[12] *Ibid.*, p. 81.

War. The damage to United States men in war service was comparatively slight, yet the number listed as disabled was over one hundred and ninety thousand. These figures, however, cover all types
of defects and many diseases; relatively few were crippled.[13] Injuries to arms, hands, and legs exceed those to other parts of the
body, and exceed also those necessitating amputation according to
official British and Canadian statistics cited by Devine and Brandt.[14]

Industrial Cripples.—Statistics of the vocational rehabilitation
services of American states cover 77,000 disabled adult persons from
1921 to 1935. In the latter year 9,422 were retrained for employment and 40,000 were in process of rehabilitation.[15] The origin of
disability among the 9,422 cases was given as 18 per cent employment accident, 7 per cent public accident, 25 per cent other accident, 42 per cent disease, and 8 per cent congenital. These figures
include injuries to sight and hearing and certain chronic illnesses,
as well as crippled conditions. The official classification by nature
of disability is stated as follows:[16]

"Most of the disabled persons for whom the service is available suffer
from major physical disabilities. Ordinarily it is the major physical impairment that results in inability to follow a former occupation. The
usual disabilities are orthopedic. Sixty-one per cent of the cases rehabilitated in 1935 suffered from orthopedic disabilities. The extent of disability due to cardiac conditions and tuberculosis is not as obvious as the
disability from amputation or paralysis. The State services have done less
for the tubercular and cardiac groups than for others. The number of persons rehabilitated in 1935, classified by nature of disability, was as follows:

DISABILITY	PERCENTAGE OF CASES	DISABILITY—continued	PERCENTAGE OF CASES
Hand	8.0	Vision	7.0
Hands	.4	Hearing	7.1
Arm	6.3	Miscellaneous	6.1
Arms	.3	Head	.3
Foot	4.0	Cardiac	1.6
Feet	1.0	Tuberculosis	5.0
Leg	34.0	Back	4.6
Legs	7.0	Total	100.0
Multiple	7.3		

[13] Kessler—*op. cit.*, pp. 145–146; and reports of the United States War Department and United States Administrator of Veterans' Affairs.

[14] Devine, Edward T., and Brandt, Lilian—*Disabled Soldiers and Sailors Pensions
and Training*, especially pp. 14–17; Carnegie Endowment for International Peace,
Preliminary Economic Studies of the War, No. 12, Oxford University Press, 1919.

[15] United States Department of the Interior, Office of Education—*Vocational
Rehabilitation of the Physically Handicapped*, p. 19; Vocational Education Bulletin No.
190, Vocational Rehabilitation Series No. 25, Government Printing Office, 1936.

[16] *Ibid.*, pp. 24–25.

"The following table indicates the educational background of the cases being served by State rehabilitation departments:

SCHOOLING	PERCENTAGE OF CASES
None	1.5
Grades 1–6	13.4
Grades 7–9	35.8
Grades 10–12	17.0
Other	32.3
Total	100.0"

Treatment for Crippled Children.—The child who is deformed or crippled is in need of specialized medical or surgical treatment. Partial or even complete cure may be possible in some cases, and in all instances there should be some degree of alleviation. To provide properly for such treatment, the disabled child must first be discovered and then cared for either in a special hospital or in the home. Cripples will escape attention until every state provides for notification and registration of all cases, as well as for accessible clinical and hospital facilities and home nursing service.

In 1930 there were hospital facilities in the United States in three hundred and twenty-five institutions for somewhat over eleven thousand crippled children. Long waiting lists were reported as facilities were still far from adequate.[17]

The next essential need is for appropriate education, both cultural and vocational. Many of the profound cases, requiring continuous attention of physicians or nurses, will have to receive their training at the hospital. Others, after treatment, can be returned to their own homes, or if necessary placed out in family homes, and can attend public schools. In general it is deemed wise to avoid the institutionalization of the crippled child where possible and to let him have the advantages of a normal upbringing and the social contacts which public schools afford. It is important, however, that each case should be studied on the basis of its individual needs and reactions, so that the type of environment best adapted to its education and progress may be provided. Not until recent years have special classes for crippled children been provided in public schools. In a number of cities special arrangements have been made for their transportation to and from school, for physical, nutritional, and

[17] White House Conference on Child Health and Protection—*op. cit.*, pp. 152–153.

medical care, and for appropriate recreation in conjunction with their instruction.

Vocational instruction similarly requires careful individualization. For though a wide variety of occupations may be open to the child who has lost the use of one of his limbs, the opportunities are considerably reduced where both arms or hands are deformed, paralyzed, or amputated, and still another group of occupational limitations prevail for the wheelchair cripple. Individualization is likewise necessary in providing for recreation and training for social contacts. The least handicapped children can be trained for transfer to regular public school classes.

In recent years many agencies have become interested in the problems of crippled children, and in developing clubs, hospitals, and other special facilities for this group. Notable among the laymen's organizations are the Rotary and Kiwanis Clubs, the Shriners and Elks, and the American Legion. Foundations and universities have promoted specialized researches, and the International Society for Crippled Children, founded in 1921, has served as a clearing house of information on this subject.

The prospects of adequate care have been materially improved by the passage of the Social Security Act in 1935, which authorizes Federal assistance to states for the care of crippled children. This portion of the Social Security Act (Title V, Part 2) is administered through the recently formed Crippled Children's Division in the Children's Bureau of the United States Department of Labor. The annual appropriation of $2,850,000 from Federal funds, to be matched by state, local, or private funds administered by an approved official state agency, seeks to provide in rural as well as urban areas the essential facilities for diagnosis, hospitalization, medical, corrective, or surgical treatment, and aftercare.

Only four-fifths of the states had laws providing public funds for medical care of crippled children prior to the passage of the national Social Security Act, but by June 30, 1937, all states had submitted plans for approval under this act. Some states extend their legislation to cover children who are blind, deaf, or suffering from cleft palate, harelip, or cardiac ailments.

Policies are now being devised quite generally among the states to discover all crippled children, with the aid of nurses, social workers, physicians, hospitals, schools, welfare agencies, birth certificates, and special investigations. Orthopedic clinics and specialized aftercare, including social case work, are planned to supplement hospitalization, special educational facilities, and vocational rehabilitation.[18]

Vocational Rehabilitation for Adults.—Prior to the World War vocational rehabilitation for adult cripples had been provided only sporadically, chiefly by private agencies. The development of workmen's compensation legislation, covered in a later chapter, stimulated and directed the demand for appropriate measures to reeducate the victims of industrial accident. The Federal Board for Vocational Education was established in 1917, and in 1920 a Federal act made possible grants to states, to be matched by state funds, for the purpose of vocational rehabilitation of disabled persons.

Meanwhile in Europe as a result of the War there was much progress in general surgery, in plastic surgery, and the invention of prosthetic devices. Specialized studies were made of the types of occupations available to the victims of each type of injury or amputation. In the United States the War Risk Insurance Act of October 6, 1917, provided treatment for the disabled, and the Vocational Rehabilitation Act of June 27, 1918, transferred this work to the supervision of the Federal Board for Vocational Education. In 1921 the Veterans' Bureau took charge of such reëducational work for soldiers and sailors, which was continued until 1928, and provided opportunity for disabled veterans unable to return to their previous occupations to learn a new trade at the expense of the Federal government.[19] Altogether over 128,000 men completed such retraining programs. As less than 60 per cent of the applicants for this training had received more than a grammar school education prior to enlistment, their instruction was primarily in the manual trades. Nearly 40 per cent were trained for industry, 16 per cent for professional service, 13 per cent each for trade, clerical occupations, and agriculture.

Vocational rehabilitation for the general population has been greatly facilitated by a special provision in the Social Security Act of 1935 which authorizes grants to states on the basis of population, following Federal approval of their legislation and contingent upon the matching of Federal funds by the states. Vocational education

---

[18] Hood, R. C.—"Crippled Children," *Social Work Year Book 1937*, pp. 112–117; Russell Sage Foundation, 1937.

[19] Kessler—*op. cit.*, pp. 181–187.

has now been transferred to the United States Office of Education for administration, and within the states is operated by a special division of the State Board of Education. The increase of the Federal appropriation to states to $1,938,000 annually should make possible improvements in the scope and quality of the services rendered by each state. Although the Federal funds cannot be used to meet subsistence costs of clients during the period of retraining, many states are already prepared to do this. Official statistics for 1935 give the cost of training as $300 per client, and reports note a general increase in earning capacity upon the part of persons who have enjoyed the benefits of vocational retraining.[20]

Prevention.—Prevention of physical disabilities requires measures for bringing causative factors under social control. The chief cause of childhood disabilities is disease, the province of preventive medicine. Inherited deformities involve the social control of heredity. Most adult cripples, however, are victims of industrial or traffic accidents, war, or accidents in the home or public places. These can be reached only by comprehensive programs, covered in later chapters. As cure, education, and vocational rehabilitation are preventives of dependency, specialized research and appropriate programs in these fields may properly be included among the devices for social control.

QUESTIONS FOR DISCUSSION OR EXAMINATION

1. Social statistics of the crippled and disabled.
2. What are the relative roles of heredity, disease, and accident in the causation of crippled conditions?
3. Outline methods of prevention of physical disabilities.
4. What social provision for this group is made by Federal and state governments?
5. In what specific ways does the social problem of the child cripple differ from that of the adult?

PROBLEMS FOR INDIVIDUAL STUDY

1. Critical analysis of each detail of Federal provision for crippled veterans.
2. Critical analysis of contemporary Federal-state programs and practices for vocational rehabilitation.
3. An historical or biographical study of the social pathology of deformity.

[20] Details of method will be found in *Vocational Rehabilitation of the Physically Handicapped;* Vocational Education Bulletin No. 190, Vocational Rehabilitation Series No. 25, Government Printing Office, 1936.

4. The history of social provision for crippled and deformed persons.
5. A social audit of schools and hospitals for cripples in your state or some other selected state.

SUGGESTIONS FOR SUPPLEMENTARY READINGS

Abt, Henry E.—*The Care, Cure and Education of the Crippled Child;* International Society for Crippled Children, 1925.

Amar, Jules—*The Disabled;* Library Press (London), 1918.

American Medical Association—*Practical Suggestions on Poliomyelitis;* American Medical Association, 1935.

American National Red Cross—*The Program of the American Red Cross with the Military and Naval Services and for Disabled Veterans;* ARC 296, May, 1936.

American Occupational Therapy Association—*Bibliography on Occupational Therapy,* 1934: and *Occupational Therapy and Rehabilitation,* published bimonthly.

American Rehabilitation Committee—*Rehabilitation Review,* published bimonthly.

Crane, Arthur G.—*Education for the Disabled in War and Industry;* Teachers College, Columbia University, 1921.

Devine, Edward T., and Brandt, Lilian—*Disabled Soldiers and Sailors Pensions and Training;* Carnegie Endowment for International Peace, Preliminary Economic Studies of the War No. 12, Oxford University Press, 1919.

Eaton, Allen, and Harrison, Shelby M.—*A Bibliography of Social Surveys,* References on "Crippled, Disabled, and Handicapped," pp. 81–83; Russell Sage Foundation, 1930.

Eaves, Lucile—*Gainful Employment for Handicapped Women;* Women's Educational and Industrial Union (Boston), 1921.

Faries, John Culbert—*The Economic Consequences of Physical Disability;* Red Cross Institute for Crippled and Disabled Men, 1918.

Federal Board for Vocational Education—Bulletins.

Friedrich, A. A.—"Veterans," *Encyclopaedia of the Social Sciences,* Vol. 15; The Macmillan Company, 1935.

Gillin, John Lewis—*Social Pathology,* Chapter 4, "Disablement"; The Century Co., 1933.

Harris, Garrard—*The Redemption of the Disabled: A Study of Programmes of Rehabilitation for the Disabled of War and of Industry;* D. Appleton and Company, 1919.

Hathway, Marion—*The Young Cripple and His Job;* Social Service Monograph No. 4, University of Chicago Press, 1928.

Hood, R. C.—"Crippled Children," *Social Work Year Book 1937;* Russell Sage Foundation, 1937.

Howett, Harry H.—*Progress in the Education of Crippled Children;* International Society for Crippled Children, 1928.

International Society for Crippled Children—*The Crippled Child,* published bimonthly.

Jones, D. Caradog, editor—*The Social Survey of Merseyside*, Vol. Three, Chapter 15, "Sub-Normal Types: The Physically Defective and the Sick"; University Press of Liverpool, Hodder & Stoughton Ltd., 1934.

Keesecker, Ward W.—*Digest of Legislation for Education of Crippled Children;* United States Department of the Interior, Office of Education, 1929.

Kessler, Henry H.—*The Crippled and the Disabled;* Columbia University Press, 1935.

La Dame, Mary—*Securing Employment for the Handicapped;* Welfare Council of New York City, 1927.

Lord, Elizabeth Evans—*Children Handicapped by Cerebral Palsy: Psychological Factors in Management;* The Commonwealth Fund, 1937.

Mangold, George B.—*Social Pathology*, Chapter XI, "The Physically Handicapped," and Chapter XII, "Education, Care and Treatment of Handicapped"; The Macmillan Company, 1932.

Massachusetts Board of Education—*Special Report of the Board of Education Relative to Training for Injured Persons;* House No. 1733, 1917.

Massachusetts Department of Public Welfare—*Final Report Relative to the Number and Care of Crippled Children;* House No. 401, December, 1931, 1932.

McMurtrie, Douglas C.—*Reconstructing the Crippled Soldier;* Red Cross Institute for Crippled and Disabled Men, 1918.

McMurtrie, Douglas C.—*Rehabilitation of the War Cripple;* Red Cross Institute for Crippled and Disabled Men, 1918.

Paeuw, Léon de—*The Vocational Re-education of Maimed Soldiers;* Princeton University Press, 1918.

Queen, Stuart Alfred, and Mann, Delbert Martin—*Social Pathology*, Chapter XXIII, "The Crippled and Disabled"; Thomas Y. Crowell Company, 1925.

Reeves, Edith—*Care and Education of Crippled Children in the United States;* Russell Sage Foundation, 1914.

Scheidemann, Norma V.—*The Psychology of Exceptional Children*, Vol. II, Chapter II, "The Cerebrally Birth Injured Child," Chapter III, "The Post-Encephalitic Child," Chapter V, "The Albinistic Child," and Chapter XI, "The Congenitally Syphilitic Child"; Houghton Mifflin Company, 1937.

Solenberger, Edith Reeves—"Crippled Children," *Social Work Year Book 1929;* Russell Sage Foundation, 1930.

Solenberger, Edith Reeves—*Public School Classes for Crippled Children;* United States Department of the Interior, Office of Education, 1918.

Sullivan, Oscar M., and Snortum, Kenneth O.—*Disabled Persons: Their Education and Rehabilitation;* The Century Co., 1926.

Toronto Child Welfare Council—*Report of a Survey of Physically Handicapped Children in Toronto;* Child Welfare Council, Toronto, 1924.

United States Office of Education—*Publications—Vocational Education;* Misc. 229 Rev. November, 1936, issued by the United States Department of the Interior, Office of Education, Vocational Education.

Upson, Lent D., and Matson, Opal V.—*Crippled Children in Michigan;* Detroit, 1931.

Veterans Administration—*Federal Laws Relating to Veterans of Wars of United States, Annotated, August 1, 1932;* Senate Document No. 131, 1932.

Watson, Frederick—*Civilization and the Cripple;* John Bale, Sons and Danielsson, Ltd. (London), 1930.

White House Conference on Child Health and Protection—*The Handicapped Child,* "The Crippled," pp. 119–193; The Century Co., 1933.

White House Conference on Child Health and Protection—*Special Education: The Handicapped and the Gifted,* "The Crippled," pp. 19–112; The Century Co., 1931.

Wright, Henry C.—*Survey of Cripples in New York City;* New York Committee on After-Care of Infantile Paralysis Cases, 1920.

Wright, Lucy, and Hamburger, Amy M.—*The Education and Occupations of Cripples, Juvenile and Adult: A Survey of All the Cripples of Cleveland, Ohio, in 1916, under the Auspices of the Welfare Federation of Cleveland;* Red Cross Institute for Crippled and Disabled Men, Series 2, No. 3, 1918.

CHAPTER XII

ALCOHOLISM AND INEBRIETY

Habitual abuse of alcohol is unquestionably a handicap to industrial efficiency and social relations. There is a popular tendency to look upon this as a moral delinquency exclusively, but because of its origin and effects alcoholism may properly be treated among the handicaps.

Definitions and Types.—The pathologic condition described as alcoholism occurs not only in inebriates but also in individuals who are constant temperate drinkers, for alcoholism is a diseased condition caused by the abuse of alcohol. Excessive use may injure stomach, liver, kidneys, or arteries, or by slowing the activity of the leucocytes may reduce resistance to invading bacteria. Among constant drinkers many diseases may be complicated in their course and treatment by the physiological effect of the frequent use of alcohol.

Inebriety is the term used popularly to designate drunkenness, but by the medical profession the term more generally refers to a condition of periodic or constant alcoholic intoxication. There is need to distinguish the social drinker from the pathologic inebriate. The former drinks because it is the custom of the group with which he associates and he may find the use of alcohol an aid to social intercourse. With him drinking is merely a social habit from which he can refrain when he has sufficient incentive to do so. The large majority of nonpathologic drinkers are of the "social" type.

Clinical specialists differ somewhat in their classification of the pathologic types. The following major classifications seem still to be justified by medical and social experience:

"(a) The first group comprises men originally of normal health of mind and body, but who through overwork, domestic or business trouble, coupled perhaps with poor hygiene, unsanitary homes or poorly cooked and ill-chosen food, have lowered their power of resistance. With frequent indulgence in alcohol or drugs self-control gradually has been destroyed, and the patient becomes powerless to discontinue his habit. The craving for narcotics (narcomania) becomes all-absorbing. Under ordinary conditions, he is unable to overcome the habit. Cases of this type studied at

188

the Foxborough State Hospital almost invariably have displayed further symptoms of mental abnormality. This is the most curable class of pathologic inebriates.

"(b) A second group, whom physicians often treat apart, are the 'periodic drunkards,'—men ordinarily temperate or even abstinent, who at periods some weeks or even months apart are seized with a mania for drunkenness which may be continuous through a number of days. This period is followed by complete sobriety for weeks or months. This form of dipsomania, which is sometimes simulated by wilful drunkards, is more rare than other forms of inebriety, and is often classed technically as a variety of insanity.

"(c) The last group comprise the defectives and degenerates among drunkards. Alcoholism of the patient . . . may in some of these cases have brought on directly or indirectly the low mental or physical condition. But it is equally true in other cases that imbecility, insanity or other forms of defectiveness or degeneracy have preceded and have been responsible for the excessive use of alcohol. The physicians in charge of the largest houses of correction and other institutions in Massachusetts to which drunkards are sent are inclined to assert that the large majority of habitual drunkards in their care are men of less than normal mentality. To this class must be added a considerable group of men past their prime of life, in whom the habit of drinking has intensified as the period of mental and physical decline (involution) has set in. Resistance in such cases is constantly lessened, and inebriety may become chronic. The reduction of mental power characteristic in all members of this group renders cure improbable." [1]

Extent of Alcoholism and Inebriety.—Much less is known about the extent of these handicaps than of the others previously considered. No attempt has been made to take a census of their number and distribution, and thus one is forced to rely upon the records of hospitals concerning the treatment of alcoholism, the reports of relief agencies concerning the number and percentage of cases in which "drink" was a factor in the causation of poverty, and court and prison records of arrests, sentences, and imprisonments for drunkenness.

Hospital statistics are of little value in indicating the volume of alcoholism, first, because presumably most cases which come under medical treatment are taken care of in the home, and secondly, because an unknown percentage of cases are classified in hospital statistics under some other category. In the latter case this may be done either to protect the family reputation or because alcoholism

[1] Special Report of the Board of Trustees of the Foxborough State Hospital—*Drunkenness in Massachusetts, Conditions and Remedies*, pp. 25–26; House Document No. 1390, 1910.

is associated with other diseases. The following may serve as an example of the counts of alcoholics made from hospital records:

"During the seven decades from 1864 to 1936 there were admitted to the Boston City Hospital 45,567 persons suffering from various stages of physical incompetency related in some manner to the excessive use of alcohol. These cases constitute one twentieth of the total number of all admissions since the hospital has been in existence, and as such form one of the largest groups for which it has had to provide care. This figure does not include cases received at the South Department (for contagious disease) or at the East Boston and Haymarket Square relief stations, nor does it include persons who were brought to the main hospital principally because of medical or surgical conditions and in addition were suffering from alcoholism. Therefore the figure given above is minimally representative and deals only with cases of obvious alcoholism, including delirium tremens. . . .

"The annual total of all patients admitted has steadily increased, and the ratio of patients with alcoholism to total admissions has likewise increased, so that on an absolute as well as on a relative basis the problem of alcoholism at the hospital is now greater than ever before. . . .

"The majority of alcoholic patients admitted are males, and these outnumber females in the proportion of 7:1. Males are admitted in largest numbers between the ages of 36 and 40, and females between 41 and 45." [2]

The Relation to Poverty.—Booth, in his social survey of London, found that in thirteen to fourteen per cent of the poor in East London the poverty was the result of "drink or thriftlessness" but failed to separate these two quite dissimilar factors. Rowntree, in his study of York, considered drink a predominant factor in secondary poverty.[3] Warner's *American Charities*, from the reports of charity organization societies in five cities during the early eighteen nineties, ascribed from 4.9 to 21.9 per cent of poverty to drink.[4]

More revealing and exact are recent studies by the Family Welfare Society of Boston and the United Charities of Chicago, which instead of listing major causes list all cases in which alcoholism was a factor. The Chicago study, covering 15,456 "situations presented" in 3,152 families given intensive treatment during the

[2] Moore, Merrill, and Gray, M. G.—*The Problem of Alcoholism at the Boston City Hospital*, pp. 3–4, and 25; reprinted from *The New England Journal of Medicine*, Vol. 217, No. 10, pp. 381–388, September 2, 1937.

[3] Booth, Charles—*Life and Labour of the People in London*, Vol. I, pp. 146–148; Macmillan and Co., Limited, 1902. Rowntree, B. Seebohm—*Poverty; A Study of Town Life*, p. 142; Macmillan and Co., Limited, 1908.

[4] Revised and reissued by Queen and Harper as follows: Warner, Amos Griswold, Queen, Stuart Alfred, and Harper, Ernest Bouldin—*American Charities and Social Work*, Table IV, opposite p. 46; Thomas Y. Crowell Company, 1930.

year 1936, lists 217 involving alcoholism.[5] The Federal Emergency Relief Administration from a five per cent sample of schedules secured in a survey of the occupational characteristics of the urban relief population of May, 1934, estimated that among 1,363,900 handicapped persons, sixteen years of age and over, 5,700 were suffering from alcoholism.[6] There is, however, no indication of the role played by alcoholism or drunkenness in producing the other handicaps and illnesses found, whether mental or physical.

The Relation to Crime.—Equally unsatisfactory as an index of volume of alcoholism and inebriety are the statistics of crime and criminals. American states vary greatly in their practices regarding arrests for drunkenness and within each state practices of the municipal police are frequently dissimilar. Even in states with the strictest practice in this regard intoxicated persons are not arrested in their own homes or clubs but only when found in a drunken condition in public places. An arrest is seldom made even under the latter circumstances if the man has a taxicab fare or friends to see him home. In many states intoxicated persons are not arrested unless their "public drunkenness" is accompanied by disturbance of the peace, disorderly conduct, drunken driving, or other infractions of law. In rural communities and villages arrests for drunkenness are infrequent.

The statistics of arrests in Massachusetts for the year ending December 31, 1935, show that out of a total of 187,560 arrests 93,151 were on the charge of drunkenness, or approximately one-half. The table does not indicate, however, the role of excessive drinking in offenses against the person and against property, nor in the remaining offenses against public order such as disorderly conduct, disturbing the peace, nonsupport, violation of traffic rules and of motor vehicle laws.[7] It should be recognized that the number of arrests for drunkenness fails to indicate the number of individuals arrested in the course of the year. Yet this is important,

[5] Statistical Department, United Charities of Chicago—*Situations Presented on Total Under Care Cases—Year 1936;* Mimeographed Table, released March 3, 1937.

[6] *Disabilities in the Urban Relief Population, May 1934,* Appendix A, Table VI, pp. g–h (Preliminary Report), Research Bulletin Series I, No. 6; Division of Research, Statistics and Finance, Federal Emergency Relief Administration, May 22, 1935.

[7] *Annual Report of the Commissioner of Correction for the Year ending December 31, 1935,* Table 51, pp. 107–108; Public Document No. 115, The Commonwealth of Massachusetts.

for the same individual may be arrested on this charge more than once. The percentage of repeaters among pathologic inebriates is large.

The abuse of alcohol plays a contributory role in many crimes other than public drunkenness. It can never be sole cause of any crime since the physical and social conditions attendant upon its use and the physical and mental condition of its user are factors of importance. Crime causation is multiple. The abuse of alcohol may be associated with feeblemindedness or dull mentality, with mental disorder or psychopathic conditions, or with convulsive disorders, when the so-called alcoholic crime is committed. In other cases alcohol may have been used by "normal" persons to give them courage to commit premeditated crimes. In still other cases alcohol by dulling the sensibilities, or relaxing the controls, leads to crimes which the men if sober would not have committed. Clearly the consequences of drunkenness are costly to society. The volume of criminality could be reduced if drunkenness could be prevented, and still further reduction would be possible if the associated factors leading to alcoholism and crime were dealt with simultaneously.[8]

Alcoholism and Heredity.—Many studies a generation ago reached the conclusion that alcoholism is an inherited character. More recently as knowledge of human heredity develops, students of this subject fail to find evidence that alcoholism behaves like a Mendelian unit character even when found recurring in the same family for many generations. No study has yet properly segregated the pathologic inebriate from other types and differentiated among the pathologic inebriates those in whom there is feeblemindedness, epilepsy, or mental disease from those who, apart from their habit, appear to be normal.

Many medical specialists in the field of alcoholism have concluded, like Dr. Irwin H. Neff,[9] that in all cases of pathologic inebriety, as distinguished from social drunkenness, there appears to be present a neurosis or psychosis and evidence throughout the patient's life

[8] Adler, Herman—"The Relation of Alcohol and Crime," Chapter XII of Emerson, Haven, editor—*Alcohol and Man: The Effects of Alcohol on Man in Health and Disease;* The Macmillan Company, 1932. Healy, William, and Bronner, Augusta—*Delinquents and Criminals, Their Making and Unmaking;* The Macmillan Company, 1926. Koren, John—*Alcohol and Society;* Henry Holt and Company, 1916. Committee of Fifty—*The Liquor Problem,* Prepared for the Committee by John S. Billings, C. W. Eliot, H. W. Farnam, J. L. Greene, F. G. Peabody; Houghton Mifflin Company, 1905.

[9] Former Superintendent of the Norfolk State Hospital in Massachusetts.

history of the presence of a constitutional diathesis or predisposition to abuse alcohol whenever it is used at all. Yet even this attitude is qualified as may be seen, for example, from Richard R. Peabody's statement, "It does not appear that the original impulse to drink is much, if any, stronger in the chronic alcoholic than it is in the hard drinker."[10] Clearly where specialists disagree there is indication of need for further study. Determination of the hereditary nature, if any, of the diathesis is dependent upon the prior demonstration of the existence of such a diathesis.

Experimentation upon animals leaves equal uncertainty as to the effect upon offspring of parental abuse of alcohol. C. R. Stockard's experiments from 1909 to 1916 upon guinea-pigs produced defective offspring whether the alcohol was administered to normal males or to females. This experiment was conducted with controls and produced 5.9 per cent of defectives where normal males were mated with alcoholic females, and 4.9 per cent when alcoholic males were mated with normal females. There seemed to be evidence further of a slight reduction of fertility through the administration of alcohol and of higher mortality among the offspring.[11] These findings, though widely quoted as definitive, failed of confirmation when repeated by the National Institute for Medical Research in England. For studies there by Miss F. M. Durham over a period of nine years, and with proper controls, failed to confirm Professor Stockard's findings either as to decrease of progeny, still births, decreased weight, deformities, or injury to germ plasm.[12]

Raymond Pearl commenting upon his own studies in alcoholizing domestic fowl, and covering similar experiments by Danforth, and experiments by Nice on white mice, and by Hanson and MacDowell

[10] Peabody, Richard R.—*Psychotherapeutic Procedure in the Treatment of Chronic Alcoholism*, p. 2; reprint from *Mental Hygiene*, pp. 109–128, Vol. XIV, No. 1, January, 1930.

[11] Stockard, Charles R.—"The Effects of Alcohol in Development and Heredity," Chapter V of Emerson, Haven, editor—*Alcohol and Man: The Effects of Alcohol on Man in Health and Disease;* The Macmillan Company, 1932. Stockard, C. R.—"Hereditary Transmission of Degeneracy and Deformities by the Descendants of Alcoholized Mammals," "Alcohol and Narcotics"; Special Number *Interstate Medical Journal*, St. Louis, Vol. xxiii, No. 6, June, 1916, pp. 385–403. Stockard, C. R., and Papanicolau, G. N.—"A Further Analysis of the Hereditary Transmission of Degeneracy and Deformities by the Descendants of Alcoholized Mammals"; *American Naturalist*, 1916.

[12] *Report of the Medical Research Council for the Year 1929-30*, p. 20, cited by Brasher, C. W. J., in "Inebriety and the Social Problem Group," Chapter IV of Blacker, C. P., editor—*A Social Problem Group?;* Oxford University Press, 1937.

on white rats, concludes that "The racial effect of alcohol is preponderantly either beneficial or, at the worst, not harmful." At most there appears to be only a slight reduction in fertility and possibly, in the case of MacDowell's experiment, a slight reduction in activity and ability to learn.[13]

Although the need of further studies of these types is still indicated there is no certainty so far that alcoholism of parents among the animals experimented upon affects the germ plasm or produces degeneration.

Another approach to this same subject has been made in the statistical researches of Karl Pearson's biometric laboratory in England. The first study by Miss Elderton and Professor Pearson, in 1910, covering data of the Edinburgh Charity Organization Society, concludes that alcoholism in parents is not a source of mental defect in offspring and that there is no marked relation between intelligence, physique, or disease of the offspring with parental alcoholism.[14] A second study in the same year by Miss Barrington and Professor Pearson attempts to distinguish the roles of environment and heredity in producing the characteristics of the children of extreme alcoholics. Data were secured from the Langho Inebriate Reformatory, but unfortunately provided full information for only two hundred and seven female inebriates. Since no woman is committed to this reformatory until she has had at least four convictions for inebriety, the population studied was doubtless abnormal —a judgment confirmed by the fact that the percentage of prostitution and mental defect in the group was very high.[15]

In 1912, Heron published a second study of extreme alcoholism in adults, on data from one hundred and sixty-six male and eight hundred and sixty-five female inebriates in British inebriate reformatories, and among the women found 54 per cent mentally defective, 2 per cent insane, 5 per cent epileptic. The police records of these women showed half of them to give evidence of immorality. The major value of this study lies in its evidence of the

[13] Pearl, Raymond—*The Racial Effect of Alcohol;* Department of Biometry and Vital Statistics, School of Hygiene and Public Health, Johns Hopkins University, No. 96, April, 1924.

[14] Elderton, Ethel M., and Pearson, Karl—*A First Study of the Influence of Parental Alcoholism on the Physique and Ability of the Offspring;* Galton Laboratory for National Eugenics, Memoir X, 1910.

[15] Barrington, Amy, and Pearson, Karl (with Dr. David Heron)—*A Preliminary Study of Extreme Alcoholism in Adults;* Galton Laboratory for National Eugenics, Memoir XIV, 1910.

interplay of many types of handicaps and the caution which it immediately suggests to be necessary before ascribing any mental, physical, or social abnormalities of their progeny to the alcoholism of parents. For it is quite clear that the parental alcoholism may be but a symptom of mental defect or abnormality and that the latter, wherever hereditary, might produce similar defects in offspring even if the parental generation had never made use of alcohol.[16]

Inheritance charts are available from a variety of sources in which one or more of the following handicaps—insanity, feeblemindedness, epilepsy, and neurosis—is found, with or without antecedent cases of alcoholism, among the ancestors or siblings of the alcoholic.[17] Moreover, family charts are rare in which extreme alcoholism is not associated with one or more of these defects. This creates a tentative presumption that extreme alcoholism or the predisposition thereto is not itself hereditary, but rather that it is symptomatic of physical or mental weakness or disease. In other words, the defect or neurosis is antecedent to the alcoholism.

Other Causes of Alcoholism.—Disease and accident, though important causes of other handicaps, are seldom a direct cause of alcoholism. The indirect role of disease is, however, large, for case histories show that many men and women start drinking to excess to forget pain. Others, especially among the poor and among women inebriates, are found to have acquired the habit through the use of patent medicines with high alcohol content. Since an ever increasing dosage is necessary to maintain a given sedative effect, the habit of inebriety may be confirmed before the patient is brought to the attention of a competent physician.

Evidence seems to indicate that most persons who drink to excess are social rather than pathologic inebriates. But it seems probable, from studies of case histories, that some who begin drinking to excess, because it is the custom of their group, acquire a habit which becomes confirmed. Thus many who begin as social drinkers may later use alcohol for its sedative effects under conditions of intense or prolonged business or domestic worry, extreme fatigue, insomnia,

[16] Heron, David—*A Second Study of Extreme Alcoholism in Adults, with special reference to the Home Office Inebriate Reformatory Data;* Galton Laboratory for National Eugenics, Memoir XVII, 1912.

[17] Brasher, C. W. J.—*op. cit.,* particularly pp. 84–93. Davenport, Charles B.—"The Effects of Alcohol on Animal Offspring," Chapter V–B of Emerson, Haven, editor—*Alcohol and Man: The Effects of Alcohol on Man in Health and Disease,* pp. 120–125; The Macmillan Company, 1932.

or other ills, physical, mental, or social. Apparently, therefore, drunkards can be created by the individual's response to the impact of adverse circumstances among human material which shows no evidence of prior pathologic predisposition. Further and more intensive studies are, however, necessary to isolate these factors and determine their relative importance.

Treatment for Inebriety.—Society's usual "treatment" for public drunkenness is arrest followed by a court sentence of fine, probation, or imprisonment. Arrest protects the individual from continuing his debauch and society from the nuisance of his presence while intoxicated. When sober he may be released with an admonition— which in chronic drinkers is unlikely to deter from further inebriety. Or, brought before the court, he may be fined—a penalty unlikely to change his habits because easy for the rich and impossible for the poor unless the fine is met by friends or paid in easy instalments to the probation officer under suspended sentence. Commonly he is sent to jail for nonpayment of fine which is virtually imprisonment for poverty. Probation is sometimes effectual for the first or second offense in the case of social drinkers, but is of no lasting value for treatment of the pathologic inebriate. Imprisonment for either type is costly and usually futile as a means of reform. Nevertheless, it is temporarily necessary for many who are dangerous when drunk—usually cases mentally abnormal—and a poor but essential expedient for many pathologic inebriates pending adequate social provision for hospitalization.

Alcoholism and pathologic inebriety are diseases requiring specialized medical and mental treatment. To punish a man for being ill by arrest, fine, or imprisonment is an absurdity and an anachronism. Yet today medical treatment of inebriety is rare except for the well-to-do. Systematic provision is unavailable at public expense and is limited chiefly to cases taken to city hospitals because of accident while intoxicated—or to emergency hospitals or hospitals for the insane because of delirium tremens or other abnormalities sufficiently obvious to be recognized by the police. Such cases are not welcome in general hospitals and are usually discharged too early to effect cure. Essential to the cure of a maximum number of inebriates is the public provision of specialized hospital colonies for pathologic inebriates sufficient in number to take care of all cases whether through voluntary self-commitment or commitment by the court on the certification of qualified physicians.

Early in the present century some beginnings had been made for such treatment in England, Germany, Switzerland, and Australia. In the second decade, New York, Pennsylvania, Iowa, and a few other states or cities established hospitals for inebriates. Massachusetts made the most notable experiments first at Foxborough State Hospital and subsequently in a specially erected group of hospital and colony buildings at Norfolk. The following account is based chiefly on Massachusetts experience, which unfortunately was abandoned as unnecessary following the adoption of the Eighteenth Amendment to the Constitution of the United States.

The means by which hospital treatment restores the inebriate to health and to economic productivity vary necessarily with the case, but certain rules are almost universally applicable. Physical health may be built up by proper nourishment, sanitary conditions, regular hours, and out-of-door work and recreation. Diseases of the body, which sometimes largely condition inebriety, should be cured by proper medical care. All this, however, has been done for many years by the better prisons and reformatories without curing chronic inebriety. For in addition to rebuilding the body it is essential to strengthen the will to resist alcohol and to prepare an environment favorable to the free play of this will.

The mental treatment of patients takes the form of daily interviews, whether in the office of the superintendent and assistant physicians or in the field, workshop, or recreation rooms. The interest of the patient in his case is sought and coöperation in the cure solicited. If such coöperation can be secured the patient's case is a hopeful one. If, after the strength of body has been restored, the mind still fails to respond to the suggestion of cure, the chances of lasting improvement are very slight. For this very reason voluntary cases are ordinarily hopeful in that they imply the consent of the patient. This further accounts for the less frequent curability of the prison rounder type in many of whom mental deficiency or abnormality, or years of acquired depravity, render mental response difficult or impossible.

Shortly after the admission of the patient to the hospital, when the effects of his excesses have subsided, there comes a period of restlessness, characteristic of convalescence, in which the patient wishes to be released. Despite repeated experiences to the contrary, he commonly believes he will not drink again, at least not in excess. In this trying period the educative process is begun.

The patient is trained to regularity of habit, a recognized bulwark against intemperance. He is helped to see the situation and its remedies and is induced to coöperate. An occupation is found for the patient, which will keep his interest and his health and better prepare him for employment upon his withdrawal from the hospital.

Many patients have been casual laborers. For these the hospital should become so far as possible a trade school, where the patient may become proficient at a trade in which the work is regular and the remuneration adequate. Men already skilled at a trade can often be kept at that work at the hospital, or may at the discretion of the superintendent be put to work at something entirely different, thus to awaken fresh interest and give them a new grasp on life. Out-of-door work such as farming, horticulture, grading of lawns, care of poultry, live stock, and stables, erection of buildings, and construction of sidewalks and roads, is often desirable as a therapeutic measure, and at the same time can be conducted to the ultimate profit of the hospital.

Hospital treatment is desirable, in that it permits the reconstruction of the drunkard apart from his old associates and influences, but at best a hospital is an artificial environment and therefore a protracted stay for most patients is inadvisable. On the other hand, there is danger of a too sudden return to an environment away from the sustaining influences of the hospital. This danger has been met by the establishment of out-patient departments.

Aftercare of Cases.—The first duty of the out-patient physician is to become acquainted with the patients while in the hospital. The next requisite step is a visit to the patient's home while he is yet in the hospital. This is done both as a means for acquiring added working data relative to the case and, quite as important, for the purpose of instructing the family in the nature of the disease, inebriety, thus preparing them for the proper reception of the patient upon his return home. In this way querulousness or its opposite, weak indulgence of the drunkard by wife, mother, or other members of the household, has been changed into intelligent aid, based upon an understanding of the patient's strength or weakness.

Protection of the patient from the presence of alcohol on the family table or premises, or from old, destructive associations will render the determination made in the hospital more possible of fulfilment, even though other conditions remain to some degree adverse. Beyond the protection of the patient lies the formation of a truly constructive environment. Through the family or the out-patient physician work should be found ready for the patient on his exit from the hospital, so that no period of unemployment and consequent discouragement may destroy the newly acquired self-mastery. Sometimes conditions require a new trade, but in general it is believed that a patient is not cured who is unable to return to his original industry and remain abstinent. The effort is made, however, to place the patient in a social environment in which helpful influences predominate.

Often some individual is found who will represent the out-patient physician during his absence. Meanwhile visits to the out-patient physician or visits to the hospital at requisite intervals by the patient keep alive the influence of the hospital until the patient is firmly established in the outer world and abstinence has become habitual. Sometimes a patient has been overconfident of his powers and has left the hospital too soon. In such case no effort is made to retain him for there is no advantage in restraining a patient when he is determined to leave; he is no longer amenable to cure. If, however, the out-patient physician finds him after an unsuccessful battle with the old environment, he may be able to persuade him to return to the hospital, and thereafter a permanent cure may be effected.

The out-patient physician thus is the link between the hospital and the outer world. He continues the treatment after the patient has left the hospital and prevents miscarriage of the hospital's efforts.[18]

Prevention of Inebriety.—Much crime, handicap, and poverty have been shown to be due directly or indirectly to the abuse of alcohol. Attempts to prevent such abuse through national prohibition legislation proved premature and impracticable. Private ownership of breweries, distilleries, and licensed establishments for retail trade stimulates consumption. In a competitive world profits depend upon the volume of sales. It is implicit in our present economic system that producers and distributors alike should seek to increase their sales by finding new customers and by encouraging overconsumption.

[18] Special Report of the Board of Trustees of the Foxborough State Hospital—*Drunkenness in Massachusetts, Conditions and Remedies;* House Document No. 1390, 1910. *Report of the Commission to Investigate Drunkenness in Massachusetts;* House Document No. 2053, 1914. See also works of Kerr, Cutten, Emerson, and Hare in the list of references at the end of this chapter.

To reduce drunkenness as distinguished from temperate drinking the major device, aside from more general and effective education in personal hygiene and self-control, would be elimination of the profit motive. This means the substitution of public ownership and management for private, or else the Scandinavian system of turning over the monopoly of sales to limited-dividend corporations established for the purpose of reducing alcohol consumption. The former device is more promising. Inherent in either plan would be the concomitant development, as in Sweden, of "substitutes for the saloon." These would take the form of universally accessible centers for adult education and recreation, skilfully organized to overcome the boredom which lies behind much intemperance. In so far as constructive leisure-time interests can be aroused and opportunities for their fulfilment made available to all, nonpathologic or "social" types of drunkenness can be materially reduced. It should be recalled, however, when relatively normal people drink excessively it is an outgrowth of fatigue, poor health, worry, or unhappiness and the desire to "escape from it all." When such people find it impossible to drink temperately, help may be needed from social workers, physicians, or others, and should be rendered available.

A supplementary device to eliminate excessive drinking, which would require further experimentation before it can be recommended without qualification, is to license the drinker. The license might be withdrawn from persons who drink to excess, precisely as motor licenses are withdrawn from reckless drivers. Since it would be repugnant to most temperate drinkers to have to show a license before the sale could be consummated, this device could not be put into practice in America until voters are impressed with its necessity. Apparently, therefore, the major means for the reduction of drunkenness rests in the withdrawal of the trade from private hands and the establishment of a government monopoly with carefully controlled conditions of sale, supplemented by the establishment of special hospitals for the cure of inebriates who are at present injured rather than helped by jail sentences.[19]

[19] Detailed practical suggestions for the application in the United States of measures similar to those above outlined will be found in the separate report by Henry W. Anderson, published in *Report on the Enforcement of the Prohibition Laws of the United States*, pp. 89–109; House Document No. 722, National Commission on Law Observance and Enforcement, Government Printing Office, January 7, 1931. Anderson's report was approved by Roscoe Pound and several others on the Commission.

QUESTIONS FOR DISCUSSION OR EXAMINATION

1. The relation of drunkenness to (a) poverty, and (b) crime.
2. Is alcoholism hereditary?
3. What are the recommended methods of treatment of pathological inebriety?
4. Is it "a man's own business" whether he shall get drunk? Under what circumstances and in what form would you recommend social intervention and treatment?
5. By what detailed social policy should inebriety be prevented?

PROBLEMS FOR INDIVIDUAL STUDY

1. The history of (a) punitive, or (b) curative treatment of inebriety, in some selected state.
2. Critical examination of procedure in your city for (a) arrest, (b) detention, (c) trial, and (d) punishment of public drunkards.
3. A study of Scandinavian policies for liquor control.
4. A comparative and critical study of American systems of liquor control, for any two states, or for any selected state before, during, and after Federal prohibition.
5. A critical analysis of the literature on the relation of alcoholism to heredity.

SUGGESTIONS FOR SUPPLEMENTARY READINGS

Billings, John S., editor—*The Physiological Aspects of the Liquor Problem;* Committee of Fifty, Houghton Mifflin Company, 1903.

Blacker, C. P., editor—*A Social Problem Group?;* Oxford University Press, 1937.

Bruno, Frank J.—*The Theory of Social Work*, Chapter VII, "Alcohol"; D. C. Heath and Company, 1936.

Calkins, Raymond—*Substitutes for the Saloon;* Committee of Fifty, Houghton Mifflin Company, 1901.

Carter, Henry—*The Control of the Drink Trade in Britain: A Contribution to National Efficiency during the Great War 1915–1918;* Longmans, Green and Co., second edition, 1919.

Carver, Thomas Nixon—*Government Control of the Liquor Business in Great Britain and the United States;* Carnegie Endowment for International Peace, Preliminary Economic Studies of the War No. 13, Oxford University Press, 1919.

Catlin, E. G.—"Alcoholism," *Encyclopaedia of the Social Sciences*, Vol. I; The Macmillan Company, 1930.

Cutten, George B.—*The Psychology of Alcoholism;* The Walter Scott Publishing Co., Ltd., 1907.

Dodge, Raymond, and Benedict, Francis G.—*Psychological Effects of Alcohol;* Carnegie Institution of Washington, Publication No. 232, 1915.

Durham, F. M., and Woods, H. M.—*Alcohol and Inheritance;* H. M. Stationery Office, 1932.

Emerson, Haven, editor—*Alcohol and Man: The Effects of Alcohol on Man in Health and Disease;* The Macmillan Company, 1932.

Feldman, Herman—*Prohibition: Its Economic and Industrial Aspects;* D. Appleton and Company, 1930.

Fisher, Irving, and Brougham, H. Bruce—*The "Noble Experiment";* Alcohol Information Committee, 1930.

Fisk, Eugene Lyman—*Alcohol: Its Relation to Human Efficiency and Longevity;* Funk & Wagnalls Company, 1917.

Great Britain—*Report from the Select Committee on Patent Medicines,* Ordered by The House of Commons, to be printed, 4th August, 1914; T. Fisher Unwin, 1914.

Great Britain, Report of the Advisory Committee, Central Control Board (Liquor Traffic)—*Alcohol, Its Action on the Human Organism;* H. M. Stationery Office, 1918.

Hare, Francis—*On Alcoholism: Its Clinical Aspects and Treatment;* P. Blakiston's Son & Co., Inc., 1913.

Kerr, Norman—*Inebriety or Narcomania: Its Etiology, Pathology, Treatment and Jurisprudence;* H. K. Lewis & Co., Ltd., third edition, 1894.

Koren, John—*Alcohol and Society;* Henry Holt and Company, 1916.

Koren, John—*Economic Aspects of the Liquor Problem;* Committee of Fifty, Houghton Mifflin Company, 1899.

McDougall, William—*The Effects of Alcohol and Some Other Drugs during Normal and Fatigued Conditions;* H. M. Stationery Office, 1920.

Miles, Walter R.—*Alcohol and Human Efficiency;* Carnegie Institution of Washington, Publication No. 333, 1924.

Miles, Walter R.—*Effect of Alcohol on Psycho-Physiological Functions;* Carnegie Institution of Washington, Publication No. 266, 1918.

National Commission on Law Observance and Enforcement—*Report on the Enforcement of the Prohibition Laws of the United States;* House Document No. 722, Government Printing Office, January 7, 1931.

Pearl, Raymond—*Alcohol and Longevity;* Alfred A. Knopf, 1926.

Pearl, Raymond—"Alcohol: Biological Aspects," *Encyclopaedia of the Social Sciences,* Vol. 1; The Macmillan Company, 1930.

Rivers, W. H. R.—*The Influence of Alcohol and Other Drugs on Fatigue;* Edward Arnold, 1908.

Schmeckebier, Laurence F.—*The Bureau of Prohibition: Its History, Activities and Organization;* Institute for Government Research, Service Monographs of the United States Government No. 57, The Brookings Institution, 1929.

Shadwell, Arthur—*Drink, Temperance and Legislation;* Longmans, Green and Co., third edition, 1915.

Shadwell, Arthur—*Drink in 1914–1922: A Lesson in Control;* Longmans, Green and Co., 1923.

Social Science Research Council—*Sources of Information Concerning the Operation of the Eighteenth Aemndment;* Social Science Research Council, 1928.

Starling, Ernest H.—*The Action of Alcohol on Man;* Longmans, Green and Co., 1923.

Webb, Sidney and Beatrice—*The History of Liquor Licensing in England, Principally from 1700 to 1830;* Longmans, Green and Co., 1903.

Wines, Frederic H., and Koren, John—*The Liquor Problem in Its Legislative Aspects;* Committee of Fifty, Houghton Mifflin Company, 1898.

CHAPTER XIII

DRUG ADDICTION

Drug addiction is a handicap numerically less frequent than alcoholism but more rapid and disintegrating in its effects upon its victim. By many specialists the term is used to cover only the habitual use of opium and its derivatives, morphine, heroin, codeine, and laudanum. The vast majority of addicts either smoke or eat opium, take morphine or heroin in the form of powders or by injection, using a hypodermic needle, or by snuffing. The cocaine habit and the use of marihuana or of hashish, because they do not create similar pathological conditions in the body and as their habitual use is relatively easy to overcome, are properly differentiated medically from addiction to opium, but should be included in the discussion of the social pathology of the use and abuse of drugs.

History.—The use of drugs probably antedates human history. Terry reports that the earliest recorded medicinal use of opium dates from about 4000 B.C., and that coca was known in prehistoric times in South America and was used by Inca priests and nobility. Morphine has been known since its discovery in 1803 by Derosne, alkaloid cocaine since its discovery by Niemann in 1859, and heroin since Dreser's experiments in 1898. The hypodermic syringe was invented in 1845. Although the use of drugs is of ancient origin, both for medicinal purposes and for the state of mind and sensations which they create, their dangers in use have not been appreciated until relatively recent times. Terry states that the first known anti-opium edict is said to be that of Yung Cheng in 1729; but in the main the campaign against drug addiction is a phenomenon of the present century.[1]

Extent.—The widest use of drugs is to be found in Asiatic countries. Estimates of the number of drug addicts in this country literally range from less than one hundred thousand to several million. So wide a range is obviously an indication of the lack of accurate

---

[1] Terry, Charles E.—"Drug Addiction," *Encyclopaedia of the Social Sciences,* Vol. 5, pp. 242–252; The Macmillan Company, 1931: also see his article on "Drug Addiction," *Social Work Year Book 1929;* Russell Sage Foundation, 1930.

counts. Since census enumerations do not cover this subject, the
estimates have been based upon local counts, chiefly records of
clinics and hospitals, and upon such knowledge as is available concerning importations, manufacture, and sale, both legal and illicit.

"The mobilization of man power following our entrance into the World
War was a means of furnishing the country with valuable data concerning
various diseases of young men and the conditions which disable. Data on
addiction to narcotics were among the information thus obtained. Up to
May 1, 1919, there had been recommended for rejection because of various mental and nervous diseases, 72,323 men out of a number approximated at 3,500,000. Among those recommended for rejection, only 3,284
were drug addicts. Col. Pearce Bailey, chief of the section of neurology
and psychiatry, in commenting on this, states that some persons particularly interested in drug addiction had warned them to be prepared for
500,000. He also intimates that there was very little traffic in drugs in the
camps in this country and in France, as practically no cases of drug addition were reported among the soldiers. He points out that access to drugs
by the soldier was not easy, and 'addicts, if they had been in France cut
off from the drug, would have been found inevitably in the hospitals.'

"The Army rate, if applied to the entire population of this country as
shown by the 1920 census, would give a total of approximately 99,500 addicts in round numbers. . . ." [2]

The most frequently quoted estimate is that of Kolb and Du Mez
of the United States Public Health Service, published in 1924. The
authors studied local narcotic surveys and clinic reports from Tennessee, Pennsylvania, New York City, and elsewhere, together with
United States Army findings and the Treasury Department survey.
They next considered the volume of annual importations to ascertain how many addicts could be maintained on the average daily
dose of morphine given at clinics ($7\frac{1}{4}$ grains). They then concluded:

"The evidence seems to show that a maximum estimate for the number
of addicts in the United States at the present time would be 150,000.
The estimates based on actual counts and on the available supplies of narcotics, together with the conditions reported by the physicians interviewed, point to about 110,000, which number is believed to be nearly
correct.

"The number of addicts has decreased steadily since 1900. Before this
decrease set in there may have been 264,000 addicts in this country.
. . .

[2] Kolb, Lawrence, and Du Mez, A. G.—*The Prevalence and Trend of Drug Addiction in the United States and Factors Influencing It*, p. 3; United States Public Health
Service, Reprint No. 924 from the Public Health Reports, May 23, 1924, Government Printing Office, 1924.

"The average daily addiction dose of the opiates in terms of morphine sulphate or heroin hydrochloride is not less than 6 grains. The dose of cocaine hydrochloride is practically the same.

"The quantities of narcotics imported by this country at the present time are believed to be only slightly in excess of the amounts required to supply medicinal needs. . . .

". . . To-day addicts use the alkaloids or their derivatives almost exclusively. Cocaine hydrochloride was used alone by a large number of addicts prior to 1915, but is now used only in conjunction with the opiates except in a few cases.

"The proportion of the delinquent type of addict is gradually increasing. This is apparently not due to an increase in the number of this type, but to a gradual elimination of normal types." [3]

A study of the distribution of narcotism in 1935, by the United States Commissioner of Narcotics, concludes:

"Whereas it has been believed in the past that the probable number of nonmedical drug addicts in the United States approximated one person in every thousand of the population, a recent survey discloses that this figure no longer obtains in many sections of the country. . . .

"In South Carolina the number of addicts known to the authorities still approximates one to every thousand of the population. Although there is less than one addict to every thousand of the population in some sections of the country, the converse is true regarding a few sections, there being in the latter sections more than one addict known to the authorities in each thousand of the population. . . .

"In a further inquiry into the problem of addiction, the Bureau of Narcotics, during the calendar year 1935, examined the records of 1,397 of the persons investigated in connection with violations of the narcotic laws who had been questioned as to their personal use of drugs. Of these 946 were found to be addicted to some form of opium or coca derivative, the other 451 giving no evidence of addiction.

"Of the 946 addicts, 757 were males and 189 females. The average age of the 946 persons was 40 years, the males averaging 41 and the females 35. As to race, 775 were white, 88 Oriental, 78 colored, and 3 American Indian, while in two instances the race was not reported. As to education, 520 had attended only grade school, 211 had reached high school but not college, and 153 had received some college or university training. Sixty-two failed to indicate what education they had received. The criminal records of the 946 addicts included 545 charges of felony, 468 misdemeanors, and 1,887 violations of either Federal or State narcotic laws." [4]

Causes of Drug Addiction.—There is no certainty that the predisposition to the abuse of drugs is inherited. There is a probability

[3] *Ibid.*, pp. 24–25.
[4] Bureau of Narcotics, U. S. Treasury Department—*Traffic in Opium and Other Dangerous Drugs for the Year Ended December 31, 1935*, pp. 2–4; Government Printing Office, 1936.

that persons who in their hereditary constitution are defective in inhibitions or intelligence would be more susceptible, but no definitive statement on hereditary sources of drug addiction will be possible until further researches have been made. Children born to mothers who are drug addicts display the withdrawal symptoms of drug addiction within two or three days after birth. In these cases the drug addiction, though constitutional because derived from the mother, is not hereditary.

The drug addict usually gives evidence of being a psychopathic or inferior personality, but there is still inadequate evidence as to how generally neuropathic or psychopathic conditions precede use. It is still widely held that some persons who would be rated normal have acquired the drug habit unwittingly through the use of patent medicines containing drugs, or out of bravado, to experiment with their effects. Others, when drugs have been administered by physicians to deaden the pain of disease or accident, have acquired the habit to relieve the distress following the cessation of the opiate, because the administration of the drug has been too prolonged.[5] Opiates are still the most effective means of relief from severe pain, and are widely used by physicians in both acute and chronic maladies.

Many persons who professionally handle drugs—physicians, dentists, and pharmacists—are to be found among addicts, some having made use of the accessible drugs to overcome their own excessive fatigue. Although an unknown but presumably small percentage of such educated users are apparently able to employ their drug in moderation, others succumb.

Another condition of drug addiction lies in the competition among illicit traffickers, who seek to improve their sales and profits by finding new recruits. Drug users likewise encourage the habit in their associates and thus many a non-user becomes an addict by imitating the practices of his companions. Others yield under the adverse conditions of imprisonment. Opiates and cocaine are widely used by prostitutes and others of the "underworld" as a means to overcome misery and to forget. Marihuana is sold in the form of candy and cigarettes and its use by children as well as adults is said

[5] See Lindesmith, A. R.—"A Sociological Theory of Drug Addiction"; *American Journal of Sociology*, Vol. XLIII, No. 4, January, 1938: and Hall, Margaret E.—"Mental and Physical Efficiency of Women Drug Addicts"; *Journal of Abnormal and Social Psychology*, Vol. 33, No. 3, July, 1938.

to be cultivated by producers and distributors.[6] Ease of access obviously facilitates increases in the volume of addiction.

Effects: Personal and Social.—Personal disorganization is an almost invariable effect of drug addiction. As in the case of alcohol, an ever increasing dosage is essential to attain a given anaesthetic

[6] Marihuana is not included in the statistical estimates of drug addiction by the Federal Bureau of Narcotics. It is the only widely used drug grown within the United States and can be cropped in virtually every state. Of it the Bureau writes: "A problem which has proved most disquieting to the Bureau during the year is the rapid development of a widespread traffic in Indian hemp, or marihuana, throughout the country. Attention is called to the fact that over 195 tons of marihuana, in the form of plants, flowering tops, and cigarettes, have been confiscated and destroyed by the various States during 1935. . . . The States of New York, California, and Florida deserve high commendation for the work they have done on the marihuana problem." *Traffic in Opium and Other Dangerous Drugs for the Year Ended December 31, 1935*, p. v.

The report of the following year states: ". . . The weed now grows wild in almost every State in the Union, is easily obtainable, and has come into wide abuse. The situation is especially fraught with danger because the abuse of this drug is being carried as a new habit to groups which have not been heretofore contaminated by drug addiction. . . .

"The reports received in the Bureau of Narcotics covering the seizures of the drug by State and municipal authorities throughout the country during 1936 clearly establish that the cannabis problem is one of increasing national significance. Seizures were made in 12 States from which none had theretofore been reported. A total of 31 States reported seizures of varying quantities of the drug and destruction of considerable areas of the growing plants. . . .

"A total of 377 seizures were reported, involving 386 tons of growing plants and dried bulk marihuana and 15,715 cigarettes. This was an increase of 191 tons, or almost 97 per cent, over the 195 tons reported during 1935, and clearly indicates the rapidity with which the traffic is expanding. . . .

"The movement for adoption of the uniform State narcotic drug act which has led to its enactment by 29 States since its introduction in 1933 to December 31, 1936, while focusing attention also on the perils of the illicit uses of opium, coca leaves, and their derivatives, has been particularly effective in making known the need for adequate legislation for the control of production, possession, sale, and use of cannabis. That there is an aroused public opinion which recognizes the menacing potentialities of illicit use of the drug is evident from the numerous requests for information concerning the evils of cannabis addiction and the extent of suppressive legislation. All of the 48 States and the Territory of Hawaii now have legislation of some nature for the control of cannabis. Of these, 37 control or license production; 44 control possession; and all 48 control sale. Twenty-nine States include control and regulation of cannabis in the uniform State narcotic drug act. Among these are Mississippi and Wisconsin, in which States the act became effective during 1936. Eleven States have special cannabis acts and eight include cannabis in their general narcotic laws. . . .

"The Marihuana Tax Act, bringing the traffic in marihuana under Federal Control, was signed by the President on Aug. 2, to become effective Oct. 1, 1937." Bureau of Narcotics, U. S. Treasury Department—*Traffic in Opium and Other Dangerous Drugs for the Year Ended December 31, 1936*, pp. 57–59; Government Printing Office, 1937.

effect. Craving may lead to desperation and even mania. Addicts tend to become moody, disorderly, and neglectful of their personal and social obligations. Their lives become centered about their habit. There may be fear of discovery, fear of the consequences of their habit, loss of self-respect, or a hardness of character in which nothing matters except to secure the drug irrespective of the means. Social ostracism of addicts occurs in some social groups. The Bureau of Narcotics reports on marihuana as follows:

". . . The toxic effects produced by its active narcotic principle appear to be exclusively on the higher nerve centers. While its effects are variable with different individuals, it usually produces first an exaltation with a feeling of well-being, a happy jovial mood, an increased feeling of physical strength, and a general euphoria. There is also a stimulation of the imagination followed by a more or less delirious state characterized by vivid kaleidoscopic visions, sometimes of a pleasing and sensual kind, but occasionally of a gruesome nature. Accompanying this delirious state is a remarkable loss in spatial and time relations; persons and things in the environment look small; time is interminable; seconds seem like minutes and hours like days.

"The principal effect of the drug is upon the mind which seems to lose the power of directing and controlling thought. Its continued use produces pronounced mental deterioration in many cases. Its more immediate effect apparently is to remove the normal inhibitions of the individual and release any antisocial tendencies which may be present. Those who indulge in its habitual use eventually develop a delirious rage after its administration, during which time they are, temporarily at least, irresponsible and prone to commit violent crimes. . . .

"A gang of seven young men, all under 20 years of age, who for more than 2 months terrorized central Ohio with a series of about 38 stickups, were arrested in Columbus, Ohio, on robbery charges. They confessed that they operated while 'high' on marihuana.

"One of the youths admitted that he had smoked 'reefers' on and off for at least 2 years, and said that when he went with the others on stickups he was 'ready to tear anybody apart' who opposed him. He claimed the practice of smoking marihuana first started among his friends about 4 or 5 years previously, while most of them were still in high school. In describing his crimes he said: 'If I had killed somebody on a job, I'd never have known it.' This was verified by the officer obtaining the confessions, who explained that the hardest problem was to get these youths to remember who committed the stick-ups, or when or where they happened. When police told them how a filling-station attendant reported a robber threatened to beat his brains out with a revolver butt, one admitted he was the robber, but had forgotten his own words.

"It is almost impossible for them to break off the habit when they could still get 'tea' so easily, they claimed. 'When you try to break off you get jumpy, your hands shake, and you hear the least little noise. A dopey feeling comes when you're going down, and you get mopey. You get so you smoke a "stick" a day, and you can't stop.' " [7]

Because law makes it an offence to supply the drug addict with his drug, addiction tends to make a criminal of the user. Persons who cater to the needs of the victims of this habit may be subject to both Federal and state penalties. The illegal traffic, whether for importation, production, wholesale distribution, or retail trade, is highly organized and crafty, and, like the rum-runners and boot-leggers of the period of Federal prohibition of the liquor traffic, its agents frequently violate criminal laws other than those directly pertaining to the traffic in order to attain their ends.

"The following may be cited as an example of the criminal records encountered in connection with enforcement of the narcotic laws:

"On April 18, 1936, narcotic agents and detectives of the New York City narcotic squad arrested Charles Ash (alias Jim Ash, alias 'Doc,' alias Jimmie Strong, alias Charles T. Bean, alias Thomas Hastings, alias Par-ker), Joseph Imbelli (alias Joseph Stern, alias Imbello), and Patsy Napoli-tano (alias Frank Nappi and other aliases) for possession of 130 grains of smoking opium and a complete smoking opium outfit. Ash had in his possession a loaded revolver.

"All of these defendants were addicts, and had long and varied crim-inal records. At the time of arrest, Ash was wanted for hold-up of a Washington bank, and was at liberty under a $2\frac{1}{2}$-year parole from Sing Sing prison. He was described as a dangerous criminal, usually armed, and an habitual opium smoker. His record extended back to 1922, and included convictions and sentences served for about eight different of-fenses, including narcotic law violations, theft of four automobiles, and safe blowing. Napolitano when arrested was at liberty under a 7-year parole from Sing Sing prison. He had a record of about 15 arrests on various charges, such as assault, robbery, and burglary.

"Ash was allowed to plead guilty and was given a suspended sentence in order that he could be removed to Washington, D. C., in connection with the bank-robbery case. Imbelli was sentenced to 20 months in Sing Sing prison, the sentence suspended, with the direction that he be re-turned to prison for 20 months for violation of parole. Imbelli had a rec-ord of 21 arrests since 1919, most of which were for burglary, and he had been convicted to 5 previous sentences in penitentiary. Napolitano was sentenced to $7\frac{1}{2}$ years in Sing Sing prison, the sentence suspended and defendant ordered returned to prison for $7\frac{1}{2}$ years for violation of parole. His criminal record dated from 1920 and included 14 serious offenses, such as grand larceny, burglary, assault, counterfeiting, etc." [8]

[7] *Ibid.*, pp. 60 and 67.
[8] *Ibid.*, p. 70.

Symptoms and Pathology.—Although drug addiction is a vice in the sense that it is an abuse of the self, experience shows that from the point of view of treatment it should be regarded as a disease. Much harm has been done to habitués and cure interfered with by the still general practice of making treatment difficult except through commitment to penal institutions. The symptoms and pathology of drug addiction have been described as follows:

> "A Narcotic Drug addict is an individual in whose body the continued administration of opiate drugs has established a physical reaction or condition or mechanism or process which manifests itself in the production of definite and constant symptoms and signs and peculiar and characteristic phenomena appearing inevitably upon the deprivation or material lessening in the amount of the Narcotic drug and capable of immediate and complete control only by further administration of the drug of the patient's addiction. In general, the symptoms, signs and phenomena consist of a sense of restlessness and depression followed by yawning, sneezing, excessive mucous secretion, sweating, nausea, uncontrollable vomiting and purging, twitching and jerking, internal cramps and pain, marked circulatory and cardiac inefficiency, irregularity of pulse going from extremes of slowness to extremes of rapidity, with loss of tone, face drawn and haggard, pallor deepening to grayness, exhaustion, collapse and, in some cases, death." [9]

The symptoms of excessive use of cocaine include loss of appetite and weight, sleeplessness, twitching of facial muscles, local anaesthesias, hallucinations, and both physical and mental deterioration. The primary symptoms upon withdrawal are muscular weakness and prolonged sleep.

Treatment.—Medical treatment for drug addiction necessarily varies from case to case with reference to the type of drug used, the purpose for which the drug was taken, and the mental and physical make-up of the individual, as well as the amount regularly used. The standardization of treatment methods within our penal institutions is responsible for much needless cruelty to patients, and often actual physical danger. Immediate withdrawal of opium and its derivatives causes intense agony to the user, while immediate withdrawal of cocaine can usually be accomplished with entire safety. For the opium addict withdrawal symptoms are most intense two days after the process begins. Specialists differ as to whether with-

---

[9] *Special Report on Drug Addiction*, p. 5, quoting a report to the American Public Health Association in 1919 by Dr. C. E. Terry, Dr. Oscar Dowling, Dr. Ernest S. Bishop, and Lucius P. Brown; State Commission of Prisons, State of New York, December 2, 1924.

drawal should be abrupt, rapid, or gradual. But in the main it appears to be increasingly agreed that for the opium addict the process can be accomplished with least disturbance to the system if, in the case of a heavy user, from two weeks to one month is allowed. Unfortunately our institutions find it necessary usually to complete the withdrawal within a week, thus seriously endangering the health of persons accustomed to heavy dosage through the shock and agony suffered.

"The treatment of drug addiction automatically divides itself into three phases, involving first, the detoxication or physical rehabilitation stage; second, the emotional stabilization and reëducational phase; and third, the social placement and community supervision phase.

"The problem of institutional treatment, however, must take into account the diverse motives or underlying reasons for seeking treatment; the incidence of intercurrent diseases and defects in such a group; the great differences in the types of personalities involved; and the need for protecting the institutional community against the weaknesses and cupidity of its component individuals.

"There are, of course, some persons addicted to the use of habit-forming drugs who sincerely desire to throw off the so-called slavery of the drug, but this sincerity vanishes when withdrawal symptoms appear. There are those who seek treatment through coercion by friends, or relatives, the individual having little sincerity or desire to throw off the habit. Then, too, there are those who seek treatment because of their desire to impress the court or court official. Others seek treatment because an institution offers a convenient refuge from the police; because of a desire to reduce the daily dose of the drug, thus lessening the expense of maintaining themselves in a future daily supply; and still others, because of their need for maintenance and support.

"The intercurrent diseases observed among these people embrace the whole category of medicine, and their needs involve provision for the ambulant, semi-ambulant, bedridden, and convalescent sick. The diverse personalities involved point to the need for appropriate classification and groupings as a necessary corollary to treatment, based upon firsthand knowledge of the antecedent, social, educational, industrial, and economic background, together with an analysis of the character traits of the individual. The appropriate classification and grouping of these people within an institution is important for rehabilitation purposes and for the safety and protection of the institutional community and the community at large." [10]

Registration.—Universal and effective treatment requires registration of addicts, such as is provided in some of the Asiatic coun-

[10] Treadway, Walter L.—*Drug Addiction and Measures for Its Prevention in the United States,* pp. 13–14; United States Public Health Service, Division of Mental Hygiene (Mimeographed A–748).

tries. It has not yet proved possible in America, and will be exceedingly difficult since the illicit nature of traffic and the penal treatment of cases inevitably foster secrecy and evasion.

Commitment.—Institutional treatment is necessary for a considerable number of weeks or months in order to effect cure. For the patient needs continuous oversight and a controlled environment, which is rarely possible in the home. In most states today specialized institutional treatment is possible only through commitment under the penal code. To send a man to prison for drug addiction, which is definitely a disease, is the equivalent of imprisonment for tuberculosis or any other disease. Naturally most addicts, even if they desire cure, are unwilling to incur criminal status in order to secure it. Similarly treatment of such cases in hospitals for the insane through legal commitment upon the certification of two physicians would be revolting to many addicts desirous of cure and to their families, and would involve conditions in treatment which would not ideally favor recovery.

Hospital Colonies.—The cure of addicts—so far as that may prove possible—is dependent upon the establishment in each of the more populous states of one or more hospital colonies devoted exclusively to the treatment of such cases. Voluntary self-commitment should be possible at such institutions in addition to certification of cases to the institutions by physicians. Addicts who have fallen into the hands of the police for minor infractions of law could properly be placed on probation on the understanding that they will undergo the treatment at the hospital as one of the conditions of such probation. Thus only those addicts who have committed serious crimes would remain to be treated in prison hospitals.

Individualization.—Essential to effective treatment in such hospital colonies would be latitude to their medical staffs in the individualization of their cases. Medical discretion would be necessary to determine the degree of rapidity of withdrawal of the drug in each case. Individualization requires careful study of the physical and mental nature of the individual; of his personality and emotional make-up, his aptitudes and interests; of the causes of his habit, its effect upon his mind and physique; of his home, his social and industrial environment; and of the factors in each that are favorable or unfavorable to cure.

"Psychopathic characters and persons in general whose personalities deviate from the normal are especially susceptible to opiate addiction and to relapse after cures. The most important phase of treatment for them is not the physical withdrawal of opium, but a reorientation of their personalities so that they do not again feel the necessity for seeking relief from the stresses of life by resorting to opiates. The rebuilding of personality cannot be accomplished within a few weeks, and in many cases cannot be accomplished at all." [11]

Cure of drug addiction involves not only understanding of the patient and his disease, but also treatment and cure of any other diseases from which he may be suffering, so that these other diseases may not militate against his recovery. Since many persons take drugs because of the pain of uncured illnesses, some of the patients will have to be transferred to other hospitals to cure, if possible, the cancers or other difficulties from which they may suffer. The remainder, after cure of their prior and concomitant illnesses and of the injuries caused by the use of the drug, must be built up to sturdy health, normal weight, and normal habits of activity and sleep.

Retraining.—Meanwhile it is necessary to elicit the genuine co-operation of the patient in his own cure. This involves profound changes in his mental attitude and habits, and emotional retraining or redirection. Treatment succeeds best where some deep-lying interest can be discovered in the individual's make-up, for the sake of which he will make sustained effort to cure himself. Such interests vary from patient to patient. In one it will be a life-long ambition to excel in his job or profession. For another it may be an invention or an art which commands his devotion. For another the incentive is personal loyalty to wife, child, mother, or patron. For yet another the appeal may be that of religion. Much insight and discrimination is needed to discover and use to its full the unique incentive operative in each case.

Occupational and Social Training.—Meanwhile, normal habits of time distribution, effort, and physical activity must be built, by means of occupations properly adapted to case needs. Ideally, the hospital colony should comprise both a farm for healthful and profitable outdoor work when season and weather permit, and one or more workshops for interesting and profitable indoor occupations. Under clever administration appropriate work about the premises can also be provided for the electrician, carpenter, plumber, gar-

[11] Kolb, Lawrence—"The Treatment of Opiate Addiction, with Special Reference to Withdrawal Therapy," *Hospital News*, Vol. 3, No. 23, p. 38; United States Public Health Service, December 1, 1936.

dener, bookkeeper, and a wide variety of other specialized occupations. In general the first purpose of the occupational assignment is therapeutic. The profit to be gained from such activities, though a secondary consideration, is nevertheless important since the cost to the state of treatment per patient can be materially reduced by an administration which makes a skilful adjustment between the therapeutic and financial objectives.

Treatment of the above type was provided in Massachusetts at the Norfolk State Hospital for a few years prior to 1918. California, under an act of 1927, made somewhat similar provision. A Federal act of 1928 provided for the establishment of two farms for the treatment of narcotic addicts convicted under Federal law. Voluntary commitment is possible. Training is available in industrial employments leading to self-support. These hospitals located at Lexington, Kentucky, and at Fort Worth, Texas, are under the direction of the United States Public Health Service.

"The object of the Lexington, Ky., farm is to rehabilitate, restore to health, and train to be self-supporting and self-reliant those who are admitted thereto. In addition, the control, management, and discipline are to be maintained for the safekeeping of the individual and the protection of American communities. Shops are being established to afford occupation, vocational training, and education. Experiments are to be carried on to determine the best methods of treatment and research in this field and the results are to be disseminated to the medical profession and the general public. In short, the functions of the institution will assume the character of a treatment and research center and of an educational, industrial, vocational, and rehabilitation center, with certain custodial features superimposed.

"The fundamental background for establishing the narcotic farms represents more than the mere housing or domiciliary care of drug addicts or their individual treatment. These institutions must, because of the functions which they are expected to perform, be represented as medical centers, with all those diversified facilities which the broad activities and interests of modern medical science and the treatment of the physically and mentally sick entail. The problem of the treatment of drug addiction in its present stage involves a chemicopharmacologic, biochemical, psychobiologic, and medical approach. These institutions represent even more than individual services for those admitted; for in their conception they are an aspect of further specialization in the evolution of public policies that aim toward a partial solution of a particular problem confronting society.

"These facilities, established for the confinement and treatment of persons addicted to habit-forming drugs, represent a form of specialization bearing a direct relationship to policies of law enforcement and the protection of American communities; to special problems in penal and correctional procedure; to safeguarding the uses of narcotic drugs in medical practice; to research and the quest for more accurate and fundamental knowledge concerning the nature of drug addiction and related phenomena; and to those instinctive demands ever present in the American people that the sick and afflicted shall be set in the way of strength and hope." [12]

Preventive Measures.—Since little is known of the relation of heredity to the formation of the drug habit, specific measures for prevention through social control of heredity are not yet indicated, though a little might be accomplished indirectly through the devices recommended for the prevention of procreation among those who are mentally diseased or feebleminded as a result of heredity.

The drug addiction which grows out of bravado, or the experimental seeking for the overrated euphoric effects, and the social use of drugs by normal persons can in part be prevented by education. In the public schools, as well as in adult education, it can be made clear in physiology classes or those on civic problems that habit-forming drugs cannot be used in safety. The so-called euphoric effects are either temporary or wholly illusory and followed inevitably by intense discomfort, which, when the drug becomes unavailable or available in inadequate quantities, becomes torture. Such discomfort or agony becomes the rule rather than the exception among users in any country which drastically curbs the sale of habit-forming drugs. The association of the drug evil with criminality is largely due to the fact that the psychoneurotic addict in desperation will commit crime in order that his pain may be relieved, though it grows further out of the changes in personality and disintegration of character which the constant use of drugs occasions in a large percentage of its victims.

Popular warning against the use of patent medicine without medical prescription is possible in school textbooks on physiology and the social sciences, as well as through such informational devices as posters, leaflets, motion pictures, or the radio. There is still widespread use of "headache cures," "cold cures," "consumption cures," and a wide variety of other so-called cures which contain dangerous drugs. Though they may temporarily relieve pain they

[12] Treadway, W. L.—*Dedication and Opening of the Lexington Narcotic Farm*, pp. 4–5; United States Public Health Service, Reprint No. 1698 from the Public Health Reports, Vol. 50, No. 31, August 2, 1935, Government Printing Office, 1935.

fail to get at the source of the difficulty and are likely to injure the user. Social case work agencies, medical clinics, and visiting nurses, where they find such preparations in use, are often able to inform and warn the user and arrange for appropriate medical treatment. A good fraction of our population, however, is still wholly unaware of the dangers which they are running in the use of patent medicines of which they have learned through advertising or through the advice of their associates.

The Committee on the Costs of Medical Care found that:

"The development of the drug store into a department store for many commodities has made the services of pharmacists readily available to the people without unduly high costs for prescribed medicines. But it has surely not retarded the growth of sales of secret-formula medicines, purchased by the patient for a self-diagnosed disease or condition. The annual sales of such 'patent medicines' amount to $360,000,000, most of which is money wasted. This is ten per cent of the total spent for all medical services and commodities." [13]

They further recommended that:

"State and Federal legislation should be enacted to prevent the sale of drugs and medicines with secret formulas. These laws should require that the label on *all* medicines disclose the kind and the quantity of all ingredients for which therapeutic properties are claimed and the disclosure of the same information in all literature accompanying the medicine or used in advertising it. Furthermore, all manufacturers of drugs and medicines should be permitted to operate only under licenses granted annually by the Federal government upon the fulfillment of prescribed conditions with respect to personnel, equipment, sanitary surroundings, and standardization of finished products." [14]

Another major source of the habit lies in the prescriptions of physicians. Pending the discovery of safer devices for the alleviation of intense pain, opium and its derivatives will have important medicinal uses. More general recognition among the profession that such use beyond a ten-day period is reasonably certain to form a habit difficult and, in longer use, impossible for the patient to break, would lead to greater precaution in its prescription and earlier withdrawal—except for certain cases like incurable cancer in which

[13] Final Report of the Committee on the Costs of Medical Care—*Medical Care for the American People*, p. 29; Publications of the Committee on the Costs of Medical Care, No. 28, University of Chicago Press, 1932.
[14] *Ibid.*, pp. 136–137.

there is no other means equally effective of alleviating long, intense suffering.

Social Control through Legislation.—Control of the legitimate traffic, and prevention and punishment of illicit traffic, are the chief methods of contemporary prevention. Federal narcotic legislation began with the Pure Food and Drugs Act of 1906. The Harrison Narcotic Act of 1914, which became law May 1, 1915, safeguards the importation, manufacture, distribution, and sale of opium and coca leaves and their derivatives. It has been subsequently amended and amplified. The Narcotic Control Board was established by the United States Government in 1922 to determine the amounts of drugs to be imported. In 1924, a supplementary act forbade the importation of opium for the manufacture of heroin.

Every state government today has laws regulating the distribution of opium and coca leaves and their derivatives or preparations from them, and limits their distribution to licensed jobbers, manufacturers, and retailers. Possession of such drugs without a prescription authorized by law is a violation of Federal law and of the laws of most states. Such legislation narrowly specifies the conditions of use and prescription by physicians, veterinarians, pharmacists, and others. By 1937 there were twenty-nine states which had adopted the Uniform State Narcotic Act, which is integrated with the Federal law and supplements it at certain points.

International Commissions.—Since most of the habit-forming drugs are imported from other countries, international drug control is indispensable to supplement national, state, and local enforcement. Beginning with the International Opium Commission at Shanghai in 1909, and The Hague Opium Convention of 1912, governing transportation primarily, the problem was taken up by the League of Nations which adopted a resolution intended to restrict production to medical and scientific purposes. A second conference was held at Geneva on this problem in 1924–25. The first joint annual meeting of committees of the World Conference on Narcotic Education and International Narcotic Education Association was held in New York City in 1927. A conference on the Limitation of the Manufacture of Narcotics met in Geneva in 1931. There now exists a Permanent Central Opium Board and an Opium Advisory Committee of the League of Nations.

Although these many conferences have accomplished a great deal in calling the attention of the world to the problem of narcotism and mark a sharp departure from the *laissez faire* of earlier centuries, the international control of production and transportation still falls far short of adequate. This is attested by the volume of drug addiction in each of the countries represented by member nations in these agreements. The pressure of selfish interests associated in an economically profitable traffic, and the difficulty of enforcing prohibitions of production in rural territory have rendered treaties only partially effective. A year's supply for a single drug addict makes a parcel of insignificant size. The ease with which goods of such small dimension but high potency and money value can be imported, concealed in other shipments, makes enforcement of laws relating to importation exceedingly difficult.

The Federal Bureau of Narcotics reports upon its experience in this regard as follows:

"Thus, Federal officers were able to seize from illicit channels, in 1935, about 511 kilograms of narcotic drugs, as compared with $3\frac{1}{3}$ tons seized or purchased as evidence during the fiscal year 1931, when smuggling was rampant. In 1935, seizures of morphine and heroin showed increases over 1934 of $27\frac{1}{2}$ per cent and $19\frac{2}{5}$ per cent, respectively, however; and cocaine showed a decrease of $63\frac{2}{5}$ per cent.

"Our figures show an increase in criminal violations detected from 4,742 in 1934 to 5,200 in 1935; convictions increased from 1,816 in 1934 to 2,065 in 1935." [15]

The illicit sale of drugs is reported to be a highly organized, unscrupulous, dangerous, but profitable racket. Through his underworld agents the drug trafficker, like the bootlegger in the period of the Federal prohibition amendment, reaches his clients, eluding as long as possible the pursuit by Federal and state enforcement officers and local police. In spite of legal penalties of great severity such traffic will continue as long as it is profitable. It is therefore clear that such detective and punitive measures as are now available for the prevention of this traffic must for effectiveness be supplemented by devices to reduce the buying public. The solution involves the continuation and perfection of all existing measures, and improvement in their enforcement; prevention, so far as possible, of the formation of the habit; and the discovery, cure in appropriate hospitals, and aftercare of all present or future addicts, even though such cure must be provided at public expense.

[15] *Traffic in Opium and Other Dangerous Drugs for the Year Ended December 31, 1935*, p. III.

QUESTIONS FOR DISCUSSION OR EXAMINATION

1. Distinguish the types of drug addiction and outline the estimates of the extent of addiction in the United States.
2. What are the causes of drug addiction?
3. Outline the individual and social pathology of drug addiction.
4. What are the contemporary measures for medical and social treatment of addicts?
5. Outline a comprehensive social policy for the prevention of (a) drug traffic, (b) drug addiction.

PROBLEMS FOR INDIVIDUAL STUDY

1. An outline of the world history of drug addiction and methods of international prevention and control.
2. A critical analysis of the social provision for registration, punishment, and curative treatment of addicts in some selected state.
3. A study of the history and contemporary social problems relating to the production, distribution, and use of patent medicines.
4. A history of Federal policies relating to narcotic drugs.
5. A critical study of the literature on the relation of drug addiction to poverty and crime.

SUGGESTIONS FOR SUPPLEMENTARY READINGS

Bishop, Ernest S.—*The Narcotic Drug Problem;* The Macmillan Company, 1920.

Buell, Raymond Leslie—*The International Opium Conferences, with Relevant Documents;* World Peace Foundation Pamphlets, Vol. VIII, Nos. 2–3, 1925.

Bureau of Narcotics, U. S. Treasury Department—*Traffic in Opium and Other Dangerous Drugs for the Year Ended December 31, 1935;* Government Printing Office, 1936.

Bureau of Narcotics, U. S. Treasury Department—*Traffic in Opium and Other Dangerous Drugs for the Year Ended December 31, 1936;* Government Printing Office, 1937.

Dunn, Wie T.—*The Opium Traffic in Its International Aspects;* Columbia University Press, 1920.

Eisenlohr, L. E. S.—*International Narcotics Control;* The Macmillan Company, 1935.

Great Britain, Ministry of Health—*Report of Departmental Committee on Morphine and Heroin Addiction;* H. M. Stationery Office, 1926.

Lindesmith, Alfred Ray—*The Nature of Opiate Addiction*, Doctoral Dissertation; University of Chicago, 1937.

Terry, Charles E.—"Drug Addiction," *Encyclopaedia of the Social Sciences*, Vol. 5; The Macmillan Company, 1931.

Terry, Charles E., and Pellens, Mildred—*The Opium Problem;* The Committee on Drug Addictions in collaboration with The Bureau of Social Hygiene, Inc., 1928.

The Traffic in Habit-Forming Narcotic Drugs, Statement of the Attitude of the Government of the United States with Documents Relating Thereto; Government Printing Office, 1924.

United States Public Health Service—*Conference on Legitimate Requirements of Narcotic Drugs, Washington, D. C.*, August 12, 1930; United States Public Health Service, Public Health Reports, October 3, 1930.

United States Public Health Service—Public Health Reports.

Walton, Robert P.—*Marihuana: America's New Drug Problem;* J. B. Lippincott Company, 1938.

Williams, Edward Huntington—*Opiate Addiction: Its Handling and Treatment;* The Macmillan Company, 1922.

Willoughby, Westel W.—*Opium as an International Problem, The Geneva Conferences;* The Johns Hopkins Press, 1925.

CHAPTER XIV

CHRONIC DISEASE

Definitions.—Diseases are divided for convenience into two groups, the acute and the chronic. Acute diseases are of short duration and have a limited course which ends in early recovery or death. They are not necessarily severe. Chronic diseases may be obscure in their onset and develop slowly but their course runs over many months or years. By the damage which they do to organs or tissues, bodily functions are disturbed.

Although almost all of the infectious diseases fall in the category of the acute, it has already been seen that in a small percentage of cases their sequelae may take the form of permanent impairment of vision, hearing, or mind, or lead to bodily impairments which fall in the category of chronic ailments. Parasitic diseases, such as hookworm and ascaris, are commonly classified among the chronic diseases because of their long duration. Degenerative diseases of the heart, kidneys, tissues, and circulatory system are chronic, and thus heart disease, nephritis, cancer, and arteriosclerosis are termed chronic. Disorders of the glands if of long duration, as in the case of goiter, fall in the chronic class. So also do diseases developing from local foci of infection (pus pockets), as for example an infected sinus, diseased teeth or tonsils, since the poisons draining into the system may cause lasting injury to heart, kidneys, or other organs, or to bones and joints. Tuberculosis and syphilis are considered among the chronic ailments because of their long course and the many kinds of damage which they may do to the body in case they fail of complete cure in the early stages.

Chronic diseases, though always of long duration, are not invariably disabling. Perrott and Holland state that "a large volume of chronic disease prevalent in the population is of a low order of severity." [1] The Massachusetts survey of chronic diseases estimated that of 500,000 persons with chronic disease in Massachusetts 45

[1] Perrott, George St. J., and Holland, Dorothy F.—*Chronic Disease and Gross Impairments in a Northern Industrial Community*, p. 9; reprinted from *The Journal of the American Medical Association*, Vol. 108, May 29, 1937.

per cent, or 225,000, were partially disabled, and nearly 5 per cent, 22,500 persons, totally disabled. Of 138,000 cases of rheumatism in Massachusetts 70 per cent were getting no medical care.[2] Thus rheumatism and certain minor circulatory diseases such as hemorrhoids, varicose veins, superficial cancers, sinus infection, neuritis or neuralgia, internal ulcers, and parasitic infections in persons of high resistance do not necessarily confine their victims to home or hospital, and in some instances would seem to result in no appreciable diminution of the quality or quantity of work performed. Some victims of chronic disease through their high quality of mind make the necessary adjustments and develop their personal controls to such a point that their suffering is not apparent to others, and their output may equal or exceed the average in their occupation or profession.

Extent of Disabling Chronic Disease.—The National Health Survey of 1935–36 is the most comprehensive study available on the prevalence of chronic diseases of a disabling type. Its examination of over two million persons in 81 cities led to the discovery that 46 persons in every 1,000 suffered from chronic disabling disease, when that term was defined to include all persons who lost a week or more from work, school, or other usual activities during the year as a result of a disease of more than three months' duration. From the point of view of frequency, heart disease and arteriosclerosis combined led the list with 8.5 annual cases per 1,000 persons, disabled for one week or longer. Rheumatism was second with 5.9, nervous diseases 5.5, orthopedic conditions 2.6, nephritis and other kidney diseases 2.5, gall bladder diseases 2.2, and tumors nonmalignant or unspecified 2.0. Asthma and hay fever combined came to 1.4, as did also tuberculosis. There was one case per 1,000 each for sinusitis, hernia, ulcer of the stomach or duodenum, and cancer, and less than one case per 1,000 for diabetes, hemorrhoids, and thyroid diseases.[3]

Viewing chronic disease as an industrial handicap, this survey would indicate that one person in every twenty suffers annually the loss of a week or more from work as a result of chronic disease of some

[2] Bigelow, George H., and Lombard, Herbert L.—*Cancer and Other Chronic Diseases in Massachusetts*, pp. 16, 18; Houghton Mifflin Company, 1933.

[3] *The National Health Survey: 1935–36—An Estimate of the Amount of Disabling Illness in the Country as a Whole*, especially p. 8; Division of Public Health Methods, National Institute of Health, U. S. Public Health Service (Preliminary Reports, The National Health Survey, Sickness and Medical Care Series, Bulletin No. 1), 1938.

sort and that fully half of these are victims of heart disease, arteriosclerosis, rheumatism, nervous diseases, or diseases of the kidney or gall bladder.

The findings for the National Health Survey confirm those of the Massachusetts Department of Public Health made in 1929 to 1931. The Massachusetts study similarly was made by means of a house-to-house canvass in 51 cities and towns. That of 1929 interviewed persons of all ages, while in the two following years only individuals over 40 were interviewed. Altogether 75,000 records were gathered, from which it was estimated that 500,000 persons, or 12 per cent of the population of Massachusetts, were suffering from chronic disease. Rheumatism led with 138,000 cases of which 5,600 were totally disabled. Heart disease was second with 84,000 cases and 2,600 disabled; arteriosclerosis 64,000 cases, 1,800 disabled; digestive diseases 29,000 cases, 500 disabled; eye and ear diseases 24,000 cases, 350 disabled; apoplexy 16,000 cases, 3,800 disabled; tuberculosis 16,000 cases; diabetes 15,000 cases, 800 disabled; cancer 11,500 cases.[4]

Death Rates from Chronic Disease.—An examination of mortality rates, however, displays that more than half of the deaths are caused by chronic diseases. The death rate from all causes per 100,000 population in the registration area for 1934 was 1,143. The leading cause of death was disease of the heart, for which the rate that year was 267.6. The second important grouping, covering cancer and other malignant tumors, had a rate of 131.5. Third in importance was nephritis, 85.6 (slightly under the figure for the combined acute diseases, influenza and pneumonia, 88.8). Fourth among the chronic diseases was listed cerebral hemorrhage and softening, 80.2. Tuberculosis followed with a rate of 53.5, and diabetes mellitus with 29.1.[5]

A study of trends indicates a rapid decrease since the beginning of this century in mortality from the acute diseases and an increase in the mortality from chronic degenerative diseases. Thus within the registration area death rates have declined for diphtheria, measles, scarlet fever, typhoid fever, and whooping cough. But the rate for diseases of the heart has nearly doubled from 137.4 in 1900,

[4] Bigelow, George H., and Lombard, Herbert L.—*op. cit.*, pp. 18, 24–26, 199.

[5] This abbreviated statement often includes in one category several of the diseases of the detailed International List. Thus under diseases of the heart are included numbers 90–93, 94a, and 95 from the International List. *Statistical Abstract of the United States 1936*, p. 83; Government Printing Office, 1936.

and for cancer from 64 in 1900, and has more than doubled for diabetes which in 1900 was 11.0. The rate has increased less notably for nephritis and cerebral hemorrhage. On the other hand, tuberculosis, a chronic disease of infectious type, has been strikingly reduced from a mortality rate of 195.2 in 1900 to 53.5 in 1934.[6]

The mortality figures are prepared directly from reports of physicians, whereas the health survey figures were gathered from householders. There is thus a greater possibility of diagnostic accuracy in the data concerning death rates. Nevertheless, these latter have limitations in value as an indication of the role of chronic disease as a handicap because, first, there is an unknown percentage of error in diagnoses; second, where the individual is suffering from a combination of illnesses the subordinate ones are not listed in the death certificate; third, old age diseases predominate among those above listed as causes of death, whereas the illnesses which interfered with productivity during life may remain unrecorded. The mortality statistics suggest the wide prevalence of incipient and unrecognized chronic disease in the working population. An examination of mortality tables through past generations indicates the rapid increase in recent decades of the degenerative diseases corresponding with a notable lengthening of the life span. The chronic diseases that show highest death rates are diseases of old age.

Intensive Surveys.—Where intensive surveys of chronic disease have been made, based upon medical diagnosis and the reports of physicians and hospitals rather than of householders, the findings make clear the heavy incidence and social cost of the degenerative diseases. Thus, the Boston Council of Social Agencies, in 1927, enumerated cases of chronic disease among the hospitals and social service agencies of that city. Their attention was confined to the limited group in which medical and nursing care were required. Altogether they found 4,316 chronic cases known to these agencies during the sixteen-month period of the survey, of which 55.7 per cent were ambulatory. By diseases, they are distributed as follows: [7]

---

[6] See mortality statistics issued annually by the Bureau of the Census; also Sydenstricker, Edgar—"The Vitality of the American People," Chapter XII of *Recent Social Trends in the United States*, Vol. 1; McGraw-Hill Book Company, Inc., 1933.

[7] Boston Council of Social Agencies—*Report on Chronic Disease in Boston, Mass.: 1927*, p. 14; Boston Council of Social Agencies, c. 1927.

Diagnosis	Number
Heart Disease	845
Organic Nervous and Mental Disease	553
Cancer and Other Malignant Tumors	534
Arthritis	467
Arteriosclerosis (Varicose veins and other diseases of circulatory system)	427
Non-pulmonary Tuberculosis	196
Fractures and Burns	138
Infantile Paralysis	135
Venereal Disease	129
Old Age (Senility and Senescence)	115
Disease of Digestive System (Ulcer of the stomach, hernia, etc.)	97
Chronic Nephritis	89
Disease of Bones and Organs of Locomotion (Osteomyelitis, etc.)	80
Diabetes	50
Non-venereal Disease of the Genito-urinary System	49
Chorea	49
Asthma	46
Chronic Alcoholism	42
Disease of Skin	40
Disease of Eye and Ear	38
Empyema	31
Chronic Bronchitis	29
Epilepsy	17
Others	120
	4,316

The Boston study of more profound cases of chronic disease may be contrasted with the highly specialized findings of the Life Extension Institute whose hundred thousand physical examinations, tabulated by Sydenstricker and Britten, were limited to native-born white males, largely in the prime of active life, practically all of whom belonged to the more prosperous economic groups. Their findings by way of contrast serve to indicate primarily the minor chronic ailments, and to show their predominance in this group over the conditions which handicap to the point of requiring absence from work and hospitalization. Chronic and degenerative disease is here disclosed in its incipient stages in the middle years of life.

Eyes and Ears	
Defective vision—uncorrected	*27%
Defective hearing	13
Nose and Throat	
Enlarged, cryptic, buried tonsils	45
Hypertrophic rhinitis (enlarged turbinates)	37

* " The percentage here used is not the total number of cases of a particular condition found divided by the total examinations, but is the mean of the percentage found in the head office examinations, and the percentage found in the field. This procedure was followed by Sydenstricker and Britten because they found significant differences between the two sets of examinations which they did not wish to bury in a straight average. Certain unimportant or infrequent conditions are omitted."

Teeth

    Heavy dentistry (X-ray recommended) 39%

    Slightly infected gums 18

    Carious teeth, septic roots. 15

    Pyorrhea, definite 6

Heart and Pulse

    Functional murmur or irregularity 6

    Enlargement 2

    Mitral regurgitation 2

Blood Vessels

    Arterial thickening—slight 14

    Arterial thickening—moderate. 3

    Varicose veins. 6

    Varicocele 9

Respiratory

    Frequent colds 16

Stomach and Abdominal

    Constipation 34

    Hemorrhoids 13

    Acid stomach 11

    Gastric disturbances 8

    Hernia 6

Genito-Urinary

    Prostate enlarged, tender 8

Brain and Nervous

    Neurasthenia and "nervousness". 7

    Abnormal reflexes 8

Endocrine Disturbances

    Goiter and hypothyroidism 2

Miscellaneous

    Chronic skin affections. 10

    Dizziness. 8

Urinalysis (given to 79,126 men)

    Albumin (slight, definite or marked) 22

    Pus 13

    Sugar—trace or marked . . . . 7 [8]

Distribution of Chronic Disease by Age.—The degenerative diseases are peculiarly a phenomenon of advancing years. There are, however, several types of chronic disease to be found among children other than blindness, deafness, deformity, and epilepsy treated in earlier chapters. Conspicuous among these are tuberculosis, rheumatic heart conditions, and parasitic affections. The White House Conference on Child Health and Protection estimated that

[8] Mills, Alden B.—*The Extent of Illness and of Physical and Mental Defects Prevailing in the United States*, p. 40; Committee on the Costs of Medical Care, Publication No. 2, 1929: citing from tabulation made by Edgar Sydenstricker and Rollo H. Britten for the Milbank Memorial Fund, "information here used is taken from typewritten manuscript of 'A General View of Physical Impairment in a Group of One Hundred Thousand Men,' furnished by the authors."

there were in the United States 400,000 tuberculous children, and
850,000 suspected cases of tuberculosis, as well as 450,000 children
with cardiac limitations.[9] There are also considerable numbers
suffering from goiter, malaria, and venereal diseases. Examination
of researches made on this problem in Cattaraugus County, New
York, in 1925–26, in Massachusetts in 1924, in Philadelphia, North
Carolina, and elsewhere reveal that "the incidence of manifest
tuberculosis among school children varies from .5 per cent to 3.5
per cent." [10]

Heart disease in children, chiefly rheumatic, displays an incidence
of roughly seven cases per thousand, according to studies made in
four of our largest cities.[11]

In southern states hookworm infestation has been found to range
in incidence among white school children from less than five per cent
in some of the larger towns to ninety-five per cent in the heavily
infested rural communities. Among Negro children the rate is
relatively slight. A study of ascaris in Wise County, Virginia, in

[9] White House Conference on Child Health and Protection—*The Handicapped Child*, p. 4; The Century Co., 1933.

[10] *Ibid.*, pp. 200–212, citing Myers, J. Arthur—"Findings in 4,500 Children Examined for Tuberculosis"; *American Review of Tuberculosis*, Vol. 16, October, 1927: Chadwick, Henry D., and McPhedran, F. Maurice—*Childhood Type of Tuberculosis;* National Tuberculosis Association, 1930: Douglas, Stephen A.— *The Organization of a Rural Tuberculosis Service;* Milbank Memorial Fund, 1930: Opie, Eugene L., Landis, H. R. M., McPhedran, F. Maurice, and Hetherington, H. W.—"A Survey to Determine the Prevalence of Tuberculous Infection in School Children"; Henry Phipps Institute of the University of Pennsylvania, 1929: Chadwick, Henry D., and Zachs, David—"The Incidence of Tuberculosis Infection in School Children"; *New England Journal of Medicine*, Vol. 200, February 14, 1929: McCain, P. P.—"A Report of the Study of 25,048 School Children for Tuberculosis"; *Southern Medical Journal*, Vol. 22, April, 1929: Korns, John H.—"Tuberculosis Infection in School Children"; *American Review of Tuberculosis*, Vol. 24, No. 5, November, 1931.

[11] *Ibid.*, pp. 229–250, citing Clark, Taliaferro—"Heart Disease a Public Health Problem"; *U. S. Public Health Reports*, Vol. 44, October 11, 1929: New York State Medical Society—*Report of the Committee to Make a Study of Heart Disease in the State of New York;* presented at Albany, New York, May 21, 1928: Robey, William H.—"A Cardiac Survey of Children in Boston Public Schools"; *The Nation's Health*, Vol. 9, December 15, 1927: Detroit Department of Health— "Report of Children with Heart Disease"; *City Health* (Annual Report), Detroit, Michigan, Department of Health Bulletin, Vol. 14, January, 1930: Halsey, Robert H.—"Heart Disease in Children of School Age"; *Journal of the American Medical Association*, Vol. 77, August 27, 1921: New York Tuberculosis and Health Association—*The Health of a Thousand Newsboys in New York City; A Study Made in Coöperation with the Board of Education;* Heart Committee, New York Tuberculosis and Health Association, Inc., 1925.

1928, showed almost sixty per cent of children and thirty per cent of adults suffering from this parasite, the more severe cases being among children under twelve. Other southern studies show much lower rates.[12]

In the earlier adult years of life the more prevalent chronic diseases are tuberculosis and the early stages of venereal disease. Heart difficulties are becoming common and increase with years. The degenerative diseases of the arteries, heart, kidneys, and tissues affect primarily the upper age level though manifesting themselves often in the middle years of life and sometimes earlier.[13] In the upper age levels also one finds the sequelae of uncured venereal disease, of excesses, whether overwork, overeating, alcohol addiction, fatigue, faulty habits of nutrition, sleep, or exertion, resulting in permanent impairments.

Distribution by Sex, Race, and Location.—Sex distribution shows definitely a higher incidence of venereal disease and alcoholism and their sequelae among males. Industrial diseases and poisonings, and organic injuries growing out of accidents and surgery are also more predominant among males. The gynecological group of chronic ailments exclusively female is accompanied also by higher rates for females than males in the incidence of cancer, tuberculosis, and most degenerative diseases.

Susceptibilities of different races and peoples to chronic disease are usually shown in relatively high rates for tuberculosis among Negroes, Indians, Puerto Ricans, Irish, and Italians, and much lower rates among the Jews. Venereal disease rates appear from many studies to be relatively high among Negroes and Indians, while the Negroes show relative immunity to hookworm infection.

Rural-urban comparisons usually show higher rates for chronic nervous diseases, tuberculosis (associated with dusty trades, congested housing, and excesses), venereal diseases, and heart diseases

[12] *Ibid.*, pp. 250–262, citing Smillie, Wilson G.—*Intensity Surveys of Hookworm Infestation;* Williams & Wilkins Company, 1927: Smillie, Wilson G.—"Intensity of Hookworm Infestation in Alabama: Its Relationship to Residence, Occupation, Age, Sex and Race"; *Journal of the American Medical Association*, Vol. 85, December 19, 1925: Cort, W. W., Otto, G. F., and Spindler, L. A.—"Investigations of Ascaris Lumbricoides and Associated Intestinal Helminths of Man in Southwestern Virginia"; *American Journal of Hygiene*, Vol. 11, January, 1930: Stiles, C. W.—"Decrease of Hookworm Disease in the United States"; *U. S. Public Health Service Report*, Vol. 45, August 1, 1930.

[13] Bigelow, George H., and Lombard, Herbert L.—*op. cit.*, pp. 41–45: and Sydenstricker, Edgar—*op. cit.*

in cities; while pellagra, and the intestinal parasitic diseases appear to be primarily rural.[14]

Geographical distribution of diseases shows a higher incidence of goiter in the region of the Great Lakes; while leprosy, fortunately rare, is found chiefly in seaboard communities, being an importation and not endemic in temperate climates. Pellagra, hookworm, and ascaris are rare except in southern states.

The Social Pathology of Chronic Disease.—Many who are described as shiftless or lazy are the victims of disease. Hundreds of thousands of the poor whites of the South were cured of "shiftlessness" when it was discovered that they were suffering from the hookworm disease which could be controlled by simple means. The work of the Rockefeller Foundation in combating this disease throughout the world is one of the outstanding examples of well-organized and efficient philanthropy. Local sanitary authorities and physicians were taught, by the agents of the Foundation, how to carry on the work in both the prevention and the cure of this disease.[15]

Some of the so-called lazy may be suffering from anemia or other malnutrition diseases, from incipient tuberculosis, chronic digestive disorders, or poisons draining from decayed teeth or other internal sources of infection. Still others may be handicapped by mental or emotional conflicts or nervous disease. All persons classified as lazy or shiftless should therefore be subjected to physical and mental examinations to ascertain whether the cause lies in disease or in faulty training.

Chronic disease may be a cause of poverty because of (1) the absorption of a large percentage of limited incomes in the purchase of medical or surgical care, hospitalization, nursing, and medicine; or (2) the loss of time, and consequently income, from work; or (3) industrial inefficiency and consequent low income or dismissal occasioned by the disease; or (4) economic disorganization of the family resulting in dependency. Boston statistics on the duration of chronic ailments show that:

"Of the 4,316 patients, 3.7 per cent. were recognized at the time of the study as having been ill less than 3 months; 9.4 per cent. from 3 to 6

[14] Sorokin, Pitirim, and Zimmerman, Carle C.—*Principles of Rural-Urban Sociology*, Chapter VI; Henry Holt and Company, 1929.

[15] See Reports of the Rockefeller Foundation, and Heiser, Victor—*An American Doctor's Odyssey;* W. W. Norton & Company, Inc., 1936.

months; 13.5 per cent., 6 months to one year; 13.1 per cent. from 1 to 2 years; 9.7 per cent. from 2 to 3 years; 8.2 per cent. from 3 to 4 years; 6.7 per cent. from 4 to 5 years. No data were available for 11.1 per cent. . . . Eighty-five and two-tenths per cent. were known to have been ill more than three months. Of the 894 chronic heart patients only 29 were ill less than 3 months. The 534 cancer patients had but 33 in the short-term group. The 196 non-pulmonary tuberculosis cases showed but 2." [16]

Nearly half, or 44.6 per cent, were between the ages of fifteen and sixty. Illness of such duration means not only unemployment during the period of hospitalization, but also peculiar difficulty in securing employment after the more severe symptoms of the illness have been allayed. Persons below fifteen or over sixty years of age with chronic ailments are inevitably an economic burden upon relatives or the community.

Perrott and Sydenstricker, in a house-to-house canvass of 12,000 white families in 1933 found "that wage-earning families reduced to poverty during the depression suffered to a greater extent from disabling illness than their more fortunate neighbors. Individuals in families supported by public or private relief exhibited a higher illness-rate than any other group. This finding was true for children as well as for adults, and in general for respiratory and non-respiratory illnesses, with the exception of the communicable diseases of childhood." [17]

Perrott and Griffin in their study of urban relief population in 1934 reported:

"In the F.E.R.A. survey, 21 per cent of all relief persons 16 years of age and over reported handicaps which they considered serious. In the group of wage-earning age, that is, 16 to 64 years, 12 per cent of those who were employed at nonrelief work and 11 per cent of those who were employed on work projects had disabilities, 15 per cent of those who were seeking work, and 27 per cent of those who were not seeking work. . . .

". . . In Dayton, Ohio, the occupational survey included nonrelief as well as relief persons and showed that the prevalence of disabilities among relief persons was three times as great as among nonrelief persons. This differential was associated chiefly with differences in the economic status of the two groups." [18]

[16] Boston Council of Social Agencies—*Report on Chronic Disease in Boston, Mass.: 1927*, p. 18.

[17] Perrott, G. St. J., and Sydenstricker, Edgar—"Causal and Selective Factors in Sickness"; *The American Journal of Sociology*, Vol. XL, No. 6, p. 808, May, 1935.

[18] Perrott, G. St. J., and Griffin, Helen C.—*An Inventory of the Serious Disabilities of the Urban Relief Population*, pp. 234–235; reprinted from *The Milbank Memorial Fund Quarterly*, Vol. XIV, No. 3, July, 1936. See also *National Health*

There is some correlation between certain types of chronic disease and criminalism, though further researches are necessary to distinguish cause and effect. Rector concludes that some crimes against the person are quite definitely an outgrowth of venereal disease. In a survey for the National Society of Penal Information, he states:

"Probably more prison inmates are afflicted with syphilis and gonorrhea than with any other ailments. While accurate statistics were not obtainable for this survey, owing to the lack of any system of record keeping in many prisons, it was found in those prisons where attention is given to this subject that from two to 50 per cent or more of the inmates give a positive Wassermann test indicating that they have had syphilis. . . .

". . . In the U. S. civil prisons examination for these infections was made a routine procedure only after a survey made late in 1926 which showed the high incidence of the disease among the inmates. In this survey 21.8 per cent of the inmates in the U. S. Penitentiary, Atlanta, Ga., were found infected; 18.44 per cent at Leavenworth, Kansas, and 19.5 per cent at McNeil Island, Washington. . . .

"The percentage of infected female prisoners is generally greater than the males. In such states as Kansas and Nebraska where infected females are committed to the reformatory for treatment, the percentage of infection runs high. In one such institution, only four out of 49 females committed were free from venereal disease, giving 92 per cent as infected. . . .

"It is a well-known fact that crimes have been committed by persons who have been infected with syphilis but apparently normal and without criminal tendencies. Business executives with large responsibilities have suddenly impaired the financial standing of their organizations by foolish acts. Railroad engineers have been guilty of running past danger signals and causing loss of life and property. In these instances the actions have been caused apparently by syphilitic cerebrospinal involvement that had lain dormant until manifested in abnormal or criminal acts." [19]

The use of alcohol and drugs by prescription or in self-medication, directly or in the form of patent medicines, to escape the pains or suffering caused by chronic illness may precipitate alcoholic crimes or those associated with drug addiction. Vagrancy and begging are common misdemeanors among the lodging house population or group known as "homeless men," among whom the percentage of chronic disease appears from certain researches to be relatively

Survey 1935–36—Disability from Specific Causes in Relation to Economic Status; Division of Public Health Methods, National Institute of Health, U. S. Public Health Service (Preliminary Reports, The National Health Survey, Sickness and Medical Care Series, Bulletin No. 9), 1938.

[19] Rector, Frank L.—*Health and Medical Service in American Prisons and Reformatories,* pp. 163, 166, and 167; The National Society of Penal Information, Inc., 1929.

high. Irritability, discouragement and other mental attitudes associated with chronic disease appear from case records to be a cause of these misdemeanors in some. Similarly, prostitution in some women may be associated with mental attitudes growing out of chronic disease.

Each chronic disease has one or more characteristic mental attitudes so frequently associated with it that they are listed as symptoms in textbooks on differential diagnosis. Such attitudes as irritability, rage, emotional instability, indifference, or egocentricity engrafted in the personality of the individual may, if uncorrected, materially affect all social relations. Involution may reach the point where the invalid is entirely preoccupied with himself and his aches. Thus many persons as a result of chronic disease alienate associates and employers, and greatly reduce the scope and quality of their social contacts.[20]

Causes of Chronic Disease.—Heredity seldom appears as primary cause of chronic disease. Except for specific types of hereditary malformations, chorea, blindness, deafness, and mental disease of a chronic nature already considered in earlier chapters, few if any of the chronic diseases give evidence of direct transmission. This statement needs qualification, however, because many studies of families in which tuberculosis, cancer, and diabetes, for example, frequently recur have led some specialists to infer that factors or groups of factors producing susceptibility or predisposition may exist in such families. This position is warmly disputed by other specialists, and until further and more careful data have been assembled the question must remain open. There still appears to be no probability of direct transmission though there is a possibility that certain stocks may have constitutional susceptibility to one or more of these diseases. In any individual so far as we know, the native constitution may render him open to the conditions in his development and environment which may produce one or more chronic diseases to which his brother or neighbor, differently constituted, would be relatively immune.

Trauma does not figure largely as a causative factor except in the case of the degenerative diseases, in the form of progressive

---

[20] An excellent group of case histories will be found in Thornton, Janet, in collaboration with Knauth, Marjorie Strauss—*The Social Component in Medical Care: A Study of One Hundred Cases from the Presbyterian Hospital in the City of New York;* Columbia University Press, 1937.

impairment of internal organs through long continued misuse. Internal injuries, through undue strain from heavy lifting or excessive exercise, may lead to impairment of organs and tissues, and to chronic orthopedic difficulties. Hernia is a chronic disease which would fall in this category. Internal injuries through accident or unskilful surgery also belong in the traumatic group.

Toxic factors are not prominent. Yet there are some chronic diseases of the heart and kidneys, as well as cirrhosis of the liver, which are traceable to alcoholism. Several of the industrial poisons produce chronic ailments, as for example lead poisoning in painting, pottery glazing, printing, and the storage battery industry which may produce palsy, convulsions, paralysis, brain disorders, and other lasting illnesses. Benzene fumes in rubber manufacture and many other industries may produce anemia. Chrome poisoning from chromium plating may cause ulcers and permanent damage to the nasal septum. Carbon disulphide in rubber vulcanization may produce paralysis. Turpentine poisoning may cause kidney disorders. Inhalation of industrial dusts over long periods may increase susceptibility to tuberculosis. Manufacture of the phosphorus match causes decomposition (or necrosis) of the jaw bone.[21]

Over thirty industrial disease groups are named in the revisions of the Workmen's Compensation Act of Michigan, made in 1937, and in the Rhode Island revision of 1936.[22]

Several of the chronic diseases are sequelae of acute infectious diseases of childhood or adult life, as for example scarlet fever or measles. Others, such as tuberculosis and the venereal diseases, are known to be transmitted by bacteria. Since in these latter groups of diseases the germs maintain their virulence under some conditions outside of the human body, there is possibility of their transmission not only by direct contact but also indirectly.[23]

[21] Hamilton, Alice—*Industrial Poisons in the United States;* The Macmillan Company, 1925. Armstrong, Barbara Nachtrieb—*Insuring the Essentials*, pp. 202–223; The Macmillan Company, 1932.

[22] Labor Law Information Service, prepared by (Charles F. Sharkey, Chief)— *Occupational-Disease Legislation in the United States, 1936: With Appendix for 1937;* United States Department of Labor, Bureau of Labor Statistics, Bulletin No. 652, Government Printing Office, 1938.

[23] Parran estimates "that half the victims of syphilis are innocently infected." There appears to be abundant evidence of the possibility of transmitting this disease through the use of common drinking utensils, towels, et cetera. Parran, Thomas—"Why Don't We Stamp Out Syphilis?"; *The Reader's Digest*, July,

Another group of chronic diseases, pellagra, scurvy, beriberi, and rickets, develop because of the absence in diet of specific vitamins or food elements. They can be cured in time, if not too far advanced, by proper medication and control of the diet. Diabetes and goiter, and also many chronic digestive and kidney disorders, are in quite different ways related to diet, and cured or aided by its control. Some chronic allergic disorders may prove remediable in the same manner, or by desensitization.

The focal infections of teeth, sinus, tonsils, or other parts of the body resulting in rheumatic heart disorders or arthritic conditions can in varying degrees be prevented, relieved, or cured by removal of the source through dentistry or surgery, and in the case of sinusitis by migration to a dry climate.

Heart disease and rheumatism have been seen to exceed other chronic ailments. Among children a majority of cardiac disorders are rheumatic in origin and a low percentage congenital.[24] Cabot states that the streptococcus which may show itself in the throat (tonsillitis), in the brain (chorea), in the joints (rheumatism), when in the heart produces inflammation of the heart valves or endocarditis.[25] Among young men and those of middle age is found also the syphilitic heart. Among elderly people the arteriosclerotic heart which enlarges and "compensates" because of its loss of elasticity. The nephritic heart is also associated with high blood pressure because the diseased kidney fails to eliminate poisonous waste products in the blood.[26]

Unquestionably also unfortunate habits of thought play some part in developing or aggravating chronic diseases. Worries, frictions, grief, and shock often figure prominently in the precipitation or development of chronic ailments or render minor chronic diseases disabling. The improvement of mental attitudes and of the emo-

1936. Although the germs of venereal disease may retain their virulence outside of the human body for perhaps only an hour or two in dark, moist places, the germs of tuberculosis have been shown by experiments to retain their virulence for over a month in masses of sputum lodged in relatively damp, dark places. Rosenau, Milton J.—*Preventive Medicine and Hygiene*, Chapter III; D. Appleton-Century Company, sixth edition, 1935.

[24] Goodman, Morris, and Prescott, Josephine W.—*Heart Disease among Adolescent School Children of New York City*, pp. 6–8; reprinted from *The Journal of the American Medical Association*, Vol. 103, July 21, 1934.

[25] Cabot, Richard C.—*A Layman's Handbook of Medicine*, p. 68; Houghton Mifflin Company, 1916.

[26] *Ibid.*, pp. 70–73.

tional life is stressed by many competent physicians and medical social workers and may be a leading factor in cure.[27]

Although specific causative factors have been isolated above for convenience in the discussion of the etiology of chronic disease, it is necessary to recognize here as elsewhere that all causation is multiple involving the play of specific environmental influences as well as the above specific causative factors upon an individual so constituted by heredity and by his habits and experience since birth that he shall be responsive.

Prevention and Cure.—The social control of the causative factors just mentioned would go far in the direction of the elimination of chronic disease. General programs for the prevention of needless accidents and disease, and for the control of toxic factors, for social security and the prevention of poverty, covered in later chapters, would contribute to the reduction of cases which grow out of infectious diseases, malnutrition, and accidents. Universal education in personal and mental hygiene, periodic medical and dental examinations for all citizens and their families, improved sanitation, and the elimination of dangerous industrial processes would prevent a still wider group of specific ailments.

Cure is largely dependent upon prompt discovery of ailments in their incipient stages. Where infectious diseases of the venereal or tubercular groups and malnutrition are discovered to have caused illness in one member of a family, it has of late proved highly advantageous to arrange for the examination of all other members of the household, exposed to the infection or subject to the same dietary, in order to prevent the spread of the disease to them. This practice has lately developed in certain progressive communities, and in the case of venereal disease the individual's personal contacts outside of the home have also been sought in order to prevent the establishment of fresh centers of infection.[28]

Victims of the infectious diseases in varying degree require isolation, quarantine, disinfection of premises, and special training with regard to prophylaxis and their social contacts. In all ambulatory cases, the protection of the patient, and the good of society, require periodic check-up by physician or clinic at intervals specified by the physician and rigidly adhered to in order to ascertain the progress

[27] Thornton, Janet—*op. cit.*
[28] Wheeler, Ralph E.—*Epidemiology and the Control of Syphilis;* reprint from *The Milbank Memorial Fund Quarterly,* Vol. XV, No. 1, January, 1937.

of the disease and make possible any needed change in medication, dietary, or labor. If the disease takes an unfavorable turn hospitalization or a surgical operation will in some cases prove necessary. Although these recommendations may seem obvious, the studies of chronic disease so far made would seem to indicate that a very large proportion of persons suffering from chronic disease fail to continue their treatments properly, whether through poverty, indifference, or hopelessness, and thus reduce their own chance of recovery while greatly increasing the social cost of their care.

Perrott has called attention to the implications of the aging population, as follows:

"If we assume no progress in prevention and control, the various causes of ill health will assume different relative importance in years to come, some increasing and some decreasing. For example, by 1980 an increase of 76 per cent may be expected in the total days of disability due to the cardiovascular-renal diseases, 15 per cent in disability due to rheumatism, 15 per cent in digestive diseases, and 22 per cent in accidents; on the other hand, disability due to the acute communicable diseases will decrease by 25 per cent even if no further progress is made toward their control." [29]

The Milbank Conference of 1937 presented the following summary of deliberations on this problem:

"The problems of chronic disease alleviation and prevention are many and complex. The aging of the population will increase the relative importance of these problems in the general disease picture of the nation. Each extension of social benefits tends to uncover disabilities and discomforts which hitherto were suffered in silence.

"Disease processes that underlie most health problems of adult life are characterized by insidious onset and gradual impairment. The attending disability seriously interferes with the usefulness of the individual during his most productive years. Not infrequently life is terminated before the individual has had the opportunity fully to discharge his responsibilities to forbears and offspring.

"The greatest need at the present time is a better understanding of the factors which determine man's physical, psychological, and economic adjustment to his environment. Perhaps in these factors may be found the preventive and remedial measures which may be exploited for the benefit of the individual and society at large.

[29] Discussion by George St. J. Perrott in "Report of Round-Table on Health Problems of Adult Life" by Joseph W. Mountin, M.D., p. 48 of *New Health Frontiers: Proceedings of the Fifteenth Annual Conference of the Milbank Memorial Fund Held on April 29 and 30, 1937, at the New York Academy of Medicine;* Milbank Memorial Fund, 1937.

"Despite the unsatisfactory state of our knowledge as regards many aspects of chronic diseases, it is believed that health agencies should give some consideration to these increasingly important problems of adult life. For some time to come study and experimentation should be the dominant elements in any extension of the health program in this field. Specific measures for the control of syphilis and of tuberculosis, both diseases of adult life, are accepted as important parts of the public health program and generally incorporated in it. The campaign against these two diseases, which constitute major health problems among adults, and for which we have tried measures of prevention and treatment, needs to be intensified and made more effective. The fact that the tuberculosis death rate has been greatly reduced should call for greater rather than less effort in its prevention, for further gains will be more hardly won. And one of the by-products of a sound anti-syphilis campaign may well be a measurable decrease in the mortality from diseases of the circulatory system, a problem which has become the subject of much public concern." [30]

Summary.—Prevention involves (1) increasing specialization on chronic disease by physicians and social workers; (2) progressive mastery of chronic diseases of all types through research—medical and social; (3) accessibility to competent medical examination and prompt treatment by all cases irrespective of income; (4) coördination of the scattered medical and hospital services, now available, into a unified system, and the provision of additional laboratories, hospital beds, clinics, medical social service, et cetera, where needed; (5) education of the public in personal hygiene and nutrition in such a manner as to prevent the faulty behavior habits (excesses or neglect) out of which deterioration often begins; and (6) comprehensive public policies to curb the causative factors of each chronic disease at its specific sources.

QUESTIONS FOR DISCUSSION OR EXAMINATION

1. Compare chronic diseases with other types of handicap with reference to their (a) extent, and (b) prevention.
2. Outline programs for the prevention of (a) the chronic diseases of childhood, (b) the infectious diseases of middle life, and (c) the degenerative diseases of later life.
3. What effects have you observed of chronic illness upon (a) personality and character? (b) upon family life? (c) upon family income? (d) upon social relationships?
4. Submit arguments for and against the provision of complete medical service at public expense to (a) wage-earners, (b) middle class families.

[30] *Ibid.*, pp. 57–58.

PROBLEMS FOR INDIVIDUAL STUDY

1. What records are kept in your state or city of chronic diseases? What measures are necessary to make these records more complete? Why haven't these measures been taken?
2. Outline the history of measures, both public and private, taken in your city or state to combat (a) tuberculosis, or (b) venereal diseases, or (c) rheumatism and heart diseases.
3. What provision is made in your city or state for the care of persons chronically ill? What deficiencies are noted? How can they be overcome?
4. What is, and what should be, the distribution of function and responsibility for chronic diseases (a) between public and private agencies? (b) between Federal, state, and local units of government?
5. Prepare summary and appraisal of health surveys made in some selected city, rural county, district, or state.

SUGGESTIONS FOR SUPPLEMENTARY READINGS

Adair, Frank E.—*Cancer;* J. B. Lippincott Company, 1931.

Baker, S. Josephine—*Child Hygiene;* Harper & Brothers, 1925.

Barker, Lewellys F., and Sprunt, Thomas P.—*The Degenerative Diseases;* Harper & Brothers, 1925.

Bigelow, George H.—*The Cancer Program in Massachusetts;* Williams & Wilkins Company, 1929.

Bigelow, George H., and Lombard, Herbert L.—*Cancer and Other Chronic Diseases in Massachusetts;* Houghton Mifflin Company, 1933.

Boas, Ernst P.—*The Significance of Research in Prevention and Care of Chronic Illness;* Committee on Chronic Illness of the Welfare Council of New York City.

Boas, Ernst P., and Michelson, Nicholas—*The Challenge of Chronic Diseases;* The Macmillan Company, 1929.

Bossard, James H. S.—*Social Change and Social Problems,* Part V; Harper & Brothers, revised edition, 1938.

Boston Council of Social Agencies—*Report on Chronic Disease in Boston, Mass.: 1927;* Boston Council of Social Agencies, c. 1927.

Boyd, Mark F.—*Preventive Medicine;* W. B. Saunders Company, third edition, 1928.

Bruno, Frank J.—*Illness and Dependency;* Committee on the Costs of Medical Care, Miscellaneous Contributions No. 9, March 1, 1931.

Carpenter, Niles—*Hospital Service for Patients of Moderate Means: A Study of Certain American Hospitals;* Committee on the Costs of Medical Care, Publication No. 4, 1930.

Chapman, Frank E.—*Hospital Organization and Management;* The Macmillan Company, 1924.

Coburn, Alvin F.—*The Factor of Infection in the Rheumatic State;* Williams & Wilkins Company, 1931.

Committee on the Costs of Medical Care—*Medical Care for the American People;* University of Chicago Press, 1932.

Craig, Frank A.—*Diseases of Middle Life*, Vols. I and II; F. A. Davis Company, 1926.

Davis, Michael M.—*Clinics, Hospitals and Health Centers;* Harper & Brothers, 1927.

Davis, Michael M.—*Paying Your Sickness Bills;* University of Chicago Press, 1931.

Davis, Michael M.—*Public Medical Services: A Survey of Tax-supported Medical Care in the United States;* University of Chicago Press, 1937.

Davis, Michael M., and Jarrett, Mary C.—*A Health Inventory of New York City;* Welfare Council of New York City, 1929.

Davis, Michael M., and Lehmann, Marcella R.—"Medical Care," *Social Work Year Book 1937;* Russell Sage Foundation, 1937.

Downs, Jean, and Price, Clara R.—*Tuberculosis Control in the Mulberry District of New York City;* reprinted from *The Milbank Memorial Fund Quarterly,* Vol. XV, No. 4, October, 1937.

Dublin, Louis I., and Lotka, Alfred J.—*Twenty-Five Years of Health Progress;* Metropolitan Life Insurance Company, 1937.

Emerson, Haven, director—*The Cleveland Hospital and Health Survey Report,* eleven monographs; The Cleveland Hospital Council, 1920.

Emerson, Haven, Pincus, Sol, and Phillips, Anna C.—*Philadelphia Hospital and Health Survey, 1929;* Philadelphia Hospital and Health Survey Committee, 1930.

Falk, I. S., Klem, Margaret C., and Sinai, Nathan—*The Incidence of Illness and the Receipt and Costs of Medical Care Among Representative Families, Experiences in Twelve Consecutive Months during 1928–1931;* Committee on the Costs of Medical Care, Publication No. 26, University of Chicago Press, 1933.

Gillette, John M., and Reinhardt, James M.—*Current Social Problems,* Part Three; American Book Company, 1937.

Goldwater, S. S.—*The Hospitalization of the Chronically Ill;* Committee on Chronic Illness of the Welfare Council of New York City.

Hamilton, Alice—*Industrial Poisons in the United States;* The Macmillan Company, 1925.

Haslam, J. F. C.—*Recent Advances in Preventive Medicine;* P. Blakiston's Son & Co., Inc., 1930.

Hoffman, Frederick L.—*Some Final Results of the San Francisco Cancer Survey;* Prudential Press, 1929.

Jarrett, Mary C.—*Chronic Illness in New York City,* 2 vols.; published for the Welfare Council of New York City by Columbia University Press, 1933.

Jarrett, Mary C.—*The Care of the Chronically Ill in New York City;* presented to the Hospital Survey for New York by the Committee on Chronic Illness of the Welfare Council of New York City, 1936.

Jarrett, Mary C.—*Report on the First Year's Work of a WPA Project for a Demonstration and Study of Home Care of Chronic Patients in New York City, October, 1935 to October, 1936;* Welfare Council of New York City, 1937.

Lord, Frederick T.—*Diseases of the Bronchi, Lungs, and Pleura;* Lea & Febiger, second edition, revised 1925.

Love, Albert G., and Davenport, Charles B.—*Physical Examination of the*

First Million Draft Recruits: Methods and Results; Government Printing Office, War Department Bulletin No. 11, March, 1919.

Mangold, George B.—*Social Pathology,* Chapter XIII, "Sickness," Chapter XIV, "Care of Disease," and Chapter XV, "Health Promotion"; The Macmillan Company, 1932.

Milbank Memorial Fund—Quarterly Bulletins and Publications.

Mills, Alden B.—*The Extent of Illness and of Physical and Mental Defects Prevailing in the United States;* Committee on the Costs of Medical Care, Publication No. 2, 1929.

Moore, Harry H.—*American Medicine and the People's Health;* D. Appleton and Company, 1927.

Moore, Harry H.—"Health and Medical Practice," Chapter XXI of *Recent Social Trends in the United States,* Vol. II; McGraw-Hill Book Company, Inc., 1933.

Moore, Harry H.—*Public Health in the United States;* Harper & Brothers, 1923.

Muntz, Earl E.—*Urban Sociology,* Part III; The Macmillan Company, 1938.

Nelson, Nels A., and Crain, Gladys L.—*Syphilis, Gonorrhea and the Public Health;* The Macmillan Company, 1938.

Newsholme, Sir Arthur—*Evolution of Preventive Medicine;* Williams & Wilkins Company, 1927.

Newsholme, Sir Arthur—*Medicine and the State;* Williams & Wilkins Company, 1932.

Peebles, Allon—*A Survey of Statistical Data on Medical Facilities in the United States;* Committee on the Costs of Medical Care, Publication No. 3, 1929.

Pemberton, Ralph—*Arthritis and Rheumatoid Conditions;* Lea & Febiger, 1929.

Phelps, Harold A.—*Contemporary Social Problems,* Chapter VII, "Social Hygiene"; Prentice-Hall, Inc., 1932.

Queen, Stuart Alfred, and Mann, Delbert Martin—*Social Pathology,* Part III; Thomas Y. Crowell Company, 1925.

Rosenau, Milton J.—*Preventive Medicine and Hygiene;* D. Appleton-Century Company, sixth edition, 1935.

Schereschewsky, J. W.—*The Course of Cancer Mortality in the Ten Original Registration States for the 21-Year Period 1900–1920;* United States Public Health Service, Public Health Bulletin No. 155, Government Printing Office, June, 1925.

Schmeckebier, Laurence F.—*The Statistical Work of the National Government,* Chapter IX, "Deaths, Diseases, and Accidents"; The Institute for Government Research, The Johns Hopkins Press, 1925.

Sinai, Nathan, and Mills, Alden B.—*A Survey of the Medical Facilities of the City of Philadelphia: 1929: Being in Part a Digest of the Philadelphia Hospital and Health Survey, 1929;* Committee on the Costs of Medical Care, Publication No. 9, July, 1931.

Sydenstricker, Edgar—*Hagerstown Morbidity Studies,* Nos. I–VIII; United States Public Health Service, Reprints 1113, 1116 of 1926; 1134, 1163, 1167, 1172 of 1927; 1225, 1227, 1229 of 1928.

Sydenstricker, Edgar—*Health and Environment;* McGraw-Hill Book Company, Inc., 1933.

Sydenstricker, Edgar—"The Vitality of the American People," Chapter XII of *Recent Social Trends in the United States*, Vol. I; McGraw-Hill Book Company, Inc., 1933.

Thornton, Janet, in collaboration with Knauth, Marjorie Strauss—*The Social Component in Medical Care: A Study of One Hundred Cases from the Presbyterian Hospital in the City of New York;* Columbia University Press, 1937.

Waite, H. H.—*Disease Prevention;* Thomas Y. Crowell Company, 1926.

Wallace, James—*The Providence Health Survey: A Study of the Health Activities and a Study of the Services for Organized Care of the Sick;* American Public Health Association, 1929.

Whipple, George Chandler—*Vital Statistics;* John Wiley & Sons, Inc., 1923.

White House Conference on Child Health and Protection—*The Handicapped Child*, "Internal Conditions," pp. 197–267; The Century Co., 1933.

Wood, Thomas D. (prepared under direction of)—*Health Education;* Report of the Joint Committee on Health Problems in Education of the National Education Association and the American Medical Association, 1924.

Wood, Thomas D., and Rowell, Hugh Grant—*Health Supervision and Medical Inspection of Schools;* W. B. Saunders Company, 1928.

Woodbury, Robert Morse—*Workers' Health and Safety: A Statistical Program;* The Macmillan Company, 1927.

Wyatt, Bernard Langdon—*Chronic Arthritis and Rheumatoid Affections;* Wm. Wood & Co., 1930.

CHAPTER XV

THE SOCIAL CONTROL OF HEREDITY

In the late nineteenth century and the early years of the twentieth there was much concern over what was often termed "hereditary degeneracy." The attention of social workers and governmental agencies had been focused on this problem by Dugdale's study of the Jukes in 1877, and somewhat later (1888) by M'Culloch's study of the Tribe of Ishmael.[1] The rediscovery of the Mendelian laws of heredity at the beginning of the present century led to their wide application to "degenerate" stocks, naively at first, but with increasing refinement of methods and discrimination in more recent years. Since contemporary theories and practices in the social control of heredity have grown out of these earlier studies, it is important to review them briefly before considering measures for the prevention of the birth of the hereditarily unfit.

The Jukes.—When, in 1874, Dugdale was appointed to inspect county jails in New York State he came across in one county several persons among the prisoners who were blood relations. This led him to a careful examination of the family history, leading back to persons who had settled in that county in the early eighteenth century. To avoid any possibility of the identification of the family he gave to them the fictitious name of Jukes. Altogether he studied seven hundred and nine persons, of whom five hundred and forty were of Juke blood and one hundred and sixty-nine of "X" blood, or persons with whom Jukes had married or cohabited. He estimated that at the time of his study there had been altogether some twelve hundred persons descended from the original six sisters of Juke blood.

In each generation, among the seven hundred and nine persons studied, there had been a high percentage of pauperism and criminality. One hundred and eighty persons had received public relief. There had been one hundred and forty criminals and offenders, of

---

[1] Dugdale, Richard L.—*The Jukes;* G. P. Putnam & Sons, 1877. M'Culloch, Oscar C.—"The Tribe of Ishmael: A Study in Social Degradation"; *Proceedings of the National Conference of Charities and Correction*, Fifteenth Annual Session, 1888.

whom sixty were habitual thieves and fifty were common prostitutes. Seven persons had been murdered by Jukes. It was estimated that between 1800 and 1875 the family had cost the state of New York over one million three hundred thousand dollars.[2]

The Tribe of Ishmael.—In the eighteen eighties M'Culloch studied a somewhat similar family in Indiana, reaching about two hundred and fifty separate households. The central family had arrived in Indianapolis about the year 1840. Its founder had married a "half-breed" woman, and three of his sons had mated with three sisters of another pauper family. Through a half century the descendants had lived by stealing, begging, and as gypsies. This group showed rather less of criminality and more of pauperism than the Jukes family. Licentiousness was common in both families.[3]

These studies were assumed to show the hereditary nature of various types of social degradation, criminalism, pauperism, and licentiousness. The influence of environment and parental example upon children was, however, abundantly illustrated in both texts. Although the hereditary nature of degeneracy was freely discussed in this period, the mechanism of heredity was not understood.

The Mendelian Law of Heredity.—Eugenics, the study of the social control of racial qualities, both physical and mental, received the attention of many thinkers since Plato. Galton had published his work on hereditary genius in 1869 and his inquiries into the human faculty in 1883. He used the term "eugenics" in the latter volume.[4]

Meanwhile, in the eighteen sixties, an Austrian monk, Gregor Johann Mendel, by cross breeding garden peas discovered formulae of heredity which remained in obscurity until their rediscovery at the beginning of the present century. In essence the Mendelian law of heredity is based upon the conception of organisms as collections of separate units which remain units throughout the generations. Certain such "unit characters" among plants were found to be dwarfism, smoothness of stem, and color of flowers or seeds. Mendel had found that by crossing dwarf peas with tall the succeeding

[2] Dugdale, Richard L.—*ibid.*

[3] M'Culloch, Oscar C.—*op. cit.*

[4] Galton, Francis—*Hereditary Genius: an Inquiry into Its Laws and Consequences;* Macmillan and Co., Limited, 1869: *English Men of Science: Their Nature and Nurture;* Macmillan and Co., Limited, 1874: *Inquiries into Human Faculty and Its Development;* Macmillan and Co., Limited, 1883: *Record of Family Faculties;* Macmillan and Co., Limited, 1884: *Natural Inheritance;* Macmillan and Co., Limited, 1889: *Eugenics: Its Definition, Scope, and Aims* (Sociological Society Papers, Vols. I and II); 1905.

generation would all be tall. Tallness was termed a dominant character and dwarfism recessive. He found, however, that self-fertilization of the second generation produced one-fourth with the recessive character of dwarfism. After years of painstaking research he arrived at the formulae: Parent stock with the dominant character mated with dominants produce dominants. DD x DD ∞ DD. Recessives similarly breed true. RR x RR ∞ RR. Hybrids are produced from the mating of one parent with the dominant character and the other, recessive. Hybrids, though appearing normal, produce in the ratio of one dominant to two hybrids and one recessive. DR x DR ∞ DD + 2 DR + RR. The mating of hybrids with dominants produces half dominants and half hybrids. DD x DR ∞ DD + DR. The mating of hybrids with recessives produces half hybrids and half recessives. DR x RR ∞ DR + RR.

"In brief the 'Mendelian Law of Alternative Inheritance' or of hereditary 'splitting' consists of the following principles:

"(a) *The Principle of Unit Characters.* The heritage of an organism may be analyzed into a number of characters which are not further divisible; these are the so-called 'unit characters' (de Vries).

"(b) *The Principle of Dominance.* When contrasting unit characters are present in the parents they do not as a rule blend in the offspring, but one is dominant and usually appears fully developed, while the other is recessive and temporarily drops out of sight.

"(c) *The Principle of Segregation.* Every individual germ cell is 'pure' with respect to any given unit character, even though it come from an 'impure' or hybrid parent. In the germ cells of hybrids there is a separation of the determiners of contrasting characters so that different kinds of germ cells are produced, each of which is pure with regard to any given unit character. This is the principle of segregation of unit characters, or of the 'purity' of the germ cells. Every sexually produced individual is a double being, double in every cell, one-half of its determiners having been derived from the male and the other half from the female sex cell. This double set of determiners again becomes single in the formation of the germ cells only once more to become double when the germ cells unite in fertilization." [5]

Early Studies of Heredity of Feeblemindedness.—A study of over three hundred families represented by children in the training school for feebleminded at Vineland, New Jersey, was published by Goddard in 1914.[6] Direct ancestry and siblings of each generation

[5] Conklin, Edwin Grant—*Heredity and Environment in the Development of Men*, p. 99; Princeton University Press, revised fifth edition, 1923.

[6] Goddard, Henry Herbert—*Feeble-mindedness: Its Causes and Consequences;* The Macmillan Company, 1914. This study was previously discussed in Chapter VI.

were examined as far back as records could be found. Feeblemindedness was found by the author to be hereditary in half the cases examined and possibly hereditary in an additional twenty per cent. Where types of mating could be ascertained feeblemindedness appeared to occur in the family histories like a true Mendelian recessive to normality. Kohs, analyzing Goddard's data, submitted the following table to justify this statement:

HEREDITY OF FEEBLEMINDEDNESS

(Mendelian)

Type of Mating [a]	Number of Matings	Total Offspring	Dead and Mentality Unde- termined	Feebleminded Offspring		Normal Offspring	
				Actual Findings	Theoretical Expectation	Actual Findings	Theoretical Expectation
FF–FF	144	749	267	476	482	6	none
FF–NF	122	698	327	193	185½	178	185½
FF–NN	18	66	32	none	none	34	34
NF–NF	33	212	66	39	36½	107	109½
NF–NN	7	27	4	none	none	23	23
Totals	324	1,752	696	708	704	348	352

[a] "FF indicates an individual who is feeble-minded. None of the sperm or egg cells produced possess the determiner or the combination of determiners or factors which makes for normal-mindedness. NF represents a normal individual, half of whose germ cells are capable of transmitting normality, and half not. NN represents a normal individual, all of whose germ cells transmit the potentiality for normal mental development."

"The close correspondence between actual findings and theoretical expectation in the above table is most remarkable and strongly confirms the assumption that feeble-mindedness is a distinct hereditable condition. On the one hand, 708 feeble-minded individuals were found, when one would theoretically expect 704, and on the other hand, 348 normals were found, when one would theoretically expect 352. No controlled experiments could yield any greater conformity between accepted theory and actual results." [7]

The findings are commonly criticized on the grounds that feeble-mindedness could not be determined by clinical tests for the generations no longer living, but solely by their reputation and institutional history. If the mental condition could have been determined for the six hundred and ninety-six persons in the category "dead and mentally undetermined" the "actual findings" with regard to heredity might have diverged widely from the "theoretical expectation."

[7] Kohs, Samuel C.—"The Borderlines of Mental Deficiency," p. 282; *Proceedings of the National Conference of Charities and Correction*, 1916.

The Kallikaks.—When, in 1912, Goddard published his study termed *The Kallikak Family* he traced in detail a stock in which feeblemindedness had occurred for many generations. The degenerate family was stated to be the result of a casual mating between a normal man of distinguished antecedents and a feebleminded woman. The record proceeds to show that the male ancestor subsequently married a normal woman of good family and produced descendants notable for their performance in public and professional life. From the casual mating with the feebleminded woman 480 descendants were traced of whom the investigators pronounced 143 mentally deficient, 3 epileptic, and 43 normal. The rest were of unknown mentality. Their social history showed 24 confirmed alcoholics, 3 criminals, 33 sexually immoral, and 8 keepers of houses of ill fame.[8]

This study is usually criticized today on the grounds that the paternity of the feebleminded child born to the feebleminded female ancestor cannot be definitely determined. If Martin Kallikak was the father of the child that bore his name, feeblemindedness must have operated as a dominant rather than a recessive character. The paternity of the offspring of those of the feebleminded who are promiscuous in their sexual habits is difficult and often impossible to ascertain even in living generations. Ascription of paternity in past generations contains much possibility of error. Moreover, even the most careful investigator cannot determine from available records, with scientific accuracy, whether or not it was mental defect in past generations which produced the pauperism, criminality, or other peculiarities of behavior of which there remains documentary evidence. Goddard's investigations of the Kallikaks and the Vineland families were of scientific value primarily for their data on the living generations, which could be examined and tested. Their indication of the prevalence of social inadequacies, throughout many earlier generations, within these same families is, however, significant.

The Jukes in 1915.—When Dugdale made his study of the Jukes in the eighteen seventies, mental tests had not been developed. Rediscovery of Dugdale's list of the family names borne by the Jukes led to a reëxamination of the data, and a detailed study of the subsequent generations was made by Arthur H. Estabrook of the

[8] Goddard, Henry Herbert—*The Kallikak Family;* The Macmillan Company, 1912.

Eugenics Record Office. Altogether the case histories of 2,820 people were investigated by Estabrook and his associates, including those previously considered by Dugdale. Of these, 2,094 were of Juke blood, and 726 were persons with whom members of the Juke family had married or mated. The text comprises data for each individual of each generation.[9]

When this study was published in 1916 there were 1,258 living members of the Juke family, residing in twenty states and in Canada. A few were prosperous and respected citizens. Many more were steady workers and doing fairly well. But nearly half were found to be socially inadequate. Nine per cent of the matings were consanguineous (as contrasted with 22 per cent among the Nams) [10] thus supplying determiners for Jukes traits from both parents. Among the female Jukes of marriageable age 51 per cent were classified as having been prostitutes, which is not an appreciable decrease in the licentiousness characteristic of the family in Dugdale's earlier study.[11]

Estabrook concludes that half of the Jukes were and are feeble-minded. He estimates the loss to society caused by their mental deficiency, crime, prostitution, syphilis, and pauperism at over two million dollars. He found that "all of the Juke criminals were feeble-minded," and that "pauperism is an indication of weakness, physical or mental." On the other hand he noted that "removal of Jukes from their original habitat to new regions is beneficial to the stock *itself*, as better social pressure is brought to bear on them and there is a chance of mating into better families." It was found also that "one in four of the Jukes is improved socially by care in Children's Institutions," but that penal institutions have little beneficial influence upon persons of defective mentality. Social neglect is evidenced by the fact that "out of approximately 600 living feeble-minded and epileptic Jukes, there are now only 3 in custodial care." [12] The highly detailed evidence from Estabrook's restudy of the Jukes, in which all statements are carefully qualified, makes it seem probable that in this particular family feeblemindedness is in some manner hereditary and that criminalism and pauperism as

[9] Estabrook, Arthur H.—*The Jukes in 1915;* Carnegie Institution of Washington, 1916.

[10] Estabrook, Arthur H., and Davenport, Charles B.—*The Nam Family: A Study in Cacogenics;* Eugenics Record Office, Cold Spring Harbor, N. Y., Memoir No. 2, 1912.

[11] Estabrook, Arthur H.—*The Jukes in 1915,* p. 56.

[12] *Ibid.,* p. 85.

such are not. Licentiousness was thought by Estabrook to be hereditary: a finding not confirmed; for family traditions, habits, and mores
might exert upon the younger generations, defective in intelligence,
sufficient influence to account for their social inadequacies and
types of misbehavior.

Dwellers in the Vale of Siddem.—Other researches made in
the second decade of this century found many types of degeneracy of
possibly hereditary origin. The Dwellers in the Vale of Siddem—who
like the Jukes and Nams of New York, the Tribe of Ishmael in Indiana, the Kallikaks of New Jersey, and a long list of other degenerate familes studied, were of native stock—had settled in Minnesota
over a century ago in a valley where many lived by lawless practices
seldom disturbed by the police. Of 1,619 residents of this valley
(excluding 892 unclassified) 156 were normal, 199 feebleminded, 34
insane, 15 epileptic, 96 nervous, 24 migrainous, 12 paralyzed, 47
tubercular, 134 alcoholic, 125 sexually immoral, 15 criminalistic,
87 had died in infancy, 27 died young, and 17 miscarriages are
recorded. The above classifications overlap, for the same individual
might be listed under several headings. The 15 criminals had mostly
been guilty of felony, as misdemeanors "more often passed unnoticed." Of the 199 persons known to be mentally defective "only
about five per cent. have been cared for in the institution for the
feeble-minded or by any sort of supervision or guardianship!" [13]

Of the fourteen children of the epileptic Corey and the insane
Tildy Yak, nine were insane and one feebleminded. In the next
generation there were ten who were feebleminded, two of whom were
also alcoholic and one a migrainous epileptic. Only two were known
to be normal.[14] It is sometimes queried whether it is not "degeneracy" which is inherited rather than feeblemindedness. The discovery of the role of heredity is, however, rendered difficult if not
impossible among such degenerates by the frequency of promiscuity.
Half the heredity of each child remains in doubt.

Biological versus "Social" Heredity.—Even if there had been
much more detailed analysis of individual case histories it would be
impossible still to make sharp distinctions between biological and
social heredity as causes of the condition and behavior of persons
born within these groups. Many a daughter in becoming a prostitute

---

[13] Rogers, A. C., and Merrill, Maud A.—*Dwellers in the Vale of Siddem*, pp. 76–
79; Richard G. Badger, The Gorham Press, 1919.
[14] *Ibid.*, pp. 27–28.

has either imitated her own mother or been trained by her mother for prostitution. Boys who steal may have imitated their fathers or other relatives, or may have been commanded to steal on the threat of a beating if unsuccessful. Nevertheless, heredity may be assumed to play some part in the production of handicap wherever feeble-mindedness, mental disease, or epilepsy recur in generation after generation.[15]

Changing Concepts of Human Heredity.—Many of the family studies in the first fifteen years of this century concluded that feeble-mindedness is inherited as a recessive unit character according to the Mendelian law of heredity. Later researches noting occasional births of normal children to feebleminded parents of "tainted" stock called attention to the possibility that there might be more than one type of hereditary feeblemindedness, each recessive to normality. The research among the Hill Folk suggested that feeblemindedness was not a unit character but a composite term for traits which might take various forms. Thus: "We may find one case of feebleminded-ness wherein the individual is cruel and keen in the pursuit of mis-chief, but unable to learn, and another case in which he is kind and learns quite readily, but is shiftless and devoid of judgment and the ability to apply his knowledge." [16] English studies, however, finding mental defectives among the offspring of insane or epileptic parents were inclined to attribute hereditary feeblemindedness to abnormal-ity in the germ plasm.

The following hypotheses are found in recent works in this field: that mental defect is due (1) to some lack in the germ plasm; or (2) to injury to the germ plasm; or (3) to a number of factors rather than one. In elaboration of the third hypothesis, it may be said that the recent postulate of the role of genes in human inheritance presup-poses the possibility of an almost infinite range of different combina-tions. Chance may determine their combination. Hundreds of genes may be necessary to make up any given individual's mentality —even a defective mentality.

Modern genetics recognizes that the germ cells from each parent, or gametes, in uniting to form a new single cell, or zygote, contain a number of rod-shaped parts termed chromosomes. Of the forty-

[15] See, however, Case, Irene, and Lewis, Kate—"Environment as a Factor in Feeblemindedness"; *American Journal of Sociology*, March, 1918.

[16] Danielson, Florence H., and Davenport, Charles B.—*The Hill Folk: Report on a Rural Community of Hereditary Defectives*, p. 9; Eugenics Record Office, Cold Spring Harbor, N. Y., Memoir No. 1, 1912.

eight chromosomes in the nucleus of such new cell, twenty-four have come from each parent, contained in the sperm and ovum. In the zygote one chromosome of each of the twenty-four pairs has come from each parent. The chromosomes appear to be the bearers of heredity. Each chromosome, according to postulate, contains many submicroscopic particles termed genes, each pair of genes being derived one from each parent. Conceivably mental deficiency might be determined by a governing or dominant gene or by a combination of genes.[17]

Heredity and Mental Disease.—Researches in the inheritance of mental abnormalities show much the same history. Earlier genetic studies dealt with insanity as if it comprised all mental diseases and as if their origin was unitary. Subsequently the Mendelian theory was tested with reference to specific mental disorders, after eliminating traumatic, toxic, and syphilitic types. Rosanoff and Orr, for example, examined large numbers of cases of insanity in a New York State hospital and stated that they found evidence, among 1,097 offspring of 206 matings, that mental disease behaved like a Mendelian recessive.[18]

Myerson, after a study of 1,547 cases at Taunton Hospital, together with a survey of the literature, arrived at the following conclusions concerning the vertical transmission of certain mental diseases:

"1. That the paranoid diseases tend to paranoid states, perhaps finally to dementia praecox states.

"2. That the manic-melancholic diseases are in the main followed by manic melancholic diseases, but in a certain number, especially of doubtful cases by dementia praecox. . . .

"3. That the involutional and senile state if paranoid, trend towards paranoid states and dementia praecox.

"4. That the manic-depressive states of involution and senium trend towards manic-depressive and dementia praecox, especially the latter.

"5. That dementia praecox in an ancestor trends towards dementia praecox in the descendants with a certain scattering incidence of imbecility. This imbecility seems to me to be in part at least of the Kraepelinian congenital or very early dementia praecox.

[17] Theories of the inheritance of mental deficiency are discussed in Chapters V and X of Davies, Stanley Powell—*Social Control of the Mentally Deficient;* Thomas Y. Crowell Company, 1930.

[18] Rosanoff, A. J., and Orr, Florence I.—*A Study of Heredity of Insanity in the Light of the Mendelian Theory;* Eugenics Record Office, Cold Spring Harbor, N. Y., Bulletin No. 5, 1911.

"6. Neither for organic disease or alcoholic disease can anything definite be said. Wherever good histories are obtained other and more definite psychopathic factors are found. . . .

"Paranoid characters remain very persistent, and so do manic-depressive characters even though a certain number of cases follow this drift. This may be stated, that when the disease gets worse from generation to generation it ends in dementia praecox, but this is not always the case and there must be a huge number of mild cases of mental disease in the descendants of the insane, who represent an upward trend, a recovery trend. Rare indeed is that mingling of stocks whereby a mental disease persists unaltered for more than two generations." [19]

It is now apparent that insanity is not a single simple defect inherited according to Mendelian law, but rather that there are many types of mental disease some few of which are inheritable. Of these Castle lists dementia praecox and Huntington's chorea.[20] Myerson though naming other possibilities is critical of current theories of heredity.[21] The fact of inheritance is widely accepted. The method and incidence of mental inheritance clearly require further research.

Heredity and Epilepsy.—Some types of epilepsy are also presumably hereditary. The early studies of Davenport and Weeks [22] as well as field studies, such as *Dwellers in the Vale of Siddem*,[23] reflected the simple assumptions of their period. Occasional association of epilepsies with insanity, feeblemindedness, and alcoholism were also uncovered. Thus Brown's Ohio study, previously mentioned, which followed 36 family histories in which there were 111 epileptics, covered altogether 4,792 persons, among whom were 51 psychotics, and 17 mental defectives. Of the 36 patients, whose family histories constituted this study, 64 per cent had epileptic relatives, and 78 per cent had relatives with a psychosis; 25 per cent had mentally deficient relatives; all but 11 per cent had one or more relatives who were epileptic, insane, or mentally deficient.[24] Until epilepsy is

---

[19] Myerson, Abraham—*The Inheritance of Mental Diseases*, pp. 222–223; Williams & Wilkins Company, 1925.

[20] Castle, W. E.—*Genetics and Eugenics*, p. 379; Harvard University Press, fourth edition, 1930.

[21] Myerson, Abraham—*op. cit.*

[22] Davenport, Charles B., and Weeks, David F.—*A First Study of Inheritance in Epilepsy;* Eugenics Record Office, Cold Spring Harbor, N. Y., Bulletin No. 4, 1911.

[23] Rogers, A. C., and Merrill, Maud A.—*op. cit.*

[24] Brown, Ralph R.—*A Study of the Mental and Physical Traits of the Relatives of Epileptics;* reprinted from *The Journal of Applied Psychology*, Vol. XIV, No. 6, December, 1930.

broken down into clearly defined subcategories which can be traced in field studies as well as in the hospital, it will be impossible to isolate the type or types which are hereditary. Meanwhile, it is reasonable to assume that inheritance plays a role in the causation of a significant but uncertain percentage of epilepsy.

Hereditary Physical Defects.—In addition to the mental defects and diseases, a small percentage of blindness, and a third of all cases of deafness also are apparently transmitted.[25] There are some types of hereditary deformity or physical abnormality so pronounced as to reduce the employability of their victims and thus produce handicaps. Albinism, which is also associated with limited vision, is one example of such abnormality. Haemophilia, or free bleeding, is another. Their victims are, however, fortunately exceedingly few. Serious congenital deformities of hereditary origin are numerically insignificant in comparison with the transmitted types of feeblemindedness or mental disease.

The Predicament of Eugenics.—The difficulties of determining the hereditary nature of any human defect have been shown to be great. (1) The mental condition of former generations cannot be ascertained from the records of their illnesses, their reputations, or evidences of dullness, shiftlessness, or rage. Differential diagnosis is becoming increasingly exact. Hence accurate genetic studies must begin with living generations. (2) Human beings cannot be experimented upon like rabbits and guinea pigs, so both heredity and environing conditions are seldom under control. There is often serious doubt as to the paternity of degenerate offspring in spite of the assertions of the mother—whether or not she may be feebleminded—thus making half of the heredity always open to question. (3) Most difficult of all, however, is the fact that human generations are so long. It will take a century of close study to assemble accurate scientific data on as few as six generations. (4) Meanwhile the complexity of human inheritance has been made increasingly apparent as the simple formulae of the Mendelian law of heredity have been modified in their application to human inheritance by recent findings.

Social Control of Heredity.—The gross number of cases of handicap presumably ascribable to heredity is large. The devices through which the state may prevent undesirable births comprise (1) euthanasia, (2) education, (3) marriage laws, (4) facilitation of birth control, (5) segregation, and (6) sterilization. Each of these measures,

[25] See Chapters IX, X, and XI.

to be wholly efficient, must be preceded by competent scientific research and accompanied by registration of cases conducted in such a manner as to locate presumptive hereditary defects.

Euthanasia.—From time to time arguments are offered in the public press and in scientific journals for the elimination of some group of the unfit by means of euthanasia or "mercy killing." Most frequently this is urged for "monstrous births," grossly misshapen or idiotic infants, or for persons suffering from incurable and agonizing illness. But in its extreme form, as expressed by McKim, it would apply to virtually all types of hereditary and incurable handicap. McKim states his position as follows:

> "I would limit the multiplication of the organically weak and the organically vicious, restricting the plan, however, to the *very* weak and the *very* vicious *who fall into the hands of the State, for maintenance, reformation, or punishment.* The surest, the simplest, the kindest, and most humane means for preventing reproduction among those whom we deem unworthy of this high privilege, is a *gentle, painless death;* and this should be administered not as a punishment, but as an expression of enlightened pity for the victims— too defective by nature to find true happiness in life—and as a duty toward the community and toward our own offspring. . . .
>
> "The painless extinction of these lives would present no practical difficulty: in carbonic acid gas we have an agent which would instantaneously fulfil the need." [26]

Proponents of euthanasia commonly point out not only that the state now takes the lives of certain felons through capital punishment, but also indirectly causes loss of lives of persons physically and mentally fit when it drafts them for military service and engages them in either defensive or offensive warfare. It may be added that by indirection the state is responsible for additional deaths through inadequate or poorly enforced legislation to curb preventable disease or accident.

Few scientists today seriously advocate euthanasia as a means to the social control of heredity. Its opponents may argue (1) on Christian grounds— "thou shalt not kill"—and deplore both capital punishment and wars as anachronisms and uncivilized. Commonly also it is argued (2) that some of the handicaps deemed incurable at the beginning of this century have since proved curable. Euthanasia would almost inevitably destroy some who if allowed to live, might be

[26] McKim, W. Duncan—*Heredity and Human Progress,* pp. 188 and 193; G. P. Putnam's Sons, 1900.

cured or helped through the progress of medicine and surgery. (3) The handicapped provide experimental material through which, with no harm to the patient, science continuously makes discoveries of importance both to the patients and to the normal population. (4) Euthanasia does violence to our nobler sentiments—of considerateness, mercy, altruism, won with difficulty in the most recent centuries of human progress. In the words of Hobhouse, "The 'right to live' is a consequence of the ethics of personality and is not recognized by the savage." [27] (5) Destruction of the hereditary handicapped is not necessary to eugenics because their breeding can be prevented through segregation or sterilization.

Education.—Popular education in the discoveries of human biology and heredity is doubtless desirable at all times. When, however, it comes to advising citizens upon mating, infinite pains should be taken to make all necessary qualifications of statement, and to express reasonable doubts. Presumably, if this were done, certain cacogenic matings among persons who are themselves mentally normal but carriers of hereditary defects might be prevented by clinical advice. The same would be true of persons potential to the transmission of hereditary blindness, deafness, or physical deformity. On the other hand, a majority of applicants at the clinic could have their minds put at rest by assurance that the "taint" they fear presumably is not hereditary, or that mating is possible for them if voluntary sterilization or other reasonable precautions are taken to prevent offspring. It should be borne in mind, however, that eugenics is a rapidly developing science in which each decade sees old theories discarded and new theories added to its mass of accepted principles. Its findings are slow to reach the general population. If theories honestly held a generation ago had at that time been forced upon the public through education, marriage laws, or forced sterilization, much needless hardship might have occurred. Obviously no one can tell whether equal strides will be made by this science in the next generation or which theories now held will later be disproved.

Marriage Laws.—Up to the present marriage laws have accomplished little as a device to prevent the birth of undesirables. First, because the state laws in operation restrict only the matings of persons who are themselves feebleminded or actively insane, instead

---

[27] Hobhouse, L. T.—*Morals in Evolution*, p. 339; Henry Holt and Company, fourth edition, 1923.

of covering also normal persons who are carriers of these taints. Second, because offspring are possible from extramarital sex relationships. And third, because the office issuing the marriage license, and the persons performing or witnessing the ceremony, are supplied neither with knowledge of the laws of heredity nor adequate data concerning the heredity of the applicants.

If it were possible to extend marriage laws to cover carriers of hereditary defect, and if the approval of a competent bureau of specialists in eugenics following adequate analysis of each applicant and his heredity could be required before the granting of a marriage license, conceivably many undesirable matings could be prevented. In a democracy such laws would be deemed an unwarrantable interference with personal liberty, prior at least to the remote period in which there may be universal education in sound eugenics.

Birth Control.—The spread of authentic information on the subject of birth control would unquestionably lead to some reduction of handicap among families which would otherwise have defective children. But knowledge of the means to birth control is least likely to be applied efficiently by the largest group of the hereditarily handicapped—the feebleminded and the marginal group "endowed" with subnormal intelligence. Legalization of responsible instruction by medical clinics and medical officials of institutions and public relief staffs throughout our forty-eight states in the methods of birth control would, however, serve not only to prevent too numerous progeny among the normal but would also prevent many an unfortunate birth and consequent heartbreak in families with hereditary types of insanity, blindness, deafness, and deformity. Effectiveness in this measure is of course dependent upon the availability of scientific research with regard to the history of the transmission of the presumptive hereditary defect in such families. The facilitation of competent instruction in birth control is one of the more important means towards prevention of the transmission of hereditary defects among persons who are themselves normal but carriers.[28]

Segregation.—At present the most general device for the prevention of procreation among the hereditarily unfit is segregation.

[28] Himes, Norman E.—*Medical History of Contraception;* Williams & Wilkins Company, 1936. Robinson, Caroline Hadley—*Seventy Birth Control Clinics;* Williams & Wilkins Company, 1930. *Medical Aspects of Human Fertility;* National Committee on Maternal Health, Inc., 1932.

It is exceedingly costly because it involves public care of female cases throughout the adolescent and adult years until the turn of life is reached, at costs ranging from $200 to $500 or more per person per year. For males it may involve institutional care for life. Actually, relatively few cases of hereditary defectiveness are under such continuous supervision today. Idiots and most imbeciles do not find mates even when not under institutional care. It is the large group of morons with a sprinkling of high grade imbeciles, and the much larger group of normal persons who are carriers, that are mainly responsible for the perpetuation of hereditary mental defectiveness. Public institutions of many types, whether almshouses, prisons, hospitals, or schools, reach a portion of the hereditary defectives, physical and mental, for brief periods. If detailed scientific examination were made of the heredity of all such institutional cases it is possible on grounds of social protection that all save those who are themselves normal (though carriers of the defect) could be permanently detained. This, however, would be a colossal public burden and in many instances would be far from a desirable procedure, in view of the fact that most handicapped persons are harmless when at home if properly trained, and because also there are simple and inexpensive means available to protect society from the birth of their potential defective offspring.

Sterilization.—The least expensive means of social control of heredity is sterilization. It has been legalized in twenty-nine American states, [29] as well as in Denmark, Esthonia, Finland, Germany, Norway, Sweden, and in parts of Canada, Mexico, and Switzerland. Sterilization is accomplished by means of a relatively simple surgical operation which severs and seals the tubes through which the ova or spermatozoa pass. The patient is not unsexed by this operation. Altogether 27,869 sterilizations under state laws have been performed in public institutions within the United States to January 1, 1938. [30] Of these there were 12,180 in California; 2,916 in Virginia; 1,915 in Kansas; 1,815 in Michigan; 1,459 in

[29] Sterilization laws are in force in the following twenty-nine American states: Alabama, Arizona, California, Connecticut, Delaware, Georgia, Idaho, Indiana, Iowa, Kansas, Maine, Michigan, Minnesota, Mississippi, Montana, Nebraska, New Hampshire, North Carolina, North Dakota, Oklahoma, Oregon, South Carolina, South Dakota, Utah, Vermont, Virginia, Washington, West Virginia, and Wisconsin.

[30] *Human Sterilization Today;* Human Betterment Foundation, Pasadena, California [1938].

Minnesota; 1,218 in Oregon; and the remainder distributed among twenty-three other states.

The legality of compulsory sterilization under proper safeguards and by state authority was upheld in 1927 by the United States Supreme Court in the case of *Buck vs. Bell*.[31] The Human Betterment Foundation estimates on the basis of California experience that by this practice of sterilizing approximately one-half of the feebleminded before they have been paroled from the institution and about one in six of the insane, a saving has been effected which exceeds $2,000,000 yearly in that state alone.[32] Meanwhile the paroled defectives have been able to live normally and have escaped the burden of families which with their meager incomes they would in most instances be unable to support. The state is spared the economic and social cost of children who might otherwise be brought up incompetently by feebleminded parents, and of the other burdens which a new generation of defectives from this source would entail.

Important though such legal sterilization may be, it can prevent only a small percentage of undesirable births. Most of the hereditary feebleminded come from moron parents who may never be institutional cases or from normal persons who are carriers. Most other hereditary handicaps occur in families in which parents are of normal mentality. Prevention in these latter groups can be accomplished only by education, voluntary sterilization, or birth control.

The Committee of the American Neurological Association for the Investigation of Eugenical Sterilization recommended in 1936 that any law concerning sterilization be voluntary rather than compulsory, and applicable not only to patients in state institutions but also to those in private institutions and at large in the community. Such selective sterilization is to be considered in cases of the following diseases: (1) Huntington's chorea, hereditary optic atrophy, familial cases of Friedreich's ataxia, and certain other disabling degenerative diseases recognized to be hereditary; (2) feeblemindedness of familial type; (3) dementia praecox (schizo-

---

[31] The decision was handed down on May 18, 1927. The opinion of the United States Supreme Court delivered on May 2, 1927, by Mr. Justice Holmes includes the following statement: "It is better for all the world, if instead of waiting to execute degenerate offspring for crime, or to let them starve for their imbecility, society can prevent those who are manifestly unfit from continuing their kind. The principle that sustains compulsory vaccination is broad enough to cover the cutting of the Fallopian tubes. . . . Three generations of imbeciles are enough." Davies, Stanley Powell—*op. cit.*, pp. 112–113.

[32] *Human Sterilization Today*, p. 4.

phrenia); (4) manic-depressive psychosis; (5) epilepsy. This admirable study is well supported by evidence.[33]

The controversy between advocates of compulsory sterilization and those who would place sterilization solely on a voluntary basis is acute. Its compulsory application is urged (1) on the grounds that society must protect itself from undesirable births or they will in time outnumber eugenic births. Many but not all of the studies of degenerate families and of family histories of institution inmates show fertility rates higher than the average or higher than those among the more gifted or better educated population.[34] (2) Compulsion makes possible sterilization of persons who would not avail themselves of the opportunity to protect themselves and society by undergoing a voluntary operation. (3) Compulsion may be safeguarded by limiting the application of the law to cases of feeblemindedness or insanity in public institutions, hospitals, colonies, or prisons, and by requiring review of the hereditary nature of each defect by a competent committee of eugenists before the operation is ordered. (4) California experience is reported to show that sterilization, though freeing the individual of one of the possible consequences of illicit sex relationships, does not increase sexual promiscuity, preclude normal sex relationships, nor harm the patient in any way. (5) Compulsory sterilization reduces institutional costs by making segregation for eugenic reasons unnecessary, thus permitting the restoration of the patient to the community after his training or cure make that possible. (6) The patient's interests can be safeguarded and his social restoration facilitated by means of parole under supervision and where necessary by repeated visits to outpatient clinics.

Advocates of voluntary sterilization (1) fear that compulsory operations will be applied in many states for other than eugenic

[33] Committee of the American Neurological Association for the Investigation of Eugenical Sterilization (Abraham Myerson, James B. Ayer, Tracy J. Putnam, Clyde E. Keeler, and Leo Alexander)—*Eugenical Sterilization: A Reorientation of the Problem*, pp. 179–181; The Macmillan Company, 1936.

[34] This position is, however, warmly disputed. For a convenient summary of data see *ibid.*, pp. 24–58. Although one can agree with Notestein and others that the "lower classes increase more rapidly than the upper" the persons with low income or humble condition should not be confused with the biologically unfit. See Notestein, Frank W.—"The Differential Rate of Increase among the Social Classes of the American Population"; *Social Forces*, Vol. XII, No. 1, October, 1933, and *The Relation of Social Status to the Fertility of Native-Born Married Women in the United States*, reprinted from *Problems of Population* (edited by G. H. L. F. Pitt-Rivers); George Allen & Unwin Ltd.

purposes to the disadvantage of the patient. The operation once performed cannot always be undone—yet it may be performed in error. (2) They consider that too little is yet known about human heredity and about the heredity of individual cases to warrant many of the operations performed. (3) They note how markedly the conceptions regarding human heredity have changed within the past generation and anticipate equal advances and changes of judgment of specialists in coming generations. (4) Voluntary sterilization, if accompanied by careful eugenic training among adults and by the provision of accessible and competent clinics, may be made to reach the noninstitutional cases of defect and the still larger group of normal persons who are carriers of hereditary defect. It may thus protect the racial stock as well as it would be protected by compulsory sterilization. (5) Compulsory sterilization would involve an unwarrantable invasion of personal liberty if applied to persons of normal mentality. Under present conditions it could not be justified for normal carriers of mental defect or abnormality since careful outbreeding on their part, or birth control in case of inbreeding, would prevent defective offspring. Similarly sterilization for the mentally normal blind, deaf, or deformed of hereditary strains should be voluntary rather than compulsory, since these groups can readily be taught how to avoid perpetuation of their hereditary defect.

Heredity and Individualization in Treatment.—The uniqueness of the individual is increasingly recognized as one of the major points of attack in the overcoming of handicaps and incapacities. It is apparent that measures for any handicapped group must for effectiveness be adapted to individual variations, peculiarities, interests, needs, and the individual's unique social context as represented by his home, family, and associations.

Many attitudes and habits with roots deep in the individual's heredity require change. Handicaps cannot be eliminated until each of the victims and their parents and children are reached, studied, and understood. The conditions of their disabilities, the causes so far as ascertainable, the influences of their daily associations and environment are significant, as well as the interests, ambitions, and needs, fancied or actual, of each case. Lasting amelioration of the condition of any individual is largely dependent upon intelligent coöperative response and effort on his part. Forces within the individual as well as within his environment have to be set in operation. The building of self-respect and self-dependence is essential as a major dynamic of permanent rehabilitation. Thus education and cure are not veneers to be applied by legislation, but involve a remaking of personality and character in a remade environment from which the obstructive or thwarting elements have been removed and in which facilitating elements have been substituted.

QUESTIONS FOR DISCUSSION OR EXAMINATION

1. Under what conditions if any would you justify "mercy killings"? Why? How would you answer counter-arguments?
2. Should state laws provide for compulsory as well as voluntary sterilization? Why and how?
3. Outline a marriage law which would be strictly eugenic in its application. Why is such a law impossible at present?
4. Should the feebleminded persons whose feeblemindedness resulted from disease or accident be sterilized? Why or why not?
5. Should compulsory sterilization laws be extended to cover the deaf, blind, deformed, inebriate, and drug addict?
6. Should sterilization, either compulsory or voluntary, be extended to cover any class of normal persons who are carriers of hereditary defects? Why and how?
7. Comment upon the following quotation from Hooton's *Apes, Men, and Morons:*

"Now it seems to me perfectly clear that what we must do, in some way or other, is to encourage a sit-down reproductive strike of the busy breeders among the morons, criminals, and social ineffectuals of our population. Probably compulsory sterilization alone would serve in the case of the insane and the mentally deficient, but it is very difficult to enforce such a measure in a democracy, unless it has been preceded by an educational campaign which has reached all of the teachable and socially-minded individuals of the electorate. Probably the only effective method of obtaining the desired result would be to establish in our secondary schools and colleges courses of applied human biology which would disseminate knowledge of the facts of heredity and of the relation of man's organism to his behavior."

PROBLEMS FOR INDIVIDUAL STUDY

1. Outline the history of the eugenic legislation of your state.
2. Compare the marriage laws or sterilization laws of your state with those of some other selected state.
3. What provision is there in your state by either public or private agencies for education in eugenics? For advice *re* mating?
4. Summarize and compare selected studies of family heredity.

SUGGESTIONS FOR SUPPLEMENTARY READINGS

Baur, Erwin, Fischer, Eugen, and Lenz, Fritz—*Human Heredity* (translated from the third German edition, 1927, by Eden and Cedar Paul); The Macmillan Company, 1930.

Blacker, C. P., editor—*A Special Problem Group?;* Oxford University Press, 1927.

Blacker, C. P.—*The Chances of Morbid Inheritance;* H. K. Lewis & Co., Ltd., 1934.

Carr-Saunders, A. M.—*Eugenics;* Henry Holt and Company, 1926.

Committee of the American Neurological Association for the Investigation of Eugenical Sterilization (Abraham Myerson, James B. Ayer, Tracy J. Putnam, Clyde E. Keeler, and Leo Alexander)—*Eugenical Sterilization: A Reorientation of the Problem;* The Macmillan Company, 1936.

Conklin, Edwin Grant—*Heredity and Environment in the Development of Men;* Princeton University Press, revised fifth edition, 1923.

Cotton, H. H.—*The Defective, Delinquent, and Insane;* Princeton University Press, 1921.

Danielson, Florence H., and Davenport, Charles B.—*The Hill Folk: Report on a Rural Community of Hereditary Defectives;* Eugenics Record Office, Cold Spring Harbor, N. Y., Memoir No. 1, 1912.

Davenport, Charles Benedict—*Heredity in Relation to Eugenics;* Henry Holt and Company, 1911.

East, Edward M.—*Heredity and Human Affairs;* Charles Scribner's Sons, 1929.

Estabrook, Arthur H.—*The Jukes in 1915;* Carnegie Institution of Washington, 1916.

Estabrook, Arthur H.—"The Tribe of Ishmael," pp. 398–404 of *Eugenics, Genetics and the Family;* Williams & Wilkins Company, 1923.

Estabrook, Arthur H., and Davenport, Charles B.—*The Nam Family: A Study in Cacogenics;* Eugenics Record Office, Cold Spring Harbor, N. Y., Memoir No. 2, 1912.

Estabrook, Arthur H., and McDougle, Ivan E.—*Mongrel Virginians: The Win Tribe;* Williams & Wilkins Company, 1926.

Fasten, Nathan—*Principles of Genetics and Eugenics;* Ginn and Company, 1935.

Field, James Alfred—*Essays on Population;* University of Chicago Press, 1931.

Gates, R. Ruggles—*Heredity in Man;* The Macmillan Company, revised edition, 1929.

Gosney, E. S., and Popenoe, Paul—*Sterilization for Human Betterment;* The Macmillan Company, 1929.

Haldane, J. B. S.—*Heredity and Politics;* W. W. Norton & Company, Inc., 1938.

Hankins, Frank Hamilton—*An Introduction to the Study of Society*, Chapter VI, "The Biological Factors in Social Life: Variation and Heredity"; The Macmillan Company, 1928.

Himes, Norman E.—*Medical History of Contraception;* Williams & Wilkins Company, 1936.

Hogben, Lancelot—*Genetic Principles in Medicine and Social Science;* Williams & Norgate, Ltd., 1931.

Holmes, Samuel J.—*A Bibliography of Eugenics;* University of California Press, 1924.

Holmes, Samuel J.—*Human Genetics and Its Social Import;* McGraw-Hill Book Company, Inc., 1936.

Hooton, Earnest A.—*Apes, Men, and Morons;* G. P. Putnam's Sons, 1937.

Huntington, Ellsworth—*Tomorrow's Children: The Goal of Eugenics;* John Wiley & Sons, Inc., 1935.

Jennings, H. S.—*The Biological Basis of Human Nature;* W. W. Norton & Company, Inc., 1930.

Jennings, H. S.—*Genetics;* W. W. Norton & Company, Inc., 1935.

Landman, J. H.—*Human Sterilization: The History of the Sexual Sterilization Movement;* The Macmillan Company, 1932.

Laughlin, Harry H.—*Eugenical Sterilization in the United States;* Psychopathic Laboratory of the Municipal Court of Chicago, 1922.

Laughlin, Harry H.—*Eugenical Sterilization: 1926;* The American Eugenics Society, New Haven, Conn., 1926.

Lidbetter, E. J.—*Heredity and the Social Problem Group;* Edward Arnold, 1934.

Lindsey, Arthur Ward—*A Textbook of Genetics;* The Macmillan Company, 1932.

Myerson, Abraham—*The Inheritance of Mental Diseases;* Williams & Wilkins Company, 1925.

Pearl, Raymond—*Studies in Human Biology;* Williams & Wilkins Company, 1924.

Popenoe, Paul, and Johnson, Roswell H.—*Applied Eugenics;* The Macmillan Company, revised edition, 1933.

Reuter, Edward Byron—*Population Problems;* J. B. Lippincott Company, revised edition, 1937.

Ryan, J. A.—*Human Sterilization;* National Catholic Welfare Conference, 1927.

Schiller, F. C. S.—*Social Decay and Eugenical Reform;* Constable & Co., Ltd., 1932.

Schwesinger, Gladys C.—*Heredity and Environment;* The Macmillan Company, 1933.

Shull, A. Franklin—*Heredity;* McGraw-Hill Book Company, Inc., 1931.

Stockard, C. R.—*The Physical Basis of Personality;* W. W. Norton & Company, Inc., 1931.

Thompson, Warren S.—*Population Problems;* McGraw-Hill Book Company, Inc., second edition, 1935.

Walter, Herbert Eugene—*Genetics;* The Macmillan Company, third edition revised, 1930.

Whitney, Leon F.—*The Case for Sterilization;* Frederick A. Stokes Company, 1934.

CHAPTER XVI

CONTROL OF DISEASE AND ACCIDENT

Social Control of Environment.—More cases of handicap have been seen to be ascribable to acquired illnesses—bacterial, traumatic, or toxic—than to hereditary traits. It is clear also that in cases of hereditary handicap, where the deterioration occurs after birth as for example hereditary types of mental abnormality, illnesses, abuse of alcohol, and unhygienic modes of living may be precipitating factors, or the immediate occasion of the handicap. The prevention of all handicaps thus necessitates the elimination of needless diseases and accident and of the misuse of toxic agents. The cure or improvement of the existing handicapped is equally dependent upon social control of these factors and their milieu.[1]

Traumatic Handicaps: Résumé.—Among the nonhereditary cases of mental handicap accident has been seen to play a small but important role. For example, some children born normal have had their mental development arrested because of a fall or blow upon the head. This may cause serious concussion and permanent interference with mental functioning, due to injury to the brain structure. Similar results occasionally occur from the improper use of forceps at time of birth. Prevention of future cases of these types depends upon the universal development of greater skill in the delivery of infants, as well as upon more general and effective instruction of mothers, nurses, and others in the prevention of accidents to children. A small percentage of mental disease and of epilepsy is also of traumatic origin.

Accident is a much more prominent cause of physical handicaps. Fully twenty-two per cent of blindness is traumatic in origin, whether caused by explosives, blows, or foreign substances in the eye, spattered alkalis such as lye, potash, and ammonia, spattered acids—

[1] Other precipitating or conditioning factors, such as poverty and economic worries, broken homes and domestic worries, unwholesome conditions of housing, industry, recreation, and the general physical and social milieu are outlined in Parts III and IV.

nitric, sulphuric, or other, exposure to overintense light, heat, or cold, or progressive nearsightedness from eyestrain due to insufficient illumination. Deafness is rarely the result of accident, but many cases of impaired hearing in later life are caused by explosions, especially in war periods where high explosives are continually utilized. War equally takes its toll in total blindness and the making of cripples through mangling and amputation. The vast majority of cripples are made so by accident, which is the outstanding causative factor of this handicap.

Statistics of Accidents.—The National Health Survey of 1935–36 included a study of accidents as a cause of disability. A house-to-house canvass was made of some 800,000 families, including 2,300,000 persons in 84 cities and 23 rural areas in 19 states. The total surveyed population was so distributed as to give a sample which was designed to be representative of cities in the United States according to size and region.[2] Their general findings were as follows:

"Accidental injury is one of the principal causes of disability in the United States today. Approximately 30,000 accidents occur daily, the victims of which are disabled (unable to pursue work or usual activities) for one or more days. This means that during one year there are 10,000,-000 such accidents. As a result of these accidents, which disabled persons for varying periods of time, there are on an average day in excess of 500,000 persons who are kept from their usual pursuits as a result of injury through accident. . . .

"Accidents vary in severity; some causing only temporary disability, some causing permanent disability, and others resulting in death. This report does not consider the minor accidents, which are included in the totals given in the preceding paragraph, but deals with (a) accidents of a serious nature which resulted in a disability of at least 7 days during the year covered by the canvass and (b) permanent impairments which have been left by accidents over the lifetime of the population. At present, the main body of data available and that on which the major portion of this

---

[2] *The National Health Survey: 1935–36—Accidents as a Cause of Disability;* Division of Public Health Methods, National Institute of Health, U. S. Public Health Service (Preliminary Reports, The National Health Survey, Sickness and Medical Care Series, Bulletin No. 3), 1938. This project was carried out under the general direction of Dr. L. R. Thompson, Director, National Institute of Health, George St. J. Perrott, Project Director, and Clark Tibbitts, Field Director. Others responsible for the technical aspects of the study were Selwyn D. Collins, Principal Statistician, and Rollo H. Britten, Senior Statistician. The major part of the responsibility for the preparation of this bulletin (No. 3) was assumed by Arch B. Clark of the survey staff.

report is based, is from 8 of the surveyed cities.[3] However, the following preliminary figures are presented for the entire surveyed population:

"Number of persons canvased (81 cities) 2,308,585
Number of persons disabled by accidents on day of visit 9,268
Per cent of persons disabled by accidents on the day of visit . . . 0.4
Number of accident cases disabling for one week or longer during
  survey year 37,899
Annual frequency of accidents disabling one week or longer, per
  1,000 persons 16.3

"Accidents, as reported in the total surveyed population, accounted for 7.6 per cent of the persons disabled on the day of the visit and comprised 8.5 per cent of all illnesses during the survey year which were disabling for a week or more. They also accounted for 7.6 per cent of the total days of disability from all causes. As a cause of disability, accidents were exceeded only by influenza and grippe in annual frequency of occurrence.

"Accidents are one of the principal causes of death, 6.9 per cent of all deaths reported by the total surveyed population were the result of accidental injury, deaths from accidents being exceeded only by diseases of the heart, cancer and pneumonia (all forms).[4] Furthermore, the annual mortality rate from accidents in the country at large exceeds that of any nation in the civilized world." [5]

Over three hundred thousand white and colored persons, canvassed in the eight cities for which accident data have been tabulated in detail, "reported 5,515 accidental injuries which were disabling for a week or more during the year. This amounted to an annual frequency rate of 17.6 per 1,000 persons, which is slightly higher than that of the entire surveyed population." [6] Twelve out

---

[3] "The eight cities (Atlanta, Ga.; Cincinnati, Ohio; Dallas, Texas; Fall River, Mass.; Newark, N. J.; Oakland, Calif.; St. Paul, Minn.; and Seattle, Wash.) were selected for detailed preliminary tabulations as being reasonably representative of large cities, excluding metropolitan areas. The population surveyed in these cities (312,686) was 38 per cent of the population surveyed in all cities from 100,000 to 500,000, and 13 per cent of the population surveyed in the 81 cities. It will be noted that two of the eight cities were in the East, two in the Central area, two in the West, and two in the South. It is planned that later reports will give corresponding information for the whole area surveyed." *Ibid.*, pp. 1 and 11.

[4] "The mortality rate for the entire population as reported by the Bureau of the Census for the calendar year 1935 followed this same order by cause of death. The census rates for these causes were: diseases of the heart 244.9; cancer and other malignant tumors, 111.0; pneumonia (all forms) 81.8; accidents 78.4. Bureau of the Census; *Vital Statistics—Special Reports*, Vol. 5; Number 14, page 37." *Ibid.*, pp. 1 and 12.

[5] *Ibid.*, p. 1.

[6] *Ibid.*, p. 2.

of every 1,000 persons in these eight cities were found to possess some permanent physical impairment as the result of accidental injury. The prevalence of permanent impairments due to accidents, disabling and nondisabling combined, classified according to the nature of the impairment and the place of occurrence of the accident were as follows: [7]

	RATE PER 1,000 PERSONS					
			Place of Occurrence			
NATURE OF IMPAIRMENT	Total	Home	Public Place		Occupational	Unspecified
			Auto	Other		
All permanent impairments due to accidents	12.4	2.9	1.2	1.7	5.9	.7
Lost members:						
Hand, arm, foot, leg, or combination	1.2	.1	.2	.3	.5	.1
Fingers, one or more	5.0	1.0	.2	.3	3.4	.1
Impaired members:						
One foot or leg	2.6	.8	.4	.6	.6	.1
One hand or arm	.9	.3	.1	.1	.3	.1
Serious combinations, spine or entire body	1.1	.3	.1	.2	.4	.2
All other [a]	1.6	.4	.2	.2	.7	.1

[a] Other trunk impaired, unspecified members lost or impaired, impaired fingers, and lost or impaired toes.

Fifty per cent of these conditions were found to be "due to occupational accidents, 25 per cent to home accidents, 15 per cent to injuries received in public places other than by motor vehicle, and 10 per cent to automobile accidents. . . . Occupational accidents were the most important cause of loss of members, causing 70 per cent of the lost fingers and 45 per cent of the losses of other members. For impaired members, home accidents were a cause of equal importance with occupational accidents."

The percentage distribution of permanent physical impairments, due to accident, disabling and nondisabling combined, according to place of occurrence was presented in the National Health Survey in the following table: [8]

[7] *Ibid.*, p. 8.
[8] *Ibid.*, pp. 9–10.

NATURE OF IMPAIRMENT	PERCENTAGE DISTRIBUTION BY PLACE OF OCCURRENCE [a]				
	Total	Home	Public Place		Occupational
			Auto	Other	
All permanent impairments due to accidents	100	25	10	15	50
Lost members:					
Hand, arm, foot, leg, or combination	100	9	18	27	45
Fingers, one or more	100	20	4	6	70
Impaired members:					
One foot or leg	100	33	17	25	25
One hand or arm	100	38	12	12	38
Serious combination, spine or entire body	100	30	10	20	40
All other [b]	100	27	13	13	47

[a] Excluding unspecified place.
[b] Other trunk impaired, unspecified members lost or impaired, impaired fingers, and lost or impaired toes.

Prevention of Accidents.—To eliminate preventable handicaps, it is therefore necessary not only to control heredity as already outlined but also to reach the sources of traumatic disabilities. Most accidents are preventable. The ratio of industrial accidents is being reduced continuously through safety engineering stimulated by labor legislation and workmen's compensation acts.[9]

Domestic accidents are difficult to prevent by legislation aside from those essential paragraphs in building and housing laws which deal with heating, lighting, fire protection, gas, electricity, elevators, and soundness of construction. Adult education in the hazards of the home, and training of children by parents and schools, in specific dangers and means of avoiding them are the major recourse.

Accidents in public places include drownings, falls, conflagrations, shipwrecks, and a variety of other major disasters [10] to be prevented primarily by the safeguarding of transportation by sea, land, or air, by prevention of war and other major disasters where possible, the elimination of hazards in public places, and the education of individuals to exercise reasonable caution.

[9] See Part III, Chapter XXII. A convenient statistical summary of accidents in building, highway, and railroad construction, and the specific means to their prevention, will be found in Kossoris, Max D., and Kjaer, Swen—*Causes and Prevention of Accidents in the Construction Industry, 1936;* reprint (Serial No. R. 801) from *Monthly Labor Review*, August, 1938.

[10] See Part IV, Chapter XXX.

Automobile injuries and fatalities increase from year to year as the number of cars and drivers and the speed of traffic increase. Devices for the control of traffic and the licensing of drivers at best merely curb the mounting toll of deaths and injuries. It is questionable whether the volume of accidents from this source can be materially reduced until the public is ready to accept legislative limitation of the speed at which any pleasure or business car may be driven to thirty-five or forty miles per hour, permitting the use of cars of higher speeds only for public protection and specially licensed emergency use.

Disease as Cause of Handicaps: Résumé.—Earlier chapters have shown that certain diseases (some of which are infectious and others chronic) are responsible for a fair percentage of cases of permanent handicap such as blindness, deafness, and mental disorder, and presumably a lower percentage of feeblemindedness and crippled conditions. A brief review of this factor may help the visualization of the role of disease.

There are preventable diseases, such as scarlet fever, which are still sometimes named as the cause of a very small percentage of cases of mental handicap. Others, such as meningitis, which sometimes brings arrest of mental development or abnormality as one of its consequences, are being more tardily brought under social control while undergoing intensive and presumably promising research.[11]

Many cases of blindness and deafness are consequences of scarlet fever, measles, and the less common meningitis. Deafness in early childhood may also develop out of common colds and the consequent clogging of ear passages. The potential seriousness of common childhood diseases is still imperfectly recognized by most parents. Tuberculosis of the bones and joints, rickets, and infantile paralysis are responsible for many cases of physical deformity.

The effects of glandular secretions and the chemical conditions of the blood stream upon mentality are being subjected to close scientific scrutiny by specialists in each of the types of mental handicap. The discovery many years ago of the relation of the thyroid gland to cretinism has resulted in a degree of control of factors which produced that type of feeblemindedness, so that now such cases, if treated early enough, may continue to develop in mentality. In this general field of scientific research there is no promise as yet of

---

[11] Rosenau assigns ratios to various diseases as factors in the production of mental disorder. Rosenau, Milton J.—*Preventive Medicine and Hygiene;* D. Appleton-Century Company, sixth edition, 1935.

the cure of cases now deemed incurable, but it is conceivable that it will ultimately lead to the prevention of some types of subnormality and abnormality traceable to glandular conditions.

Diseases, both infectious and chronic, produce also an immense volume of temporary handicap or disability which in the winter months withdraws fully six million people each day from work, school, or other usual activities.[12] Thus programs for disease prevention may reduce the volume of both permanent and temporary handicap.

Statistics of Disease.—The National Health Survey of 1935–36 included an estimate of the amount of disabling illness in the country as a whole.

"Illnesses which disabled for a minimum of one week occurred at a rate of 172 per 1,000 persons canvassed, in the 12 months preceding the survey date. Applied to the population of the country as a whole, this rate gives an estimated total of 22 million illnesses disabling for a week or longer, or about 16 such illnesses for each death occurring in 1935, the approximate survey year. This figure is to be taken as a minimum, since illnesses of short duration are not included, and illnesses, like deaths, cannot be completely enumerated.

"In the small town of 5,000 persons, this rate represents some 800 cases; in the city of medium size (100,000 population) approximately 17,000 cases; in the large city of 500,000 population, 86,000 cases. These estimates express in minimum terms the problem of illness which must be met annually by the combined efforts of the physician, the health officer, the welfare administrator, the bedside nurse, the public health nurse, and other medical and public health workers. . . .

"The amount of disability for the average child under 15 years of age is somewhat under one week per year. The frequency of illness is high in childhood, but the average duration per case is low compared with that for the average adult case. The average old person is disabled nearly 5 weeks annually, the result of both high frequency of illness, and a long average duration per case among the aged. Adults of the ages 15 to 64 years are disabled approximately 9 days per person per year. In this age period, illnesses are less frequent than in childhood or old age, but this lower frequency is accompanied by an average duration per case

[12] "This estimate is arrived at by applying to the population of the whole country the results obtained in the National Health Survey (1935–36), in which 4.5 per cent of more than 2,300,000 persons surveyed in urban areas were reported as being disabled on the day of the canvass. . . . The survey took place during the months of November, 1935, to March, 1936. A record of the illnesses present on the day of the visit therefore refers to a varying day, but each family enters into the picture only once." *The National Health Survey: 1935–36—An Estimate of the Amount of Disabling Illness in the Country as a Whole*, p. 1; Division of Public Health Methods, National Institute of Health, U. S. Public Health Service (Preliminary Reports, The National Health Survey, Sickness and Medical Care Series, Bulletin No. 1), 1938.

which exceeds that of childhood, although definitely lower than that of the average case among persons over 65 years of age. . . .

"*The relative importance of various diseases as causes of illness.*—The frequency and severity rates . . . are averages based on all illnesses disabling for a week or more without consideration of cause. Diseases vary widely in severity. The average case of disabling illness due to a chronic disease resulted in 138 days of disability—almost two and one-half times as long as the average duration per case of illness of all causes. Illnesses due to chronic disease occurred with about the same frequency as acute respiratory diseases, yet the duration of the average chronic case was over 7 times as long as the average case of respiratory disease.

"We find, then, that chronic disease alone accounts for more than 6 of the total of 10 days of incapacity from disabling illness experienced by the average person in a year. The respiratory diseases account for one day of disability per person; next in order of importance are infectious diseases and accidents, each with a rate of seven-tenths of a day per person." [13]

The annual frequency of illnesses disabling for one week or longer is shown in the table on this and the following page. It will be noted that the venereal diseases are excluded because of incompleteness of data, but that accidents, chronic illnesses, and specific diseases of eye and ear (though previously covered) are retained in this table to facilitate comparison of data.[14]

Diagnosis [a]	Annual Cases Disabling for One Week or Longer per 1,000 Persons	Number of Cases
All diagnoses	172.4	397,978
Infectious and parasitic		
Measles	8.9	20,483
Mumps	5.6	12,950
Chickenpox	4.5	10,362
Whooping cough	3.2	7,430
Scarlet fever	2.8	6,482
German measles	1.3	2,927
Malaria	0.8	1,867
Local infection, blood poisoning	0.8	1,782
Diphtheria	0.4	840
Erysipelas	0.2	436
Typhoid fever	0.2	353
Smallpox	0.1	242
Other	0.8	1,929
Respiratory (except chronic)		
Influenza and grippe	18.1	41,752

[a] If an illness was due to more than one cause, the classification is according to the condition which was of longest duration.

[13] *Ibid.*, pp. 3–4.   [14] *Ibid.*, Appendix Table 1, pp. 7–8.

DIAGNOSIS	ANNUAL CASES DISABLING FOR ONE WEEK OR LONGER PER 1,000 PERSONS	NUMBER OF CASES
Tonsillitis [including tonsillectomies and quinsy]	9.9	22,855
Coryza (head colds) and colds unspecified	7.2	16,708
Pneumonia	4.7	10,935
Bronchitis and chest cold	3.3	7,674
Throat affections except of tonsils	2.3	5,398
Pleurisy	1.0	2,325
Digestive (except chronic)		
Appendicitis	5.1	11,766
Indigestion and allied conditions	3.0	6,844
Diarrhea, enteritis, and colitis	0.9	1,971
Diseases of mouth, teeth, and gums	0.5	1,222
Puerperal state		
Live births	13.9	32,144
Still births and abortions	1.1	2,438
Complications of childbirth and pregnancy	0.3	694
Accidents		
Automobile	3.2	7,480
Other	12.5	28,917
Chronic diseases (disabling for a week or more)		
Heart disease and arteriosclerosis	8.5	19,710
Rheumatism	5.9	13,609
Nervous diseases	5.5	12,627
Orthopedic conditions	2.6	5,868
Nephritis and other kidney diseases	2.5	5,744
Gall bladder diseases	2.2	5,108
Tumors, non-malignant or unspecified	2.0	4,573
Asthma and hay fever	1.4	3,300
Tuberculosis, all forms	1.4	3,228
Sinusitis	1.1	2,613
Hernia	1.0	2,303
Ulcer of stomach or duodenum	1.0	2,233
Cancer	1.0	2,200
Diabetes	0.9	2,061
Hemorrhoids	0.7	1,670
Goiter and other thyroid	0.6	1,447
Other	7.6	17,552
All other		
Skin diseases	2.1	4,902
Diseases of ear and mastoid process	1.9	4,389
Miscellaneous circulatory diseases	1.3	3,025
Diseases of eyes	0.9	2,157
General, not appearing above	0.3	739
Homicides and suicides, including attempted	0.2	436
Ill-defined and unknown	3.2	7,277

Prevention of Disease.—The past century has witnessed phenomenal progress in the social control of disease. Medical science, and more particularly bacteriology, epidemiology, immunology, physiology, and pathology, by their progressive mastery through research of the nature of the body and its functions, of the sources, courses, and prevention of disease, have made possible the virtual elimination in the United States of many scourges of past generations. Thus yellow fever, smallpox, cholera, and typhus, forms of pestilence which periodically swept the cities of our eastern seaboard in the early eighteen hundreds, have been virtually eliminated by preventive medicine. Typhoid is no longer common, and many other diseases, through the discovery of the specific bacteria through which they are transmitted, have been greatly reduced in their incidence.[15]

The achievements of medical research have been paralleled by measures, both private and public, to curb the spread of disease and promote personal and public hygiene. Few human ills have been combated by so wide a variety of agencies and with such evidence of relative effectiveness. Sanitary engineering has developed to the point where the water supply for most urban dwellers is of protected purity, where the disposal of sewage and household wastes is vastly superior to that of earlier generations. Less efficient measures govern the safety and health of industrial workers in the establishments which employ them but nevertheless progress has been made in this field. School children generally have the benefit of periodic medical examination and instruction in personal hygiene. Hospital and nursing services have become widely available. Within the past generation many types of clinics and dispensary service have been rendered accessible to a portion of our population. Federal, state, and local departments of health inaugurate or supervise these many services, and together with the universities, medical schools, and foundations conduct researches which lead to still further control of disease. Private organizations, whether for the prevention of tuberculosis or other diseases, for the maintenance of hospitals and nursing services, or for educational propaganda or experimentation, have made noteworthy contributions to the program.

[15] For the history of pestilence in New York City see Ford, James, with the collaboration of Morrow, Katherine, and Thompson, George N.—*Slums and Housing, with Special Reference to New York City: History, Conditions, Policy,* Vol. I, pp. 378–380; Harvard University Press, 1936.

Social Policy for Prevention of Disease.—Nevertheless, the statistics of contemporary disease rates make it clear that the social control of disease is still in its early stages. The volume of both temporary and permanent handicaps growing out of disease is huge in spite of the progress of preventive medicine and public hygiene. Further reduction of its volume involves simultaneous activity in the following eight fields: (1) Registration of all cases of preventable or chronic illness, and of all mortality by causes. (2) Research to discover the causes of all types of illness, their course, modes of transmission, and cure. (3) Control by law, directed to remove the sources of disease and prevent its transmission. (4) Enforcement of legislation through established Federal, state, or local departments of health, and through special departments or commissions on city planning, housing, industrial hygiene, sanitary engineering, et cetera. (5) Measures especially in the recreational field for the building up of personal resistance to disease. (6) Public health insurance to bring health services within the reach of citizens of modest means. (7) Universal education in personal and public hygiene for both children and adults. (8) Organization and coördination of all health services in such manner as to make competent medical examination and complete treatment available when necessary to every citizen.

Registration and Research.—Complete morbidity and mortality records are necessary in order that precautionary measures to avert the spread of disease and to ensure prompt cure may be taken. Such records are needed also to discover epidemics in the initial stages and mass efforts to keep them from developing. The statistical data gleaned from registration cards are essential to research specialists, since the correlation of diseases with other factors, whether occupation, race, sex, age, dietary, or otherwise, may lead to further discoveries as to their etiology or control. Mortality statistics in America today are relatively complete. Morbidity statistics, except for a few of the more serious preventable diseases, fall far short of adequacy, and will tend to remain so until coördinated health services and health insurance become universally available, and make possible the diagnosis of specialists in all cases of serious illness.

Although medical research is relatively advanced in America and well endowed by many foundations, medical schools, and public departments, specialists agree that much more rapid progress in the mastery of disease could be made if the laboratories, facilities, and staffs were greatly increased. Lack of resources still retards or thwarts promising endeavor. Limited facilities may be responsible for the delay in arriving at the complete mastery of infantile paralysis, meningitis, cancer, and many other diseases.

Health and Sanitary Legislation.—To prevent disease or its spread the causative factors must in each instance be brought under social control as soon as they are understood. Sanitary legislation for the protection and purification of water supplies, the safe disposal of sewage, the collection and disposal of refuse, the draining of standing water, the elimination of dumps and other nuisances, wherever ably undertaken, have been reflected in declining mortality rates and in reduction of certain diseases such as typhoid fever and malaria. Less general and efficient have been measures for the segregation of noxious industries under health and zoning legislation; for the elimination of unwholesome housing through building codes, health, and city planning legislation; for the elimination of food poisoning or adulteration through pure food and drug acts and health inspection of the factories, retail establishments, and restaurants in which food products are made or sold; for the elimination of dangerous industrial processes, or for the protection of the worker through factory or labor laws. Only slight inroads have been made upon industrial accidents, disease, and fatigue. Thus, though the causes of disease have been increasingly reached in recent generations, only a small fraction of preventable disease is curbed at the source. Unsafe water may be characteristic only of rural communities, villages, small towns, and the outskirts of large cities. Unsafe milk and food to some extent invade urban communities as well. The industrial diseases and those associated with conditions of housing have still been but slightly touched in the progress of sanitary legislation.

Health Administration and the Enforcement of Legislation.— The passage of a law is no guarantee of its enforcement. Most state or local boards of health are handicapped in administration by the inadequacy of funds at their disposal. They are consequently understaffed and thereby limited in the inspections which they can make and in other details of enforcement. Prompt inspections upon complaint, and periodic, regular inspection of all sources of potential danger are requisite safeguards of the health of citizens. Health departments through inadequate appropriations may also be unable to pay salaries sufficiently high to secure well-trained and competent service. Political appointments and deficiencies in civil service rules or examinations may mean inexpert service where expertness is needed. The laws under which the departments operate may confer inadequate powers for the elimination of nuisances, for the control of carriers of disease, for the vacation or demolition of buildings unfit for human habitation.

Rules or practices governing vaccination and inoculation; quarantine and isolation of contagious diseases; disinfection, fumigation, and prophylaxis; or for the prevention of specific diseases, such as syphilis, may be so antiquated or limited in value as to be nugatory or severely limited in their effectiveness. The prevention of disease can be accomplished only through the provision of adequate financial resources for administrative departments of health, housing, city planning, zoning, and industrial hygiene, and through policies which will ensure expertness of staff and prompt progressive adaptation of measures to the findings of medical research.

Constructive Legislation and the Building of Resistance to Disease.—The best regulatory legislation of the types just considered may go far in the building of a wholesome environment. Enforced laws regarding vaccination and innoculation may also confer artificial immunity to specific diseases such as smallpox, diphtheria, and typhoid fever. Resistance is, however, mainly built up by improvement in the bodily tone and in the phagocytic power of the blood. The chief means to this end is to make possible for all citizens a sufficiency of sunshine, fresh air, exercise, sleep, and an adequate well-rounded diet.

City planning legislation at its best can provide for the segregation of industrial and commercial districts from residential districts. Within the residential districts city planning and housing legislation can so control the layout of streets, blocks, lots, and dwellings that all rooms used for living purposes may have adequate sunshine, fresh air, and the amenities of attractive grounds or gardens. The existence of slums with dark, damp, filthy, and sunless quarters attests the limited application of such constructive legislation. City planning and recreation legislation have made within the past generation an attempt to provide accessible breathing spaces in the form of neighborhood parks, and playgrounds for supervised play, within easy access of each dwelling. This accepted policy is, however, slow of realization because in the compactly built areas of our cities the prices of land may be prohibitive. Increasing concern with regard to municipal architecture is beginning to result in the construction of new schools and new buildings for recreational uses which are amply oriented for sunlight and fresh air, within grounds adequate for their prospective recreational use. Here again there is a considerable lag between realization of the need and the incorporation of these principles in public buildings.

Wholesome food is being made available at modest prices for school lunches, but little is directly done by public authority for the promotion of adequate nutrition of adults except through poor relief, minimum-wage legislation, and through education. Measures for the elimination of noise and other factors which interfere with privacy and sleep are in the main nonexistent except for the removal of elevated railways and electric cars from some of the streets of our more progressive cities, and rare measures in housing legislation to ensure soundproofing, and the type of apartment planning which is conducive to privacy. Public measures for the building of resistance are thus relatively underdeveloped.

Health Education and Health Service.—Education in physiology and personal hygiene has been promoted with increasing skill in the public schools of America especially during the past two generations. Such systematic instruction has been supplemented in leading schools by gymnastic training, by instruction in public hygiene and home economics, and by periodic medical examination. Adults have widely benefited by the educational propaganda of Federal, state, and local health authorities, and private organizations operating on a national, state, and local basis, such as the American National Red Cross, the National Tuberculosis Association, the General Federation of Women's Clubs, and the National Congress of Parents and Teachers. Yet the unhygienic modes of living of the mass of our population, the widespread use of nostrums and patent medicines without medical prescription, and the high disease rate attest the insufficiency of current educational services for adults.

The individual citizen can be reached only through health services accessible within his own community. The elimination of preventable disease renders necessary the ultimate universal provision of community services for (1) competent diagnosis, (2) cure, and (3) prevention, for all citizens irrespective of their incomes and capacity to reimburse for services rendered. At present some communities through combined public and private services meet a fair percentage of needs in all four categories, reasonably well.

The trend is toward the establishment of community health centers, coördinating public and private diagnostic and advisory services, equipped with essential laboratories, providing educational services in the form of lectures, exhibits, motion pictures, demonstrations, and pamphlet literature, as well as clinics, dispensaries, and headquarters for visiting nursing services. Diagnostic functions ideally comprise periodic annual check-up or preventive examination for citizens by groups of specialists, as well as prompt diagnosis of illness in its incipient stages. In addition to general medical clinics, specialized clinics for maternity cases, or pediatric, venereal, tubercular, cardiac, surgical, mental, dental, or other groups of cases have demonstrated their value in larger communities. Close coöperation of such clinics with private medical practitioners, and with hospitals and out-patient services, is essential to facilitate both cure and prevention of disease.

To make the transition from the chaotic and sporadic medical services commonly characteristic of American communities today to the universal provision of specialized, coördinated services of a type that will cure all curable disease and prevent all preventable disease is a project of colossal magnitude requiring wise leadership and persistency through long years. Equally difficult are the economic devices to render such services universally available irrespective of each citizen's earning capacity and consequent ability to pay for his diagnosis, medicines, hospital bed, convalescence, and nursing fees. These latter aspects of the problem will be treated in more detail as an aspect of "social security" in a later chapter.

Venereal Disease and Social Hygiene.—Venereal diseases have already been shown to operate as causative factors in the production of many types of handicap. Syphilis in the mother if not treated in early pregnancy may be transmitted to the foetus.[16] By some

---

[16] The Surgeon General of the United States, Dr. Thomas Parran, writes: "Most obstetrical clinics now take routine Wassermanns. This practice must be extended to private patients as well. If treatment of a pregnant woman with active syphilis is started before the fifth month of her pregnancy she has nine chances out of ten of giving birth to a healthy child. Without treatment, the child is likely to be stillborn or so diseased or deformed as to require constant care to live at all. Even more unfortunate, however, are those who seem normal at birth but later develop the dreaded symptoms. Within the last few weeks I have seen juvenile paretics who started out in life as normal children but have degenerated into almost vegetable-like existence. I saw only yesterday a beautiful young girl—intelligent, charming, utterly good—who is slowly going blind because her mother was untreated sixteen years ago. These congenital cases

specialists it is considered to be a cause of mental retardation. Though the percentage of syphilitics who become insane is relatively small, syphilis is still a primary cause of about seven per cent of mental disorder. Venereal disease may also produce cases of blindness, of deafness, and of deformity.[17]

Aside from these interrelations with other handicaps venereal diseases are among the most damaging of chronic diseases, and consequently of poverty and of early death. They are also a common cause of sterility. The United States Public Health Service estimates that there are from 500,000 to 1,000,000 new cases of syphilis in this country each year and that possibly one person in ten eventually suffers from this disease.[18]

Though often innocently acquired by the wife from her husband, by the child from father or mother, or even from infected drinking glasses, towels, bed linen, or toilets, the major source of transmission is illicit sexual intercourse and prostitution. Hence prevention of these diseases involves the usual controls over infections and contagious diseases already outlined, and particularly registration, prompt and free Wassermann tests, and clinic treatment, health tests prior to marriage, and protection of associates. The United States Public Health Service, in addition to its active promotion of these measures, has in recent years succeeded in bringing this subject into the open by means of increasingly effective programs for adult education in sex hygiene.

Because venereal diseases are spread chiefly by sexual promiscuity, suggested measures for reducing promiscuity require study. Peoples vary considerably in their sexual mores and taboos,[19] and there are

respond poorly to treatment. Five months' treatment during pregnancy is better than five years' treatment after the birth of the child. No mother objects to silver nitrate in her baby's eyes, which protects it against blindness from gonorrhea. She would not object to a blood test for syphilis or to treatment for syphilis if she understood its importance to her baby. Indeed, her own infection might have been prevented if the state in which she lived had required a blood test before marriage." Parran, Thomas—"Why Don't We Stamp Out Syphilis?" p. 72; *The Reader's Digest*, July, 1936, condensed from the *Survey Graphic* of July, 1936.

[17] This was discussed in Chapters IX, X, and XI. See also Best, Harry— *Blindness and the Blind in the United States*, p. 138; The Macmillan Company, 1934.

[18] See their current publications. Also Parran, Thomas—"No Defense for Any of Us"; *Survey Graphic*, Vol. XXVII, No. 4, April, 1938.

[19] See, for example, Mead, Margaret—*Coming of Age in Samoa;* W. Morrow and Company, 1928, and Mead, Margaret—*Growing Up in New Guinea;* W. Morrow and Company, 1930: also Margold, Charles W.—*Sex Freedom and Social Control;* University of Chicago Press, 1926.

wide variations in the folkways among the various racial, economic, and cultural groups of our own population. Premarital sexual intercourse and postmarital promiscuity, especially for the male, are condoned in many circles and advocated in some. The influence of church and state is chiefly towards continence prior to marriage and strict monogamy within the institution of marriage. Since, however, prostitution has existed from early historical times it is not indicative of a breakdown of earlier social organization but rather of a failure to make behavior conform to rules or ideals that are more or less widely accepted.

Prostitution is punished by the state as a crime. The male patron is, however, seldom reached by the law. Surveys of commercialized vice in this country have found relatively low mentality and brief schooling among inmates of houses of ill-fame and among streetwalkers or other prostitutes who have been sent to jail. No statistical study can cover the entire group for any one city and hence these findings may not be representative.[20]

From the local surveys of prostitution at present available it appears that few persons enter prostitution solely for economic reasons. Society's attitude toward the unmarried mother may, in conjunction with other factors, cause her to enter this profession.[21] Some women report seduction by employers or associates as the precipitating factor. A few have been victims of "white slavery" and forced into prostitution. More commonly women have entered prostitution as the cumulative result of loose sexual relationships with their associates, or casual acquaintances of the rooming-house, commercial dance hall, or street. Relatively few of the statements considered to be reliable report that the beginning was deliberate. Once the profession has been entered there is some scattered evidence that it is more easily dropped by the street-walker than by the employees of establishments for commercialized vice. There are some records of exploitation of the latter group and of hierarchies of persons grafting upon their earnings.

[20] Fernald, Mable R., Hayes, Mary H. S., and Dawley, Almena—*A Study of Women Delinquents of New York State;* D. Appleton-Century Company, 1920. Kneeland, George J.—*Commercialized Prostitution in New York City;* D. Appleton-Century Company, 1913. Reckless, Walter C.—*Vice in Chicago;* University of Chicago Press, 1933. Thomas, William I.—*The Unadjusted Girl;* Little, Brown, and Company, 1928. Waterman, Willoughby C.—*Prostitution and Its Repression in New York City, 1900–1931;* Columbia University Press, 1932.

[21] Kammerer, Percy Gamble—*The Unmarried Mother: A Study of Five Hundred Cases;* Little, Brown, and Company, 1918.

American cities, since about 1912, have largely eliminated the protected areas or "red light districts." Where such police measures are well executed the volume of prostitution has apparently been reduced, though scattered and driven under cover. Whether or not the vigorous prosecution of commercialized vice increases the volume of other illicit sexual relationships, as has been claimed, is not statistically demonstrable. The many pathological problems of public morals associated with prostitution—pandering, perversions, pilfering, drug addiction, etc.—are hedged with deceit and evasions. This fact tends to limit the more scientific data to penal and medical records, supplemented by case histories which are, however, subject to all of the limitations characteristic of such evidence.

European experience demonstrates the impossibility of preventing the spread of venereal disease by compulsory medical treatment of each prostitute.[22] Public policies to reduce prostitution are largely limited to the raiding of houses of ill-fame and of "houses of call," and the prosecution of soliciting in the street or elsewhere. Public regulation and supervision of commercialized recreations have some value, yet all such measures are of limited practical efficacy unless the exploiters of prostitutes can be apprehended and sentenced.

Since venereal disease may be acquired also through casual illicit sexual relationships the volume can be further reduced only in so far as family, church, school, and other public agencies can devise and put into practice a type of sex education which will increase continence, moral self-control, the sublimation of the sexual drives, and the ideals of strict monogamy and marital loyalty. Comprehensive policies for public recreation may succeed in bolstering the programs for law enforcement and education previously mentioned.[23]

Toxic Factors as Cause of Handicap: Résumé.—The abuse of alcohol and of drugs has been shown to play a fairly large role in the production of certain forms of handicap. Alcoholism presumably aggravates some types of epilepsy. The relationship of alcoholism to mental disease is much more clear since over 9 per cent of all first admissions and over 7 per cent of readmissions to hospitals for the

[22] Flexner, Abraham—*Prostitution in Europe;* D. Appleton-Century Company, 1914.

[23] Davis, Katharine Bement—*Factors in the Sex Life of Twenty-Two Hundred Women;* Harper & Brothers, 1929. Hamilton, G. V., and Macgowan, Kenneth—*What Is Wrong with Marriage?;* Albert & Charles Boni, 1929. Tufts, James Hayden—*America's Social Morality*, Chapters VI and XVIII; Henry Holt and Company, 1933.

insane in Massachusetts are for alcoholic types of insanity.[24] Leaving out of consideration the temporary mental disturbances of delirium tremens, usually cared for in the home or in emergency hospitals, the alcoholic psychosis most common in our hospitals for the insane is alcoholic hallucinosis. There are also forms of alcoholic delusional insanity and of dementia.

A small percentage of blindness is caused by the abuse of tobacco or by the taking of wood alcohol or beverages containing methylated spirits to produce intoxication. Many accidents result from alcoholic intoxication because alcohol taken in excess and carried by the blood stream to the brain renders the nerve cells of the brain torpid and thus reduces inhibitions, discrimination, and locomotor control.

Less than one per cent of the cases of insanity in our hospitals involve drug addiction. Nevertheless, the abuse of drugs as well as of alcohol may obscure symptoms and aggravate the conditions of mental disease having their origin in other causes and may cause accidents which result in physical handicap. Either alcohol or drugs may be taken by the victim, when he feels that he is losing his grip, to help him forget his worries or mistakenly to stimulate energy or courage. Such use may be continued to a point which will make cure or even improvement of an abnormal mental condition impossible.

Since confirmed alcoholics, inebriates, and drug addicts may also be classified as handicapped in meeting their social and economic obligations, their presence in the population warrants measures for the prevention of the abuse of toxic agents.

Prevention and Control of Toxic Factors.—Prevention of handicap caused by toxic factors involves the following special measures:

(1) Central recording of pathologic cases that come under public jurisdiction in state or municipal boards of public welfare, mental diseases, education, correction, or probation.

(2) Promotion of research in toxicology; the pathology and therapy of alcoholism, inebriety, and drug addiction; their causes, physical, mental, and social; and controls.

(3) Regulatory legislation regarding importation, production, transportation, and sale of alcohol, drugs, and poisons; the licensing of legitimate dealers and perhaps also of users.

[24] Dayton, Neil A.—*The First Year of the New Standard Nomenclature of Diseases in Massachusetts Mental Hospitals;* reprinted from *The American Journal of Psychiatry,* Vol. 92, No. 3, November, 1935.

(4) Administrative authorities, Federal, state, and local, with definite and appropriate powers conferred by law, ample funds, and competent staffs.

(5) Governmental ownership and operation of production and sale where private industry cannot be controlled by regulatory legislation.

(6) Constructive legislation to provide wholesome substitutes for the social factors which now precipitate abuse of alcohol and drugs. Such legislation comprises labor laws to protect workers from excessive strain or fatigue, building and housing laws to make possible wholesome living conditions, and public recreational policies to bring opportunities for socially desirable uses of leisure time within the reach of all citizens.

(7) Education for children and adults in the findings of science with reference to the physical, mental, and social effects of the use of alcohol and drugs. Clinical consultation service where needed.

(8) Hospital colonies for the treatment of pathologic inebriates, and special hospitals for drug addicts, to make possible curative treatment for the victims of these handicaps without the stigma of prison terms.

Progressive reduction of these handicaps thus depends upon accurate knowledge supplemented by regulatory, administrative, educational, constructive, and curative services, properly coördinated in a comprehensive social policy.

QUESTIONS FOR DISCUSSION OR EXAMINATION

1. Outline the findings of the National Health Survey as to the place of occurrence of permanent impairments due to accident.
2. Outline social policies for the prevention of (a) accidents, (b) disease, (c) inebriety and drug addiction.
3. How would you justify the emphasis upon the importance of (a) more complete registration? (b) more extensive and intensive research?
4. Why is progress so slow in the prevention of preventable disease and accident? How can it be accelerated?
5. In how far and by what arguments can you justify social interference with man's use of alcohol and drugs?

PROBLEMS FOR INDIVIDUAL STUDY

1. Assemble contemporary accident data for your state, and outline recommendations for (a) recording, (b) research, (c) prevention.
2. Compare the disease data for your city with those of some other selected city, and seek reasons for differences discovered.

3. Examine and evaluate the contemporary reports of your state and municipal boards of health and the laws under which they operate.
4. Compare the health, accident, or liquor laws of your state for 1900 (or some earlier date) with those now in force. What have been the sources of progress, retrogression, or change?
5. Outline the medical services available in your city and compare with the Bellevue-Yorkville district of New York City, or with the Cleveland Health Survey of 1920, or with some other local health survey.
6. Write a review and critical appraisal of some one of the books in the following list of references.
7. Prepare an annotated bibliography of the studies and reports on (a) accidents, (b) diseases, (c) medical facilities, or (d) liquor and drug control, for your city or state.

SUGGESTIONS FOR SUPPLEMENTARY READINGS

American Public Health Association—*Bibliography on Public Health and Allied Subjects;* September, 1934.
Bache, Louise Franklin—*Health Education in an American City;* published for the Milbank Memorial Fund by Doubleday, Doran & Company, Inc., 1934.
Binder, Rudolph—*Health and Social Progress;* Prentice-Hall, Inc., 1925.
Bossard, James H. S.—*Social Change and Social Problems,* Part V; Harper & Brothers, revised edition, 1938.
Committee on the Costs of Medical Care—*Medical Care for the American People;* University of Chicago Press, 1932.
Committee on the Costs of Medical Care—*Surveys of Organized Medical Service;* Committee on the Costs of Medical Care, Abstracts of Publications Nos. 17 to 21, 1932.
Davis, Michael M.—*Clinics, Hospitals and Health Centers;* Harper & Brothers, 1927.
Davis, Michael M., and Jarrett, Mary C.—*A Health Inventory of New York City;* Welfare Council of New York City, 1929.
Dinwiddie, Courtenay—*Child Health and the Community—An Interpretation of Coöperative Effort in Public Health;* The Commonwealth Fund, 1931.
Dublin, Louis I.—*Health and Wealth;* Harper & Brothers, 1928.
Dublin, Louis I., and Lotka, Alfred J.—*Twenty-Five Years of Health Progress;* Metropolitan Life Insurance Company, 1937.
Eaton, Allen, and Harrison, Shelby M.—*A Bibliography of Social Surveys;* Russell Sage Foundation, 1930.
Ferrell, John A., Smillie, Wilson G., Covington, Platt W., and Mead, Pauline A.—*Health Departments of States and Provinces of the United States and Canada;* United States Public Health Service, Public Health Bulletin No. 184, Government Printing Office, revised edition, 1932.
Ferrell, John A., and Mead, Pauline A.—*History of County Health Organizations in the United States 1908-33;* United States Public Health Service, Public Health Bulletin No. 222, Government Printing Office, March, 1936.

Frankel, Lee K., with the collaboration of Bunzel, Bessie—*The Health of the Worker;* Funk & Wagnalls Company, 1924.

Gardner, Mary Sewall—*Public Health Nursing;* The Macmillan Company, revised edition, 1936.

Goldberg, Rosamond W.—*Occupational Diseases;* Columbia University Press, 1931.

Green, Howard Whipple—*Health Councils;* Committee on the Costs of Medical Care, Miscellaneous Contributions No. 12, 1932.

Haggard, Howard W.—*Man and His Body;* Harper & Brothers, 1938.

Heinrich, Herbert W.—*Industrial Accident Prevention—A Scientific Approach;* McGraw-Hill Book Company, Inc., 1931.

Hiscock, Ira V., editor—*Community Health Organization;* The Commonwealth Fund, revised edition, 1932.

Hiscock, Ira V.—*District Health Administration;* The Science Press Printing Company, 1936.

Holbrook, Stewart H.—*Let Them Live;* The Macmillan Company, 1938.

International Association of Industrial Accident Boards and Commissions—*Proceedings;* published annually as bulletins of the U. S. Bureau of Labor Statistics.

Jarrett, Mary C.—*Chronic Illness in New York City,* 2 vols.; published for the Welfare Council of New York City by Columbia University Press, 1933.

Jordan, Edwin O.—*A Textbook of General Bacteriology;* W. B. Saunders Company, ninth edition, 1929.

Love, Albert G., and Davenport, Charles B.—*Physical Examination of the First Million Draft Recruits: Methods and Results;* War Department Bulletin No. 11, Government Printing Office, March, 1919.

McCombs, Carl E.—*City Health Administration:* The Macmillan Company, 1927.

McLaughlin, Allan J.—*The Communicable Diseases;* Harper & Brothers, 1923.

Messner, C. T., Gafafer, W. M., Cady, F. C., and Dean, H. T.—*Dental Survey of School Children, Ages 6–14 Years Made in 1933–34 in 26 States;* United States Public Health Service, Public Health Bulletin No. 226, Government Printing Office, May 1936.

Milbank Memorial Fund—Quarterly Bulletins.

Mills, Alden B.—*The Extent of Illness and of Physical and Mental Defects Prevailing in the United States;* Committee on the Costs of Medical Care, Publication No. 2, 1929.

Moore, Harry H.—*American Medicine and the People's Health;* D. Appleton and Company, 1927.

Moore, Harry H.—*Public Health in the United States;* Harper & Brothers, 1923.

Mustard, Harry S.—*An Introduction to Public Health;* The Macmillan Company, 1935.

National Safety Council—*Transactions;* published annually.

Newsholme, Sir Arthur—*Evolution of Preventive Medicine;* Williams & Wilkins Company, 1927.

Newsholme, Sir Arthur—*International Studies on the Relation between the Private and Official Practice of Medicine with Special Reference to the Prevention of Disease,* in three volumes; George Allen and Unwin Ltd., 1931.

Newsholme, Sir Arthur—*Medicine and the State;* Williams & Wilkins Company, 1932.

Perrott, George St. J., and Holland, Dorothy—"Chronic Diseases and Gross Impairments in a Northern Community"; *Journal of the American Medical Association,* May 29, 1937.

Prescott, Samuel C., and Horwood, Murray P.—*Sedgwick's Principles of Sanitary Science and Public Health, Revised;* The Macmillan Company, 1935.

Reed, Louis S.—*Health Insurance: The Next Step in Social Security;* Harper & Brothers, 1937.

Rice, Thurman B.—*The Conquest of Disease;* The Macmillan Company, 1927.

Rosenau, Milton J.—*Preventive Medicine and Hygiene;* D. Appleton-Century Company, sixth edition, 1935.

Sand, Rene—*Health and Human Progress: An Essay in Sociological Medicine;* The Macmillan Company, 1936.

Schmeckebier, Laurence F.—*The Public Health Service: Its History, Activities and Organization;* Institute for Government Research, Service Monographs of the United States Government No. 10, The Johns Hopkins Press, 1923.

Schmeckebier, Laurence F.—*The Statistical Work of the National Government,* Chapter IX, "Deaths, Diseases, and Accidents"; The Institute for Government Research, The Johns Hopkins Press, 1925.

Smiley, D. F., and Gould, A. G.—*Community Hygiene;* The Macmillan Company, revised edition, 1935.

Smillie, Wilson G.—*Public Health Administration in the United States;* The Macmillan Company, 1935.

Sydenstricker, Edgar—*Health and Environment;* McGraw-Hill Book Company, Inc., 1933.

U. S. Bureau of Labor Statistics—*Statistics of Industrial Accidents in the United States to the End of 1927;* Bulletin No. 490, 1929.

Vernon, H. M.—*Accidents and Their Prevention;* The Macmillan Company, 1937.

Wallace, James—*The State Health Departments of Massachusetts, Michigan, and Ohio;* The Commonwealth Fund, 1930.

White House Conference on Child Health and Protection—*Public Health Organization;* The Century Co., 1932.

Winslow, C.-E. A.—*A City Set on a Hill;* Doubleday, Doran & Company, Inc., 1934.

Winslow, C.-E. A.—"Communicable Diseases, Control of," *Encyclopaedia of the Social Sciences,* Vol. 4; The Macmillan Company, 1931.

Winslow, C.-E. A.—*The Evolution and Significance of the Modern Public Health Campaign;* Yale University Press, 1923.

Winslow, C.-E. A., and Zimand, Savel—*Health Under the "El": The Story of the Bellevue-Yorkville Health Demonstration in Mid-Town New York;* published for the Milbank Memorial Fund by Harper & Brothers, 1937.

PART III

POVERTY AND ECONOMIC HAZARDS
THE DISORGANIZATION AND PATHOLOGY
OF ECONOMIC RELATIONSHIPS

CHAPTER XVII

EXTENT AND CONDITIONS OF POVERTY

Definitions.—The term poverty implies inadequate resources. Since, however, most persons find their means insufficient to meet their own rapidly multiplying desires, it is proper to restrict the term. It is reasonable to classify as poor any family whose income is insufficient to provide adequate food, clothing, shelter, or other necessaries of life adequate in amount and kind to maintain health. Thus, poverty in one sense of the term is "economic insufficiency." [1] Some, but not all of the families with insufficient incomes receive aid from public or private sources. This latter group is known as the "dependent poor." In their case poverty would be defined as "economic dependence."

Virtually all of the dependent group suffer from economic insufficiency, though some few secure public relief who could get along without it. Many persons with inadequate incomes, however, fail to become dependents through pride, ignorance, or the unavailability of relief. Poverty in the sense of economic insufficiency is thus a more inclusive category than is economic dependence.

Current Misconceptions.—By many persons who are well above the poverty line, the poor are visualized in terms of the street beggar.

---

[1] This term was used by Jacob H. Hollander in his excellent study entitled *The Abolition of Poverty;* Houghton Mifflin Company, 1914. At best the terms "adequacy" and "economic insufficiency" suffer from inescapable subjectivity. The victim of "inadequacy" measures his condition in terms of his standard of life (defined by Alfred Marshall as "activities adjusted to wants") which has its basis in the contemporary culture complex, and in the traditions, habits, and attitudes of his immediate family and associates, as well as in his own training and ambitions. The standard of adequacy remains subjective even when reduced to terms of "health and efficiency." For though the health and efficiency of each individual are social desiderata and wide deviations therefrom are measurable, many and perhaps most marginal cases are highly subjective in that by a change in personal attitudes they might be removed from the "inadequate" group to that labeled "adequate." The most useful compilations of contemporary literature on family needs and budgets will be found in Eliot, Thomas D.—*American Standards and Planes of Living;* Ginn and Company, 1931: Williams, Faith M., and Zimmerman, Carle C.—*Studies of Family Living in the United States and Other Countries;* U. S. Department of Agriculture, Miscellaneous Publication No. 223, Government Printing Office, 1935; and Zimmerman, Carle C.—*Consumption and Standards of Living;* D. Van Nostrand Company, Inc., 1936.

Poverty is still often confused with vice and criminality, with filth and degeneracy, with shiftlessness and indolence and is deemed the penalty of moral obliquity. The poor are said to receive their just deserts. Some assume that poverty is inevitably implicit in our moral and economic order. "Ye have the poor with you always" is accepted by such as an injunction rather than as a statement of historical fact. The tendency of the well-to-do victims of these misconceptions is to face the problem of the poverty of others with either loathing, indifference, or begrudging alms. Ignorance of the true nature and effects of poverty has been responsible for the survival of *laissez faire*, and for delay through the two millenniums of the Christian era in effecting a comprehensive public policy for prevention.

Social surveys from the time of Charles Booth have revealed that few among the poor are beggars or degenerates. Even those few might have been deflected from mendicancy if wisely aided during their early and impressionable years. The variety of human types among the poor appears to be as wide as it is among an equal number of the population above the poverty line. They include some men and women of talent, refinement, and high character, as well as many of the ignorant and dissolute, and a still larger mass of persons whose attainments are neither unusually high nor low. The percentage of persons suffering from physical or mental handicap is, however, higher among the poor than in the general population because such handicaps, by reducing earning capacity, lead to dependency.

Conditions of Poverty.—For all of the poor, whether or not dependent upon relief, poverty means hardship. If relieved in time, the diet though meager may be sufficient; but undernourishment is common. Restricted income means that clothing, furniture, and utensils cannot be replenished when they wear out. Many suffer seriously from inappropriate or insufficient clothing during the winter season. In cities their homes are in the oldest and least sanitary tenements or shacks of their community and generally consist of one, two, or three rooms, of which only one is heated even in the winter months. Life ordinarily lacks comfort and even privacy; for among the chronic poor several persons must often sleep in the same room or even in one bed. Life may be lived in constant fear of creditors, of hunger, of eviction, of the almshouse, and a pauper's grave. In rural regions many of these dangers are sometimes accentuated because of the unavailability of organized relief.

In both city and country years of poverty may break health and spirits, and so handicap the growing child in physique, training, and attitude that normal life and happiness may be rendered unattainable.[2]

The Extent of Dependency.—The actual volume of dependency is not known. Many families and individuals are aided, and sometimes entirely supported, by relatives whose gifts are not recorded. Much help is received from neighbors; for the poor understand distress and often share the little they have. Fraternal organizations do not publish particulars of the aid which they give to members in straitened circumstances. Many church organizations render no public account of their assistance to distressed parishioners. Employers, trade unions, immigrant societies, and casual givers each make unrecorded contributions.

There remain therefore as sources of information on the extent of dependency only the reports of public welfare departments and of organized private welfare service. Since the same individual may apply to more than one of these agencies in any given year, or to the same agency more than once, official figures which in some instances count applications rather than individuals may give an exaggerated picture of the number of dependents. It is, however, a safe assumption, in view of the large volume of unrecorded relief, that the amount of temporary dependency is larger than the figure obtained from such official records.

Official figures of public relief in the United States for recent years show that the volume of dependency varies widely according to local circumstances. There have been communities in which the whole population has been dependent for its income upon employment in a local mine or factory. When the mine or factory has closed down all families have been thrust upon relief. In our largest cities somewhat over 15 per cent of the population have been recorded as in receipt of public aid. Among smaller communities some have fallen well below and some are far above this percentage of public dependence. For example, in May, 1934, although the per-

[2] The conditions of poverty are well described in Devine, Edward T.—*Misery and Its Causes;* The Macmillan Company, 1913, and more recently in Cavan, Ruth Shonle, and Ranck, Katherine Howland—*The Family and the Depression;* University of Chicago Press, 1938. Social surveys (see Part I, Chapters II and III) and casebooks reveal the wide variety of forms which they take. Recent conditions of poverty in England are presented in *Men without Work*, a Report made to the Pilgrim Trust; Cambridge University Press, 1938.

centage of families on relief to total families in seventy-nine cities was around 15 per cent, the ratio in Burlington, Vermont, was only 6 per cent, and in Gastonia, North Carolina, Gloversville, New York, Oakland, California, and Portsmouth, New Hampshire, only 7 per cent. Yet at the other end of the scale Butte, Montana, showed 67 per cent of its total families on relief.[3]

Estimates of public expenditures for relief by the Federal, state, and local governments for the four years 1933 to 1936, inclusive, place the total cost at sums ranging as high as $13,000,000,000.[4] However, the official figures as reported to the Federal Relief Administration, from January, 1933, through June, 1936, gave a grand total of $4,394,274,293, of which over $2,929,307,125 consisted of Federal funds and the remainder of state and local funds.[5] In addition, the Civil Works Administration spent well over one billion dollars and the Works Progress Administration, up to December 31, 1936, over $3,500,000,000. But these latter expenditures together with a large percentage of those of the Civilian Conservation Corps and the Rural Resettlement Administration and all of those of the Public Works Administration have included supplies as well as reimbursed services and utilities of social value. Unquestionably several billion dollars would have to be deducted from total expenditures in order to arrive at those which might properly be considered "relief." The continuing expenses for emergency relief of the local units of government since June, 1936, belong, however, almost wholly under the cost of relief.

The total number of individuals and families helped is not known, but at the peak of public relief in February, 1934, the number of different households aided by Federal, state, and local governments was reported to be 7,879,000, making a total of 27,606,000 persons or over 20 per cent of our population as estimated in the Census of 1930.[6]

---

[3] Mueller, John H.—"Some Social Characteristics of the Urban Relief Population," p. 65; *Social Forces*, October, 1936.

[4] Alsop, Joseph, Jr., and Catledge, Turner—"Our Biggest Business—Relief"; *The Saturday Evening Post*, Vol. 209, No. 40, April 5, 1937.

[5] *Monthly Report of the Federal Emergency Relief Administration, June 1 through June 30, 1936* (final issue), p. 171; Government Printing Office, 1937.

[6] Burns, Arthur E., and Williams, Edward A.—*A Survey of Relief and Security Programs*, p. 3; Works Progress Administration, May, 1938. These authors estimate expenditures for the relief, work, and security programs from January, 1933, through December, 1937, at over thirteen billion dollars of which the Federal government supplied 74 per cent. *Ibid.*, p. 67.

In recent years of economic depression private charities have largely confined their efforts to advisory social work as distinguished from relief. In cases needing special care they have on occasion supplemented the funds available from public sources. They still continue to be the sole support of many thousands of families.

When, as is sometimes the case, 40 per cent of the workers in a community are unemployed but only 15 per cent are receiving public relief, it is safe to assume that a large portion of the remaining unemployed are not subsisting wholly on savings but are receiving aid from friends, relatives, fraternal organizations, churches, and other sources the donations of which are not recorded. This may be true also of many families who have only part-time employment or who are engaged at poorly remunerated labor. It is thus conservative to assume that at times in the depression years 1930–38 one-fourth of our families have been supported, in part or in full, by the remaining three-fourths.

Poverty as Economic Insufficiency: Brookings Institution Studies, 1929.—To give a precise picture of the extent of poverty in the sense of economic insufficiency is even more difficult. When the Brookings Institution showed that in 1929, the year of the peak of prosperity, one-tenth of 1 per cent of the families of America received practically as much income as 42 per cent of the families at the bottom of the scale, it revealed much concerning *relative* poverty. The 42 per cent comprised about twelve million families whose incomes that year were less than $1,500 each. Half of this latter group, or six million families, had annual incomes of less than $1,000.[7]

Unquestionably many of the rural families with incomes of less than $1,000 were able to live wholesomely on their meager budgets. Doubtless many other families dwelling in southern cities or in small towns throughout America, in spite of incomes of less than $1,000, found it possible to keep above the poverty line. For it costs less to live in the country than in the city, and money usually stretches much farther in the South and West than in the North and East. In villages, small towns, and to a less degree in cities, many a minister, teacher, industrial worker, or small shopkeeper has demonstrated that by thrift and careful planning a standard of living acceptable to prevailing custom can be maintained for a not-too-

[7] Leven, Maurice, Moulton, Harold G., and Warburton, Clark—*America's Capacity to Consume*, pp. 55–56; The Brookings Institution, 1934.

large family with a money income not much over $1,000 per year. Yet on the other hand large numbers of families with incomes exceeding $1,500, if residing in northern cities, did without things necessary for health and well-being, because there were too many mouths to feed, or because of illness or unwise expenditures.

Excluding the rural population, the Brookings Institution found that about 13 per cent of non-farm families of two or more persons in the United States received in 1929 an annual income of less than $1,000.[8] They gave by these percentages a rough indication of the size of the urban group which in prosperous years is considerably below the poverty line—since the number in poverty who receive above that sum would presumably much more than counterbalance the number who are not in poverty though receiving less.

Not far from the poverty line, however, were a large percentage of the sixteen million families with incomes under $2,000 who constituted 59 per cent of all families. Of gross American savings only 1.6 per cent of the total national income saved was ascribable to this group. Nineteen million families, or 71 per cent of the total, had incomes of less than $2,500. These comprised 5,169,-000 farm families and 14,399,000 urban families.[9] In the words of Harold G. Moulton, they "spend practically all their income for bare necessities. These families therefore are practically without conveniences or luxuries." [10]

Poverty at Higher Income Levels.—Families with incomes well above $1,500 and even up to $2,500 a year often suffer hardship either (1) because they cannot find within the community wholesome housing within their rent-paying capacity; or (2) because through ignorance of food values and markets they cannot properly nourish the family on an expenditure which should be adequate for its food needs; or (3) because too large a percentage of income is invested in accessories, recreation, dissolute living, or even savings; or (4) because past emergencies have been met by borrowing, frequently at usurious rates, forcing the use of much of the present income to meet interest payments; or (5) because the family is unduly burdened with instalment payments for furniture and clothing,

---

[8] *Ibid.*, p. 231.

[9] Moulton, Harold G.—*Income and Economic Progress*, pp. 37, 40, and 69; The Brookings Institution, 1935.

[10] Moulton, Harold G.—"Economic Progress without Economic Revolution"; *Fortune*, November, 1935—see p. 10 of reprint by the Maurice and Laura Falk Foundation of Pittsburgh.

or payments towards the purchase of a house or shop; or (6) because of expensive illnesses or accidents; or (7) because of dependents outside the immediate family circle; or (8) because of too many children.

Housing as Index.—In every community the families with lowest incomes are forced by circumstances to live in the oldest and least sanitary dwellings. Relatively few of the wage-earning population of America find it possible to live in houses that are safe, sanitary, wholesome, convenient, comfortable, and with adequate provision for decency, space needs, and privacy. In New York City, for example, over two million persons or thirty per cent of the population live in dwellings erected prior to this century.[11] They have to put up with the inferior standards of sanitation, planning, and construction of the preceding century, which means apartments of not more than three rooms, in dark, malodorous tenement houses usually without central heat or private toilets or baths within the apartment, and with their sole outlook upon a cheerless slum. In the South and West the day laborer's allowance for rent usually makes possible only a dismal, crowded dwelling in an undesirable neighborhood and lacking many of the modern conveniences.

The real property inventory conducted in 1934 by the United States Department of Commerce in sixty-four cities of varying size, but covering at least one city in each of the forty-eight states, examined over one million four hundred thousand residential buildings housing over seven million seven hundred thousand persons. Findings are briefly summarized as follows:

"According to final figures, 34,841 buildings, or 2.3 per cent of the structural units in the 64 cities were in the 'unfit for use' class, and 235,-353, or 15.8 per cent in the class needing structural repairs. The combined group are, therefore, 18.1 per cent of the total. The number of dwelling units in each class would be about 1.4 greater, if the ratio of dwelling units to structures in these classes is average. It is almost certainly higher.

"The summary shows that 16.8 per cent of the occupied dwelling units (not structural units) were crowded or worse, that 13.5 per cent of all

[11] There are in New York City approximately 67,000 old-law tenement houses erected prior to 1900. These contain 500,000 apartments. In addition there are over 300,000 single-family dwellings and 160,000 two-family dwellings, a large percentage of which were erected prior to this century. It is conservative to state that the number of persons dwelling in substandard tenements or houses is over two million. Ford, James, in collaboration with Morrow, Katherine, and Thompson, George N.—*Slums and Housing, with Special Reference to New York City: History, Conditions, Policy*, Vol. I, p. 298; Harvard University Press, 1936.

dwelling units lacked private indoor toilets, 20.2 per cent had neither bathtubs nor showers, 8.1 per cent lacked modern lighting, and 5.0 per cent were without running water.

"It cannot be demonstrated that these percentages are overlapping ·and refer to the same houses, but to a large extent they undoubtedly do. The figures vary widely from city to city, but in every city bad housing is present. . . .

"The percentages of crowding are illuminating. The only cities with less than 10 per cent are Portland, Oreg., with 7.3 per cent, San Diego with 8.6 per cent, Lansing with 9 per cent, Syracuse with 9 per cent, Seattle with 9.5 per cent, and Williamsport with 9.7 per cent. At the high end are Charleston with 40.4 per cent of crowded homes, Atlanta with 30.3 per cent, Santa Fe with 35.4 per cent, Columbia with 32.4 per cent, Birmingham and Jackson, with 27.2 per cent, Paducah with 28.4 per cent, and Knoxville with 28.1 per cent. . . .

"The picture emerging will be of nearly a fifth of our urban population living in dilapidated houses, generally crowded, and typically lacking private indoor toilets and bathtubs. Nearly half of these substandard homes are also without electric lights and about a quarter of them have no running water. More fortunate than this class are a borderline group who live in structurally sound homes, needing paint and other minor repairs, and lacking baths and water closets." [12]

Certainly families that cannot afford to provide a sanitary and wholesome home and neighborhood in which to bring up their children may be described as poor.

Malnutrition as Index.—Many families cannot earn enough to meet the cost of their food requirements. Others of the poor are uninformed concerning food values so that even though the percentage of income expended for food is sufficient to provide for adequate nourishment ignorance leads to a poorly rounded dietary. A number of studies of food expenditures by the poor have revealed that too little is spent for milk for growing children—whose breakfasts often consist merely of bread and tea or coffee—and too little for fresh vegetables and fruits.[13] Since, however, malnutrition may be an evidence of ignorance or carelessness, and may even occur in well-to-do families, it is a less satisfactory index of the extent of poverty than is housing. Personal factors such as indifference,

[12] Wood, Edith Elmer—*Slums and Blighted Areas in the United States*, pp. 84, 85, and 86; Federal Emergency Administration of Public Works, Housing Division Bulletin No. 1, Government Printing Office, 1935.

[13] Gibbs, Winifred S.—*The Minimum Cost of Living;* The Macmillan Company, 1917. Eliot, Thomas D.—*op. cit.*, especially Chapter VII. Boudreau, F. G.— *The International Campaign for Better Nutrition;* reprinted from *The Milbank Memorial Fund Quarterly*, Vol. XV, No. 2, April, 1937.

response to fashion, interests, training, and associates largely influence expenditures for clothing and sundries. Hence these too do not serve well as an index of economic insufficiency. The details of family budgets and standards of living will however be treated in later chapters.

Secondary Poverty.—Many a family with an income which would be sufficient to provide the necessaries of life is in what Rowntree has termed "secondary poverty," [14] because money needed for food or clothes has been spent on drink or gambling, or on recreation, education, or savings. Some years ago a community in the Connecticut Valley was shocked to see several children in an immigrant Polish family going to school, in the chill winds of late October, barefoot and dressed in flimsy summer garments. A collection of warm clothing was taken up for the family. Yet a few months later the father paid $5,000 in cash for the purchase of a farm. He had kept the family in "secondary poverty" in order to achieve his life's ambition. Similarly, children are sacrificed to save money for the purchase of a store or tenement, for education, or other purposes which are in themselves often highly praiseworthy. At the other end of the moral scale we find heavy expenditures for drink, movies, and lotteries, reducing an income which would otherwise be adequate, and resulting in underfeeding or curtailments elsewhere in the budget.

Debts.—The burden of past debts holds large numbers of families in poverty when their incomes would otherwise be ample to meet their needs. Unemployment, illness, help rendered to relatives or neighbors, unwise investment, or frivolous expenditure may have occasioned the debt. Families of low income having no securities to use as collateral cannot borrow, as the well-to-do can, from banks, at 5 or 6 per cent interest, but must ordinarily have recourse to the pawnbroker, usurer, or loan shark. Their few prized possessions, and even necessary clothing and furniture, may never be retrieved from the pawnbrokers. There are abundant recorded instances of families wrecked by borrowing at usurious rates from the loan sharks.[15] Even the remedial loan associations organized by philanthropy may legally charge 36 per cent per year on small

[14] Rowntree, B. Seebohm—*Poverty; A Study of Town Life;* Macmillan and Co., Limited, 1901.

[15] Nugent, Rolf—"Family Debt," *Social Work Year Book 1937;* Russell Sage Foundation, 1937, gives a brief description of conditions and submits useful references to literature.

loans.[16] Furniture and clothing purchased on instalments may be taken back by the seller if payments are not kept up, so that both the payments already made and the goods are lost. Mortgage foreclosures on owned homes for which families have made years of sacrifice may likewise reduce to dependence families once well above the poverty line.

The group suffering from poverty in the sense of economic insufficiency, which in prosperous periods is certainly not less than 12 to 15 per cent of our population, becomes very much larger in periods of depression. Unemployment, reduced salaries and wages, loss of investments (whether securities, equities, or savings), the requests or demands for aid from relatives so that they may be spared the shame of "going on relief" have during the nineteen thirties brought poverty, or the daily fear of poverty, to fully a third of our population, and "relative poverty" through shrinkage of capital and incomes to a large percentage of the remainder.

Approach to the Pathology of Economic Relationships.—Since economics is the science of the production and distribution of wealth, poverty, or the lack of income adequate to meet family needs, may be viewed as a problem of the pathology of economic relationships. It has been seen that handicap is not exclusively a problem of heredity or disease. Similarly, poverty is never exclusively a problem of economic relationships. In both fields personal attitudes and behavior, as conditioned by training and experience, by the physical and social environment, and by personal will and character, interact with and modify economic circumstances. It will be found, however, that to some extent the economic factors can be isolated for study, and that policies for social control of economic conditions can affect the volume and incidence of poverty. Hence we turn first to the consideration of causative factors.

QUESTIONS FOR DISCUSSION OR EXAMINATION

1. Define and distinguish poverty, dependence, economic insufficiency, pauperism, indigence, penury, destitution.
2. Is poverty necessarily (a) an evil? (b) pathological? (Define both terms.) Is the cult of poverty by certain religious groups (a) an evil? (b) pathological?
3. Is dependence upon relatives a problem in social pathology? Why? Why not? or Under what conditions?

[16] Robinson, Louis N., and Stearns, Maude E.—*Ten Thousand Small Loans;* Russell Sage Foundation, 1930.

4. What standards of reference would you use to determine the presence or absence of poverty? Why?
5. Under what circumstances if any would secondary poverty not be a problem in social pathology?
6. Define (a) disorganization of economic relationships, (b) pathology of economic relationships. Can you think of instances of one of these in which the other is not present?

PROBLEMS FOR INDIVIDUAL STUDY

1. Assemble and interpret all available data *re* poverty in your own city or some selected city or state.
2. Compare data *re* extent of poverty in works of Hunter, Parmelee, Kelso, Hollander, or other selected volumes.
3. Account for variations in dependency rates (as given in Federal, state, and local documents) for two or more contrasted states, counties, cities, or wards.
4. A critical examination of studies of income distribution.
5. The pathology of economic relationships and its association with other pathologic conditions from analysis of case records or casebooks (*e.g.* Southard, E. E., and Jarrett, Mary C.—*The Kingdom of Evils;* The Macmillan Company, 1922).

SUGGESTIONS FOR SUPPLEMENTARY READINGS

Angell, Robert Cooley—*The Family Encounters the Depression;* Charles Scribner's Sons, 1936.

Bossard, James H. S.—*Social Change and Social Problems,* Part III; Harper & Brothers, revised edition, 1938.

Cavan, Ruth Shonle, and Ranck, Katherine Howland—*The Family and the Depression;* University of Chicago Press, 1938.

Devine, Edward T.—*Misery and Its Causes,* Chapter I, "Poverty and Maladjustment"; The Macmillan Company, 1913.

Eaton, Allen, and Harrison, Shelby M.—*A Bibliography of Social Surveys,* References on "Dependency," pp. 88–89, and on "Relief," pp. 259–260; Russell Sage Foundation, 1930.

Eliot, Thomas D.—*American Standards and Planes of Living,* especially Chapter II; Ginn and Company, 1931.

Ford, James—*Social Problems and Social Policy,* Chapters XIX and XX; Ginn and Company, 1923.

Gillette, John M., and Reinhardt, James M.—*Current Social Problems,* Chapters VIII–XI; American Book Company, 1937.

Gillin, John Lewis—*Poverty and Dependency,* Chapters II–IV; The Century Co., 1921.

Great Britain—*Report of Royal Commission on the Poor Laws and Relief of Distress,* Report (1 vol.) with evidence and appendices (33 vols.); H. M. Stationery Office, 1909–10.

Haber, William, and Stanchfield, Paul L.—*Unemployment, Relief and Economic Security: A Survey of Michigan's Relief and Unemployment Problem,*

Chapter II; Second Report of the State Emergency Welfare Relief Commission, Lansing, 1936.

Hollander, Jacob H.—*The Abolition of Poverty*, Chapter I, "The Nature of Poverty," and Chapter III, "The Distribution of Income"; Houghton Mifflin Company, 1914.

Hopkins, Harry L.—*Spending to Save: The Complete Story of Relief;* W. W. Norton & Company, Inc., 1936.

Kelso, Robert W.—*Poverty*, Part I; Longmans, Green and Co., 1929.

King, Willford Isbell—*The Wealth and Income of the People of the United States;* The Macmillan Company, 1922.

Leven, Maurice, Moulton, Harold G., and Warburton, Clark—*America's Capacity to Consume;* The Brookings Institution, 1934.

National Bureau of Economic Research—*Income in the United States: Its Amount and Distribution, 1909–1919;* Harcourt, Brace and Company, Inc., 1921.

National Industrial Conference Board—*The Cost of Living in the United States, 1914–1936;* National Industrial Conference Board, 1936.

Parmelee, Maurice—*Poverty and Social Progress*, Chapters VI–VIII; The Macmillan Company, 1917.

Queen, Stuart Alfred, and Mann, Delbert Martin—*Social Pathology*, Chapter XII, "Poverty—Income and Standards of Living"; Thomas Y. Crowell Company, 1925.

Rowntree, B. Seebohm—*Poverty; A Study of Town Life*, Chapter III, "The Standard of Life," and Chapter IV, "The Poverty Line"; Macmillan and Co., Limited, 1901.

Sorokin, Pitirim, and Zimmerman, Carle C.—*Principles of Rural-Urban Sociology*, Chapter III, "The Status of the Farmer-Peasant Class Among Other Social Classes"; Henry Holt and Company, 1929.

Southard, E. E., and Jarrett, Mary C.—*The Kingdom of Evils*, pp. 390–415; The Macmillan Company, 1922.

United States Bureau of the Census—*Special Report: Relief Expenditures by Governmental and Private Organizations, 1929 and 1931;* Government Printing Office, 1932.

Watson, J. P.—*Economic Backgrounds of the Relief Problem*, especially Chapters 1, 2, and 12; Bureau of Business Research, University of Pittsburgh, 1937.

Webb, Sidney and Beatrice—*The Prevention of Destitution*, Chapter I, "Destitution as a Disease of Society"; Longmans, Green and Co., 1911.

Williams, Faith M., and Zimmerman, Carle C.—*Studies of Family Living in the United States and Other Countries;* U. S. Department of Agriculture, Miscellaneous Publication No. 223, Government Printing Office, 1935.

Wolman, Leo—"Consumption and the Standard of Living," Chapter I of *Recent Economic Changes in the United States*, Vol. I; published for the National Bureau of Economic Research, Inc., by McGraw-Hill Book Company, Inc., 1929.

Wood, Edith Elmer—*Slums and Blighted Areas in the United States;* Federal Emergency Administration of Public Works, Housing Division Bulletin No. 1, Government Printing Office, 1935.

Zimmerman, Carle C.—*Consumption and Standards of Living;* D. Van Nostrand Company, Inc., 1936.

CHAPTER XVIII

EXAMPLES OF CLASSIC THEORIES OF POVERTY CAUSATION

Early Theories of Poverty.—For many centuries leading thinkers and humanitarians have given thought to the causes of poverty; but until the latter part of the eighteenth century little evidence was adduced in support of their arguments. Histories of economic thought and of economic conditions trace criticisms of the methods of remuneration of labor far into the past.[1] Histories of political theory and social practice uncover early concern with the problems of poverty, slavery, serfdom, and labor, as well as with the forms of social organization and of social policy.[2]

Beginning with the era of social investigation each writer in turn offered some major solution for the pathologic conditions which his researches uncovered, or devoted his later life to specific reforms deemed by him to be of paramount importance. Davies urged minimum-wage legislation. Eden, like Adam Smith and Nassau Senior, sought poor law reform. Le Play argued for paternal authority within monogamic marriage institutions. Booth urged the withdrawal of his "Class B" from competition with Classes C and D and their colonization, and in his later years promoted old age pensions. Engel, Rowntree, and others sought a variety of reforms.[3]

The Search for Fundamental Causes.—Three of the earlier studies which still influence thought and attitudes are those of Thomas Malthus, Karl Marx, and Henry George. Because they offer panaceas, and because they represent schools of thought seriously followed by large numbers of people, they deserve examination here.

The Malthusian Theory.—Malthus, in his *Essay on Population*, first published in England in 1798, noted the tendency of population

---

[1] Gide, Charles, and Rist, Charles—*A History of Economic Doctrines from the Time of the Physiocrats to the Present Day* (authorized translation from the second revised edition of 1913 under direction of William Smart, by R. Richards); D. C. Heath and Company, 1915. See also footnote 10 of Part I, Chapter II.

[2] See works of Barnes and Becker, Dunning, Hearnshaw, Lecky, and McIlwain mentioned in the list of references which follow this chapter.

[3] See Part I, Chapter II.

to increase in geometrical ratio while the means of subsistence and especially food increased in only arithmetical ratio.[4] The natural consequence of such a law of population was noted to be famine except where peoples were periodically decimated by war or pestilence. Malthus made clear in his later writings that through the moral factor of restraint this law of population could be curbed in its operation.

In his second and revised edition of 1803, Malthus closed his "general deductions" with the statements:

"If a country were never to be overrun by a people more advanced in arts, but left to its own natural progress in civilisation; from the time that its produce might be considered as an unit, to the time that it might be considered as a million, during the lapse of many thousand years, there might not be a single period when the mass of the people could be said to be free from distress, either directly or indirectly, for want of food.   In every state in Europe, since we have first had accounts of it, millions and millions of human existences have been repressed from this simple cause, though perhaps in some of these states an absolute famine may never have been known.

"Must it not then be acknowledged by an attentive examiner of the histories of mankind, that, in every age and in every state in which man has existed or does now exist,

"The increase of population is necessarily limited by the means of subsistence:

"Population invariably increases when the means of subsistence increase,* unless prevented by powerful and obvious checks:

"These checks, and the checks which keep the population down to the level of the means of subsistence, are moral restraint, vice, and misery?

". . . I think it appears that in modern Europe the positive checks to population prevail less and the preventive checks more than in past times, and in the more uncivilised parts of the world.

"War, the predominant check to the population of savage nations, has certainly abated, even including the late unhappy revolutionary contests; and since the prevalence of a greater degree of personal cleanliness, of better modes of clearing and building towns, and of a more equable distribution of the products of the soil from improving knowledge in political economy, plagues, violent diseases, and famines have been certainly mitigated, and have become less frequent.

[4] Malthus, Rev. T. R.—*An Essay on Population*, two volumes; E. P. Dutton & Co. (no date). He expressed the principle as follows: "Taking the whole earth, instead of this island, emigration would of course be excluded; and, supposing the present population equal to a thousand millions, the human species would increase as the numbers, 1, 2, 4, 8, 16, 32, 64, 128, 256, and subsistence as 1, 2, 3, 4, 5, 6, 7, 8, 9. In two centuries the population would be to the means of subsistence as 256 to 9; in three centuries as 4096 to 13, and in two thousand years the difference would be almost incalculable." Pp. 10–11.

"With regard to the preventive check to population, though it must be acknowledged that that branch of it which comes under the head of moral restraint, does not at present prevail much among the male part of society, yet I am strongly disposed to believe that it prevails more than in those states which were first considered; and it can scarcely be doubted that in modern Europe a much larger proportion of women pass a considerable part of their lives in the exercise of this virtue than in past times and among uncivilised nations. But however this may be, if we consider only the general term which implies principally a delay of the marriage union from prudential considerations, without reference to consequences, it may be considered in this light as the most powerful of the checks which in modern Europe keep down the population to the level of the means of subsistence."[5]

Specialists in problems of population dispute whether in countries of primitive agriculture like China or India the tendency can be noted for population to increase with greater rapidity than the means of subsistence. In our western civilization, however, the rapid progress in the science of agriculture—in seed selection, fertilization, cultivation, and the manufacture and use of agricultural machinery—has increased the output per capita even though population has greatly increased. It is thus proved possible for an ever declining percentage of the population to feed the nation.[6]

Penrose, in his brilliant work entitled *Population Theories and Their Application*, states:

"From the standpoint of its serviceability for the interpretation of modern conditions, the Malthusian scheme suffers on the one hand from an undue emphasis on the limitation of the supply of land, and on the other from inadequate stress on the possibilities opened up by industrialization and international trade. Both of these shortcomings are to a considerable extent in turn the outcome of a tendency to underestimate the importance of inventions and improvements in the arts. In the time of Malthus the limitation of the supply of land was more important for particular communities than it is now, and industrialization and international trade were still of relatively small dimensions.

". . . The Malthusian vision of an ever present tendency for reproduction to outstrip production no longer need haunt us. There is

[5] *Ibid.*, pp. 314–315. *"By an increase in the means of subsistence, as the expression is used here, is always meant such an increase as the mass of the population can command; otherwise it can be of no avail in encouraging an increase of people."

[6] Cf. Taussig, F. W.—*Principles of Economics*, Vol. II, Chapters 52 and 53; The Macmillan Company, 1913: East, Edward M.—*Mankind at the Crossroads;* Charles Scribner's Sons, 1926: and Chase, Stuart—*Men and Machines;* The Macmillan Company, 1935.

no inexorable law, inherent in the processes through which the reproduction of the race is attained, leading mankind to disaster. It is not the niggardliness of Nature but the irrationality of Man that stands in the way of a working solution of the population problems that arise out of the inevitable disparity between the distribution of population and the distribution of natural resources."[7]

In recent years also population growth has been curbed through later marriages, birth control, and possibly also increasing sterility, to a degree never contemplated by Malthus. There are, to be sure, abundant instances of families, both urban and rural, that are too large to be supported adequately on the income of the breadwinner. But the general poverty within the nation cannot be ascribed to the Malthusian hypothesis.

The Marxian Theory.—Marx, trained in law and Hegelian philosophy, found the origin of poverty in human exploitation. His theory was brought to the attention of the world first in *The Communist Manifesto* which he wrote jointly with Frederick Engels in 1848. The explanation of poverty was much amplified and refined in his three-volume work *Das Kapital*, the first volume of which appeared in 1867.[8] There are three main propositions commonly accredited to him by both his followers and his enemies on which his account of the source of poverty rests. These are stated here without Marx's own careful qualifications.[9] The first is a theory of value—that the exchange value of goods depends on the amount of socially necessary labor time required to produce them. The second is the "iron law of wages"—that workers, though they produce everything, are paid only the bare cost of living, only enough to keep them alive and working and able to reproduce another generation of workers. The third is the doctrine of surplus value—that the worker creates by his labor more value than he receives, which value is appropriated by capitalists in the form of rent, interest, and profits.

"The value of labor-power is determined, as in the case of every other commodity, by the labor-time necessary for the production, and conse-

[7] Penrose, E. F.—*Population Theories and Their Application: With Special Reference to Japan*, pp. 13 and 336; Food Research Institute, Stanford University Press, 1934.

[8] Marx, Karl—*Capital: A Critical Analysis of Capitalist Production* (translated from the third German edition, by Samuel Moore and Edward Aveling, and edited by Frederick Engels); The Humboldt Publishing Co. (no date).

[9] Some of the qualifications are summarized in Harris, Abram L.—"The Marxian Right to the Whole Product," pp. 147–198 of *Economic Essays in Honor of Wesley Clair Mitchell;* Columbia University Press, 1935.

quently also the reproduction, of this special article. So far as it has value, it represents no more than a definite quantity of the average labor of society incorporated in it. Labor-power exists only as a capacity, or power of the living individual. Its production consequently presupposes his existence. Given the individual, the production of labor-power consists in his reproduction of himself or his maintenance. For his maintenance he requires a given quantity of the means of subsistence. Therefore, the labor-time requisite for the production of labor-power reduces itself to that necessary for the production of those means of subsistence; in other words, the value of labor-power is the value of the means of subsistence necessary for the maintenance of the laborer. Labor-power, however, becomes a reality only by its exercise; it sets itself in action only by working. But thereby a definite quantity of human muscle, nerve, brain, etc., is wasted, and these require to be restored. This increased expenditure demands a larger income. If the owner of labor-power works to-day, to-morrow he must again be able to repeat the same process in the same conditions as regards health and strength. His means of subsistence must, therefore, be sufficient to maintain him in his normal state as a laboring individual. His natural wants, such as food, clothing, fuel, and housing, vary according to the climatic and other physical conditions of his country. On the other hand, the number and extent of his so-called necessary wants, as also the modes of satisfying them, are themselves the product of historical development, and depend, therefore, to a great extent on the degree of civilization of a country—more particularly on the conditions under which, and consequently on the habits and degree of comfort in which, the class of free laborers has been formed. In contradistinction, therefore, to the case of other commodities, there enters into the determination of the value of labor-power an historical and moral element. Nevertheless, in a given country, at a given period, the average quantity of the means of subsistence necessary for the laborer is practically known.

"The owner of labor-power is mortal. If, then, his appearance in the market is to be continuous, and the continuous conversion of money into capital assumes this, the seller of labor-power must perpetuate himself, 'in the way that every living individual perpetuates himself, by procreation.' The labor-power withdrawn from the market by wear and tear and death must be continually replaced by, at the very least, an equal amount of fresh labor-power. Hence the sum of the means of subsistence necessary for the production of labor-power must include the means necessary for the laborer's substitutes, i.e., his children, in order that this race of peculiar commodity-owners may perpetuate its appearance in the market.

"In order to modify the human organism, so that it may acquire skill and handiness in a given branch of industry, and become labor-power of a special kind, a special education or training is requisite; and this, on its part, costs an equivalent in commodities of a greater or less amount. This amount varies according to the more or less complicated character of the labor-power. The expenses of this education (excessively small in the case of ordinary labor-power) enter *pro tanto* into the total value spent in its production.

"The value of labor-power resolves itself into the value of a definite quantity of the means of subsistence. It, therefore, varies with the value of these means, or with the quantity of labor requisite for their production. . . .

"The labor-process, turned into the process by which the capitalist consumes labor-power, exhibits two characteristic phenomena. First, the laborer works under the control of the capitalist, to whom his labor belongs; the capitalist taking good care that the work is done in a proper manner, and that the means of production are used with intelligence, so that there is no unnecessary waste of raw material, and no wear and tear of the implements beyond what is necessarily caused by the work.

"Secondly, the product is the property of the capitalist, and not that of the laborer, its immediate producer. Suppose that a capitalist pays for a day's labor-power at its value; then the right to use that power for a day belongs to him just as much as the right to use any other commodity, such as a horse that he has hired for the day. To the purchaser of a commodity belongs its use, and the seller of labor-power by giving his labor does no more in reality than part with the use-value that he has sold. From the instant he steps into the work-shop the use-value of his labor-power, and therefore also its use, which is labor, belongs to the capitalist. By the purchase of labor-power the capitalist incorporates labor as a living ferment with the lifeless constituents of the product. . . .

"We know, however, from what has gone before that the labor-process may continue beyond the time necessary to reproduce and incorporate in the product a mere equivalent for the value of the labor-power. Instead of the six hours that are sufficient for the latter purpose, the process may continue for twelve hours. The action of labor-power, therefore, not only reproduces its own value, but produces value over and above it. This surplus-value is the difference between the value of the produce and the value of the elements consumed in the formation of that product; in other words, of the means of production and the labor-power. . . .

"During the second period of the labor-process—that in which his labor is no longer necessary labor—the workman, it is true, labors—expends labor-power; but his labor, being no longer necessary labor, he creates no value for himself. He creates surplus-value, which, for the capitalist, has all the charms of a creation out of nothing. This portion of the working-day I name surplus labor-time, and to the labor expended during that time I give the name of surplus-labor. It is every bit as important, for a correct understanding of surplus-value, to conceive it as a mere congelation of surplus labor-time, as nothing but materialized surplus-labor—as it is, for a proper comprehension of value, to conceive it as a mere congelation of so many hours of labor, as nothing but materialized labor. The essential difference between the various economic forms of society—between, for instance, a society based on slave-labor and one based on wage-labor—lies only in the mode in which this surplus-labor is in each case extracted from the actual producer, the laborer. . . .

"The rate of surplus-value is, therefore, an exact expression for the degree of exploitation of labor-power by capital, or of the laborer by the capitalist." [10]

The widespread class hatred, which has existed since the popularization of this theory, largely rests upon its plausible doctrine of the exploitation of man by man.

As stated in *The Communist Manifesto:*

"But does wage labor create any property for the laborer? Not a bit of it. It creates capital, i. e., that kind of property which exploits wage labor, and which cannot increase except upon condition of begetting a new supply of wage labor for fresh exploitation. Property, in its present form, is based on the antagonism of capital and wage labor. . . .

"The average price of wage-labor is the minimum wage, i. e., that quantum of the means of subsistence, which is absolutely requisite to keep the laborer in bare existence as a laborer. What, therefore, the wage-laborer appropriates by means of his labor, merely suffices to prolong and reproduce a bare existence. We by no means intend to abolish this personal appropriation of the products of labor, an appropriation that is made for the maintenance and reproduction of human life, and that leaves no surplus wherewith to command the labor of others. All that we want to do away with, is the miserable character of this appropriation, under which the laborer lives merely to increase capital, and is allowed to live only in so far as the interest of the ruling class requires it." [11]

Yet no one of these three propositions is wholly correct. It is easy to demonstrate that the exchange value of land, antiques, or works of art does not depend upon the amount of socially necessary labor time required to produce them. The error ascribed to Marx lies in his overemphasis upon labor cost as a determinant of value, and his failure to estimate properly the role of supply and scarcity in their relation to demand and utility.

The "iron law of wages" may be correct as a statement of tendency. But it may be affirmed with equal accuracy that the wage-earner's weekly, daily, or hourly wage will purchase more of the necessaries of life today than in the days of Karl Marx. This increase in "real" wages has been accomplished in part by trade unionism, in part by the increasing enlightenment of employers, in part by the per capita increase in output made possible by the developing use of machinery and of other inventions, and in part by labor and welfare legislation. The corollary of this Marxian theory that "the poor are getting poorer and the rich richer" does not hold. The

[10] Marx, Karl—*op. cit.*, pp. 92–93, 102–103, 118–119, and 124.
[11] Marx, Karl, and Engels, Frederick—*The Communist Manifesto;* Socialist Co-operative Publishing Association, 1901.

condition of the poor has improved somewhat over the days when they were clothed literally in rags and owned no change of clothes. But the disparity in wealth between the rich and poor has been continuously increasing, stayed only temporarily by periods of commercial and industrial depression.

There is only partial truth also in the doctrine of surplus value. The capitalist must get more than wages for his labor, or else large-scale industry will cease. In the absence of profits to the producer the volume of distributable goods would decline and with it the laborers' share. Until all capital is collectively owned, the individual capitalist, to be induced to continue his operations, must receive interest on his investment in the business and profits for the risks undertaken. Much that labor visualizes as theft is earned and essential to the continuance of production. On the other hand monopoly gains, the foisting of worthless articles upon the consumer, the gains of fraud, favoritism, and special privilege, in so far as they occur cannot be justified. The present industrial order puts a premium upon selfishness by increasing the capitalist's rewards when he pays employees less than he could afford to pay them. It thus obviously contributes to the volume of poverty and should be changed when a better system can be rendered practical. Such matters must, however, be considered in more detail in later chapters.

The Theory of Henry George.—In his volume entitled *Progress and Poverty*, first published in 1879, Henry George explained poverty in the following terms:

> "The poverty which in the midst of abundance, pinches and embrutes men, and all the manifold evils which flow from it, spring from a denial of justice. In permitting the monopolization of the natural opportunities which nature freely offers to all, we have ignored the fundamental law of justice—for so far as we can see, when we view things upon a large scale, justice seems to be the supreme law of the universe. But by sweeping away this injustice and asserting the rights of all men to natural opportunities, we shall conform ourselves to the law—we shall remove the great cause of unnatural inequality in the distribution of wealth and power; we shall abolish poverty; tame the ruthless passions of greed; dry up the springs of vice and misery; light in dark places the lamp of knowledge; give new vigor to invention and a fresh impulse to discovery; substitute political strength for political weakness; and make tyranny and anarchy impossible." [12]

[12] George, Henry—*Progress and Poverty: An Inquiry into the Cause of Industrial Depressions and of Increase of Want with Increase of Wealth*, pp. 489–490; Henry George, 1888.

After considering a variety of causes of poverty and their suggested remedies, Henry George offers the following as the "true remedy":

> "There is but one way to remove an evil—and that is, to remove its cause. Poverty deepens as wealth increases, and wages are forced down while productive power grows, because land, which is the source of all wealth and the field of all labor, is monopolized. To extirpate poverty, to make wages what justice commands they should be, the full earnings of the laborer, we must therefore substitute for the individual ownership of land a common ownership. Nothing else will go to the cause of the evil—in nothing else is there the slightest hope.
>
> "This, then, is the remedy for the unjust and unequal distribution of wealth apparent in modern civilization, and for all the evils which flow from it:
>
> "*We must make land common property.*
>
> "We have reached this conclusion by an examination in which every step has been proved and secured. In the chain of reasoning no link is wanting and no link is weak. Deduction and induction have brought us to the same truth—that the unequal ownership of land necessitates the unequal distribution of wealth. And as in the nature of things unequal ownership of land is inseparable from the recognition of individual property in land, it necessarily follows that the only remedy for the unjust distribution of wealth is in making land common property." [13]

A major criticism of the present economic order by George's followers lies in his observation that it is the presence of population that is responsible for increases in the value and rent of land; yet these values created by all of us are appropriated by persons who hold deeds to property. Actually, however, these "unearned increments" to land values are socially created and justly belong to the community and not to the individual who receives them. Collectively they constitute a colossal annual income, which if restored to their rightful owners or creators in the form of a single tax upon land rents could be used by the municipality for the good of all.

Contemporary economics, however, asserts that the problem is not so simple as it has been made to appear. It recognizes that a considerable fraction, and sometimes all, of the increments to urban site values are not literally earned by the present owner, in other than the legal sense. Yet exceptions are noted where the owner by building better than his neighbors is responsible for increasing the values not only of his own lot but of others in his vicinity. In the case of agricultural land it is even more difficult than in the case of urban sites to determine what share of the increase in land values

[13] *Ibid.*, pp. 295–296.

is due to the owner's cultivation and fertilization of the land. Attempts at progressive increment taxation, as well as attempts to levy taxes solely upon land, while removing taxes from the improvements upon it, have not always met with success. Such taxes have created so many new problems that economists accepting the principles of Henry George warn against a policy that is too hasty or that is "rough and grasping." For such a policy will frighten investors, obstruct initiative, and thus reduce the volume of distributable wealth—thereby defeating one of the major purposes of the single tax. Some conclude that it would be simpler and more effective to proceed at once to the direct ownership of land by city, state, and nation, and thus ensure to the public all future increments in land values.

No Panacea for Poverty.—It is clear that although there is some important truth to be drawn from each of these three classic theories, each requires some qualification of statement, and no one of them is sufficient in itself to explain all poverty. Each draws attention forcibly to a single factor or group of factors which operates in a social context in which there are myriad other factors. Poverty cannot be explained by reference to any single cause, correspondingly there is no panacea, *i.e.* no single specific, the application of which will cure all the ills of our body politic.

QUESTIONS FOR DISCUSSION OR EXAMINATION

1. What further arguments and evidence can you supply in support of the theories of Malthus, Marx, and George? Against?
2. Would it be possible by (a) better and more extensive education, (b) applied eugenics, to eliminate the necessity for social control of the rate of normal births? or of industrial production? or of land?
3. What sources of poverty would not be reached by (a) universal birth control? (b) elimination of the exploitation of labor by employers? (c) the levying of all taxes upon land? (d) public ownership of all land? (e) public ownership of all means of production? (assuming for purposes of discussion that each of these is practicable).

PROBLEMS FOR INDIVIDUAL STUDY

1. Analysis of the writings of Malthus, Marx, or George, with special reference to the causation of poverty.
2. Analysis of selected contemporary works in (a) population theory, (b) radical social theory, (c) single tax, or (d) land nationalization, with special reference to the causation of poverty and the practicability of their proposals.

3. Study of contemporary attitudes, with reference to these theories in their bearing upon poverty, among selected groups: *e.g.* (a) trade unionists, (b) industrial unionists, (c) business men, (d) professional men, (e) students of economics.
4. A critical examination of the literature on some one of the following— (a) increment taxation, (b) land taxation in Canada or Pittsburgh, (c) some phase of the problem of population increase, (d) decline of population in selected areas, (e) the "iron law of wages," (f) disparities in wealth or income, (g) entrepreneurs' gains—in relation to the problem of poverty.
5. Trace the development of the theories of poverty in some selected country and century.

SUGGESTIONS FOR SUPPLEMENTARY READINGS

Aschrott, Paul Felix—*The English Poor Law System Past and Present* (translated from the German by Herbert Preston-Thomas); Knight & Co. (London), 1888.

Ashley, W. J.—*An Introduction to English Economic History and Theory*, three volumes; G. P. Putnam's Sons, 1901–03.

Barnes, Harry Elmer, and Becker, Howard—*Social Thought from Lore to Science*, two volumes; D. C. Heath and Company, 1938.

Bonar, James—*Malthus and His Work;* The Macmillan Company, 1925.

Cheyney, Edward P.—*An Introduction to the Industrial and Social History of England;* The Macmillan Company, revised edition, 1920.

Cunningham, William—*The Growth of English Industry and Commerce During the Early and Middle Ages;* Cambridge University Press, fifth edition, 1910.

Cunningham, William—*The Growth of English Industry and Commerce in Modern Times*, two volumes; Cambridge University Press, sixth edition, 1919.

Day, Clive—*Economic Development in Modern Europe;* The Macmillan Company, 1933.

Dorau, Herbert B., and Hinman, Albert G.—*Urban Land Economics;* The Macmillan Company, 1928.

Douglas, Paul H.—*Real Wages in the United States, 1890–1926;* Houghton Mifflin Company, 1930.

Drahn, Ernst—*Marx-Bibliographie;* Deutsche Verlagsgesellschaft für Politik und Geschichte (Charlottenburg), 1920.

Dunning, William Archibald—*A History of Political Theories*, three volumes; The Macmillan Company, 1902–20.

East, Edward M.—*Mankind at the Crossroads;* Charles Scribner's Sons, 1926.

Ely, Richard T.—*French and German Socialism;* Harper & Brothers, 1883.

Ely, Richard T., and Morehouse, Edward W.—*Elements of Land Economics;* The Macmillan Company, 1924.

Geiger, George Raymond—*The Philosophy of Henry George;* The Macmillan Company, 1933.

Geiger, George Raymond—*The Theory of the Land Question;* The Macmillan Company, 1936.

George, Henry—*Complete Works* (Memorial edition, ten volumes, including the *Life of Henry George*, by Henry George, Jr.); Doubleday, Page & Co., 1898–1901.

George, Henry—*A Perplexed Philosopher;* Charles L. Webster & Company, 1892.

George, Henry—*Progress and Poverty;* Henry George, 1888.

George, Henry—*Social Problems;* Kegan Paul, Trench & Co. (London), 1884.

Gide, Charles, and Rist, Charles—*A History of Economic Doctrines from the Time of the Physiocrats to the Present Day* (authorized translation from the second revised edition of 1913 under direction of William Smart, by R. Richards); D. C. Heath and Company, 1915.

Gray, B. Kirkman—*A History of English Philanthropy;* P. S. King & Son, Ltd., 1905.

Haig, Robert Murray—*The Exemption of Improvements from Taxation in Canada and the United States;* a Report prepared for the Committee on Taxation of the City of New York, 1915.

Haney, Lewis H.—*History of Economic Thought. A Critical Account of the Origin and Development of the Economic Theories of the Leading Thinkers in the Leading Nations;* The Macmillan Company, third edition, 1936.

Hayes, Carlton J. H.—*A Political and Social History of Modern Europe;* The Macmillan Company, 1927.

Hearnshaw, F. J. C., editor—*The Social and Political Ideas of Some Great Mediaeval Thinkers;* George G. Harrap & Company Ltd., 1923.

Hearnshaw, F. J. C., editor—*The Social and Political Ideas of Some Great Thinkers of the Sixteenth and Seventeenth Centuries;* George G. Harrap & Company Ltd., 1926.

Hearnshaw, F. J. C., editor—*The Social and Political Ideas of Some Representative Thinkers of the Revolutionary Era;* George G. Harrap & Company Ltd., 1931.

Hearnshaw, F. J. C., editor—*The Social and Political Ideas of Some Representative Thinkers of the Age of Reaction and Reconstruction 1815–65;* George G. Harrap & Company Ltd., 1932.

Jorns, Auguste—*The Quakers as Pioneers in Social Work* (translated by Thomas Kite Brown, Jr.), Chapter One, "Poor Relief"; The Macmillan Company, 1931.

Kautsky, Karl—*The Economic Doctrines of Karl Marx* (translated by H. J. Stenning); The Macmillan Company, 1937.

Lecky, W. E. H.—*History of European Morals from Augustus to Charlemagne*, two volumes; D. Appleton and Company, third revised edition, 1925.

Leonard, E. M.—*The Early History of English Poor Relief;* Cambridge, at the University Press, 1900.

Le Rossignol, James E.—*Orthodox Socialism: A Criticism;* Thomas Y. Crowell Company, 1907.

McIlwain, Charles Howard—*The Growth of Political Thought in the West;* The Macmillan Company, 1932.

Mackay, Thomas—*A History of the English Poor Law;* P. S. King & Son, Ltd., 1899.

Malthus, Rev. T. R.—*An Essay on Population*, two volumes; E. P. Dutton & Co. (no date).

Marx, Karl—*Capital: A Critical Analysis of Capitalist Production* (translated from the third German edition, by Samuel Moore and Edward Aveling, and edited by Frederick Engels), Vol. I; The Humboldt Publishing Co. (no date), (also published by Swan, Sonnenschein and Co., 1889).

Marx, Karl—*Capital: A Critique of Political Economy* (translated from the second German edition by Ernest Untermann), Vols. II and III; Charles H. Kerr & Company, 1909.

Marx, Karl—*Das Elend der Philosophie;* Druck und Verlag von J. H. W. Dietz (Stuttgart), 1885.

Marx, Karl, and Engels, Frederick—*The Communist Manifesto;* Socialist Co-operative Publishing Association, 1901.

Odum, Howard W., and Jocher, Katharine—*An Introduction to Social Research;* Henry Holt and Company, 1929.

Palgrave, R. H. Inglis, editor—*Dictionary of Political Economy* (corrected edition, with appendix, 1906–09), three volumes; The Macmillan Company (new edition, edited by Henry Higgs), 1926.

Parsons, Talcott—*The Structure of Social Action; A Study in Social Theory with Special Reference to a Group of Recent European Writers;* McGraw-Hill Book Company, Inc., 1937.

Penrose, E. F.—*Population Theories and Their Application: With Special Reference to Japan;* Food Research Institute, Stanford University Press, 1934.

Post, Louis F.—*The Taxation of Land Values;* Bobbs-Merrill Company, 1915.

Queen, Stuart Alfred—*Social Work in the Light of History;* J. B. Lippincott Company, 1922.

Rogers, James E. Thorold—*Six Centuries of Work and Wages; the History of English Labor;* G. P. Putnam's Sons, 1884.

Salter, F. R.—*Karl Marx and Modern Socialism;* The Macmillan Company, 1921.

Smith, Adam—*An Inquiry into the Nature and Causes of the Wealth of Nations* (edited by Edwin Cannan), two volumes; G. P. Putnam's Sons, 1904.

Taussig, F. W.—*Principles of Economics*, Vol. II, Chapter 43, "Urban Site Rent," Chapter 64, "Socialism," Chapter 65, "Socialism," and Chapter 68, "Taxes on Land and Buildings"; The Macmillan Company, 1913.

Toynbee, Arnold—*Lectures on the Industrial Revolution of the 18th Century in England;* Longmans, Green and Co., ninth impression, 1927.

Twentieth Century Fund, Committee on Taxation—*Facing the Tax Problem; A Survey of Taxation in the United States and a Program for the Future;* Twentieth Century Fund, Inc., 1937.

Usher, Abbott Payson—*An Introduction to the Industrial History of England;* Houghton Mifflin Company, 1920.

Wagner, Donald O.—*Social Reformers: From Adam Smith to John Dewey;* The Macmillan Company, 1934.

Watson, Frank Dekker—*The Charity Organization Movement in the United States*, Chapter II, "Foreign Antecedents"; The Macmillan Company, 1922.

Webb, Sidney and Beatrice—*English Local Government: English Poor Law*

History: Part I, The Old Poor Law; Longmans, Green and Co., 1927: *Part II, The Last Hundred Years,* two volumes; published by the authors, 1929.

Webb, Sidney and Beatrice—*The History of Trade Unionism;* Longmans, Green and Co., 1911.

Young, Arthur Nichols—*The Single Tax Movement in the United States;* Princeton University Press, 1916.

CHAPTER XIX

STUDIES OF THE SOURCES OF DEPENDENCY

Reason for Prior Consideration of Dependency.—To ensure a correct understanding of poverty in the sense of economic insufficiency, and to distinguish economic factors from other factors producing poverty, it is necessary first to visualize the group with which we are dealing. Many of the families with incomes insufficient for their needs have become dependent for support upon the associated private agencies of their community. The latter have diagnosed their ills case by case and have often attempted to summarize their findings for all the families under their care in tables of "causes of poverty" or of "situations presented." Though their summaries tend to stress the immediate occasions or the precipitating factors of dependency and sometimes merely their presenting symptoms, they help to provide a useful frame of reference for the consideration of the pathology of economic relationships. For they reveal much concerning the nature of human distress, the varied forms it takes, the multiplicity and the overlappings of human ills, and the consequences of the imperfections in social organization.

Sources of Data.—All of the data in this chapter have been assembled by private agencies primarily concerned with the diagnosis and rehabilitation of families which have become dependent. Whether known as charity organization societies, united charities, family welfare societies, or by other names, they represent the core of the group responsible for the development in the past two generations of the principles of social diagnosis and social case work. Their forms and methods are treated in later chapters, but here it should be understood that the findings which follow are not the result of casual observation or a single interview, but rather the fruit of protracted relationships with the dependent families in question and of the analysis of many clues and much pertinent data relating to each case.

Early "Classic" Analysis of Causes of Dependency.—A generation ago students of this subject received much of their training from

315

Warner's *American Charities*, first published in 1894.[1] It contains many tables compiled from the reports of private charitable agencies. What appeared to be the major immediate factor precipitating poverty was given as its "cause." The role of each such major factor in the production of poverty in two thousand cases was indicated by percentages. Thus, in the early nineties, from the reports of charity organization societies in Baltimore, Boston, Buffalo, Cincinnati, and New York City, twenty-three major "causes" were listed. To drink was ascribed from 4.9 per cent of poverty (Buffalo 1889–90) to 21.9 per cent (Boston 1891–92); to shiftlessness and inefficiency were attributed from 1.8 per cent to 14 per cent; to crime and dishonesty from 0 to 3 per cent; to roving disposition from 0 to 5.4 per cent. These factors were totalled under a heading entitled "causes indicating misconduct" which were found to account for from 7.5 per cent to 32.5 per cent of all dependency.

The remaining factors, except for a few "not classified," were listed as "causes indicating misfortune." To imprisonment of bread winner was traced from 0 to 2.4 per cent. Orphanhood and abandoned children accounted for from 0 to 1.6 per cent; neglect by relatives 0 to 2 per cent; no male support, including death of husband and desertion, from 4 to 19.4 per cent; lack of employment from 9.7 per cent to 32.5 per cent; insufficient employment from 0 to 11.9 per cent; poorly-paid employment from .3 to 8.7 per cent; unhealthy or dangerous employment from 0 to .8 per cent; ignorance of English from 0 to 1.1 per cent; accident from 2.3 to 5.5 per cent; sickness or death in the family from 14.6 to 29.5 per cent; physical defect from 1 to 8.7 per cent; insanity from .5 to 1.8 per cent; old age from 0 to 7.1 per cent; large families from 0 to 4.5 per cent; nature of abode from 0 to 2.2 per cent.[2]

Limitations of this Method.—The excuse for submitting these figures here is that they reflect the attitudes of case workers at that period. The tendency to ascribe poverty to misconduct has long since been outgrown because of the recognition that misconduct is itself often a result of unfortunate circumstances over which the individual at the time of dependency has little, if any, control. Moreover, the misconduct of the individual applicant for relief is the misfortune of

---

[1] Revised and reissued by Queen and Harper as follows: Warner, Amos Griswold, Queen, Stuart Alfred, and Harper, Ernest Bouldin—*American Charities and Social Work;* Thomas Y. Crowell Company, 1930.

[2] *Ibid.*, Table IV, opposite p. 46.

all who are dependent upon him for support. So the distinction between these two categories is no longer made.

The number of cases covered in these studies was much too small to have made sound statistical conclusions possible even if the causes of the poverty had been scientifically determined. For only about two thousand applicants had been analyzed in the twelve reports from the five cities on which the table was based. The major criticism, however, relates to the strictly subjective nature of the record made in each instance. Ordinarily the history of a family seeking relief will reveal the presence of a half dozen or more of the "causes" listed in this table. Two investigators analyzing the same case might in such circumstances disagree as to the major causes. If an elderly man with a large family becomes intoxicated, and in that condition suffers an accident and loses his job, the bias of the investigator will determine whether the "cause" of his poverty is old age, large family, drink, accident, or unemployment. A temperance reformer will allot a larger percentage of cases to drink than will be so assigned by a person without such a bias. A socialist might ascribe the majority of cases to inadequate wages.

A further statistical limitation of this method lies in the fact that the data were not gathered primarily for statistical purposes but had been gleaned from case records obtained for another purpose— namely to provide appropriate charitable assistance. Further investigation of these families by trained statisticians using standard definitions and schedules might have revealed additional precipitating factors. Moreover, if to this analysis of the cases of private agencies had been added those dealt with in the same year by public agencies of relief, old age and feeblemindedness would certainly have been more prominent. Restriction of the study to families actually destitute [3] would have yielded still another distribution.

Values of this Method.—Nevertheless, these studies may have had real value in calling attention to the prominence of certain factors in case histories of dependency. Though statistically unimportant they have the merit of revealing the relatively high frequency in case records of drink, inefficiency, lack of male support, and unemployment, sickness or death in the family. It is clear, furthermore, that in the large majority of cases the poverty was occasioned by

---

[3] Some of the families aided by the charity organization societies or family welfare societies are not destitute but for other reasons are in need of advice and the types of assistance which social workers can render.

conditions over which it would seldom have been possible for the family to have had control without the assistance of some competent agency which because of its wider experience could serve as adviser.

Though one cannot hope for data of statistical value from the further employment of this device, it is useful in indicating points of attack upon the problem of dependency. The factors listed do largely precipitate distress. To the person seeking aid, the difficulty is generally visualized as "lack of money," the threat of eviction because the rent has gone too long unpaid, the lack of food for the next meal and of means with which to purchase it. These, however, are symptoms rather than occasions of poverty.

Early Refinements of Method.—Recognizing the interplay of the causes of dependency A. M. Simons,[4] in a study of cases of the Bureau of Associated Charities in Chicago, followed the suggestion of Warner "to consider the influences resulting in destitution in each case as making up ten units, and [to] indicate the relative force of each cause by a proportionate number of units." The effect of this method in Simons' study was to top the list with "lack of employment." Intemperance and sickness were nearly on a parity for second place in the stockyards district, but took a very different distribution in Englewood as revealed by the following table: [5]

	STOCKYARDS DISTRICT	ENGLEWOOD
Lack of employment	456	499
Intemperance	157	105
Sickness	154	95
Incompetence	61	36
Desertion of breadwinner	51	22
Laziness	34	160
Old age	33	54
Death of breadwinner	33	29
Pauper association	17	0
Insanity	4	0

A table like this, based upon a highly subjective evaluative procedure, lacks the exactness required of science. One may be justified also in suspecting bias where, for example, 160 points are ascribed to laziness in Englewood as against 34 in the stockyards district. Nevertheless, the outstanding roles of intemperance, sickness, and

---

[4] Simons, A. M.—"A Statistical Study in Causes of Poverty," pp. 615–616; *American Journal of Sociology*, Vol. III, No. 5, March, 1898.
[5] *Ibid.*

lack of employment are again indicative of prevalent conditions of life among the applicants for relief even though the table does fail to reveal fundamental causes.

Listing by "Problems."—The executive of an agency for family social work or public welfare administration may find practical value in noting for each applicant each one of the factors in the above list or in one much more elaborate. There may be only two or three factors present in some cases and a dozen or more in others. The advantage of listing each of these factors wherever it may be present, and of determining in the monthly and annual office records the number of cases in which each appears, would be to discover those conditions of poverty which are most frequently present, whether or not they are causes. Variations might be noted from week to week, or month to month, in their incidence, and if necessary changes in organization, staff, or assignments can be made to meet the discovered trends. For example, changes in the liquor laws should be reflected in the number of cases showing drink as a factor. Increased vigor in police administration might be reflected in a larger percentage of cases involving imprisonment of the breadwinner. More general substitution by the courts of probation for imprisonment should involve reduction of this latter factor. The volume of frank or uncomplicated unemployment cases would increase with the oncoming of hard times and decrease as the community emerges from depression.[6]

A contemporary example of this type of record kept solely "for reference purposes," is that of the Family Welfare Society of Boston. The distribution is as follows:

PROBLEMS (Under Care Only) [7]

	1931	1932	1933	1934	1935	1936
Unemployment	1,653	3,353	3,522	2,665	1,769	1,458
Physical disability	1,384	1,893	2,131	2,358	2,504	2,348
Desertion	182	324	226	187	186	161
Nonsupport	247	291	274	234	234	243
Alcoholism	267	307	311	312	357	314
Old age	466	546	473	447	485	526

[6] The Boston table which follows fails to indicate this because the public welfare agencies increasingly took care of unemployment cases.

[7] Malcolm S. Nichols, General Secretary, in a letter dated April 16, 1937, states: "We do not publish this widely, but we keep these figures each year for reference purposes. I realize that they are quite inadequate in giving any clear picture of the so-called causes of dependency."

Chicago's Analysis of "Situations Presented."—In much greater detail the United Charities of Chicago has listed 15,456 "situations presented" in 3,152 families given intensive treatment during the year 1936 (excluding about 7,000 other families which received short time care). Of 3,216 instances of economic factors 1,406 were unemployment, 716 indebtedness, 241 insufficient wage, 230 partial unemployment, 193 legal entanglement, 164 the difficulties of small tradesmen, and 266 were unspecified.

The distribution of 4,164 situations involving physical factors was as follows: 1,154 instances of chronic illness not covered elsewhere in the list, 604 involving defective teeth, 445 maternity, 387 acute illness, 311 instances of defective eyesight, 226 malnutrition diagnosed by physician, 158 old age, 155 venereal disease diagnosed by physician, 134 tuberculosis, 96 convalescence, 81 accident, 72 deafness or defective hearing, 19 blindness, 13 death in family, and 309 "other physical factors."

Of 987 instances of mental factors, 290 were of suspected mental disturbance, 220 of diagnosed mental disturbance, 217 alcoholism, 142 diagnosed mental defectiveness, 65 suspected mental defectiveness, 44 epilepsy, and 9 of drug addiction. There were also 370 instances of emotional factors; 254 were in adults and 116 in children.

Social and behavior factors were noted in 5,025 instances: 933 were listed as difficulties in parent-child relationships, 854 domestic discord, 662 undistributed adult behavior factors, 576 difficulty with relatives, 415 undistributed behavior factors in children, 346 illegitimacy, 288 nonsupport, 241 inadequate parental care, 209 bad housekeeping, 203 irregular sex relationship, 77 imprisonment, 68 juvenile delinquency or truancy, 57 unmarried pregnant women, 48 parole or probation, 39 illegal marriage, and 9 placement factors.

Of 1,694 instances of community factors 508 were inadequate recreation, 353 bad housing, 349 inadequate vocational guidance or training, 163 inability to speak English, 124 alien, 76 inadequate educational facilities, 56 illiteracy, 55 nonresident, and 10 undistributed.[8]

The Chicago study has the value of revealing still further the great complexity of poverty causation. Categories are seen to overlap. Each can obviously be still further distributed into subcatego-

[8] Statistical Department, United Charities of Chicago—*Situations Presented on Total Under Care Cases—Year 1936;* Mimeographed Table, released March 3, 1937.

ries. A given family may suffer from many ills any one of which might either produce or prolong dependency. Rehabilitation clearly involves within each case the overcoming of many factors.

The Search for Deeper Causes.—The interweaving of proximate causative factors may be better understood if we look back of any given situation to its causes in turn. The lack of employment may be examined in this manner. One man may be discharged because he talked back to the boss. Did he do this because the boss was unfair, or because he had a quarrel with someone else earlier in the day which put him in a vicious mood? Did he lack proper training in self-control or in judgment? Is he a borderline psychopathic case?

Another man is unemployed because he went on strike. A third because of a lockout. A fourth because he came to work drunk. A fifth because cancellation of orders caused the shop to close down. A sixth because the factory was unable to secure long-term credit. A seventh because the factory is no longer able to sell in its former European market. An eighth because of illness. And so on through an exceedingly long list. For each of these the anterior causes should be sought.

Back of each of these factors and interpenetrating them lie others. Each specified difficulty has many roots in the economic, political, and social order, in the individual personality and its biological and social heredity. At the base will be found the individual's heredity of which little is known except where there is a recognizable hereditary defect—and the social and biological factors which determined the parental mating and the matings of preceding generations. But there exist equally those influences of environment, experience, and training up to the moment of unemployment which made the employer and employee react as they did. Any attempt to specify a unitary cause would make unwarranted abstractions from among a complexity of causes. A strictly linear presentation of causes would fail of accuracy because of the subtleties and complexities of their interrelations.

The Circular Presentation of Causative Factors.—The complexity of causation is made more apparent if one may temporarily depart from linear to circular presentation, following the method of Dr. J. B. Hurry in his volume entitled *Poverty and Its Vicious Circles.*[9] Here is discussed the "process by which a primary disorder

[9] Hurry, Jamieson B.—*Poverty and Its Vicious Circles;* J. & A. Churchill, second and enlarged edition, 1921.

provokes a reaction which aggravates such disorder." Poverty, it is shown, tends to become self-perpetuating.

Thus a low income may mean that the family will be unable to pay the rent necessary for wholesome sanitary quarters and will put up with crowded, insanitary housing which will result in reduced resistance to disease or positive ill health, which in turn makes the breadwinner lose his job and sink more deeply into poverty. The vicious circle in this instance is displayed by Dr. Hurry as

poverty—defective housing—ill health—unemployment—increased poverty—Other examples are as follows:

poverty—defective feeding—malnutrition—lower wages—poverty
poverty—defective clothing—less eligibility—poverty
poverty—defective education—inefficiency—poverty
poverty—alcoholism—inefficiency—loss of situation—poverty
poverty—diminished credit—borrowing—high interest—poverty
poverty—recklessness—numerous family—poverty
poverty—purchase of small quantities—enhanced cost—poverty
poverty—improvidence—want of reserve—acceptance of first vacancy—poverty
poverty—misery—loss of energy—poverty
poverty—crime—loss of situation—poverty
poverty—pawning—high interest—poverty
poverty—helplessness—inability to bargain—low wages—poverty
poverty—employment of wife—increased competition—low wages—poverty

It would be easy to add to this list by multiplying instances of human tragedy. Long continued poverty interferes with the education of children and thus with their ultimate employability. It forces upon them the unfortunate and sometimes dangerous associations of the slum which may lead to delinquency, drunkenness, prostitution, or a variety of other evils which reduce employability and income. It may cause worry and anxiety which may lead to physical or mental disease and thus increase poverty. In the absence of outside aid to break the vicious circle at some strategic point, the effects of poverty are cumulative and inescapable. In the words of Solomon: the destruction of the poor is their poverty.

Multiple Causation.—When one considers the circular theory of poverty causation in conjunction with the linear theory, it becomes at once apparent that each is only a partial explanation. Causation is multiple. The present condition or total situation grows out of past conditions or total situations, in a social process that is dynamic —never static. Since, however, the human mind is balked by infinite complexity, one is forced in a program for the prevention of poverty to concentrate major attention and effort upon factors which recur frequently.

Social Control of Causative Factors.—It has already been seen that prevention of any pathologic condition should if possible be accomplished by discovery of its causes and by preventing them from operating further. Where, however, causation is so complex each chain and each vicious circle of poverty may be attacked at any point; whether it be disease or defective housing or poor feeding; whether it be unemployment or the factors which produce it; whether it be anxiety, low income, defective education, the pawn-shop, the employment of women, or the slum.

Since human interests in reform are as diverse as the causes of poverty themselves, it has proved possible to organize simultaneous attacks upon many fronts. Thus, the elimination of defective hous-ing, which might seem to the uninitiated to be a unitary field of interest, actually is distributed among many interests. Some are concerned exclusively with sanitation; others with remodelling; still others with model housing through limited-dividend corpora-tions; some with restrictive legislation, with tenant education, with government housing, with slum elimination, and so on. There is surprisingly little overlapping of interest among these advocates. Hence, these many phases can be attacked each by its own group. Results may be useful in case there is proper provision for coördina-tion of diverse programs into one unitary system of reform.

Similarly, the elimination of malnutrition may be approached from the angle of home economics, dietary research in food values, the visiting housekeeper, school lunches, the dispensary, and the visiting nurse, as well as from the angles of agricultural production, distribution of food products, or education in physiology and hygiene. All of these approaches have merit. Effective social plan-ning requires a coördination of attack. Each other so-called cause may likewise be met by a variety of specialists and agencies.

Detailed and penetrating analysis demonstrates that each case of poverty is a resultant of the interplay of factors in individual heredity and training with factors in the immediate environment of the individual—his family, home, neighborhood, and shop—and with other factors deep in our physical, biological, economic, political, and social order. A social policy for the elimination of poverty must thus draw its data from a wide range of sciences—not merely from economics, political science, and social work, but also from biology, physiology, pathology, psychology, sociology, and an immense list of applied sciences and arts, such as pedagogy, medicine, engineering, agriculture, commerce, and industry.

QUESTIONS FOR DISCUSSION OR EXAMINATION

1. What are the limitations and values of the (a) Warner, (b) Simons, (c) Chicago methods of analyzing the causes of poverty?
2. What evidences of pathology of (a) economic relationships, (b) family relationships, (c) group relationships, (d) physical and mental handicaps, do you note from the Warner and Chicago studies? Which appear to be the more prominent factors?
3. Submit argument for and against misconduct as a cause of poverty.
4. Show points at which each "vicious circle of poverty" might be broken. How?
5. Show how each factor might be related to heredity, environment, and training.

PROBLEMS FOR INDIVIDUAL STUDY

1. Examine and appraise studies of the causes of poverty which have been made in your city or state.
2. Submit critical review of one or more of the books in the following list of references.
3. Apply to the problem of dependency the methods of social control outlined by Ross, Lumley, or others.
4. Analyze and summarize selected works on causation.
5. From case records of a local social agency, or from casebooks (*e.g.* Southard and Jarrett, Cannon, Breckinridge) tabulate "causes" of dependency and give your reasons for assigning (a) relative priority in time, and (b) relative priority in importance.

SUGGESTIONS FOR SUPPLEMENTARY READINGS

Brandt, Lilian—*Five Hundred and Seventy-four Deserters and Their Families;* Charity Organization Society, New York City, 1905.

Breckinridge, Sophonisba P.—*Family Welfare Work in a Metropolitan Community: Selected Case Records;* University of Chicago Press, 1924.

Cannon, Mary Antoinette, and Klein, Philip, editors—*Social Case Work: An Outline for Teaching: With Annotated Case Records and Sample Course Syllabi;* published for the New School of Social Work by Columbia University Press, 1933.

Carlisle, Chester Lee—*The Causes of Dependency Based on a Survey of Oneida County;* State of New York, State Board of Charities, Division of Mental Defect and Delinquency, The Bureau of Analysis and Investigation, Eugenics and Social Welfare Bulletin No. XV, Albany, 1918.

Devine, Edward T.—*Misery and Its Causes;* The Macmillan Company, 1913.

Fawcett, Henry—*Pauperism: Its Causes and Remedies;* The Macmillan Company, 1871.

Ford, James—*Social Problem and Social Policy*, Chapter XXI, "Analysis of the Causes of Dependency"; Ginn and Company, 1923.

Gillin, John Lewis—*Poverty and Dependency*, Chapters VI–IX; The Century Co., 1921.

Great Britain—*Report of Royal Commission on the Poor Laws and Relief of Distress*, Report (1 vol.) with evidence and appendices (33 vols.); H. M. Stationery Office, 1909–10.

Hunter, Robert—*Poverty;* The Macmillan Company, 1904.

Hurry, Jamieson B.—*Poverty and Its Vicious Circles;* J. & A. Churchill, second and enlarged edition, 1921.

Karpf, Maurice J.—*The Scientific Basis of Social Work*, especially Part II; Columbia University Press, 1931.

Kelso, Robert W.—*Poverty*, Part II; Longmans, Green and Co., 1929.

Lumley, Frederick Elmore—*Means of Social Control;* The Century Co., 1925.

MacIver, R. M.—*The Contribution of Sociology to Social Work;* Columbia University Press, 1931.

Mangold, George B.—*Social Pathology*, Chapter III, "Poverty," and Chapter IV, "Abolition of Poverty"; The Macmillan Company, 1932.

National Conference of Social Work—*Proceedings*.

Ross, Edward Alsworth—*Social Control. A Survey of the Foundations of Order;* The Macmillan Company, 1901.

Social Science Research Council—*Studies in the Social Aspects of the Depression: Research Memoranda, prepared under the direction of the Committee on Studies in Social Aspects of the Depression*, thirteen volumes; Social Science Research Council, 1937.

Southard, E. E., and Jarrett, Mary C.—*The Kingdom of Evils;* The Macmillan Company, 1922.

Warner, Amos Griswold, Queen, Stuart Alfred, and Harper, Ernest Bouldin—*American Charities and Social Work*, Chapters III–V; Thomas Y. Crowell Company, fourth edition, 1930.

Watson, Frank Dekker—*The Charity Organization Movement in the United States;* The Macmillan Company, 1922.

Wilson, Robert S.—*The Short Contact in Social Case Work: A Study of Treatment in Time-Limited Relationships in Social Work*, Vol. I, *General Theory and Application to Two Fields*, Vol. II, *Selected Short Contact Case Records;* National Association for Travelers Aid and Transient Service, 1937.

CHAPTER XX

THE CAUSES OF POVERTY—COMPREHENSIVE INVESTIGATIONS AND ECONOMIC FACTORS

Economic Factors and Dependence.—The preceding analysis of case studies of the factors which precipitate dependence has served to show the importance of the economic situation of the breadwinner. Low income, casual labor, intermittent earnings, unemployment, industrial accident, and occupational disease are all direct evidence of pathologic economic relationships of which dependence may be a consequence. If, however, the earnings of the breadwinner are insufficient to provide for his old age, for the costs of family illnesses, for the support of his widow in case of his death, for the education and well-being of his children, economic factors are in part chargeable with the dependence which may follow. Furthermore, hours of work that are too long, speed that is too intense, surroundings that are unwholesome, employer attitudes that irritate, performance by men, women, or children of work unsuited to their age, sex, physical condition, or capacity, show economic factors in conjunction with others, producing a chain of pathologic consequences expressed, not only on occasion in handicap or poverty, but also in the disorganization of family and group life.

Booth's "Poverty Line."—Several of the social surveys of urban populations have noted the factors in city life which push families below the poverty line.[1] The largest undertaking of this sort, Charles Booth's *Life and Labour of the People in London*, amassing its evidence in the eighteen eighties and eighteen nineties, discovered somewhat over thirty per cent of the population of London in poverty, which Booth defined in the following manner:

"By the word 'poor' I mean to describe those who have a sufficiently regular though bare income, such as 18s. to 21s. per week for a moderate family, and by 'very poor' those who from any cause fall much below this standard. The 'poor' are those whose means may be sufficient, but are barely sufficient, for decent independent life; the 'very poor' those whose

[1] A classified list is available in Eaton, Allen, and Harrison, Shelby M.— *A Bibliography of Social Surveys;* Russell Sage Foundation, 1930.

means are insufficient for this according to the usual standard of life in this country.   My 'poor' may be described as living under a struggle to obtain the necessaries of life and make both ends meet; while the 'very poor' live in a state of chronic want. . . .

"The eight classes into which I have divided these people are:

A. The lowest class of occasional labourers, loafers, and semi-criminals.

B. Casual earning —'very poor.'

C. Intermittent earnings \
D. Small regular earnings / together the 'poor.'

E. Regular standard earnings—above the line of poverty.

F. Higher class labour.

G. Lower middle class.

H. Upper middle class." [2]

Booth's Causes of Poverty.—The causes of poverty are thus described:

"Questions of employment—Lack of work or low pay—Questions of habit, idleness, drunkenness, or thriftlessness—Questions of circumstance, sickness, or large families.   Under these heads fall all the causes of poverty.   To throw some light on the proportion which these troubles bear to each other, and so on to the ultimate question of what cure can be found, I have attempted to analyze four thousand cases of the poor and very poor known to selected School Board visitors in each district, . . . It would not be safe to generalize very confidently from an analysis of this sort unless it can be supported by other evidence.   The figures have, however, statistically one great element of value.   They are representative of all the poor in the districts from which they are drawn, and not only of those who apply for relief. . . .

"Of the 4000 cases, 1600 heads of families belonged to Classes A and B (the 'very poor'), and of them 60 [4 per cent] are admitted loafers— those who will not work.   After these come 878 [55 per cent] whose poverty is due to the casual or irregular character of their employment, combined more or less with low pay; then 231 [14 per cent] whose poverty is the result of drink or obvious want of thrift, and finally 441 more [27 per cent], who have been impoverished by illness, or the large number of those who have to be supported out of the earnings.

"Of the remaining 2,400 cases from Classes C and D, there are 1,600 who are poor because of irregular earnings, or low pay [68 per cent], 300 whose poverty can be directly traced to drink or thriftless habits [13 per cent], and 500 with whom the number of their children or the badness of their health is the cause [19 per cent].   No loafers are counted here.   The amount of loafing that brings a man's family down part way to destitution is not very noticeable, or may perhaps pass as irregular employment. Such men live on their wives.

[2] Booth, Charles—*Life and Labour of the People in London*, Vol. I, p. 33; Macmillan and Co., Limited, 1902. Booth's methods of study were sketched in Part I, Chapter II.

"It may be observed that the proportion of Classes C and D who owe their poverty to questions of employment is greater, while that of those owing it to questions of circumstance is less, than with the very poor, while drink accounts for about the same proportion in both tables. In the case of very poor, low pay and casual or irregular work are combined, and account for 55 per cent. With the 'poor' these causes can be separated, and we have 43 per cent whose poverty is traced to the irregularity of their work, and 25 per cent whose poverty is traced to their low pay." [3]

Economic factors appear to predominate among the London population of Booth's classic research.

Rowntree's Findings.—Rowntree, in *Poverty; A Study of Town Life*, followed but amplified Booth's method in York, England, in the year 1901. As has been seen, he found 9.91 per cent in primary poverty in the sense that their total earnings were insufficient to obtain the minimum necessaries for the maintenance of merely physical efficiency. But in addition to these there were 17.93 per cent in secondary poverty, *i.e.* "families whose total earnings would be sufficient for the maintenance of merely physical efficiency were it not that some portion of them is absorbed by other expenditure, either useful or wasteful." Two-thirds of the families in primary poverty were brought there by the death or desertion of the breadwinner, or by illness or old age. Low wages accounted for 12.6 per cent, unemployment for 8.7 per cent, casual labor for 5.1 per cent, and large families for 7.3 per cent. The relative prominence of factors producing secondary poverty could not be ascertained by Rowntree; but he states that "there can be but little doubt, however, that the predominant factor is drink." Betting, gambling, and ignorant or careless housekeeping were also frequent. [4]

Later English Studies.—Subsequent studies of other industrial cities in England have recorded somewhat lower percentages. First was a volume entitled *Livelihood and Poverty*, in which A. L. Bowley and assistants examined the economic conditions in workingclass families of five of the smaller industrial cities of England. Ten years later, in 1925, the same cities were reëxamined by Bowley in a volume entitled *Has Poverty Diminished?* It was noted that the weekly wages of unskilled workers had nearly doubled in ten years, while

---

[3] *Ibid.*, pp. 146–148.
[4] Rowntree, B. Seebohm—*Poverty; A Study of Town Life*, pp. 111, 117, x, 45–46, and 142; Macmillan and Co., Limited, edition of 1908. For brief sketch of Rowntree's method see Chapter II.

the cost of maintaining the minimum standard had risen around seventy per cent. The result was a very marked reduction of poverty in families in which the man is normally earning and has full time employment. Yet it was found that one child in every six was at some period of his young life below the poverty line.[5]

When London was restudied in 1928 by Sir Hubert Llewellyn Smith and associates, striking changes were observed in the factors producing poverty as compared with the end of the past century. For the average weekly time-rates of wages had increased from 110 to 120 per cent since 1890, while the money cost of the principal necessaries was estimated to have increased only from 80 to 87 per cent. Such an increase of one-third in the real earnings of the worker would be sufficient, other things equal, to raise all members of Charles Booth's Classes C and D above the poverty line, and to reduce the percentage of population in poverty from 30 per cent to less than 8 per cent. Moreover, the development of old-age pensions and unemployment insurance eases considerably the financial distress not only of the poor but also of all groups near the poverty line. Though dependency still exists, primary poverty has diminished due to changes in economic and social conditions and the social legislation of the intervening period. The contemporary trend is to redefine terms and factors both economic and personal.[6]

American Investigations of Poverty.—The many general social surveys made in America have not displayed the detailed special interest in the factors precipitating poverty which has characterized the foregoing English studies. The Pittsburgh survey was concerned primarily with labor problems, that of Springfield, Illinois, with appraisals of agencies, those of Cleveland [7] with analysis of a variety of other special problems related to poverty, but in no instance following closely the British method.

State boards have on occasion made intensive analyses of dependency. For example, such a survey in Oneida County, authorized by the New York State Bureau of Analysis and Investigation of the

---

[5] Bowley, A. L., and Burnett-Hurst, A. R.—*Livelihood and Poverty;* G. Bell and Sons, Ltd., 1915. Bowley, A. L., and Hogg, Margaret H.—*Has Poverty Diminished?* especially pp. 20–25; P. S. King & Son, Ltd., 1925.

[6] *The New Survey of London Life and Labour,* Vol. I, *Forty Years of Change,* especially Chapter I, "Introduction," Chapter III, "Cost of Living," and Chapter IV, "Wages, Hours of Labour and Earnings," by Sir H. Llewellyn Smith; P. S. King & Son, Ltd., 1930.

[7] See Part I, Chapter III.

State Board of Charities, emphasized hereditary and mental factors rather than those primarily economic.[8]

The number of specialized investigations under private auspices is large, whether the emphasis be upon heredity, mental condition, behavior, personal or social characteristics, wages, conditions of employment, or case histories. The depression years precipitated studies by colleges, foundations, social workers, government departments, special commissions, and research agencies with or without the use of unemployed workers assigned by the E.R.A., C.W.A., or W.P.A.

Michigan's Relief Population: 1933-35.—The studies published by the State Emergency Welfare Relief Commission of Michigan and directed by William Haber, Administrator, are notable for their comprehensiveness.[9] Findings concerning the economic factors in public relief cases of Michigan for the depression period are as follows:

". . . From July, 1933 through December, 1935, an average of more than 651,000 persons per month were cared for by the Emergency Relief Administration at an average monthly cost of $4,978,000. In December, 1934, when the relief load was at its peak, over 890,000 persons—18 per cent of the state's population—received aid. . . .

"Michigan's industrial specialization makes some future unemployment inevitable. Since 1910 the state has changed from a dominantly agricultural to a highly specialized industrial state. The great mass of the population is now concentrated in the industrial centers and dependent on wages for a livelihood; farmers and independent proprietors, who are relatively immune to unemployment, make up a decreasing percentage of the total population. The risk of unemployment is exceptionally great in this state because its industries are specialized rather than diversified. The dominant industry—automobile manufacturing—is by the nature of its operations specially subject to conditions which are found to some extent in all large scale industries—seasonal unemploy-

[8] The State Board of Charities of New York made a detailed study of the causes of dependency of children and adults in public institutions for the year 1914-15 covering 636,565 cases of dependency or 6.5 per cent of the population of the state. The Oneida County study, which includes briefs of case records for 880 cases and much intensive study of selected cases and their backgrounds, is as follows: Carlisle, Chester Lee—*The Causes of Dependency Based on a Survey of Oneida County;* State of New York, State Board of Charities, Division of Mental Defect and Delinquency, The Bureau of Analysis and Investigation, Eugenics and Social Welfare Bulletin No. XV, Albany, 1918.

[9] Haber, William, and Stanchfield, Paul L.—*Unemployment, Relief and Economic Security: A Survey of Michigan's Relief and Unemployment Problem;* Second Report of the State Emergency Welfare Relief Commission, Lansing, 1936. See also ten monographs of Michigan Census of Population and Unemployment.

ment, displacement of workers by technological change, and restricted employment of workers who are past middle age.

"Seasonal unemployment, especially, was very prevalent in Michigan's manufacturing industries between 1920 and 1929 but its effects were partly concealed by the general expansion of the state's industries. During the years from 1920 through 1931, 40 per cent of the workers employed in the month of peak production in the Detroit area were jobless in the month of minimum employment. This difference represented at least a short period of unemployment for a yearly average of over 76,000 workers. Special studies of the automobile industry have shown that labor turnover rates are exceptionally irregular from month to month, and that even workers who survive seasonal lay-offs often suffer a marked reduction in working hours and weekly earnings. . . .

"The need for public relief and welfare activities will be abnormally great for many years to come because of conditions which have existed during the depression. Many workers who are still physically sound have, through prolonged unemployment, lost much of the skill and habituation to work which they need to compete successfully in the labor market. In some cases the psychological effect of prolonged idleness may have led to unemployability. In others physical handicaps which might have been corrected in their early stages have become permanent because of the worker's inability to pay for necessary medical care.

"Another group whose prospects for employment are slight are the workers in the age group from 50 to 70 years of age, who in many industries find themselves unable to find work at all or are limited to a few months' work during the peak season of the year. Michigan's industrial structure calls for a high percentage of young workers of the semi-skilled and unskilled class but the population as a whole is constantly becoming older. New occupations and industries are not likely to create a demand for older workers rapidly enough to prevent a serious problem of unemployment among them.

"The financial effects of the depression wiped out the savings and other resources of many families which will have no chance to build a new financial reserve. Many families which, before 1929, had every prospect of a comfortable and independent old age have lost their savings through bank failures and business losses; others have lost their homes; still others have exhausted all resources in an unsuccessful attempt to 'stay off relief.' Many of these cases involve workers, now too old to build a new reserve, who may remain permanently dependent on public funds.

"Michigan's relief problem has been most acute in the upper peninsula and the northern half of the lower peninsula. Many problems in these areas will demand special adjustments even after industrial recovery is accomplished. Many northern counties were declining in population before 1930, because of the exhaustion of the timber and mineral resources exploited in their original development. Private lumbering and mining are unlikely to employ more than a fraction of the population who formerly found work in these industries. A critical economic situation in these areas is indicated by high rates of tax delinquency and local financial resources which are inadequate to maintain proper standards of education, welfare, and other social services. Economic planning for improved land use, with emphasis on reforestation, seems to promise an ultimate solution—but in the immediate future thousands of workers have no prospect of earning an income which will make them independent. . . .

"Unemployment has not been the only cause which has led to the growing need for emergency relief. About one-fifth of the cases on the rolls, or between 40,000 and 45,000, were unemployable persons and families with no able-bodied wage-earner. In normal times many of these people might have received aid from relatives and friends. Others would have been cared for by private agencies and local treasuries. Among them are aged persons, disabled veterans of industry, widows with children of school and pre-school age, and others who have no prospect of ever earning wages. The emergency relief program has cared for many of them because no other provision was available. . . .

"The great majority of the persons who have received relief are members of family groups. The average relief population of 708,600 persons per month during the second fiscal year included 678,500 persons in families and about 30,000 unattached single persons. These one-person cases represented 16 per cent of the cases receiving relief but only 4.2 per cent of the individuals who received aid. . . .

"A careful classification of the 192,000 cases which were on Michigan's relief rolls at the end of January, 1935, showed that 37,364 contained no employable person. These 'unemployable' cases made up 19 per cent of all relief cases. The remaining 81 per cent of all cases were classified as needing aid only because they could not find work. . . .

"The dividing line between employable and unemployable persons is indistinct and even the best classification must yield an approximate, rather than an exact figure. A given type of physical disability may disqualify a worker for certain occupations, but not for others. Almost every individual is capable of some sort of useful work, but many may require special training and treatment to make them employable. Old age may make one man unemployable at 55, while another is physically sound at 70. Some workers who seem physically employable may actually be unemployable because of physical handicaps or psychological states of mind which cannot be recognized until they are actually tried out on a job. Finally, the actual prospects of employment are determined not only by ability and willingness to work but by special conditions in the labor market, such as the reluctance of employers to hire elderly men or slightly handicapped workers when younger workers are available. . . .

". . . Out of every thousand workers on the relief rolls in March, 76 were professional workers, proprietors, office workers, and salesmen; 107 were skilled workers in building and construction trades; and 63 were skilled workers in manufacturing and other industries. These three groups, combined, account for about one-quarter of the workers shown in the table. About 223 out of each thousand were semi-skilled workers and 166 were unskilled laborers in manufacturing, transportation, and construction. A representative sample of a thousand workers selected in proportion to the state total would also have included 55 farm laborers, 44 farmers, 64 workers from occupations connected with domestic and personal service, and 202 employable persons without previous work experience. . . .

". . . These inexperienced persons included 29,810 persons between 16 and 24 years of age—young workers who had been unable to find regular work since leaving school—and 10,081 inexperienced persons who were over 25 years of age. Of this latter group, over 95 per cent were women—presumably forced to seek work for the first time because of economic reverses during the depression.

"Many of the families on the relief rolls contain more than one able-bodied worker. The 197,614 workers on the rolls in March were concentrated in 137,049 of the families on the relief rolls. . . .

". . . About 129,400 employable persons, or almost exactly two-thirds of the state total, were located in urban areas—i.e. in communities of more than 2,500 inhabitants. . . .

"Large families of five or more members have been more numerous in the relief population than in the general population of the state. . . .

"Nearly three-quarters of the cases receiving emergency relief in Michigan in October, 1933, were so-called normal families, consisting of husband and wife, with or without children or other related and unrelated persons. The most frequent type—57 per cent of all cases—consisted of husband, wife, and their children. Thirteen per cent of the cases consisted of husband and wife without children, and an additional 4 per cent consisted of normal families with other persons. Altogether, 74 per cent of the cases included a married pair, usually with children. The majority of the husbands in the husband-wife-children type were well below middle age.

"About one case in eight was a 'broken family,' consisting of a man with his children or a woman with children. Families composed of woman and children accounted for two-thirds of the broken families, or 8 per cent of all cases. The man-children type accounted for 4 per cent of all cases. About one-sixth of the broken families contained other related or unrelated persons.

"Fourteen per cent of the cases were non-family persons (a man or woman, without spouse or children). About two-thirds of the non-family cases (9 per cent of the total) were single men. Single women accounted for 3 per cent of the cases, and men with persons other than spouse or children constituted 2 per cent. A large proportion of the non-family men were in the younger age groups. . . .

"Broken families were much more common in the urban relief population (13 per cent) than in rural areas (8 per cent). Non-family cases, especially those of the man-alone type, were more common in the rural relief population. . . .

"A very large proportion of the persons on Michigan's relief rolls are children of school and pre-school ages, and a relatively small proportion are between 25 and 44 years of age. In October, 1933, 41.0 per cent of the persons on Michigan's relief rolls were children under sixteen years of age. Less than 31 per cent of the population of the state, at the time of the 1930 census, were under sixteen years of age. Persons between 25 and 44 years of age, on the other hand, make up only 25.2 per cent of the persons on the relief rolls as compared with 31.8 per cent of the persons in the general population. . . .

"The Relief Census of October, 1933, showed that 48,547 of the 607,824 persons on Michigan's emergency relief rolls, or 8 per cent, were Negroes. White persons constituted 91.4 per cent of the total, and only 3,523 persons, or 0.6 per cent, were of other races. This last group comprised about 1,200 Mexicans, 2,000 American Indians, and a few orientals. Negroes and other races make up a much smaller proportion of Michigan's relief population than is true for the country as a whole. . . .

"There is a considerable amount of evidence that foreign born whites have been more seriously affected by unemployment than native born whites. Statistics for the state as a whole are not available, but a study of the Detroit relief rolls in March, 1934, showed that 43 per cent of the heads of relief families were foreign born whites, though the 1930 census found that only 39 per cent of the family-heads in Detroit's general population were foreign born. Native born whites, who constituted 53 per cent of the city's family-heads in 1930, accounted for only 31 per cent of the heads of relief families." [10]

Federal Investigations of the Recipients of Relief.—The research bulletins of the Federal Emergency Relief Administration (F.E.R.A.) and its legatee and successor the Works Progress Administration (W.P.A.) contain elaborate summarizations concerning the Federal relief population. Never before have so many data been gathered concerning public dependents. Yet the findings chiefly cover numbers, geographical distribution, contrasts between urban and rural population, sex, race, color, and prior occupations of persons out of work, rather than the causes of their poverty—or more specifically, of their unemployment.

Transients.—Of the few published researches which consider causes, the following brief summaries may be pertinent. Among 24,268 unattached transients registered for relief in thirteen cities in April, 1935, reasons for beginning migration were given as follows: seeking work 75 per cent, promised job 2 per cent, adventure 8 per cent, ill health 2 per cent, migratory occupation 3 per cent, domestic difficulties 3 per cent, inadequate relief 1 per cent, visits 4 per cent, personal business 1 per cent. Altogether economic factors are ascribed for 81 per cent of transiency among single men and women. Among 1,769 transient family groups in the same

[10] *Ibid.*, pp. 1, 2–4, 18, 22, 57, 62, 64, 67, 71, 74–75, 76–77, and 80–81.

month, 68 per cent were seeking work, 11 per cent began migration because of ill health, 5 per cent for visits, 4 per cent because of promised jobs, 3 per cent because of inadequate relief, 2 per cent each because of migratory occupations or domestic difficulties. Thus 72 per cent of this specific group of dependents appear to have their predicament actuated by conditions primarily economic.[11]

Rural Cases.—W.P.A. studies of rural relief population in 1935 revealed that:

"About 1,000,000 rural cases received general relief in October 1935. This total was lower than that for any other month in the history of the F.E.R.A. reporting service except September 1933, when relief rolls had been temporarily reduced to about a million cases by seasonal agricultural employment, and December, 1933, when the expanding C.W.A. program also temporarily reduced rural relief to about a million cases. The October 1935 case load was 40 per cent less than that of October 1934. . . .

"The reasons for the continued intensity of rural relief in these states [12] in the face of a general decline are found in such factors as (a) the depletion of soil fertility and of natural mining and lumbering resources leaving a stranded yet increasing population (Kentucky and West Virginia), (b) stranded populations of laborers from agriculture and from the oil fields (Oklahoma), (c) the after-effects of the drought of last year and partial crop failure this year (North Dakota and Oklahoma), (d) stranded miners (Utah), and (e) a fairly general failure of local governments in these states to provide adequate funds for the care of 'unemployables. . . .'

" 'New' cases continued to come on to the relief rolls in rural areas in large numbers. Of the 215,000 relief cases opened in nine agricultural areas during March, April, May, and June of 1935, about 43 out of every 100 had not been known previously to the agency accepting the case. . . .

"Many of these 'new' cases were families who had held on to their independence during the depression but who were continually drawing on their personal resources and being forced into dependence upon public relief. Many others had been dropped from the lists of local public

[11] Webb, John N.—*The Transient Unemployed: A Description and Analysis of the Transient Relief Population*, p. 117; Works Progress Administration, Division of Social Research, Research Monograph III, 1935.

[12] "About 255,000 cases, or more than one fourth of all rural cases, were located in four states, Kentucky, Oklahoma, Texas, and West Virginia. Five states with high proportions of the general rural population on relief were Kentucky, Oklahoma, West Virginia, North Dakota, and Utah, each with a relief rate of more than 16 per cent as compared with an average of 8 per cent for all states combined." *Changes in the Rural Relief Population through October 1935;* Works Progress Administration, Research Bulletin H–6, January 14, 1936.

or private agencies, while others had moved or been transferred to a different emergency relief agency." [13]

Urban Cases.—No such convenient résumé is available for the causes of poverty or unemployment in urban areas.[14] Nevertheless a F.E.R.A. summary for 1,500,000 relief cases in seventy-nine cities for May, 1934 (conducted by sampling 202,000 relief households) showed 73 per cent in which all persons of working age were unemployed and 10 per cent with no employable person in the household. Over half the families had only one employable member. One-fourth of the families were of Negro "or other racial extraction." The average size of white families was 3.8 persons and of Negro families 3.4 persons.

Although neither a statistical average nor a mode gives a true picture of the range of problems within the group, the following description has the merit of suggesting several sources of urban poverty:

"The typical unemployed person on urban relief rolls in May 1934 was a white man 38 years of age who was the head of a household. He had not completed an elementary school education, but had, on the average, 10 years' experience at the occupation he considered his customary or 'usual' one. This occupation varied considerably with the type of community in which he lived, but was most frequently a semiskilled or unskilled occupation in the manufacturing or mechanical industries. Perhaps the most significant fact about the average urban worker on relief in May 1934 was that he had lost the last job at his usual occupation in the winter of 1931–32.

"The largest single group (34 per cent) of unemployed men on urban relief rolls had formerly been employed in unskilled occupations. One-fourth of the total had worked in skilled and another fourth in semiskilled occupations. . . .

"The average unemployed woman, on relief and seeking work, was 5 years younger than the average man. She had a slightly better education

[13] *Ibid.*, pp. 1 and 7.
[14] See, however, Palmer, Gladys L., and Wood, Katherine D.—*Urban Workers on Relief. Part I—The Occupational Characteristics of Workers on Relief in Urban Areas: May 1934;* Works Progress Administration, Division of Social Research, Research Monograph IV, 1936: and Wood, Katherine D.—*Urban Workers on Relief. Part II—The Occupational Characteristics of Workers on Relief in 79 Cities: May 1934;* Works Progress Administration, Division of Social Research, Research Monograph IV, 1936. See also *The National Health Survey: 1935–36—Characteristics of the Urban Unemployed;* Division of Public Health Methods, National Institute of Health, U. S. Public Health Service (Preliminary Reports, The National Health Survey, Population Series, Bulletin No. D), 1938.

but had worked for a shorter period at her customary occupation. She had lost the last job at her usual occupation in the fall of 1932 and had not had a nonrelief job of 1 month or more for approximately $1\frac{1}{2}$ years. . . .

"The evidence of the study demonstrates in general the cumulative effects of prolonged unemployment. The longer persons are out of work, the worse their chances are for reëmployment at their customary occupation or, in fact, at any type of job. Although the majority of unemployed workers on relief stay on relief for relatively short periods of time, there appears to be a residual group of long-time unemployed who are the core of a permanent unemployment problem. This group will not be able to qualify for unemployment benefits under the provisions of the Social Security Act. Some of the workers of this group live in specialized industrial centers which have been characterized by steadily declining employment opportunities in recent years. Others were formerly employed in occupations which are now obsolescent. Still others are too old to secure employment readily in the occupations in which they were formerly employed, or for which they have been trained, and are too young to secure old age assistance. Together they constitute a group of workers who are 'stranded' in every sense of the word." [15]

QUESTIONS FOR DISCUSSION OR EXAMINATION

1. Booth suggested state colonization of "Class B" as a major means to the solution of the problem of poverty in London. Would such a plan be (a) practical? (b) just? In your judgment what form would colonization best take? What factors producing poverty would remain operative after "Class B" is withdrawn?
2. Is one justified in assuming from the findings of Bowley and Smith (a) that the problem of poverty is already largely solved? (b) that its solution may be left to social evolution?
3. Distinguish economic factors from other factors in the findings of the Michigan relief survey.
4. Compare causative factors of (a) transiency, (b) poverty in farming areas, (c) poverty in urban areas.
5. How do you account for the discrepancies between these findings and those of (a) the classic theorists? (b) case-counting studies?

PROBLEMS FOR INDIVIDUAL STUDY

1. Critical analysis of some one of the works in the following list of references.
2. Detailed study of conditions, causes, and distribution (geographical, economic, social) of poverty in your own city, county, or state as revealed by public records of relief.
3. Contrast (a) two selected cities, or (b) two selected states, or (c) urban and rural areas, with reference to the volume, types, and sources of poverty.

[15] *Monthly Report of the Federal Emergency Relief Administration, June 1 through June 30, 1936* (final issue), pp. 116–120; Government Printing Office, 1937.

4. Study trends of poverty for a selected area over a period of time that is covered by adequate records.
5. Compare the findings of Chapters XIX and XX with the texts of Malthus, George, or Marx.

SUGGESTIONS FOR SUPPLEMENTARY READINGS

Angell, Robert Cooley—*The Family Encounters the Depression;* Charles Scribner's Sons, 1936.

Armstrong, Louise V.—*We Too Are the People;* Little, Brown, and Company, 1938.

Beck, P. G., and Forster, M. C.—*Six Rural Problem Areas: Relief—Resources—Rehabilitation;* Federal Emergency Relief Administration, Division of Research, Statistics and Finance, Research Monograph I, 1935.

Booth, Charles—*Life and Labour of the People in London,* seventeen volumes; Macmillan and Co., Limited, 1902.

Bowley, A. L., and Burnett-Hurst, A. R.—*Livelihood and Poverty;* G. Bell and Sons, Ltd., 1915.

Bowley, A. L., and Hogg, Margaret H.—*Has Poverty Diminished?;* P. S. King & Son, Ltd., 1925.

Brunner, E. deS., and Lorge, Irving—*Rural Trends in Depression Years; A Survey of Village-centered Agricultural Communities, 1930–1936;* Columbia University Press, 1937.

Cavan, Ruth Shonle, and Ranck, Katherine Howland—*The Family and the Depression;* University of Chicago Press, 1938.

Chapin, F. Stuart, and Queen, Stuart A.—*Research Memorandum on Social Work in the Depression;* Committee on Studies in Social Aspects of the Depression, Social Science Research Council, Bulletin 39, 1937.

Collins, Selwyn D., and Tibbitts, Clark—*Research Memorandum on Social Aspects of Health in the Depression;* Committee on Studies in Social Aspects of the Depression, Social Science Research Council, Bulletin 36, 1937.

Cross, W. T., and Cross, D. E.—*Newcomers and Nomads in California;* Stanford University Press, 1937.

Davenport, Donald H., and Croston, John J.—*Unemployment and Prospects for Reëmployment in Massachusetts: With Particular Reference to Manufacturing Industries;* Graduate School of Business Administration, Harvard University, Business Research Studies No. 15, 1936.

Elderton, Marion, editor—*Case Studies of Unemployment;* University of Pennsylvania Press, Industrial Research Studies No. XII, 1931.

Federal Emergency Relief Administration—publications.

Haber, William, and Stanchfield, Paul L.—*Unemployment, Relief and Economic Security: A Survey of Michigan's Relief and Unemployment Problem;* Second Report of the State Emergency Welfare Relief Commission, Lansing, 1936.

Hopkins, Harry L.—*Spending to Save: The Complete Story of Relief;* W. W. Norton & Company, Inc., 1936.

McCormick, Thomas C.—*Comparative Study of Rural Relief and Non-Relief Households;* Works Progress Administration, Division of Social Research, Research Monograph II, 1935.

MacNeil, Douglas H.—*Seven Years of Unemployment Relief in New Jersey, 1930–36.* Committee on Social Security, Social Science Research Council, 1938.

Massachusetts—*Report on the Census of Unemployment in Massachusetts as of January 2, 1934;* Massachusetts Department of Labor and Industries, Division of Statistics, Public Document No. 15 (Labor Bulletin No. 171), 1935.

Millett, John D.—*The Works Progress Administration in New York City;* published for the Committee on Public Administration of the Social Science Research Council by Public Administration Service (Chicago), 1938.

Niceforo, Alfredo—*Les classes pauvres: Recherches anthropologiques et sociales;* V. Giard & E. Brière (Paris), 1905.

Palmer, Gladys L.—*Recent Trends in Employment and Unemployment in Philadelphia;* Works Progress Administration, Philadelphia Labor Market Studies Report No. P–1, December, 1937.

Palmer, Gladys L., and Wood, Katherine D.—*Urban Workers on Relief. Part I—The Occupational Characteristics of Workers on Relief in Urban Areas: May 1934;* Works Progress Administration, Division of Social Research, Research Monograph IV, 1936.

Pruette, Lorine, editor—*Women Workers Through the Depression: A Study of White Collar Employment Made by the American Woman's Association;* The Macmillan Company, 1934.

Rice, Stuart A., editor—*Methods in Social Science;* Committee on Scientific Method in the Social Sciences of the Social Science Research Council, University of Chicago Press, 1931.

Rowntree, B. Seebohm—*Poverty; A Study of Town Life;* Macmillan and Co., Limited, 1908.

Sanderson, Dwight—*Research Memorandum on Rural Life in the Depression;* Committee on Studies in Social Aspects of the Depression, Social Science Research Council, Bulletin 34, 1937.

Sellin, Thorsten—*Research Memorandum on Crime in the Depression;* Committee on Studies in Social Aspects of the Depression, Social Science Research Council, Bulletin 27, 1937.

Smith, Sir H. Llewellyn (Director)—*The New Survey of London Life and Labour,* nine volumes; P. S. King & Son, Ltd., 1930–35.

Social Science Research Council—*Studies in the Social Aspects of the Depression: Research Memoranda, prepared under the direction of the Committee on Studies in Social Aspects of the Depression,* thirteen volumes; Social Science Research Council, 1937.

Stouffer, Samuel A., and Lazarsfeld, Paul F.—*Research Memorandum on the Family in the Depression;* Committee on Studies in Social Aspects of the Depression, Social Science Research Council, Bulletin 29, 1937.

Thompson, Warren S.—*Research Memorandum on Internal Migration in the Depression;* Committee on Studies in Social Aspects of the Depression, Social Science Research Council, Bulletin 30, 1937.

United States Office of Education—*Youth: A Contemporary Bibliography;* Prepared by the Committee on Youth Problems, Circular No. 152, United States Office of Education, 1935.

Vaile, Roland S.—*Research Memorandum on Social Aspects of Consumption in the Depression;* Committee on Studies in Social Aspects of the Depression, Social Science Research Council, Bulletin 35, 1937.

Watson, J. P.—*Economic Backgrounds of the Relief Problem;* Bureau of Business Research, University of Pittsburgh, 1937.

Whetten, N. L., Darling, H. D., McKain, W. C., and Field, R. F.—*Rural Families on Relief in Connecticut;* Department of Sociology, Connecticut State College (Storrs), Bulletin 215, January, 1937.

White, R. Clyde, and White, Mary K.—*Research Memorandum on Social Aspects of Relief Policies in the Depression;* Committee on Studies in Social Aspects of the Depression, Social Science Research Council, Bulletin 38, 1937.

Williams, James Mickel—*Human Aspects of Unemployment and Relief with Special Reference to the Effects of the Depression on Children;* University of North Carolina Press, 1933.

Wood, Katherine D.—*Urban Workers on Relief. Part II—The Occupational Characteristics of Workers on Relief in 79 Cities: May 1934;* Works Progress Administration, Division of Social Research, Research Monograph IV, 1936.

Works Progress Administration—publications.

CHAPTER XXI

SOCIAL CASE WORK AND POOR RELIEF

Historical Sources.—In every field of human endeavor current attitudes and practices have their roots deep in the past. The treatment and prevention of poverty exemplify this principle at every point. Christian charity draws its rules and justifications from both the New Testament and the Old, as well as from interpretations by the early Christian Fathers, the Scholastics, and subsequent leaders and commentators.[1] Contemporary federations of Jewish welfare agencies still respect, quote, and apply many principles of giving that were stated in the earlier books of the Old Testament, the Talmud, and subsequent Rabbinical writings. So strong are these traditions that the destitute Orthodox Jew of today can usually still demand (rather than request) aid of others of his race and be sure that subsistence will be provided by them.[2]

The principles of public relief were drawn by the American colonies from the laws and practices of England of the seventeenth and eighteenth centuries, which in turn were derived from the common law of the Anglo-Saxons and the earliest statute laws. Louisiana laws incorporate much that proceeds from the early laws and practices of France, but in all other states the English tradition prevails.[3]

[1] Gray, B. Kirkman—*A History of English Philanthropy: From the Dissolution of the Monasteries to the Taking of the First Census;* P. S. King & Son, Ltd., 1905. Kerby, William J.—*The Social Mission of Charity: A Study of Points of View in Catholic Charities;* The Macmillan Company, 1921. Lecky, W. E. H.—*History of European Morals from Augustus to Charlemagne,* two volumes; D. Appleton and Company, third revised edition, 1925. Loch, C. S.—*Charity and Social Life;* Macmillan and Co., Limited, 1910. Peabody, Francis Greenwood—*Jesus Christ and the Social Question;* The Macmillan Company, 1930. Queen, Stuart Alfred—*Social Work in the Light of History,* Part IV; J. B. Lippincott Company, 1922. Uhlhorn, Gerhard—*Christian Charity in the Ancient Church;* Charles Scribner's Sons, 1883. Watson, Frank Dekker—*The Charity Organization Movement in the United States;* The Macmillan Company, 1922.

[2] Bogen, Boris D.—*Jewish Philanthropy: An Exposition of Principles and Methods of Jewish Social Service in the United States;* The Macmillan Company, 1917: and Frisch, Ephraim—*An Historical Survey of Jewish Philanthropy: From the Earlier Times to the Nineteenth Century;* The Macmillan Company, 1924.

[3] Kelso, Robert W.—*The History of Public Poor Relief in Massachusetts, 1620–*

Effects of Tradition.—The continuity of tradition is daily exemplified by individuals in their reactions to the distress suffered by themselves or others. It reveals itself in conceptions of both rights and duties. It affects behavior whether the constellation of ideas takes the form of "noblesse oblige" or "workingmen of the world unite!"

In public councils as in private life the heavy hand of tradition is constantly felt. The "crust of custom" is hard to break, though the need may be great. The mental stereotypes [4] of some legislators can be traced in the *Congressional Record* or observed at sessions of state legislatures or city councils. Eminently reasonable proposals for change in social policy for the poor—for providing the media essential to rehabilitation or development—may be condemned by quoting an ancient principle or practice. It is, however, in judicial decisions that the domination of the past over the present is most readily traced, since the sources of each decision in past laws and past decisions are cited, and may in turn be examined until the judgments have been followed back over many centuries. Tradition is reflected in the prevalent resistance to change in state and Federal constitutions. It develops an aura and authenticity of its own, supported by emotional reactions. It may serve to prevent or postpone certain types of social disorganization—especially the disorganization of social institutions—and too rapid social change. But its conservatizing force tends to persist unduly and if unbroken or uncorrected will retard or prevent rational and needed improvements.

Almsgiving.—Throughout human history until the past century poverty, like other evils, almost universally has been assumed to be inevitable. It has been met outside of the poorhouse chiefly by the giving of alms. The effect of almsgiving has been to perpetuate the evil rather than to remove it. It gives to the recipient relief from immediate discomfort and, temporarily, the illusion of security. It virtually does the same for the smug donor, but it relieves neither of the probability of future discomfort.

There is a close parallel between the early history of poor relief

1920; Houghton Mifflin Company, 1922. Queen, Stuart Alfred—*op. cit.*, Part III. Wisner, Elizabeth—*Public Welfare Administration in Louisiana;* University of Chicago Press, 1930. Also works of Leonard, Mackay, and Webb cited in Chapter XVIII.

[4] See Young, Kimball—*Source Book for Social Psychology*, Part Four; Alfred A. Knopf, 1927, and Young, Kimball, editor—*Social Attitudes;* Henry Holt and Company, 1931.

and that of medicine. The patient suffering pain was until recently given an opiate to make him forget his torment. Today medicine is a science and the source of the pain is ascertained and, when possible, removed.

The almsgiving of the past two thousand years has served as the opiate for poverty. Whether it took the form of the largess of the Roman Emperor, pennies in the cup of the blind mendicant, or a dime to the street beggar for "a cup of coffee," it gave no thought to the causes and removal of the difficulties of the poor, but merely perpetuated the distress while temporarily relieving it. This abuse became so general that in 1893 Robert Treat Paine of Boston was led to list indiscriminate almsgiving as one of the four leading causes of poverty.[5]

Skilful beggars are still known to refuse good jobs if they can make a better living at begging. Their number is large in cities where begging is tolerated. They swarm in many cities of Europe and Asia—so that it has been remarked that a community "may have as many poor as it will pay for." Large numbers of persons are found willing to be parasites upon others wherever it is made easy to do so.[6]

The Movement for Charity Organization.—Until the latter part of the nineteenth century charitable relief of the poor was chaotic. In each of our cities large numbers of private agencies had funds at their disposal for the relief of the poor, but each worked independently of the others. Persons in need, and many others as well, made a practice of going from one agency to another to request aid, and each agency correspondingly tended to provide less than full maintenance. In such circumstances relatively little could be accomplished towards the restoration of families in need to self-support. Funds were thus inefficiently used and dependency was perpetuated.

[5] "Pauperism in Great Cities: Its Four Chief Causes," read at the International Congress of Charities, Correction and Philanthropy, at Chicago, June 12, 1893.

[6] Recent trends in the prevention of begging can be followed by consulting Cobb, W. Bruce—"Begging," *Social Work Year Book 1929;* Russell Sage Foundation, 1930, and Moore, MacEnnis—"Transiency and Non-Residence," *Social Work Year Book 1937;* Russell Sage Foundation, 1937, together with the references to literature submitted by each. Where enforcement is competent and discriminating, work refusal becomes rare among the ablebodied. See Warner, Amos Griswold, Queen, Stuart Alfred, and Harper, Ernest Bouldin—*American Charities and Social Work,* pp. 107–110; Thomas Y. Crowell Company, fourth edition, 1930, and recent studies by the Works Progress Administration, *i.e.* *Surveys of Job Refusals by Relief Clients Reported in Six Communities* (*March to June,* *1935*), Research Bulletin, Series I, No. 15.

These difficulties were recognized by Thomas Chalmers in Glasgow, Scotland, Joseph Tuckerman in Boston, and others early in the nineteenth century. But there was a lag of nearly fifty years between the recognition of the problem and efficient organization to meet it.[7]

The beginning of the charity organization movement in its present form occurred with the establishment of the Charity Organization Society of London, England, in 1869, and in this country with the Charity Organization Society of Buffalo, New York, in 1878, though the latter was preceded by one in Germantown, Pennsylvania, in 1873.[8] Other cities in England and America following these models established similar organizations, in the decades following, sometimes with the same name but often with similar names such as Associated Charities, United Charities, or Federation of Charities. These have largely changed their names in the twentieth century to that of Family Welfare Society or some equivalent term. Altogether America now has over two hundred organizations of this type that are members of the Family Welfare Association of America, and one may be found in practically every city of more than fifty thousand population, and sometimes in communities much smaller.

Initially, the charity organization movement was chiefly concerned with the prevention of the overlapping of relief and the repression of mendicity, which was the current term in that period for begging. These aims were to be accomplished in the main through making a thoroughgoing investigation of each applicant prior to relief and by the maintenance through the charity organization society of a central registration bureau—later termed Social

---

[7] See Watson, Frank Dekker—op. cit., Chapters II and III, and his references. Also Chalmers, Thomas—The Christian and Civic Economy of Large Towns (first written in 1826, abridged and with an introduction by Charles R. Henderson in 1900); Charles Scribner's Sons, 1900: and Tuckerman, Joseph—On the Elevation of the Poor; a selection from his reports as minister at large in Boston (with an introduction by E. E. Hale); Boston, 1874. Other foreign precursors of one detail or another of charity organization include Sir Thomas Bernard of London, the London Mendicancy Society (1805), the Edinburgh Society for the Suppression of Mendicity (1813), William Allen and Elizabeth Fry of the Society of Friends, the London Metropolitan Visiting and Relief Association (1813), the Society of St. Vincent de Paul which originated from the charitable methods of Frederick Ozanam and Sylvain Bailly in Paris in 1833. These can be traced through works of Gray, Jorns, Loch, and others in the list of references following this chapter.

[8] Bosanquet, Helen—Social Work in London, 1869 to 1912; John Murray (London), 1914, and Watson, Frank Dekker—op. cit.

Service Exchange—containing the names and addresses, and other identifying information concerning each case which applied for aid to any one of the coöperating agencies. The maintenance of such a list made it possible for each agency to refuse aid to an applicant who was being looked after by another agency. This not only served to prevent overlapping of aid to any given family but conserved the funds of each coöperating agency so that fuller service could be rendered to each needy family in its direct care.

The charity organization society was seldom a merger of existing agencies, but tended everywhere to become a service agency for the purpose of coördination, diagnosis, and treatment, drawing its funds for relief of families chiefly from preëxisting sources, and utilizing its own funds primarily for the salaries of its staff, who were trained social workers. The evolution of the charity organization society to its present form as family welfare society has been guided throughout by many of the keenest minds in the field of social work.

Organized charity at first assumed each applicant to be an imposter until he demonstrated that he was one of the "worthy poor." The treatment in the eighties and nineties was sometimes so searching and exacting that a contemporary poet described it as

"Organized charity scrimped and iced
In the name of a cautious, statistical Christ."

Nevertheless the organization of charity, though at first perforce overstressing the repression of mendicity and the discouragement of parasitism, developed its own correctives and emerged as the scientific but human family social work of today.

Principles of Social Case Work.—The original *principle of investigation* developed into the science and art of social diagnosis, which was defined by Mary Richmond as "the attempt to make as exact a definition as possible of the situation and personality of a human being in some social need—of his situation and personality, that is, in relation to the other human beings upon whom he in any way depends or who depend upon him, and in relation also to the social institutions of his community." [9]

The early *principle of repression* outgrew the hounding of the sturdy beggar and was replaced by sympathetic treatment with reference to the applicant's needs. Evil may be "repressed" but not the person who is suffering from the evil—whether drunkenness, gambling,

[9] Richmond, Mary E.—*Social Diagnosis;* Russell Sage Foundation, 1917.

or prostitution. In general the word repression is outgrown since evil is largely overcome with "good," *i.e.* the substitution of constructive interests for those primarily destructive.

The *principle of individualization* emerged from the discovery that cases could not properly be labeled, and treated categorically as widows, drunkards, etc. Instead, it is now realized that each applicant represents a unique problem to be dealt with according to his own needs, aptitudes, ambitions, and the circumstances of his family and environment.

The *principle of coöperation* developed to the point where it no longer involved mere collaboration with other agencies to prevent overlapping of relief, but joined their services in a common plan for making over each member of the applicant's family according to need. Coöperation with the client and each member of his family in the solution of their problem has also largely replaced the paternalism and the dictatorial methods of earlier times.

The *principle of adequacy* displaced the earlier English principle of less eligibility [10] and meant material aid to the family of an amount and kind sufficient to make conditions of living wholesome during the period of treatment and to remove all factors which might thwart recovery.

The *principle of rehabilitation* made restoration to self-support the aim of family social work on the material side, and wholesome family life and constructive participation in industry, neighborhood, and community, goals to be sought wherever the applicant or members of his family were mentally and physically capable.

Definition of Family Social Work.—Family social work is now recognized to "consist of those processes which develop personality through adjustments consciously effected, individual by individual, between men and their social environment." [11] Charitable relief has

[10] The English poor law of 1834 affirmed the principle that persons or families receiving aid should be maintained at a standard less eligible or desirable than that of the least well paid independent self-supporting worker. It was assumed that if the standards should be made higher the lower paid workers would drop their jobs and apply for relief. This and the other principles of English poor law together with subsequent changes are ably outlined in Webb, Sidney and Beatrice—*English Poor Law Policy;* Longmans, Green and Co., 1910. The principle of adequacy can, however, replace that of less eligibility once social diagnosis and the other essential principles of social case work are discriminatingly applied.

[11] Richmond, Mary E.—*What Is Social Case Work?;* Russell Sage Foundation, 1922.

thus become a mere means to an end—not an end in itself. Personality development is both the ideal and the end-product of the services of scientifically trained social workers.

Limitations of Family Social Work in Practice.—Few agencies of social work in any given community live up to all of the standards of their profession in their daily practice. Limitations of funds mean that the staff will be inadequate, and the case load too heavy, so that the diagnosis will not be as thorough as it should be. The level of relief may be inadequate for rehabilitation. Thus insufficient contributions to a community's welfare agencies may prolong dependency.

A large percentage of families helped in most of our cities are looked after by church denominations, many of which have not yet learned to make use of the organized agencies for family social work. They still give alms, though often in a kindly and sympathetic manner. Because of their lack of technical knowledge, and failure to coöperate they may not succeed in rehabilitating their needy parishioners and thus may render them continuing charges upon charity.

Public relief as a rule does not yet recognize social case work as its province. Its traditional emphasis has been upon material aid rather than upon restoration of the individual and his family to creative social living. Many municipal departments of public welfare fail to coöperate with the organized private agencies of their communities. Some city welfare departments refuse to make use of the Social Service Exchange, confidential in nature, which has been the primary means in recent years of preventing needless overlapping of relief on the one hand and of facilitating the coöperation of agencies in case treatment upon the other. Failure to make use of it almost inevitably means imperfect diagnosis, and is likely consequently to result in inferior treatment.[12]

Municipal and state boards of public welfare do not yet, as a rule, secure their staff members from among the trained graduates of schools for social work. Appointment on both boards and staffs still tends to be political in nature. The inevitable result is a type of relief which may rob the applicant of self-respect, maintain him and his family at a dangerously low standard of life, thus failing to restore them to self-support. Public relief in so far as it is admin-

[12] See publications of the Committee on Social Service Exchange of Community Chests and Councils, Inc.; also Woodberry, Laura G.—*The Central Index;* 1929.

istered by politicians and untrained staffs needlessly perpetuates poverty. There are probably millions of persons on relief rolls who under wise guidance and skilled social work would be capable of being restored to independence.

The Beginnings of Public Relief.—In mediaeval times the poor had been aided, if at all, by the nobility, churches, and monasteries. The first legislation in England was undertaken to suppress vagrancy, and was passed in 1349, known as the Statute of Labourers.[13] Further measures were passed under Henry VIII [14] in the sixteenth century. It was not until the Act of 1572, which created the office of the Overseer of the Poor, and the Acts of 1597 and 1601,[15] which placed upon the overseers the obligation of devising means for the relief of the poor, that groups of the poor other than the vagrant and beggar were recognized in English law. The principles established comprised (1) local responsibility for the poor of the community, (2) the provision of work for the ablebodied and for children, (3) relief for those profoundly handicapped or infirm, (4) the levying of taxes to accomplish these purposes. Children were generally apprenticed, families often separated. But the principle had become established in British law that the poor should be supported by the local community out of funds raised through taxation. It is noteworthy that economic crises precipitated this early legislation. The Statute of Labourers was passed following the ravages of the Black Death. The vagrancy laws of Henry VIII followed the corn riots, and the Elizabethan law of 1597 followed three years of extreme scarcity of corn and consequent starvation of many of the poor. [16]

Beginnings of Public Poor Relief in America.—The English colonists brought to America the principles of public poor relief established in the home country. These principles became firmly established in statute law and in practice. The poor were legally entitled to relief. The responsibility for their care rested with the local government. Persons in distress who had not acquired local settlement were returned to the community from which they had come. Children who were dependent were indentured or placed out in private families where they could work for their keep. Adults

[13] 23 Edward III, Cap. 1.
[14] 27 Henry VIII, Cap. 25, 1536.
[15] 39 Elizabeth, Cap. 3, followed by 43 Elizabeth, Cap. 2, 1601.
[16] See especially Kelso, Robert W.—*op. cit.*, Chapter I.

were often similarly placed out for work, or, if incompetent, boarded in private homes. Though some few almshouses had been established prior to seventeen hundred, aid generally took the form of "outdoor relief," which was the name given to relief in the home. Those who were able to work were made to do so whether young or old. There was much relief "in kind," which ranged from the provision of food to occasional instances of community provision of home, farm, or cow. At first the problems of each poor family were taken up for discussion in town meeting. But by 1691 Boston, following the English practice, had elected overseers of the poor. [17]

The Nineteenth Century.—From the eastern states the pioneers who settled first in the Northwest Territory, and later west of the Mississippi, carried these principles of English law and practice to the remainder of the country. The nineteenth century, however, witnessed the abandonment of indenture and the development of differentiation of the many subgroups of the poor for treatment. There was some crude experimentation in the relative merits of indoor or institutional relief as compared with outdoor or home relief, with temporary abandonment in some communities of the latter. More notable progress was made in the latter part of the century by the establishment of state boards of charity, later known as state boards of public welfare. The various groups of the handicapped were increasingly treated in separate institutions either by the state board of public welfare or by specialized boards or commissions. States also assumed the burden of those of the poor who lacked local settlement. [18]

Evolution of the Almshouse.—Meanwhile the local community, or according to state law and practice the county, continued to care in the traditional manner for the local poor. The almshouse tended to become the receptacle in which were placed all but the temporary poor and those cared for by the state. In it were found, and in many parts of America still are found, persons of all ages and both sexes, immigrant or native, including often many who are feebleminded or mentally diseased, some who are deaf, blind, crippled, or epileptic.

[17] *Ibid.*, Chapters II–V.
[18] Breckinridge, Sophonisba P.—*Public Welfare Administration in the United States: Select Documents;* University of Chicago Press, second edition, enlarged and revised, 1938. Odum, Howard W.—*An Approach to Public Welfare and Social Work;* University of North Carolina Press, 1926. Odum, Howard W., and Willard, D. W.—*Systems of Public Welfare;* University of North Carolina Press, 1925.

Vagrants may also be received. The almshouse itself is still usually directed by some political appointee untrained in social work.

The trend definitely is towards specialization in the treatment of persons who have become dependent. In our more progressive states and cities what was once the almshouse is being made over into two separate institutions. The first a receiving station for diagnosis and temporary residence pending placement in a specialized institution, and the second a home and infirmary for the aged poor.[19]

Twentieth Century Trends.—In the twentieth century the state boards of public welfare or state boards of control have greatly extended their provision for specialized treatment. In addition to the education and hospitalization of each group of the handicapped, special provision has been made increasingly by state authority for the placing out of dependent children in carefully selected and appropriate private homes, or as in New York State in institutional homes of the cottage type which are the modern outgrowth of the orphan asylums of earlier days.

The twentieth century has witnessed also the development of social security legislation, certain types of which originated prior to the Federal Social Security Act of 1935 and often are administered by the state board of public welfare, or by new state boards created largely upon its recommendation. Thus widows' pensions and mothers' aid, old-age pensions, and pensions for the blind were outgrowths of, but in many ways improvements upon, the poor relief legislation of prior centuries. The details will, however, be treated in later chapters.

Federal Measures for the Relief of the Poor.—In recent years the entire field of public relief for the poor has undergone striking change through the invasion by the Federal government of a field of service originally recognized as strictly local. The economic depression beginning late in 1929 had within two years so profoundly overtaxed community resources available for the relief of distress, both public and private, that the necessity for Federal intervention as a means of equalizing or better distributing the economic burden became apparent.

An official Federal report of the trends in public relief expenditures from 1910 to 1935 includes the following summary:

[19] Johnson, Alexander—*The Almshouse;* Charities Publication Committee, Russell Sage Foundation, 1911. See also *Proceedings* of National Conference of Social Work.

"During the recent depression, which has been of greater intensity and longer duration than any previous depression in the history of the United States, the relief of unemployment and distress has been a major national problem. The tremendous increase in the extent of need and the assumption by the Federal Government of a substantial share of the responsibility for meeting the need have focused attention on the administration of relief during the depression years and have made the general public aware of the issues involved.

"Although much has been written concerning the scope and nature of the contemporary relief problem, little is known of the extent of the burden in the United States in the decades preceding the depression of the 1930's. The purpose of this study is to give as much perspective as possible to recent developments by viewing them in relation to long-time trends. The report is restricted to aid extended to families and individuals outside of institutions and does not include foster-home care or welfare services. The relief burden has been measured, in so far as possible, in terms of the amount of aid distributed to relief cases rather than in terms of the cost of relief plus its administration.

"The term *relief* is a generic one covering many types and forms of aid. Since this report has been compiled from secondary sources, it has not been feasible to standardize terminology. Different terms designating the same or similar forms of relief have been used in the original sources and have been retained in the present discussion. *Outdoor relief* is an inclusive term in general use, referring to all types of relief extended to families and individuals outside of institutions. *Wage assistance* is a term devised especially for this report to refer to assistance of a modified relief character, extended in the form of wages to persons employed on the work programs operated during 1933, 1934, and 1935 by the Civil Works Administration, the Civilian Conservation Corps, the Works Progress Administration, and other agencies participating in the Works Program. . . .

". . . The following basic tendencies may be noted.

"1. The forms of public relief have tended to become more and more differentiated through the enactment of special legislation.

"2. There has been a progressive tendency to widen the base of governmental responsibility for relief beyond the local units, first through State and then through Federal participation.

"3. At least since 1910 there has been a strong underlying upward trend in relief expenditures. The very great increase in expenditures in the depression years represents a sharp acceleration of a tendency manifest throughout the preceding two decades.

"4. The increase in both public and private relief expenditures has been far greater than the growth in population.

"5. The rate of increase of public relief expenditures, at least in large urban areas, has greatly exceeded that of all governmental expenditures combined.

"6. While expenditures for general public relief have increased steadily, the most rapid expansion in public relief prior to the depression occurred in aid to dependent children.

"7. There is little evidence that the introduction of aid to special classes, such as the aged, the blind, and dependent children, has resulted in the past in reduction of the general relief burden. Although there has been some shifting of cases from general relief rolls to the rolls of agencies providing statutory relief, to a considerable extent the special types of assistance have tapped new reservoirs of need. The influx of new cases to the general relief rolls, combined with rising standards of care, has largely offset such absorption as has occurred.

"8. Following the 1921–1922 depression, relief expenditures did not return to the predepression level. There was a temporary recession from the depression peak but relief expenditures continued to mount in subsequent years.

"9. There have been wide regional and local variations in the relative proportions of public and private relief, but public agencies bore an important share of the burden long before the onset of the recent depression. Since the assumption of a share of the responsibility for relief by the Federal Government in 1932 the proportion of the burden borne by private agencies has been very slight.

"10. Work relief and work projects in the recent depression have assumed a new and increasing importance as a means of assisting the destitute unemployed.

"11. The expansion in expenditures for outdoor relief has, since 1932, been relatively greater in rural and town areas than in urban areas. . . .

"In 1933, 1934, and 1935 wage assistance constituted a very important part of the total public assistance structure. Expenditures for all forms of relief and wage assistance in this period totaled approximately $5,375,000,000. Of this amount more than 65 per cent was for emergency relief, 30 per cent was for wage assistance, and less than 5 per cent was for categorical relief.

"During the 3-year period there were frequent changes in Federal programs inaugurated for the relief of unemployment and distress, involving important shifts in emphasis from emergency relief to wage assistance and vice versa. There was also a very close interplay between the case loads of the emergency relief and the wage assistance programs. Hence, changes in one form of aid can be interpreted only in the light of changes in the other.

"The following data are indicative of the effect on the public assistance structure of changes in program development. In January 1933 emergency relief constituted 91 per cent of the total expenditures for outdoor public assistance, and wage assistance had not yet been developed as a means of meeting the needs of the unemployed. In January 1934 emergency relief had shrunk to 17 per cent of the total while wage assistance constituted 81 per cent. Emergency relief again accounted for the major share of expenditures in January 1935, with wage assistance only 10 per cent of the total.

"Throughout the 3-year period expenditures for categorical relief were fairly stable and constituted a very small proportion of the total burden. . . .

"Categorical Relief. During 1933, 1934, and 1935 relief to the aged, to the blind, and to dependent children was administered by State and local agencies operating outside the sphere of Federal financial or administrative control. Since there was no country-wide collection of monthly statistical data relating to categorical relief for this period, monthly estimates of total expenditures for these types of aid have been prepared for this study from information available from miscellaneous sources. . . .

"From the estimates it appears that approximately one-quarter of a billion dollars was expended in the United States during the 3-year period for relief to the aged, to the blind, and to dependent children. Of this total amount, the aged received about 48 per cent, the blind 8 per cent, and dependent children 44 per cent." [20]

The virtual withdrawal of the Federal government from assistance to the states in their policies of direct relief in 1936 had been preceded by the gradual substitution of emphasis upon work relief:

"The growth of the work relief movement since 1930 has been one of the significant and perhaps enduring features characterizing the depression period. The 'work principle' as a technique of mitigating the hardships arising from unemployment gained widespread support from local relief authorities in the early years of rapidly advancing unemployment. By the end of 1932 many States had established emergency relief administrations, some of which actively supported the diverse work relief programs of the local political units. Following the establishment of the Federal Emergency Relief Administration in May 1933 the work relief programs of the local governments received the financial assistance of the Federal Government through Federal grants to the States. Since 1933 the Federal Government has coöperated in, or has directly operated, several extensive work relief programs with monthly employment ranging from 1,300,000 to over 4,200,000. The cumulative growth of this work relief movement, from the uncoördinated and sporadic local programs to the vast work relief programs of the Federal Government, has been accompanied by a wide variety of policies governing wages and hours of work. A summary of these policies will be presented in the following pages.

"For purposes of this summary the term 'work relief' will refer to those work projects which are undertaken primarily for the purpose of affording employment to the destitute unemployed while the social and economic value of the completed work relief projects is of secondary importance, i. e., work undertaken primarily in response to a demand for employment and only secondarily to a demand for the project. Need is the primary basis for determining eligibility for employment on such projects, with ability and fitness for the specific work next in importance. Need is usually established by the 'means' test, although in some instances unemployment status alone has been sufficient. Thus the standards of

[20] Geddes, Anne E.—*Trends in Relief Expenditures, 1910–1935,* pp. xi, xiii–xv, and 74; Works Progress Administration, Division of Social Research, Research Monograph X, Government Printing Office, 1937.

project selection and employment on work relief differ from those applied to regular public works and private work. [21]

"Under this definition of work relief the wage and hour policies of the following programs will be included in this summary: the local work relief programs in existence prior to May 1933; [22] the work relief projects initiated by local relief administrations but largely financed by Federal Emergency Relief Administration grants from May through November 1933; the Civil Works program operated by the Federal Government during the winter of 1933–1934; the Emergency Work Relief Program sponsored by the Federal Emergency Relief Administration in coöperation with the States, April 1934–December 1935; and the program of the Works Progress Administration. [23]

"The work relief movement, inaugurated by local public authorities (and by private agencies in some instances), has developed into a national policy of providing work to the destitute unemployed." [24]

[21] "This definition of work relief is tentative since the distinction between 'work relief' and 'public works' is difficult to draw with precision. Under the above definition work relief is designed to provide employment, whereas public works are executed primarily to acquire the finished project. Both purposes, however, are present in emergency public works. Generally speaking, emergency public works projects are those that have been delayed in the past through lack of funds or those that were planned for future development but which are currently undertaken to mitigate present unemployment. In either case, the completed public project, or the social capital, is the primary consideration in the prosecution of the project; the desire to relieve unemployment or to take advantage of available funds, or both, merely time the undertaking. On the other hand, work relief projects do not overlook the value of the completed work; in fact, as the programs develop, increasing emphasis is usually placed on the quality of the projects. Hence, from the standpoint of ends to be achieved, the distinction between regular public works and work relief is primarily a matter of emphasis."

[22] "In view of the definition adopted here, some qualification concerning some of the early local work relief activities deserves mention. In some instances the establishment of work relief programs was motivated not by an enlightened awareness of the nature of the unemployment problem and the needs of the unemployed but by the desire to provide a 'work test' as a condition for the receipt of relief. In these cases the work offered was a deterrent designed to discourage application for relief rather than a method of meeting the relief problem through the provision of work."

[23] "The other agencies coöperating in the Works Program, financed by funds appropriated by the Emergency Relief Appropriation Act of 1935, do not come entirely within the limits as defined. The primary emphasis of the Public Works Administration since its establishment in 1933 has been the completion of projects. Similarly this aim predominates in the programs of the Bureau of Public Roads, the Resettlement Administration, and other coöperating agencies. It must be emphasized that differentiation of programs is not without its theoretic difficulties. These difficulties are most apparent in the classification of the several parts of the present Works Program. The Civilian Conservation Corps affords peculiar difficulties of classification and is not included in this summary."

[24] Burns, Arthur E.—"Work Relief Wage Policies, 1930–1936" in *Monthly Report of the Federal Emergency Relief Administration, June 1 through June 30, 1936* (final issue), pp. 22–23; Government Printing Office, 1937.

Relative Merits of Private and Public Agencies of Relief.— Contrasting private agencies for relief with governmental agencies one notes that: (1) the former may be capable of somewhat greater elasticity or adaptability. For the latter cannot change their methods without prior change in the statute law upon which they are based. Timid and unimaginative executives or boards, however, make few changes in either type of agency; while bold executives may not feel hampered by law. (2) Private agencies may have somewhat more latitude in experimentation with new methods since not directly responsible either to politicians or to the people. (3) Private agencies can generally provide service to the poor of a more personal type. Friendship and sympathetic understanding are needed by many of the poor and facilitate rehabilitation. On the other hand public agencies tend to have (1) larger and more certain resources at their command; (2) can distribute the economic burden of relief more widely through the power of taxation; (3) can enforce their decisions more readily, due to the powers of compulsion lodged with the various units of government—but especially the police powers of the state.

Distribution of Function between Private and Public Agencies.—Six centuries ago all charitable relief was private. Adoption of relief functions by government under Elizabethan laws still left most of the aid for the poor to private charity. Until very recent times the division of field between public and private agencies took either one of two forms: (1) either each agency looked after all cases that happened to apply first to it, or (2) the private agency tended to take the temporary or remediable cases, leaving (or turning over) to public agencies the less hopeful chronic cases—or at least those which failed to arouse its interest or sympathy. Since the early nineteen thirties there has been a most decided trend toward leaving the actual relief of economic distress to public agencies and supplementary aid, whether economic or (as is usually the case) moral and personal, to private agencies. Nevertheless the division is seldom sharp. Relief though a public prerogative is often so inadequate or poorly administered that private agencies must help in so far as they can. Social case work though essentially the technique of private agencies is fortunately finding its way into public relief via the employment in public service of trained social workers who largely frame its rules and standards, and direct their application.[25]

---

[25] Note, for example, the influence of the Children's Bureau and of the Department of Labor upon both relief and social security legislation.

Close and detailed coöperation between these two groups of agencies is now locally maintained in many cities through the local council of social agencies or welfare council in which both are represented and in which questions of jurisdiction, responsibility, and coöperation in both the treatment and prevention of poverty are freely discussed and followed by appropriate action.

QUESTIONS FOR DISCUSSION OR EXAMINATION

1. Discuss the role of tradition in its relation to social change.
2. Outline the history (a) of private charity, (b) of public relief.
3. What are, and what should be, the relative fields of public relief and private charity?
4. What are, and what should be, the respective roles of local, state, and Federal governments in the relief of the poor?
5. By what arguments would you justify "the right to relief"?

PROBLEMS FOR INDIVIDUAL STUDY

1. Search for the roots of current philanthropic attitudes and relief practices in (a) Christian documents, (b) Jewish documents, or (c) early English law.
2. Analysis of references to tradition in (a) the *Congressional Record*, (b) selected court decisions, (c) legislative documents, (d) discussions at the National Conference of Social Work.
3. Trace origins of the "right to live," "right to relief," "right to work."
4. Analysis of Federal, state, or municipal reports on relief.
5. The contributions to social theory and/or social practice of (a) Chalmers, (b) Tuckerman, (c) Ozanam, (d) Elizabeth Fry, or others.

SUGGESTIONS FOR SUPPLEMENTARY READINGS

Abbott, Edith—"Public Assistance," *Social Work Year Book 1937;* Russell Sage Foundation, 1937.

Bogen, Boris D.—*Jewish Philanthropy;* The Macmillan Company, 1917.

Bosanquet, Helen—*Social Work in London, 1869 to 1912;* John Murray (London), 1914.

Bossard, James H. S.—*Social Change and Social Problems*, Part VIII, "Problems of Social Work"; Harper & Brothers, revised edition, 1938.

Breckinridge, Sophonisba P.—*Public Welfare Administration in the United States: Select Documents;* University of Chicago Press, second edition, enlarged and revised, 1938.

Clarke, John J.—*Social Administration, Including The Poor Laws;* Sir Isaac Pitman & Sons, Ltd., 1922.

Colcord, Joanna C.—*Cash Relief;* Russell Sage Foundation, 1936.

Colcord, Joanna C., Kopolvitz, William C., and Kurtz, Russell H.—*Emergency Work Relief;* Russell Sage Foundation, 1932.

De Schweinitz, Karl—*The Art of Helping People Out of Trouble;* Houghton Mifflin Company, 1924.

Emminghaus, A., editor—*Poor Relief in Different Parts of Europe;* Edward Stanford (London), 1873.

Feder-Leah, Hannah—*Unemployment Relief in Periods of Depression;* Russell Sage Foundation, 1936.

Federal Emergency Relief Administration—publications.

Ford, James—*Social Problems and Social Policy,* Chapters XXIII–XXVI, and XXX; Ginn and Company, 1923.

Frankel, Emil—*Poor Relief in Pennsylvania: A State-Wide Survey;* Commonwealth of Pennsylvania, Department of Welfare, Bulletin No. 21, 1925.

Frisch, Ephraim—*An Historical Survey of Jewish Philanthropy;* The Macmillan Company, 1924.

Geddes, Anne E.—"Federal Agencies in Social Work," *Social Work Year Book 1937;* Russell Sage Foundation, 1937.

Gillin, John Lewis—*Poverty and Dependency,* Part Three, "Historical Institutions and Methods of Dealing with Dependents"; The Century Co., 1921.

Gray, B. Kirkman—*A History of English Philanthropy;* P. S. King & Son, Ltd., 1905.

Heffner, William Clinton—*History of Poor Relief Legislation in Pennsylvania, 1682–1913*; Holzapfel Publishing Company (Cleona, Pa.), 1913.

Hogg, Margaret H.—*The Incidence of Work Shortage;* Russell Sage Foundation, 1932.

Hopkins, Harry L.—*Spending to Save: The Complete Story of Relief;* W. W. Norton & Company, Inc., 1936.

Isakoff, Jack F.—*The Public Works Administration;* University of Illinois Press, 1939.

Johnson, Arlien—*Public Policy and Private Charities: A Study of Legislation in the United States and of Administration in Illinois;* University of Chicago Press, 1931.

Jorns, Auguste—*The Quakers as Pioneers in Social Work* (translated by Thomas Kite Brown, Jr.); The Macmillan Company, 1931.

Karpf, Maurice J.—*The Scientific Basis of Social Work;* Columbia University Press, 1931.

Kelso, Robert W.—*The History of Public Poor Relief in Massachusetts, 1620–1920;* Houghton Mifflin Company, 1922.

Kelso, Robert W.—*The Science of Public Welfare;* Henry Holt and Company, 1928.

Kerby, William J.—*The Social Mission of Charity;* The Macmillan Company, 1921.

Klein, Philip—*A Social Study of Pittsburgh,* Part Two; Columbia University Press, 1938.

Kurtz, Russell H.—*The Public Assistance Worker;* Russell Sage Foundation, 1938.

Lee, Porter R.—*Social Work as Cause and Function;* Columbia University Press, 1937.

Libbey, Betsey—"Family Social Work," *Social Work Year Book 1937;* Russell Sage Foundation, 1937.

Loch, C. S.—*Charity and Social Life;* Macmillan and Co., Limited, 1910.

McLean, Francis H.—*The Family Society;* American Association for Organizing Family Social Work, 1927.

Marshall, Dorothy—*The English Poor in the Eighteenth Century;* George Routledge & Sons, Ltd. (London), 1926.

Millett, John D.—*The Works Progress Administration in New York City;* published for the Committee on Public Administration of the Social Science Research Council by Public Administration Service (Chicago), 1938.

Millspaugh, Arthur C.—*Public Welfare Organization;* The Brookings Institution, 1935.

National Conference of Social Work—*Proceedings.*

Odum, Howard W.—*An Approach to Public Welfare and Social Work;* University of North Carolina Press, 1926.

Odum, Howard W., and Willard, D. W.—*Systems of Public Welfare;* University of North Carolina Press, 1925.

P E P (Political and Economic Planning)—*Report on the British Social Services: A Survey of the Existing Public Social Services in Great Britain with Proposals for Future Development;* P E P (London), 1937.

Queen, Stuart Alfred—*Social Work in the Light of History;* J. B. Lippincott Company, 1922.

Richmond, Mary E.—*Social Diagnosis;* Russell Sage Foundation, 1917.

Richmond, Mary E.—*What Is Social Case Work?;* Russell Sage Foundation, 1922.

Schneider, David M.—*The History of Public Welfare in New York State, 1609–1866;* University of Chicago Press, 1938.

Sheffield, Ada Eliot—*Social Insight in Case Situations;* D. Appleton-Century Company, 1937.

Stafford, Paul Tutt—*State Welfare Administration in New Jersey;* New Jersey Department of Institutions and Agencies (Trenton), 1934.

Stevenson, Marietta—*Public Welfare Administration;* The Macmillan Company, 1938.

Uhlhorn, Gerhard—*Christian Charity in the Ancient Church;* Charles Scribner's Sons, 1883.

United States Bureau of the Census—*Paupers in Almshouses: 1923;* Government Printing Office, 1925.

Veeder, Fredric R.—*The Development of the Montana Poor Law;* University of Chicago Press, 1938.

Warner, Amos Griswold, Queen, Stuart Alfred, and Harper, Ernest Bouldin—*American Charities and Social Work;* Thomas Y. Crowell Company, fourth edition, 1930.

Watson, Frank Dekker—*The Charity Organization Movement in the United States;* The Macmillan Company, 1922.

Webb, Sidney and Beatrice—*English Poor Law Policy;* Longmans, Green and Co., 1910.

Wisner, Elizabeth—*Public Welfare Administration in Louisiana;* University of Chicago Press, 1930.

Works Progress Administration—publications.

CHAPTER XXII

ECONOMIC HAZARDS AND SOCIAL SECURITY

Life's Hazards.—There are five major hazards of life which every family must face: sickness, accident, unemployment, old age, and the death of the breadwinner. Each is an economic hazard because it involves the possibility of a reduction or cessation of the family income. The wealthy may be able to save against these contingencies. Families with only moderate income cannot save enough to make their permanent security certain. Wage-earning families must live in chronic fear of exhaustion of their meager resources from sickness, accident, or unemployment, and of spending their declining years in the almshouse. Few wage-earners even among the skilled can save enough out of their small incomes to guarantee protection of their families from recourse to charity in the case of incurable illness or early death.

Social Pathology of Incapacitation.—Whether the worker is incapacitated by illness, accident, old age, or unemployment, or suffers death, many pathologic conditions arise in his relationships, economic and social. First, his economic output ceases, reducing the volume of distributable wealth. Second, industry loses a trained or experienced worker who must be replaced by another at perhaps considerable cost until the training is completed. Third, the women and older children of the worker's household will either have to go to work or become dependent upon relief. Their work may injure health or wholesome family relationships, and their availability at low wages may lead to the dismissal of male labor. Fourth, the family's plane of living is almost inevitably reduced, which not infrequently means poorer educational opportunities for the children, fewer or inferior social contacts, and a lower quality of citizenship.

Social Security Legislation as Preventive of Dependence.— As a means to the elimination of poverty, social security legislation has a unique function. In no direct way does it put a stop to the operation of the fundamental causes of poverty.[1] It is, however,

---

[1] Indirectly, however, it leads to efforts to prevent disease, accident, and unemployment in order to reduce the economic burden of social insurance.

designed to reduce economic insufficiency for the individual by maintaining him or his family during life's crises at a subsistence level.[2] It adds nothing directly to the volume of national wealth. Instead it serves in a moderate way to redistribute existing wealth. It thus may help to reduce or prevent individual dependency— though to do so over a long period it must avoid hampering economic enterprise by its financial policies and administration.

Potentials of Social Security.—Virtually all dependency, whether in periods of prosperity or depression, involves one or more of these hazards. They take their toll in the cases of poverty ascribed to heredity, handicap, incapacity, low income, disaster, or war. Yet plans for social security, which spread the burden of meeting these risks, are properly undertaken primarily for the ablebodied workman and his family, to prevent avoidable dependency. If the security afforded to labor by social insurance is ample, universal in its coverage, ably administered, and soundly financed, most employable wage-earners may be safeguarded from suffering dependency under normal economic conditions, at any time in life—without special recourse to the supplementary devices for prevention described in other chapters. By means of social insurance most families now above the poverty line can be kept for life from falling below it.

For at its best, social security legislation may perform the miracle of conferring relative solvency upon millions who daily tread the brink of insolvency. It may provide a subsistence income, as long as needed, to the victims of life's tragedies, under conditions that confer no stigma and that are consistent with self-respect. It may displace pauperism and its connotations with benefit payments or annuities to which the recipient or his family have contributed both directly and indirectly and which they can justly feel that they have earned by their work, their contributions, and their citizenship.

Beginnings of Social Security Legislation.—When, in 1935, the Social Security Act was passed by the Federal Congress to meet this problem the United States had already had experience with a wide variety of types of social insurance. Lagging a full generation behind Europe, American states first provided, through workmen's compensation acts, for benefits in case of industrial accident. The first such legislation passed in Maryland in 1902 was followed by

---

[2] The comfort level has seldom, if ever, been reached by the states through any of their systems of social insurance. A major purpose of Federal grants-in-aid is to make the subsistence level possible.

other states until in 1937 most industrial workers in forty-six states and in Federal branches as well were protected in case of injury received while engaged at their occupation.

Extent of Industrial Accidents.—Statistics of industrial accident are still far from complete. From European evidence, which is less fragmentary than our own, it has been estimated that there is one industrial accident for every eleven workers and one fatal accident each year for each eighteen hundred men employed.[3] An American actuary, in 1924, estimated that industrial accidents each year in the United States caused twenty-five thousand deaths, an equal number of permanent disabilities, and about two million temporary injuries of more than three days' duration.[4] Rates are relatively high in mining, especially coal mining, and in structural steel erection, for example, and very much lower in most branches of manufacturing.

Needs of the Victims of Accident.—Fatalities make provision for dependents necessary. Permanent disabilities necessitate provision for life for the disabled worker and his family. Minor and temporary injuries require medical service and an adequate income until the worker is reëmployed. Injuries resulting in loss of members involve the same needs but often also vocational rehabilitation.[5]

Limitations of Workmen's Compensation Acts.—In highly varying degrees the American states have provided by special acts for these contingencies. The acts differ greatly in their coverage, the amounts of compensation offered, and the duration of the benefits. With few exceptions they are limited to injuries arising in the course of employment and deny compensation where there has been misconduct or negligence on the part of the employee. Agricultural workers, domestic employees, and workers in small shops in which only one or two are employed are normally excluded from the benefits of these acts. The compensation for major injuries is still usually too small or of too brief duration to prevent ultimate dependency. Although in recent years the states have increasingly included in their provisions compensation for occupational diseases, a large percentage of states still lack this service.

To protect workers from all industrial hazards and to prevent dependency from this source, it is obvious that American workmen's

[3] Armstrong, Barbara N.—*Insuring the Essentials*, pp. 173–174; The Macmillan Company, 1932.

[4] Downey, Ezekiel Henry—*Workmen's Compensation;* The Macmillan Company, 1924.

[5] See Chapters XI and XVI.

compensation laws would have to be extended to cover all wage-earners irrespective of occupation or size of plant. Adequate medical aid is needed in each case. Compensation and benefits should maintain the worker and his family at an adequate plane of living for the duration of the disability, retraining the worker if necessary for another occupation. Each such act should provide for an insurance fund under state safeguards, within which all employers are insured, and with administration of benefits through a competent state commission or board adequately financed. Following its researches and findings, the state commission should be enabled to devise and enforce among all firms strict requirements for the prevention of both occupational disease and accidents.[6]

Accidents Not Yet Covered.—The problem of poverty resulting from accident would not, however, be wholly eliminated even if workmen's compensation acts were brought up to these standards. For most accidents in this country still occur in the home or the street, and will be compensated for, if at all, only after expensive law suits which the poor cannot afford. This problem might be overcome by including provision for medical service and benefits for such accidental injuries within a system of public health insurance. Costs may thus be shared by employer, employee, and the government. This essential branch of security legislation, which is still held in abeyance in America, will be discussed later.

Early Legislation for Widows' Pensions.—America's second venture in social security legislation was in the field of widows' pensions. Previously, death of the male breadwinner had meant dependency of his widow and children or else a job for the woman and consequent neglect of children, or even separation of the children from their living parent. The first legislation of this type was an act passed in Missouri in 1911, followed later in the same year by Illinois.[7] Like workmen's compensation acts, widows' pensions and

---

[6] An admirable detailed study of conditions and recommendations will be found in Armstrong, Barbara N.—*op. cit.*, as well as in current publications of the American Association for Labor Legislation, and the United States Department of Labor. See, for example, *Workmen's Compensation in the United States as of July 1, 1938;* reprint (Serial No. R. 815) from *Monthly Labor Review*, September, 1938, and Dawson, Marshall—*Adequacy of Benefit Payments under Workmen's Compensation;* reprint (Serial No. R. 813) from *Monthly Labor Review*, September, 1938.

[7] "As early as 1906 the juvenile courts of some counties of California granted aid to children in their own homes, and in 1911 the State began to reimburse counties for such aid given to half orphans. An Oklahoma law of 1908 provided for 'school scholarships' to be paid by counties upon recommendation of the

mothers' aid laws were noncontributory, but unlike workmen's compensation their benefits were met solely from public funds. In some states they were administered by courts, in others by special commissions, and in still others by state boards of public welfare.

At their best they became state aid for women who had been deprived of male support and who had children dependent upon them. The pension was made available not as compensation for the loss of the husband but virtually as a salary to the mother to make it possible for her to keep her family together and rear her own children without the necessity of securing outside work.

Such legislation in Massachusetts, for example, was lodged with the State Board of Charities, subsequently reorganized as the State Board of Public Welfare. Under the direction of the highly competent State Commissioner of Public Welfare standards were developed for the handling of all such cases which involved thoroughgoing social diagnosis to ascertain needs, and continuing social work of an appropriate advisory nature. For convenience the detail of the administration was decentralized among the local boards of public welfare, who as a condition of receiving state aid which amounted to one-third of the local bill for such pensions,[8] were required to make the requisite investigations and carry out the rules set by the State Board. By this means local boards of public welfare were for the first time familiarized with the principles of scientific diagnosis and case work which, bit by bit, they increasingly applied to cases that were not on pension but on relief. Mothers' aid thus became a device for the much needed training of local boards, while at the same time it made possible a change in status of mothers with dependent children from that of pauper to that of pensioner.

Limitations of State Legislation for Mothers' Aid.—The major criticisms of this branch of social security, which by 1935 was incor-

school authorities to children whose widowed mothers needed their earnings. A Michigan law of 1911 also authorized payment from school funds to enable children of indigent parents to attend school. The first definite legal provision of aid to mothers of dependent children was passed by the Missouri Legislature in 1911, applying only to Jackson County (in which Kansas City is located), and later in the same year extended to the city of St. Louis. The first state-wide mothers' aid law was enacted in Illinois in 1911." Bogue, Mary F.—*Administration of Mothers' Aid in Ten Localities*, p. 4; United States Department of Labor, Children's Bureau, Publication No. 184, Government Printing Office, 1928. See also Davis, Ada J.—"The Evolution of Mothers' Pensions in the United States"; *American Journal of Sociology*, Vol. XXXV, No. 4, January, 1930.

[8] The state met the full costs in case the mother had no "legal settlement."

porated in the legislation of all but two states, are its frequent failure
to reach all eligible families, and the relative inadequacy of its payments. The average monthly grants per family in 1931 ranged in
size from $69.31 in Massachusetts to $4.33 in Arkansas.[9] The purpose of such acts is defeated except where benefits are sufficient in
size to permit healthful, wholesome living. Children moreover have
usually been forced to go to work when they would have been able
to profit by further education. Another weakness of virtually all of
the state laws is that they have forced the mother to exhaust her
savings before she can acquire eligibility to the pension, whereas it
is often definitely to the state's advantage that she should continue
to own her own home, if she has one, and maintain her insurance
policy or savings account, if she happens to possess one, against
future contingencies.

Federal Inclusion of Mothers' Aid.—The inclusion of mothers'
aid in the Federal Social Security Act of 1935 tends to obviate many
of these limitations by providing more substantial pensions, more
uniform standards, and extension of coverage to include responsible
relatives other than the mother. The emphasis has thus shifted in
the Federal Act from the mother to the child. There are at least a
million dependent children in this country, according to estimates of
the Social Security Board. A "dependent child" is defined by the
Act as "a child under the age of 16 years who has been deprived of
parental support or care by reason of the death, continued absence
from the home, or physical or mental incapacity of a parent, and
who is living in the home of his father, mother . . . " or other
specified relatives. No child may be excluded from the benefits of
the Act on the grounds of residence if he "has lived in the State for
1 year immediately preceding application, or was born in the State
within such year, provided the mother has lived in the State for
1 year immediately preceding the child's birth."

> "What the Social Security Act does is to offer to the States Federal
> help in fulfilling an obligation to which they have long been committed,
> but which many of them have found hard to support.
> "The system of grants-in-aid by which Federal funds are made avail-
> able to the States is equally well established. The Federal Government
> has for many years made grants of this sort to assist the States in public

[9] Abbott, Grace—"Mothers' Aid," *Social Work Year Book 1937;* Russell Sage
Foundation, 1937. Average benefits per family with dependent children under
the Federal Social Security Act amounted to $32.06 for the month of January,
1938.

projects ranging from road building and fighting forest fires to financing certain educational measures.

"Both in its purpose—the support of dependent children in their own homes—and in its method—Federal grants-in-aid—the Social Security Act thus follows well-tried American precedents. It is new only in the sense that grants-in-aid are now made available for social welfare.

"In setting up any plan for public assistance under the Social Security Act, the State must take the initiative. As with grants-in-aid for other purposes, so here also the Federal Government stands ready to help— when the State so elects. Each State decides for itself whether it wishes to take part in the program; if it does, it makes its own plan within the broad requirements of the act. Needs and resources vary from State to State; the Social Security Act gives every State opportunity to set up a plan in line with local conditions.

"After its plan is approved by the Social Security Board, the State continues to carry the major responsibility for its efficient operation. It determines how and by whom its plan shall be administered, how State and local funds are to be raised, to whom and how much assistance shall be given.

"To States with approved plans the Federal Government makes grants for aid to dependent children equal to one-third of the State's total expenditures both for assistance and administration, estimating its contribution on maximum monthly payments of $18 for the first child and $12 for each additional child in the same home. These figures simply place an upper limit on the amounts taken as the basis for computing Federal grants. The State is entirely free to set its own rate of individual payments, either higher or lower; they may be made to depend upon the needs and resources of the family and the funds which State and local governments will be able to provide with Federal aid." [10]

Provision for Maternal and Child Health.—Beginning with the Sheppard-Towner Act, passed by the Federal Congress in 1921, another tributary to American experience in the field of social security developed. Unlike its predecessors, it provided for neither compensation nor pensions, but by means of Federal grants-in-aid facilitated state programs for maternal and child health. It operated for seven years and involved Federal grants to states to the extent of $1,240,000.[11] The Act was found constitutional by the United States Supreme Court in the case of *Massachusetts vs. Mellon*.[12]

[10] *Aid to Dependent Children under the Social Security Act*, pp. 3–4; The Social Security Board, Informational Service Circular No. 6, March, 1937.

[11] Douglas, Paul H.—*Social Security in the United States: An Analysis and Appraisal of the Federal Social Security Act*, pp. 196–200; McGraw-Hill Book Company, Inc., 1936.

[12] 262 U. S. 447.

Altogether forty-five states took advantage of the Federal grants in this earlier period, which made possible extensive advisory and medical service to women during pregnancy, and educational, medical, and dental services for young children. The decline during these seven years of infant mortality is doubtless in part traceable to this Act though rates for maternal mortality failed to show an appreciable decline. When the Federal grants were discontinued in 1929 the states generally continued their share of the service but their appropriations had declined about fifty per cent by the fifth year of the depression period.

The Social Security Act of 1935 revived this important service at many times its original scale. For the annual appropriation is $3,800,000. Each of the forty-eight states is to receive $20,000 each year if it will match that sum. A further sum of $1,800,000 is assigned for distribution among states in accordance with their relative number of live births. The state is required to match the Federal funds. An additional $980,000 is available without matching for allotment by the Secretary of Labor in accordance with special needs. States must provide for administration or supervision efficiently through state health agencies and render reports to the Federal government. In effect this section of the Federal Social Security Act increases the volume of local maternal and child health services severalfold, and makes possible health units and demonstration services in rural and other needy areas.

Old Age as Hazard.—Old age is a contingency for which the worker, at present wage rates, can seldom fully prepare. The increasing speed and strains of industrial life have at some points so reduced the work span that workers find themselves unable to continue at their accustomed occupations when still in their forties or fifties. Many are unable thereafter to find remunerative employment fitted to their capacities. Unless support is available from one or more of his children without unduly reducing their own plane of living, the almshouse or public relief has until recently been the only recourse for the aging worker.

History of Old-Age Security.—Provision for security against old age developed late in this country and by 1929 only eight American states had old-age pension systems to supplement the ubiquitous almshouse. Nevertheless through the early years of the depression the movement for old-age pensions gathered momentum so that by 1934 there were twenty-eight states with legislation of this type and some 231,000 persons in receipt of pensions.[13] Most of the acts were far from adequate in all particulars. In several states men and women could not receive pensions until seventy years of age though their work opportunities and incomes might have been exhausted many years earlier. Five of the acts were of the optional type so that pensions were not provided in counties where the authorities were unwilling to adopt them. The average monthly pension in December, 1934, was only $16.16, which would be insufficient for the needs of most elderly persons. Not more than forty per cent of the population of this country dwelt in counties in which such pensions were available. Some additional persons did, however, enjoy pensions for soldiers or retirement allowances accorded to public servants.

Federal Grants for Old-Age Pensions.—In 1930, 5.4 per cent of our population was over sixty-five years of age, or one person in every twenty. The Federal Social Security Act of 1935 drawing its line (after January 1, 1940) at sixty-five years of age provided for old-age security through two devices: first, by Federal aid to states for old-age pensions; and second, by a Federal system for old-age annuities on a contributory basis. Pensions are based upon the needs of the aged while annuities are based upon their earnings. Since the former is designed to continue and improve existing state pension legislation and to extend the system to other states, it will be considered first.

Federal grants to states for old-age pensions are made available for persons over sixty-five years of age—but not below—at a rate not to exceed $15 per month per person, to supplement an equal contribution by the state, or by the state and local government. The state may grant more than $15 but the Federal contribution may not exceed this sum. Federal aid is available only to states in which the pension law is mandatory and administered or supervised by a state agency. One may qualify for a pension by continuous residence within the state during the last year prior to the receipt of the pension and by residence in the state during five of the preceding nine years. Although aged persons in almshouses or other public institutions may not receive Federal aid for pensions such aid is possible for persons in private institutions. Negroes and others are not to be deprived of pensions by any specific requirement the state may have concerning citizenship. The state must file with the Federal Social Security Board reports on its administration of the Act.

[13] Douglas, Paul H.—*op. cit.*, pp. 7–10.

By means of this section of the Federal Social Security Act state pensions to the needy aged will be practically doubled. Provision for old-age pensions had extended by December, 1938, to every American state. It seeks to cover all persons over sixty-five years of age who lack both means and employment and who are not in need of care in public institutions, until the Federal annuity system, which will make its first payments in 1942, succeeds in displacing pensions by earned annuities for those who are eligible and whose resources are sufficient. As the percentage of our population over sixty-five years of age becomes greater from decade to decade, the Federal burden for pensions will probably never fall below $100,000,000 per year. Moreover, future legislation may reduce the age for eligibility or increase the Federal grant.[14]

Federal Old-Age Insurance.—The policy of grants-in-aid to states for their old-age pension systems is supplemented in the Social Security Act of 1935 by a system of Federal old-age insurance operated directly by the Federal government. This is a contributory system supported by contributions of employers and employees, the former through a payroll tax and the latter by deductions from their wages. The taxes are levied on all business, irrespective of the number of employees, but not on the proportion of income which is in excess of $3,000 a year from any one employer. Exceptions are made, however, of domestic service in private homes, of agricultural labor, of certain types of casual labor, and of philanthropic, educational, or governmental service. Equal contributions are drawn from employers and employees. At the outset employees pay 1 per cent of their wages which is increased gradually until in 1949 it will reach 3 per cent. This contribution is matched by the employer through the payment of a tax. These sums become an old-age reserve account in the Federal Treasury. To this account Congress is authorized under specified conditions to appropriate annual sums from the general revenue.

Beginning in 1942 employees who have contributed to this account and who have reached the age of sixty-five years may receive monthly annuities for life in case they have been employed during each of the preceding five years and have received in all $2,000 or more in wages or salary. Persons in occupations which come under the Federal Act who were over sixty years of age, when the Act went

---

[14] It is estimated that by 1980 old-age insurance will reduce old-age pensions sixty per cent. *Ibid.*, pp. 155–156.

into effect, and who are ineligible for annuities, will receive in a lump sum three and one-half per cent of the gross earnings of the intervening period. The same percentage is paid to the estate of those who die.

The monthly annuities to be received for life by insured employees range from a minimum of $10 per month to a maximum of $85, calculated in the following manner: on the first $3,000 of insured earnings, $5 for each thousand; for the next $42,000, $5 for each six thousand; and thereafter $5 for each twelve thousand of insured earnings, over the total period of employment under this Act. Thus, in the lower salary ranges illustrative benefits are as follows:

	YEARS OF EMPLOYMENT AFTER 1936			
AVERAGE MONTHLY SALARY	10	20	30	40
$50	$17.50	$22.50	$27.50	$32.50
100	22.50	32.50	42.50	51.25
150	27.50	42.50	53.75	61.25
200	32.50	51.25	61.25	71.25
250	37.50	56.25	68.75	81.25

The major advantage of this Act, both individual and social, is that once it is in full operation it will substitute earned retirement allowances for unearned pensions for all individuals that come under its provisions. It is now possible for the worker to save for his old age without appreciable difficulty to him or his family and with the government's guarantee against the loss of his savings. As old-age insurance, unlike old-age pensions, provides no "means" test, the worker is not discouraged from making additional savings and investments wherever he is able to do so. For his annuity is due him because of his weekly contributions and by virtue of his years of work in insured occupations.

Limitations of Federal Security to the Aged.—On the other hand, the annuities received in the earlier years of the operation of this Act will for many persons be inadequate to meet the cost of their living, especially if there are dependents, and supplementary funds from pensions or other sources will be necessary. There cannot be universal security against dependency in old age until all classes of the population are included within this or supplementary acts. Under certain economic conditions, also, the employer is likely to recoup his tax either by reduction of wages or by increasing prices to the consumer. Wherever this occurs practically the full cost of the insurance will be met by the employee in his capacity

either of consumer or worker.[15] There remains also the possibility
that inflation of the dollar may in some subsequent period render
the earned benefits or annuities grossly inadequate for the worker's
needs thus defeating the honest intention of the Act. Such eventualities may have to be met by special large supplementary appropriations from public treasuries.

In spite of these criticisms and limitations, together with the
exceedingly difficult financial and administrative problems which
relate to the accumulation and investment of the colossal old-age
reserve account,[16] the degree of security afforded by this Act is
decidedly greater than that obtainable by the worker prior to
its passage. The principle of collective insurance under public
direction and guarantee has become established in America—be-
latedly as compared with most of the civilized nations, but yet with
reasonable initial effectiveness. All major nations have found it
necessary from time to time to make changes in their social insurance
legislation as a result of experience in its operation as well as changes
in economic conditions. It is reasonably certain that the Federal
Social Security Act, like these others, will undergo changes. For
universal protection against old-age poverty such amendments
should be directed toward extending the benefits of the Act to
classes not now covered, toward making annuities adequate in
amount wherever and whenever conditions may make that necessary
for the prevention of old-age dependency, and toward providing
financial, actuarial, and administrative soundness in each detail
of the operation of the Act.[17]

Studies of Insurance against Sickness.—Although illness is the
hazard which strikes each family most frequently,[18] it is not yet
covered by social insurance legislation in America either by the

[15] *Ibid.*, pp. 55–65.

[16] The official estimate places the probable size of the old-age reserve account
in 1980 at $46,942,700,000. *Report of Senate Committee on Finance*, 74th Congress,
1st Session, Senate Calendar No. 661, Report No. 628, p. 9.

[17] See especially Schneider, Margaret Grant—*More Security for Old Age: A
Report and a Program* (Factual Report by Margaret Grant Schneider—A Program
for Action by the Committee on Old-Age Security); Twentieth Century Fund,
Inc., 1937. Also Dechamp, Cyrille—"The Investment of Compulsory Social
Insurance Funds"; *International Labour Review*, Vol. XXXVII, No. 3, March,
1938: and Clague, Ewan—"Statistical Problems in the Administration of Social
Security"; *Journal of the American Statistical Association*, Vol. 32, No. 199, Septem-
ber, 1937.

[18] Cf. Bruno, Frank J.—*Illness and Dependency;* Committee on the Costs of Medical Care, Miscellaneous Contributions No. 9, March 1, 1931.

Federal government or the states. Several states have in recent years appointed commissions to study the subject. It was studied also by the President's Committee on Economic Security which drew the recommendations on which the Federal Social Security Act is based. The health provisions were withdrawn from submission to Congress because the program had not yet been sufficiently matured and because also of disagreement among the medical profession, some of whose members regarded the provisions as savoring unduly of "state medicine."

Many European nations have had long and reasonably successful experience with public health insurance. The need for it is apparent in this country because of the impossibility for the wage-earner under existing wage rates to meet the cost of protracted illness either of himself or members of his family or to pay for the services of specialists.

Extent of Illness.—Reports of the Committee on the Costs of Medical Care, which conducted extensive researches in this field over a period of years, reveal that the average family suffers 3.8 illnesses per year of an average duration of 7.1 days per person.[19]

"It is frequently said that people have, on the average, one illness a year (exclusive of dental and eye care and preventive services). This average conceals the fact that for a general population (all incomes combined) 47 out of 100 persons have no illness during a year, 32 have one illness, somewhat more than 18 have two or three illnesses, and 2 have four illnesses or more. Families composed of one and two persons quite uniformly record two illnesses each, and families with three persons show approximately three illnesses each, regardless of income. But among larger families there is a striking difference in the number of illnesses reported; the wealthy report proportionately more illness as the size of the family increases, while the poor report only slightly more illness for a large family than for a small one. In the larger families of the poor, more illness remains unrecognized or unattended. These findings suggest that at least part, if not all, of the variation in incidence for the several economic classes is spurious and is determined by economic criteria in the definition of illness. They indicate the degree of neglect of illness among lower income groups rather than true variation in incidence." [20]

"During a prosperous period (1928–1930) estimates made in the

---

[19] Falk, I. S., Klem, Margaret C., and Sinai, Nathan—*The Incidence of Illness and the Receipt and Costs of Medical Care among Representative Families, Experiences in Twelve Consecutive Months during 1928–1931*, pp. 47 and 79; Committee on the Costs of Medical Care, Publication No. 26, University of Chicago Press, 1933.

[20] *Ibid.*, p. 4 of Abstract of Publication No. 26.

Summary Volume of the Committee on the Costs of Medical Care are that the maximum annual wage-loss was less than a billion dollars, whereas the amount actually expended for medical care by families with incomes of less than $2,500 a year was about one and one-half billion.

"Among the lower paid wage-earners, conditions are different. These families (with incomes of less than $1,200 a year) spend a larger proportion of their income for medical care than the better paid people, but the actual amounts expended per family are smaller, partly because they secure some care at reduced fees and partly because they receive a considerable amount of care, particularly in hospitals, without any payment. The studies of the Committee on the Costs of Medical Care indicated that in 1928–1931 the average charges for care of sickness by families with $1,200 income was $49.17. The 6,000,000 families with incomes of less than $1,200 per year, therefore, spent nearly $300,000,000 for medical care. The 10,000,000 wage-earners in these families may be estimated to have suffered an average wage-loss of about $25 per year because of sickness, or about $250,000,000 for the group. The wage-loss due to sickness in this group thus appeared to be about five-sixths of their expenditures for medical care.

"For families with incomes of between $1,200 and $2,500, the expenditure for medical care was about $1,200,000,000. There are about 14,000,000 families in this group and about 20,000,000 wage-earners. The wage-loss in this group, averaging $32 per wage-earner per year would have been about $610,000,000, or a little over half the expenditures for medical care." [21]

Need of Public Health Insurance.—Although minor illnesses of brief duration may be taken care of satisfactorily by the employed wage-earner out of his annual budget, a protracted illness usually means dependency, especially if it involves loss of wages in addition to the cost of medical care. Hence to prevent dependency from this source it is necessary that workers when well and working should be able to contribute a reasonably small percentage of their wage to a central insurance fund under government supervision to which the government and employers likewise contribute. Such a fund should make possible both the continuation of at least fifty per cent of wages during the period of the employee's illness and the requisite medical service for himself or members of his family in case of the latter's illness, together with funeral benefits. Such insurance should be open on a voluntary basis to persons who are self-employed as well as to others of low income who are not covered by the compulsory features of the act. Chronic illness may be made an

[21] Davis, Michael M.—*The American Approach to Health Insurance*, pp. 7–8; reprinted from *The Milbank Memorial Fund Quarterly*, Vol. XII, No. 3, July, 1934.

adjunct either to health insurance, or may be included as the "invalidity" section of the old-age insurance law.

Problem of State Medicine.—Essential to public health insurance legislation is the provision of such medical service as is necessary both to cure the illness and prevent, so far as possible, future illness in the individual beneficiary and among the citizenry at large. Unless such service can be rendered preventive as well as curative the collective financial burden entailed will be needlessly great.

Reduction of this burden also makes speediest possible cure essential, particularly in view of the fact that malingering is not uncommon; for many persons, to get a vacation from unpleasant work, will feign illness, refuse to coöperate in cure, or protract the convalescence as long as possible where wages continue and medical cost is free. To obviate such difficulties it is essential that the nature of the disability be ascertained by physicians in the employ of the state—competent and thorough in diagnosis. The patient may then select his practitioner from private practice, who in turn may command also the services of specialists where clearly necessary and approved. Speedy cure and able supervision can be made to forestall much malingering. Until such standards can be guaranteed, public health insurance would involve too serious a financial burden and would be inadvisable.

Provision for this type of insurance has been opposed by certain branches and members of the medical profession who feel that there may be a loss either of dignity or of income to that profession if a large percentage of its membership become employees of the government. Actually, however, public health insurance need make relatively few members of the medical profession full-time employees of the government, permitting private practitioners to be listed on the government's panel for medical service, to be paid out of the insurance funds for each specific service rendered.

Today much less is spent on medical service by industrial workers than by persons with higher incomes.[22] It is safe, however, to assume that the families with lower incomes failed to have adequate medical attention because they could not afford it. Proper medical service supported by health insurance would mean a much larger employment of physicians than is now possible under private payments—as well as a much better chance that the physician will be paid.

---

[22] Sinai, Nathan, and Klem, Margaret C.—*The Costs of Medical Care: Preliminary Report;* Committee on the Costs of Medical Care, 1930.

Resistance of the medical profession to the socialization of medicine is natural and commands respect wherever it is leveled at the
debasement of standards. Professional integrity and advance require
untrammeled research, the fostering of professional skill, and that
kind of understanding personal relationship with the families of
patients which facilitates the knowledge of personal traits, tendencies, and reactions, and elicits the full coöperation of the patient
in his cure. These values are endangered when medical service is
socialized; but with the coöperation of the medical profession they
could presumably be maintained, safeguarded, and developed under
wisely framed provisions in public health insurance legislation.

Model Act for Health Insurance.—All of the essentials of efficient, workable health insurance legislation, suggested above, appear
to be incorporated in the model act drawn up in 1935 by the American Association for Social Security. It provides for compulsory
state-wide systems covering all employees with incomes of $3,000 or
less per year, except (for reasons of expediency) agricultural labor
and shops with less than four employees (who may however enter
on a voluntary basis). The plan is contributory, raising a fund
equal to 6 per cent of payrolls each year; one and one-half per
cent of payrolls to be appropriated by the state and four and one-
half per cent divided between employers and their employees.
Benefits after a five-day waiting period would run for six months
at from 50 to 75 per cent of the beneficiary's usual wage according
to the number of dependents. Medical service would cover all
members of the family and include physician, dentist, clinic, hospital, laboratory, and specialist if needed. Fiscal problems would be
handled through the governmental administrative office, but medical matters are left to medical direction. The former certifies disability; but the beneficiary's family physician may treat him and be
reimbursed from the insurance fund. Federal grants are called for by
this plan so that Federal standards may ensure quality of service.

Health Provisions of Social Security Act.—Pending the solution
of these difficulties and controversies and the establishment of a
system of collective health insurance which will cover all members
of the lower income groups, the Federal Social Security Act has
provided at certain strategic points for the protection of health and
prevention of disease. Not only has it stabilized or increased the
incomes of the aged, the unemployed, and of mothers with dependent
children, thus facilitating the employment of physicians where

needed, but it has also supplemented maternity benefits by an annual appropriation of $2,850,000 for crippled children, $1,500,000 for homeless and neglected children, and $10,000,000 for public health. It has thus stimulated state activity for improved health and for disease prevention among both children and adults.

The principle of Federal grants-in-aid is utilized to assist state promotion of Federally-approved plans. The aid for crippled children, of whom sufferers from infantile paralysis comprise a large group, is to be used for locating cases and for providing medical, corrective, and surgical treatment, diagnosis, hospitalization, and aftercare. The grants for child welfare services are primarily for rural areas, though available in part to supplement the present provisions for homeless, neglected, or delinquent children in urban areas. State pensions for the blind are supplemented by matched grants of Federal money up to a total of $30 per month for combined Federal-state aid.

The appropriation for public health allows $2,000,000 to the United States Public Health Service for research, which is concerned primarily with the prevention and control of diseases, and $8,000,000 to be distributed to the states on the basis of population, financial needs, and special health problems. In this instance, also, since there is urgent need in rural areas, the funds are being used largely for the employment of county health officers, for maintaining adequate public health services, the training of personnel, and the promotion of local health work.

A degree of security against another costly aspect of disease has been provided by continuing under the Social Security Act the Federal grants for vocational rehabilitation, which the states since 1920 have had access to, wherever the Federal funds have been matched dollar for dollar. These funds are appropriated for "vocational rehabilitation of persons who, by reason of a physical defect or infirmity, whether congenital or acquired by accident, injury, or disease, are incapacitated for remunerative occupation; rendering such persons fit for remunerative occupation." [23] No provision, however, is yet made by the Act to meet the cost of living of its beneficiaries during the period of retraining.

Valuable though these provisions are, the major problem— the prevention of dependency through sickness among the low-

[23] *Summary of Provisions of the Social Security Act Relating to Federal Grants to States for Public-Welfare Purposes;* Government Printing Office [no date].

income groups of the population—is still only partially reached. This is the most serious deficiency in the social insurance legislation of this country.

Need for Insurance against Unemployment.—The hazard of unemployment is too uncertain in its incidence and too costly in its duration for the individual worker to face unaided. Even in normal years the average unemployment among industrial workers is as high as eight per cent.[24] Although some unemployment is the fault of the employee, most of it grows out of conditions wholly beyond his personal control. To prevent the type of dependency involved in unemployment the cost of maintaining the jobless man and his family must be widely distributed. The workshop is too small a unit to carry this cost because economic conditions may force it to close its doors. The industry is an inappropriate unit because some industries are dependent upon season or fashion and others feel compelled to release the majority of their employees during depression periods. The state is too small a unit to carry the burden of unemployment insurance by itself since recent experience has demonstrated that the percentage of unemployment may be four times as great in one state as in another during a given year.[25] Thus neither the worker, the workshop, the industry, nor the state can be relied upon to take full responsibility for unemployment insurance.

Unemployment Provisions of the Social Security Act.—Social insurance against unemployment to be adequate must distribute the burden among the forty-eight states. This was done by the Federal Social Security Act of 1935 which, except for the brief experience of the State of Wisconsin, was America's first venture into this branch of social security. The Wisconsin Act of 1932 is unusual in type in that it establishes company funds. Though this method, originally known as the "American Plan," may continue at the option of any state under the Federal Act of 1935, the drift is toward the pooling of funds under public administration. A major purpose of the Act, which centralizes funds but decentralizes administration, is to encourage states to enact unemployment compensation legislation.[26]

[24] *Report of the Committee on Economic Security*, p. 1, quoting an average for the years 1922–29; Government Printing Office, 1935.

[25] Michigan suffered four times as much unemployment of gainful workers as South Dakota in 1930. Michigan's per cent was 13.9 as against 3.9 for the latter state. Douglas, Paul H.—*op. cit.*, p. 40.

[26] "Approved unemployment compensation programs are in existence in every

A Federal excise tax on payrolls is levied upon all employers of eight or more workers in industry and commerce—1 per cent of wages paid by employers in 1936, 2 per cent in 1937, and 3 per cent in 1938 and thereafter. The employer may credit against the Federal tax, up to 90 per cent of the tax, contributions required to be paid by him to unemployment funds under an approved state unemployment compensation law. This "tax offset" feature of the Federal Act is designed to safeguard the employers of each state against any disadvantage in interstate commercial competition; for such advantage would be inevitable if all American employers were not equally taxed, whether or not the state in which they did business had yet enacted unemployment compensation.

Excluded from the operation of the Act are the smaller plants with less than eight employees, agricultural labor, domestic service in private homes, employees of Federal and state governments and their subdivisions and instrumentalities, and charitable nonprofit corporations, and unfortunately also the transient or migratory worker, the self-employed, and certain types of casual laborers.

The Social Security Board must approve any state law for unemployment compensation submitted to it if the law provides that:

"(1) All compensation is to be paid through public employment offices in the State or such other agencies as the Board may approve;

"(2) No compensation shall be payable with respect to any day of unemployment occurring within two years after the first day of the first period with respect to which contributions are required;

"(3) All money received in the unemployment fund shall immediately upon such receipt be paid over to the Secretary of the Treasury to the credit of the Unemployment Trust Fund established by section 904;

"(4) All money withdrawn from the Unemployment Trust Fund by the State agency shall be used solely in the payment of compensation, exclusive of expenses of administration;

"(5) Compensation shall not be denied in such State to any otherwise eligible individual for refusing to accept new work under any of the following conditions: (A) if the position offered is vacant due directly to a

State at the present time. Benefits are now available to the eligible unemployed in 24 States and the District of Columbia. With the exception of Wisconsin, these programs came into operation early in 1938 at a time when unemployment had reached very high levels. During the first week in April over 800,000 unemployed were receiving unemployment compensation benefits in 22 States and the District of Columbia.

"Other States will begin benefit payments during the second half of 1938, and in 1939 all States will have unemployment-compensation programs in operation." Burns, Arthur E., and Williams, Edward A.—*A Survey of Relief and Security Programs*, p. 65; Works Progress Administration, May, 1938.

strike, lockout, or other labor dispute; (B) if the wages, hours, or other conditions of the work offered are substantially less favorable to the individual than those prevailing for similar work in the locality; (C) if as a condition of being employed the individual would be required to join a company union or to resign from or refrain from joining any bona fide labor organization;

"(6) All the rights, privileges, or immunities conferred by such law or by acts done pursuant thereto shall exist subject to the power of the legislature to amend or repeal such law at any time." [27]

Coördination with Public Employment Services.—The merits of the policy of paying insurance benefits through public employment offices are many. In so far as the coördination of public employment exchanges with unemployment insurance succeeds in increasing the number of such exchanges, improving the quality of their administration, and the scope of their listings of available jobs, the Social Security Act can progressively prevent unemployment and greatly reduce its duration in the very process of paying benefits. For it is possible to require each of the unemployed who register for insurance benefits to register at the same time for new jobs. Compensation can be withheld if eligible individuals refuse to accept appropriate new work. Malingering or the tendency to take a vacation on the dole can be largely prevented. Skilful administration can in ordinary circumstances find new employment for the worker much more rapidly than he has ever in the past been able to find it for himself.

On the other hand the worker is protected under Section 5 from needlessly unwholesome conditions of labor, from incurring the opprobrium of his fellows through being forced to work as a "scab," and from certain kinds of duress with regard to labor organization, as well as from "yellow-dog" contracts.

Limitations of Unemployment Compensation.—Definite limits are set to unemployment compensation by the state laws. There is usually a waiting period of a specified number of weeks before the benefits begin and a limited number of weeks during which the benefits may be enjoyed. The size of the benefits received by each worker is generally determined with reference to the length of his previous employment; but his benefit check will always be less than his customary wage. Latitude is allowed to the states on these matters subject, however, to Federal approval of the standards

[27] *The Federal-State Program for Unemployment Compensation*, pp. 2–3; The Social Security Board, Informational Service Circular No. 5, December, 1936.

which they set. There is nothing in the Act to prevent any state from securing larger contributions from the employer than those exacted by the Federal excise tax. The state may, furthermore, require employee contributions, and may, itself, contribute from its own funds through any appropriate type of taxation. Larger benefits and longer periods of duration of such benefits will be possible in states which take advantage of this option. Under the present Federal tax offset it is calculated that benefits will usually run only from ten to twenty weeks. It is estimated that an additional two per cent, whether provided from employer, employee, or the state, might make possible twenty-six weeks of benefits after a four-week waiting period. [28]

Federal Policy for Social Security.—The Federal Social Security Act thus accustoms American states and their citizens to the principle and practice of social insurance and may protect, partially at least, twenty million or more of our industrial workers from danger of dependency when out of work. Progressive changes in Federal and state legislation are inevitable to extend coverage to groups not now covered, to increase the size and duration of benefits, and to perfect administrative details. Development and coördination of public employment exchanges, and certainty of employment on public works for ablebodied workers whose unemployment benefits have ceased before new private employment is found, are essential supplements to this Act as devices to prevent dependency among ablebodied unemployed workmen.

It has been seen that social insurance does not directly prevent life's hazards—whether unemployment, accident, disease, old age, or death—but that it can be made to prevent the dependency which might grow out of them. Social security legislation is thus secondary prevention as contrasted with programs of economic planning, eugenics, or education, for example, which are primary forms of prevention. Current writings on social insurance deal primarily with questions of finance and adminstration which are not pertinent to this discussion except in so far as the social security of the worker is dependent upon them. It should be made clear, however, that the volume of our national distributable wealth might be seriously reduced if the government's financial or social policies at any time

---

[28] *Ibid.*, p. 11. This problem is well covered in Burns, Eveline M.—"Unemployment Compensation in the United States"; *International Labour Review*, Vol. XXXVII, No. 5, May, 1938.

become so ill-advised that they injure our financial and credit structure, frighten the investor, cramp the taxpayer, or discourage sound undertakings of a commercial or industrial nature.

The wisest social policy is one which provides ample security for all who need it, while distributing fairly the burden occasioned by any hazard. Avoidance of every type of abuse, whether waste of public funds or loss of personal initiative, should be assured by competent administration. European countries after a generation or more of security legislation have progressed far in guaranteeing these essentials. Competent continuing research into the effects and limitations of American social security legislation through its initial years can provide guidance for the modification of Federal and state laws where needed, until each worker and his family are rendered reasonably secure from all types of dependency occasioned by life's major hazards.

QUESTIONS FOR DISCUSSION OR EXAMINATION

1. Which types of social insurance should be contributory? Which types should be supported exclusively by government? Why?
2. What responsibilities and functions in each type of social insurance rest with (a) the Federal government? (b) the state? Why?
3. What is the justification in social insurance of contributions to the insurance fund (a) by the employer? (b) by the employee?
4. What extensions (a) in types of insurance, (b) in coverage are essential to prevent the dependency now occasioned by each of the five major hazards?
5. What are the merits and shortcomings of the "American Plan" and the tax offset system of unemployment insurance?

PROBLEMS FOR INDIVIDUAL STUDY

1. Trace the history of employer's liability and workmen's compensation legislation with reference to the concepts and principles involved.
2. Analyze the arguments and evidence presented before your state legislature, or legislative hearings, for and against any one of the types of social security discussed in this chapter.
3. Analyze the local administration and procedure governing old-age pensions and insurance, or any other type of social security legislation.
4. Study any one of the five hazards in some selected state or city to ascertain how effectively it is being met by social security legislation and by other measures.
5. Study the arguments for and against state medicine as submitted in medical literature, and compare with the recorded experience of countries in which health insurance is in operation.

SUGGESTIONS FOR SUPPLEMENTARY READINGS

American Association for Labor Legislation—*American Labor Legislation Review*, published quarterly.

American Association for Social Security—*Annual Proceedings*, and *Social Security* (monthly).

Armstrong, Barbara N.—*Insuring the Essentials;* The Macmillan Company, 1932.

Bakke, E. Wight—*Insurance or Dole?;* Yale University Press, 1935.

Bittermann, Henry J.—*State and Federal Grants-in-Aid;* Mentzer, Bush & Company, 1938.

Bogue, Mary F.—*Administration of Mothers' Aid in Ten Localities, with Special Reference to Health, Housing, Education, and Recreation;* United States Department of Labor, Children's Bureau, Publication No. 184, Government Printing Office, 1928.

Booth, Charles—*Old Age Pensions and the Aged Poor;* Macmillan and Co., Limited, 1899 and 1906.

Brown, J. Douglas—*The Development of the Social Security Act: A Selected List of References;* Princeton University Press, 1936.

Burns, Eveline M.—*Toward Social Security: An Explanation of the Social Security Act and a Survey of the Larger Issues;* McGraw-Hill Book Company, Inc., 1936.

Carroll, Mollie Ray—*Unemployment Insurance in Germany;* The Brookings Institution, revised edition, 1930.

Chaney, Lucian West—*Statistics of Industrial Accidents in the United States to the End of 1927;* U. S. Bureau of Labor Statistics, Bulletin No. 490, Government Printing Office, 1929.

Committee on Economic Security—*Report to the President of the Committee on Economic Security;* Government Printing Office, 1935.

Commons, John R., and Andrews, John B.—*Principles of Labor Legislation,* Chapter VIII, "Social Insurance"; Harper & Brothers, revised edition, 1936.

Davis, Michael M.,—*Public Medical Services; A Survey of Tax-supported Medical Care in the United States;* University of Chicago Press, 1937.

Douglas, Paul H.—*Social Security in the United States: An Analysis and Appraisal of the Federal Social Security Act;* McGraw-Hill Book Company, Inc., 1936.

Downey, Ezekiel Henry—*Workmen's Compensation;* The Macmillan Company, 1924.

Dublin, Louis I., and Vane, Robert J., Jr.—*Causes of Death by Occupation;* U. S. Bureau of Labor Statistics, Bulletin No. 507, Government Printing Office, 1930.

Eastman, Crystal—*Work-Accidents and the Law;* Charities Publication Committee, Russell Sage Foundation, 1910.

Epstein, Abraham—*The Challenge of the Aged;* Vanguard Press, Inc., 1928.

Epstein, Abraham—*Facing Old Age: A Study of Old Age Dependency in the United States and Old Age Pensions;* Alfred A. Knopf, 1922.

Epstein, Abraham—*Insecurity; A Challenge to America;* Random House, third revised edition, 1936.

Falk, I. S.—*Security against Sickness;* Doubleday, Doran & Company, Inc., 1936.

Francis, Bion H., and Harwood, Sumner—*Accident and Health Insurance, from the Victim's Point of View;* American Institute for Economic Research, 1938.

Great Britain—*Report of the Royal Commission on National Health Insurance;* H. M. Stationery Office, 1926: and *Minutes of Evidence Taken before the Royal Commission on National Health Insurance;* H. M. Stationery Office, 1925.

Harris, Joseph H., editor—*Social Security: A Symposium;* entire issues of the *National Municipal Review;* March and April, 1936.

Henriques, J. Q.—*A Citizen's Guide to Social Service;* George Allen and Unwin Ltd., 1938.

Hopkins, Harry L.—*Spending to Save: The Complete Story of Relief;* W. W. Norton & Company, Inc., 1936.

Industrial Relations Counselors, Inc.—*Unemployment Compensation: A Chronological Bibliography of Books, Reports, and Periodical Articles in English, 1891–1927* (by Linda H. Morley, librarian): Industrial Relations Counselors, Inc. (New York), 1928.

Industrial Relations Counselors, Inc.—Unemployment insurance series.

International Labour Office—*Compulsory Sickness Insurance: A Comparative Analysis of National Laws and Statistics;* International Labour Office Studies and Reports, Series M, No. 6, 1927.

Key, V. O.—*The Administration of Federal Grants to the States;* Public Administration Service (Chicago), 1937.

McCleary, G. F.—*National Health Insurance;* H. K. Lewis & Co., Ltd., 1932.

Macdonald, Austin F.—*Federal Aid: A Study of the American Subsidy System;* Thomas Y. Crowell Company, 1928.

Massachusetts Bureau of Statistics—*Report of a Special Inquiry Relative to Aged and Dependent Persons in Massachusetts in 1915;* 1916.

Massachusetts Commission on Pensions—*Report on Old Age Pensions;* 1925.

Millis, Harry Alvin—*Sickness and Insurance;* University of Chicago Press, 1937.

Millis, Harry A., and Montgomery, Royal E.—*Labor's Risks and Social Insurance;* McGraw-Hill Book Company, Inc., 1938.

New York, State of—*A Study of the Medical Needs of Recipients of Old Age Assistance in New York City in 1934;* State of New York, Department of Social Welfare, Publication No. 21, Albany, 1937.

New York State Commission on Old Age Security—*Old Age Security;* New York State Commission on Old Age Security, Legislative Document No. 67, Albany, 1930.

Orr, Douglass W., and Orr, Jean Walker—*Health Insurance with Medical Care. The British Experience;* The Macmillan Company, 1938.

P E P (Political and Economic Planning)—*Report on the British Social Services: A Survey of the Existing Public Social Services in Great Britain with Proposals for Future Development;* P E P (London), 1937.

Reed, Louis S.—*Health Insurance: The Next Step in Social Security;* Harper & Brothers, 1937.

Riesman, David—*Medicine in Modern Society;* Princeton University Press, 1938.

Rubinow, I. M.—*Social Insurance, with Special Reference to American Conditions;* Henry Holt and Company, 1916.

Rubinow, I. M.—*The Quest for Security;* Henry Holt and Company, 1934.

Schneider, Margaret Grant—*More Security for Old Age: A Report and a Program* (Factual Report by Margaret Grant Schneider—A Program for Action by the Committee on Old-Age Security); Twentieth Century Fund, Inc., 1937.

Social Security Board—publications.

Stewart, Maxwell S.—*Social Security;* W. W. Norton & Company, Inc., 1937.

U. S. Bureau of Labor Statistics—*Occupational-Disease Legislation in the United States, 1936: With Appendix for 1937;* Bulletin No. 652, Government Printing Office, 1938.

U. S. Bureau of Labor Statistics—*Unemployment Benefit Plans in the United States and Unemployment Insurance in Foreign Countries;* Bulletin No. 544, Government Printing Office, 1931.

U. S. Bureau of Labor Statistics—current publications.

Warbasse, James Peter—*Cooperative Medicine;* The Cooperative League, revised edition, 1938.

Williams, Gertrude—*The State and the Standard of Living;* P. S. King & Son, Ltd., 1936.

Wyatt, Birchard E., and Wandel, William H.—*The Social Security Act in Operation: A Practical Guide to the Federal and Federal-State Social Security Programs;* Graphic Arts Press, Inc., 1937.

CHAPTER XXIII

UNEMPLOYMENT: CAUSES, TREATMENT, AND PREVENTION

Extent.—In periods of relative prosperity, such as the nineteen twenties, at any given time there probably were at least two million persons in the United States seeking work. In part, this is because of the seasonal nature of many jobs, the ever present change in markets and demand, or other economic factors, and in part because of reasons more personal. In periods of profound economic depression that number may increase by millions.[1] Obviously the number found unemployed depends upon the definitions used and the methods of collecting the data. In the absence of compulsory universal registration of the unemployed all estimates are crude.

"According to the voluntary registration in the National Unemployment Census of November 16–20, 1937, the number of totally unemployed, including persons on emergency relief work, was 7,822,912.

"The enumerative test census which followed this voluntary registration, and which actually covered 1,950,000 persons by house-to-house canvass, indicated that the voluntary census had been 72 per cent complete, so that allowance for this variation would give a projected maximum total of 10,870,000 who regarded themselves as unemployed, at the time of the unemployment census. The number of emergency relief workers included in the voluntary record as unemployed was 2,001,877. The number of females who reported themselves as totally unemployed or on emergency relief work in the voluntary registration and who are included in the above totals was 1,996,699.

"The number in the 48 States and the District of Columbia registered as totally unemployed and wanting work (not including persons on emergency work) was 5,821,035. The registration was as low as 3,091 in Nevada and as high as 763,322 in New York. Slightly over one-half of the 5,821,035 unemployed wanting work (2,925,415) were in 8 States— New York (763,322), Pennsylvania (566,437) Illinois (338,055), Ohio (304,682), California (258,005), Massachusetts (248,484), Texas (229,254), and New Jersey (217,176).

[1] Cf. Wolman, Leo—"Labor," Chapter VI of *Recent Economic Changes in the United States*, Vol. II; published for the National Bureau of Economic Research, Inc., by McGraw-Hill Book Company, Inc., 1929. Estimates and their sources are summarized in Hopkins, Harry L.—*Spending to Save;* W. W. Norton & Company, Inc., 1936.

"Persons who registered as partly employed and wanting more work numbered 3,209,211, of whom 2,641,660 were males and 567,551, females. That the voluntary registration of these partly unemployed was only 57 per cent complete was indicated by the subsequent test census. The Middle Atlantic States, including New York, New Jersey, and Pennsylvania, had the largest number partly unemployed, totalling 715,158, of which number 580,934 were males and 134,224 were females." [2]

Social Pathology of Unemployment.—Whether the extent of unemployment in the United States be large or small the effect upon the jobless man or woman and upon the family may be profound. The immediate effect of cessation of income upon the domestic economy is to force the use of capital or savings to procure the daily necessaries of life—chiefly food, since the replacement of clothing and utensils must usually be deferred until there is a steady income. When savings are exhausted, or if there are no savings, the urgent needs may be met by borrowing from relatives, friends, or loan companies, or by the pawning of articles that have sufficient value, thus seriously burdening the future for the sake of present requirements. When these resources are also exhausted dependency upon private charity or public relief is the only alternative until work is found and the first pay check received. To well-organized and highly adaptable personalities a crisis of this sort may be a challenge which will lead to useful developments in resourcefulness, initiative, courage, and effort which will master the circumstances to the lasting advantage—economic and moral—of the family. To poorly organized and unadaptable personalities and to most persons suffering from fatigue, ill health, or lack of self-confidence, the effects of loss of work are likely to be disintegrating or demoralizing. Such conditions tend to be reflected in time throughout the family and to become cumulative through malnutrition, the reduction of social contacts, and the decline in the mode of living as reflected in dress, housing, and recreation.

Protracted unemployment may reduce the man's employability through reduced health, the loss of industriousness and of self-confidence, nervous or mental impairment produced in part by incessant worry, or the changes in attitude toward work which grow out of dependency. Individuals vary widely in their reactions, but harmful

[2] Data are from National Unemployment Census, Washington, press releases of January 2, 3, and 8, 1938, cited in "National Unemployment Census, 1937," p. 355; *Monthly Labor Review*, Vol. 46, No. 2, February, 1938.

effects of unemployment are general. The problem is particularly
serious for young men and women unable to find work when their
schooling is completed.[3]

Causes and Types.—Unemployment, which has already been
shown to be a major cause of poverty, is induced in turn by an immense variety of factors which lie in the personalities of the individual
worker and his employer, in the industrial and social order, and in the
interactions between them. Some men are unemployed because they
are unemployable—due to factors already discussed under handicap,
personal incapacity, and personal hazards. Others are employable
but dismissed because of such personal factors as insubordination,
or strikes of workers on the one hand, or the obdurateness or selfishness of the employer on the other. Many lose their jobs as a
result of man-displacing machinery, or the inability of the management to purchase advantageously, to secure credit, to collect moneys
owed, to invest wisely, or to market its product either in this country
or abroad. Thus unemployment may be traceable to new inventions; executive incapacity; speculation; shifts in industry, agriculture,
mines, transportation, or markets; changes in credit structure;
effects of competition, tariffs, taxation, or law; and to downward
trends in the business cycle. The employable man is not long unemployed in prosperous periods, but he may be one of the most
tragic victims of a depression. Unemployment and consequent
dependency are usually not the fault of the employable unemployed.

Prevention.—The elimination of unemployment as a cause of
poverty involves the devices for prevention of handicap, maladjustment, undesirable habits, physical or mental sickness, ignorance,
and other forms of incapacity already considered.[4] But the unemployment which has been produced by conditions within the contemporary economic order has to be reached through national
economic planning. Whenever a willing and efficient worker is
unable to find employment both government and the industrial
system are at fault.

[3] Cavan, Ruth Shonle, and Ranck, Katherine Howland—*The Family and the
Depression;* University of Chicago Press, 1938. Social Science Research Council—
*Studies in the Social Aspects of the Depression: Research Memoranda, prepared under the
direction of the Committee on Studies in Social Aspects of the Depression,* thirteen
volumes; Social Science Research Council, 1937; and their bibliographies.
Angell, Robert Cooley—*The Family Encounters the Depression;* Charles Scribner's
Sons, 1936.
[4] See Part II.

Assuming the perpetuation of the present system of private owner-ship of property and industry, the solution must be found either through the wise and farsighted coöperation of industry and govern-ment, or else through an extensive increase of forced interference with, and control of, industry by government. If some branches of industry under wise leadership can be rendered coöperative in disposition, drastic regulation and control may not be universally necessary.

Technological Unemployment.—Much attention has been paid in recent years to technological unemployment—the displacement of men by machinery. This problem in America is more than a century old. In each country it dates from the beginning of the industrial revolution in which steam-driven machinery replaced the more primitive sources of power—the muscles of men and of beasts, and the earlier devices to utilize power from rivers, wind, or tide. The industrial revolution, beginning in the latter part of the eighteenth century in England and the early nineteenth century in America, made possible the congregation of large numbers of workers under one roof at work upon machines propelled by central power. It led at once to a rapid increase in the division of labor, which in human terms meant that the individual worker instead of creating a com-plete product now worked at only a small part of the finished product. Such specialization has developed continuously through-out the past century.

Side by side with the development in the volume of power har-nessed by man there has been a continuous succession of discoveries in the fields of physics and chemistry, each applied with increasing skill in the fields of engineering and mechanics. The number of patents issued by the United States Patent Office per decade has doubled in the past half century. They amounted, in the decade from 1880 to 1890 to 208,000, from 1900 to 1910 to 314,000, and from 1920 to 1930 to 421,000.[5] This in turn has meant the constant replacement of old machinery with new, and a corresponding ad-vance both in the productivity of labor and in the per capita volume of manufactured goods.

Each new marketable invention has, however, tended to cause temporary unemployment for individual workers while the new

[5] A useful summary of "The Influence of Invention and Discovery" by W. F. Ogburn will be found in Chapter III of *Recent Social Trends in the United States*, Vol. I; McGraw-Hill Book Company, Inc., 1933.

machinery is being installed. It has caused more lasting unemployment for those unable to master the operation of the new machine, and who must find work elsewhere within their capacities. It has permanently displaced persons whose work can be done wholly by machinery. A machine which can be tended by one worker, or a handful of workers, may in some instances do efficiently what has previously been done by hundreds.

Recent instances cited by the Institute of Economics of Brookings Institution reveal that:

"Seven men now do the work which formerly required 60 to perform in casting pig iron; 2 men now do the work which formerly required 128 to perform in loading pig iron; 1 man replaces 42 in operating open-hearth furnaces.

"In machine and railway repair shops 1 man replaces 25 skilled machinists with a gang of 5 or 10 semiautomatic machines; 4 men can now do in 3 to 7 hours what it formerly took 8 men 3 weeks to perform in repair work on locomotives, due to the oxyacetylene torch. Fifteen years ago it took 15 to 30 hours to turn one pair of locomotive tires; now it takes 8 hours to turn 6 pairs with same number of men by use of modern processes.

"A brick-making machine in Chicago makes 40,000 bricks per hour. It formerly took one man 8 hours to make 450.

"The most up-to-date automatic bottle-making machine makes in 1 hour what it would take more than 41 workers to make by hand in the manufacture of 4-ounce oval prescription bottles. In 25 and 40 watt electric bulbs the man-hour output of the automatic machine is more than thirty-one times that of the hand process.

"In New York from 1914 to 1925 the number of workers in the paper-box industry decreased 32 per cent, while the output per wage earner increased 121 per cent.

"Thousands of skilled musicians with a life's training behind them are being thrown out of employment by the advent of the talking movie. In the field of news transportation the Simplex and the Multiplex machines have eliminated the need for trained telegraphers and to-day by the mere process of typing a message at the sending office, the message is automatically printed at the receiving office. Many thousands of trained telegraphers have been made unnecessary during the past few years as a result of this new device. In the printing trades new inventions in typesetting threaten to make possible the setting of type in innumerable offices scattered as many as 500 miles away by the manipulation of keys in a central plant." [6]

[6] By Isador Lubin in the Hearings before the Committee on Education and Labor, United States Senate, Seventieth Congress, Second Session, pursuant to S. Res. 219, *Unemployment in the United States*, p. 500; Government Printing Office, 1929.

Replacement of Displaced Labor.—Viewing the displacement of men by machinery over the past century it is apparent that invention which displaces men at one job creates work for them in another. The number of employees in transportation increases, though railroads, airplanes, and motorcars replace the stagecoach and sailing vessel. The number of employees in manufacture increases even though mill products take the place of those of the handworker. The machine creates more work by reducing unit costs and thus finding a wider market for its products. New inventions create new wants and new demands, so the appearance of the telephone, radio, typewriter, or any other salable invention means new occupational opportunities.[7]

Although labor displaced by technological improvements has very largely secured reëmployment throughout the century and a half which has followed the industrial revolution, the displaced worker has suffered serious temporary hardship. If he possessed a skill and training for which there was no longer a demand he has often been forced down into the ranks of unskilled labor. Many of the younger men have been able to acquire new skills but others have been unable to make such an adjustment. Special studies have revealed that less than half are reabsorbed in the old industry, that a few never succeed in finding full-time remunerative occupation, that some are forced to turn from manufacturing to transportation, trade, or domestic occupation, and that often a majority will have to suffer three months or more of unemployment before full-time work is found.[8]

Measures to Absorb Displaced Labor.—To keep unemployment at a minimum, this natural process must be guided. The essential

[7] See *Recent Economic Changes in the United States* (Report of the Committee on Recent Economic Changes, of the President's Conference on Unemployment), especially final chapter of Vol. II by Wesley C. Mitchell, pp. 876–879; published for the National Bureau of Economic Research, Inc., by McGraw-Hill Book Company, Inc., 1929.

[8] For general discussion see: *Recent Social Trends in the United States*, Vol. I, especially Chapter V, "Trends in Economic Organization" by Edwin F. Gay and Leo Wolman, and Chapter VI, "Shifting Occupational Patterns" by Ralph G. Hurlin and Meredith B. Givens. *Recent Economic Changes in the United States*, Vol. I, Chapter II, "Industry—Changes in New and Old Industries" by Dexter S. Kimball; Vol. II, Chapter VII, "Management" by Henry S. Dennison, and the final chapter by Wesley C. Mitchell. Haber, William, and Stanchfield, Paul L.—*Unemployment, Relief and Economic Security: A Survey of Michigan's Relief and Unemployment Problem*, especially Chapter IV; Second Report of the State Emergency Welfare Relief Commission, Lansing, 1936. *Employment Statistics and Conditions*, especially pp. 187–191; U. S. Bureau of Labor Statistics, Bulletin No. 616, Handbook of Labor Statistics, 1936 edition.

means are: (1) Through making all available jobs known to the worker, at or even before dismissal. This is a new province for public employment exchanges. (2) By reasonable reduction of the hours of labor for those who have jobs so as to distribute work among more workers. This program would reduce dependency somewhat, but fails to increase the total output and thus fails to reduce poverty in the sense of economic insufficiency. (3) Through creating new opportunities for the employment of labor. A nation-wide program at this time, to eliminate all slums and provide decent housing for all wage-earners would serve this purpose not only for the building trades but also for the factories from which they buy, the transportation agencies which convey, and the commercial and recreational establishments in which the reëmployed workers would spend.[9]

Shorter Hours.—Shorter working hours, however, whether produced by the plan of spreading work or by specific legislation are continuously being demanded. When achieved, they may bring some difficult problems to our social and political order unless accompanied by comprehensive social planning which will provide constructive outlets for the worker's interests and energy during his increased leisure. In the absence of such anticipatory planning the discontent derived from boredom or from debilitating recreations will reduce social well-being.

The constructive recreation which such a social policy involves for the mass of our population would, however, create new jobs. For it would provide occupations for teachers in all branches of adult education, and occupations for directors and assistants in all the arts, sports, and recreational facilities which the program might comprise. In addition, there are many opportunities for the wage-earning population to develop leisure-time hobbies or subsidiary occupations, especially for example in crafts, practical arts, or home gardening, which if wisely directed would expand the total mass of national wealth and would directly raise the plane of living of each family thus engaged.

Reversion to earlier and more primitive types of industry is economically and socially inadvisable. Technological unemployment can be made merely temporary. Adjustment of economic and social life to overcome the hardships occasioned by new invention is wholly feasible. Since technological improvements can provide

---

[9] Wagner, Robert F.—"The Ideal Industrial State"; *The New York Times Magazine*, May 9, 1937.

more distributable goods per hour of human labor applied to their production, and a larger per capita output,[10] it is clear that the advance of science and invention can be made a means to the elimination of poverty if properly controlled. This can be accomplished, however, only by so distributing the enhanced production that all persons will receive their reasonable share. Thus in the long run society and all who comprise it may share in the evergrowing output of a dynamic technology.

Seasonal Unemployment.—The balance of the unemployment of the ablebodied is due in the main to defects in industrial organization, or to executive or managerial mistakes within the individual plant. In the former group would fall seasonal unemployment even though this condition is in part traceable to fashion or other vagaries in consumer demand. Thus in the automobile industry "the season decided upon for the introduction of new models will occasion a sharp rise in production over the slack period of the preceding months caused by declining sales of the old model."[11] In the Detroit area, which is dominated by the automobile industry, "an average of forty per cent of the workers employed in the period of peak production between 1920 and 1935 suffered at least one month of seasonal unemployment during the year. Most of these workers faced longer periods of seasonal unemployment, ranging from two to eleven months.[12]

A few of the examples cited by the Brookings Institution may serve to exemplify the seasonal aspect of unemployment in a variety of other industries. Thus in the men's clothing industry "an investigation of eight representative plants in three large markets showed that over a period of three years the equipment was utilized on the average but 69 per cent of the possible working time. One plant was used 58 per cent of the time, a condition which might safely be said to characterize hundreds of others. Similar instances could be cited in the shoe industry where sales in some months of the year run as high as 250 per cent above the average and in others as low as 87 per cent below. In printing the case of one large and important plant can be cited which employs 2,700 people in rush seasons and drops to 1,500 in dull."[13]

---

[10] *Recent Social Trends in the United States*, Vol. I, p. 232.
[11] Haber, William, and Stanchfield, Paul L.—*op. cit.*, p. 145.
[12] *Ibid.*, p. 147.
[13] *Unemployment in the United States*, p. 495.

Measures to Overcome Seasonal Unemployment.—Industries with a high sense of social responsibility have increasingly demonstrated that it is possible to iron out the peaks and valleys in the employment curve, reducing overtime work in one season of the year and building up employment in what had previously been the slack season.

"One large organization employing over 3,000 workers, which had formerly to concentrate its production within seven months of the year, found, after exerting the proper effort, that it was possible to secure orders for its goods sufficiently far in advance to make possible the employment of its labor force for almost 50 weeks each year. This firm, by giving special discounts and even special low prices for orders placed 3, 4, and 5 months in advance, had no difficulty in overcoming the hesitancy of merchants towards placing advance orders.

"Other firms have found that by producing staples for stock it was possible to employ labor during those months when normally there would be little to do. One large packing firm in Brooklyn, N. Y., which sells most of its products between the months of September and January, had found through past experience that during the last four months of the year it was necessary to increase the average working force of the first eight months by over 600 per cent. This firm, which employed an average of 200 people between January and September, used to employ from thirteen to fourteen hundred people during the months September to January. It was thought that this situation could not be overcome because of the fact that their product was highly perishable. An experiment with so simple a device as a cold-storage warehouse showed that their product could be produced and packed regularly throughout the year and delivered as the market required during the late fall and winter months. As a result of this discovery this firm now employs some 800 people regularly throughout the 12 months of the year. Moreover, they have found it possible to produce a product of higher quality, to furnish continuous work to their employees, and develop a better morale in every branch of their business." [14]

The findings and recommendations of the United States Department of Commerce on seasonal operations have already contributed to more effective planning for stabilizing the use of labor forces. Some progress is being made in the fields of housing and construction by spreading consumer demand throughout the year, so as to reduce seasonality in the building trades. Special attention has been devoted in northern climates to the creation of profitable winter work in these occupations. The combining of two seasonal industries, such

[14] *Ibid.*, p. 498.

as the retailing of ice and coal, is another excellent example of an effective attack upon this problem.

"Some organizations, in order to furnish regular employment to their laborers, have developed side lines which dovetail with their regular products. Thus, for example, one manufacturer of shovels, whose market demands shipments during the summer, has taken on the production of sleds, which are sold in the winter. One of our largest manufacturers of ink and glue, unable to keep labor employed during the winter months because weather conditions made it impossible to ship these products because of freezing while being transported, recently took on the production of pens and pencils, which could be moved during those months when their main products could not. . . .

"The determination to keep labor regularly employed has led to the discovery that many things can be done during what were considered necessary slack periods which had never before been attempted. Thus, for example, it has always been the policy of the railroads to lay their rails only in the summer months. The determination of some of our railroad systems to keep their trackmen steadily employed led them to experiment with laying rails in winter. They found that rails could be more cheaply and efficiently laid in the winter than in the summer months and as a result these systems are doing most of their rail-laying work in winter and using the same forces for replacing ties, ditching, and clearing the right of way in the summer. The railroads found also that by budgeting their equipment repairs it was possible to keep most of the men in the mechanical department steadily employed throughout the year. Statistics presented . . . by two large railroad systems showed that the labor turnover in this line of work, which formerly averaged more than 25 per cent, has been reduced to less than 10 per cent." [15]

Errors of Management as Cause.—Executive unwisdom, ignorance or incapacity, and the mistaken policies which flow therefrom, are also a frequent cause of the shutting down of plants or the permanent reduction of labor forces. The principle of *laissez faire* is so deeply ingrained in American thought with regard to the ownership and operation of industry that any individual or group with sufficient funds or credit can initiate or take over virtually any legitimate field of production. Thus, many a plausible personality becomes an industrial executive and employer of labor, only to demonstrate subsequently his incompetence through the inappropriate location or size of his establishment or through unskilful buying, selling, or financial arrangements, or through ineffectual internal management. In any one of these instances the hardworking

[15] *Ibid.*, pp. 498–499.

employee who accepts work in good faith will find himself sooner or later unemployed.

Extension of Economic Control.—America has traditionally believed that progress is dependent upon the free play of initiative. But such opportunity and freedom have left many an abandoned mine, oil well, mill, factory, and workshop in their wake. The extension of public control over the initiation of productive enterprise or over the personal qualifications for industrial management is hazardous and may, on occasion, interfere with socially desirable developments. Yet such control can properly be exercised through the financial and credit structure. This is primarily a function for Federal and national agencies supervising loans or securities. Unwise undertakings in manufacture or commerce can be prevented by the establishment and enforcement of carefully drawn criteria governing investment in industrial enterprise by banks, trust companies, and all other financial agencies enjoying Federal or state supervision.

Obvious and rational fields for governmental control are those which involve speculation, the credit structure, transportation, and foreign markets. In each of these, government in recent years has increasingly attempted regulation in the public interest. But each is susceptible to refinements and extension in policies of control so that the nation's business may be conducted still further to the advantage of the consumer. For in the long run the interest of the entrepreneur is not inconsistent with that of the consumer.

Conceivably, securities legislation can be so developed that fraudulent investments, and needless mulcting of the public will be almost wholly eliminated without curbing legitimate socially-useful and promising enterprise.[16] The credit structure requires control to eliminate needless losses, protect values, and facilitate desirable enterprise. Transportation needs a more reasonable freight-rate structure so that no properly located industry may suffer from discrimination. All desirable modes of transportation should be encouraged, thus helping to raise the consumer's standard of living by means of minimum charges for the goods he purchases.[17] Both

[16] The Securities and Exchange Commission now operates under the authority of the Securities Act of 1933, the Securities Exchange Act of 1934, and the Unlisted Trading Act of 1936. When the present gaps in its service are filled by supplementary legislation it will be able to operate through the entire life cycle of all securities in so far as the protection of the public renders that necessary.

[17] See Vol. III of the Publications of the President's Conference on Home

the importation and exportation of goods would profit by public facilitation in a manner consistent with national well-being, which may be construed to cover safety, national economic self-sufficiency in whatever may prove to be a reasonable degree, as well as international reciprocity, friendship, and coöperation.[18]

Such principles are recognized and are already in partial operation. Their limitations in current practice, though often political in origin, are largely the result of their newness. Many lessons have to be learned from experience, and in a republic changes cannot be made readily until key persons and key groups can be reached and public opinion for change can be cultivated. The elimination of the unemployment which may be the outgrowth of defects in Federal control in any of these four fields is dependent upon the speed and skill with which progress can be made in well-judged policies of control consistent with the totality of national economic planning.

Industrial Crises and Depressions.—The third major type of unemployment of the ablebodied is that which grows out of general industrial crises and depressions. It is usually termed cyclical unemployment. Like technological unemployment its origins are in part traceable to the industrial revolution, for in its present form it is a phenomenon of large-scale industry. Like seasonal unemployment, it is in part traceable to executive unwisdom, since errors in judgment on the part of capitalists and entrepreneurs have caused the overcapitalization and overproduction which precede it.

Crises in American history have been of two major types, the financial panic and the industrial depression. The former is of shorter duration and has its origin in problems of money, banking, credit, and investment. Industrial depressions, on the other hand, originate in overexpansion in the fields of manufacturing or transportation and, in the more severe cases, may last for years. The two may overlap and there is some degree of repercussion upon industry by financial panic or upon financial conditions by industrial depression. Each shows relative periodicity, for throughout the past century there has been more or less regular recurrence, roughly taking the form of a twenty-year interval between major depressions, with minor crises every ten years. Such periodicity, however, is subject

Building and Home Ownership entitled *Slums, Large-Scale Housing and Decentralization*, pp. 181, 199–200, and 202; 1932.

[18] Taussig, F. W.—*Principles of Economics*, Vol. I, Book IV; The Macmillan Company, 1911.

to vagaries that are inevitable where a multiplicity of factors operate as causes.

Theories of the Causation of Depressions.—Since industrial depressions are the major cause of extensive long-continued unemployment, they have been subjected to wide study and analysis. Theories of causation range all the way from Jevons' theory, which relates them to sun spots, to those which emphasize producers' or consumers' demand, money, prices, saving, capitalization, or credit, and those which find the source in factors of individual and group psychology.

It is apparent that such crises follow periods of excessive general optimism in which capitalization and production expand rapidly. There comes a point where production exceeds demand, factories are overstocked, curtail their production and their orders, and begin to lay off workers. Dismissals reduce the purchasing power of workers now unemployed and their families. Earnings on investments shrink which retards the sale of consumers' goods to the investing public. The declining values of stocks and the declining trade which have followed industrial retardation lead to general pessimism, which in turn accentuates the downward swing of economic activity. This leads to additional dismissals of labor in trade, transportation, and domestic service as well as in virtually all types of industry.

There is still no universally acceptable answer to the problem of prevention of crises. Whether industrial crises could be stopped by a greater degree of governmental control of industry is again not certain, even though the Federal government has at its command devices through which it may regulate credit, savings, securities, money, and prices. Depression, major source of periodic dependency, cannot be rendered preventable until further researches point the way. The economic insufficiency which grows out of retarded production requires more fundamental solutions than have yet been discovered—solutions which presumably will deal simultaneously with industrial, trade, financial, and psychological factors.

There is also no wholly clear way to speed recovery once the depression has occurred. It has become an accepted practice to promote desirable public works during depression periods in order to give an income to labor and to keep active the firms which fill the government's orders. Yet such devices do not appear to keep a depression from running its full term, nor have they served to revive optimism generally among producers and investors. When,

in a period like that of the year 1937, one leading group of economists recommends the raising of prices, and another reduced prices
but increased wages, a third financial control, a fourth stable money,
and a fifth a colossal public investment in the stimulation of a single
industry by means of a universal public program to displace all substandard housing with new and decent housing [19]—it is apparent that
there is as yet no agreement as to the solution.

Public Works Reserve as Expedient.—The widespread dependency during depression periods can be eased by unemployment insurance, as well as by public works through which dismissed workmen can be temporarily reëmployed. Unemployment insurance
in its present form, as has been seen, may be expected to tide large
numbers of industrial workers over three or four months of unemployment. Beyond that point, in a protracted depression, their
benefits if continued must be supplied by special Federal grant [20]
or else work must be created for them. The Swedish plan [21] of post-
poning certain types of public work for development in such a period,
makes possible normal employment for the "cyclical unemployed"
at normal wages if they are not eligible for such insurance, or after
the insurance benefits are exhausted. Dependency may thus be
averted—and by devices much less costly and vastly more wholesome than public relief.

Such "reserve" public works require careful advance planning,
so that idle labor may be absorbed during periods of industrial
depression. They may well comprise not only the myriad ventures
in conservation, road building, parks, forests, waterfronts, monu-
mental building, and others with which our populace is now familiar,
but also developments in economic, social, and historical research,
in scientific experimentation, and in the arts as recently encouraged
by the Works Progress Administration. There is in America so

[19] Current recommendations are best traced in the articles and reviews published in the leading professional journals of the economists and statisticians.
The more important of the earlier theories will be found in standard works on
economics.

[20] Cf. Douglas, Paul H.—*Social Security in the United States: An Analysis and Appraisal of the Federal Social Security Act*, pp. 296–298; McGraw-Hill Book Company,
Inc., 1936.

[21] A vivid discussion of the Swedish plan will be found in Parts V and VI of
Davis, Maxine—*They Shall Not Want;* The Macmillan Company, 1937. Many
useful bibliographical references will be found on pp. 405–412 of that book.
See particularly *Social Problems and Policies in Sweden;* entire issue of *The Annals
of the American Academy of Political and Social Science*, Vol. 197, May, 1938.

much of hazard to be replaced by safety, so much of ignorance to be superseded by knowledge, so much of ugliness to be destroyed and of beauty to be protected and developed, that national wealth and well-being can be greatly enhanced by discriminating development of public works in each of these directions during depression periods. The attendant stimulation to the industries from which the public agencies must buy their materials, and to the transportation and commercial agencies which convey and purvey them, though vastly important, is but secondary in significance to this larger objective.

Pending the extension of unemployment insurance to cover all workers, and the solution of the larger economic problems, of which unemployment is a derivative, much can be done to prevent needless distress among the workers.

Public Employment Offices.—The next major essential is an effective nation-wide system for the placement of labor. The ups and downs of consumer demand, as well as internal conditions within industry, make some unemployment of labor through dismissals inevitable. A network of public labor exchanges, immediately cognizant of all vacancies, would make it possible to reduce to a minimum the number of days of idleness for each dismissed worker. As demand for labor is often highly localized it is necessary to have each local exchange informed of the national as well as the local market for labor. There is no inherent reason why labor services in America should not ultimately be rendered as highly efficient as those of England or Sweden. In view of the public interest at stake, and particularly of the protection of funds which would otherwise have to be devoted to the public care of dependents, the organization and operation of such exchanges is a legitimate public function even though many, but not all, of the private exchanges would be eliminated by government ascendancy in the placement of industrial labor. Government would thus make itself responsible for maximum continuity of employment.

The present status of public employment agencies is indicated in the following official summary:

"Public employment agencies, sometimes designated free public employment offices, are agencies supported by a public body—State, county, city, town, or village. Such agencies are primarily established for the purpose of furnishing employment to workers and labor to employers.

"The first free public employment office in the United States was a municipal agency established in 1890 at Cleveland, Ohio. Later the idea became a definite movement which was taken up by various States, through their legislative bodies. The movement spread until at the present time the majority of the States have provided for the establishment of public employment offices. The growth of these institutions in the United States may be attributed in part to the alleged abuses which have grown up around private agencies. At the same time social utility and economic developments, as well as the belief that obtaining employment for the unemployed is a proper exercise of public authority, have played a powerful and important part in the establishment of public employment agencies.

"As established, however, not all these agencies were functioning units. While enabling acts were adopted, some of the States made no appropriations for the maintenance of an up-to-date, efficient organization, and as a result the work of seeking to bring about contacts between the 'jobless man' and the 'manless job' has been seriously handicapped. With the adoption of Federal-State coöperative relations in the maintenance and operation of State employment offices under the Federal act of 1933, public employment agencies in the United States entered a new stage of development.

"The principle of impartial administration was enunciated when the Supreme Court of Illinois, [*Mathews* v. *People*, 202 Ill. 389, 67 N. E. 28.] as early as 1903, declared that whenever the public undertakes to conduct an employment office the services rendered must be without discrimination. An act of the Illinois legislature (acts of 1899, p. 268), which the court declared unconstitutional, forbade public employment agencies to furnish names of applicants for work to employers whose workmen were on strike. . . .

"The Federal Government entered the field of public employment service in 1907. By an act of the Congress of that year (34 U. S. Stat. L. 898) a division of information in the Bureau of Immigration and Naturalization (Department of Commerce and Labor) was established . . .

"In 1913, when the Department of Labor was created as a separate executive department, the division of information of the Bureau of Immigration was transferred to it. . . .

"The Federal Labor Service was organized in 1915, and was engaged mostly in the distribution of farm labor. . . . In January 1918, the Service was taken from the Bureau of Immigration and set up as a separate agency in the United States Department of Labor. . . .

"At the Seventy-first Congress (1931), a bill creating a coöperative national employment system was passed by both the House and Senate only to meet a presidential veto. Later in the same session, however, the Department of Labor (46 U. S. Stat. L. 1575) was granted an appropriation of $500,000 for its Employment Service. As a result of the appropriation thus obtained an enlarged Federal Employment Service was established at once with offices in every State of the Union. This system continued until it was abolished early in 1933.

"Shortly afterwards, on June 6, 1933, a national employment system was established by an act (48 Stat. L. 113) passed at the special session of the Seventy-third Congress.

"This law created a United States Employment Service in the Department of Labor and supplanted a former Federal employment service, with offices in every State, conducted independently of the State employment service.

"The new law established a national employment system in coöperation with the various States, including the Territories of Hawaii and Alaska. An appropriation of $1,500,000 was provided for the fiscal year ending June 30, 1934, and $4,000,000 for each fiscal year thereafter, up to and including the fiscal year ending June 30, 1938. Thereafter the amount of the appropriation is to be determined by the Congress, as may be deemed necessary.

"In order to obtain the benefits of any appropriations, a State must accept the provisions of the national act and designate a State agency with necessary powers to coöperate with the United States Employment Service. Seventy-five per cent of the amounts appropriated are to be apportioned by the director among the several States in the proportion which their population bears to the total population of the United States. No payment shall be made to any State until an equal amount has been appropriated and made available for that year by the State. By an act of May 10, 1935, it was provided that in the apportionment of the amount, at least $10,000 must be granted to each State.

"The United States Employment Service is charged with the duty of promoting and developing a national system of employment offices for men, women, and juniors 'who are legally qualified to engage in gainful occupations'; to maintain a veterans' bureau, a farm placement service, and a public employment service for the District of Columbia; and to assist in establishing public employment offices in the several States and political subdivisions thereof in which there shall be located a veterans' employment service. The Federal agency is charged also with the duty to 'assist in coördinating the public employment offices throughout the country and in increasing their usefulness by developing and prescribing minimum standards of efficiency, assisting them in meeting problems peculiar to their localities, promoting uniformity in their administrative and statistical procedure, furnishing and publishing information as to opportunities for employment and other information of value in the operation of the system, and maintaining a system for clearing labor between the several States.'

"The law provides for the appointment of a Federal Advisory Council. This board is to be composed of representatives of employers and employees and the public for the purpose of formulating policies and the determining of problems relating to employment. The Federal director is required to form State advisory councils, similarly organized.

"Before any applicant is referred to a place for employment, notice of any strikes or lock-outs must be given.

"All States desiring to receive benefits under the act must submit detailed plans to the director, and must also make such reports concerning any operations and expenditures of money as the director may require. The franking privilege for free transmission of official mail matter is extended to the United States Employment Service and to all State employment systems operating under the provisions of the act.

". . . With the enactment of several laws during 1937, all of the States and the two Territories have become affiliated with the United States Employment Service. . . .

"At the present time in the United States there are 42 States which have enacted legislation directly or indirectly regulating the operation of private employment offices. In most of the States provisions are made for the licensing and bonding of such agencies. In addition to the private employment agencies conducted for profit, agencies are also established by various philanthropic organizations, trade-unions, and associations of employers. Agencies created for the placement of professional workers such as teachers, nurses, etc., are also numerous. . . .

"One of the reasons given for the establishment of public employment agencies is the alleged abuses practiced by many of the private agencies. Some of the more common of the fraudulent methods were enumerated by the United States Bureau of Labor in 1912 as follows:

"1. Charging a fee and failing to make any effort to find work for the applicant.

"2. Sending applicants where no work exists.

"3. Sending applicants to distant points where no work or where unsatisfactory work exists, but whence the applicant will not return on account of the expense involved.

"4. Collusion between the agent and employer, whereby the applicant is given a few days' work and then discharged to make way for new workmen, the agent and employer dividing the fee.

"5. Charging exorbitant fees, or giving jobs to such applicants as contribute extra fees, presents, etc.

"6. Inducing workers, particularly girls, who have been placed, to leave, pay another fee, and get a 'better job.'

"In addition to the abuses alleged, the charge of inadequacy has also been lodged against the private employment agencies." [22]

Industrial Retraining.—The mere provision of a national network of labor exchanges is, however, not enough in itself to eliminate unemployment of the ablebodied. Trends in consumer demand cause declines in some industries and ultimate abandonment of others. Technological improvements may displace many kinds of skilled labor permanently with machines. Industrial relocation— whether caused by shifts in the production of raw materials, or the

[22] Labor Law Information Service, prepared by the (Charles F. Sharkey, Chief)—*Laws Relating to Employment Agencies in the United States, As of July 1, 1937*, pp. 1–7; U. S. Bureau of Labor Statistics, Bulletin No. 630, Government Printing Office, 1937.

combinations of materials used, or by availability of cheaper power or labor, or by changes in the market—will lead to much unemployment of skilled workmen in the communities which have been abandoned. Many of these workers for personal or family reasons, or otherwise, will be unable to follow the industry to its new location. Since there will be no further demand for their specific skill in the local market, industrial retraining for skilled operations for which there is a demand should be accessible to them, and preferably before their original job ceases.

To render the retraining process efficient it should be adapted to individual capacities and needs. This involves vocational analysis, through aptitude and personality testing, to precede vocational retraining, guidance, and placement. Our larger cities are well equipped in the main with opportunities for the vocational education of children, and are increasingly making such resources available in the evening hours to adults, often at quite nominal charges. But what is everywhere lacking is the efficient coördination of vocational analysis, guidance, and education or retraining, with reference to the incidence of vocational demand. These may properly remain functions of state and local governments preferably with Federal subsidization and its attendant standard-setting and supervision. Vocational placement through the network of national labor exchanges is now recognized to be primarily a Federal function so that this service may be integrated with unemployment insurance and may facilitate needed migrations of labor. Coördination and high general standards of service in this fourfold process of analysis, guidance, education, and placement, may be made to contribute to the reduction of dependency and the increase of national productivity.

QUESTIONS FOR DISCUSSION OR EXAMINATION

1. What effects of unemployment upon the jobseeker and his family have you personally observed or learned of from competent witnesses? Can you justify your conclusion that these "effects" were produced by unemployment?
2. What solutions do you see for (a) technological unemployment, (b) seasonal unemployment, (c) cyclical unemployment, (d) the unemployment due to errors in industrial management?
3. After reviewing Part II and this chapter, what solutions do you see for the problem of the "unemployable"?
4. In how far can the social objectives (Part I, Chapter IV) be attained by the policies to eliminate or mitigate unemployment, outlined in this chapter?

5. Would it be (a) desirable, (b) practicable, to nationalize and unify all employment services, public and private? Why? or Why not?

PROBLEMS FOR INDIVIDUAL STUDY

1. Analyze and compare available statistical studies of employment and unemployment with reference to (a) the definitions employed, (b) the methods utilized to secure the data.
2. Study the trends of (a) technological unemployment, (b) seasonal unemployment, or (c) cyclical unemployment to discover what evidence there may be of the effects of public policies for control.
3. Study and appraise the work and methods of local (a) public employment offices, (b) vocational retraining opportunities, or (c) agencies for vocational analysis and guidance.
4. Analyze (a) the available data concerning unemployment in some selected city or state, and (b) the methods now employed there to cope with unemployment, and (c) submit your recommendations for improvement of the local services.

SUGGESTIONS FOR SUPPLEMENTARY READINGS

Angell, Robert Cooley—*The Family Encounters the Depression;* Charles Scribner's Sons, 1936.

Atkinson, Raymond C., Odencrantz, Louise C., and Deming, Ben—*Public Employment Service in the United States;* Public Administration Service (Chicago), 1938.

Ayres, Leonard P.—*The Economics of Recovery;* The Macmillan Company, 1933.

Bakke, E. Wight—*The Unemployed Man;* E. P. Dutton & Co., 1934.

Beveridge, W. H.—*Unemployment; A Problem of Industry;* Longmans, Green and Co., new edition, 1930.

Bingham, W. V.—*Aptitudes and Aptitude Testing;* Harper & Brothers, 1937.

Bossard, James H. S.—*Social Change and Social Problems*, Part IV, "Problems of Socio-Economic Security"; Harper & Brothers, revised edition, 1938.

Bursk, J. Parker—*Seasonal Variations in Employment in Manufacturing Industries;* University of Pennsylvania Press, 1931.

Calkins, Clinch—*Some Folks Won't Work;* Harcourt, Brace and Company, Inc., 1930.

Cavan, Ruth Shonle, and Ranck, Katherine Howland—*The Family and the Depression;* University of Chicago Press, 1938.

Commons, John R., and Andrews, John B.—*Principles of Labor Legislation*, Chapter VI, "Unemployment"; Harper & Brothers, revised edition, 1936.

Creamer, Daniel B.—*Is Industry Decentralizing?;* University of Pennsylvania Press, 1935.

Davenport, Donald H., and Croston, John J.—*Unemployment and Prospects for Reëmployment in Massachusetts: With Particular Reference to Manufacturing Industries;* Graduate School of Business Administration, Harvard University, Business Research Studies No. 15, 1936.

Davison, Ronald C.—*The Unemployed, Old Policies and New;* Longmans, Green and Co., 1929.

Davison, Ronald C.—*What's Wrong with Unemployment Insurance;* Longmans, Green and Co., 1930.

Dearborn, Walter F., and Rothney, John W. M.—*Scholastic, Economic and Social Backgrounds of Unemployed Youth;* Harvard University Press, 1938.

Dennison, Henry S., and Galbraith, J. K.—*Modern Competition and Business Policy;* Oxford University Press, 1938.

Dennison, Henry S., Filene, Lincoln, Flanders, Ralph E., and Leeds, Morris E.—*Toward Full Employment;* McGraw-Hill Book Company, Inc., 1938.

De Schweinitz, Dorothea—*How Workers Find Jobs;* University of Pennsylvania Press, 1932.

Douglas, Paul H., and Director, Aaron—*The Problem of Unemployment;* The Macmillan Company, 1931.

Elderton, Marion, editor—*Case Studies of Unemployment;* University of Pennsylvania Press, Industrial Research Studies No. XII, 1931.

Family Welfare Association of America—*The Effect of Economic Unemployment on Family Life;* Family Life and National Recovery Series, Family Welfare Association of America, 1935.

Feldman, Herman—*Problems in Labor Relations;* The Macmillan Company, 1937.

Feldman, Herman—*The Regularization of Employment;* Harper & Brothers, 1925.

Fitch, John A.—*Vocational Guidance in Action;* Columbia University Press, 1935.

Griffitts, Charles H.—*Fundamentals of Vocational Psychology;* The Macmillan Company, 1924.

Haber, William, and Stanchfield, Paul L.—*Unemployment, Relief and Economic Security: A Survey of Michigan's Relief and Unemployment Problem;* Second Report of the State Emergency Welfare Relief Commission, Lansing, 1936.

Hansen, Alvin H.—*Full Recovery or Stagnation?;* W. W. Norton & Company, Inc., 1938.

Hansen, Alvin H., Petrowski, Nelle M., and Graves, Richard A.—*An Analysis of Three Unemployment Surveys in Minneapolis, St. Paul, and Duluth;* University of Minnesota Press, 1932.

Hexter, Maurice Beck—*Social Consequences of Business Cycles;* Houghton Mifflin Company, 1925.

Hobson, J. A.—*The Economics of Unemployment;* The Macmillan Company, revised edition, 1931.

International Labour Office—*Technical Progress and Unemployment;* International Labour Office, 1938.

Kahn, D. C.—*Unemployment and Its Treatment in the United States;* American Association of Social Workers, 1937.

Keller, F. J., and Viteles, M. S.—*Vocational Guidance Throughout the World; A Comparative Study;* W. W. Norton & Company, Inc., 1937.

King, Willford I.—*The Causes of Economic Fluctuations;* The Ronald Press Company, 1938.

Klein, Philip—*The Burden of Unemployment;* Russell Sage Foundation, 1923.

Lee, Edwin A., editor—*Objectives and Problems of Vocational Education;* McGraw-Hill Book Company, Inc., 1938.

Lescohier, Don D.—*The Labor Market;* The Macmillan Company, 1919.

Lindley, Betty and Ernest K.—*A New Deal for Youth;* The Viking Press, 1938.

Loucks, William N.—*The Stabilization of Employment in Philadelphia;* University of Pennsylvania Press, 1931.

Massachusetts—*Report on the Census of Unemployment in Massachusetts as of January 2, 1934;* Massachusetts Department of Labor and Industries, Division of Statistics, Public Document No. 15 (Labor Bulletin No. 171), 1935.

Mills, Frederick Cecil—*Statistical Methods: Applied to Economics and Business;* Henry Holt and Company, revised edition, 1938.

Mitchell, Wesley Clair—*Business Cycles;* National Bureau of Economic Research, Inc., 1927.

The National Health Survey: 1935–36—Characteristics of the Urban Unemployed; Division of Public Health Methods, National Institute of Health, U. S. Public Health Service (Preliminary Reports, The National Health Survey, Population Series, Bulletin No. D), 1938.

National Resources Committee—*Public Works Planning;* Government Printing Office, December, 1936.

National Resources Committee—*Technological Trends and National Policy;* Government Printing Office, June, 1937.

Nourse, Edwin G., and Drury, Horace B.—*Industrial Price Policies and Economic Progress;* The Brookings Institution, 1938.

Parker, Willard E.—*Books About Jobs. A Bibliography of Occupational Literature;* published for the National Occupational Conference by the American Library Association, preliminary edition, 1936.

Pennsylvania State Emergency Relief Administration—*The Unemployment Relief Digest* (a monthly bulletin presenting in compact form the substance of recently published material concerning unemployment and the administration of relief); State Emergency Relief Administration, Department of Research and Statistics, Harrisburg, Pennsylvania.

Pigou, A. C.—*The Theory of Unemployment;* The Macmillan Company, 1933.

Pilgrim Trust, A Report made to the—*Men Without Work;* Cambridge University Press, 1938.

President's Conference on Unemployment—*Business Cycles and Unemployment;* McGraw-Hill Book Company, Inc., 1923.

President's Conference on Unemployment—*Recent Economic Changes in the United States,* two volumes; published for the National Bureau of Economic Research, Inc., by the McGraw-Hill Book Company, Inc., 1929.

Pribram, Karl—"Unemployment," *The Encyclopaedia of the Social Sciences,* Vol. 15; The Macmillan Company, 1935.

Robinson, Joan—*Essays in the Theory of Employment;* The Macmillan Company, 1937.

Scott, J. W.—*Self-Subsistence for the Unemployed: Studies in a New Technique;* Faber & Faber (London), 1935.

Slichter, Sumner H.—*Modern Economic Society;* Henry Holt and Company, 1931.

Slichter, Sumner H.—*Towards Stability: The Problem of Economic Balance;* Henry Holt and Company, 1934.

Snyder, Carl—*Business Cycles and Business Measurements;* The Macmillan Company, 1927.

Social Science Research Council—*Studies in the Social Aspects of the Depression: Research Memoranda, prepared under the direction of the Committee on Studies in Social Aspects of the Depression,* thirteen volumes; Social Science Research Council, 1937.

Taussig, F. W.—*Principles of Economics,* Vol. I, Chapter 29, "Crises and Industrial Depression," Chapter 30, "Financial Panics," and Vol. II, Chapter 41, "Overproduction and Overinvestment"; The Macmillan Company, 1911–13.

United States Department of Labor, Bureau of Labor Statistics—*Monthly Labor Review,* and other publications.

United States Office of Education—*Youth;* prepared by the Committee on Youth Problems, Bulletin, 1936, No. 18–I, United States Office of Education, Government Printing Office, 1936.

Williams, James Mickel—*Human Aspects of Unemployment and Relief with Special Reference to the Effects of the Depression on Children;* University of North Carolina Press, 1933.

Works Progress Administration, National Research Project on Reëmployment Opportunities and Recent Changes in Industrial Techniques—publications.

CHAPTER XXIV

LOW INCOME: THE CONTROL OF ECONOMIC FACTORS

Low Wages and Income as Cause of Poverty.—Poverty is obviously the lack of adequate wealth or income. Above the subsistence minimum personal attitudes determine what constitutes adequacy. Personal handicaps or incapacities may prevent an individual from producing, and thus earning an income sufficient to meet his needs. Or wages too low to meet the needs of a family of average size may be the outgrowth of conditions deeply rooted in the economic system. The problem of the abolition of poverty, therefore, largely resolves itself into control of personal factors and their social milieu on the one hand, and the control of economic factors on the other. We now turn to the latter.

Economic Insufficiency Unnecessary.—The United States is a country of rich and abundant natural resources. Under properly controlled development of these resources, with well-considered policies for their conservation, it is quite generally and credibly concluded that a reasonable living could be rendered available to the present population and for a considerable period to come. There is sufficient wealth latent in America to eliminate poverty in the sense of economic insufficiency, if skilfully produced and distributed.

It is not true, however, as some of the less well informed street orators assume, that the seizure and an equal distribution of the wealth of our multimillionaires and capitalists would produce an adequate income for all. The man of the street may visualize the capitalist's income as spent on costly yachts and motorcars, lavish clothes and food, mansions, travel, and other consumers' goods. Actually, however, the greater part of his income is reinvested in such a manner as to make further production and improvements in production possible. If his annual income were seized and distributed among the propertyless, wornout machinery could not be replaced, buildings could not be repaired, and improvements in methods of production, which reduce the unit cost of goods, would cease. Investment of capital is essential to the continuance of corporate industry. Failure to invest means reversion to handicrafts and peasantry. Crude expropriation (without provision for capital from other sources, either small investors or socialized wealth) would thus mean universal poverty within a few months or years.

Uneven Distribution of the National Wealth and Income.— Estimates of the Brookings Institution for the year 1929 place our national wealth (based upon money valuation of "farms, mines, railways, factories, stocks of goods, etc.") at around four hundred and sixty billion dollars, or $3,700 per capita. The national income in that year was estimated at $80,882,000,000, or $625 per capita. Under our system of uneven distribution twenty per cent of the income went to 220,000 families or only eight-tenths of one per cent of the population.[1]

This uneven distribution of wealth and income appears unfair. Yet unless capital—the means of production and distribution—is socialized under public ownership and operation uneven distribution is probably, for the present, essential in order to continue large-scale production. If all persons inheriting wealth or receiving incomes larger than their legitimate personal needs require possessed excellent judgment in investment and always gave first consideration to the needs of mankind, there would be no occasion, unless on grounds of absolute justice, to protest against disparities in wealth. Such capitalists would, by hypothesis, be wise trustees of their excess wealth and would use it invariably in the public interest. Poverty would cease. Sufficient income for health, happiness, and welfare would be allotted to all.

Pathologic Aspects of Distributive System.—Actually, however, most men, capitalists included, show limitations or lapses in judgment and in character. A large portion of the nation's wealth is accumulated at the expense of the consumer or of the worker or both. Most employers fear to raise wages, even when they can afford to do so, on the grounds that labor, ignorant of the business, will resist reductions when conditions of the market change and the employer faces a loss. But many maintain hard terms with labor for reasons less creditable. The consumer too is often exploited by foisting upon his ignorance goods which are not durable or serviceable. Usually goods tend to be sold at whatever price the market

---

[1] Moulton, Harold G.—*Income and Economic Progress*, pp. 73–75, and 78; The Brookings Institution, 1935. Stewart, Maxwell S.—*Income and Economic Progress*, p. 11; Public Affairs Committee (Washington), Public Affairs Pamphlet No. 1.

will bear, irrespective of their quality. The present industrial order puts a premium upon selfishness, often conferring its prizes, its largest incomes, upon its most ruthless members—those who are least considerate of the worker, of the buying public, and of social welfare.

Communism as Solution.—Such conditions will have to be met either by the extension and improvement of social legislation within the present industrial order or else by some radical change in the direction of benevolent dictatorship, state socialism, or communism.

To consider the latter first, communism involving dictatorship of the proletariat appears to many wage-earners to be the most promising solution. But as a device for the elimination of poverty communism under proletarian operation offers no promise of efficiency, because the wage-earners who make up the proletariat lack training and experience in the operation of big business and of public affairs.

If, to secure expertness in management, communism should commandeer the services of present experts in business, industry, banking, engineering, and so on, one of two things is likely to happen. Either, like labor within the present industrial order, such experts will practice sabotage which will wreck the new state; or else, being convinced of the futility of communism, they will seize the power and substitute their limited control for proletarian democracy. It is more probable, in view of the history of revolutions, that their services would not be commandeered and that as "dangerous persons" lacking proletarian sympathies they would be imprisoned or executed, leaving the new communist state to be operated as best it might be by proletarian theorists. In time, through high concentration of powers and concomitant sacrifice of many principles of democracy and of community of ownership, and with much display of force and regimentation of labor, the communist government might, as in Russia, succeed in bringing about a degree of recovery. There is every presumption, however, that it would take more than one generation to restore standards of living as high as those which prevailed prior to the revolution.

If communism can abolish poverty at all, it can do so only after a long period of general suffering and at the expense of democracy and liberty. A tragic error of revolution as a device for social amelioration lies in its attempt to achieve its ultimate good, visualized as elimination of the exploitation of man by man and substitution of just distribution of property and income, by means which are themselves evil—class hatred, bloodshed, uncompensated expropriation, imprisonments and executions of opponents, universal suspicion, regimentation, and reduction of freedom of choice and action.

Dictatorship as Solution.—Many minds, in their discouragement with contemporary conditions and with radical alternatives, turn to "benevolent" dictatorship as a solution of the problem of poverty. It is argued, reasonably enough, that a dictator possessing both judgment and an interest in serving his people could so order the industrial system as to put a stop to exploitation of men and resources and provide for a decent standard of living and adequate universal education. Assuming that such dictators could always be found and proved sufficiently acceptable, so that their positions would not have to be maintained by force, this might be deemed a major solution for the problem of poverty.

It is, however, unbelievable that a nation like our own, which has stressed throughout its history the principles of personal liberty and democracy, could find, install, and retain even a benevolent dictator without opposition and the use of force. Moreover, dictatorships fall sooner or later into sinister hands. There is no device to prevent this except the use of force. But most serious of all is the fact that dictatorships, even though benevolent, rest upon enforced conformity to the dictator's will. The citizens are reduced to the status of children from whom obedience is exacted. Freedom of thought and action is sacrificed. Citizens are robbed of all moral responsibility save that of conformity to an external will. This is the morality of the slave, not of the master. Dictatorship, even at its best, would deprive the population of self-government, self-direction, and freedom of choice which are the very essence of character. It would secure the material values of life—adequate food, clothing, and housing for all—at the expense of life's deeper values.

Evolutionary Collectivism as Solution.—State socialism arrived at in a democracy by a well-ordered evolutionary process is worthy of more serious attention. This is a process by which the government acquires the means of production, land and capital, and becomes capitalist, entrepreneur, and landlord, in trust for its citizens. Through gradual substitution of public ownership for private, the exploitation of man by man could be progressively reduced while continuing the republican form of government.

As employer the government would be in a position to pay a

fair wage to labor and to maintain a decent plane of living for all. As universal landlord it would receive all rents and thus would secure for public use all those increments to land values which are socially created and "unearned" by their present recipients.   As producer and salesman, the government would be in a position to manufacture durable goods or goods of sound quality, and thus the present too-prevalent exploitation of the consumer would cease. In the framing of its economic policy the government could put a stop to the abuse of natural resources—an abuse which in private hands already threatens their exhaustion.   The fertility of soil could be maintained, forests restored, a large percentage of mines and oil wells could be closed until future needs bring them again into use.   Effort could be concentrated where it would count most for the provision of a universal wholesome standard of living.

Difficulties Involved in Public Ownership and Operation.— The popular tendency to confuse evolutionary socialism with revolutionary proletarian communism is partially responsible for the slow progress that has been made in socializing capital.   There is, however, another major difficulty—that of maintaining in public operations an efficiency as great as that obtained in the best of private enterprise.   State socialism can develop wholesomely only where it can employ competent, skilled, honest, and loyal service. The history of Federal and state bureaucracy often fails to reveal such virtues.   Public ownership in a democracy tends to a greater or less degree of inefficiency through political exploitation with its attendant evils of patronage, graft, favoritism, routine-mindedness, and incompetence.

As compared with private enterprise at its best government ownership and operation suffers from many handicaps.   Its overhead is much more costly.   The time of large staffs is consumed in making detailed reports to higher officials, budgets, and publicity statements; in hearings, speeches, and field representation; in public records and itemized documents which no private business would need to prepare.   This is a heavy, continuous burden necessitated by law and tradition and by responsibility to the populace.

Individual executive salaries in government are low.   Collectively they are high.   Since the lower ranges of office labor are paid much higher wages than private industry pays, the total wage and salary overhead of any public project is heavy.

It is difficult for the government to get expert service in each of its branches. Experts command higher salaries in the competitive world outside. Government service means insecurity for executives and experts because of administration changes and frequent reorganization. The government may have to content itself, in normal as distinguished from emergency periods, with second-rate personalities in positions which should be held by experts. Greater security of clerical staffs may also mean relative inefficiency, for many employees "go to seed on the job."

Civil service, though indispensable in routine departments to prevent favoritism, sorely complicates government operation in any complex business. Once the government enters business, civil service reduces the range of choice in hiring and makes firing exceedingly difficult. To discharge an incompetent worker who has powerful political backing may endanger the position of the executive or lead to curtailment of his budget.

Efficiency in business operations necessitates quick decisions, rapid execution, ample budgets, and a competent staff. It requires highly trained, experienced executives. No one of these requirements can be guaranteed in government operations. Except in emergency periods the most competent of private executives feel they cannot exchange their large incomes for the low regular salaries which government pays. They may fear, also, the opprobrium which conspicuous government executives almost inevitably incur, developed by the opposition press.

Private enterprise can keep alert and adapt itself quickly to new situations by picking the ablest available subexecutives and staff, and by holding over them the threat of dismissal if their competence or energy declines. Government is more likely to make its choices only from second-rate ability, and to incur serious delays in dismissal or to be unable to dismiss when an employee demonstrates incompetence. Quick decisions and rapid execution are impossible for the government, because of the necessity of waiting for the approval of still higher officials in the governmental hierarchy.

The budget may be ample at the start, but to keep it sufficient for continuing operations the executive may be forced to spend an undue percentage of his time in reaching and winning the approval of members of Congressional committees concerned with the budget and other key persons of influence within the Cabinet or Congress.

In letting contracts and subcontracts, private enterprise has a free hand in determining upon the lowest competent bidder and in practicing every proper economy throughout the period of construction. There is always danger in government operations that there will not be so free a hand in bargaining, or that in one administration or another executives will feel it necessary to arrange the bids so that contracts will go to political favorites.

The most dangerous spot of all is management. Although management might be of the highest quality under some political administrations, it is quite certain in others to become a field for the exercise of favoritism. It might readily become a device for vote control. Even if this contingency were avoided, there is danger that a well-conceived policy would from time to time be changed, to the disadvantage of the public treasury, as a result of local political pressure for special favors. When selfish interests flood Congress and administrative departments with letters and telegrams, or when prominent politicians lobby for favors, some governmental executives would not have backbone enough to resist, and a less advantageous managerial policy might become firmly entrenched.[2]

How Difficulties in Government Ownership Can Be Overcome.—Nevertheless, the abolition of poverty may make it necessary to extend government ownership whenever the best available regulatory measures are demonstrably ineffectual. Public operation should therefore be rid as far as possible of its existing handicaps and be rendered sound and efficient. Aside from perfecting the civil service and governmental budgetary control, it is clear that higher salaries should be paid to executives and experts in governmental service, decreasing the disparities which now exist when compared with private industry. Still more important is special training for public officials, in backgrounds as well as techniques, in the fundamental principles of political and economic science as well as in the details of engineering, or statistical research, or administration, as the case may be. Planning and the framing of any economic policy is dependent upon a rigorous training in the amassing, winnowing, and interpretation of evidence, and in discrimination and judgment. Its execution requires thorough understanding of men and of issues, past and present, of trends and timeliness, of individual and social psychology, of public opinion and the relative merits of

[2] The preceding eight paragraphs have been borrowed with slight modification from Ford, James—"Is Government Housing Desirable"; *Review of Reviews*, September, 1936.

devices to win response, of all means of self-expression—combined with practical idealism in service for the public good. Graduate schools that can provide such training for carefully selected men and women apprenticed in public employ will be able to create a demand for their output. The entrance of government upon the domains of economic planning and public ownership involves solid preparation for government service as a career. The scope of political manipulation can thus be reduced in large part, though probably never entirely, to elective offices, and certain routine fields already preëmpted by politics. Expert and qualified service should, however, be safeguarded by vigorous maintenance of nonpartisan organizations of citizens interested to serve for the public as watchdogs of public employment, administration, and expenditure— thereby bolstering alertness, incentive, expertness, and probity by their backing.

Evolutionary Collectivism.—Evolutionary state socialism, as thus described, is vastly more economic and efficient than revolutionary communism and yet could be made to preserve the values of democracy. Unlike communism it could utilize the services of present capitalists in the management of its public enterprises, and could avoid excessive costs of compensation for the properties socialized by providing jobs, or where necessary, pensions, to present owners. The process of socialization of capital could be performed gradually according to need, beginning probably with those natural resources which are in danger of exhaustion, and extending to the industries which are most exploitative in character, where regulatory legislation fails properly to protect either the worker or the consumer.

Principle of Choice in Determining What Operations to Socialize.—It is conceivable, however, that the adoption of the policy of socializing refractory industries would bring enough of trade and manufacture to a sense of their trusteeship that the state would be able to control the industrial system with a quite limited application of public ownership.[3] Thus not only farms, private dwellings, small shops, professions, and coöperative communities might be operated to entire satisfaction under private ownership, but also

[3] For a realistic presentation of difficulties which may prove to be insuperable see Arnold, Thurman W.—*The Folklore of Capitalism;* Yale University Press, 1937. See also Willcox, O. W.—*Can Industry Govern Itself?;* W. W. Norton & Company, Inc., 1937.

many large industries and commercial establishments might under private ownership continue as recognized agents of the state. A limited collectivism might thus be possible once the principle were established and applied that any trade or industry would be taken over by the government in case of continued exploitation of its workers or buying public or other misbehavior. In case poverty cannot be abolished under the existing social and industrial order evolutionary extension of public ownership is the only safe resort, and the only one which will protect and conserve America's established principles of liberty and democracy.

Policies Essential to Elimination of Economic Insufficiency.— If more radical procedures are to be averted, the challenge definitely presents itself to our present system of government and our present industrial order to find solutions which will make them unnecessary. These would include, *first*, thoroughgoing policies for the conservation of natural resources so that coming generations will not be plunged in poverty by their exhaustion; *second*, policies to increase the volume of the nation's distributable wealth through the improvement at every point of the system of production; *third*, policies for the elimination of all needless wastes in the process of production; *fourth*, policies for the elimination of waste in the distribution of goods; *fifth*, policies for the elimination of waste in human effort through redistribution of labor and talents to positions where each can be applied most productively; *sixth*, policies for the redistribution of wealth in such a way as best to serve humanity; *seventh*, policies for the redistribution of income in such a way that an adequate minimum wage may be available for all laborers and their dependents; *eighth*, policies for the elimination of consumer exploitation, through the maintenance of reasonable standards of quality, safety, wholesomeness, and durability for all products; *ninth*, policies that will encourage, stimulate, and foster experimentation, invention, and the general utilization of the findings of scientific research; *tenth*, policies for the protection and development of wage-earner credit and thrift; *eleventh*, policies for the fostering of sound wage-earner organization, both for protection of labor from the aggression of employers and for the fulfilment of labor's economic and cultural interests in a manner consistent with the interests of the general public.

National Economic Planning.—The name now gaining currency for coördinated centralized policies to govern the production and distribution of wealth or goods and services is national economic planning. It comprises other measures in the field of finance, tariff, taxation, agriculture, trade, and transportation not touched upon above, but all of which have their bearing upon the volume of wealth and the equity of its distribution. It has ramifications in international relations, in political structure, in historical traditions, in folkways and mores, and in individual psychology.

National economic planning is thus a colossal ideal which, in a civilization as complex as ours, must gain momentum in spite of imperfect knowledge, in spite of delays in determining fundamental principles, in spite of uncertainties as to the exact effects of existing measures—whether for currency or crop control, processing taxation, strike mediation, international trade, or others of its almost infinite components. For control has to be exercised on the basis of such little scientific knowledge as may be at hand and such judgment and experience as may be available in public councils.

Inevitably, national economic planning is a process of trial and error to be perfected laboriously from week to week, from year to year, by discoveries as to the consequences of present statutes or by more penetrating thought and research in basic policy. The coördination of its many branches similarly must be ever changing to accommodate plans to changes in details, in conditions, and in administrative personalities. Nevertheless, in spite of incredible difficulties continuous centralized planning is required to mass effort, perfect organization, improve functioning, conserve gains, eliminate inconsistencies or needless duplications, and to fill in gaps in the program, though always primarily to increase national economic strength and welfare.

The eleven major policies outlined as of primary importance for the reduction of poverty—in the sense of economic insufficiency—are but phases, important though they may be, of such national economic planning. Achievement in these eleven fields is dependent upon correlation of effort, as well as upon the detailed measures through which each policy is executed.

QUESTIONS FOR DISCUSSION OR EXAMINATION

1. Arguments for and against (a) communism, (b) dictatorship, (c) evolutionary socialism, (d) limited extension of public ownership, as means to the abolition of poverty.
2. Arguments for and against continuing disparities in wealth and income.

3. What personal evidence have you of (a) the exploitation of labor, (b) the exploitation of the consumer, (c) other pathologic aspects of the industrial or distributive system?
4. What are the inefficiencies characteristic of the public ownership and operation of industrial processes? How can they be overcome?

PROBLEMS FOR INDIVIDUAL STUDY

1. Critical review of any of the works in the following list of references.
2. Critical analysis of both favorable and unfavorable accounts of contemporary examples of (a) communism, (b) dictatorship, or (c) public ownership.
3. Study of civil service for a selected unit of government showing (a) history, (b) purposes, (c) achievements, (d) limitations, (e) recommendations for improvement.
4. Problem study: Can exploitation of labor be eliminated without the socialization of industry?

SUGGESTIONS FOR SUPPLEMENTARY READINGS

Armstrong, Hamilton Fish—*"We or They": Two Worlds in Conflict;* The Macmillan Company, 1937.

Arnold, Thurman W.—*The Folklore of Capitalism;* Yale University Press, 1937.

Barnes, Major J. S.—*Fascism;* Henry Holt and Company, 1931.

Beard, Charles A.—*An Economic Interpretation of the Constitution of the United States;* The Macmillan Company, reissue, 1935.

Bossard, James H. S.—*Social Change and Social Problems,* Part III, "Social Well-Being and Problems of Income"; Harper & Brothers, revised edition, 1938.

Callender, Clarence N., editor—*The Crisis of Democracy; The Annals of the American Academy of Political and Social Science,* Vol. 169, September, 1933.

Clark, Harold F.—*Life Earnings in Selected Occupations in the United States;* Harper & Brothers, 1937.

Cole, G. D. H., Webb, Sidney, Steed, Wickham, Salter, Sir Arthur, Blackett, P. M. S., and Hogben, Lancelot—*What Is Ahead of Us?;* The Macmillan Company, 1937.

Coyle, David Cushman—*Roads to a New America;* Little, Brown, and Company, 1938.

Daugherty, Carroll R.—*Labor Problems in American Industry;* Houghton Mifflin Company, 1933.

Davis, Jerome—*Contemporary Social Movements;* The Century Co., 1930.

Edwards, Lyford P.—*The Natural History of Revolution;* University of Chicago Press, 1927.

Elliott, W. Y.—*The Pragmatic Revolt in Politics;* The Macmillan Company, 1928.

Fitch, John A.—*The Causes of Industrial Unrest;* Harper & Brothers, 1924.

Florinsky, Michael T.—*Fascism and National Socialism: A Study of the Economic and Social Policies of the Totalitarian State;* The Macmillan Company, 1936.

Foster, William Trufant, and Catchings, Waddill—*The Road to Plenty;* Houghton Mifflin Company, Pollak Foundation Series, No. 11, 1928.

Gulick, Luther, and Urwick, L., editors—*Papers on the Science of Administration;* Columbia University Press, 1937.

Hardman, J. B. S., editor—*American Labor Dynamics;* Harcourt, Brace and Company, Inc., 1928.

Hollander, Jacob H.—*The Abolition of Poverty;* Houghton Mifflin Company, 1914.

Hubbard, Joseph B.—*Current Economic Policies;* Henry Holt and Company, 1934.

King, Willford Isbell—*The National Income and Its Purchasing Power;* National Bureau of Economic Research, Inc., 1930.

Laski, Harold J.—*Communism;* Henry Holt and Company, 1927.

Laski, Harold J.—*Democracy in Crisis;* University of North Carolina Press (expanded version), 1933.

Lee, Murray G.—*The Government's Hand in Business;* Baker, Voorhis & Co., 1937.

Leven, Maurice, Moulton, Harold G., and Warburton, Clark—*America's Capacity to Consume;* The Brookings Institution, 1934.

Mayo, Elton—*Human Problems of an Industrial Civilization;* The Macmillan Company, 1933.

Moulton, Harold G.—*Income and Economic Progress;* The Brookings Institution, 1935.

National Industrial Conference Board—*Differentials in Industrial Wages and Hours in the United States* (by M. Ada Beney); National Industrial Conference Board, 1938.

Parmelee, Maurice—*Farewell to Poverty;* John Wiley & Sons, Inc., 1935.

Perlman, Selig—*A Theory of the Labor Movement;* The Macmillan Company, 1928.

Pfiffner, John M.—*Public Administration;* The Ronald Press Company, 1935.

Pigou, A. C.—*Socialism versus Capitalism;* The Macmillan Company, 1937.

Pipkin, Charles W.—*Social Politics and Modern Democracies,* two volumes; The Macmillan Company, 1931.

President's Conference on Unemployment—*Recent Economic Changes in the United States,* two volumes; published for the National Bureau of Economic Research, Inc., by the McGraw-Hill Book Company, Inc., 1929.

Public Affairs Committee—*Our Government—For Spoils or Service?;* Public Affairs Pamphlets No. 3, 1936.

Queen, Stuart Alfred, Bodenhafer, Walter Blaine, and Harper, Ernest Bouldin—*Social Organization and Disorganization,* Part III, "Institutions"; Thomas Y. Crowell Company, 1935.

Robbins, Lionel—*Economic Planning and International Order;* The Macmillan Company, 1937.

Roos, Charles Frederick—*NRA Economic Planning;* The Principia Press (Bloomington, Ind.), 1937.

Schloss, David F.—*Methods of Industrial Remuneration;* Williams & Norgate, Ltd., third edition, 1898.

Seager, Henry R.—*Principles of Economics;* Henry Holt and Company, revised edition, 1923.

Slichter, Sumner H.—*Modern Economic Society;* Henry Holt and Company, 1931.

Soule, George—*A Planned Society;* The Macmillan Company, 1932.

Tawney, Richard Henry—*Poverty as an Industrial Problem;* The Ratan Tata Foundation, London School of Economics, 1914.

Tawney, R. H.—*The Sickness of an Acquisitive Society;* The Fabian Society and George Allen and Unwin Ltd., 1920.

Thomas, Norman—*After the New Deal, What?;* The Macmillan Company, 1936.

Todd, Arthur James—*Industry and Society;* Henry Holt and Company, 1933.

United States Department of Commerce, Division of Economic Research—*National Income in the United States 1929–35;* Government Printing Office, 1936.

Williams, Whiting—*Mainsprings of Men;* Charles Scribner's Sons, 1925.

Wooddy, Carroll H.—*The Growth of the Federal Government, 1915–1932;* McGraw-Hill Book Company, Inc., 1934.

CHAPTER XXV

LOW INCOME: THE INCREASE OF DISTRIBUTABLE WEALTH

Prerequisites of Abolition of Poverty.—To prevent poverty, in the sense of economic insufficiency, it would be necessary simultaneously to build up, so far as possible, the volume of distributable wealth and to distribute the general income more carefully. If national wealth is the dividend, and population the divisor, then the quotient will be the per capita wealth of the nation. Unless this is substantial, and economic life so ordered that it will not decrease, there will be poverty. Unless also it is distributed with utmost care there will be poverty. For the problem cannot be solved unless a wholesome standard of living can be guaranteed to each worker and his family.

Conservation of Natural Resources.—The first essential in building up a lastingly high per capita wealth is the conservation of natural resources. Without it any program would be futile since the depletion of forests, mines, oil wells, and soil fertility in one generation would, in the absence of new inventions, mean a reduced standard of living and relative poverty for the next.

Some of our natural resources are now being exploited with undue rapidity. In the early history of this country land, forests, and mineral resources were so abundant in proportion to the people's needs, and soil so rich, that they seemed inexhaustible. Within the past half century, after all free homesteading land had been taken up, the tradition of "mining" the land continued practically unabated. "The nitrogen, phosphorus, potassium, sulphur and other elements of fertility removed from the soil in the crops and animals or animal products sold from farms have not been restored except in limited areas. Leaching of the elements of soil fertility by the rain and their removal in the drainage waters has continued and has in some areas perhaps even been accelerated by the destruction of the original forest or grass cover." [1]

[1] *Recent Social Trends in the United States,* Vol. I, pp. 93-94; McGraw-Hill Book Company, Inc., 1933.

The range area of the United States is reported to have been depleted fully 52 per cent from its virgin condition, "using depletion in the sense of reduction in grazing capacity for domestic live stock. Practically this means that a range once capable of supporting 22.5 million animal units can now carry only 10.8 million. On nearly 55 per cent of the entire range area, forage values have been reduced by more than half." [2]

The original forests which covered some eight hundred million acres of land two centuries ago have been reduced to about five hundred million acres of either forests or cut-over land, and only about one hundred million acres now bear virgin saw timber. Until quite recently it was estimated that the annual cut, waste, and fire destruction was four times the annual growth. The rate of depletion is still only partially retarded.[3]

Mineral resources, though still far from exhaustion, are so carelessly mined as to involve prodigious waste. By Stuart Chase, the annual "known waste" in coal is estimated at seven hundred and fifty million tons, in water power fifty million horse-power, in oil one billion barrels, in natural gas six hundred billion cubic feet.[4]

Prevention of Wasteful Exploitation of Resources.—Each year of continuing depletion of resources means reduced distributable wealth for future generations. Increasing poverty is threatened. No solution is possible through leaving these vast resources in private or corporate hands since the investor's interest is in immediate profits. Public interference and firm control of the uses of land, water, mineral supplies, vegetation, wild life, and fisheries is indispensable to avert future general poverty. Where education in crop rotation, cultivation, fertilization, erosion prevention, and reforestation prove sufficient to maintain or replace fertility and forests, extension of public ownership may not prove necessary. But where education and regulation prove ineffectual, extension of public ownership, especially in the field of forestry, is a clear necessity.

Wherever private ownership operates in a manner inimical to

---

[2] Clapp, Earle H.—"The Major Range Problems and Their Solution: A Résumé" in *The Western Range*, p. 3; Letter from The Secretary of Agriculture transmitting in response to Senate Resolution No. 289 a Report on the Western Range—A Great but Neglected Natural Resource, Senate Document No. 199; Government Printing Office, 1936.

[3] *Recent Social Trends in the United States*, Vol. I, p. 115.

[4] Chase, Stuart—*The Tragedy of Waste*, p. 264; The Macmillan Company, 1929.

public well-being the first obvious essential is an adequate visualization of the situation. All resources must be known and charted: the methods and rates of exploitation determined. The second stage in public policy is control by law. With experience, public regulation of private exploitation, the development of public opinion, and the eliciting of the coöperation of the extractive industries in the public program may prove sufficient.

Where regulation has been given fair trial and has failed, natural resources should revert to public ownership. The latter makes possible the concentration of the extractive processes where geographically and economically most appropriate, and the conservation or replenishment of the remainder.

Increase of Production.—The total mass of distributable wealth can be greatly increased also through improvements in the system of production. It may seem superfluous to outline methods of increasing the volume of farm products in a nation in which many crops are not harvested or are ploughed under because of the lack of an adequate market. The elimination of poverty, however, requires an annual production of each crop sufficient to provide ample food and a varied dietary for each member of our population. Though this aim is to be met chiefly by improvements in the system of distribution, adequate standards in food, clothing, housing, and culture cannot be made available to all and maintained from year to year without many improvements in agricultural production as well.

A planned agricultural economy for maximum output per unit of labor would involve the raising of each crop in the most appropriate soil and climate under methods of cultivation which are scientific—involving crop rotation and the use as needed of machinery, fertilizers, and chemicals for insect control. Most farming operations are still unscientific in that they yield a needlessly low volume of high-grade product per unit of effort. Rural poverty, the absence of leisure time for the pursuit of cultural interests, and the much-too-general persistence of peasant standards in our contemporary civilization among poor whites as well as Negroes and immigrants, are traceable to prevalent systems of agriculture as well as to conditions of marketing. The answer may lie in building and perfecting the comprehensive educational program of our Federal and state departments of agriculture, state agricultural colleges and experiment stations, the policies for rural resettlement, farm credit, and marketing, in full collaboration with a developing national economic plan.

Prevention of Inefficiency in Manufacture.—There are abundant examples of inefficiency in the secondary industrial process known as manufacture, which takes over the products of the land and makes them into prepared foods, drugs, utensils, paper, furniture, building materials, machinery, or other goods. Outmoded methods of manufacture are widely characteristic of small shops and mills which in large part yield an insufficient annual income to their owners and workers. A planned economy which would utilize this scattered and wasted effort, under conditions where modern machinery and skilled management could apply it to best advantage, would increase prodigiously the volume of production per worker and per consumer.

Idle Patents.—The volume of distributable wealth could presumably be greatly increased by the utilization of patents for improved processes which for one reason or another are shelved or not yet in use. Doubtless a large percentage are idle because a backer cannot be found. Others have been purchased by leading industrial corporations to prevent their utilization. In a well-organized social order it would be impossible for a handful of individuals to deprive the mass of the population of potential utilities in this manner or to rob the inventor of the fruits of his discovery. The lag between discovery and general use is a source of tragedy to the inventor and needless deprivation to the potential consumer. Means should be found to give promising inventions a trial.[5]

Social Control of Inventions.—The stimulation of invention from public as well as private sources might increase rapidly the discovery of new materials and processes. For example, the building industry is still largely dependent upon traditional materials— lumber, brick, stone, and steel, and upon processes of construction which show few of the economies of the machine age. The stimulation of experimentation in the manufacture of synthetic building materials and new processes of construction might bring the prefabricated house, of three or four fully equipped rooms, within the reach of that third of our population who are now condemned by circumstances to dwell in housing grossly substandard and unwholesome. Over a hundred million dollars have been spent by the

[5] See Ogburn, W. F.—"The Influence of Invention and Discovery," Chapter III of Vol. I, *Recent Social Trends in the United States.*

Federal government in its program for the housing of industrial workers by present inefficient and outmoded methods. Conceivably the investment of a small fraction of this sum in the invention or testing of new materials and processes would make possible a superior type of single-family housing at lower unit cost and with much lower ultimate expenditure by the public treasury.[6]

A general recognition that the products of invention belong to mankind might facilitate the rapid development of devices which increase the volume of distributable wealth. The public program in question might comprise: *first*, the stimulation of invention through specialized education and publicity; *second*, the provision of public experimental laboratories; *third*, reasonable salaries to persons whose projects are promising, to cover the period of their experimentation, to be supplemented by providing the equipment necessary for their researches, and special pensions for their later years; *fourth*, legislation to prevent the "killing" of patents by private individuals or corporations—restoring each patent to the government or owner after the expiration of a reasonable number of months or years in which the corporation has demonstrated that it will not make use of it; *fifth*, the possibility of sale of such patents or discoveries by the government to private industry, after proper advertising that is reasonably effective in reaching potential purchasers; *sixth*, the utilization of funds thus acquired by the government to finance its own experimental laboratories or develop its own manufacture for patents which private industry fails to utilize, or which, as in the case of some costly drugs or medicines, offer no profit in private sale and require subsidized distribution.

By some such policy, thus briefly suggested, it should be possible without undue burden upon the government to make available to the general population a vast array of goods and services not now available which will help materially in their escape from poverty.

Wastes in Production.—The volume of distributable wealth can be further increased by elimination of needless wastes in production, distribution, and human effort. Wastes in production were studied at great length many years ago by a special committee of the Federated American Engineering Societies. Their findings

[6] Developments in prefabrication are covered in current architectural journals. See, for example, *The Architectural Forum*, October, 1936, and April, 1937. See also Federal Housing Administration—*Recent Developments in Dwelling Construction;* Technical Bulletin No. 1, revised June 1, 1936, Government Printing Office, 1936.

are still largely pertinent. Waste was found to be attributable to (1) faulty management of materials, plant, equipment, and men; (2) interruptions of production caused by the idleness of materials, plants, equipment, or men; (3) intentional restrictions of production whether caused by owners, management, or labor; and (4) lost production caused by ill health, physical defects, and industrial accidents. It was found that over fifty per cent of the responsibility for waste in six industries studied was chargeable to management and less than twenty-five per cent to labor. [7] To management are ascribable the losses occasioned by waiting for work and material, haphazard planning, speculative purchasing of raw materials, defective control of design, lack of standardization of products, lack of essential equipment, faulty labor control with consequent high labor turnover, faulty sales policies leading to cancellation of orders, and deterioration or obsolescence of idle materials, plants, and equipment.

To eliminate such wastes planned managerial control should extend to every factor and activity within the plant "reaching materials, design, equipment, personnel, production, costs and sales policies and coördinating these factors to a common objective." [8] Much research is needed to base productive capacity upon demand, to reduce wastes from cancellations of orders, and to curtail the privilege of returning goods ordered and received, to correlate production schedules with sales policies, and to maintain workable relations with labor.

Business is all too frequently conducted in a manner which is shockingly unbusinesslike and governed by "hunches," prejudices, and chance opportunities and contacts. The elimination of this type of waste rests with owners and their executives. In so far as business and industry can be taught to recognize that their function is a public trust to be performed in the public service with maximum care and skill, the problem can be met within the existing industrial order.

If industry could be rendered aware of the fact that the violation of such trust, through wastes and imperfections in the service rendered, is a primary source of the demand for the socialization of

---

[7] Federated American Engineering Societies, Committee on Elimination of Waste in Industry—*Waste in Industry*, p. 9; McGraw-Hill Book Company, Inc., 1921.

[8] *Ibid.*, p. 24.

industry, chambers of commerce and manufacturers' associations might feel impelled to solve the problem. The trend toward government interference and to public ownership is, by now, so general and so strong that there can be little question that public enterprise will sooner or later replace private ownership and operation wherever the latter fails sufficiently to consider the interest of either labor or the consumer. If capital and industry can recognize this condition in time, and improve their methods sufficiently, America may escape extensive collectivism and any hardships which the transition period might entail.

The challenge is now definitely before the world of industry and power, but is as yet grasped by few. Meanwhile little can be done by the Federal government to eliminate wastes of the types just outlined except through the extension and perfection of its information and statistical services, the facilitation of types of industrial combination necessary to reduce wastes, and the framing of measures for the protection of labor.

Wastes in Distribution.—There are many needless wastes in the contemporary system of distribution. Federal tariff policy, for example, may artificially stimulate industry in locations where it has no justification. Tariffs on imported necessaries of life reduce the purchasing power of the consumer's dollar for other desirable goods. Viewed on strictly economic, as distinguished from political and nationalistic grounds, the removal of tariff barriers and the development of free international trade would have the initial effect of increasing the amount of goods which the annual income of most American laborers could buy. Nevertheless, until free trade becomes general, the "pauper" competition of importations of necessaries, produced by foreign labor with vastly lower standards of living, may on nationalistic grounds justify the retention of many of the tariffs on imported necessaries, for protection of the American wage-scale. On international or humanitarian grounds—or on the basis of a world economy as distinguished from a national economy—tariff barriers have no ultimate justification and can be defended only so long as the probability of international wars renders national industrial self-sufficiency essential.

Distributive wastes include also losses in transportation whether by sea or land, by merchant marine, railroad, truck, or airplane. Defects in service cause losses to the producer through delays, breakage, shrinkage of bulk, spoiling of perishable goods, or otherwise. They usually increase the unit cost of the product to the buyer. This field is definitely one for action on the part of producers' organizations, shippers, and government alike. Research, followed by judicious and appropriate extension of public control, is resulting in gradual improvements in our colossal network of transportation services and may thus progressively reduce wastes. Judicious decentralization of functions that are strictly local within a system of highly centralized public control, competently informed, and empowered by law, will conceivably keep wastes from this source low without much immediate extension of public ownership.

Other wastes in distribution include excessive overhead costs for both commercial and consumer credit, costs of inappropriate advertising—in fact costs of all advertising and carrying charges on goods that are of little or no value to the consumer purchaser—and excessive costs for display and delivery of goods.

Perhaps the most serious of all the wastes caused is that of deterioration. Goods may decay or deteriorate for any of a large number of reasons, some of which are traceable to management and others to the buying public. Miscalculation of demand may lead the manager to overpurchase. Inadequate storage or display space, imperfect equipment for refrigeration or protection from dampness or heat, from insects or from fire, cause huge aggregate losses on goods which never reach the consumer. The latter consequently tends in the long run to meet this loss by paying higher unit prices for the goods he actually buys. Though many department stores reduce progressively their prices on damaged or slow-moving stock until a purchaser can be found, and although others may unload such stock at sacrifice prices to inferior cut-rate firms, thus giving the consumer opportunity to purchase at a price satisfactory to himself, there is still enormous loss to both the producer and the consumer from needless deterioration. This may be particularly apparent in the handling of perishable foods, such as fruits and vegetables.

Prevention of Wastes in Distribution.—A well-organized social economy, after applying every effort to the prevention of such losses, would find a means to make ripe perishables accessible at reasonable prices to families at or near the poverty line. It is not clear whether this can be accomplished without public interference. The presumption is against it, because of the immense difficulty of organizing the very large numbers of provision merchants, large and small, immigrant and native, under a unified system of self-operated control. Moreover, the spread of management training among all provision merchants would be rendered exceedingly slow if not impossible by the ignorance or lack of adequate schooling on the part of large numbers of the keepers of basement or small neighborhood shops in the industrial quarters of our cities. Rigorous sanitary inspection of shops, under health and food laws properly enforced, can eliminate the worst of such shops and the most dangerous of the goods which they carry, but cannot succeed in getting rid of all unwholesome food nor in preventing wastes.

Consumer Organization.—In the absence of organization for the control of food distribution in the public interest, the chief means for consumer self-protection would appear to be coöperative organization. Modern coöperation is essentially democratic. Its effective practice dates from the adoption of a specific business and social policy drawn up in 1844 by a group of twenty-eight flannel weavers in Rochdale, England. This policy, with minor changes, is now applied by coöperators throughout the world.

The Rochdale principles were: (1) open membership with shares of low denomination—usually at £1 or $5 each and payable by instalments, so as to be within the reach of all; (2) limitation of the amount of shares to be held by any one member, to prevent wide inequality in financial status of members; (3) democratic government, each member to have but one vote, irrespective of the number of shares that he or she may hold; (4) pure goods, fair measure, and sale at prevailing market price, to avoid arousing needlessly the destructive hostility of local merchants; (5) cash sales, to avoid loss through delayed payments and uncollectable accounts, to reduce bookkeeping costs, and to ensure wholesale purchase of stock for cash on most advantageous terms; (6) payment of not more than five per cent interest on shares, the rest of the profits, after deduction for depreciation and reserve, to go partly to an educational fund, partly to charity, and the remainder to be distributed to purchasers whether members or not, in proportion to their trade at the store. Today, coöperative trade in Great Britain, though still dominated by wage-earners, amounts to over a billion dollars per year. [9]

[9] Fay, C. R.—*Cooperation at Home and Abroad;* P. S. King & Son, Ltd., 1920. Gide, Charles—*Consumers' Cooperative Societies;* Alfred A. Knopf, 1922. Warbasse, James P.—*Cooperative Democracy;* The Macmillan Company, 1923.   Baker, Jacob—*Co-operative Enterprise;* Vanguard Press, Inc., 1937.   Elliott, Sydney R.— *The English Cooperatives;* Yale University Press, 1937. See also publications of the American Institute of Cooperation, Washington, D. C., the International Co-

Through the coöperative movement in European countries organized consumers have been able to establish their own standards and grades for goods consumed, to buy in the most advantageous market, to make expensive advertising unnecessary through membership loyalty to the store and advertising by word of mouth rather than by billboards and newspaper pages. They have been able to keep the overhead costs of bad debts and collections to an absolute minimum by prohibiting credit beyond the amount of the value of the shares of stock held. They have been able to keep down the cost of delivery either by charging extra for each delivery or by inducing "cash and carry" trade as a matter of loyalty to the shop. They have kept losses from deterioration at a minimum, both by agreeing in members' meetings upon a limited number of brands to be carried—thus keeping stock from being too multifarious and slow-moving—and by charging whatever price is necessary, no matter how low, to dispose of perishable goods.

In the countries where the coöperative movement is most highly developed, as in England, the massed purchasing power of some twenty million individuals has made it possible to establish and maintain fair prices of goods. More significant still is the success of the British coöperative movement in maintaining a trade union minimum wage for labor in private factories from which they buy— a power which they can enforce through the threat of establishing their own rival factory wherever producers will not come to their terms.

Considerable additional waste in our distributive system may lie in the large number of intermediaries who have to be supported between the producer and the consumer. These include buyers, jobbers, wholesalers, and salesmen, who are looked upon by the coöperative movement as leeches upon the consumer. It may be argued by traditional economics that these intermediaries could not exist for long unless they serve a useful purpose. Nevertheless, in coöperative enterprise the road from producer to consumer has often been made much shorter, with consequent saving to the latter in spite of reasonable prices to the former. For consumer organizations make it possible for their representatives to deal directly with the producer or the producer's coöperative organization. The goods may thus reach the consumer more quickly and

operative Alliance, London, and of the Cooperative Union, Manchester, England.

with less loss from breakage and deterioration and some, though not all, intermediate profits are eliminated.

The resurgence of the coöperative movement in recent years in America suggests the possibility of considerable savings in the wastes of distribution. For success, such coöperation requires loyalty to the coöperative association of which one is a member, not only during the early and most difficult years but also throughout its history. This loyalty must be expressed in concentrating the family's trade through the coöperative store, in attendance at business meetings, and in the study and practice of the Rochdale principles of coöperation. Otherwise the consumers' representative—the salaried manager of the store—will sooner or later become a self-seeking dictator to the disadvantage of the members, or will buy them out and replace the benefits of coöperation with the traditional less desirable features of profit-seeking trade. Coöperation is possible only to the "coöperative man." It will succeed if wisely guided and if facilitated by appropriate special legislation in each of our forty-eight states. Relaxation of the insistence upon the study and practice of coöperative principles is the nemesis of this movement. The utilization of this device to eliminate wastes in distribution is thus dependent upon continuously wise leadership.[10]

Wasteful Distribution of Talent.—There is much needless waste occasioned by the faulty distribution of human effort. If each person could be employed at the tasks for which he is best equipped by nature, the total volume of wealth would be much increased. It would be still further increased if he should be trained to make the best possible use of his native talent and were then placed where his work would count for most. There would be still further increases if he were equipped with the best possible tools for the type of work at which he would be engaged.

Under existing conditions, as has already been shown, few men have opportunity to discover their native capacities. Even where abilities are discovered, those who possess them are seldom properly trained and placed. Boys or girls leaving school are likely to take the first job that is offered and are usually constrained, by their poverty or by their lack of initiative, to continue at such work rather than to risk unemployment while seeking a job more appropriate to their talents or interest. Even those few who succeed in

[10] Daniels, John—*Cooperation: An American Way;* Covici Friede, 1938.

leaving the home town for a more favorable labor market are still limited in their choice of occupation by lack of vocational analysis, vocational education, and vocational placement based upon their native abilities.

Most persons appear to have many and various talents sufficient in number and type so that they are capable of being trained for more than one occupation. The findings of the science of genetics make it clear that each individual is also unique in his combination of traits and capacities.[11] It is possible, to say the least, that out of this "margin of uniqueness" there is some special contribution to human welfare which could be made by each person. It is probable that each would contribute vastly more to the total volume of distributable wealth if his capacities could first be ascertained and if special training were given to him with reference to them.

On the other hand, it must be recognized that the placement of labor should be determined also by demand, that is, by the need, actual or potential, for the kind of services which one can perform. Since men have varied abilities and since employment requirements may already be met in certain of the fields in which individuals are capable of serving, it may be socially desirable that one's major training be built about others of his native capacities.

Hence the presumptive capacities of each individual should be periodically ascertained by analysis. Intensive education might be given him for appropriate training in fields for which there is an active demand. He would still have opportunity through evening schools [12] to keep alive and develop some if not all of his other capacities, so that with shifting demand for labor or with display on his own part of exceptional competence he would be likely in time to build his workaday life about his deepest interests and special gifts. His technical training should be so combined with training in economic geography and the labor market that he would be able roughly to gauge the preferable geographical locations for his employment. An adequate system of vocational placement, in coöperation with a national system of public employment offices, should make it possible to keep him informed of shifts in the labor market and of vocational opportunities for men possessed with his

[11] Quoted in an earlier chapter—see Part II, Chapter V.

[12] In Metropolitan Boston a list of about four thousand such approved courses is compiled annually by the Prospect Union Educational Exchange, Cambridge, Massachusetts, under the title *Educational Opportunities of Greater Boston: A Selective List of Day and Evening Classes and Home Study Courses for Adults.*

type of skill, thus giving him a chance to improve his condition when circumstances warrant.

A complete nation-wide system of vocational analysis would have the additional advantage of discovering individuals with executive or managerial capacity [13] or with special aptitude for public service. It seems likely that these latter occupations require all-around ability combined with special traits of temperament, personality, and character.

Training for Leadership.—Since a policy for the elimination of poverty will inevitably make heavy demands upon commerce and industry and each of the units of government, Federal, state, and municipal, this program in all its ramifications could readily absorb all of the executive ability that can be discovered and trained. It is presumably true that there is always room at the top for persons who can demonstrate greater talent than has been shown by their predecessors. But for each highly competent executive there are required large numbers of subexecutives, salesmen, promoters, research experts, accountants, editors, bankers and other specialists in finance, and so on through a lengthy list, upon whose outstanding capacities in their specialized fields the executive or the government officer is exceedingly dependent. The prevention of waste of human effort is thus largely contingent also upon the discovery and training of leadership, and upon increasing greatly the number of men of initiative and judgment who can create profitable employment for the less gifted remainder of the population.

QUESTIONS FOR DISCUSSION OR EXAMINATION

1. How can wasteful exploitation of natural resources best be prevented?
2. How can inefficiency in manufacture best be overcome?
3. How can the fruits of inventions best be brought under social control and abuse of patents obviated, without reduction of inventiveness?
4. How can wastes in production best be prevented?
5. How can industry develop a sense of trusteeship for the common welfare?
6. How can wastes in distribution be prevented?
7. What are the sources of economic strength in the coöperative movement?
8. How can wasteful distribution of human talent be overcome?

---

[13] "Seven distinct aptitudes have been isolated and can be measured. . . . Two others can be approximated, and some evidence of the existence of six additional ones has been obtained. Major executives score high in a wide range of these diverse characteristics." O'Connor, Johnson—*Psychometrics: A Study of Psychological Measurements*, pp. xxii, *et seq.*; Harvard University Press, 1934.

PROBLEMS FOR INDIVIDUAL STUDY

1. Report on existing measures and achievements—Federal, state, or municipal—to conserve natural resources.
2. Report on evidences of social pathology and social disorganization within a selected trade or industry.
3. Analysis of (a) the trends of invention, (b) the social consequences of invention, or (c) the social control of invention.
4. Analysis of the principles of consumer coöperation, and their application in some selected coöperative society or in the coöperative organizations of a selected area.

SUGGESTIONS FOR SUPPLEMENTARY READINGS

Baker, O. E.—"Agricultural and Forest Land," Part 2 of Chapter II, "Utilization of Natural Wealth," *Recent Social Trends in the United States*, Vol. I; McGraw-Hill Book Company, Inc., 1933.

Berle, Adolf A., Jr., and Means, Gardiner C.—*The Modern Corporation and Private Property;* The Macmillan Company, 1933.

Black, John D., and Black, A. G.—*Production Organization;* Henry Holt and Company, 1929.

Carver, Thomas Nixon—*Essays in Social Justice;* Harvard University Press, 1925.

Chase, Stuart—*The Economy of Abundance;* The Macmillan Company, 1934.

Chase, Stuart—*Government in Business;* The Macmillan Company, 1935.

Chase, Stuart—*The Tragedy of Waste;* The Macmillan Company, 1929.

Clark, Colin—*National Income and Outlay;* The Macmillan Company, 1937.

Copeland, Morris A.—"The National Income and Its Distribution," Chapter XII of *Recent Economic Changes in the United States*, Vol. II; published for the National Bureau of Economic Research, Inc., by McGraw-Hill Book Company, Inc., 1929.

Cowling, Ellis—*Cooperatives in America: Their Past, Present and Future;* Coward-McCann, 1938.

East, Edward M.—*Mankind at the Crossroads;* Charles Scribner's Sons, 1926.

Fairchild, Henry Pratt—*Profits or Prosperity?;* Harper & Brothers, 1932.

Fay, C. R.—*Cooperation at Home and Abroad;* P. S. King & Son, Ltd., 1920.

Federated American Engineering Societies, Committee on Elimination of Waste in Industry—*Waste in Industry;* McGraw-Hill Book Company, Inc., 1921.

Gay, Edwin F., and Wolman, Leo—"Trends in Economic Organization," Chapter V of *Recent Social Trends in the United States*, Vol. I; McGraw-Hill Book Company, Inc., 1933.

Gide, Charles—*Consumers' Coöperative Societies;* Alfred A. Knopf, 1922.

Goodrich, Carter, Allin, Bushrod W., and Hayes, Marion—*Migration and Planes of Living; 1920–1934;* University of Pennsylvania Press, 1935.

Gragg, Mabel Taylor, in collaboration with Borden, Neil H.—*Merchandise Testing as a Guide to Consumer Buying;* Publications of the Graduate School of Business Administration, George F. Baker Foundation, Harvard University, Vol. XXV, No. 6, Business Research Studies No. 22, 1938.

Hellman, Florence S.—"A Selected List of Recent References on Economic Planning, with a Section on Economic Councils"; Library of Congress, Division of Bibliography, 1935.

Hobson, J. A.—*The Science of Wealth;* Henry Holt and Company, 1911.

Holcombe, Arthur N.—*Government in a Planned Democracy;* W. W. Norton & Company, Inc., 1935.

Houser, J. David—*What the Employer Thinks;* Harvard University Press, 1927.

Johnson, Gerald W.—*The Wasted Land;* University of North Carolina Press, 1937.

Laidler, Harry W.—*Concentration of Control in American Industry;* Thomas Y. Crowell Company, 1931.

Laidler, Harry W.—*A Program for Modern America;* Thomas Y. Crowell Company, 1936.

Lewisohn, Sam A.—*The New Leadership in Industry;* E. P. Dutton & Co., 1926.

Macartney, C. A.—*Social and Economic Planning;* League of Nations Union (London), No. 383, 1935.

McNair, Malcolm P., and Lewis, Howard T., editors—*Business and Modern Society;* Harvard University Press, 1938.

Martin, P. W.—"Some Aspects of Economic Planning," pp. 313–354 of *Economic Essays in Honor of Wesley Clair Mitchell;* Columbia University Press, 1935.

Merriam, Charles E.—*The Role of Politics in Social Change;* Oxford University Press, 1936.

Mills, Ogden L.—*What of Tomorrow?;* The Macmillan Company, 1935.

Nourse, Edwin G., and Associates—*America's Capacity to Produce;* The Brookings Institution, 1934.

O'Connor, Johnson—*Psychometrics: A Study of Psychological Measurements;* Harvard University Press, 1934.

Ogburn, W. F.—"The Influence of Invention and Discovery," Chapter III of *Recent Social Trends in the United States,* Vol. I; McGraw-Hill Book Company, Inc., 1933.

Page, Kirby—*Individualism and Socialism;* Farrar & Rinehart, Inc., 1933.

Parmelee, Maurice—*Farewell to Poverty;* John Wiley & Sons, Inc., 1935.

Pigors, Paul—*Leadership or Domination;* Houghton Mifflin Company, 1935.

Ryan, John A.—*Distributive Justice: The Right and Wrong of Our Present Distribution of Wealth;* The Macmillan Company, revised edition, 1927.

Taylor, Horace—*Contemporary Problems in the United States,* two volumes; Harcourt, Brace and Company, Inc., fifth annual revision, 1936–1937.

Tryon, F. G., and Schoenfeld, Margaret H.—"Mineral and Power Resources," Part 1 of Chapter II, "Utilization of Natural Wealth," *Recent Social Trends in the United States,* Vol. I; McGraw-Hill Book Company, Inc., 1933.

Tugwell, Rexford G.—*The Battle for Democracy;* Columbia University Press, 1935.

Tugwell, Rexford Guy, Munro, Thomas, and Stryker, Roy E.—*American Economic Life and the Means of Its Improvement;* Harcourt, Brace and Company, Inc., revised edition, 1930.

Van Hise, Charles—*The Conservation of Our Natural Resources;* The Macmillan Company, revised edition (under the editorship of Loomis Havemeyer), 1930.

Van Kleeck, Mary—*Creative America; Its Resources for Social Security;* Covici Friede, 1936.

Warbasse, James P.—*Cooperative Democracy;* The Macmillan Company, 1923.

Zimmermann, Erich W.—*World Resources and Industries;* Harper & Brothers, 1933.

CHAPTER XXVI

LOW INCOME: THE REDISTRIBUTION OF WEALTH

The Uneven Distribution of Wealth.—Many argue that the chief cause of poverty is the uneven distribution of wealth since the poor, in spite of our large national income, are persons with inadequate means. In a nation in which a majority of the population can leave at death no property to their families and descendants, save for a few personal effects of slight value, while others leave estates valued at millions of dollars, the disparity in property ownership is apparent.

Nevertheless, as has already been pointed out, both the wealth and the income of the well-to-do are largely invested in ways which make continuance of industrial plants and machinery and increased production possible. Without the services which they render as the unofficial custodians of the greater part of the national income the whole nation would shortly be plunged into general poverty. Assuming therefore that the system of private ownership of capital and private exploitation of industry, commerce, and finance must be continued until a system clearly better, and at least equally productive, can be devised, our problem is to determine how it is possible under the existing system to redistribute wealth in such a manner as may best serve humanity through the values it creates.

Measures for Redistribution.—Such a program involves consideration of a variety of devices to recapture for the public treasury, and thus presumably for the general advantage, the excess in large fortunes.

The first group of measures seeks by taxation to seize excess personal wealth or income and to use it for the public welfare. It comprises progressive income taxes, progressive inheritance taxes, luxury taxes, and either land taxation or devices for the social appropriation of certain increments to land values.

A second group of measures operating at the opposite end of our economic structure is concerned with improvements in our methods of industrial remuneration. Of these the most promising device appears to be minimum-wage legislation, so framed that each indus-

436

trial worker may receive an income sufficient to make possible a reasonable standard of living for himself and his family.

A third group of measures, refusing to accept industrial regulation, would meet the problem by some type of government subsidy to workers, either through the family allowance system, rent subsidies, or other unearned benefits.

A fourth group of measures approaches the problem from the point of view of the workingman as consumer rather than as producer, and seeks to protect him from exploitation in his purchase of goods and credit. This program comprises legislation with regard to weights and measures, standards and brands, labels and advertising, as well as laws to prohibit or check usury, eliminate the loan shark, and encourage sound agencies for credit and thrift.

A fifth group of devices, alleviative rather than fundamental, but still in the mass not unimportant, comprises measures initiated by the employer for the welfare of his employees.

Lastly there are many programs which provide for the workingman and his family, at public expense, facilities and services which he would otherwise have to meet out of his income or do without— covering fire, police, and health protection, free public schooling, adult education, parks, playgrounds, libraries, museums, and a lengthy list of other recreational and cultural opportunities.

Unless a solution can be found within the present industrial order for the hardships it occasions to those whose wealth is least and whose incomes are low, it is inevitable that one form or another of collectivism will sooner or later displace it. It is therefore essential that the nature and potentials of these alternatives to socialism should be fairly appraised.

Should Wealth Be Equalized?—Few persons, even among the leaders of radical thought, argue for complete equalization of wealth. For it is now recognized that men are not "born equal" in intelligence or capacity. The range in native intelligence is from idiocy to genius. Moreoever the contribution which each person may make by his labor is dependent not only upon his mental endowment but also upon the conditions of his effort—the appropriateness of the medium of his service. Men who hold important offices or carry heavy responsibilities may, on occasion, be more productive if they dwell in large houses, have employees, motor cars, and other facilities which poor men would term luxuries. Such extra facilities are not for "show" but are apparatus necessary to

the job in question, and hence may be publicly owned and transferred with the office to the next incumbent. Persons less gifted can
perform their less responsible services just as effectively if they live in
smaller quarters and have access to a considerably lower proportionate share of the state's distributable wealth.

The extreme inequalities in either wealth or income which America displays are justified by few who have given the matter real
thought. For it is readily seen that some persons fortuitously
receive incomes much larger than would be necessary to stimulate
their utmost creative effort, while at the other end of the scale
there are highly capable persons whose productivity is definitely
thwarted by the smallness of the reward for their labor. The latter
include not only many professional workers who are unable to
purchase tools needed in their labor, whether instruments, books,
adequate laboratories, or offices, cars, clothes, or travel, but also
competent laboring men, farmers, and shopkeepers who are unable
to provide adequate homes and higher education for themselves
and their more gifted children. Disparities in wealth are clearly
too pronounced.

Optimum Standards of Living.—Ideally, each individual should
receive that income which would make it possible for him and all
members of his family to live on their most creative level. This does
not mean equality of income, but rather equality of opportunity in
the sense that all wealth or income factors which now block any
individual's development should be removed. A Thoreau may make
his best contribution to American literature when possessing only a
primitive log cabin, meager self-made furniture, and a small library
of well-chosen books. A John Ruskin may have to be surrounded
with costly works of art to attain greatest productivity.

All persons need housing that is sanitary, safe, and wholesome,
with enough rooms to provide all necessary privacy for each member
of the family. All persons should have enough food, wholesome,
palatable, and in sufficient variety to nourish them properly and
give them good health and zest for work. All persons require sufficient clothing to provide for health and comfort in each season, and
to meet the reasonable demands of their occupation and social
groups. Without such universal minimum standards of life their
productivity and their contribution to total national wealth, are
restricted, and development, to attain their full potentials, is
thwarted.

The social obligation of an enlightened nation to its citizens does not end here, since each citizen's income should provide for his own security from dependency in case of ill health, accident, old age, unemployment, and for the family's security in the event of his death, until social provision against these eventualities has been rendered both universal and adequate. Moreover such recreation as is necessary to develop the body and keep it fit is essential to all, irrespective of age or sex. The income should make it possible to meet all obligations of social life and to participate properly in the activities of professional associations, church, and state. It should provide education for each member of the family as long as he can profit by it so that skills and capacities may be continuously developed. Hence, it should make possible the purchase of necessary books, periodicals, equipment, and travel.

Family needs in these regards vary greatly, but what is known as the minimum standard of decency is the lowest standard at which the factors thwarting development can be removed. Even this standard is usually unattainable in the homes of unskilled labor. Unquestionably a fair percentage of our population, especially in the professions and executive or subexecutive positions, would require appropriately individualized "luxury" standards to make possible their maximum output. Presumably few attain them.

Private Sources of Supplementation.—Recognizing this problem many employers have attempted to supplement the meager wages paid their employees by welfare work, pensions, and other devices under their own control. Though this has sometimes been done to bind the employee to the plant and sap his bargaining power for increased wages, it has often been undertaken with earnestness and good faith. It can never be a general solution, however, both because some employers will be unwilling to undertake it and because employers on the margin of production will be quite unable to do so.

Private philanthropy also has, in a definite sense, supplemented industrial wages by its medical charities, settlement houses, and other endowed institutions for health, recreation, and culture. Such services may genuinely ease or positively help the lives of their recipients. But since there is no guarantee or even likelihood of universality in these supplementary services, they cannot offer a solution of the problem of the redistribution of wealth. They are alleviative, not fundamental; temporarily helpful, but not a major factor in the ultimate policy for the banishment of poverty.

Public Policy for Redistribution by Taxation of Incomes.—
Universality of provision for citizens' needs therefore necessitates
public intervention. Such a policy involves the regulation of industrial remuneration, the reduction of excessive disparities in wealth,
and the effective redistribution of the surpluses socially expropriated.
Since the former are in many details dependent upon the forms taken
by the latter, it is better to examine first the program for the control
of surplus wealth and income.

The major device for both Federal and state governments to recapture excess wealth is the progressive income tax. This may bring
to the public treasury a reasonable percentage of income at the
medium ranges, a much larger percentage in the upper ranges, but
no tax at all from the laborer. Obviously such measures are dependent upon the government's success in discovering actual income and
in collecting its share. The share of income exacted from the rich is
not determined with reference to the needs of the family that receives it (aside from the standard allowance made for dependents),
but solely with reference to the amount of that income. If the government appropriates too large a percentage of the incomes of the
most highly competent entrepreneurs or investors, the former may
be deprived of their incentive to produce and the latter may turn
from investment in socially necessary private production to investment in tax-free government bonds. In either instance the further
production of wealth is restricted. In extreme cases it might be put
to a stop altogether.

If necessary, for fiscal reasons, it is probable that a much larger
percentage of the higher incomes could be taken by the government
of this country, following the precedents of England and France. It is
impossible, however, to gauge with a high degree of accuracy how
largely entrepreneurs and investors would be deflected from socially
valuable enterprise by such a procedure. If less damaging alternative fiscal devices can be perfected, enterprise and thus wealth production would suffer no danger of retardation, while fiscal needs
might be met equally well. Ideally, income taxes should be sufficiently progressive to provide needed revenue but should never
thwart socially desirable expansion of production.

Taxation of Inheritances.—Progressive inheritance taxes of both
the Federal and state governments seek to exact a percentage of
wealth rather than of income. Less immediate damage is done to
enterprise by public expropriation of the major part of large in-

herited fortunes than by the seizure in the form of taxes of an equal percentage of income. Inherited wealth possibly does actual harm to irresponsible recipients. Incentives to effort might be greater on the part of many beneficiaries of wills if no person were to receive a lump sum of more than $200,000 or an annuity of more than $10,000, from any one source or even from all sources combined. The testator by such limited gifts or annuities would be able to protect those whom he holds dear from poverty, and from the dangers to character inherent in the possession of unearned capital or income. Colossal difficulties would have to be surmounted to put such a plan in practice, to establish comity between Federal and state taxation, to prevent violations of the spirit of the law by the establishment of trusts or gifts prior to death, and so to individualize its application while following the letter of the law that neither the government nor the beneficiary would suffer.

The major arguments against the extreme limitation of inheritance noted above would be: *first*, that it might reduce the incentives of our capitalists and industrialists, many of whom work chiefly to build a family fortune; *second*, that it would force the sale of family-owned plants to meet the government taxes and correspondingly might induce loss in good will, in the competence of management, and in output; *third*, that it would largely preclude the use of inheritances as private capital and thus might rob society of many ingenious or useful enterprises; *fourth*, that it would reduce the number and size of private foundations for research and social welfare, the perpetuation of which still seems essential in certain fields of experimentation and social action.

The whole social process leading to maximum wealth production combined with justice in distribution would thus seem to involve discovery of sound means of making inheritance taxes and income taxes increasingly progressive while keeping them from becoming unduly so.

Luxury and Personalty Taxation.—Luxury taxes if they could yield enough revenue to permit the untaxing of necessaries, might accomplish a little in the direction of the redistribution of wealth. But they are difficult to define and apply. A motor car may be a necessary for one family and a luxury for another. No effective and equitable means has yet been found for individualizing taxation. Attempts to accomplish this same end by means of taxation of personal property, which may be quite unrelated to income, likewise tend to be both exceedingly difficult and unfair.

Land and Increment Taxation.—The municipal government can contribute to the process of the redistribution of wealth chiefly through its policy with reference to the taxation of land and improvements. Many huge fortunes and large percentages of other fortunes have been derived from and perpetuated by the rent of land. In urban communities, as distinguished from agricultural areas, increases in land values and income from the sale of the land, though legally "earned," are from the broad social and economic point of view largely if not wholly unearned. In so far as the municipality can actually distinguish those increments to land values which are socially created—that is, created by the presence of population, by the increase of population, or by the efforts of others rather than the owner—it would wisely and justly seize them for the common treasury.[1]

The expedient of untaxing improvements, thus deriving all taxation from the land, has so far never worked out to entire satisfaction. Increment taxation to date has been timid and has brought to the public treasury only a small fraction of the unearned income of land. Obviously further research is necessary to find ways to bring to the municipal treasury the whole of the unearned increment to land values without frightening legitimate investment in land, or stampeding or mulcting recent bona fide investors. If it can be done it may have the beneficent result of preventing too rapid extension of municipal ownership and management. For the only alternative is rapid municipalization of land which would, when rented by the municipality, bring to its coffers all subsequent increases in land rental and thus the income which is derived from the socially created increments to its value.

Assuming that by progressive inheritance and income taxes, increment and luxury taxes, government succeeds in securing a reasonable percentage of excess fortunes and unearned wealth without robbing industry of its incentive to productiveness, the problem yet remains to determine how such funds can best be utilized to level up standards of living at the lower end of our economic scale.

Governmental Measures to Raise Living Standards.—The first essential for any unit of government, Federal, state, county, or municipal, is to make sure that its own wage-scales are adequate

---

[1] See Chapter XVIII. Also Taussig, F. W.—*Principles of Economics*, especially Vol. I, Chapter 43 on "Urban Site Rent," and Vol. II, Book VIII on "Taxation"; The Macmillan Company, 1911–13.

for unskilled and semiskilled labor. Altogether well over three million of the persons engaged in gainful occupations are direct employees of one branch or another of government.[2] By determining what constitutes the minimum wage essential to wholesome and developmental living, and by establishing such wage as the minimum wage for all government employees for the area to which each given standard applies, the Federal and local governments could not only eliminate poverty for the seven per cent of our population in gainful occupations which they directly employ but would also set proper standards for private industry to follow.

Since the cost of living is not uniform throughout the nation, but varies with geographical location and climate, the minimum wage should be determined with reference to a standard budget scientifically worked out. The cost of the factors which make up this budget should be ascertained for each community and periodically revised in accordance with changes in prevailing prices. Relatively little attention has been paid to this problem up to this time by state, county, and municipal governments. Through the establishment of scientifically determined minimum wages for labor by each type of government, and through the rigorous enforcement of such standards material progress in the reduction of poverty is now possible.

Services at Public Expense as Supplementation of Wages.—
At the same time each unit of government can promote higher standards of living for everyone by providing at public expense certain services for which the family now pays out of its wage. Such services would include, in addition to the prevalent free public schooling, opportunities for continuing adult education in both vocational and cultural subjects. To supplement the state agricultural and mechanical colleges, state and municipal universities, and public evening schools, there is needed the type of university extension now afforded by the Extension Division of the Massachusetts State Board of Education,[3]

[2] *Statistical Abstract of the United States 1936*, pp. 156–157, and 333; Government Printing Office, 1936. If to this total are added the employees of the W.P.A., C.C.C., N.Y.A., and R.F.C. for their various work projects the number of Federal employees alone in March, 1938 was over 4,400,000 and the total for all units of government over 6,000,000. U. S. Bureau of Labor Statistics—*Employment and Pay Rolls*, p. 6 of Serial No. R751; Government Printing Office, March, 1938.

[3] James A. Moyer, Director of the Division of University Extension, Department of Education of the Commonwealth of Massachusetts, in a letter dated April 22, 1937, states that there are roughly two hundred and twenty correspondence courses now offered in addition to about five hundred courses that are offered in classes in the various cities and towns of the state.

which will make possible correspondence courses for individuals anywhere in the state and group courses as well on any subject for which a half-dozen class members can be found. This task will not be completely accomplished until any person, irrespective of geographical location, shall find it possible at public expense to develop any capacity with which he may have been endowed and to secure as much education as his mentality permits.

Living standards can be raised also by a wide variety of recreational opportunities of types which each of our units of government is already beginning to provide. National, state, and municipal park and forest systems with free well-supervised camp sites, beaches, interconnecting highways, playgrounds, recreation piers, gymnasiums, and facilities for outdoor sport have made a good beginning. They are meagerly supplemented by sporadic municipal art centers, auditoriums, operas, symphonies, pageants, and drama. The service of human needs has been met only scantily.

The problem will not be solved until each individual can secure at public expense any recreational or cultural opportunity essential to his health, his well-being, or his development. The highest type of civilization cannot be attained until all factors which block development have been removed and until each individual is provided at each stage in his life with the opportunity and the incentive not only for good health, which is the precondition of growth, but also the opportunity to take the next steps in his own development.

The third point at which the family's minimum wage can wisely be supplemented from the government's enhanced income lies in the field of social security. Few families, if any, have incomes sufficient to meet all the calamities which might befall them. But the distribution of the burden entailed by the possibilities of early death, accident, prolonged illness, undeserved unemployment, or major disasters, is possible through social insurance on a nation-wide scale, as has already been indicated. The mere pensioning of public employees who have been retired is not enough. The only reasonable way to prevent the types of poverty which grow out of the individual assumption of all such risks is to spread the risk under competent government direction and meet it in part, where necessary, through public subsidization.

Any remainder of funds which the government may secure, through the types of taxation mentioned, will be needed in its programs for research and invention, and its policies for the prevention of poverty at the source through conservation, stimulation of invention, vocational analysis and placement, or otherwise, as has already been outlined.

Subsidization of Rehousing.—Further study may be necessary of devices to subsidize out of the public treasury certain specific needs of the industrial worker's family. Frequently, for example, it is recommended that the rehousing of our slum population be left entirely to private capital on the condition that the government subsidize the worker's rent to a point which will make possible the provision by the private builder of housing with sound standards. It is recognized that the rent-paying capacity of the industrial worker is now too low to make possible the replacement of slum dwellings with wholesome, durable housing. Yet the elimination of such dwellings is essential to his health and development and in all probability to public security as well.

It is conceivable that in time the application of the many measures for increasing the volume of distributable wealth, and for perfecting its redistribution, mentioned elsewhere in these pages, will so raise laborers' wages that they can pay for adequate housing. But certainly the burden of demolishing present slums, which were created through no fault of the wage-earners themselves, should be met out of public funds. The argument for rent subsidies has grown out of fear or pessimism with regard to public ownership or a blind adherence to the tradition of private exploitation. Rent subsidies might create a dangerous precedent, and if used in stimulation of the private rebuilding of slum areas would almost inevitably lead to the acceptance of standards in subsidized housing lower and less desirable than those which government units would be able to maintain under a system of direct construction and operation.

It would be vastly safer and more politic for governments to meet the inevitable need for their aid in the process of slum rebuilding by undertaking to condemn and buy up slums on a system of compensation which would never exceed present exchange value as determined by the market for private sales, and to turn over the land either on lease or at nominal cost—its housing value—to private enterprise to rebuild according to detailed government specifications and under public supervision as to design, structure, prices for materials, wages to building labor, and tenancy. In this way the government would escape the continuing contribution involved in rental subsidies and would take its "loss" or expense once for all in its outlay for buying and demolishing the insanitary buildings and in writing down the cost of the land. In so doing the government would merely be meeting the cost of its own past tragic neglect. The trend, however, is toward the costlier expedient of public construction and operation of large housing projects under local housing authorities enjoying Federal stimulation, subsidization, and control of standards.[4]

Family Allowance System.—Another type of subsidy widely recommended is known as the family allowance system. Under it various European governments subsidize large families by an annual payment to the laborer, in addition to his wage, for each child beyond a given number. As a device to increase population in countries where the birth rate is declining, or man power—"cannon fodder"— is wanted for future expected wars, the family allowance system is "justified" on grounds of expediency. It cannot be recommended even on humanitarian grounds as an American public policy because in so far as it would encourage breeding at the bottom of our biologic scale it would increase rather than diminish the percentage of permanent dependents in our society.[5]

Minimum-Wage Legislation.—So far we have considered how government can redistribute wealth through the supplementation of the incomes of the lower paid groups of our population. It is possible, however, for government to extend this principle to private industry by means of regulatory legislation. The primary means to this end is known as minimum-wage legislation.

Under normal economic conditions, all poverty save that of the handicapped and misfit elements of our population, might conceivably be eliminated by means of enforcing upon private industry a minimum wage for each worker sufficient properly to support himself and his family.[6] By normal economic conditions, however, is meant conditions free from such disasters as economic depression, flood, drought, war, and their aftermaths, and an economic system capable of putting all ablebodied labor to useful work and keeping it

[4] For more detailed treatment of this problem see Ford, James, in collaboration with Morrow, Katherine, and Thompson, George N.—*Slums and Housing, with Special Reference to New York City: History, Conditions, Policy;* Harvard University Press, 1936. See also Post, Langdon W.—*The Challenge of Housing;* Farrar & Rinehart, Inc., 1938.

[5] Arguments pro and con are briefly offered in Armstrong, Barbara N.— *Insuring the Essentials,* Part II, Section XII; The Macmillan Company, 1932.

[6] For summaries of present status see Commons, John R., and Andrews, John B.—*Principles of Labor Legislation;* Harper & Brothers, revised edition, 1936. Also Armstrong, Barbara N.—*ibid.*

continuously employed. Such a criterion of normality may seem fanciful in view of contemporary conditions and problems, but is not beyond attainment by a well-organized and highly civilized nation.

The minimum wage in question, as has been previously stated, is one that would provide adequate food for all members of the family; clothing to meet seasonal, climatic, and reasonable social demands; wholesome housing, including adequate light and heat; decent furnishings and equipment; and such education and recreation as are necessary for the well-being and continuing development of each member of the household. In money terms for a family of four or five persons it might range as high as $2,000 per annum in certain northern cities and conceivably as low as $1,000 for certain of the semirural and industrial workers of the South.

The wage should be determined on the basis of standard budgets, local living costs, and group needs. In framing it, supplementations of income through free schooling, recreation, medical service, or otherwise, must be taken into consideration. Because of the wide variations in living costs in different parts of America and between country and city, the setting of minimum-wage standards would appear to be a state function rather than one for the Federal government. Nevertheless, the latter through its devices for research and information should ultimately prove capable of establishing principles applicable to the nation as a whole by the use of standard budgets which can be adapted to local use in terms of the local costs and modes of living. The failure of the N.R.A. to do so was one of the causes of the opprobrium with which its rules were met.

The type of minimum-wage legislation which is needed would induce a leveling up of the wages of most unskilled and much semi-skilled labor. This, however, is obviously impractical except where profits are large, unless at the same time the volume of distributable wealth can be increased by devices of the types already considered. There can be no high universal minimum to labor unless labor and industry jointly create it by their efforts. Although successful monopolies and the most successful of competitive corporations could, if necessary, pay more than they now do to the poorest paid workers in their employ, the marginal competitors could not. The establishment and maintenance of a universal high minimum is therefore dependent upon a relatively high degree of national economic planning for the production and conservation of wealth, the reorganization of industry, and elimination or salvaging of waste. Such a comprehensive policy for industrial reorganization is not beyond the possibility of achievement, but will be unattainable in a democracy until attacked with vastly greater skill and insight than has as yet been displayed in public economic programs.

The history of minimum-wage legislation in America to date is characterized by earnest though limited attacks on the problem by twenty-five states, and within them in relatively few industries. Except for the Federal effort through the N.R.A. the principle had scarcely been applied to male labor outside of Oklahoma until the passage of the Fair Labor Standards Act of 1938.

"More popularly known as the 'Wages and Hours Law,' the Fair Labor Standards Act of 1938 was passed in the closing days of Congress and was signed by President Roosevelt, June 25, 1938. . . .

"Although during the first year the minimum wage prescribed by the law is fixed at 25 cents an hour and the maximum hours permitted are 44 per week, the purpose of the act is to set a minimum wage level of 40 cents an hour and to reduce the maximum hours of work to 40 per week as rapidly as is economically feasible without substantially curtailing employment. After the law has been in effect for 1 year the minimum wage level will automatically be raised to 30 cents an hour and the hours of work will be reduced to 42. After 2 years the law provides for a maximum 40-hour workweek and after 7 years for a minimum hourly rate of 40 cents. Workers, however, do not necessarily have to wait 7 years in order to be covered by a 40-cent minimum wage, as upon recommendation of an industry committee, the Administrator may at any time issue an order establishing a minimum hourly rate ranging up to 40 cents.

"The number of workers whose wages will be affected by the law cannot be determined with any degree of accuracy. It will depend largely upon the wage orders issued by the Administrator providing for minimum wages above the 25-cent minimum set in the law. Estimates indicate that a minimum rate of 40 cents and employment conditions similar to those which prevailed last August when industry was more active would result in increased earnings to upwards of a million factory wage earners. . . .

"Workers employed in industries engaged in interstate commerce or in the manufacture of goods shipped in interstate commerce are covered by the Fair Labor Standards Act of 1938. . . .

"The wage and hour provisions of the law do not apply to—

"(a) workers employed in a bona fide executive, administrative, or professional capacity, workers engaged as outside salesmen, and employees in retail and service establishments, the greater part of whose business is within the State.

"(b) workers employed as seamen, employees engaged in the transportation of persons and mail by air, employees of suburban or interurban electric street railways, and employees of local trolley or motorbus carriers.

"(c) agricultural workers and those engaged in fishing, including the canning, packing, marketing, and distributing of fish and other sea foods.

"(d) workers employed in connection with the publication of weekly or semiweekly newspapers with a circulation of less than 3,000, the major part of which is within the county where it is printed and published.

"(e) workers engaged in handling, packing, storing, ginning, compressing, pasteurizing, drying, preparing in a raw or natural state, or canning any agricultural commodity for marketing, or in making cheese or butter if employed within the area of production of the raw materials.

". . . workers are entitled to receive compensation at the rate of not less than one and one-half times their regular rate for all hours in excess of the maximum permitted by law.

". . . the Administrator is required to establish as quickly as feasible the highest minimum wage possible for each industry. . . .

"The Administrator must appoint for each industry an industry committee consisting of an equal number of representatives of employers, workers, and the public. After careful study of the industry and its problems, with due regard for the economic and competitive conditions in the industry, the committee must recommend to the Administrator the highest minimum wage for the industry possible without substantially curtailing employment within the industry.

". . . the industry committee may recommend reasonable classifications within an industry and recommend separate minimum wage rates which must be the highest for each classification without substantially curtailing employment in that classification and without giving a competitive advantage to any group in the industry. No minimum wage rates can be fixed solely on a regional basis or on the basis of age or sex of employees. The industry committees and the Administrator are required to consider among other relevant factors the following:

"(a) Competitive conditions as affected by transportation, living, and production costs.

"(b) The wages established for work of like or comparable character by collective labor agreements negotiated between employers and employees by representatives of their own choosing.

"(c) The wages paid for work of like or comparable character by employers who voluntarily maintain minimum-wage standards in the industry.

". . . if after a public hearing and opportunity for interested parties to be heard the Administrator finds that the recommendations of the committee are not justified, he may reject them and either refer the question back to the same committee for further study or appoint a new industry committee.

". . . all wage orders must be based upon recommendations of an industry committee.

". . . learners and apprentices, persons handicapped by age or physical defects, and messengers employed exclusively in delivering letters and messages are exempt from the application of the minimum-wage provisions of the law under conditions determined by the Administrator. . . .

"No producer, manufacturer, or dealer can ship or deliver for shipment in interstate commerce goods produced in establishments where oppressive child labor conditions have prevailed within 30 days prior to shipment. . . .

"Oppressive child labor means the employment of children under 16 years of age and the employment of minors of 16 to 18 years of age in occupations found and declared hazardous by the Chief of the Children's Bureau. An employer may protect himself from the illegal employment of minors by securing employment certificates issued in accordance with regulations established by the Children's Bureau of the U. S. Department of Labor. . . .

"Children under 16 employed in agriculture when not legally required to attend school, children employed as actors in motion picture or theatrical productions, and children working for their parents in any occupation other than manufacturing or mining are exempt. . . .

". . . children between 14 and 16 years of age may be granted permits for work in occupations other than manufacturing and mining if the Chief of the Children's Bureau finds that such employment will not interfere with their schooling or impair their health and well-being. . . .

". . . children employed in local trades and services who constitute nearly three-fourths of the total number of minors employed in the United States are not covered by the law. . . .

"The Fair Labor Standards Act creates within the Department of Labor a Division of Wages and Hours in charge of an Administrator appointed by the President of the United States subject to the approval of the Senate. The child labor provisions of the Act will be administered by the Children's Bureau of the U. S. Department of Labor. . . .

"Employers who willfully violate the wage and hour provisions of the law or the wage orders fixed by the Administrator will be prosecuted in the courts and are subject to a fine of not more than $10,000 or imprisonment for not more than 6 months or both, provided, however, that no person can be imprisoned for a first offense. . . .

". . . employees, individually or through representatives, can institute court proceedings to collect the differences in wages to which they are entitled due to violations of the law and an equal amount as damages. The employer is also liable for the costs involved in prosecuting the case. . . .

". . . employers are prohibited from wilfully discharging or in any other manner discriminating against employees who serve on industry committees or who file complaints or testify on alleged violations of the law." [7]

[7] Adapted from "The Fair Labor Standards Act of 1938," pp. 1–5; *Labor Information Bulletin*, Vol. V, No. 7, July, 1938.

A minimum wage which would provide a decent living standard cannot be paid to laborers by private industry unless they earn it themselves by their own efforts within that industry. Thus the problem of the worker who is inefficient but not too handicapped to work at all is one to be handled by the government in retraining colonies where men may work for as large a percentage of the cost of their care as they are capable of. Some can be made productive and returned to the competitive world. The remainder will require oversight and assistance for life.

The decision of the United States Supreme Court in 1937, finding state minimum-wage legislation constitutional, has removed the chief political obstruction to minimum-wage legislation.[8] The economic obstructions, difficult though they may be, have the merit of bringing forcibly to attention the problems of the productivity of labor on the one hand and those of marginal industry on the other. If minimum-wage legislation is to be made effectual in the accomplishment of its purpose, industry will no longer be left to the operation of strictly economic forces, but will be subjected to increasing public regulation. Sharper distinctions will be made between unproductive labor and labor which "earns its keep" or is sufficiently productive to warrant the payment of the minimum wage established by state law. Separate policies will be devised for each. Marginal industries which can not afford to pay the state's minimum may be crowded out at first, but the problems which they face will need to be subjected to study. This will have to lead to types of economic regulation designed to facilitate all necessary production at economic levels. It is too early to prognosticate concerning the forms which such legislation should take, but it is reasonable to insist that all labor employed must both earn and receive the state's minimum wage,

[8] "As a result of the United States Supreme Court decision holding minimum-wage laws constitutional, much legislation was adopted by the States. In four jurisdictions (Arkansas, District of Columbia, Minnesota, and Puerto Rico) minimum-wage laws which were already on the statute books were revived and made effective. Such laws were also amended or reenacted in Colorado (ch. 189), Connecticut (p. 286), Massachusetts (ch. 401), Minnesota (ch. 79), New York (ch. 276), and Wisconsin (ch. 333). New minimum-wage laws were adopted in Arizona (ch. 20, 2d Spec. Sess.), Nevada (ch. 207), Oklahoma (p. 387), and Pennsylvania (No. 248). The Oklahoma law was made applicable to men, as well as to women and minors." U. S. Bureau of Labor Statistics— *State Labor Legislation, 1937: Including Workmen's Compensation Legislation*, p. 8; Bulletin No. 654, Government Printing Office, 1938. See also Stitt, Louise, and Smith, Florence P.—"Progress of State Minimum-Wage Legislation, 1937," pp. 194–195; *Monthly Labor Review*, Vol. 46, No. 1, January, 1938.

that legislation regarding credit and industrial combination must sufficiently revise economic structure to facilitate socially desirable economic functions while making possible sound investments and reasonable profits to the entrepreneur.

Measures to Protect the Consumer.—The remaining means to the more effective distribution of wealth lies in deflecting to the consumer, income which has been misappropriated by either the producer or the usurer. Some of the worker's income is needlessly wasted by the purchase of foods, drugs, utensils, and clothes so poor in quality as to be practically worthless. Still more of his income is needlessly lost through imperfectly regulated instalment buying, which deprives him of both his furniture and the instalments already paid thereon when he is unable to meet a given payment. Another large fraction may be absorbed by the loan shark or usurer who entangles him in high interest payments and ruins him under burdens too heavy to carry. Yet another high percentage goes to industrial or burial insurance at premiums that are disproportionately high.

Any poor man's income would go much further in the purchase of necessaries—and the needed minimum wage to be established by legislation might be made correspondingly lower—if these four groups of consumer exploiters could be eliminated or controlled by well-enforced legislation, and all consumers thereby protected.[9]

The percentage of our national wealth, viewed in terms of raw materials, which is utilized in the manufacture of nondurable or otherwise worthless or unwholesome goods, must be very considerable. Quite aside from the gigantic costs of war, one must consider the deflection of man power from constructive uses to the production of abused drugs and intoxicants, patent medicines, adulterated foods, gambling, betting, speculation, those forms of commercialized recreation which are unwholesome, crime and commercialized vice, quackery, and needless fashions or luxuries. In *The Tragedy of Waste* Stuart Chase estimated the total minimum wasted man power as the labor of eight million persons.[10] Even if the volume of wasted man power were half this amount or less, it is clear that its reëm-

[9] Nugent, Rolf—"Family Debt," *Social Work Year Book 1937;* Russell Sage Foundation, 1937. Mr. Nugent offers also an excellent summary of recent literature on financing the consumer, the regulation of the small loan business, instalment selling, and credit unions. See also Taylor, Maurice—*The Social Cost of Industrial Insurance;* Alfred A. Knopf, 1933, and the publications of the Massachusetts Savings Bank Life Insurance.

[10] Chase, Stuart—*The Tragedy of Waste;* The Macmillan Company, 1929.

ployment in the creation of true social values could greatly increase the grand total of distributable wealth and be made to raise the living standard of the wage-earning population.

QUESTIONS FOR DISCUSSION OR EXAMINATION

1. Should labor be rewarded according to (a) need? (b) effort? (c) productivity?
2. Discuss the relative merits of the various measures suggested for the redistribution of wealth. Should wealth be equalized?
3. Discuss the optimum standard of living. Can it be attained through minimum-wage legislation?
4. In how far and by what means can commercial exploitation of the consumer be prevented?

PROBLEMS FOR INDIVIDUAL STUDY

1. Discuss recommendations of this chapter *re* (a) taxation, (b) minimum-wage legislation, or (c) protection of the consumer, with business men of your acquaintance. Distinguish their emotional reactions from their arguments supported by evidence. What difficulties (a) of principle, (b) of practical application, emerge? (These residual problems may be assigned to members of the class for further research or for class discussion.)
2. Break down the business man's complaint against "government interference with business" into its elements or component parts and evaluate the various means by which each difficulty might be overcome.
3. Must one conclude that poverty cannot be abolished within the capitalist system? That socialism is inevitable? That dictatorship is inevitable? That communism, dictatorship, or state socialism give evidence of being more effective means to the abolition of poverty?
4. Would the prejudice, intolerance, selfishness, exploitative impulses, wastefulness, apathy, etc., which now militate against the changes in policy proposed in the last three chapters, cause less difficulty under communism or dictatorship than under a democracy accompanied by a capitalistic industrial order under governmental regulation?

SUGGESTIONS FOR SUPPLEMENTARY READINGS

Adams, Thomas S., Chairman—Report of the Committee on Taxation in *Home Finance and Taxation*, pp. 102–268; The President's Conference on Home Building and Home Ownership, Vol. II, 1932.
Armstrong, Barbara N.—*Insuring the Essentials;* The Macmillan Company, 1932.
Arnold, Thurman W.—*The Folklore of Capitalism;* Yale University Press, 1937.
Babson, Roger W.—*The Folly of Installment Buying;* Frederick A. Stokes Company, 1938.
Beyer, William C., Davis, Rebekah P., and Thwing, Myra—*Workingmen's*

Standard of Living in Philadelphia (A Report of the Bureau of Municipal Research of Philadelphia); The Macmillan Company, 1919.

Bossard, James H. S.—*Social Change and Social Problems*, Part III, "Social Well-Being and Problems of Income"; Harper & Brothers, revised edition, 1938.

Broda, Rudolf—*Minimum Wage Legislation in Various Countries;* U. S. Bureau of Labor Statistics, Bulletin No. 467, Government Printing Office, 1928.

Catlin, Warren B.—*The Labor Problem;* Harper & Brothers, revised edition, 1935.

Commons, John R., and Andrews, John B.—*Principles of Labor Legislation;* Harper & Brothers, revised edition, 1936.

Douglas, Paul H.—*Real Wages in the United States, 1890–1926;* Houghton Mifflin Company, 1930.

Douglas, Paul H.—*Wages and the Family;* University of Chicago Press, 1925.

Douglas, Paul H., Hitchcock, Curtice N., and Atkins, Willard E.—*The Worker in Modern Economic Society;* University of Chicago Press, 1923.

Eliot, Thomas D.—*American Standards and Planes of Living;* Ginn and Company, 1931.

Estey, James Arthur—*The Labor Problem;* McGraw-Hill Book Company, Inc., 1928.

Ford, James, in collaboration with Morrow, Katherine, and Thompson, George N.—*Slums and Housing, with Special Reference to New York City: History, Conditions, Policy,* two volumes; Harvard University Press, 1936.

Hamilton, Walton, and May, Stacy—*The Control of Wages;* The Macmillan Company, 1923.

Heer, Clarence—"Taxation and Public Finance," Chapter XXVI of *Recent Social Trends in the United States,* Vol. II; McGraw-Hill Book Company, Inc., 1933.

Hewett, William Wallace—*The Definition of Income and Its Application in Federal Taxation;* Westbrook Publishing Company, 1925.

Hollander, Jacob H.—*The Abolition of Poverty;* Houghton Mifflin Company, 1914.

Houghteling, Leila—*The Income and Standard of Living of Unskilled Laborers in Chicago;* University of Chicago Press, 1927.

Hubachek, F. B.—*Annotations on Small Loan Laws;* Russell Sage Foundation, 1938.

King, Clyde L.—*Public Finance;* The Macmillan Company, 1935.

Lauck, W. Jett—*The New Industrial Revolution and Wages;* Funk & Wagnalls Company, 1929.

Leven, Maurice, Moulton, Harold G., and Warburton, Clark—*America's Capacity to Consume;* The Brookings Institution, 1934.

Lynd, Robert S.—"The People as Consumers," Chapter XVII of *Recent Social Trends in the United States,* Vol. II; McGraw-Hill Book Company, Inc., 1933.

Lyon, Leverett S., Homan, Paul T., Terborgh, George, Lorwin, Lewis L., Dearing, Charles, and Marshall, L. C.—*The National Recovery Administration: An Analysis and an Appraisal;* The Brookings Institution, 1935.

McMahon, Theresa S.—*Social and Economic Standards of Living;* D. C. Heath and Company, 1925.

McNair, Malcolm P., and Lewis, Howard T., editors—*Business and Modern Society;* Harvard University Press, 1938.

National Industrial Conference Board—*The Cost of Living in the United States, 1914–1936* (by M. Ada Beney); National Industrial Conference Board, 1936.

National Industrial Conference Board—*Wages, Hours, and Employment in the United States, 1914–1936* (by M. Ada Beney); National Industrial Conference Board, 1936.

Parmelee, Maurice—*Farewell to Poverty;* John Wiley & Sons, Inc., 1935.

Peixotto, Jessica B.—*Getting and Spending at the Professional Standard of Living. A Study of the Costs of Living an Academic Life;* The Macmillan Company, 1927.

Post, Langdon W.—*The Challenge of Housing;* Farrar & Rinehart, Inc., 1938.

Robinson, Louis N., and Stearns, Maude E.—*Ten Thousand Small Loans;* Russell Sage Foundation, 1930.

Ryan, John A.—*Distributive Justice: The Right and Wrong of Our Present Distribution of Wealth;* The Macmillan Company, revised edition, 1927.

Ryan, John A.—*A Living Wage. Its Ethical and Economic Aspects;* The Macmillan Company, 1906.

Ryan, John A.—*Social Reconstruction;* The Macmillan Company, 1920.

Ryan, John A.—*The Supreme Court and the Minimum Wage;* The Paulist Press, 1923.

Simons, Henry C.—*Personal Income Taxation: The Definition of Income as a Problem of Fiscal Policy;* University of Chicago Press, 1938.

Smith, Reginald Heber—*Justice and the Poor;* Carnegie Foundation for the Advancement of Teaching, Bulletin No. 13, 1919.

Stecker, Margaret Loomis—*Intercity Differences in Costs of Living in March 1935, 59 Cities;* Works Progress Administration, Division of Social Research, Research Monograph XII, Government Printing Office, 1937.

Stecker, Margaret Loomis—*Quantity Budgets for Basic Maintenance and Emergency Standards of Living;* Works Progress Administration, Division of Social Research, Series I, No. 21, 1936.

Streightoff, Frank Hatch—*The Standard of Living among the Industrial People of America;* Houghton Mifflin Company, 1911.

Taussig, F. W.—*Principles of Economics,* Vol. II, Book V, "The Distribution of Wealth," Book VI, "Problems of Labor," Book VII, "Problems of Economic Organization," and Book VIII, "Taxation"; The Macmillan Company, 1913.

Taylor, Maurice—*The Social Cost of Industrial Insurance;* Alfred A. Knopf, 1933.

Tugwell, Rexford Guy, Munro, Thomas, and Stryker, Roy E.—*American Economic Life and the Means of Its Improvement;* Harcourt, Brace and Company, Inc., revised edition, 1930.

Twentieth Century Fund, Committee on Taxation—*Facing the Tax Problem: Survey of Taxation in the United States and a Program for the Future;* Twentieth Century Fund, Inc., 1937.

Waggaman, Mary T.—*Family Allowances in Foreign Countries;* U. S. Bureau of Labor Statistics, Bulletin No. 401, Government Printing Office, 1926.

Williams, Faith M.—"An Analysis of Recent Urban Budgets and Studies of Family Living" in *Household Management and Kitchens*, pp. 104–143; The President's Conference on Home Building and Home Ownership, Vol. IX, 1932.

Williams, Faith M., and Zimmerman, Carle C.—*Studies of Family Living in the United States and Other Countries;* U. S. Department of Agriculture, Miscellaneous Publication No. 223, Government Printing Office, 1935.

Williams, Gertrude—*The State and the Standard of Living;* P. S. King & Son, Ltd., 1936.

Wolman, Leo—"Consumption and the Standard of Living," Chapter I, Vol. I, and "Labor," Chapter VI, Vol. II of *Recent Economic Changes in the United States;* published for the National Bureau of Economic Research, Inc., by McGraw-Hill Book Company, Inc., 1929.

Wolman, Leo, and Peck, Gustav—"Labor Groups in the Social Structure," Chapter XVI of *Recent Social Trends in the United States*, Vol. II; McGraw-Hill Book Company, Inc., 1933.

Zimmerman, Carle C.—*Consumption and Standards of Living;* D. Van Nostrand Company, Inc., 1936.

PART IV

SOCIAL PATHOLOGY OF FAMILY
AND GROUP LIFE

CHAPTER XXVII

PATHOLOGY OF FAMILY RELATIONSHIPS

The Family.—Throughout human history the family has tended to be the primary social group which has made possible for its members more intimate relationships and more continuous association than is provided by any other primary group (neighborhood or village), or any secondary group (club, professional organization, or city), or any other institutionalized groups (church, school, or government). As a social institution the monogamic family is, in varying degrees, intrenched in the mores and enforced by religious, legal, and social-moral sanctions to induce conformity.

Functions of the Family.—A major function of marriage is the begetting and the rearing of children. Within the limitations of prevailing mores and law there are recognized secondary or contributory functions of the family—to provide shelter, alimentation, and protection for all its members; to serve as primary unit for the ownership of land or other property, and for work and the accumulation of wealth; to begin the process of education of the young, transmitting the customs and systems of ideas (moral, religious, industrial, and governmental) of the larger social groups; to regulate sex relationships and confer status upon the individual.

The Family in Transition.—No human institution or organization is or can be static. In the large literature relating to the family one can follow, for example, through recent centuries in Western Europe and America, the reduction of the family from a kinship group in which are many generations and cousins to a marriage group of husband, wife, and children; the decline and in some urban areas the virtual disappearance of patriarchal domination; later marriages and fewer children; emancipation of women from their former subordination; increasing release of children from parental control.

These phenomena are not evidences of social disorganization, as is so frequently assumed, unless the criterion employed is one of domination by the male head of the family, with corresponding subordination and lack of freedom of choice and action by its other members. They are rather evidences of the intrusion within the

459

family group of the ideals of democracy, freedom, and equality—of the paramount ethical value of personality—ideals which in this same period have in varying measure entered the fields of political and economic thought and practice. To some specialists these are mere evidences of cyclical trends; to others they appear as transition phenomena which may be leading in the contemporary mores to the reorganization of the family.

Social Pathology of the Family.—For convenience the pathologies of relationships within the family or between the family and other social groups may be sketched under the headings (1) biological, (2) physiological, (3) psychological, (4) pedagogical, (5) demotic, (6) economic, (7) legal, (8) moral. All of these will be found to deal with matters of sociological significance but for convenience the category (9) sociological will be utilized for the discussion of some of the major problems which overlap many of the more specialized approaches.

Biological Considerations.—From the point of view of the evolution of the race or of humanity, a major social function of marriage is to make possible sound progeny and improved quality of stock. The results are pathological in so far as the stock declines in quality. The pursuit of optimal standards presupposes continuous improvement in the quality of births and (adducing a political criterion) a quantity of offspring sufficient to meet efficiently the rational needs of industry and the state.

Our earlier study of hereditary handicaps has shown that applied eugenics still fails to cause marked retardation in the rate of increase of defective stocks. Until sterilization is accepted and applied as a rational social policy for institutional cases or those cases of mental abnormality or subnormality that are hereditary in nature, supplemented by voluntary sterilization for hybrid carriers, this pathologic condition cannot be greatly reduced unless effective devices prove practicable to promote outbreeding by means of placing-out, resettlement, or otherwise.[1] Failure of families of sound biologic stock and supernormal inherited qualities to average three or more children—so as to reproduce the parental generation and the requisite ratio in the population of persons of potential quality—is also

[1] Part II, Chapter XV. Outbreeding further makes possible profound changes in attitudes and behavior. Waller, in another connection, notes that the cyclic aspect of family life can be altered by change of culture, by culture conflict, or by change of social class. Waller, Willard—*The Family: A Dynamic Interpretation,* pp. 121–122 and *passim;* The Cordon Company, 1938.

a problem in social pathology.[2] A social policy to encourage larger families in this group might incorporate not only appropriate biological education and propaganda directed to this end but also economic facilitation of early marriage, adequate housing, and medical services for this group to overcome its present relative economic disadvantage. Sweden's methods warrant close analysis to determine in how far they are applicable to this country.[3]

Physiological Considerations.—The sickness of any member of a household tends to limit the activities and relationships of other members as well as to reduce the contacts and services of the member who is ill. Methods of reducing the volume of illness and of acquired handicaps have already been outlined.[4] Within this category should be mentioned, however, the fact that venereal diseases may lead either to infection of the children or to sterility, and in either case are among the more profoundly pathologic conditions from which families suffer. Their presence may be an evidence of marital unfaithfulness which may occasion profound emotional disturbance in the mate and among the children, with often serious consequences to mental or nervous health or to domestic stability. But fidelity, in combination with other factors, may also cause emotional disturbance. Sexual incompatibilities and abnormalities are physiological factors difficult to reach but inimical to family welfare. Preventive social policy involves both adequate sex education and competent medical advice and treatment at public health centers with regard to any of these personal problems.[5]

Psychological Considerations.—Mental and emotional abnormalities are conspicuous factors in case records of unstable and disrupted families. Sometimes the origins are of types previously considered.[6] Often the basis for the mental abnormalities appears to be found in sexual incompatibilities with consequent frustration and nervous illness. The unavoidable intimacies of family life may pre-

[2] Lorimer, Frank, and Osborn, Frederick—*Dynamics of Population;* The Macmillan Company, 1934. See also *The Annals of the American Academy of Political and Social Science*, Vol. 188, November, 1936, especially articles by Lotka, Alfred J., and by Notestein, Frank.

[3] Ohlin, Bertil, editor—*Social Problems and Policies in Sweden;* entire issue of *The Annals of the American Academy of Political and Social Science*, Vol. 197, May, 1938: see especially article by Myrdal, Gunnar—"Population Problems and Policies."

[4] Part II, Chapter XVI.

[5] Folsom, Joseph Kirk, editor—*Plan for Marriage;* Harper & Brothers, 1938.

[6] Part II, Chapters VII and VIII.

clude escape from hurts, fears, and worries of innocent origin but cumulative incidence. Thus the misunderstood child, wife, or husband may withdraw or contend—but in either case there is less-than-optimum cohesiveness if not actual disruption. Psychoanalysts have traced consequences in the field of criminality,[7] as well as in the divorce courts and psychopathic wards.

Preventives, other than those considered earlier include provision for social diagnosis and case work for each member of such households, as well as psychological analysis and treatment for each neurotic or psychotic member.[8]

Pedagogic Considerations.—Most parents lack adequate training for rearing their children. The majority of parents have had not more than a grammar school education, which means little development of the capacity for judgment, and possibly also, little specific training of their own personal characters—though it should of course be recognized that character is not necessarily a function either of the degree of schooling or of economic status. Scoldings, warnings, and punishments which they crudely administer to their children largely fail properly to guide them. If their own personalities are unorganized, and force is their only means to domination, the parents will be unable to help the child to organize its own character. Often the parental example is itself unwholesome for the child to witness. The child's affection (or hate) for its parent may lend to the example a peculiar cogency and serve strongly as suggestion (or counter-suggestion) for its own behavior.

Preventives lie in lengthening the period of education and in improving its adaptation to life's prospective needs. Undereducation may mean ignorance of sex and social hygiene with consequent mistakes in behavior. It may mean ignorance of domestic science and family budgeting with consequent needless disruptions over cooking or spending. It may mean that untrained labor is the only means to livelihood with consequent inadequacy in the family standard of living, associated with ill health, debt, and other disruptive factors.

---

[7] Works of Healy, William—*e.g. Mental Conflicts and Misconduct;* Little, Brown, and Company, 1917.

[8] Mowrer, Ernest R.—*Family Disorganization;* University of Chicago Press, 1927. Mowrer, Ernest R., with the collaboration of Mowrer, Harriet R.—*Domestic Discord;* University of Chicago Press, 1928. Mowrer, Harriet R.—*Personality Adjustment and Domestic Discord;* American Book Company, 1935. Thomas, William I.—*The Unadjusted Girl;* Little, Brown, and Company, 1928. Waller, Willard—*op. cit.*

It may mean parental incompetence and a new generation equally incompetent. Each of these pathologic conditions requires appropriate measures of instruction either before leaving school or in continuation classes preceding marriage. Parent-teacher associations, social work, and the various agencies for adult education fill in this gap pending universal and systematic provision for these needs in the standard public school curriculum.

Demotic Constitution of Family in an Industrial Society.— From the Federal Census of 1930 it appears that three-fifths of our population fifteen years of age or older is married. One-third of the men and one-quarter of the women are single. Over 10 per cent of the women and less than 5 per cent of the men are widowed. Slightly over 1 per cent of each are divorced.

MARITAL CONDITION OF PERSONS 15 YEARS OF AGE AND OVER [9]

(Continental United States–1930)

CLASS	MALES 15 YEARS AND OVER		FEMALES 15 YEARS AND OVER	
	Number	*Per Cent*	*Number*	*Per Cent*
All classes	43,881,021	100.0	42,837,149	100.0
Single	14,953,712	34.1	11,306,653	26.4
Married	26,327,109	60.0	26,170,756	61.1
Widowed	2,025,036	4.6	4,734,207	11.1
Divorced	489,478	1.1	573,148	1.3
Unknown	85,686	.2	52,385	.1

Comparing urban communities with rural for 1930, one finds a higher percentage of divorced persons in urban communities for both the white and Negro populations.[10] The upward trend in

---

[9] *Statistical Abstract of the United States 1936*, p. 46; Government Printing Office, 1936. "The excess of married men over married women in 1930 was 156,353, as compared with 530,333 in 1920. The excess of married men is due mainly to the fact that there is a large number of foreign-born married men present in the United States who have left their wives in their native countries. The rapid reduction of this excess is due to the restriction of immigration, and perhaps also to the fact that many of the wives came in as nonquota immigrants prior to the census of 1930. The excess of widows over widowers is due primarily to the greater longevity of women than of men. This excess is made still greater by the fact that men usually marry at later ages than women, so that even aside from the greater longevity of women, the marriage is more likely to be broken by the death of the husband than by the death of the wife." U. S. Bureau of the Census—*Fifteenth Census of the United States: 1930. Population. Marital Condition*, p. 837; Government Printing Office, 1933.

[10] *Statistical Abstract of the United States 1936*, p. 47.

divorce, which now ends one marriage in every six, and the effects of depression upon both marriage and divorce are indicated in the following table.

MARRIAGES, DIVORCES, AND ANNULMENTS [11]

(Number and Ratio of Divorces to Marriages, Continental United States)

CALEN-DAR YEAR	MARRIAGES, NUMBER	TOTAL NUMBER	DIVORCES				NUMBER OF DIVORCES PER 1,000 MARRIAGES	NUMBER OF ANNUL-MENTS a
			Granted to Husband		Granted to Wife			
			Number	Per Cent	Number	Per Cent		
1890	542,537	33,461	11,625	34.7	21,836	65.3	62	....
1923	1,229,784	b165,096	52,999	32.2	111,480	67.8	134	....
1928	1,182,497	b195,939	55,065	28.6	137,277	71.4	166	4,237
1929	1,232,559	b201,468	57,148	28.7	142,187	71.3	163	4,408
1930	1,126,856	b191,591	52,554	27.7	137,309	72.3	170	4,370
1931	1,060,914	b183,664	49,591	27.2	132,612	72.8	173	4,339
1932	981,903	b160,338	42,335	26.5	117,375	73.5	163	3,903

a Statistics for annulments were collected for the first time in 1926.
b Includes divorces for which the libellant was not reported. Percentages, however, are based on the total number for which libellant was reported.

A study [12] of age groupings reveals a much larger percentage of children in rural areas.

AGE DISTRIBUTION, 1930	URBAN POPULATION		RURAL POPULATION	
	Total Urban	Per Cent of Total	Total Rural	Per Cent of Total
Under 5 years	5,626,360	8.2	5,818,030	10.8
5 to 9 years	6,211,141	9.0	6,396,468	11.9
10 to 14 years	5,949,693	8.6	6,055,184	11.3
15 to 19 years	6,015,411	8.7	5,536,704	10.3
20 to 44 years	29,071,885	42.2	17,951,362	33.4
45 to 64 years	12,490,762	18.1	8,924,219	16.6
65 years and over	3,523,535	5.1	3,110,270	5.8
Unknown	66,036	0.1	27,986	0.1

Well over half the families have no young children, i.e. under ten years of age.

[11] Ibid., p. 93. For recent estimates see Stouffer, Samuel A., and Spencer, Lyle M.—"Recent Increases in Marriage and Divorce"; American Journal of Sociology, Vol. XLIV, No. 4, January, 1939.
[12] Statistical Abstract of the United States 1936, p. 19.

FAMILIES

(Number of Children under 10 Years of Age, for the United States, 1930) [13]

ITEM	PER CENT				
	All Classes	Native White	Foreign-Born White	Negro	Other Races
Families having—					
No children under 10	58.8	58.3	61.8	59.0	43.3
1 child under 10	19.2	19.9	18.2	16.7	17.2
2 children under 10	11.8	12.1	11.1	10.3	14.8
3 children under 10	6.0	5.9	5.3	6.8	12.1
4 children under 10	2.8	2.7	2.4	4.3	8.0
5 children under 10	1.0	.9	.9	2.1	3.4
6 or more	.3	.3	.3	.8	1.1

Society has an interest in the age distribution of members of families since an excess of young children or of aged people means a burden too great for the breadwinner to support and thus possible dependency. Widowhood and its economic equivalents, divorce and desertion, as well as orphanhood and illegitimacy, also involve greater likelihood of dependency.

Childhood Dependency.—Childhood dependency develops out of such conditions of family life as orphanhood, parental neglect or incompetence, or low income. All children normally are dependent upon their parents or immediate relatives for support. If such support is withdrawn or becomes too meager, the children, and perhaps also the family, must be cared for by public relief or private philanthropy. Cruelty and miseducation by parents, and delinquency on the part of either parent or child, also justify public interference, which may mean public support for the child.

In the middle of the past century our larger American cities had many homeless children who with difficulty fended for themselves to secure their food, and who slept in vacated buildings, under doorsteps or bridges, or in parks. They were victims of utter social neglect. Through the work of Charles Loring Brace and other pioneers, the institutional care and later the placing of dependent children in private homes have been arranged, so that waifs are now seldom seen. The adolescent tramps, both boys and girls, a few years ago were a recrudescence of this problem which has since been met for older boys by the Civilian Conservation Corps and for others

[13] *Ibid.*, p. 50.

by various types of public and private aid. In December, 1933, the number of children placed in institutional homes was approximately 140,350. The number in private foster homes was 102,577.[14]

A generation ago when families went upon relief it was customary in a surprisingly large number of public and private agencies to remove the children and put husband and wife to work. It is now the practice to keep the family together and provide work for the man if he is capable. In case of his death or illness, mothers of good character who have legal settlement are generally entitled to widows' pensions or mothers' aid, which makes it possible for them to support themselves and their families until the children are capable of self-support. The mother thus becomes the state's agent for the guardianship and rearing of her own children. Of five million cases on relief in the United States in December, 1934, there were 333,500 composed of women with children under sixteen years of age—altogether 6.6 per cent of the nation's relief load.[15]

When parents are cruel to their children, exploit them, neglect them, or serve as evil examples because of their immoral practices, children may be withdrawn by private agencies or by the state and placed in homes where the influences will be wholesome. Such withdrawal, though meaning dependency during childhood, may prevent adult dependency.

Many children make a poor start in life because of unhappiness in the home. It may be because of ever present financial worry, or the personal incompatibility of parents or of brothers and sisters. Continual scolding may drive to the unfortunate influences of the street a child who might otherwise be a coöperative member of the household. Families may be too large, mothers anxious and worried, and the food supply meager or uncertain. Sleep may be interfered with by the necessity of having several children sleep in the same room or even the same bed. There may be no source of comfort or beauty either within the home or in the slum which surrounds it. Wherever such conditions make the daily environment, or wherever

[14] Carstens, C. C.—"Child Welfare Services," *Social Work Year Book 1937*, p. 66, quoting the United States Bureau of the Census; Russell Sage Foundation, 1937.

[15] *Estimated Number of Cases, Unemployable by Reason of Family Composition, Receiving Emergency Relief in the United States, by States, December 1934*, p. 1; Federal Emergency Relief Administration, Division of Research, Statistics and Finance, Research Bulletin (mimeographed) D-10, March 15, 1935. See Part III, Chapter XXII for discussion of mothers' aid; also publications of the United States Children's Bureau.

irritability and belligerent attitudes are the rule, children start life under a heavy handicap. In such circumstances there is little hope of their developing the physical strength and energy or the co-operative attitudes essential in adult years for continuous and profitable employment. The seeds of adult poverty thus are often planted in childhood years, for those who have known no other life. The habit of parasitism may even be learned from parental example.[16] Though many families in poverty or upon relief succeed in "keeping their heads up" and maintaining surprisingly high standards in spite of their predicament, a high percentage of children in homes of the poor suffer in some degree from conditions of the sorts which have just been described.

To these must be added desertion—which is the poor man's divorce—and illegitimacy, each of which appears frequently in case records of dependent families. Although desertion may be fortunate where there is utter incompatibility, in families where there are young children it may cause dependency, or else neglect because of the absence of the mother during the working hours of the day. There is still a stigma attached to illegitimacy which modern social legislation is attempting to remove or minimize.[17]

This summary, necessarily brief, of the factors which produce neglect and dependency in childhood fails to show the continuous unrelieved and unmitigated hardship which the child suffers by day and by night, year in and year out, until it can make its escape from the home. Some never recover from the effects of an unhappy and bitter childhood. Others succeed in rising above even the most unfortunate of circumstances.

Devices for the preventive treatment are twofold. First, removal of the child to a foster home unless or until the source of its difficulty

[16] Waller, in discussing families in which begging, divorce, or religious rebellion occur generation after generation as a result of attitude transmission from parent to child, has stated: " . . . once the breeding of social deviates begins, successive generations tend to marry other deviates and to lead with them an atypical family life. . . . If culture remains constant, the life patterns of individuals may repeat themselves from one generation to the next with considerable fidelity." Waller, Willard—*op. cit.*, pp. 120 and 121.

[17] Colcord, Joanna C.—*Broken Homes: A Study of Family Desertion and Its Social Treatment;* Russell Sage Foundation, 1919. Eubank, Earle Edward—*A Study of Family Desertion;* Department of Public Welfare, Chicago, 1916. Gillin, John Lewis—*Social Pathology*, see especially Part II, "The Pathology of Domestic Relationships"; The Century Co., 1933. White House Conference on Child Health and Protection—*Dependent and Neglected Children;* D. Appleton-Century Company, 1933.

can be reached. Second, the retraining of the parents according to their need, whether in medical clinics, domestic relations courts, or by the ministrations of social case work. In some instances the causes of domestic unhappiness can be found and removed. In others a separation may be necessary. It may not always be possible to make good parents out of those who are cruel, immoral, or degraded. If it is not possible, some type of social segregation in institutions, curative or reformatory, may be indicated for them. But any comprehensive policy for the prevention of poverty must provide a fresh start for the children under influences which will confer constructive attitudes and train for efficiency in trade or industry and for normal citizenship.

To ensure the elimination of those factors which lead to childhood dependency or train children for parasitism in adult years, it is necessary for the state to take over parental functions whenever parents are incompetent. All conditions which thwart wholesome development, whether physical, cultural, or moral, should be removed where necessary by public interference. All opportunities essential to the development of the child for constructive participation in the family and community life of his adult years must be provided under public direction wherever parents fail. The only guarantee against the products of parental incompetence or neglect is the full assumption of such responsibility by the state.[18]

Economic Considerations.—Low standards of family living and earning, and the consequent low economic contribution of the family to national wealth have been treated with their correctives in Part III. The labor of women and children, long hours, unemployment, and unhealthy or unsafe industrial operations are obvious in their implications. These expressions of contemporary industrial organization, in combination with other factors, fill social case records with their consequences in family disintegration. Whether reflected in fatigue, worry, disease, or prolonged absence from home, family cohesiveness is affected, often deleteriously. Pending fundamental economic planning or reorganization the preventives rest with labor and security legislation and with social case work.

[18] Essential standards for child welfare are summarized in the Children's Charter drawn up by the White House Conference on Child Health and Protection. Their defense is covered in over forty volumes of reports issued by that Conference and published by D. Appleton-Century Company, 1930, *et seq.*

Family Economics and Malnutrition.—The family standard of living may be either a cause or an effect of poverty. Low standards of diet, clothing, housing, or culture may proceed from ignorance or apathy as well as from the economic factor of low income. But whatever standard is maintained, the health, outlook, and efficiency of children and adults alike are affected. Diet may be taken as an example of living standards, since protracted malnutrition may do lasting injury and lead to permanent dependency.

The volume of malnutrition in America is not known, but a recent British study has arrived at the tentative conclusion that "a diet completely adequate for health, according to modern standards, is reached at an income level above that of 50 per cent of the population." [19] Deficiencies among the poor are displayed in the consumption of milk, eggs, and fruit especially. Even where diet is adequate in protein, fats, and carbohydrates it is lacking in certain vitamins and minerals. Health and physique are found to improve as income increases. [20]

A recent American study is summarized as follows:

"Records of a week's food supply for families at several low income levels or on relief in five large industrial cities, in New York City, in Birmingham, in South Carolina cotton-mill villages, and in a mining district of West Virginia were collected in the spring of 1933.

"The average energy value of the food supply was nearly 20 per cent below the adequate standard of 3,000 calories per day per adult male unit for families in the five cities with a weekly income of less than $2 per person, and about one-fourth of these families had less than 2,200 calories daily. The calorie supply was similarly low for families in New York City with incomes less than $4 weekly per person. Relief families, except those on work relief in New York City, had a higher average supply of calories than the poorest non-relief groups, but 25 per cent in the five cities and 29 per cent in New York had less than 2,200 calories per adult male unit. The average caloric value of the food supply of families at the lowest income levels in the other three communities equalled or exceeded the adequate standard, owing to the general use of large quantities of fat meat, flour or other cereal foods, and sugar.

"A greatly diminished use of milk, vegetables, and fruits was associated with lower incomes in all the communities in the study. In the five cities the average supply of milk purchased by families with income less than $2 per capita per week was one-third less than minimum requirements, and average amounts of fresh and canned vegetables and fruits were

[19] Orr, John Boyd—*Food Health and Income: Report on a Survey of Adequacy of Diet in Relation to Income*, p. 5; Macmillan and Co., Limited, 1936.
[20] *Ibid.*, pp. 49–50.

about equal to minimum needs. Bread and cereals were also used in smaller amounts than is recommended for a low-cost diet. On the other hand, amounts of meat and fish, eggs, and sugary foods purchased, though less than amounts purchased by higher-income families, exceeded the quantities recommended for an adequate low-cost diet. The result was a dietary low in calcium and vitamins."[21]

Studies of malnutrition reflect lack of variety in diet. Only through specialized education can the housewife be taught food values, the markets in which to make most advantageous purchases, the cereal foods with high nutritive value which can be used as meat substitutes—well-known to the Italians and Orientals—and the ways consistent with low expenditure of preparing meals for interest, variety, and nutrition.

Whether future studies reveal a malnutrition rate for America of 5 per cent or 50, the problem is serious. Two policies are required to meet it, first to raise the annual incomes of labor as discussed in previous chapters, and second to train homemakers in the selection, purchase, and preparation of foods so that a rounded dietary may be provided that will meet the needs of each member of the household. This latter type of training should be available for children before leaving public school, as well as through adult education.

Legal Considerations.—The pathology of family relationships is reflected in the number and types of cases before our civil courts, not only petitions for legal separation, divorce, and legal custody of children, but also family suits regarding inheritances, nonsupport, and other matters relating to income or property. They are reflected in criminal courts directly in cases involving sex crimes—rape, incest, perversions, adultery, and abortions—and more or less directly in many other crimes and misdemeanors ranging from drunkenness to murder. Some degenerate families miseducate their children, training them for begging, theft, or prostitution. Some professional crimes among persons of normal intelligence are undertaken and executed as family enterprises.

Clearly in each instance the individual needs to be reached by social diagnosis and case work systematically provided from the appropriate source or sources—whether a welfare society, domestic re-

[21] Wiehl, Dorothy G.—*Diets of Low-Income Families Surveyed in 1933*, pp. 20–21; United States Public Health Service, Reprint No. 1727 from the Public Health Reports, Vol. 51, No. 4, January 24, 1936; Government Printing Office, 1936.

lations court, legal aid society, public defender, probation officer, psychiatrist, or family clinic. But concomitantly the law and the courts need to be administered to the maximum advantage of both society and each individual concerned. The large literature of this subject clearly indicates society's failure often to accomplish these aims.[22]

Fundamental preventives, in addition to improvements in the system of public education, comprise thorough revision of legislation and procedures to facilitate justice or the recognition of each personality on the one hand ("equal rights" and "single standard"), and to conform law to the prevailing trends in marital and domestic relationship on the other.[23]

Moral Considerations.—Most family relationships and behavior are at times upon the subjective moral plane which is the plane of conscious purpose. All family problems are moral problems also when viewed objectively with reference to social purpose. Social case workers who serve as advisers on family difficulties note many factors which tend to reduce family cohesion or coöperation.[24] Whether estrangement between husband and wife seems to have resulted from mental or emotional abnormalities, from sexual incompatibilities or vice, from differences in age, race, religion, or background, from interference of relatives, or from marriage for reasons strictly economic, there are always factors of a moral nature involved.

This can be illustrated by taking selfishness as our example— though ignorance, lack of control, injustice, inconsiderateness, non-coöperativeness, or the desire to dominate might serve about as well, since these are overlapping categories. Contemporary marriage involves mutuality or "give and take." When either mate marries primarily for economic considerations, for unrestricted sexual indul-

[22] Smith, Reginald Heber—*Justice and the Poor;* Carnegie Foundation for the Advancement of Teaching, Bulletin No. 13, 1919. The limitations of the family clinic today are well outlined in Davis, Kingsley—"The Application of Science to Personal Relations"; *American Sociological Review,* Vol. I, No. 2, April, 1936.

[23] Groves, Ernest Rutherford, and Ogburn, William Fielding—*American Marriage and Family Relationships;* Henry Holt and Company, 1928. President's Research Committee on Social Trends—*Recent Social Trends in the United States,* two volumes; McGraw-Hill Book Company, Inc., 1933. Lichtenberger, J. P.—*Divorce;* McGraw-Hill Book Company, Inc., 1931.

[24] Colcord, Joanna C.—*op. cit.* Richmond, Mary E.—*Social Diagnosis;* Russell Sage Foundation, 1917. Other classifications will be found in Lichtenberger, J. P.—*op. cit.*, and Mowrer, Ernest R.—*Family Disorganization;* University of Chicago Press, 1927.

gence, to dominate the other, or even to make over the other against his or her will, the prospects for family cohesiveness and happiness are not good. The "spoiled child" makes a poor mate because self-centered. Yet since many persons are selfish, quarrelsome marriages are frequent.

Preventives lie in the field of moral education, already treated in earlier chapters. In so far as men and women can be trained in their childhood for considerateness, coöperation, and mutuality, marriage has a better chance of approximating the romantic ideal and the family has a chance of being a fit and wholesome environment for the growing child. Social case workers, domestic relations courts, and other advisers in marital difficulties thus attempt to develop mutuality between estranged mates by rational discussion of each of their points of disagreement, by gaining concessions from each, but particularly by securing from each recognition of the interests of the other and by developing common objectives, reciprocity, and joint participation in outside interests.

Treatment on the plane of individual morality, however, tends to make undue abstraction of these elements from the broader social context. The "control culture" of customs, beliefs, and institutions has a profound influence upon marital selection and parent-child relationships, and upon individual attitudes. There is continuous interaction between the personality and these agencies—each attempting the modification of the other. Neither the individuals in their experimental search for happiness through marriage, nor the social groups in their attempted imposition of conformity to the law or the traditional mores characteristically see far beyond the immediate issue. Thus the individual in marital relationships or divorce may face inequities in law and ostracism within the community when pursuing a course of behavior which to him is moral. Where the effects of the group upon the family are invasive or even divisive the moral issue broadens to the consideration of the possibility of change in the prevailing moral codes or in the techniques of their imposition or enforcement. This would comprise, for example, consideration of the advisability of the revision of existing law so as to establish equality of legal rights for men and women within the marriage relation; or to permit divorce by mutual consent; or to rectify the abuses of alimony, inheritance, and property ownership. Change in the mores is inevitable, but in the absence of social condonation of experiments in the relationships of the sexes, the wise guidance of each such change requires fuller knowledge than is yet available.[25]

Sociological Factors.—By way of recapitulation it may be stated that the family as a social institution appears to be in transition. Evidences of change in recent generations among our own people are: (a) the reduction in the size of families from many children to few; (b) the increasing age at time of marriage; [26] (c) the increasing economic and social emancipation of women; and (d) the corresponding reduction of dominance of the male; (e) the reduced association of children with parents in their daily tasks; and concomitantly (f) the increased freedom of children from parental domination; (g) the increasing tendency of older generations to live apart from their children (only slightly modified by the exigencies of the depression economy); exemplifying (h) the change of the family from a kinship group to a marriage group; more or less associated with (i) increasing urbanization and industrialization and consequent anonymity; and, finally, (j) the substitution of government for family or primary group control in what were once family prerogatives.

To characterize this change as the "rise of individualism" [27] may be unfortunate because of the connotations of that term. Actually the increasing independence of the individual from the family has been accompanied by increasing invasion of the state in domestic matters. Where the process is conscious it can sometimes be characterized as an increasing recognition of the ethics of personality—of the relational self [28] working for the congruous interests of the self in a medium of relative freedom of choice, but curbed by the state where the results of such freedom are deemed inimical to the general welfare. The arbitrary restraints of patriarch and mate are disappearing and for them are being substituted the more elastic judgments of the courts and the more liberal judgments of neighbors. But the process of change is uneven as may be witnessed by the differences from state to state in statute law relating to marriage, di-

[25] This subject is admirably developed in Waller, Willard—*op. cit.*, Chapters I, XXI, XXII, and *passim*.
[26] Not true in recent decades in the United States. See Ogburn, William F.—"The Family and Its Functions," Chapter XIII of *Recent Social Trends in the United States*, Vol. I, p. 680; McGraw-Hill Book Company, Inc., 1933.
[27] *E.g.* Mowrer, Ernest R.—*ibid.*, Chapter VII, "Social Forces in Family Disorganization."
[28] Part I, Chapter IV.

vorce, and rights of wives with reference to the ownership of property. The differences in attitude between city and country, North and South, Catholic and Protestant, on the matters of divorce, birth control, and the relative duties and rights of wife and husband are further witness of the hold of tradition and of cultural lag.

There are indications of trends (a) towards the recognition of marriage as a contract rather than a sacrament, associated with the relegation of the Church from its former absolutism to the function of moral adviser; (b) towards toleration of separation or divorce not only on grounds of adultery, but also for insanity, impotency, drunkenness, conviction of crime, desertion, physical cruelty, marriage by coercion, nonsupport, venereal infection, sexual perversion, and more recently mental cruelty which tends to become a thin disguise for incompatibility. Errors in judgment in mating have been found in many a case history to have caused unrelieved unhappiness which apparently could not be overcome within the marriage relationship, and a fresh start for each of the contracting parties is becoming possible by divorce.

Social control in this field clearly indicates (a) the need of better training for the responsibilities of both marriage and parenthood; (b) special attention to the problem of mental health and social adjustment of children in unhappy homes, and of all persons in homes broken by separation, desertion, or divorce; (c) the study of the conditions and trends in marriage, parenthood, and divorce to discover more effective ways to obviate the abuses of each; (d) appropriate revision and recodification of laws relating to problems of marriage and the family in each of our forty-eight states to adapt them better to contemporary social trends and changes in the mores in so far as may prove consistent with the well-being of each member of the family group and of the state.

QUESTIONS FOR DISCUSSION OR EXAMINATION

1. By what measures can the racial stock be improved?
2. By what means can the incompetence of parents, in the rearing of their own children, be overcome?
3. Is there any solution short of the assumption by the state of the whole process of child-rearing? What should be the state's policy?
4. What social measures are necessary to eliminate (a) malnutrition of children, (b) cruelty or neglect by parents?
5. What are the evidences that the family is in transition? What should be done about it? Why?

PROBLEMS FOR INDIVIDUAL STUDY

1. A study of trends in (a) marriage, (b) divorce, or (c) illegitimacy.
2. A critical examination of, and report upon, the literature on (a) the emancipation of women, or (b) the assumption by the state of the present parental functions in child training.
3. A comparative and critical study of the literature of any of the subjects treated in this chapter.
4. A critical study of measures suggested to provide training for marriage and for parenthood.
5. A detailed study of the legislation of two or more states regarding (a) marriage, (b) divorce, (c) desertion and nonsupport, (d) illegitimacy.

SUGGESTIONS FOR SUPPLEMENTARY READINGS

Adler, Felix—*Marriage and Divorce;* D. Appleton and Company, 1915.

Angell, Robert Cooley—*The Family Encounters the Depression;* Charles Scribner's Sons, 1936.

Bosanquet, Helen—*The Family;* Macmillan and Co., Limited, 1906.

Cahen, Alfred—*Statistical Analysis of American Divorce;* Columbia University Press, 1932.

Calhoun, Arthur W.—*A Social History of the American Family from Colonial Times to the Present,* three volumes; Arthur H. Clark Company, 1917–1919.

Cavan, Ruth Shonle, and Ranck, Katherine Howland—*The Family and the Depression;* University of Chicago Press, 1938.

Chapin, F. Stuart—*Contemporary American Institutions: A Sociological Analysis;* Harper & Brothers, 1935.

Colcord, Joanna C.—*Broken Homes: A Study of Family Desertion and Its Social Treatment;* Russell Sage Foundation, 1919.

Davis, Katharine Bement—*Factors in the Sex Life of Twenty-two Hundred Women;* Harper & Brothers, 1929.

Dickinson, Robert Latou, and Beam, Lura—*A Thousand Marriages: A Medical Study of Sex Adjustment;* Williams & Wilkins Company, 1931.

Dickinson, Robert Latou, and Beam, Lura—*The Single Woman: A Medical Study in Sex Education;* Williams & Wilkins Company, 1933.

Douglas, Paul H.—*Wages and the Family;* University of Chicago Press, 1925.

Elmer, Manuel C.—*Family Adjustment and Social Change;* Ray Long & Richard R. Smith, Inc., 1932.

Eubank, Earle Edward—*A Study of Family Desertion;* Department of Public Welfare, Chicago, 1916.

Flügel, J. C.—*The Psycho-analytic Study of the Family;* L. and V. Woolf, Hogarth Press (London), fifth edition, 1935.

Folsom, Joseph Kirk—*The Family: Its Sociology and Social Psychiatry;* John Wiley & Sons, Inc., 1934.

Folsom, Joseph Kirk, editor—*Plan for Marriage;* Harper & Brothers, 1938.

Freund, Ernst—*Illegitimacy Laws of the United States and Certain Foreign Countries;* United States Children's Bureau, Publication No. 42, Government Printing Office, 1919.

Goodsell, Willystine—*Problems of the Family;* D. Appleton-Century Company, revised edition, 1936.

Groves, Ernest R.—*The American Family;* J. B. Lippincott Company, 1934.

Groves, Ernest R.—*Marriage;* Henry Holt and Company, 1933.

Groves, Ernest R., and Gladys H.—*Sex in Marriage;* The Macaulay Company, 1932.

Groves, Ernest R., and Brooks, Lee M.—*Readings in the Family;* J. B. Lippincott Company, 1934.

Groves, Ernest Rutherford, and Ogburn, William Fielding—*American Marriage and Family Relationships;* Henry Holt and Company, 1928.

Hall, Fred S.—*Medical Certification for Marriage;* Russell Sage Foundation, 1925.

Hall, Fred S., and Brooke, Elisabeth W.—*American Marriage Laws in Their Social Aspects;* Russell Sage Foundation, 1919.

Hamilton, G. V., and Macgowan, Kenneth—*What Is Wrong with Marriage?;* Albert and Charles Boni, 1929.

Hathway, Marion—*The Migratory Worker and Family Life;* Social Service Monograph No. 21, Chicago, 1934.

Horowitz, Jacob I.—*Manual of Divorce and Other Matrimonial Actions;* Central Book Company, 1938.

Kammerer, Percy Gamble—*The Unmarried Mother: A Study of Five Hundred Cases;* Little, Brown, and Company, 1918.

Key, Ellen—*Love and Marriage* (translated from the Swedish by Arthur G. Chater); G. P. Putnam's Sons, 1911.

Lichtenberger, J. P.—*Divorce: A Social Interpretation;* McGraw-Hill Book Company, Inc., 1931.

Lorimer, Frank, and Osborn, Frederick—*Dynamics of Population;* The Macmillan Company, 1934.

Lumpkin, Katharine DuPre, and Douglas, Dorothy Wolff—*Child Workers in America;* Robert M. McBride & Co., 1937.

Lundberg, Emma O., and Lenroot, Katharine F.—*Illegitimacy as a Child-Welfare Problem;* United States Children's Bureau, Publication No. 66, 1920, No. 75, 1921, and No. 128, 1924.

Lynd, Robert S., and Lynd, Helen Merrell—*Middletown: A Study in Contemporary American Culture;* Harcourt, Brace and Company, Inc., 1929.

Lynd, Robert S., and Lynd, Helen Merrell—*Middletown in Transition: A Study in Cultural Conflicts;* Harcourt, Brace and Company, Inc., 1937.

Mead, Margaret—*Coming of Age in Samoa;* W. Morrow & Company, 1928.

Monachesi, Elio D., and Baylor, Edith M. H.—*Child Welfare;* Harper & Brothers, 1937.

Mowrer, Ernest R.—*Family Disorganization: An Introduction to a Sociological Analysis;* University of Chicago Press, 1927.

Mowrer, Harriet R.—*Personality Adjustment and Domestic Discord;* American Book Company, 1935.

National Committee on Maternal Health—*Medical Aspects of Human Fertility;* National Committee on Maternal Health, Inc., 1932.

National Council of Parent Education, Inc.—*Parent Education,* a journal published by the National Council of Parent Education, Inc. (New York City), beginning April, 1934.

Puttee, Dorothy Frances, and Colby, Mary Ruth—*The Illegitimate Child in Illinois;* University of Chicago Press, 1937.

Queen, Stuart Alfred, and Mann, Delbert Martin—*Social Pathology*, Part I; Thomas Y. Crowell Company, 1925.

Reuter, Edward Byron—*Population Problems;* J. B. Lippincott Company, revised edition, 1937.

Reuter, Edward Byron, and Runner, Jessie R.—*The Family: Source Materials for the Study of Family and Personality;* McGraw-Hill Book Company, Inc., 1931.

Richmond, Mary E.—*Social Diagnosis;* Russell Sage Foundation, 1917.

Sumner, William Graham—*Folkways;* Ginn and Company, 1907.

Sutherland, E. H., and Locke, H. J.—*20,000 Homeless Men;* J. B. Lippincott Company, 1936.

Terman, Lewis M.—*Psychological Factors in Marital Happiness;* McGraw-Hill Book Company, Inc., 1938.

Thomas, William I.—*The Unadjusted Girl;* Little, Brown, and Company, 1928.

Thomas, William I., and Thomas, Dorothy Swaine—*The Child in America;* Alfred A. Knopf, 1928.

United States Department of Labor, Children's Bureau—*Selected List of Publications, March 1, 1937;* Government Printing Office, 1937.

Van Waters, Miriam—*Parents on Probation;* New Republic, Inc., 1927.

Vernier, Chester G.—*American Family Laws*, Vol. I, *Introductory Survey and Marriage* (assisted by Fred A. Weller), 1931; Vol. II, *Divorce and Separation* (assisted by Benjamin C. Duniway), 1932; Vol. III, *Husband and Wife* (assisted by John B. Hurlbut), 1935; Vol. IV, *Parent and Child* (assisted by E. Perry Churchill), 1936; Vol. V, *Incompetents and Dependents* (assisted by J. Rex Dibble and Richard A. Frank); Stanford University Press, 1938.

Waller, Willard—*The Family: A Dynamic Interpretation;* The Cordon Company, 1938.

Westermarck, Edward—*The History of Human Marriage*, three volumes; Macmillan and Co., Limited, 1891 and 1921.

Williamson, Margaretta—*The Social Worker in Child Care and Protection;* Harper & Brothers, 1931.

Young, Donald, editor—*The Modern American Family;* The Annals of the American Academy of Political and Social Science*, Vol. 160, March, 1932.

Zimmerman, Carle C., and Frampton, Merle E.—*Family and Society;* D. Van Nostrand Company, Inc., 1935.

CHAPTER XXVIII

SOCIAL PATHOLOGY OF GROUP LIFE

Types of Deviation and Inadequacy.—At many points group life may fall short of standards of wholesomeness or efficiency. Pathologic conditions may be considered with reference to social life in any geographical location ranging from the dwelling, neighborhood, community, metropolitan area, and county to the larger units of state, section, nation, empire, continent, and the world. They may also be treated with reference to the types and areas of human struggle and conflict.

Conflict involves a clash between individuals or groups, with an attempt to obstruct the activities and success of the opponent. It may profitably be examined under the headings: biological, or struggle for existence; physiological, or struggle for food; economic, or struggle for wealth; political, or struggle for power; and mental, or struggle for intellectual domination.[1] For convenience, however, in order to relate our discussion to earlier chapters, conflict will be sketched briefly under the categories economic, religious and sectarian, political, race and nativity, class, and culture conflicts.

Economic Conflicts.—Pathologies of economic life have been treated in many of their aspects in Part III, which was concerned primarily with individual and social inadequacies in income and opportunity. But there remain a wide variety of forms of struggle, often pathologic in their aspects, relating to the accumulation of wealth, and the opposing interests of capital and labor, of employer and employee, of landlord and tenant, of producer and consumer. In the economic field belong also the morbid conditions which grow out of speculation in the stock market or in land. There are also pathologies developing out of adoption of divergent moral standards—between the exponents of professional ethics and of fraudulent

---

[1] See Sorokin, Pitirim—*Contemporary Sociological Theories*, Chapter VI; Harper & Brothers, 1928. Or the approach may be that of social psychology. See, for example, Young, Kimball—*Source Book for Social Psychology*, Parts IV–VI; Alfred A. Knopf, 1927. The social significance of conflict is admirably indicated in MacIver, R. M.—*Society: A Textbook of Sociology;* Farrar & Rinehart, Inc., 1937.

methods, mutuality and self-interest, freedom and constraint, equity and inequity.

Pathologic conditions begin where demonstrable damage is done to individuals, or where the process of personal development is thwarted. It has been seen from the discussion of handicap that individuals may be permanently injured by failure in competition, by prolonged worry, by industrial disease or accident, by impure food purchased on the market, by patent medicines, and the abuse of liquors and drugs. Prevention of all save worry can, in part, be accomplished by regulation through statute law, or, failing that, by public monopoly supplemented by medical and social case work and reëducation.

Struggle between employer and employee, or between landlord and tenant, appears to be implicit in an industrial order based upon private ownership of property and competitive profit-making. Organization of each group to protect its own interests appears indispensable. But the means by which each characteristically protects its interests, whether the lockout, black list, employment of scabs, industrial espionage and refusal to negotiate on the one hand, or strikes, the ca'canny policy, or sabotage on the other, inevitably result not only in serious economic wastes but also on occasion in physical injury and a wide variety of morally injurious habits as well.

Here and there one finds evidence of successful reduction of this area of conflict through welfare work, employee representation, and the type of labor legislation which sets high minimum conditions for wages, hours, and control of the physical conditions within the plant. To some extent also the potential consequences of antagonism are mitigated by mediation, conciliation, and arbitration. But unless competitive industry can be made to operate under conditions equitable to both the employer and the employee, and coöperation can be induced within all areas in which there may be identity of interest, pathologic consequences are certain.

The struggle between landlord and tenant is less acute and not highly organized. Nevertheless, rent profiteering and evictions on the part of the landlord, and tenant strikes, deliberate damage to property, and rent dodging attest that this is an area of conflict in which economic conditions and particularly the private ownership of property tend to foster habitual inconsiderateness and antagonism. This is especially true in some slum districts in which as much rent is exacted as the market will bear, while no improvements are made on property and little or nothing invested (unless at the insistence of the board of health) for upkeep. Legislative regulation in this highly complex field of economic investment has seldom proved effectual because requisite fundamental changes in property today involve expenditures which cannot be recouped in higher rents from wage-earning tenants. Suggested preventives in the form of public housing will be considered later in the section on housing.

Religious and Sectarian Conflicts.—Struggles between the world's great religions, or between sects within a given religion, have often in the world's history been supported by persecution of the nonbeliever, and by force. In spite of America's fundamental principle of freedom of worship there are still periodic local evidences of the survival of conflicts of injurious types, expressed in the occasional administration of physical injury by some local group of vigilantes, or in mental injury or hardship, resulting from attitudes of contempt, hate, or ostracism. Mistreatment of the Jew in many countries of Europe within the present century has been "justified" often on religious grounds. Preventives lie largely in such training of the intellect and the emotions as will lead to more rational interpretation and application of religious doctrines and to tolerance.

Political Conflicts.—The struggle for power which in human history has led often to usurpation, annexation, conquest, and slavery is expressed within our nation at present chiefly in party organization and conflicts at the polls. Party organization appears to be essential for the representation of diverse points of view. But the concomitant manifestations of misleading propaganda, ballot-stuffing and other cheating, brawls, patronage, graft, and corruption are pathologic in their forms and consequences. The many devices to curb or eliminate these evils, whether constitutional amendments, the initiative and referendum, the short ballot, proportional representation, municipal management, and a wide variety of other expedients are achieved through legislation.[2] Undesirable laws and ineffectual enforcement fall also in the category of the pathology of political life. Preventives may comprise many structural or functional changes in the field of community organization including,

---

[2] They can be followed in the literature of political science. Current developments may be studied in the *Political Science Quarterly*, the *National Municipal Review*, *The Annals of the American Academy of Political and Social Science*, and many other periodicals.

among others, devices for the reshaping of attitudes and for moral and civic education and training for public office.

Race Conflicts.—Struggle between races has been continuous throughout human history and has been one of the more important factors in bringing about wars. In America, race conflict in its most conspicuous form is expressed in illegal exploitation and deprivation of privileges (which may result in accommodation rather than further conflict), local race riots, Oriental exclusion, and a fortunately decreasing number of annual lynchings. Although attitudes and practices toward races which differ in color from our own vary considerably from one section to another, social groups try to prevent interracial amalgamation through marriage laws reënforced by deep-seated sentiments and their social correlates, stable mores.

Where members of the contrasting race are many in number their dwellings tend to be segregated to a limited district within the city by understanding among members of the white race if it is impossible to accomplish such segregation under the law.[3] There is a marked tendency to limit the activities of the unfavored race to unskilled labor, farming, and domestic service; to segregate them in church, school, theatre, and transportation; and to exclude them from the social activities of the white population. There are many pronounced differences in the customs with regard to the white man's treatment of the Negro, between the North and Virginia, and between Virginia and the deep South. Negroes tend on the whole to suffer fewer social disadvantages where their number and percentage in the population are low, but there are local exceptions to such generalizations. For Negroes there is unquestioned restriction of opportunity, economic, social, and cultural—other than that suffered by the wage-earning group of the white population—practically throughout America.

In general the restrictions upon Oriental races are equally severe. These races still tend to suffer in a large part of America from social discrimination and in some districts from economic discrimination as well. The American Indian has endured extreme economic exploitation, and often quite inadequate protection from Federal sources, with, however, notable exceptions in the periods of service of at least two Federal Commissioners of Indian Affairs.

[3] See, for example, Gries, John M., and Ford, James, editors—*Negro Housing;* The President's Conference on Home Building and Home Ownership, Vol. VI, 1932.

The Foreign Born.—During periods of heavy immigration of persons from European or other countries speaking languages or following religions markedly different from those prevailing in the communities in which they settled, the immigrants, though not of colorèd races, have been treated as inferiors even when in culture, productivity, and character they may have been the equals or superiors of the native population. Amalgamation with the native stock and complete social assimilation have taken two or three generations in such cases. It has taken an equally long period for many forms of social discrimination to disappear. Traces of it still persist in many communities.[4]

Preventives must be traced in the literature of the subjects of race, immigration, and community organization primarily. Adequate evidence is still lacking that the biological result of the intermixture through marriage of white with yellow, red, or black stock leads to progeny physically and mentally the equal of the white. Hence, on biological grounds, quite apart from emotional considerations and tradition, the limitations upon the mingling of such remote races lacks scientific justification. But economic discriminations, or interference with the social development of members of remote races within their own social groups are in varying degree products of such unethical traits as selfishness, narrowness, intolerance, ignorance, and racial bigotry. Pathologic conditions arising therefrom must for their elimination depend upon developments in civic and moral education, as well as in general education. Improvements in statute law have much incidental value in the correction of the more tangible abuses.

Class Conflicts.—Dividing lines are not sharp between class struggle and the conflicts already described between employers and employees, between persons affiliated with "socially correct" religious organizations and those attended by the "lower classes," or between the landowner whites and their colored tenánts. The so-called class struggle between the bourgeoisie and the proletariat, or between the propertied and propertyless, in the main overlaps the struggle between corporate capital and organized labor. This dichotomy or division of humanity into two antagonistic groups is not absolute as some of its propounders have affirmed it to be. For

---

[4] On the problem of social distance and race prejudice see the excerpts from R. E. Park, E. S. Bogardus, E. F. Young, and W. I. Thomas in Young, Kimball —*op. cit.*, Chapter XVIII. On the Negro, *ibid.*, Chapter XIX.

many members of the wage-earning group possess some property and capital that is invested and thus are not strictly of the proletariat. Also many persons with little or no property of their own share the capitalist's ideologies and vote with the capitalist group.

Moreover, it should be noted that there are many class distinctions from the social viewpoint within the group known as the capitalists. There is little prospect that the person who has recently acquired his fortune will be "recognized" by the "old families," or that the person of inferior breeding, recent immigration, insufficient culture or character, will prove socially acceptable among those whose status is assured. In older communities particularly such considerations are deemed important and often inviolable within many of the groups of families which have enjoyed social prestige for many generations. The established families, conscious of position, tend to be reclusive as well as exclusive, and many are quite unaware of any envy or hatred of them which may develop on the part of outsiders. Their only weapons as a rule are withdrawal, or nonrecognition of others, with occasional ostracism of some member of their own group who violates the customs of their set. More aggressive and less fine tactics may, however, be employed by social groups immediately below them whose members may attempt to hold their recently and hard won status by means of snobbery and slights. Similar devices are used by certain members of each social group with reference to those "outsiders" whom they consider to belong in a group below them. The only pathologic condition, unless the slights and heartaches may be considered such, lies in that there should be any social distinction other than the distinction of character.

The Marxian division of society into two contending groups, the bourgeoisie and the proletariat, though widely accepted as fact, has been shown to be incorrect. Under conditions of revolution Sorokin has shown that the division tends to be one between persons who accept the party in power and those who do not. Some members of the bourgeoisie may become communists and thus acceptable, while some members of the proletariat by resisting the new government fall into the proscribed group. Thus the so-called class struggle proves to be primarily a struggle for political supremacy.[5]

Culture Conflicts.—The socio-cultural conflicts are of two main types—struggles between coeval or parallel cultures, and struggles of the new against the old. Wars between nations or groups of

[5] Sorokin, Pitirim—*op. cit.*, p. 530.

nations may be activated by contrasting ideologies in greater or less degree, whether between Mohammedan and Christian, monarchy and republic, dictatorship and democracy, capitalism and communism, civilization and barbarism, or other contrasting systems of thought, institutions, and behavior. Overlaps of each of these categories of culture conflict with one or more of the preceding areas of conflict—religious, political, economic, or racial—should be noted. A discussion of the preventives of war will be found in a later chapter.

Culture conflicts within the community, if one excludes race and labor conflicts, are not as a rule violent in their manifestations. Seldom today is the struggle more than a battle of words and newspaper broadsides, with some use of the *index expurgatorius*, some burning of books, occasional sabotage, and sequestration of leaders or opposing intellectual groups in concentration camps as in contemporary Germany. The persecution of Jews or of communists tends to involve simultaneously factors of "race," religion, economics, and politics. The fusion of so many hates may lead to extreme mob measures. Social ostracism, or banishment (deportation), may be supplemented by physical persecution and destruction of property. These are periodically characteristic manifestations both of pogroms or Jew-baiting, and of the persecution of seditious persons or Red-baiting.

The major preventives of conflict lie in overcoming prejudice through knowledge and in the discovering and fostering of common interests. If the social objective is, however, at all times to give each individual the opportunity to take the next steps in his intellectual, moral, and social development, and if it is pursued through a program of child and adult education which will provide with increasing effectiveness for each of these needs, most culture conflicts can in a few generations be reduced to the proportions of mere friendly rivalries.[6]

---

[6] One may concede the presumptive potentialities of scientific training of character while recognizing the limitations of available methods and tests. See especially *Studies in the Nature of Character* by The Character Education Inquiry, Teachers College, Columbia University, in coöperation with The Institute of Social and Religious Research, particularly Vol. II, *Studies in Service and Self-Control* (by Hugh Hartshorne, Mark A. May, and Julius B. Maller), and Vol. III, *Studies in the Organization of Character* (by Hugh Hartshorne, Mark A. May, and Frank K. Shuttleworth); The Macmillan Company, 1929–1930. See also Hartshorne, Hugh—*Character in Human Relations;* Charles Scribner's Sons, 1932: Jones, Vernon—*Character and Citizenship Training in the Public School;* University of Chicago Press, 1936: Young, Kimball, editor—*Social Attitudes*, especially Chapter III, "Attitudes and the Redirection of Behavior" by L. L. Bernard; Henry

Crisis Situations.—Unquestionably there are values to the individual and to social groups to be gleaned from crisis situations. The areas of conflict already described have tended periodically to precipitate crises with corresponding value to the community in so far as they developed initiative, resourcefulness, and intense coöperative effort. Conflict has, however, at the same time interfered with solidarity in the larger society while intensifying it within each segregated or warring group. It has sanctioned measures against the enemy which would be deplored within the group; accentuated social distance; created or fostered alignments inimical to the general welfare; and substituted coercion for freedom of intercourse and action. The elimination of conflict is still remote, but if by measures such as have been outlined or by other means conflicts should be virtually eliminated, social policy, to avert relative stagnation, would be under the necessity of continuing these values so far as possible through the encouragement of competition and friendly rivalries. Presumably there are enough unavoidable crises, in the form of unpreventable disasters [7] and political emergencies, to keep the capacity for intense effort alive. The personal crises derived from unsolved problems, and the disparities between the aims of the individual and the means at his command continue as major sources of stimulus and effort.

Pathologies of the Physico-social Environment.— Many conditions which tend to injure the individual and the group, or to thwart development, are characteristic of specific physical environments. Pathologies of the industrial environment have been sufficiently considered. Pathologies in the recreation field or the environment of leisure hours belong primarily to the literature of community organization, and would cover the physical, mental, and moral injuries done by commercialization of pleasure. The pleasure-seeking impulses of the population are exploited for profit primarily by catering to the common denominators of the populace—their sex, love, fun, and adventure interests. Regulation by law has proved difficult and the substitution of public provision of recreational facilities to meet the leisure-time needs of the population has been tardy. Nevertheless, the major preventive of the evils of irresponsible commercial

Holt and Company, 1931: and Young, Kimball—*Source Book for Social Psychology*, especially Chapter XVIII, "Prejudice: An Outgrowth of Subjective Environment"; Alfred A. Knopf, 1927.

[7] See Chapter XXX.

domination of the leisure-time interests would appear to be the socialization of recreation where regulation after fair trial proves ineffectual.

To exemplify the pathologies and correctives employable in each of these three physical environments of the daily life, industry, recreation, and the home, a fuller treatment of the problem of housing may prove advantageous.

Family Economics and Housing.—The types of dwellings which the low-income group are able to afford are almost invariably poorly built and are not infrequently dangerous to health. Insanitary housing, by causing disease, may be responsible for the unemployment or unemployability of the tenant breadwinner, thus causing primary poverty. Or, so large a portion of his wages may be expended for drugs, medicine, and medical service for wife or children to combat such illness, that secondary poverty is induced.

The prevailing type of wage-earner housing found in our largest American cities is the tenement house. This is a structure from three to six stories high, built largely of wood but often with a brick exterior commonly sharing party walls with similar buildings to right and left and thus sharing with its neighbors a narrow court or shaft at the sides and an ugly yard at the rear. Within, there may be a dark hallway, a common toilet located in hall, cellar, or yard, and the stench from uncleanliness, insanitary plumbing, and years of careless usage and disrepair.

Housing and Disease.—Such dwellings may contribute to ill health on the part of the occupants in the following ways:

1. Through improper location on wet or imperfectly drained land, the lower stories may be damp. Dampness tends to lower resistance to disease. If the building is erected in a highly exposed position, proper heating in the winter season may be impossible for many rooms and such exposure may reduce resistance to disease.

2. Through the characteristic use of wood for interior, if not exterior, construction, tenants are exposed to a continuous fire risk. Few tenements or apartment houses have more than one fireproof means of egress, if any is provided, so each family is constantly endangered by the carelessness of all the other families in the building. A tenement-house fire may mean the possibility of death from burning or suffocation, or injury from accident. Fright may cause permanent nervous impairment.

3. Through defective structure or bad repair there may be con-

tinuous danger to life or limb from accident. Winding stairs and worn treads take their annual toll in broken limbs; rotten flooring, insecure railings of stairs, and piazzas or fire escapes insecurely attached are the cause of many injuries.

4. Through defective orientation with reference both to the points of the compass and to neighboring buildings, tenants may be deprived of sunshine and even of adequate light. Many of our cities have planned, and continue to plan, streets running due east and west. If the apartments on such streets are built up to their side lot lines, approximately half of their rooms are sunless. The absence of sunshine generally means dampness, cheerlessness, and in those thousands of flats which have no sunlighted room a reduced resistance and an increased exposure to disease.

5. Through excessive height; for high buildings may contribute to ill health, not only by increasing the fire risk and shutting out sunshine, but also by necessitating stair climbing, which is a hardship to the aged, a limitation to the play activities of the very young, and often a source of pain, if not positive danger, to pregnant women or cardiac cases.

6. Through the crowding of many families in the same building, sharing the same halls, and perhaps the same toilets, the chances of exposure to certain infections and contagious diseases are increased.

7. Through crowding of population within the tenement block or district, there is increased strain upon the nervous system. It is difficult to secure relief from the noises of traffic and of neighbors. As sleep is essential to the repair of the body after the fatigue of the day's activities, the sleeplessness entailed by crowded living must be considered one of the most serious of the sources of reduced resistance or ill health on the part of the tenement dweller.

8. Through crowding of rooms there are increased opportunities for communication of disease. Where there is crowding of lodgers in the same apartment with the family there are reduced opportunities for privacy and perhaps for the accepted decencies of life, which may be an occasion, in conjunction with other causes, for immorality with its train of sexual diseases.

9. Through inadequate plumbing, the use of unclean or defective fixtures, and the sharing of toilets by two or more families, transmission of diseases is facilitated. Lack of water supply within an apartment makes personal cleanliness and house cleaning difficult.

10. Through poor ventilation, windowless rooms, or rooms on narrow closed courts, discomfort is incurred from stale air, and probably also reduced resistance to disease.

11. Through inadequate natural lighting ill health is caused by dirt which must be seen to be removed, and by impairment of the vision through eyestrain. The chances of transmission of tuberculosis from one family to another are increased and the resistance of those members of the family who are forced to pass their days in gloomy or dark rooms is almost certain to be reduced, as human beings need sunshine for vigorous growth.

12. Through defective or imperfect equipment, health may be injured in a variety of ways. A leaky flue or defective gas fixtures may endanger the lives of the tenants from carbon monoxide. Defective electric wiring may create risk from fire or shock. Vermin and insects may infest houses in poor repair.

13. Finally, through the proximity of factories to tenements, air may be vitiated by chemical gases, mineral dust, or soot, causing throat irritation and reduced resistance to respiratory diseases.

The poor in smaller cities, suburbs, villages, and rural communities live usually in detached dwellings but may suffer the dangers of disrepair, lack of proper sanitation, and undesirable surroundings.

In comparison with the multiple dwelling the detached house can more easily be rendered conducive to high disease resistance and to good health. With a little attention to planning, it can be made structurally safe and every room can be well lighted, well ventilated, and equipped for the comfort and convenience of its occupants. For families with children it makes possible not only good health, but opportunities for supervised play activities and for protection from undesirable associates.

Neighborhood Inadequacies.—Aside from the housing in slums, many other deleterious influences are exercised by the slum. Streets, yards, and alleys are foul or ill kept; buildings are ugly and depressing. Confusion, dust, and noise are inescapable. The street life of children is beyond parental guidance and control. The shops which vend meat and groceries, and the eating and drinking establishments, have low standards of sanitation and sometimes cause illness from the inferior drink or food which they sell. Inferiority characterizes the commercial recreations. Play space is lacking where children may safely engage in wholesome recreation. Parks are rare in which children or adults may enjoy restful contact with nature. For a majority of slum dwellers there has been no escape from ugly, sordid, dispiriting surroundings.

To counteract these influences settlement houses, institutional churches, branch libraries, school centers, and occasional playgrounds have been established and have worked with creditable unselfishness, and courage, judgment, and skill. Their exponents increasingly contend that their service is often neutralized and sometimes nullified by the omnipresent counter influences which surround them. The building of industrial efficiency or of character is largely dependent upon a milieu which is wholesome, which favors the development of energy, self-confidence, and self-respect. While strong personalities, given the necessary incentive, can override or live down adverse circumstances, the majority requires a more favorable medium. Poverty may be both a cause and a result of the slum, as many of the vicious circles of poverty operate here, but clearly the elimination of all poverty and handicap involves the clearance of all slums.

Prevention.—In a relatively wealthy nation there is no necessity for perpetuating the types of dwellings which injure health and morale. City slums and suburban areas of shacks and shambles have been accepted, unthinkingly or apathetically, as a necessary evil. It is possible to eliminate them and replace them with wholesome housing and decent, respectable neighborhood developments. Recent Federal undertakings in this direction have called public attention to the problem. England, Holland, and other European countries have proceeded much further than America in the replacement of slums with sanitary low-cost housing. A well-framed public policy, executed with judgment, could within two or three generations eliminate all unwholesome housing and thereby prevent such poverty as bad housing entails. European experience indicates that a general rise in standards of living, and improvement in habits, attitudes, health, vigor, and longevity, follow the provision of improved housing for the poor.[8]

The prevention of such pathologic conditions as are traceable to insanitary and unsafe housing involves the following measures. *First,* housing legislation including building laws, sanitary laws, and zoning ordinances which will require all new construction to be sound, sani-

[8] Ford, James, in collaboration with Morrow, Katherine, and Thompson, George N.—*Slums and Housing, with Special Reference to New York City: History, Conditions, Policy,* Vol. II, Chapter XXVII; Harvard University Press, 1936.

tary, and safe, and ensure adequate light and ventilation for each house or apartment. *Second*, competent enforcement, which necessitates appropriations sufficient to make periodic inspections of all tenements and houses, new or old, to discover violations of the law and prosecute such violations. *Third*, devices to encourage detached single-family housing and to bring it within the reach of the low-rental group through facilitating (1) the location of industries in suburbs and outlying communities, and (2) large-scale suburban developments to bring down the unit cost of housing. *Fourth*, legislative encouragement of the limited-dividend type of housing company and of coöperative housing by tenants. *Fifth*, removal of taxation on improvements of a residential character for low-income groups, levying all property taxes upon the land, or else public ownership of the land for housing ventures approved and supervised by Federal, state, or municipal governments.[9]

A comprehensive program for slum elimination is also necessary. It would include, first, the devices already described for the replacement of insanitary housing. Beyond this there is needed an accurate identification of slum areas, an understanding of the trends of each, and a plan consistent with the master plan of the city for the future utilization of each area to be cleared. The worst areas should be eliminated first. Many would be found by the city planning authority to be appropriate for replacement by commerce, industry or parks, or by high-class residential developments. Others would be more appropriate for the rehousing of wage-earning families displaced by slum clearance. If clearance costs were met from public funds, private enterprise under public control or supervision would be able to meet a large percentage of the costs of rebuilding, especially if the pooling of block-ownership were made practicable by special legislation and if Federal loans or Federal guarantees of private loans for the rehousing of wage-earners under government standards were facilitated. Nevertheless, in our larger cities public housing or heavy public subsidies for government-supervised private housing by limited-dividend corporations would be necessary at the core of the slum where the very poorest now dwell. Promising beginnings in this colossal program are today being made in many American cities under Federal stimulation.[10]

footnotes[9] *Ibid.*, Vol. II.
[10] *Ibid.*, Vol. II, Chapter XXXV, and Post, Langdon W.—*The Challenge of Housing;* Farrar & Rinehart, Inc., 1938.

If, as has been estimated, one-third of the population of the United States lives in substandard dwellings, the cost of replacement with ten million wholesome, sanitary, fire-safe homes, would run to not less than twenty billion dollars and more likely to much larger figures. Granting that no great nation can afford to tolerate conditions of living that injure health, endanger life, lower efficiency, or warp citizenship, the problem should be faced of providing the needed homes, within a generation or two, by methods that are economic, practical, and yet consistent with the aim expressed above.

Doubtless many of the present substandard homes can be rendered decent places of residence by means of appropriate reconditioning. This can be done economically by private capital if its efforts are aided by guaranteed loans at low interest, as have recently been made available through the Federal Housing Administration. But the economies will be illusory unless each loan is contingent upon demonstration of the wisdom of the proposed repairs or improvements and unless the loans are limited to areas in which other dwellings are already improved or improvable by the same method. Existing knowledge does not reveal whether less or more than half of the substandard housing of America can be rendered wholesome by this means.

Easy, government-guaranteed loans, for private construction of new homes or of developments, costing, for example, $2,500 or less per house, would also serve to meet another fraction of this rehousing problem with little or no loss to public funds, where ably directed and supervised. Rural and suburban resettlement competently planned with reference to all economic factors involved, offers another outlet.

The slum, however, remains untouched by these measures. It is beyond repair and so requires wholesale demolition before decent housing can be rendered practical. The loss involved in condemnation and demolition inevitably falls to Federal, state, or local governments, since private owners can find no economic incentive to destroy and rebuild on the site of an investment once profitable but now a liability.   •

Immediate assumption by government of all the losses inevitable in the acquisition and demolition of slum properties would make possible downward revaluation of the land to a point which would interest private capital in leasing or purchasing it for housing. The government's loss would be quickly compensated by savings in costs of dependency, disease, or crime, as well as by the increased productivity—both economic and civic—of the former slum population now wholesomely housed.[11] Even where public money is necessary to subsidize a portion of the construction costs in rehousing the poorer elements of the slum population there should still be net public gain —assuming always honest, skilful, and competent planning and administration. Such subsidy if never directly repaid could properly be classed as a form of "relief" that rehabilitates present dependents and prevents future dependency. For it would confer upon the present slum population opportunities to health, self-respect, and efficiency not available to America's poor since the homesteading period of the past century.

An adaptable public housing policy, keen to discover and adopt the most economic means to slum elimination and decent housing— to secure skilled local coöperation for each project and to utilize private enterprise wherever it will competently conform to government standards of planning and operation—can remake the daily environment of the poor and replace discouragement with fresh incentive. If accompanied by economic planning to increase the nation's distributable wealth and the worker's income [12] further governmental underwriting of wage-earner housing might be unnecessary within a generation or two.

Deviation and Conflict, Considered with Reference to Geographical Units.—Neighborhoods depart from norms of wholesomeness and efficiency when they contain areas of economic blight (declining property values) or of slums. Lack of adequate and accessible parks, playgrounds, schools, libraries, churches, and transportation services to municipal, commercial, industrial, civic, and cultural centers are symptoms of inefficiency. Factors thwarting development include noxious conditions of insanitation in housing, industry, and recreation. Preventives are chiefly in the fields of regulatory legislation (health, building, housing, zoning, and public safety legislation) and in the science and art of city planning.

Community, city, and metropolitan regions depart from norms of economic and social efficiency wherever any inhabitants suffer needless ill health, or inconvenience, because of defects in the city or regional plan, or difficult economic and social adjustments

[11] Ford, James—*op. cit.*, Vol. II, Chapters XXXVIII and XLI.
[12] See *supra* Chapters XXIV–XXVI.

because of the migration of its industries or other local calamities.[13]

County, state, or section may suffer urban-rural conflicts, or conflicts between agriculture and commerce or industry. Diversity in products, traditions, and standards of living as well as race, religion, and politics may lead to antagonisms between states or groups of states, ranging from mere bickerings to civil war. The tendency of stronger groups to appropriate to themselves all economic and social privileges, may not only reduce standards of living for the less powerful group (not necessarily the minority) but lead to deep resentment and bitterness which will influence future relations deleteriously. Preventive measures fall within the fields of economic planning, and state or national planning.[14]

Lastly, nations and groups of nations throughout the world comprise all of the areas of conflict—physical and social—and all the deleterious results of imperfectly controlled heredity and environmental conditions, which have been treated in this chapter and the foregoing chapters. But to these are added trade and tariff wars, exclusive agreements, embargoes, armaments, coercion, and war. World conferences, whether on textiles, drug traffic, or the reduction of armaments; international research agencies, such as the International Labour Office; world-wide professional organizations; the League of Nations and the World Court; as well as provisions for free migration and the interchange of culture are with few exceptions the contributions of quite recent generations. They are too recent in origin to warrant more than tentative appraisal. If carefully developed and combined with the types of education for internationalism outlined in the later chapter on war, it is not inconceivable that in time friendly competition and coördination can largely replace conflict and compromise in an ever changing but increasingly integrated world plan.

QUESTIONS FOR DISCUSSION OR EXAMINATION

1. What are the values of struggle? How can these be preserved while eliminating those effects which are harmful?
2. Classify contemporary types of conflict and give examples of each.
3. By what measures can conflict be reduced or eliminated in each of these categories?

[13] Adams, Thomas—*Outline of Town and City Planning;* Russell Sage Foundation, 1935. McKenzie, Roderick D.—*The Metropolitan Community;* McGraw-Hill Book Company, Inc., 1933. Carpenter, Niles—*The Sociology of City Life;* Longmans, Green and Co., 1931.

[14] *E.g.* Publications of the National Resources Board.

4. What are the pathologic conditions of (a) housing, or (b) neighborhood environments? By what measures can these be eliminated?
5. What specific forms should education take to reduce conflicts of race, religion, or class?

PROBLEMS FOR INDIVIDUAL STUDY

1. A detailed analysis of any area of conflict—together with methods for social regulation and prevention.
2. A study of the social assimilation of immigrants from some selected foreign country.
3. A report on selected works on (a) social attitudes, (b) social distance, or (c) racial amalgamation.
4. A field study of housing conditions and measures, in some selected city.
5. A field study of labor conflicts, in some selected industry or city.

SUGGESTIONS FOR SUPPLEMENTARY READINGS

Anderson, Elin L.—*We Americans;* Harvard University Press, 1937.

Armstrong, Hamilton Fish—*"We or They": Two Worlds in Conflict;* The Macmillan Company, 1937.

Beard, Charles A.—*American Government and Politics;* The Macmillan Company, seventh edition, 1935.

Beard, Charles A.—*The American Party Battle;* The Macmillan Company, 1928.

Beard, Charles A.—*An Economic Interpretation of American Politics,* two volumes; The Macmillan Company, 1913–15.

Boeckel, Florence B.—*Between War and Peace. A Handbook for Peace Workers;* The Macmillan Company, 1928.

Brinton, Crane—*The Anatomy of Revolution;* W. W. Norton & Company, Inc., 1938.

Buell, Raymond Leslie—*The Native Problem in Africa,* two volumes; The Macmillan Company, 1928.

Bunyan, James—*Intervention, Civil War, and Communism in Russia, April–December 1918;* The Johns Hopkins Press, 1936.

Bunyan, James, and Fisher, H. H.—*The Bolshevik Revolution, 1917–1918;* Stanford University Press, 1934.

Carr-Saunders, A. M.—*World Population, Past Growth and Present Trends;* Oxford University Press, 1936.

Case, Clarence Marsh—*Non-Violent Coercion: A Study in Methods of Social Pressure;* The Century Co., 1923.

Catlin, George E. G.—*Preface to Action;* The Macmillan Company, 1934.

Chapin, F. Stuart—*Contemporary American Institutions: A Sociological Analysis;* Harper & Brothers, 1935.

Commons, John R.—*Races and Immigrants in America;* The Macmillan Company, new edition, 1920.

Coyle, Grace Longwell—*Studies in Group Behavior;* Harper & Brothers, 1937.

Cruttwell, C. R. M. F.—*A History of Peaceful Change in the Modern World;* Oxford University Press, 1937.

Dixon, Roland B.—*The Building of Cultures;* Charles Scribner's Sons, 1928.

Doob, Leonard W.—*Propaganda: Its Psychology and Technique;* Henry Holt and Company, 1935.

Doyle, Bertram Wilbur—*The Etiquette of Race Relations in the South;* University of Chicago Press, 1937.

Durkheim, Emile—*Division of Labor in Society* (translated by George Simpson); The Macmillan Company, 1933.

Edwards, Lyford P.—*The Natural History of Revolution;* University of Chicago Press, 1927.

Elliott, Mabel A., and Merrill, Francis E.—*Social Disorganization;* Harper & Brothers, 1934.

Fairchild, Henry Pratt—*Immigration: A World Movement and Its American Significance;* The Macmillan Company, revised edition, 1925.

Feldman, Herman—*Problems in Labor Relations;* The Macmillan Company, 1937.

Fisher, V. E., and Hanna, Joseph V.—*The Dissatisfied Worker;* The Macmillan Company, 1931.

Frankfurter, Felix, and Greene, Nathan—*The Labor Injunction;* The Macmillan Company, 1930.

Friedman, Lee M.—*Early American Jews;* Harvard University Press, 1934.

Garis, Roy L.—*Immigration Restriction;* The Macmillan Company, 1927.

Gillin, John Lewis—*Social Pathology;* The Century Co., 1933.

Gobbel, Luther L.—*Church-State Relationships in Education in North Carolina Since 1776;* Duke University Press, 1938.

Golder, Frank Alfred, editor—*Documents of Russian History 1914–1917* (translated by Emanuel Aronsberg); The Century Co., 1927.

Gosnell, Harold F.—*Machine Politics: Chicago Model;* University of Chicago Press, 1937.

Hart, Hornell—*The Science of Social Relations;* Henry Holt and Company, 1927.

Hartshorne, Edward Yarnall, Jr.—*The German Universities and National Socialism;* Harvard University Press, 1937.

Hicks, Granville, with the assistance of Stuart, John—*John Reed. The Making of a Revolutionary;* The Macmillan Company, 1936.

Hiller, E. T.—*The Strike: A Study in Collective Action;* University of Chicago Press, 1928.

Hocking, William Ernest—*The Spirit of World Politics;* The Macmillan Company, 1931.

Janowsky, Oscar I.—*People at Bay;* Oxford University Press, 1938.

Jones, J. Carlton, Vandenbosch, Amry, and Vandenbosch, Mary Belle—*Readings in Citizenship;* The Macmillan Company, 1932.

Klineberg, Otto—*Race Differences;* Harper & Brothers, 1935.

Laski, Harold J.—*Democracy in Crisis;* University of North Carolina Press, (expanded version), 1935.

Lippmann, Walter—*American Inquisitors;* The Macmillan Company, 1928.

Lippmann, Walter—*A Preface to Politics;* The Macmillan Company, 1933.

Lippmann, Walter—*Public Opinion;* The Macmillan Company, 1922.

Lowe, Boutelle Ellsworth—*International Protection of Labor. International Labor Organization, History and Law;* The Macmillan Company, revised edition, 1935.

Marcus, Jacob R.—*The Jew in the Medieval World;* The Sinai Press, 1938.

Mayo, Elton—*Human Problems of an Industrial Civilization;* The Macmillan Company, 1933.

Meriam, Lewis, and Associates—*The Problem of Indian Administration;* The Brookings Institution, 1928.

Merriam, Charles E.—*Chicago. A More Intimate View of Urban Politics;* The Macmillan Company, 1929.

Merriam, Charles E., and Gosnell, Harold F.—*The American Party System;* The Macmillan Company, revised edition, 1929.

Merriam, Charles E., Parratt, Spencer D., and Lepawsky, Albert—*The Government of the Metropolitan Region of Chicago;* University of Chicago Press, 1933.

Palm, Franklin C.—*The Middle Classes: Then and Now;* The Macmillan Company, 1937.

Park, Robert E., and Miller, Herbert A.—*Old World Traits Transplanted;* Harper & Brothers, 1921.

Perlman, Selig—*History of Trade Unionism in the United States;* The Macmillan Company, 1922.

Pitt-Rivers, G. H. L.—*The Clash of Culture and the Contact of Races;* George Routledge & Sons, Ltd., 1927.

Queen, Stuart Alfred, Bodenhafer, Walter Blaine, and Harper, Ernest Bouldin—*Social Organization and Disorganization;* Thomas Y. Crowell Company, 1935.

Ross, Edward Alsworth—*Social Control. A Survey of the Foundations of Order;* The Macmillan Company, 1901.

Salter, Sir Arthur, Thompson, Sir J. Arthur, Johnston, G. H., Zimmern, Alfred, Andrews, C. F., Libby, Frederick S., Atkinson, Henry A., Steed, Wickham, and others—*The Causes of War;* The Macmillan Company, 1932.

Sorel, Georges—*Reflections on Violence* (authorized translation by T. E. Hulme); B. W. Huebsch, Inc., 1914.

Sorokin, Pitirim—*Social Mobility;* Harper & Brothers, 1927.

Sorokin, Pitirim A.—*The Sociology of Revolution;* J. B. Lippincott Company, 1925.

Soule, George—*The Coming American Revolution;* The Macmillan Company, 1934.

Soule, George—*The Future of Liberty;* The Macmillan Company, 1936.

Taylor, Griffith—*Environment, Race, and Migration;* University of Chicago Press, 1938.

Thomas, Norman—*The Choice Before Us: Mankind at the Crossroads;* The Macmillan Company, 1934.

Thomas, William I., and Znaniecki, Florian—*The Polish Peasant in Europe and America;* two volumes, Alfred A. Knopf, 1927.

Wagner, Donald O.—*Social Reformers: From Adam Smith to John Dewey;* The Macmillan Company, 1934.

Whitehead, T. N.—*The Industrial Worker;* Harvard University Press, 1938.

Young, Donald—*American Minority Peoples: A Study in Racial and Cultural Conflicts;* Harper & Brothers, 1932.

Young, Kimball—*Source Book for Social Psychology;* Part Four, "Social Attitudes and the Subjective Environment"; Alfred A. Knopf, 1927.

CHAPTER XXIX

DELINQUENCY AND CRIME

Social Pathology of Crime.—No field of individual deviation has more obvious social consequences of a pathologic nature than criminality. For crime, whether murder, theft, or trespass, clearly injures persons other than the perpetrator. Organized professional criminality is also a threat to social organization. Racketeering offers a striking example of antisocial organization; but counterfeiting, blackmail, forgery, robbery, kidnapping, violation of liquor and drug laws are but a few types of professional crime in which resistance to the established order is often undertaken by organizations of professional criminals. Crime, whether or not it is organized, exemplifies rebellion against the authority of society's rules as expressed in criminal law.

The groups into which social deviates are classified overlap. The inebriate has already been discussed under the general category of the handicapped. But if the inebriate is found intoxicated in public places he may be arrested for the misdemeanor of "public drunkenness" or "disturbance of the peace" and if convicted and sentenced, becomes technically a criminal. There are types of behavior characteristic of certain stages of inebriety, epilepsy, mental disorder, and drug addition which are in violation of law and may involve arrest and sentence. Criminality in such cases—and even in cases of feeblemindedness and chronic disease—is in one sense a symptom of the more fundamental disorder. Assault by a person suffering from an epileptic seizure, a mania, or intoxication by alcohol or marihuana is still objectively a "crime against the person." Theft or prostitution by a feebleminded person, attempted suicide by the victim of chronic disease, illegal possession of drugs or liquors by addicts are technically crimes and such symptomatic actions swell the figures of criminal offenses. It is incorrect to state that the handicap is "the cause" of the crime but it is prominent among the associated factors in each such individual case whether in providing the susceptibility, the propensity, or the incentive.

Similarly, larceny may under certain conditions be symptomatic of

498

poverty. Juvenile delinquency is a common symptom of the broken home. Sex crimes may be associated with peculiarities in family relationships. Rape and brutality develop in conditions which war forces upon invading armies. Vagrancy may be an outgrowth of migration in search of employment.

Although the percentage of the mentally abnormal and subnormal who are criminals is higher than the percentage of normal persons who are criminals, it should be recognized that the vast majority of mental deviates are not criminal. Similarly, careful studies show that the percentage of criminalism among the poor is very low. Handicaps and poverty operate less as motives to crime than as conditioning factors.

Definitions.—A crime is an act or a failure to act (an omission) which is prohibited by law and punished by society through some established agency of government. The law penalizes the act or omission because it is deemed wrongful and harmful to the interests of the group. Not all wrongful acts—which in the earlier terminology include sins, vices, and torts—however, are designated as crimes. Thus among the sins, or offenses against deity, recognized by any given religion or sect, some, such as murder ("thou shalt not kill"), are crimes in contemporary civilized states while others, such as blasphemy ("thou shalt not take my name in vain"), may not be punished under the criminal code. Some vices, or forms of "self-injury in violation of natural law," are also crimes or violation of public law. Others are not. In general, solitary sexual vice is not fully covered under penal codes, while most perversions involving two or more persons are commonly reached. Public drunkenness is a crime in many states; drunkenness in the home, though equally recognized as an "injury to self in violation of natural law," is not a crime, because not so listed in statute law. No act is a crime until specific law makes it so.

Torts are wrongful acts for which the victim may claim damages before the civil courts. Under housing acts, for example, many kinds of negligence on the part of the builder or landlord make possible suit for damages by the victim in civil courts and at the same time proceedings by the state in criminal courts for violations of the criminal law. But many other wrongs actionable in civil courts are not covered in the criminal law. There are also wrongful acts that may be neither crimes, vices, nor torts, and perhaps that are not specifically included in the definitions of sin offered by the

Church. Thus much harm can be done to one's neighbors by innuendo or forms of gossip which cannot be reached by the courts.

Crimes are not necessarily wrongful acts in the absolute sense. There is always the possibility that acts innately good and socially useful will be infringements of the existing penal code and thereby technically crimes. The prophets of a new religion have often in history been subject to arrest, prosecution, and capital punishment under the laws of their period. The leaders of rebellion or revolution are technically criminals under the government which they seek to overthrow. Unless the revolution is successful they are likely to suffer capital punishment. But if successful they will be rated as heroes and may become executives under a new government which will make legal "criminals" of their former persecutors.

Delinquency is the term ordinarily used in recent years to cover the infractions of the law by juveniles—usually the line is drawn at the age of eighteen. But feebleminded adult criminals with the mental age of children are increasingly termed "defective delinquents." Often the term delinquency is used loosely for behavior which would be likely to lead to conviction in the courts in case the perpetrator were caught.

Criminology is the science which deals with crime and delinquency in their relations to social organization and the social process, and is largely concerned with the classification and etiology of crime, the nature of the criminal, and the effects of contemporary procedure. Penology is the branch of criminology which is concerned with the treatment of criminals whether penal or reformatory.

Extent of Crime.—Crime statistics are of limited value because the number of infractions of law is never known to the police. The available statistics cover arrests, sentences, and persons in prison, on probation or parole, but do not bear a constant ratio to the infractions of law. The crimes "known to the police" have been summarized since 1930 by the Federal Department of Justice from data supplied by the police. In 1935 reports from 1,423 cities comprising less than half the population of the country showed for that year 6,390 criminal homicides, 25,178 aggravated assaults, 37,967 robberies, 177,381 burglaries, 371,796 larcenies, 121,045 automobile thefts, and 4,106 cases of rape. Altogether there was a total of 744,863 major offenses exclusive of embezzlement, counterfeiting, forgery, arson, sex offenses other than rape, receiving of stolen goods, etc. Only one offender in four is apprehended, and the number of offenses not reported is unknown.[1]

For the state of Massachusetts in that same year there was a total of 187,560 arrests, of which 176,956 were male and 10,604 female. Of these 7,096 were for offenses against the person, 15,239 offenses against property, and 165,225 offenses against public order. Of offenses against the person there were 5,585 of assault. Robbery came second with 653; manslaughter third with 224; 41 arrests for murder; and miscellaneous 593. Of the 15,239 offenses against property 7,822 were for larceny; breaking, entering, and larceny 3,389; using motor vehicle without authority 838; trespass 723; stealing ride and evading fare 543; fraud 274; and miscellaneous 1,650. Of the 165,225 arrests for offenses against public order 93,151 were for drunkenness; 36,038 for violations of motor vehicle laws; and 9,350 more for violating traffic rules. Next in order were nonsupport (5,548); sex offenses (2,492); "idle and disorderly" and disturbing the peace (2,290); tramps, vagabonds, vagrants (1,195); violating liquor laws (992); carrying weapon (315); violating narcotic drug laws (178); and somewhat over ten thousand cases distributed among other offenses. A study of these figures reveals half the arrests for drunkenness and a quarter for violations of motor laws or traffic rules. Of the 187,000 arrested over 52,000 cases were dismissed, and during that year over 115,000 convicted, of whom somewhat over 13,000 or 7 per cent of those arrested were sentenced to prison.[2]

Federal statistics of state and Federal prisons and reformatories, and county and city jails show 136,810 prisoners present on January 1, 1934, and 62,251 received during the year 1934 in state and Federal prisons. On January 1st of the preceding year county and city jails had an additional population of 51,436, and received during the first half of that year 304,242 additional prisoners.[3] From such data as are available it is evident not only that arrests are made for only a minority of the infractions of law reported to the police,

[1] Sellin, Thorsten—"Crime Prevention and Treatment," *Social Work Year Book 1937;* Russell Sage Foundation, 1937. Sellin submits estimates of over 1,300,000 major offenses and 15,000,000 minor offenses a year, exclusive of liquor and motor law violations, known to the police of the United States.

[2] Massachusetts—*Annual Report of the Commissioner of Correction for the Year Ending December 31, 1935,* pp. 106–108, 109, *et seq.;* The Commonwealth of Massachusetts, Public Document No. 115 (no date).

[3] *Statistical Abstract of the United States 1936,* p. 74; Government Printing Office, 1936.

but also that, since few of those arrested are imprisoned, statistics of prisoners cover only a small percentage of the lawbreakers of any given year. The percentages of habitual and of casual lawbreakers in our population are not known, though estimated at from one to three per cent.

The Social Cost of Crime.—The annual crime bill for America is many billions of dollars per year.[4] Accurate measurement of the money cost is, however, not possible. The more significant cost of crime to society lies in the loss entailed where the personal development and constructive social participation of the criminal are thwarted, rather than in the cost of maintaining police, courts, and prisons, or in replacing the losses suffered by the victims of crime.

Causes of Crime.—In the vast literature of criminology the causes of crime have tended to be covered by three major approaches: first, general statistical studies; second, local studies analyzing specific factors; and third, case studies attempting to determine the relative weight and the interplay of the many elements in personality and environment which have some bearing upon subsequent criminality.[5]

Space does not permit a summary of the findings of the relations of crime in general, or of specific crimes, to season, weather, race,

[4] J. Edgar Hoover uses the figure $15,000,000,000. See, for example, his article "A War on Crime"; *This Week*, September 12, 1937. These larger figures include estimates of annual losses by fraud, etc., in addition to the costs of Federal, state, and local police, courts, prisons, and their officers. The National Commission on Law Observance and Enforcement concludes that any attempt at a lump-sum estimate should be avoided. To show the range they cite: "Anderson, 'The State Program for Mental Hygiene,' *Journal of Social Forces*, Vol. 1, p. 92 (1923) ($2,500,000 per day, or $912,500,000 per year); Gillin, 'Crime Is Our Most Expensive Luxury,' *Journal of Applied Sociology*, Vol. 10, p. 213 (1926) ($3,000,000,000 per year); Bower, *The Economic Waste of Sin*, p. 97 (New York, 1924) ($3,329,813,788 per year); Smith, 'Our Biggest Tax—The Cost of Crime,' *Literary Digest*, Vol. 82, p. 34 (1924) ($10,000,000,000 per year); Enright, 'Our Biggest Business—Crime,' *North American Review*, Vol. 228, p. 385 (1929) ($11,-800,000,000 to $13,000,000,000 per year); Anonymous, 'What the Criminal Costs and What to Do about It,' *American Review of Reviews*, Vol. 75, p. 431 (1927) ($13,000,000,000 per year); White House Conference on Child Health and Protection, Preliminary Report of the Committee on Youth Outside the Home and School, p. 405 (New York, 1930) ($16,000,000,000 per year); Reeve, 'Eighteen Billion a Year for Crime,' New York *Herald-Tribune*, March 22, 1931 ($18,000,000,000 per year)"; *Report on the Cost of Crime*, p. 70; Publication No. 12, Government Printing Office, 1931.

[5] In the suggestions for supplementary readings following this chapter the works of Aschaffenburg and of Bonger might be termed general statistical studies; Breckinridge and Abbott, Shaw (*Delinquency Areas*), and Thrasher offer excellent examples of local studies; the three works by Sheldon and Eleanor T. Glueck, and several by William Healy are based primarily on case studies.

religion, age, sex, marital condition, occupation, region, or the business cycle.[6] Many of the conclusions, subject to the inevitable qualifications of their local application, may, however, be gleaned from the excerpts which follow. For the purposes of the student of social policy, local studies and case studies have more immediate value.

Delinquency Areas.—Many studies have been made of the environment of the delinquent child and its relation to behavior. Outstanding in scope and quality is the report by Shaw and McKay on "Social Factors in Juvenile Delinquency," based on data for Chicago.

It covered:

"1. A series of 9,243 alleged delinquent boys (aged 10 to 16) dealt with by the juvenile police probation officers during the year 1926.

"2. A series of 8,141 alleged delinquent boys (aged 10 to 16) brought before the juvenile court of Cook County during the period 1917–1923.

"3. A series of 2,596 delinquent boys (aged 10 to 16) committed to correctional institutions by the juvenile court of Cook County during the period 1917–1923." [7]

The general findings resulting from the study were that:

"1. Juvenile delinquents are not distributed uniformly over the city of Chicago but tend to be concentrated in areas adjacent to the central business district and to heavy industrial areas. . . .

"2. There are wide variations in the rates of delinquents between areas in Chicago. . . .

"3. The rates of delinquents tend to vary inversely with distance from the center of the city. . . .

"4. The areas of high rates of delinquents in Chicago have been characterized by high rates for a long period of time. . . .

"5. In areas of high rates of delinquents a higher percentage of delinquent boys become recidivists and the average number of times recidivists appear in court is greater than among boys in areas of low rates of delinquents. . . .

"6. The location of delinquency areas is closely related to the processes of city growth. . . .

"7. Delinquency areas in Chicago are characterized by physical deterioration, decreasing population, high rates of dependency, high percentages of foreign and Negro population in the total population, and high rates of adult crime. . . .

[6] See, for example, Sutherland, Edwin H.—*Principles of Criminology;* J. B. Lippincott Company, 1934: Gillin, John Lewis—*Criminology and Penology;* The Century Co., 1926: Gault, Robert H.—*Criminology;* D. C. Heath and Company, 1932.

[7] Shaw, Clifford R., and McKay, Henry D.—"Social Factors in Juvenile Delinquency" in National Commission on Law Observance and Enforcement—*Report on The Causes of Crime*, Vol. II, p. 26; Government Printing Office, 1931.

"8. The community fails to function effectively as an agency of social control in these areas of high rates of delinquents. . . .

"9. The greatest concentrations of delinquents occur in the areas of marked social disorganization. . . .

"10. Juvenile delinquency is traditional behavior in the disorganized areas of the city. . . .

"11. There are many positive influences leading to delinquency in the disorganized areas. . . .

"12. The racial and nationality composition of the population in the areas of high rates of delinquents changed almost completely between 1900 and 1920, while the relative rates of delinquents in these areas remained practically unchanged. . . .

"13. As the older immigrant groups moved out of the areas of high rates of delinquents the rates of delinquents among the children of these groups decreased and they tended to disappear from the juvenile court. . . .

"14. The facts concerning the distribution and variation in rates of delinquents revealed in the Chicago study are confirmed by the studies in the six other cities. . . .

"15. The areas of high rates of delinquents in other cities have characteristics similar to the characteristics of the areas of high rates in Chicago. . . .

"16. Juvenile delinquency is group behavior. . . .

"17. Delinquent traditions are transmitted through group contacts. . . .

"18. The delinquent code is acquired through contacts with delinquent companions and groups. . . .

"19. Participation in the activities of delinquent groups often serves to satisfy the fundamental human desires of the boy in the delinquency area of the large city. . . .

"20. There are wide differences between the rates of broken homes in different racial and national groups, and significant differences between the rates of broken homes at different ages, among unselected school boys. . . .

"21. The rates of broken homes among delinquent boys in the Cook County juvenile court and the rates of broken homes among boys of the same age and nationality in the school population are not widely different. . . .

"22. No consistent variation was found between rates of broken homes and rates of delinquents. . . .

"23. Case studies suggest the need for greater emphasis upon the study of the subtler aspects of family situations in relation to delinquency. . . .

"24. A delinquent career is the product of a natural process of development." [8]

Factor-by-Factor Analysis.—The Gluecks in 1934 published the third of their detailed case studies under the title *One Thousand*

[8] *Ibid.*, pp. 383–393.

Juvenile Delinquents.[9] This was "a study of the boys who appeared before the Boston Juvenile Court during the years 1917 and 1922 and who were referred by the court to a children's clinic (the Judge Baker Foundation) for diagnosis and treatment recommendations. These boys averaged thirteen years of age at the time of the arrest that brought them to the attention of the Boston Juvenile Court."[10] Though the following table based on that study was prepared to show "the influence of the factor of nativity in the criminogenic complex" it serves also to reveal the distribution of forty-nine selected factors in the "vertical" or developmental history of the cases examined.[11]

In 15 of 49 factors the native born of mixed parentage were found to resemble the native born of native parentage more closely than they did the native born of foreign parentage:

FACTOR	OF MIXED PARENTAGE	OF NATIVE PARENTAGE	OF FOREIGN PARENTAGE
One or both parents attended grade school .	71.9%	72.2%	33.9%
Inadequate homes (broken or poorly supervised)	94.9%	95.0%	90.7%
Broken homes	53.9%	60.8%	35.3%
Conjugal relations of parents fair or poor . .	46.5%	52.5%	32.1%
Mother poor disciplinarian	76.0%	72.8%	69.2%
Poor physical home	45.1%	45.6%	68.4%
Average number of children in family. . . .	4.9	4.1	5.5
Illegitimate birth	6.3%	7.6%	1.5%
Early abnormal environmental experiences .	50.3%	52.9%	28.9%
Mental disease or distortion or personality difficulty	64.8%	66.9%	53.5%
Average age at first known misbehavior . .	9.4 yrs.	9.5 yrs.	8.0 yrs.
Average age at first arrest	12.2 yrs.	12.3 yrs.	11.4 yrs.
Offense committed with others	62.1%	64.4%	74.3%
School misconduct	88.4%	90.6%	82.7%
Father unskilled worker.	34.9%	38.7%	46.8%

In 5 of 49 factors the native born of mixed parentage more closely resembled the native born of foreign parentage than they did the native born of native parentage:

FACTOR	OF MIXED PARENTAGE	OF NATIVE PARENTAGE	OF FOREIGN PARENTAGE
Average disparity in ages of parents	6.5 yrs.	4.5 yrs.	6.6 yrs.
Father affectionate to boy	67.1%	57.3%	71.1%
Irregular worker	78.3%	86.7%	81.7%
In street trades	56.7%	64.8%	59.1%
Offender first-born child	19.8%	36.1%	20.1%

[9] Glueck, Sheldon and Eleanor T.—*One Thousand Juvenile Delinquents;* Harvard University Press, 1934.

[10] Glueck, Eleanor T.—*Culture Conflict and Delinquency*, pp. 2–3; reprinted from *Mental Hygiene*, Vol. XXI, No. 1, January, 1937.

[11] *Ibid.*, pp. 3–4.

In 5 of 49 factors, the native born of mixed parentage differed from the two other groups:

FACTOR	OF MIXED PARENTAGE	OF NATIVE PARENTAGE	OF FOREIGN PARENTAGE
Age of youngest parent at marriage	22.7 yrs.	21.6 yrs.	21.6 yrs.
Father poor disciplinarian	75.5%	68.3%	67.1%
Mother works out	44.6%	56.6%	36.9%
Has belonged to club	33.5%	24.1%	22.1%
Delinquency in parents	84.2%	77.0%	67.0%

In 24 of the 49 factors, the native born of mixed parentage resembled both other groups:

FACTOR	OF MIXED PARENTAGE	OF NATIVE PARENTAGE	OF FOREIGN PARENTAGE
Mother affectionate	81.5%	80.7%	83.1%
Economic condition marginal	71.2%	68.2%	67.7%
Poor neighborhood influences	82.8%	81.7%	86.2%
Social agencies interested in family	87.7%	91.4%	88.6%
Average number of agencies	4.0	3.6	3.8
Family history of mental disease or defect	89.1%	89.1%	87.2%
Delinquency in family	89.9%	87.3%	88.5%
Intelligence normal or superior	42.6%	41.7%	42.4%
No talents	95.6%	97.5%	98.7%
No prior mental examination	93.0%	90.8%	92.5%
Average age at which began work	12.8 yrs.	13.0 yrs.	12.5 yrs.
Average number of arrests	2.3	2.1	2.4
Referred to Judge Baker Foundation from Boston Juvenile Court for property crimes	71.1%	67.8%	74.0%
Average length of time between first misbehavior and first arrest	2.8 yrs.	2.5 yrs.	2.6 yrs.
Average length of time between first misbehavior and J.B.F. examination	3.4 yrs.	3.5 yrs.	3.1 yrs.
Good health at time of examination by Judge Baker Foundation	56.9%	53.0%	56.2%
Recidivism	89.0%	93.1%	87.8%
Bad habits	76.1%	76.0%	79.6%
Criminal ideations, conflicts, dissatisfactions	15.1%	13.3%	13.2%
Harmful use of leisure	89.9%	94.0%	95.1%
Bad companions	90.5%	93.2%	95.1%
Entered high school	20.8%	25.4%	16.6%
Retarded more than one year in school	60.1%	58.0%	57.1%
Left school for economic reasons	65.6%	60.7%	64.3%

Complexity of Crime Causation.—The points of agreement among leading American criminologists with regard to crime causation were compactly outlined in 1931 by a committee of the President's Conference on Home Building and Home Ownership.

"The layman and legislator, and not a few students of social problems, have a tendency toward oversimplification of the problem of crime causation. If, for example, they are particularly interested in the improvement of housing conditions, they will point to the fact that in some localities crowded tenements and 'slum areas' and a high incidence of juvenile delinquency are found together. From this they jump to the conclusion that the one is the 'cause' of the other. They ignore the fact that they have isolated but one factor out of a mass of entangled influences and assigned primary importance to that factor. If their interest lies primarily in providing playgrounds, they can readily find that some communities with inadequate recreational facilities have a higher incidence of delinquency than regions in which there are many playgrounds. And again they pass to the wished-for conclusion. If they approach the crime problem with a eugenical bias, they may point to the findings of a high incidence of mental deficiency in some prison as compared with the general population of the locality, and arrive at the conclusion that mental deficiency is a primary 'cause' of crime. It is easy for one to become a special pleader when dealing with such a complex problem as crime causation; because so many individual and social factors are involved and their interplay is so intricate and confused, one need only seize upon whatever end of the tangled skein interests him most and assign to it a primary causative value. . . .

"A few illustrations will indicate some of the intricacies of this problem of crime causation. It has been abundantly demonstrated [2] that an appreciable fraction of the youth of certain city areas become delinquent or criminal. These areas are characterized not only by a greater incidence of criminality than is found in other regions, but by such unhealthy social conditions as unattractive, crowded housing, poverty, vice, antisocial cultural traditions, etc., etc. Is it reasonable to assume that any or all of these conditions comprise the 'cause' of the relatively high incidence of criminality? On the one hand it is found that in such areas, say 10 per cent of the youths are brought to the juvenile court on delinquency petitions, while in other areas, where such conditions do not prevail, or exist to a less extent, only 2 per cent of the children are brought to court. On the other hand, however, it is also evident that, in the delinquency area, 90 per cent of the children are not brought to court. Hence, the most that can be deduced from the findings is that the complex of unhealthy elements in the delinquency area operated to bring 10 per cent of the boys to court. But can even this thesis be sustained without qualification? Standing alone it does not explain why 90 per cent of the youths were not brought to court as delinquents, though subjected to the same general conditions.

"Consider another illustration. Suppose it were found that 10 per cent of the psychotic, psychopathic, psychoneurotic and mentally defective population of any city commit crimes, while only 2 per cent of the mentally healthy population of the same place are criminalistic. Could it thereby be concluded that mental abnormality is a 'cause' of crime? On the one hand it is true that the mentally aberrant contribute a higher percentage of their number to the criminal ranks than the mentally sound; on the other hand, however, it is also true that 90 per cent of the mentally ill do not commit crimes.

"If it were consistently discovered, in a wide variety of samples, that the proportion of criminals among those who live in deteriorated areas compared to the percentage of those who live elsewhere is, say, as 10:2, and the proportion of criminals among the mentally aberrant compared to the mentally sound as 3:2, one might with some assurance say that the environmental and cultural characteristics of deteriorated areas have a greater causative force in criminality than constitutional or conditioned mental illness. But such differences in proportion have never been demonstrated. And even if the finding were made, there would remain the problem of evaluating the relative influence to be assigned to the various *elements* that together comprise the delinquency area. How, for example, would one be able to say that bad housing conditions were more conducive to antisociality than lack of playgrounds?

"This discussion emphasizes two basic concepts in all sociological inquiry: The extreme complexity of causation and the great difficulty of assigning relative *weights* to different elements in the causation complex.

"**The 'Vicious Circle' Concept.** Another difficulty involved in any causation study in this field is that of assigning the position of the 'cart' or the 'horse' to any single factor associated with another. X is in prison for burglary. On examination it is found that he is also a 'constitutionally inferior psychopathic personality' and an habitual alcoholic. Further inquiry discloses that X and his family have long been in dire poverty and residing in the vilest tenement house in a 'delinquency area.' Has X's criminality been 'caused' by his drunkenness, or have both the alcoholism and the misconduct been 'caused' by his constitutional inadequacy, or did X's habitual imbibition of alcohol aggravate his original weak inhibitory capacity? Did X become a drunkard because he couldn't stand his family's miserable economic situation, or was the drunkenness the cause of that unhealthy economic status? All these sequences may have occurred at different times in the life of X, in a series of vicious 'action-reaction' mechanisms. But even by close scrutiny of X's developmental history it would be difficult to assign *primacy* to any of the factors involved.[3] The great difficulty lies in determining what is 'primary.' Some would naturally be inclined to place the constitutional inadequacy first; but it is conceivable that that defect alone would not have caused X to become a criminal, or that without his having lived in a deteriorated neighborhood containing many 'speakeasies' X never would have become a chronic alcoholic, or that even if his inebriety preceded his criminality he never would have lapsed into crime had his economic situation been adequate, etc., etc.

"The foregoing discussion shows that, in addition to the difficulty of assigning relative *weights* to different factors in a causative complex, there is the difficulty of assigning *primacy* to any of the arcs in the series of vicious circles so often found in the lives of criminals.

"As is shown below, statistical science enables us to some extent to gauge the relative weight to be assigned to individual causes, when analyzing an adequate sample of cases and to assign primacy among them. But even such refined technique does not completely eliminate the difficulties described in these pages, if for no other reason than that each individual case in a series must first be subjected to some such analysis as described, before *mass phenomena* can be determined through mathematical statistics. This brings us to still another difficulty in causation analysis where human conduct is involved, namely, the differentiation of cause and motive.

"**Cause and Motive.** Too often it is concluded by social workers that because a person who is criminal was found to reside in a bad home and deteriorated city area, the former fact is *necessarily* 'caused' by the latter. X and Y are reared in a 'delinquency area.' X becomes a fine citizen, recognized leader, sober and law-abiding; Y turns out to be a burglar or gunman. Both were subjected to bad housing, poverty, and other undesirable situations in childhood. But, to the one, the bad environmental influences were a stimulus to legitimate, socially acceptable behavior; to the other, to illegitimate, socially repulsive conduct. In both cases, poverty or bad housing was not only a *situation* in the environment but a *motive* in the life of the individuals involved. Since the situational forces were similar, the difference in outcome in the two cases can only be attributed to the dissimilarity in the *persons* involved or to accidental factors of an unknown nature.

"Consider another case. A, a God-fearing, law-abiding bank clerk, who has never before even thought of stealing, needs money badly because of the illness of his wife or children, or the dread of impending unemployment. He embezzles funds. Is the *situation* necessarily the 'cause' of his criminality? The situation is, to be sure, the immediately determining factor; yet if A had been B he would not have stolen, even in the situation described. He would have sought some other solution of his acute and extraordinary situation, such as borrowing funds, or appealing to relatives, or letting his family go without their needs. In other words, the pressing situation would not have become a motive to misconduct. Here we see that, even in cases where the situation is the immediately precipitating stimulus, the make-up of the person (constitutional and conditioned) is still the factor that makes the real difference.

"These illustrations suggest two useful concepts in crime-causation study: (1) A 'factor,' whether personal or situational, does not become a 'cause' unless and until it becomes a 'motive,' [4] and whether it will become a motive for one form of behavior or another depends upon the constitutional and acquired make-up of the individual. (2) Every person has his individual resistance-limit. It is difficult for *all* members of any society to lead a socially acceptable existence which involves a submergence of the ego desires to the supposed common weal. But most persons are capable of sufficient resistance and inhibition (natively and through education) to meet the ordinary requirements of the legal standard of the age and place in which they live. If society raises the demands somewhat, or, through social stress, such as continued unemployment, etc., makes it more difficult to adhere to them, more persons will violate the law than before, because it thereby taps the level of those whose resistance-capacity is at present stretched almost to the breaking point.

If it raises the social taboos still higher or extends them or renders it more difficult to observe them, it further increases the number of violators of the socio-legal standard by tapping the tier of persons whose resistance-capacity is somewhat stronger than the prior group, etc.[5]

"The criminal act occurring at any one time is the outcome of constitutional and acquired, personal and situational forces, when the power of resistance has been overbalanced by the strength of the other circumstances. Hence, some men would be criminal (i.e., would violate the social conventions) in almost any 'society' however rudimentary or complex, and in almost any 'situation' in life, however ordinary or unique; others would be criminalistic in a complex society but not so in a simpler one; others would be criminal in extraordinary emergency though not in ordinary situations; still others would be criminal only in an extremely complex society and in an unusually provocative situation. Criminality is thus shown to be relative to the time, place, and occasion on the one hand and the constitutional and conditioned makeup of the individual on the other.

"The 'Natural History' Point of View. In the foregoing analysis the discussion has perhaps suggested a more or less *mechanical* interplay of forces at definite levels. In addition to the difficulty of analyzing a cross section of any person's life at the time of his commission of an offense, there is the further difficulty presented by the fact that each person is a living, constantly changing organism, a truth that requires analysis of the natural history of the individual. Only by such 'vertical' investigation can one hope to discover whether the particular response of the individual to the stimuli that apparently were operative at the time of the criminal act under scrutiny is quite typical or atypical. The need of studying the developmental history of the individual renders even more difficult the task of assigning relative weight and primacy to the various elements in any causative complex involving human conduct and misconduct. Moreover, if one were to give as great weight to unconscious motivation and forgotten experience of early childhood as is assigned by psychoanalysis, the problem would become still further complicated.

"Can We Speak of Specific 'Causes'? In view of the foregoing discussion, can we speak of any *specific* causative factor in crime, such as bad housing? Only if we recognize that (1) it is causative in but a fraction of cases and (2) only then, as part of a *complex of interacting forces*. This view, while not as simple or naive as the popular misconception of powerful and direct cause and effect relationship between bad housing, or poverty, or mental defect, or any other 'cause' and criminality, is much nearer the facts. Is it, however, a sufficient basis upon which to plan programs of social amelioration, such as better housing? Yes, because in attacking at least one of a complex of factors found to be related to delinquency and criminality, vice, poverty, etc., we may make some progress in the reduction of those evils, although much greater progress might be made if the crime problem were attacked simultaneously along the many other fronts suggested by the other factors involved in the cause-effect melange. In other words, an attack upon bad housing may be one way of breaking certain of the 'vicious circles' of modern urban life, of which delinquency and criminality are arcs.[6]

"Housing and Delinquency as a Statistical Problem. The statistical generalizations we now possess about the relation of housing and delinquency are few, and not very explicit. Studies in Chicago and other cities reveal that juvenile delinquency is most frequent (in proportion to the juvenile population) in 'areas of deterioration,' generally adjacent to the business sections of our large cities. These are regions in which the foreshadowed exit of residents and entrance of business and manufacturing discourages the maintenance of good standards of housing in the generally old structures found there. Such areas often show decrease of population, while the city as a whole may be growing rapidly. There, also, live the poorest classes, as revealed by the percentages of population receiving aid from charities. Disease and death rates are largely concentrated in these neighborhoods. Are we justified, then, in saying that bad housing itself is the principal factor, or even one factor, in producing delinquent behavior?

"As has already been pointed out, delinquency and crime have a very complicated causation. If we consider housing in this connection, we immediately see that the apparent causal relations between housing and delinquency are far from simple. Delinquents come mostly from the poorer classes. In the larger cities of the United States they are to a large degree the children of immigrant groups, i.e., Europeans, or Negroes from the southern states. But the poor and immigrants (two overlapping classes) live largely in these areas of deterioration. They may, to a certain degree, make bad housing worse by poor standards of housekeeping, again related to poverty and to ignorance of so-called 'American' standards.

"Most studies of the social effects of housing in general have relied on single indices, such as the density of population, or the number of persons per room. Even the latter is a very crude measure of housing, though possibly the most practical one so far developed for large-scale measurement. When we find high density, or a high degree of room overcrowding, associated with a high delinquency rate, comparing area with area, it suggests that there may be some causal relation. It does not prove it. This causal relation might be complex. For instance:

"Room overcrowding may cause delinquency directly;

"Poverty may be the chief cause of room overcrowding;

"Poverty alone (i.e., without room overcrowding) may be a cause of delinquency;

"Room overcrowding injures health and vitality, increasing poverty;

"Delinquency (in persons of working age) reduces industrial efficiency— which would have an effect in increasing poverty;

"Areas of bad housing generally have a dearth of good recreation facilities, which may be a causative factor in delinquency;

"Incorporated in these areas we often find the segregated districts of prostitution and gambling, factors not conducive to wholesome community and neighborhood life.

"Note that no account has here been taken either of the race and nationality factors or of the personal factors. It is tacitly assumed that the groups considered are homogeneous with the remainder of the population, and that we are dealing with two single factors, housing and delinquency. Obviously the addition of these two new factors would complicate our problem not by addition, but by multiplication.

"When, therefore, we estimate the degree to which bad housing (indicated by a single index for a whole tract) tends to occur with delinquency (indicated by a single index for a whole tract) we simplify the problem by ignoring its complexities.

"These are two methods basically related, by means of which we may disentangle these Gordian knots. That is, if we can get an accurate and sensitive index for each factor. One method is to subdivide our populations and areas to be studied till we have units which are practically homogeneous in every respect except housing. This is easy to say and hard to do. Then the relation of housing to delinquency would be studied in its relative isolation, somewhat as the physicist studies the relation of volume and pressure of a gas, while the temperature is held constant. The other method is that of partial correlation, in which the net relationship of two factors may be measured, while the others are held constant. Unfortunately the data we have do not always satisfy the requirements laid down by the mathematician as antecedent to the application of such a method.

"To a large degree we do not have even the raw materials of such studies, in the form of indices of these various factors.

"Other methods suggest themselves. Instead of taking a tract or area, let us take the house as a unit. Ascertain about each delinquent such facts about the housing of his family as are pertinent to establish its quality. Then secure the same information about the housing of an equal number of known, nondelinquents from the same general area or areas in the city, having concern of course that the nondelinquents come from approximately the same kind of economic background. What differences are noted in the housing? Could these differences be due to the mere chance of random selection? Or are they significant? The only answer the statistician can give to this question is to indicate what the probability is that the difference indicates something fundamental and not a mere chance due to the haphazard selection of a sample. This is what differentiates the work of the statistician from that of the physicist, for example. The latter may assume that his sample experiment or experiments are representative because of the invariableness of natural law. The statistician has no such security, and the best he can offer is reasonably heavy odds on his answer being as representative as all the other answers that would be given if other samples were selected.

"Does this mean that statistical methods are not useful? By no means. Statistics provide us with a kind of screen that sorts out the grossly important factors. These then can be subjected to more refined analysis by statistics. Or the method of the intensive study of individual cases can be used. For instance, an analysis of the manner in which housing has affected individuals. Since all influences toward or away from crime bear upon individual minds and produce individual behavior, good or bad, it is in the ultimate analysis of individual behavior that we shall find the explanations we seek." [12]

Prevention of Criminality.—Recognizing the complexity of crime causation, preventive policies, under present conditions of limited knowledge, are reasonably directed at each of the presumptive factors—to break the "vicious circles" of community life and to redirect the individual developmental process, where needed. A few examples will suffice.

Certain crimes appear to demonstrate correlation with specific handicaps. Assault and disturbance of the peace, as well as public drunkenness, are associated very frequently with alcoholism. Violation of drug laws and also certain petty forms of crimes against property, are the more frequent crimes of drug addicts. Attempted suicide shows some relation with mental disease or with chronic disease; homicide with certain types of mental disease, of epilepsy and marihuana addiction; prostitution with feeblemindedness and probably alcoholism and drug addiction; larceny with mental handicaps of several types. Few of the handicapped are criminals, but successful social policies for the prevention and improved treatment

[12] "Housing and Delinquency" (prepared for the Committee on Housing and the Community by the Group on Housing and Delinquency, Clifford R. Shaw, Chairman, Charles Elmer Gehlke, Sheldon Glueck, A. Warren Stearns, M.D., and Edwin H. Sutherland), Chapter II of Gries, John M., and Ford, James, editors—*Housing and the Community*, pp. 13–22; The President's Conference on Home Building and Home Ownership, Vol. VIII, 1932: citing the following footnote references—"2. Shaw, C. R., and McKay, H. D., 'Social Factors in Juvenile Delinquency,' *Report on the Causes of Crime* (Report No. 13, Vol. II), National Commission on Law Observance and Enforcement, Washington, U. S. Government Printing Office, 1931, and studies therein referred to." "3. 'Vicious Circle is the process by which a primary disorder provokes a reaction which aggravates such disorder.' Hurry, J. B., *Poverty and Its Vicious Circles*, London, (J. and A. Churchill), 1917, p. xi. Adapted by Ford, J., *Social Problems and Social Policy*, Boston, Ginn and Company, 1923, pp. 581 *et seq.*" "4. For this concept we are indebted to Dr. Bernard Glueck." "5. A similar theory may be advanced from a psychological point of view in connection with 'regressions' to infantile levels. The psychoneurotic soldier who, under the stress of battle, suddenly exhibits childish emotional and physical symptoms, has reached his particular regression-point. Other soldiers require a more severe fear-arousing stimulus before they will begin to react by regression as a means of 'escape from reality.' " "6. 'Every Vicious Circle has one excellent virtue, viz., there are at least two points in its circumference at which interruption is possible. When the *locus minoris resistentiae* has been discovered, a breach must be effected and the gyration arrested.' Ford, J., *op. cit.*, p. 585."

of feeblemindedness, mental disease, convulsive disorders, alcoholism, and drug addiction would presumably be reflected in the reduction of these crimes. Similarly in so far as larceny, prostitution,
and other crimes or misdemeanors are an outgrowth of poverty,
successful policies to prevent poverty should reduce the volume of
criminality.

Where broken or unhappy homes are found to deprive a child
of needed understanding and direction at difficult times, preventive
policy may arrange either for the retraining of the parents, or the
social worker and domestic relations court may place the child in a
more suitable home.

Where bad housing drives the child or man to the streets to escape
the crowding, confusion, and dreariness of the tenement, the razing
of slums and improved housing in model communities may reduce
criminality in such cases.

Where sensational movies and the tabloid press are found to be
sources of morbid suggestion and occasional criminal action on the
part of susceptible persons, trade agreements among producers of
motion pictures and the owners and editors of journals may be made
to prevent overelaboration of the details of crime, cruelty, or depravity: otherwise public censorship of these details may be necessary. Resistance to unwholesome influences may be built by sound
education and constructive recreation. For case work largely utilizes
creative interests to crowd out morbid impulses.

Where boys' gangs engage in organized depradations—the beginning of many a criminal life, clever direction may make of the
gang a club for athletics, debating, or manual arts. Loyalty to the
gang—a virtue, though often misdirected—can by clever direction
be made subordinate to a higher loyalty—to the settlement, the
school, or the neighborhood. In a self-governing boys' club the young
delinquent may learn the nature and necessity of law, police, and
courts; for he would frame laws and enforce them in his service on
the club's police or jury. The most effective education is not by
rote or precept but is "learning by doing."

Where the love of adventure and of danger lead to robberies,
holdups, and killings, substitute uses may be found for such drives.
In so far as the criminals of adventure can be discovered in time
they may be trained for the more hazardous trades and professions.
Aviation, the navy, and the merchant marine, fire-fighting, detective
service, and the state constabulary offer constructive outlets for

bravery and resourcefulness. Individualized study under a system of vocational guidance should be able to find an appropriate vocational interest for each such case.

Punishment as a Cause of Repetition of Criminality.—Inappropriate punishments are also a "cause" of crime. Boys who are first offenders are still often sent to reform schools to pay there the penalties of juvenile pranks. First offenders among adults are still commonly sent to city jails or county penitentiaries. Yet experience increasingly indicates that only dangerous criminals—not the average drunk, street-walker, vagrant, beggar, or person now jailed for nonpayment of fines—should go to prison until admonition, probation, and the suspended sentence have first been tried. For in prison the man who was an ignorant or accidental offender associates with professionals. He learns there how to pick pockets or open safes. He makes friendships which will lead to invitations to crime after release. He may feel forced to accept such invitations because imprisonment has cost him his job, driven his family upon charity, lowered his self-respect, embittered him, or cut off opportunities for further employment. Society's failure to provide appropriate treatment is thus a cause of much recidivism and professionalism in criminality.

Adult ignorance displayed in inappropriate punishments is the product of fear and tradition. We are emerging tardily from mediaeval concepts of crime and punishment. The whipping-post, solitary confinement in "dungeon cells," and hanging are survivals of ancient misconceptions. Criminology is a young science scarcely a century old. Its modern principles have only just begun to filter through to the electorate and their representatives in the legislature and on the bench. Few thus realize that certainty of arrest and sentence is a more effective deterrent than undue severity of punishment. A century ago in England, pickpockets used to ply their trade in the crowd gathered to witness the public execution of pickpockets because their chances of being caught were slim. Murders do not increase where certainty of life imprisonment is substituted for the less certain but more severe penalty of the electric chair.

Reformation of Prisoners.—Three quarters of our prison population are repeaters. Since they have not been deflected from crime by the prevailing methods of punishment, modern penology recommends the reformation of all prisoners who can still be made over, whose vicious or antisocial attitudes and habits are not too deeply ingrained. Reformation, wherever it can be applied, is less costly and more effective than punishment undertaken exclusively for determent. The cause of the prisoner's past delinquencies is best removed by individualized treatment. His coöperation and continuing effort are necessary to make him over. Constructive interests are utilized to crowd out his antisocial attitudes. Life may be rebuilt about a new job for which he may train in prison. To prevent discouragement and reversion, employment should be waiting for him upon his release.

The modern theory of reformation affirms that prison should not break the convict's spirit but redirect it. Efficient, honorable life after release from prison is difficult if not impossible unless right attitudes and self-respect are built up before release. By persistent, skilful training, wholesome interests can be made to displace those that are unwholesome and destructive. The ex-prisoner who responds to reformatory treatment may thus emerge a new man with good habits already firmly built about the better traits of his nature, with a new resolve and will to win, embedded in (not veneered upon) his personality and character.

The penologist's policy at its best parallels the physician's. To prevent disease the sanitarian and medical specialist find the causative factors in order to destroy or circumvent them, but they meanwhile build up resistance. To prevent crime it is not enough to uproot the causes. Resistance is built by developing judgment and character so strong that antisocial behavior loses its interest and appeal. The process is strengthened by filling life with absorbing interests and activities that leave no time for idleness and mischief.

Penological Policy.—The following recommendations for the revision of present penal methods appear to emerge from the literature of contemporary penology.

1. A recognition that society has a triple responsibility with reference to crime:
    (a) to protect itself against future crime—punishment for deterrence;
    (b) to protect itself against future harm from its more dangerous criminals—punishment for disablement;
    (c) to give the criminal a chance to reform—punishment for reformation.
2. That justice should be swift and sure (determent) and involve incarceration (disablement) for dangerous, degenerate, and professional criminals under conditions that will reform before release.
3. To accomplish this all perpetrators of crime must be discovered (by

improved detective services in police departments amply endowed) and recognized in case they are repeaters (by means of fingerprint systems of identification supplemented by the Bertillon System) and taken before courts which can act promptly, efficiently, and with justice (which involves reforms of judicial procedure).

4. To facilitate individualization of cases provision is needed for ample resources for each branch of the penal system and for the training of its officers. This includes probation work for misdemeanants and institutions (lockups, jails, houses of correction, reformatories, prisons, farm colonies, hospitals) for each type of criminal. Buildings should be suitably designed for their purpose and managed in a manner that will accomplish the given objectives. Individualization further requires that criminals be turned over to competent boards of criminologists or departments of correction which shall have power to transfer them to institutions appropriate to their needs, and to recommend release under parole when the prisoner is deemed ready.[13]

QUESTIONS FOR DISCUSSION OR EXAMINATION

1. Distinguish crime, vice, sin, and tort. Cite examples of acts which may fall in two or more of these categories and of acts which may not fall in more than one.
2. Give examples of the multiple causation of crime.
3. What is the role of heredity in the causation of crime?
4. Outline methods of education to prevent crime. To reform criminals.
5. Outline methods of social control of recreation to reduce delinquency.

PROBLEMS FOR INDIVIDUAL STUDY

1. A critical analysis of theories of punishment.
2. A field study of (a) the police system, (b) the criminal courts, (c) the juvenile court, (d) the probation system, (e) the prisons, or (f) the parole system, in your city or state.
3. Examination of theories and practices in the reformation of criminals.
4. Critical analysis of selected literature on crime causation.
5. Examination of (a) statistical studies, (b) case analyses, relating criminality to mental defects or abnormalities and to poverty.

SUGGESTIONS FOR SUPPLEMENTARY READINGS

Alexander, Franz, and Staub, Hugo—*The Criminal, the Judge and the Public;* The Macmillan Company, 1931.
American Institute of Criminal Law and Criminology—*Journal of Criminal Law and Criminology;* published bimonthly.
Aschaffenburg, Gustav—*Crime and Its Repression* (translated by Adelbert Albrecht); Little, Brown, and Company, 1913.

[13] See especially among supplementary readings the works of Bates, Cantor, Gillin, Glueck, Pound, and Sutherland.

Bates, Sanford—*Prisons and Beyond;* The Macmillan Company, 1936.

Best, Harry—*Crime and Criminal Law in the United States;* The Macmillan Company, 1930.

Bonger, William Adrian—*Criminality and Economic Conditions* (translated by Henry P. Horton); Little, Brown, and Company, 1916.

Breckinridge, Sophonisba P., and Abbott, Edith—*The Delinquent Child and the Home;* Charities Publication Committee, Russell Sage Foundation, 1912.

Burt, Cyril—*The Young Delinquent;* D. Appleton and Company, 1925.

Cantor, Nathaniel F.—*Crime, Criminals and Criminal Justice;* Henry Holt and Company, 1932.

Cavan, Ruth Shonle—*Suicide;* University of Chicago Press, 1928.

Chassell, Clara Frances—*The Relation Between Morality and Intellect: A Compendium of Evidence Contributed by Psychology, Criminology, and Sociology;* Bureau of Publications, Teachers College, Columbia University, 1935.

Cummings, Homer, and McFarland, Carl—*Federal Justice;* The Macmillan Company, 1937.

Durkheim, Émile—*Le Suicide;* F. Alcan (Paris), 1897.

Elliott, Mabel A.—*Conflicting Penal Theories in Statutory Criminal Law;* University of Chicago Press, 1931.

Elliott, Mabel A., and Merrill, Francis E.—*Social Disorganization,* Chapters V, VI, VIII, XVII, and XXX; Harper & Brothers, 1934.

Fink, Arthur E.—*Causes of Crime: Biological Theories in the United States 1800–1915;* University of Pennsylvania Press, 1938.

Ford, James, in collaboration with Morrow, Katherine, and Thompson, George N.—*Slums and Housing, with Special Reference to New York City: History, Conditions, Policy,* Vol. I, Chapter XVI, "Slums and Crime Distribution," and Chapter XVII, "The Effects of Bad Housing in Terms of Crime and Other Anti-Social Behavior"; Harvard University Press, 1936.

Gault, Robert H.—*Criminology;* D. C. Heath and Company, 1932.

Gillin, John Lewis—*Criminology and Penology;* The Century Co., 1926.

Glueck, Sheldon—*Crime and Justice;* Little, Brown, and Company, 1936.

Glueck, Sheldon, editor—*Probation and Criminal Justice;* The Macmillan Company, 1933.

Glueck, Sheldon, and Glueck, Eleanor T.—*Five Hundred Criminal Careers;* Alfred A. Knopf, 1930.

Glueck, Sheldon and Eleanor—*Later Criminal Careers;* The Commonwealth Fund, 1937.

Glueck, Sheldon and Eleanor T.—*One Thousand Juvenile Delinquents;* Harvard University Press, 1934.

Glueck, Sheldon and Eleanor, editors—*Preventing Crime;* McGraw-Hill Book Company, Inc., 1936.

Goring, Charles—*The English Convict: A Statistical Study;* H. M. Stationery Office, 1913.

Gries, John M., and Ford, James, editors—*Housing and the Community,* Chapter II, "Housing and Delinquency," and Appendix I, "Crime Causation and Housing"; The President's Conference on Home Building and Home Ownership, Vol. VIII, 1932.

Halpern, Irving W., Stanislaus, John N., and Botein, Bernard—*The Slum and Crime;* New York City Housing Authority, 1934.

Healy, William—*The Individual Delinquent;* Little, Brown, and Company, 1915.

Healy, William—*Mental Conflicts and Misconduct;* Little, Brown, and Company, 1917.

Healy, William, and Bronner, Augusta F.—*Delinquents and Criminals;* The Macmillan Company, 1926.

Healy, William, Bronner, Augusta F., Baylor, Edith M. H., and Murphy, J. Prentice—*Reconstructing Behavior in Youth: A Study of Problem Children in Foster Families;* Alfred A. Knopf, 1929.

Hooton, Earnest A.—*The American Criminal,* Vol. I, *The Native White Criminal of Native Parentage;* Harvard University Press, 1939.

Hooton, Earnest A.—*Crime and the Man;* Harvard University Press, 1939.

Lawes, Warden Lewis E.—*Invisible Stripes;* Farrar & Rinehart, Inc., 1938.

Lewis, Burdette G.—*The Offender and His Relations to Law and Society;* Harper & Brothers, second edition, 1921.

Millspaugh, Arthur C.—*Local Democracy and Crime Control;* The Brookings Institution, 1936.

National Commission on Law Observance and Enforcement—*Report on the Causes of Crime,* two volumes; Government Printing Office, 1931.

New York Crime Commission—Reports.

Oliver, Alfred C., Jr., and Dudley, Harold M.—*This New America: The Spirit of the C. C. C.;* Longmans, Green and Co., 1937.

Oppenheimer, Heinrich—*The Rationale of Punishment;* University of London Press, 1913.

Pound, Roscoe, and Frankfurter, Felix, directors and editors—*Criminal Justice in Cleveland: Reports of the Cleveland Foundation Survey of the Administration of Criminal Justice in Cleveland, Ohio;* The Cleveland Foundation, 1922.

Reckless, Walter C., and Smith, Mapheus—*Juvenile Delinquency;* McGraw-Hill Book Company, Inc., 1932.

Reeder, Rudolph R.—*Training Youth for the New Social Order;* The Antioch Press, 1933.

Reeves, Margaret—*Training Schools for Delinquent Girls;* Russell Sage Foundation, 1929.

Sellin, Thorsten—"Crime," *Encyclopaedia of the Social Sciences,* Vol. 4; The Macmillan Company, 1931.

Sellin, Thorsten—"Crime Prevention and Treatment," *Social Work Year Book 1937;* Russell Sage Foundation, 1937.

Sellin, Thorsten—*Research Memorandum on Crime in the Depression;* Committee on Studies in Social Aspects of the Depression, Social Science Research Council, Bulletin 27, 1937.

Shaw, Clifford R., editor—*Brothers in Crime;* University of Chicago Press, 1938.

Shaw, Clifford R. with the collaboration of Zorbaugh, Frederick M., McKay, Henry D., and Cottrell, Leonard S.—*Delinquency Areas;* University of Chicago Press, 1929.

Shaw, Clifford R.—*The Jack-Roller: A Delinquent Boy's Own Story;* University of Chicago Press, 1930.

Shaw, Clifford R., in collaboration with Moore, Maurice E.—*The Natural History of a Delinquent Career;* University of Chicago Press, 1931.

Smith, Bruce—*The State Police: Organization and Administration;* The Macmillan Company, 1925.

Sutherland, Edwin H.—*Principles of Criminology;* J. B. Lippincott Company, 1934.

Sutherland, Edwin H., annotated and interpreted by—*The Professional Thief. By a Professional Thief;* University of Chicago Press, 1937.

Tannenbaum, Frank—*Crime and the Community;* Ginn and Company, 1937.

Thomas, William I., and Thomas, Dorothy Swaine—*The Child in America;* Alfred A. Knopf, 1928.

Thrasher, Frederic M.—*The Gang: A Study of 1,313 Gangs in Chicago;* University of Chicago Press, 1927.

Tufts, James Hayden—*America's Social Morality: Dilemmas of the Changing Mores;* Henry Holt and Company, 1933.

United States Bureau of the Census—*Prisoners in State and Federal Prisons and Reformatories;* issued annually.

United States Bureau of the Census—*Judicial Criminal Statistics;* issued annually.

United States Department of Labor, Children's Bureau—*Selected List of Publications, March 1, 1937;* Government Printing Office, 1937.

Van Waters, Miriam—*Youth in Conflict;* New Republic, Inc., 1932.

White House Conference on Child Health and Protection—*The Delinquent Child;* The Century Co., 1932.

White, William A.—*Insanity and the Criminal Law;* The Macmillan Company, 1923.

Wickman, E. K.—*Teachers and Behavior Problems;* The Commonwealth Fund, 1938.

Wilson, Helen—*The Treatment of the Misdemeanant in Indiana, 1816–1936;* University of Chicago Press, 1938.

Winfield, Percy H.—*The Province of the Law of Tort;* The Macmillan Company, 1931.

Winslow, W. Thacher—*Youth, A World Problem;* National Youth Administration, 1937.

CHAPTER XXX

MAJOR DISASTERS

Social Pathology of Disaster.—There remains one large group
of factors, erratic and infrequent in their incidence, which may produce destitution, handicap, and abnormal social relationships over
extensive areas, among rich and poor alike. These are usually
termed large-scale disasters and include floods, earthquakes, hurricanes, tornadoes, tidal waves, drought, famine, pestilence, conflagrations, and war. Within smaller areas or population groups
may be added such calamities as mine disasters, explosions, and
shipwrecks. Each includes—though in varying degrees—loss of life
or limb. Property losses may be complete where the disaster is so
extensive as to ruin the companies in which property is insured.
Dependency is unavoidable for many of the victims.

> "Disasters cause death, permanent physical injury, temporary injury,
> mental shock, personal and real property loss, some disasters including
> all of these factors.
> "Not infrequently disasters arrest and prostrate community life by
> destroying large stores of food and supplies, dislocating transportation,
> breaking off communication with the outside world, disorganizing busi-
> ness and producing extensive unemployment. They also produce prob-
> lems of family welfare brought about by the death or serious injury of
> those upon whom families are wholly or chiefly dependent for support.
> "But whether the disaster expresses itself primarily in loss of life, or
> loss of property, whether the victims be a few score or many thousands,
> its evil consequences register themselves in family life and family welfare,
> and the family must, therefore, be the unit of treatment in the adminis-
> tration of relief." [1]

The American Red Cross has rendered assistance in 1,666 domestic disasters since its inception. Between July 1, 1923, and
June 30, 1937, it has helped the victims of 1,241 such domestic calamities.[2] The following table [3] covers those cases during the twenty-

[1] *When Disaster Strikes*, p. 8; The American National Red Cross, A.R.C. 209,
revised, July, 1924.
[2] From typewritten data submitted by the Accounting and Statistical Department of the American National Red Cross, August, 1937.
[3] *Ibid.*

year period from March, 1917, to March, 1937, in which there were one hundred or more fatalities:

DATE	TYPE	LOCATION	PERSONS KILLED
April 10, 1917	Explosion	Eddystone, Pa.	125
July 1, 1917	Race riot	E. St. Louis, Ill.	100
Oct. 4–5, 1918	Explosion	South Amboy, N. J.	100
Sept., 1919	Hurricane	Corpus Christi, Texas	400
Sept., 1921	Flood	San Antonio, Texas	100
April 28, 1924	Mine explosion	Benwood, W. Va.	120
March 18, 1925	Tornado	Midwestern	796
Sept. 18, 1926	Tornado	Florida	327
March, 1927	Flood	Mississippi Valley	300
May 9, 1927	Tornado	Eastern Arkansas and Missouri	162
March 19, 1928	Dam break	Los Angeles, Calif.	407
Sept. 16, 1928	Hurricane	Florida	1,810
Nov. 13, 1928	Shipwreck	Portsmouth, Va.	115
April 21, 1930	Fire	Columbus, Ohio	322
Mar. 21–28, 1932	Tornadoes (2)	Southeastern	370
Sept. 8, 1934	Shipwreck	New Jersey Coast	137
Sept. 2, 1935	Hurricane	Florida	423
April 5, 1936	Tornado	Gainesville, Ga.	113
April 5, 1936	Tornado	Tupelo, Mississippi	201
Jan.–Feb., 1937	Flood	Ohio & Mississippi Valley	292[a]
March 19, 1937	Explosion	New London, Texas	295[a]

[a] Final reports not in. Information subject to change.

The poverty which disaster precipitates comprises much more than the loss of the breadwinner. His family may be left without the means of support. The cost of funerals and readjustment must be met. Society is deprived of the wealth he would have produced had he lived. Many survivors in most disasters are maimed or suffer disease. Many suffer anxiety or fright from which they never fully recover. Property loss is a minor phase of some calamities but widespread and complete in others. Hundreds and even thousands of families may be rendered dependent for months or years. Some remain dependents for life.

Prevention of Disasters or of Resulting Dependency.—Some disasters, such as conflagration, pestilence, and war, are largely preventable. Many of Nature's disasters, however, are wholly beyond human prevention; though it is possible through human measures to reduce the volume of dependency which they characteristically cause. Where their incidence can be foreseen this may be done either by moving the population away from the affected areas, or by protective devices. Floods, earthquakes, and hurricanes serve as examples.

Floods.—There are two major types of floods: first, those caused by the breaking of dams, and second, those in which rivers overflow. The American Red Cross records thirty-two floods between 1917 and 1937 in which five or more persons have lost their lives. The total fatalities amounted to 1,667. The following quotations from the official summary of the Mississippi Valley Flood of 1927 help one to visualize this sort of catastrophe.

"The total area of lands covered by the flood was 16,570,627 acres, or approximately 26,000 square miles. . . . The extent of the disaster is indicated by the fact that the population of the area actually flooded was 931,159, or 20.9 per cent of the total population of the counties affected to any degree. Of the sufferers, 53.8 per cent were negroes. . . .

"Agriculture suffered a heavier proportionate loss than any other industry. In addition to wiping out all seeded and growing crops in an area of 5,289,576 acres, or about 28.2 per cent of the entire agricultural acreage in the flooded counties, the water remained on the land for weeks in some sections and for months in others, making immediate replanting impossible. This created one of the many perplexing relief problems. . . .

"Live stock constitutes a large item in this total tabulation. The number of work animals, cattle, hogs, sheep and goats lost was 165,298 head, while estimated poultry losses totaled 1,010,375. . . .

"Damage to homes, farm implements, furniture and other household effects was heavy. The number of families whose homes were flooded was 162,017, of whom 40,451 owned their homes and 121,566 were tenants. A total of 8,947 of these houses were destroyed, as were 32,540 other buildings. In many cases the buildings which were inundated withstood the water's onslaught, although the contents were often a complete loss and the structures badly damaged. The number of homes thus damaged but not completely destroyed was 88,076, while 92,431 other buildings suffered a similar fate.

"Families losing household goods totaled 65,005, while 23,656 families lost farm implements, and 38,506 live stock. Those listed as losing farm implements and live stock were in most cases deprived of household effects as well. . . .

"Among the intangible results of the flood must also be listed the experiences of nearly a million persons whose normal habits of living were disrupted, of whom 325,554 were compelled to remain for a considerable time in Red Cross refugee camps and 311,922 were rationed by the Red Cross in public buildings, the second stories of their flooded homes and other temporary shelters. . . .

"The contamination of the water supply over an area of 26,000 square miles; the vast swamps with stagnant water in districts already infested with malaria; the constant prevalence in this territory of typhoid fever and certain other communicable diseases and similar conditions de-

manded prompt action on the part of all the public health agencies. The
nuisances created by thousands of dead carcasses of animals drowned by
the flood also required immediate attention.

"One of the more difficult administrative problems devolving upon
the relief organization arose from the necessity of providing a well bal-
anced diet for hundreds of thousands of the homeless and temporarily
destitute. . . .

Persons cared for during the Emergency Period	637,476
Families receiving rehabilitation aid	120,732
Acreage planted with Red Cross aid	2,199,551
Acreage replanted with Red Cross aid	245,751
Gardens planted with Red Cross aid	120,920
Estimated value of all harvested crops from Red Cross seed	$48,000,000
Estimated value of all supplies and services donated to Red Cross for relief work	$ 6,129,000
Total cash expenditures by the Red Cross	$17,498,902"[4]

Ohio and Mississippi Valley Floods of 1937.—Many floods of
large dimensions concern the American Red Cross each year. Thus
in the year ending June 30, 1937, there occurred twenty-two floods.
That of the Ohio and Mississippi Valley affected a larger number of
families and a larger area than any of its predecessors.

"With the Spring Floods of 1936 still a very vivid memory throughout
the Nation, there came the stupendous January floods in the Ohio and
Mississippi Valley. Communities still feeling the effect of the earlier
flood once again girded themselves to meet this new ravaging menace.
Again as in the previous year, urban populations bore the brunt of the
flood. In addition to industrial destruction, thousands of homes were
destroyed, many thousands damaged while in some of the affected rural
sections rich agricultural soil was eroded or left covered with heavy
sand deposits. This was particularly true throughout the lower Mississippi Valley.

"Considering the extent of the flood and the heavily populated areas
affected it is little short of miraculous that but few lives were lost through
drowning or other accidental causes directly attributable to the flood.
Exposure followed by respiratory diseases took a larger toll of life.

"West Virginia, Indiana, Ohio, Kentucky, Illinois, Missouri, Arkansas, Tennessee, Mississippi and Louisiana felt in varying degrees of intensity the effects of the unprecedented river stages. Throughout this
area residents of 182 counties sought relief from disaster. A total of 252,-
620 families were registered with the Red Cross for assistance.

"Little warning heralded the approach of the flood that created the
disaster of greatest magnitude ever administered by the Red Cross. In

[4] *The Mississippi Valley Flood Disaster of 1927: Official Report of the Relief Operations*, pp. 5–10; The American National Red Cross.

areas where normal January rainfall ranged from 3.2 inches to 3.5 inches, actual Weather Bureau measurements showed rainfall of 10.7 to 13.6. Frozen ground provided a natural run-off into the swollen rivers. The sheer extent of the disaster front may be visualized by the coincidence that at the point of the flood's origin families were returning to their homes, while farther along the path of the water families were forced to remain in concentration centers until the water had receded, while coincidently even farther south families were evacuating their homes and being taken to places of safety and shelter.

"There were many outstanding features. There was little warning, particularly at points near the headwaters. Even with warning, residents of threatened communities could not conceive a flood of such proportions and, therefore, often made inadequate preparations.

"At Cincinnati a bursted gasoline storage tank spread a film of gasoline over the rising waters. Shortly thereafter the gasoline became ignited and caused the explosion of several other tanks. This burning lake covered four square miles in this manufacturing center of the city. After a thirty-six hour fight with chemicals and hose strung along bridges of boats, the flames were extinguished.

"An almost complete exodus was necessary from the city of Paducah, Kentucky. Seventy per cent of the city was under water; and this inundation remained for thirty days.

"Louisville too experienced scattered fires and one explosion which took a toll of 15 lives.

"At Cairo, Hickman, Memphis and other points along the Mississippi, thousands of men working in shifts day and night, successfully fought to save the levees from crevasses throughout a period of three weeks. Fuse plugs of the New Madrid floodway were blown for the first time since the construction of the floodway to relieve pressure upon the Cairo levees.

"At Evansville, Indiana, 40 per cent of which was under water, certain sections of the city not inundated could not be reached due to lack of transportation facilities. This condition was shortly remedied through local construction of flat boats and the later arrival of Coast Guard units.

"Jeffersonville and Lawrenceburg, both protected by municipally-owned levees, were seriously affected when crevasses occurred in their levee systems. These crevasses created rapid currents resulting in more complete destruction of property than was experienced elsewhere throughout the flood zone.

"Public utilities were crippled in all communities along the Ohio for days. Transportation, communication and power, providing light and heat, were crippled. Thousands of families accustomed to modern facilities reverted to candle light and the usages associated therewith.

"Fortunately, even though industry was checked temporarily along the flooded riverways, little time was lost in the resumption of manufacture and workers were able to assume their normal occupations or were absorbed in other branches of the industry.

"During the interim, however, thousands of families were maintained by the Red Cross either in centers of concentration, in homes of relatives or friends or in their own homes.

"Governmental and private agencies coöperating with the Red Cross made signal contributions to the relief work. President Roosevelt definitely placed the responsibility for family relief upon the Red Cross and made available the resources and personnel of government departments where needed. The Chairman of the Red Cross during the early weeks of the disaster, presided at daily coördination meetings of government agency representatives. The W.P.A. in addition to clean-up and repair of public property, made workers available for warehouse duty, policing of camps, clerical and professional work and furnished large quantities of supplies. National Guard, Army and Navy supplies were made available and utilized. Army personnel were loaned and functioned admirably in refugee movements and placement. Equipment of the Tennessee Valley Authority was effectively brought into service. The Coast Guard with its usual efficient and splendid coöperation did yoeman service in rescue and transportation of refugees. Floating plant that could be spared by the U. S. Engineers was used for rescue work and men of this Corps with the background of experience were made available to assist in the direction of rescue activities. U. S. Weather Bureau forecasts of rainfall and river stages were an indispensable guide to rescue activities. Almost without exception, state and city governments made available their facilities for Red Cross use.

"State and city coöperation was evidenced through the endorsement of relief activities by the various governors and mayors of affected states and communities. Private agencies were very definitely helpful and coöperative. The American Legion and the Veterans of Foreign Wars, through policing, assistance in camp maintenance, fund raising, collection and distribution of clothing and foodstuffs made a contribution of immeasurable value. The Boy Scouts with their messenger and other service were indispensable. Other public and private agencies loaned experienced and trained personnel to supplement the Red Cross disaster relief staff.

"Over 9,900 workers were employed in bringing relief to flood affected families. Of this number, 1,460 were trained family workers. This number, of course, is small compared with the number of volunteer workers. . . .

"A relief fund goal of $2,000,000 was increased to $10,000,000 as the enormity of the disaster became apparent. At the termination of the fiscal year, $25,312,167.70 had been received at National Headquarters. . . .

"In addition to these actual cash contributions to the relief work, hundreds of freight cars of donated supplies of food and clothing were shipped into the disaster zone." [5]

---

[5] *Annual Report for the Year Ended June 30, 1937*, pp. 32–37; The American National Red Cross, A.R.C. 501, 1937.

MAJOR DISASTERS

Prevention of Floods.—Though excessive rainfall and accumulations of snow and ice over large areas—the source of floods—cannot be brought under human control, floods from dam breaks can be prevented by skilful engineering, and the height of river floods and their potential damage can in time be greatly reduced. Since the Mississippi flood of 1927, beginnings have been made in integrated programs for building levees to confine river water, spillways to divert it, reservoirs to retain excess water, and deeper, wider channels to convey it. The floods in New England, Pennsylvania, and the Ohio River Valley in 1936, and the Ohio-Mississippi flood of 1937 show how little by way of control has yet been accomplished.[6] The Flood Control Act of 1936, however, goes farther than previous legislation in that while continuing and expanding the engineering program it provides for prevention at the source through soil conservation. A few excerpts from a recent address by the Chief of the Soil Conservation Service, H. H. Bennett, may serve to clarify purposes and methods:

"It so happens that the same agricultural practices leading to soil conservation and erosion control also apply to upstream flood control, and when the conservationist slows down the runoff of rainwater in order to halt erosion, he is also reducing the volume and velocity of water which might otherwise contribute to floods. At the same time, he is keeping the soil on the land where it belongs, and keeping it out of the streams where it serves to reduce the water-carrying capacity of the channels. . . .

"The conservationist utilizes both vegetative and engineering practices to retard the runoff of rainwater and to hold the productive and absorbent layer of topsoil in place against the wash of rain and the drifting of wind. Without stabilization of this absorbent surface layer, land sheds water at an astonishingly accelerated rate. . . .

"At the erosion experiment station at Tyler, Texas, in a region of gentle slopes with an annual rainfall of 40 inches, clearing and cultivating the land increased the run-off 35 times and the soil losses 800 times on poorly managed land. Even on the better managed soils, the run-off was increased 25 times and the soil losses 180 times. . . .

"Only $6\frac{1}{4}$ per cent of the total annual rainfall was lost as surface runoff from land under native grass sod in the Appalachian hill section at Zanesville, Ohio. Fallow land in this area, however, shed 42 per cent of the rainfall. Under continuous corn 33 per cent of the rainfall was lost as surface run-off.

"Thus, from the findings at Zanesville, we obtain significant data on soil losses under three different types of cover. At rates I have just given,

[6] *Spring Floods and Tornadoes;* The American National Red Cross, A.R.C. 974, October, 1936.

native grass sod would protect the underlying soil so well that it would require about 5,300 years for erosion to remove 6 inches of soil, which is about the average depth of the topsoil of that region. Under continuous corn 31 years would be required for the top 6 inches to be washed away; and fallow land, of exactly the same slope and soil type, would lose its upper 6 inches of topsoil in the brief space of 33 years. . . .

"I am convinced that we can largely reduce flood hazards on numerous streams. What has already taken place on some streams where the greater part of the watershed was treated by adaptable erosion-control measures, together with the information collected from the erosion experiment stations, leads me to believe that it will be entirely practicable to reduce the peak of floods along numerous streams by as much as 15 to 20 per cent and along some streams by as much as 25 per cent, or possibly more. This, of course, can not be done over night." [7]

Nation-wide extension of this joint program might achieve elimination of floods of catastrophic proportions within a generation, while its agricultural phase would at the same time build up the sources of national wealth—soil, humus, forests, and other vegetation.

Earthquakes.—As compared with floods, earthquakes, of sufficient intensity to cause disaster, are of infrequent occurrence in the United States. Two, within the past twenty years, which have necessitated Red Cross intervention were those of Los Angeles and Orange County, California, in 1933, and Helena, Montana, in 1935. These resulted in 95 and 7 deaths respectively and the former caused extensive personal injuries and property loss.

In 1906, San Francisco suffered earth tremors so intense and frequent as to break watermains. Conflagration that ensued, together with earthquake damage, rendered about 200,000 persons homeless, nearly one-half of the population of the city.

Since earthquake disasters cause loss of life and property by destruction of buildings, the prevention of loss and dependency can be accomplished in the affected areas by requiring new construction to be earthquake proof. This means that building laws in such areas should ultimately displace types of buildings constructed of two or more materials, which because of their different vibration rates

[7] Bennett, H. H.—*Soil Conservation and Flood Control*, an address given before the Connecticut Engineering Congress, Bridgeport, Connecticut, July 25, 1936, pp. 4, 6, 7, and 9; United States Department of Agriculture, Soil Conservation Service, July, 1936. See also reports of Chief of Engineers, War Department, and *Floods in the United States*, Water-Supply Paper No. 771, U. S. Geological Survey, 1936, and publications of the Civilian Conservation Corps on Emergency Conservation Work, and of the U. S. Department of Agriculture, Bureau of Agricultural Engineering and Forest Service.

shake apart, with new buildings of monolithic construction that will sway as a unit. Chimneys, cornices, and parapets should be so constructed and bonded that in case of earthquake they will not fall into the street. Recent developments in the building legislation of California cities are beginning to incorporate such principles.[8]

Hurricanes.—Ten hurricanes recorded by the American Red Cross between 1917 and 1937 (March) killed 2,770 persons and caused much loss of property. Except for South Carolina, all occurred in the Gulf Coast states of Florida, Louisiana, and Texas. The two which were most destructive of human lives swept over portions of Florida. That of 1928 was responsible for 1,810 deaths, and the more recent ones of September and November, 1935, resulted in 423 deaths. Rarely do hurricanes reach Northern states with an intensity sufficient to do much damage. Nevertheless the hurricane, flood, and tidal wave of September, 1938 caused the loss of several hundred lives in New England and New York State and property losses estimated at over one hundred million dollars. Similar calamities had occurred in New England at least twice before—August 15, 1635 and September 25, 1815.

In the hurricane of September, 1935, ocean swells reported to be twenty feet high swept over the coral islands, which form the Keys, and destroyed all habitations. One or more members of practically every family, and scores of veterans and unemployed ex-servicemen in temporary camps, were lost. The hurricane of November 6 struck the more populous sections about Miami and Fort Lauderdale, but in this instance warnings of the coming of the storm reached residents, homes were boarded up, and families were evacuated to places of safety. Altogether, as a result of the two storms, 4,000 families had to be aided by the Red Cross with temporary shelter or donations of food and clothing. The destruction of farm crops, stock, and poultry was considerable. Reports state that 128 homes were demolished, and 3,538 homes seriously damaged.[9]

[8] Source material regarding the construction of earthquake-proof buildings can be secured from the National Lumber Manufacturers Association, Washington, D. C.; the American Institute of Steel Construction, New York City; and the American Society of Metallurgical Engineers, New York City. See also *Building Standards Monthly*, January, 1937, p. 3; *American Builder*, January, 1936, p. 52; *Coast and Geodetic Survey*, No. 579, p. 82; *Architect and Engineer*, March and April issues, 1931; and Dye, Edward R.—*Earthquake Resisting Structures;* Bulletin No. 1, Engineering Experiment Station, Montana State College, 1936.

[9] *Hurricanes 1935;* The American National Red Cross, A.R.C. 972, October, 1936.

Since hurricanes are confined, with rare exceptions, to geographically determinable areas, it is proving possible by education to induce many persons in such districts to build houses of poured concrete, which is "hurricane-proof" in the sense that it provides a larger measure of protection from future storms than anything else yet devised. Evacuation of endangered areas is sometimes, but not always, possible through U. S. Weather Bureau warnings and the coöperation of the U. S. Coast Guard and the Red Cross.[10]

Tornadoes.—According to Red Cross records, tornadoes occur more frequently than any other type of disaster. Between 1917 and 1937 they listed 125 in which five or more deaths resulted, with a total of 4,300 killed—all in Southern and Central states.

In the spring of 1936 tornadoes wrecked the business section of Gainesville, Georgia, and much of the residential section of Tupelo, Mississippi, and shortly after destroyed large portions of Greensboro, North Carolina, and Cordele, Georgia. The toll for Georgia was 166 killed, 1,008 injured, 1,742 buildings destroyed or damaged, 3,648 families aided at a cost of over $421,000. Mississippi suffered 151 deaths, 972 injured, 1,054 buildings destroyed or damaged, 1,762 families aided at a cost (prior to September 28, 1936) of $332,723.[11]

Because the swath of the tornado is narrow and the regions within which tornadoes occur are immense, preventive measures other than the encouragement of concrete construction and of cyclone cellars are impractical. Property loss may be covered by government-supervised insurance. Some loss of life is inevitable.

Drought and Famine.—The more usual causes of famine are drought or other meteorological conditions, and insect pests; or, as recently in China, drought combined with overpopulation, disorder, depredations, exactions, and ignorance of modern agricultural methods.[12] Its prevention in countries which are not over-populated may be accomplished in large part through agricultural and engineering projects for equalizing water supply to farming areas, or through general education in the appropriate branches of scientific agriculture, changes in the prevailing crops or in methods of cultivation. Where such measures are unavailing, rural resettle-

[10] *Florida Refugee Evacuation Plan;* South Florida Red Cross Safety Committee, July, 1936.

[11] *Spring Floods and Tornadoes,* p. 37.

[12] *The Report of the American Red Cross Commission to China;* The American National Red Cross, A.R.C. 270, October, 1929.

ment may prove necessary, removing farm families from the threatened or stricken area to regions where the meteorological conditions are favorable.

Drought is beginning to take on the proportions of a major catastrophe. That of 1930–31 affected so severely 1,057 counties in twenty-three states that it was termed by the American Red Cross "the greatest calamity of its kind in the country's history." [13] The droughts of 1881 and 1894 though covering as large an area were of shorter duration; but that starting in the spring of 1930, with local exceptions, lasted through until February or March of the following year, so that in February, 1931, the Red Cross was relieving 460,240 families or over 2,071,000 individuals.[14] This was more than three times the number aided in the Mississippi flood of 1927, which up to this time had been the greatest peacetime relief operation in the history of the American Red Cross.

A case of the extreme type is thus described by a Red Cross field worker:

> "In a small town here, one family I interviewed presented an abject picture. It consisted of the farmer, his wife, and three small children. He was a tenant farmer and had planted 160 acres in cotton. His share netted him $15 after a year's heart-breaking toil. Of his three cows, two were in a dying condition because of lack of feed. The single meal daily in this house consisted of three white potatoes and some beans, and but two days' supply remained in the larder. The farmer's cash resources were two pennies. He was thirty-six years old and had been farming all his life, and this is the first time he had failed. Everything he owned— mules, farm equipment, cows, personal property—was mortgaged. And his case is only one of hundreds which can be found in this farming section." [15]

Aid to the drought-stricken areas consisted in shipment of trainloads of green vegetables, mixed produce, groceries, fruits, and meats, and of feed for animals. School lunches were provided for children, yeast for pellagra control, and medical aid. Over $768,000 was expended also on garden and pasturage seed; but the major item of the $15,589,000 expended by the Red Cross was the $7,229,000 for food of which more than half was needed for Arkansas, Oklahoma,

[13] *Relief Work in the Drought of 1930–31*, p. 7; official report of the operation of the American National Red Cross (Covering Activities from August, 1930, to end of Fiscal Year, June 30, 1931), October, 1931.
[14] *Ibid.*, p. 12.
[15] *Ibid.*, pp. 42–43.

and Kentucky, with Louisiana, Texas, Missouri, Mississippi, Tennessee falling next in order in the matter of the cost of food relief.[16]

The most serious suffering occurs in regions where but a single crop is raised. The major preventives appear to be diversification in farming, and conservation of water sources through the reduction of soil erosion, together with devices to prevent exhaustion of credit—all of which are agricultural phases of national economic planning.

Dust Storms.—Dust has been termed "nature's newest agency of destruction." In the spring of 1935 portions of five Southwestern states remained for months under its dense pall. The "Dust Bowl" included portions of Colorado, Kansas, Oklahoma, Texas, and New Mexico. It covered 18,000,000 acres in all, with Liberal, Kansas as its center.[17]

Dust storms are new to this region. Its early timber had been cut to make grazing land. The pasture cropped first by the buffalo, then by cattle, and finally by sheep, yielded to large-scale cultivation. Lack of windbreaks and ever deeper ploughing opened the land to wind storms in years of drought, until in 1935 it lay under a continuous black cloud. Dust formed huge drifts upon the land. It invaded all buildings. Month followed month with no escape from choking discomfort and from darkness.

When the Red Cross was called into this area by the Federal Emergency Relief Administration, it found it necessary to arrange treatment for prevalent respiratory diseases, to educate the population in the use of dust masks, to demonstrate to all householders devices for dustproofing homes, and to establish visiting nursing and hospital care.

Official estimates quoted by Kimmel place the total area involved from 1933 to 1938 at 97,000,000 acres from which 850,000,000 tons of soil have been swept each year. Around two million people live in the area involved—including some 90,000 farm families.[18]

Poverty invaded the Great Plains, for many in the sense of sudden dependency and acute suffering, but for all in the shrinkage of property values, the breakdown of social facilities, and the imminent danger to inhabitants of the loss of their homes and lands—their

[16] *Ibid.*, p. 84.

[17] *The Dust Area Welfare Program of 1935;* The American National Red Cross, A.R.C. 957, November, 1935.

[18] Kimmel, Roy I.—"A United Front to Reclaim the Dust Bowl"; *New York Times Magazine*, August 14, 1938.

means to livelihood. In the absence of an adequate conservation program there may be danger to the nation of the abandonment of an area once classed among the most fertile.

There are many districts in the West where lands once amazingly fruitful may become in effect deserts unless both sod and moisture are scientifically conserved. The only preventive, short of practical irrigation, is agricultural planning over large areas, involving regions comprising many states. Such a policy must restore the sod through the planting of grass, forests, or other dense crops over a sufficient percentage of the land to hold the soil, which in the "Dust Bowl" at least is still rich. For those whom the land can no longer sustain, organized resettlement under governmental auspices is essential as long as our nation has need of their services in agricultural production. Coördination of three branches of the United States Department of Agriculture—the services for Forestry, Agricultural Extension, and Soil Conservation—directly or through regional authorities, in conjunction with Federal agencies concerned with water power and flood control, is necessary both to prevent similar calamities in other overcropped areas and to reclaim such regions as can be salvaged where dust storms or desert formation have already begun.

Pestilence.—In past centuries pestilence has at times eliminated large fractions of urban and rural population over broad areas covering many nations. One by one epidemic and pandemic diseases have been mastered by developments in the fields of bacteriology, pathology, medicine, and sanitary engineering. Thus cholera, typhoid and typhus fevers, the bubonic plague, smallpox, yellow fever, and malaria have been brought, in civilized nations, under such a high degree of control that their recurrence as a major disaster seems improbable. Security is obtained, however, only at the cost of continuous unrelaxed vigilance on the part of sanitary authorities. New pandemic scourges are deemed possible by many epidemiologists. The surest means to the prevention of future epidemics and pestilence rests in ample subsidization of sanitary and medical research and continuous universal cultivation of public and personal hygiene.

Conflagration.—In sharp contrast with pestilence conflagration is not a prominent cause of death. Its toll is taken primarily in property losses and temporary dependency. Every American city is built largely of wood, even though exteriors may be of brick.

Every fire in a crowded area is a potential conflagration. The infrequency of extensive conflagrations is due to the efficiency of fire-fighting forces and of municipal water service. Nevertheless in the century from 1832 to 1931 the nation suffered 142 conflagrations in each of which the property loss was a million or more dollars, 13 with a loss of from five to ten million, and 9 at ten million or more. The more extensive fires are listed below.[19]

Date		City	Buildings Destroyed	Loss
Dec. 16,	1835	New York, N. Y.	530	$15,000,000
July 19,	1845	New York, N. Y.	450	6,000,000
March,	1852	New Orleans, La.	Warehouses	5,000,000
Dec. 12,	1861	Charleston, S. C.	576	5,000,000
July 4,	1866	Portland, Me.	1,800	10,000,000
Oct. 7,	1871	Chicago, Ill.	17,430	168,000,000
Nov. 9,	1872	Boston, Mass.	776	75,000,000
	1874	Chicago, Ill.	360	5,000,000
June,	1889	Seattle, Wash.	Mercantile section	6,626,000
Nov. 9,	1889	Lynn, Mass.	319	5,000,000
	1901	Jacksonville, Fla.		11,000,000
Feb.,	1902	Paterson, N. J.	325	5,500,000
Feb. 7,	1904	Baltimore, Md.	140 acres	50,000,000
Apr. 18,	1906	San Francisco, Calif.	28,000	350,000,000
Apr. 12,	1908	Chelsea, Mass.	3,500	12,000,000
June 25,	1914	Salem, Mass.	1,600	8,000,000
Mar. 21,	1916	Paris, Tex.	1,440	10,000,000
May 21,	1917	Atlanta, Ga.	1,938	5,500,000
Oct.,	1918	Minnesota	Forest fires	9,000,000
Mar. 15,	1922	Chicago, Ill.	13	5,000,000
Dec. 8,	1922	Astoria, Ore.	30 city blocks	8,000,000
Sept. 17,	1923	Berkeley, Calif.	584	6,000,000

Conflagration is to a great extent preventable. Forest or prairie fires may destroy many villages in their path. Thus Chisholm, Minnesota, a town of about 5,000 population was destroyed in an hour's time, leaving only 65 structures standing. The forest fire which engulfed it devastated nearly 1,600 square miles.[20] Usually settlements can be protected by counter fires or other fire-fighting devices. Federal, state, and municipal park and forest services by means of watch-towers, fire-breaks, etc., and the Civilian Conservation Corps are reducing this menace and the area of loss.

Many urban fires have been destructive over extensive areas.

[19] Data supplied by the National Fire Protection Association, see Gries, John M., and Ford, James, editors—*Housing and the Community: Home Repair and Remodeling*, pp. 213–216; The President's Conference on Home Building and Home Ownership, Vol. VIII, 1932.

[20] Deacon, J. Byron—*Disasters*, pp. 108–109; Russell Sage Foundation, 1918.

That of Chicago in 1871 burned over three and one-third square miles. The San Francisco earthquake and fire of 1906 burned an area of 11.14 square miles. The Chelsea, Massachusetts, conflagration in 1908 covered 287 acres, and the Salem, Massachusetts, fire of 1914 extended over 300 acres.[21] In cities conflagrations can, in time, be entirely prevented by passing and enforcing building laws that require all new construction within the urban area to be fire-resistive. Such requirements develop slowly, however, because they increase the cost of construction of urban buildings from 50 to 100 per cent.

It is already the general practice within the heart of each of our major cities—designated on a city engineer's map as the first fire zone—to force first-class construction for all new buildings above a given height. But there are so many survivals within these areas of buildings of second-class (brick exterior but wood interior) or of third-class (entirely of wood or quick-burning construction) that the center of no city is wholly free of conflagration risk. The outer zone or zones are usually almost exclusively of second- or third-class construction.

The Baltimore conflagration of 1904 demonstrated that a major conflagration can begin in buildings of second-class construction and destroy large districts of buildings of both second- and first-class construction. For the first-class buildings in such a district, subjected to the intense heat of the conflagration, are rendered unavailable for future use by the warping of steel beams and girders, and the conflagration feeding upon the goods and furniture which they contain easily makes its way to the buildings beyond, if not carried there by flying embers.

It is estimated that in any American city a major conflagration would be possible during a dry season and on a day of high wind velocity if the fire should start in certain of the danger spots which are carefully listed by the National Board of Fire Underwriters, and if, because of delays in notification of the fire department or because of traffic jams, the fire apparatus should be twenty minutes late in arriving upon the scene of the fire. In view of such possibilities, it is reasonable to recommend the use of fire-resistive material throughout the construction of all new buildings in strictly urban districts. The rapid development in fire-proofing methods means that such requirements would cause relatively little retardation of construction. Business enterprise is likely to accommodate itself within a

[21] *Ibid.*, p. 125.

few years to the stricter provisions of the law. In normal circumstances the process of replacement of old buildings with new would proceed with sufficient rapidity to make conflagration in most growing cities unlikely within one generation and impossible within two.

Explosions.—In fifty-four explosions demanding Red Cross aid between 1917 and 1937 the total number killed was 2,228.[22] Some cases occurred in the manufacture of war materials, as at South Amboy, New Jersey, in 1918, where one hundred were killed. Many have happened in crowded factories. Thirty-two are recorded in this period for mines. Explosions are thus highly destructive of life.

Preventive measures to increase safety in manufacture have already been discussed. Policies for the prevention of mine casualties have been carried out with increasing effectiveness in recent years by the United States Bureau of Mines and special agencies of state governments and within the industry itself.

> "In the 20-year period preceding 1929, mine explosions and fire took an average toll of about 285 lives annually in the United States; since then the number of fatalities from explosions and fires has been reduced to an annual average of 114. The fiscal year 1934 established an all-time low record; only 34 fatalities resulted from explosions and fires compared with 42 fatalities from these causes during the fiscal year 1936. . . .
>
> "The reduction of fatalities due to gas and dust explosions in bituminous-coal mines from an average of 438 per year in the 5-year period 1906–10 to 65 per year in the 5-year period 1931–35, a decrease of 85.2 per cent or an average decrease of about 2.8 per cent per year, shows what can be done. . . .
>
> "The material decline in the frequency and severity of explosions during the past 5 years is believed to be due primarily to: (1) Increased activities of the various State mine inspection departments, especially in educational work, and demand for more rigid adherence to State laws and to safety practices far beyond the strict letter of the law; (2) growing realization of the economic waste of all accidents, including explosions, and more or less general acceptance by the mine operators of responsibility for accident occurrence; and (3) widespread dissemination of safety data by the United States Bureau of Mines and other safety organizations."[23]

The most prolific causes of mine fires have been found to be electricity, explosives, and open lights. The reduction in explosions

[22] Explosions in which there were less than five deaths are not included.

[23] Harrington, D., and Fene, W. J.—*Coal-Mine Explosions and Coal- and Metal-Mine Fires in the United States during the Fiscal Year Ended June 30, 1936*, pp. 15 and 17; United States Bureau of Mines, Department of the Interior, I.C. 6927, December, 1936.

is due to control of these factors and specifically to increased use of permissible explosives, safer handling, and improved ventilation.[24]

Other Types of Disaster.—Although loss of life, injury, and dependency are ascribed to other disasters—wrecks of trains, ships, buses, or airplanes, land or snow slides, riots and bombings, cave-ins of mines, collapse of theatres or other buildings—it is assumed that preventives have been indicated sufficiently in the foregoing treatment of specific disasters or elsewhere in this volume.

Prevention.—In general prevention of any catastrophe (and thereby of the poverty and handicaps it would occasion) involves research which will reveal causes, trends, and controls, and public understanding and practice of reasonable precautionary measures. Much damage resulting from earthquakes, fires, tornadoes, or hurricanes could be prevented by enforcement of appropriate construction methods. Skilful engineering programs bulk large among preventives of floods and mine disasters. But flood as well as drought and famine can largely be circumvented by scientific agriculture; pestilence by progress in bacteriology, pathology, medicine, and sanitary engineering.

Many calamities imposed upon man by natural forces beyond his control can be kept from producing death, injury, or poverty by the combined service of science and organization. Each type of disaster is individual in the problems it raises but its toll in loss of life and property is progressively reducible through the application of the findings of research and experience under well-advised agencies of social control, amply empowered.

Disaster Relief Policies and Procedure.—Because of the erratic nature of disasters and the swift manner in which they usually strike and prostrate a community, the citizens are rarely able to recover fully without outside aid. The paralyzing effect of shock and bereavement may so disorganize the survivors that outside help becomes imperative. The National Red Cross is prepared to give skilled guidance and assistance, and equipped to extend relief in calamities in which numbers of persons are plunged into suffering and helplessness.

The actual task of giving relief to victims of disasters involves two major stages: (a) the emergency period, in which "relief is usually

[24] *Ibid.*, pp. 8 and 13. See also Denny, E. H.—*Suggested Methods for the Reduction of Mine Accidents from the Viewpoint of the Safety Engineer;* United States Bureau of Mines, Department of the Interior, I.C. 6925, December, 1936.

extended on a mass basis," and (b) the rehabilitation period, in which "relief is always given on an individual family basis in accordance with standard case work practices." [25] There is no sharp division between these two periods. As rehabilitation gets under way emergency relief diminishes gradually.

> "During the emergency period immediately following a disaster, the Red Cross may supply mass relief in the essentials of medical aid, shelter, food and clothing for a period depending upon the nature and extent of the disaster, but this mass relief will be terminated at the earliest possible date and further assistance given upon the basis of the needs of each individual family. In planning the rehabilitation of the family, the Red Cross endeavors to place within the reach of the people their standards of living which existed prior to the disaster. . . .
>
> "The Red Cross does not restrict itself to particular kinds of relief but gives its aid to each family in whatever form or forms will contribute most directly to its speedy and effective rehabilitation. . . .
>
> "The basis for assistance is need, resulting from situations in the family created or aggravated by the disaster. Such assistance includes not only the basic emergency needs of medical aid, shelter, food, and clothing, but also, where necessary, the more permanent forms of relief such as household furnishings and building supplies, and likewise the services of nurses and family case workers. . . .
>
> "No attempt is made to establish any relationship between loss and award in any case. Although persons have suffered heavily in a disaster, if their situation is such that the loss can be borne, they are not proper recipients of Red Cross relief. Each person will be expected to assume as much responsibility as possible for his own rehabilitation, by using both his actual and potential resources. If he can reëstablish himself by using available capital and such credit as he is able to obtain and handle without undue hardship, he will be expected to do so without aid from the relief fund. However, if such resources are inadequate, they will be supplemented by the Red Cross. The decision as to the amount of assistance which will meet the minimum needs of the family is arrived at by a careful appraisal of all the facts in the case. . . .
>
> "The Red Cross does not make loans to disaster sufferers. Help is extended freely and creates no obligation on the part of the recipients." [26]

To be most effective, relief must be prompt and centralized. Swift mobilization of funds, supplies, and experienced relief workers to send to the aid of the sufferers is the first and indispensable step. After the more acute problem of relieving misery has been met, there remains the task of restoring welfare, which involves reuniting

---

[25] *When Disaster Strikes: Manual of Preparedness and Relief,* p. 33; The American National Red Cross, A.R.C. 209, revised, October, 1934.

[26] *Ibid.,* pp. 9–10.

separated families, the safeguarding of health of all citizens, and the assisting of afflicted families to become independent and self-supporting again. The skill and wisdom with which rehabilitation is planned and executed is an important phase of disaster relief administration.

Preparedness Organization.—For those catastrophes which are beyond the control of man and which give rise to death, injury, and poverty, it is important to have regional and local preparedness, in the form of a Red Cross Chapter. The American Red Cross has developed, out of its years of experience in disaster relief, a plan of organization for Chapters which is applicable to all types of calamities. It is simple in structure and effective in operation. It recommends that every Chapter maintain a strong Committee on Disaster Preparedness and Relief, which should be composed of the best community leadership available. The Committee is asked to make itself responsible for: "(a) preparing for disasters; (b) prevention of loss of life and property in territory with disaster hazards which are known in advance, such as floods and hurricanes; (c) taking necessary action when disaster strikes." In their pamphlet *When Disaster Strikes*, the Red Cross lists fourteen "first steps" for this Committee in the event of a disaster, and outlines organization and methods of preparedness and relief.[27]

In addition to the main Committee on Disaster Preparedness and Relief, Subcommittees on the following have proved to be necessary and adequate: Survey, Rescue, Medical Aid, Shelter, Food, Clothing, Transportation and Communication, Registration and Information, Fund Raising, and Public Information. When a disaster entails rehabilitation, a Subcommittee on Rehabilitation should also be appointed, but not until after the disaster has occurred, since the location and type of calamity should be considered in the selection of the personnel of this group. Relief procedure for each Subcommittee is given in detail.[28]

QUESTIONS FOR DISCUSSION OR EXAMINATION

1. Which types of disaster are preventable? How can they be prevented?
2. By what measures can the volume of dependency for each type of disaster be reduced?
3. Should social security legislation be extended to cover disasters specifically? On a state, national, or international basis? How may the economic burden be fairly distributed?

[27] *Ibid.*, pp. 5–6, and 15.   [28] *Ibid.*, pp. 15–50.

4. Should disaster relief take the form of "compensation for loss"? Or aid according to need? Why?

PROBLEMS FOR INDIVIDUAL STUDY

1. Analysis of a selected disaster, from data in newspapers of the period, public documents, and reports of the American Red Cross, and local social service agencies.
2. Comparison of two selected disasters, contrasting the forms of relief organization and the rehabilitation methods employed.
3. A study of rebuilding after conflagration or earthquake to ascertain how largely the community profited by its experience and opportunity, and why.
4. From detailed studies of specific disasters (*e.g.* Prince) examine evidence of changes in habits, attitudes, personality, and social relationships precipitated by emergency or catastrophic conditions.

SUGGESTIONS FOR SUPPLEMENTARY READINGS

Adams, W. W., Geyer, L. E., and Parry, M. G.—*Coal-Mine Accidents in the United States: 1934;* United States Bureau of Mines, Bulletin 397, Government Printing Office, 1936.

Adams, W. W., and Kolhos, M. E.—*Metal-Mine Accidents in the United States: 1933–34;* United States Bureau of Mines, Bulletin 398, Government Printing Office, 1936.

American National Red Cross—Annual Reports 1905 to date, and publications.

American National Red Cross—*The Report of the American Red Cross Commission to China;* The American National Red Cross, A.R.C. 270, October, 1929.

American National Red Cross—*When Disaster Strikes: Manual of Preparedness and Relief;* The American National Red Cross, revised edition, A.R.C. 209, October, 1934.

Ash, S. H.—*Explosions in Washington Coal Mines;* United States Bureau of Mines, Technical Paper 507, Government Printing Office, 1931.

Boardman, Mabel T.—*Under the Red Cross Flag at Home and Abroad;* J. B. Lippincott Company, 1915.

Bondy, Robert E.—"Disaster Relief,"—*Social Work Year Book 1937;* Russell Sage Foundation, 1937.

Brownlee, Aleta—"Disasters and Disaster Relief," *Encyclopaedia of the Social Sciences*, Vol. 5; The Macmillan Company, 1931.

Dallavalle, J. M., and Bloomfield, J. J.—*Application of the Preliminary Sanitary Survey to Flooded Areas;* United States Public Health Service, Reprint No. 1751 from the Public Health Reports, Government Printing Office, 1936.

Deacon, J. Byron—*Disasters;* Russell Sage Foundation, 1918.

Devine, Edward T.—*The Principles of Relief;* The Macmillan Company, 1905.

Downey, Fairfax—*Disaster Fighters;* G. P. Putnam's Sons, 1938.

Gumpert, Martin—*Dunant: The Story of the Red Cross;* Oxford University Press, 1938.

Lamson, Herbert Day—*Social Pathology in China;* The Commercial Press, Limited (Shanghai, China), 1934.

National Conference of Social Work—*Proceedings*, especially 1928.

O'Connor, Charles J., McLean, Francis H., Artieda, Helen Swett, Motley, James Marvin, Peixotto, Jessica, and Coolidge, Mary Roberts (compiled from studies by)—*San Francisco Relief Survey; the Organization and Methods of Relief Used After the Earthquake and Fire of April 18, 1906;* Survey Associates, Inc., Russell Sage Foundation, 1913.

Prince, Samuel Henry—*Catastrophe and Social Change, Based upon a Sociological Study of the Halifax Disaster;* Columbia University, 1920.

Queen, Stuart Alfred, and Mann, Delbert Martin—*Social Pathology*, Chapter XIX, "Disasters"; Thomas Y. Crowell Company, 1925.

Smillie, Wilson G.—*Public Health Administration in the United States*, "Disaster Relief—The Red Cross," pp. 387–395; The Macmillan Company, 1935.

Sorokin, Pitirim A.—*Social and Cultural Dynamics*, Volume Three, *Fluctuation of Social Relationships, War, and Revolution;* American Book Company, 1937.

Stewart, W. D.—*Mines, Machines and Men;* P. S. King & Son, Ltd., 1935.

Tannehill, Ivan Ray—*Hurricanes;* Princeton University Press, 1937.

Thompson, Dorothy—*Refugees;* Random House, 1938.

United States Bureau of Mines—Information circulars.

CHAPTER XXXI

WAR

Social Pathology of War.—War is potentially, and on occasion actually, a major source of handicaps and poverty. All measures and policies so far described as preventives of these pathologic conditions may be upset by war. Hence, handicaps and poverty cannot be extirpated and their recurrence made impossible unless war is abolished.

But among the pathologic results of war are also breakdowns in general social solidarity involving interruption or loss of contacts, cleavages, and fresh alignments which may amount to social disorganization, or organization on a level of reduced efficiency. Appraisal of the consequences of any given war, however, inevitably reflect the bias of the commentator. What is termed disorganization by the defeated may mean reorganization to the victor. Where wars are followed by slavery or emancipation of slaves, by domination or subjugation, by the imposition of an alien religion or culture, by decline of democratic institutions, by Sovietism, or by dictatorship, the consequences are termed evolutionary or regressive according to the standard of reference employed. Even where the consequences are approved, two questions, largely ethical in nature, yet remain: Was it worth the cost? Could the objective have been reached better by peaceful means?

Costs of war can be appraised in terms of (a) financial resources and labor diverted from other uses for the pursuit of war; (b) loss of life; (c) permanent and temporary disabilities; (d) destruction of property; (e) consequences of the financial expedients employed, *e.g.* debts and inflation; (f) dependency of refugees and families of combatants; and (g) economic effects upon investments, manufacturing, trade, and wages. Less tangibly its costs are reflected in the moral conditions of war hysteria; the condonement of hate, violence, cruelty, and deceit; sexual demoralization, whether expressed in rape and perversions or broken homes; the hounding of minorities and the elimination of freedom of speech. In addition are the social costs of malnutrition, malhygiene, the spread of diseases and commonly of epidemics, and under some war conditions the increase of juvenile delinquency. Less tangible still are the consequences of the undernourishment or abandonment of peacetime institutions sacrificed for the pursuit of war, and the delays in the perfection of institutions or practices begun prior to war.[1] Finally, there are the lingering and indeterminate costs of individual and institutional readjustment following either victory or defeat, and of the distrust, hates, realignments, loss of "face" which for generations are suffered by the populations of large areas or by whole nations.[2]

Effects upon Selection.—Of war's dysgenic nature there is still some doubt. Standing armies may not represent the "flower of youth." But it is argued that in all countries during war times the men who are most fit physically and competent mentally tend to be selected to bear arms. If the war is of long duration the last and poorest draft and the relicts tend to predominate among survivors. Such selection in a modern war may mean elimination of an undue percentage of those most fit to breed. The average quality of the stock must decline if new post-war generations descend from males unfit for military service and from a reduced ratio of the more fit who have survived the war. The inevitable result would be a higher ratio in subsequent populations of persons inheriting relatively limited capacities. Thus have argued Novicow, Jordan, Kellogg, and others. Gini, Steinmetz, and Sorokin, on the other hand, have pointed out a variety of qualifications of this argument through "positive selection" among females, as well as the tendency of the most fit among males to survive.[3]

The Cost of the World War.—Deaths of combatants in the World War are placed at from eight to ten millions. Each death represents a productive life cut short. The warring nations thereafter have had to do without the goods these men would have produced by their labor had they survived. The nations have been forced to forego as well the wealth which would have been produced by the sixty-five million combatants during the period of their military service. The number of war survivors so seriously maimed or diseased as to stop or greatly reduce their productive capacity

---

[1] *E.g.* the prostration of the South following the Civil War, or the retardation of the arts following the World War.

[2] The South following the Civil War; Alsace-Lorraine, Poland, and the countries of Middle Europe, for example.

[3] Sorokin, Pitirim—*Contemporary Sociological Theories*, Chapter VI; Harper & Brothers, 1928.

amounted to over six million among the twenty-one million persons who were wounded. The loss of their labor in production and the cost of their dependency and that of their families in itself assumes catastrophic proportions.[4]

Whether one places the cost of the World War at four hundred billion dollars—one hundred and eighty thousand dollars for each minute of its duration [5] or at half or quarter that figure, the cost is too great for ready comprehension. Aside from its continuing burdens in casualties and handicap, in broken lives and suffering, it turned much of the labor of the world from creation of goods and services of value for the consumer to the manufacture and transportation of munitions and explosives which in a brief time had served their destructive purpose. In this way the volume of the world's distributable wealth was rapidly reduced and economic insufficiency, whether on a national or per capita basis, became increasingly general among the belligerent countries of Europe. Its effects were profoundly felt even in America: our share in initial money cost, exclusive of the billions loaned to the Allies, has been estimated at between twenty-two and twenty-four billion.[6]

Viewing the invasion of northern France and Belgium in August and September, 1914, in a manner in which other major disasters have already been examined, it is found that one million five hundred thousand persons of the civilian population were driven from their homes by the advancing armies. Before the end of the War the refugee population in France was nearly two million. Similar invasions were suffered by countries to the north, south, and east of Germany. These refugees were virtually destitute, possessing little but the clothes that they wore or what they could load in the packs on their backs, in the carts which they pushed, or on the few farm animals which in their haste they were able to drive before them. With considerable skill the French government allotted the refugees among the civilian population of the remaining sections of France. Those who did not escape from the invaded regions, in-

[4] Estimates commonly used are those of the U. S. War Department and those prepared by Ernest L. Bogart in his *Direct and Indirect Costs of the Great World War* for the Carnegie Endowment for International Peace; Oxford University Press, 1919.

[5] Bogart, Ernest L.—*ibid.*, and Knight, Bruce Winton—*How to Run a War;* Alfred A. Knopf, 1937.

[6] Cf. Palmer, Frederick—"Can We Keep Out of War"; *This Week*, March 21, 1937, and *Statistical Abstract of the United States 1936*, p. 203; Government Printing Office, 1936.

cluding most Belgian civilians and over half of those in northern France, remained during four and a half years of German occupation, subject to pillage, forced labor, indignities, cruelties, malnutrition of children, and to the atrocities still characteristic of hostile armies.

The devastated area covered six hundred square miles in Belgium and seven thousand in France. The previous population of this district in Belgium was three hundred thousand, and in France five million. The size of the area was about that of Connecticut and Rhode Island combined. Approximately three per cent of France was virtually destroyed by war. The first estimate of the devastation, by Louis Dubois in December, 1918, placed the loss to France at sixty-four and a half billion francs, of which ten billion was for the destruction of agricultural land, twenty billion for buildings, five billion for furnishings, twenty billion for demolished factories and mines, and nine and a half billion for railroads and other transportation. In February, 1919, Dubois estimated the total destruction at 1197.7 billion francs, of which 35.4 was for buildings and public works, 32.4 for furnishings, tools, and equipment, 28.7 for raw materials and supplies, and 23.2 for "revenue or exploitation losses."

Two hundred and forty thousand buildings were entirely destroyed, and a hundred and seventy thousand more were damaged but reparable. Two hundred and fifty thousand acres of arable land had been rendered unavailable for subsequent use by the building of trenches and barbed-wire entanglements, by covering the fertile land with shell-holes and with showers of sand and gravel from exploded shells. Three-quarters of the million and a half acres of woods and forests had been ruined. In this region, which had produced seventy per cent of all the coal mined in France, the mines had been flooded and machinery destroyed. In the manufacturing cities, during the retreat, everything of value had been systematically removed and every factory completely demolished. In addition three thousand five hundred miles of railroad track had been torn up, forty-eight thousand five hundred cars and two thousand locomotives lost, six hundred and seventy miles of canals damaged, four hundred and fifty bridges demolished, together with sixty-five thousand six hundred miles of roads and highways.

Little that could have value for the industrial and social recovery of France was left. Similarly, Italy, in an official report of April, 1919, placed her total losses between a hundred and ten and a hundred and thirty-five billion lire. Roumania, in the same month and year, placed her material loss at over ten billion francs and injury to private individuals at sixteen billion francs. Poland's losses were estimated at seventy-three billion francs.[7]

Clearly no other type of disaster is comparable with war in its destructiveness. Yet war, unlike earthquakes, tornadoes, and other convulsions of Nature, is of human origin and presumably amenable to human control.

Trends of War.—History reveals that war has persistently recurred throughout the ages. From the point of view of participation, duration, and casualties the twentieth century has demonstrated no diminution as compared with earlier centuries.[8]

The World War was justified in part by allied organizers of the defense as "the war to prevent war." Today, however, it is clear that this purpose has failed of accomplishment. The inability of world powers and of the League of Nations to prevent aggression in Ethiopia, China, Spain, Austria, and Czechoslovakia, and the rapid extensive rearming of Europe in recent years indicate clearly enough that the factors productive of war are still operating.

Nations, while still struggling under the colossal debt burdens, direct and indirect, incurred during the World War and its predecessors, have largely rearmed to a point far exceeding that of 1914. The armament competition indicates no declining trend as yet. Such show of strength is deemed by its proponents a safeguard which will prevent wanton aggression among neighboring nations. Temporarily it may possibly serve that purpose. But it demonstrates with certainty that a future international conflict would not likely be of brief duration and that the "next world war," so actively discussed in contemporary periodical literature, might involve vastly greater destructiveness, casualties, and debt burdens than its predecessors, conceivably crippling for all time our Western civilization.

In the face of such possibilities it is absurd to refuse to consider pacific means to the elimination of war, or to assume on grounds of "inevitability" that such elimination is impossible of achievement.

[7] This account of the devastation of northern France is largely condensed from Ford, George B.—*Out of the Ruins;* The Century Co., 1919.

[8] The most comprehensive analytical treatment of this subject will be found in Sorokin, Pitirim A.—*Social and Cultural Dynamics*, Volume Three, Part Two, "Fluctuation of War in Intergroup Relationship"; American Book Company, 1937. Sorokin also submits a valuable summary and criticism of sociological theories of war in Chapter VI of his *Contemporary Sociological Theories.*

Since war has a greater potential for the creation of universal poverty and destruction of values than has any other form of human disaster, all rational devices for its prevention require analysis.

Can War be Prevented?—Study of the causes of war and the breakdown of international organization makes it immediately apparent that here, as in the case of other social problems, there is to be found a multiplicity of factors. Some have their many roots deep in history and tradition and an abundance of accumulated precedent by which both nations and international councils are bound. It takes exceptional breadth of vision, greatness of character, and dynamic courage for a nation's leaders and advisers to transcend established precedent. Other causes lie deep in personality make-up and the influences economic, political, educational, and moral to which personality responds. To prevent war such factors must be brought by some means under social control.

Economic Factors.—There is multiple causation among the economic factors to which war is imputed. Few nations are even approximately self-sufficient. Yet each considers it essential to be prepared to be so, as far as possible, in case of war. All lack certain essential raw materials. Nations also require outlets for their surplus population. They must have markets for their products to make possible reciprocal international trade. This latter need in a world greedy for revenue, leads to shortsighted tariff wars, breeders of international ill will. These three requisites, raw materials, population outlets, and the need for markets, are preponderating factors in imperialistic policies and colonial expansion, and in combination with other factors underlie most modern wars of aggression.

Conspicuous among economic factors is also the private manufacture of armaments. Nations must have munitions plants manned and active, so that emergency orders can be filled expeditiously. Individuals or corporations, and their investors and financial backers, are dependent for their livelihood upon finding markets for their products. Thus it is argued by many that throughout the world such agencies serve as fomenters of war.[9] This argument, however, re-

[9] Hudson, Manley O.—*International Regulation of Trade in and Manufacture of Arms and Ammunition* (report submitted to the Special Committee of the U. S. Senate); Government Printing Office, 1935. Lefebure, Victor—*Scientific Disarmament;* The Macmillan Company, 1931. Noel-Baker, Philip—*The Private Manufacture of Armaments;* Oxford University Press, 1937. Stone, William T.— *The Munitions Industry, An Analysis of the Senate Investigation, September 4–21, 1934;*

quires more intensive study of the data, and in terms of the total situation. Private manufacture of arms is never the sole cause of war. Extensive armaments are possible where, as in Russia, there is government ownership.

Political Factors.—A contemporary threat of outstanding significance lies in the phenomenon of dictatorship or the totalitarian state. Implicit in dictatorship is the necessity of self-perpetuation in office. Any tendency to a weakening of the dictator's control necessitates measures on his part which will reaffirm his mastery. Mistakes in internal policy, rebuffs from other nations, unemployment, depression, or other sources of opposition are likely to drive the dictator to bravado—aggressive self-assertion toward other nations, mobilization, and the threat of war. He knows that in crisis periods among his followers loyalty to nation will be identified with his own person and that his hold upon his people will be increased. His bravado and his threats may, however, at any point force him into wars of conquest, for otherwise prestige will be imperiled. Thus dictatorship, and the systems of behavior which it induces, menace world peace.

It is quite evident that none of the causes of war as revealed by the events of 1914 has yet been curbed materially in its operation. Indeed the factors precipitating war in Europe appear to have been multiplied or to have gained greater potency in the past generation due to the terms of the reparations, the allotments of territory under the Treaty of Versailles, alliances and treaties, the internal convulsions within nations expressed in revolutions, dictatorships with "dynastic ambitions" or with national unity or prestige as objective, and economic depression. With these has come intensification of the prejudices, rivalries, hates, fears, desire for revenge, and other disintegrating emotions which war and war propaganda either engendered or fostered and which subsequent events have confirmed.

In effect, the League of Nations and the World Court, movements for the limitation of armaments, reciprocal trade agreements in the

Foreign Policy Association, Foreign Policy Reports, Vol. X, No. 20, revised edition, January 21, 1935. Williams, Benjamin H.—*American Diplomacy: Politics and Practice;* McGraw-Hill Book Company, Inc., 1936. Hearings before the Committee on Foreign Affairs, House of Representatives, on the *Exportation of Arms, Munitions or Implements of War to Belligerent Nations;* Government Printing Office, 1929, and a similar hearing on the *Exportation of Arms or Munitions of War;* Government Printing Office, 1933. League of Nations—*Reduction of Armaments—Supervision of the Private Manufacture and Publicity of the Manufacture of Arms and Ammunition and of Implements of War* (A. 30. 1929. IX); Geneva, 1929.

direction of free trade,[10] international agreements for currency stabilization and for either firm control of the private manufacture of munitions or the substitution of public manufacture for private, are, all of them, mechanisms vastly important to world peace—but still essentially mechanisms. The crux of the problem of war elimination would appear to be not the multiplication of agencies and devices to prevent war, but rather the quality of the cultural milieu in which such mechanisms are established and operated.

Attitudes as Factors.—The central problem may be to create throughout the nations of the world such a profound change in the attitudes of their peoples and representatives that future war will be rendered inconceivable. The mechanisms of international amity can not function effectively in a medium of suspicion, hate, fear, and narrow national patriotism. They can probably achieve their ultimate purpose only when war is outlawed in the minds of the peoples of the world and the diplomats who represent them.

The first essential would appear to be to ground the abolition of war in the will of the peoples of the world. Today this objective rests merely in longing and wishful thinking. Will or determination, which is the dynamic of action, would better rest upon judgment. It has been seen that there is ample evidence to justify the conviction that war is a paramount evil incompatible with civilization and endangering its continuance. Another world war, more destructive than the last, would threaten all of the highest values of individual and national life. By untiring cultivation of this conviction among all citizens of all countries, the objective of world peace, and the will to strive to bring it about, might be incorporated as major elements in thought, habit, and action.

This conviction is the necessary safeguard against the evidences of mob psychology to which mankind now readily succumbs. The very expectation of war tends to bring about the event even though few may desire it. A sense of helplessness in the face of the "inevitable"—a feeling of futility—is general. It is still easy to develop a war fervor among the masses by the glory of the uniform, drill, and parades, or by spreading through propaganda the conviction that one's nation has been wronged and that it is a patriotic duty to right that wrong. It is still possible to arouse fear, hate, jealousy, intolerance, ambition, avariciousness, impatience, touchiness, or anger in

[10] Sayre, Francis Bowes—"War or World Trade—Which?"; *The New York Times Magazine*, November 22, 1936.

the individual by means of misrepresentation or appeals to narrow patriotism.

Thus there are fundamental causes in human attitudes—in points of view. It is on these that war scares, jingoism, and even war glory are based. The causes seldom if ever work singly, but combine, and in combination gather force. Unrestricted emotionalism which envelopes them precludes clear thinking, and the individual from then on lives in his world of hate or fear until the conclusion of the war makes reflection possible.

Turning from the psychological conditioning of the individual to collective attitudes and behavior, Bernard summarizes as follows: ". . . the method of redirecting collective behavior is subjectively the same as that of redirecting individual behavior, for collective behavior is merely multiple or complementary and coördinate individual behavior on a larger scale. The subjective technique is . . . the reorganization of attitudes, largely on the emotional and intellectual levels. Collective behavior in large groups or collectivities must be organized on the basis of the higher levels of attitudinal response because these responses can be conditioned at a distance or throughout a large area only by means of symbolic stimuli carried through distance conveyers, such as radio, periodicals, movies, or traveling lecturers, or by the relaying of the stimuli from one carrier to another." [11]

Moral and Pedagogical Factors.—Individuals do what seems best to them in the circumstances. Nations do the same. Ignorance may lead to destructiveness. Trained minds, however, seek precise definitions of the ultimate objective or aim of life and search for the remote consequences of all actions—not merely their immediate results.

Wars largely grow out of miseducation and the failure to educate—from information and propaganda that intentionally misrepresent motives and conditions. Oratory and newspaper headlines have often quickly created war scares and hates among peaceloving peoples. War itself has been made to appear noble, and man's higher impulses have been appealed to in order to secure his enlistment. The outstanding facts of warfare—death for millions of combatants, shattered bodies and minds, destruction of homes and of the

[11] Bernard, L. L.—"Attitudes and the Redirection of Behavior," Chapter III of Young, Kimball, editor—*Social Attitudes*, p. 70; Henry Holt and Company, 1931.

fertility of land, spread of sexual perversions, mud, lice, disease, and a regimentation which precludes self-directed moral activity—are completely overlooked or suppressed. Misconceptions are prevented by an honest study of all facts, squarely faced.

When the people of a nation are "taken in" by propaganda and misrepresentation it is because they have not been trained to reason, or because their moral natures are disorganized or unorganized. Education in school and college is still primarily a matter of acquiring and memorizing information. Judgment is still a rare human trait. Reasoning capacity has been little developed by the pedagogical process. Challenge should be encouraged, not discouraged. Independent research, and the weighing of evidence are factors in the process of developing judgment. But judgment is never highly developed in social, civic, and economic problems until all reasonable alternatives are regularly and fairly considered and tested with reference to principles, and equally with reference to life's objectives. A generation of school children and college students well trained—in each class according to capacity—in analysis, comparison, interpretation, challenge, and the periodic revision of objectives, would be able to see war or any other public problem in perspective.[12]

Suggestibility is a major factor in the response of the populace to propaganda. It is in the main a useful trait since it opens life to wider fields of interest. But uncontrolled by self-organization suggestibility makes men unthinkingly responsive to emotional appeal whether good or evil. Unorganized personalities, including also those dominated by superimposed constellations of ideas—as for example, the Nazi trooper—respond freely to oratory, to fears and hates. They are the raw material which makes up the lynching party, pogrom, riot, or war. The second defense against mob psychology, aside from the development of reasoning capacity already discussed, is therefore self-organization—the essence of character.

For character is the settled habit of the will, and organization of all of the factors of selfhood with reference to self-chosen ideals. Our agencies of moral education, whether home, school, or church, have concentrated their effort too generally upon ideals and habits and

---

[12] Such a program of training is outlined in Chapter XIV of Ford, James, and Ford, Katherine Morrow—*The Abolition of Poverty;* The Macmillan Company, 1937.

too little upon the more fundamental factor of self-organization, and the massing of the individual's effort to overcome his weaknesses and build up a more consistent and unified life dominated by rational aims. Humanity will not be safe from aggression, selfish ambitions, anger, hate, prejudice, fear, and their consequences in international relations until such training becomes general.

A difficulty lies in the prevailing narrow conception of the self. Presumably most people still naively assume that one man's gain must be another man's loss. Yet once the self is conceived in its relations and selfhood construed in terms of the world community, self-interest is recognized as identical with the interests of humanity. The broader conception of the self and of the state as elements in the human process leads naturally to the search for common interests, objectives, and ideals. Lacking this, even the internationalist may be warlike. Progress is made not by the competition, bargaining, jockeying, and compromise of parliamentary bodies or conferences of diplomats but by coöperation, interpenetration of minds, and congruous activity for common ends.

In many human relations there is evidence of movement in the direction of amity and coöperation where belligerency has previously existed. Within the period covered by human history there has been, over a large part of the earth's surface, virtual elimination of personal feuds and warfare between families through developing loyalty to tribal or local government. Wars between cities have been overcome through the development of state control and of loyalty to state. Wars between states have largely become a matter of the past through federation of these smaller units into national governments. Each has been accompanied by formal organization. It remains for man to take the next step and so to build *loyalty to humanity* that wars between nations may become a thing of the past.

Nationalism versus Internationalism.—Patriotism as a rule is narrowly construed. Children of each of our nations are still being taught that their own nation is or should be supreme and that invasion of that supremacy should be resisted by force of arms. It may not be too late to inculcate greater depth and breadth in prevailing convictions. In its negative aspect civic education can make it clear that war is a disgrace incompatible with civilized society and to be avoided by all reasonable means. In its positive aspect the teaching may stress that the morality of the state should be construed in terms as high as the morality of the individual. Men of character no longer settle their personal differences by fisticuffs. National pride need not take the form either of arrogance or of resentment at the failure of others to recognize the supremacy of one's own nation. Resentment and arrogance are as unbecoming to nations as to individuals. Conceivably nations can in time be made to take pride rather in the exercise of their responsibility to humanity, even at the expense of temporary humiliation.

Assuming the ideology that the nation exists to serve, it would become the function of individuals and states to forward the interests of humanity. Kindred ideals and a similar sense of responsibility would be recognized and encouraged in other individuals and nations. Since evil may crop up in the best-ordered world a reasonable continuation of devices for national defense would be necessary but developed as rapidly as possible in the form of international policing to preclude aggression.

If the roots of war are defects in the attitudes and character of individuals, its elimination is dependent upon universal moral education. By the development of reasoning capacity, self-organization, and the translation of these into terms of national responsibility and service of humanity, war might in time be rendered a virtual impossibility. The lack of a substantial, internationally-integrated program for changing human attitudes and for developing an ingrained determination to outlaw war, may thus be the chief deficiency in the present day policy for war prevention. To devise and execute such a program would require the consecrated efforts of gifted leaders in every nation. Peace propaganda to date has been in large degree both sentimental and superficial. The program suggested here is not propaganda but education of the habits of thought, will, and action of all persons, young or old.

Since, however, the lasting effectiveness of action depends upon accuracy of knowledge, such a program would require elaborate, well-organized, and accurate research into each of the "causes" of war and their combinations and interrelations. This injunction applies both to human attitudes and the environmental factors, economic, political, and social.[13] Shifts in policy and method may frequently be made necessary by the progressive findings of such research. At each stage the program should grow out of the best knowledge and judgment available at the time.

[13] Sorokin, Pitirim A.—*Social and Cultural Dynamics*, Volume Three, especially pp. 370–380.

International Organization.—Organization for international coöperation is a corollary of education for international coöperation. Though some treaties providing for arbitration commissions between two or more nations antedate the first Hague Conference of 1899, the deliberate movement for international measures to reduce armaments and maintain peace is credited to the Hague Conferences of 1899 and 1907. These sought to provide for the peaceful settlement of disputes between nations, to provide for inquiry and arbitration, to reduce military budgets and regulate warfare.

The League of Nations was established following the World War and the Treaty of Peace at Paris, 1919. The League was composed of the signatories to the treaty and other states admitted by a two-thirds vote of the Assembly. The permanent secretariat was established at Geneva. The first meeting of the Assembly, representing forty-one countries, occurred at Geneva, November 5, 1920. Provision was made by the Covenant for mutual protection against aggression, and maintenance of territorial integrity; for inquiry and submission of disputes for arbitration; for abrogation of treaties inconsistent with the Covenant; for steps toward reduction of armaments; for joint action to prevent traffic in women and children, epidemics, and traffic in narcotics; for full and frank interchange of information. The experience of the Hague Conferences was utilized and Article 14 of the Covenant provided for a Permanent Court of International Justice. To enforce the League's decisions, Article 16 states:

"Should any Member of the League resort to war in disregard of its covenants under Articles 12, 13, or 15, it shall *ipso facto* be deemed to have committed an act of war against all other Members of the League, which hereby undertake immediately to subject it to the severance of all trade or financial relations, the prohibition of all intercourse between their nationals and the nationals of the covenant-breaking State, and the prevention of all financial, commercial or personal intercourse between the nationals of the covenant-breaking State and the nationals of any other State, whether a Member of the League or not.

"It shall be the duty of the Council in such case to recommend to the several Governments concerned what effective military, naval or air force the Members of the League shall severally contribute to the armed forces to be used to protect the covenants of the League.

"The Members of the League agree, further, that they will mutually support one another in the financial and economic measures which are taken under this Article, in order to minimize the loss and inconvenience resulting from the above measures, and that they will mutually support

one another in resisting any special measures aimed at one of their number by the covenant-breaking State, and that they will take the necessary
steps to afford passage through their territory to the forces of any of the
Members of the League which are cooperating to protect the covenants
of the League.

"Any Member of the League which has violated any covenant of the
League may be declared to be no longer a Member of the League by a
vote of the Council concurred in by the Representatives of all the other
Members of the League represented thereon." [14]

The protocol for pacific settlement of international disputes
adopted at the fifth annual meeting of the Assembly of the League of
Nations on October 2, 1924, declared aggressive war an international crime; refusal to arbitrate constituted aggression; sanctions
of Article 16 were to be applied against the aggressor. Events of
recent years have demonstrated that through the failure of some
countries to join the League, through the withdrawal of others, and
the defiance of certain leading powers, its principles have failed to
prevail in many international issues of profound importance. [15]

Nevertheless, attitudes regarding war and international relations
are changing. Such institutions as the League may be able to survive
in periods that could not have produced them, and to contribute to
the removal of some irritants. Meanwhile increasing international
arrangements for communication, commerce, investment, travel,
health; for the control of propaganda, removal of economic barriers,
and promotion of peace contribute to the development of the habit
of mutuality and to order as a dominating ideal and may in time
crowd out the old traditional rights of states to act purely on their
own.

With Sorokin one may conclude that "One of the main—and I
am inclined to say even the main—weapons against war is the
crystallization of the system of cultural values and of social relationships. Until this is achieved, the efforts to prevent war are likely to
be fruitless." [16]

But then with MacIver it may be added "Perhaps the greatest
and certainly the hardest task that faces civilized man is to dis-

[14] *Handbook of the League of Nations, 1920–24;* World Peace Foundation Pamphlet, Vol. VII, Nos. 3–4, 1924.

[15] The same is true in greater or less degree of decisions of many other international conferences, whether the Washington Conference on Disarmament of
November, 1922, the Genoa Conference of April, 1922, the Lausanne Conferences of 1922 and 1923, and a long list of subsequent attempts.

[16] Sorokin, Pitirim A.—*Social and Cultural Dynamics*, Volume Three, p. 380.

cover how, through the co-operative application of intelligence, he can maintain, advance, and redirect to the service of common ends the elaborate complex of material means and social institutions to which, almost unwittingly, he has fallen heir." [17]

QUESTIONS FOR DISCUSSION OR EXAMINATION

1. What are the (a) biological, (b) economic, (c) political, (d) psychological, (e) pedagogical, and (f) moral factors which tend to involve nations in war?
2. Do the trends toward greater and more destructive wars render peace programs absurd? Why, or why not?
3. What is the evidence that wars produce social disorganization?
4. Can wars ultimately be reduced or abolished by moral education? Give your reasons for accepting or rejecting each of the suggestions offered in this chapter.
5. By what arguments would you meet the following statements: (a) "war is inevitable," (b) "all peace movements are sentimental and unreasonable," (c) "man's cupidity, selfishness, aggressiveness, apathy, mob-mindedness are incurable"?

PROBLEMS FOR INDIVIDUAL STUDY

1. Critical report upon any two of the following list of references.
2. Analysis of the causes and effects of some selected war.
3. Examination of arguments for and against (a) compulsory military education, or (b) pacifistic movements, or (c) nonresistance. Support your conclusions with both your reasons and your evidence.
4. A critical study of (a) isolationism, (b) war debts, (c) the World Court, (d) tariff barriers, (e) war propaganda, (f) national protection of private investments in foreign countries, (g) imperialism, (h) dictatorships vs. democracy, (i) neutrality legislation.

SUGGESTIONS FOR SUPPLEMENTARY READINGS

Allen, Devere—*The Fight for Peace;* The Macmillan Company, 1930.

American Academy of Political and Social Science—*The Annals;* many issues devoted to war and international problems, see especially July and September, 1934, July, 1936, and July, 1937.

Angell, Sir Norman—*Raw Materials, Population Pressure and War;* World Peace Foundation, World Affairs Books No. 14, 1936.

Bemis, Samuel Flagg—*A Diplomatic History of the United States;* Henry Holt and Company, 1936.

Blakeslee, George H.—*Conflicts of Policy in the Far East;* Foreign Policy Association and World Peace Foundation, World Affairs Pamphlets No. 6, 1934.

[17] MacIver, R. M.—*Society: A Textbook of Sociology*, p. 528; Farrar & Rinehart, Inc., 1937.

Bryce, James—*International Relations;* The Macmillan Company, 1922.

Buell, Raymond Leslie—*The New American Neutrality;* Foreign Policy Association, Inc., 1936.

Case, Clarence Marsh—*Non-Violent Coercion: A Study in Methods of Social Pressure;* The Century Co., 1923.

Chase, Stuart—*The Economy of Abundance;* The Macmillan Company, 1934.

Cruttwell, C. R. M. F.—*A History of Peaceful Change in the Modern World;* Oxford University Press, 1937.

Devine, Edward T., and Brandt, Lilian—*Disabled Soldiers and Sailors Pensions and Training;* Carnegie Endowment for International Peace, Preliminary Economic Studies of the War No. 12, Oxford University Press, 1919.

Dickinson, G. Lowes—*War: Its Nature, Cause and Cure;* The Macmillan Company, 1924.

Dublin, Louis I.—*The Population Problem and World Depression;* Foreign Policy Association, Inc., 1936.

Dunn, Frederick Sherwood—*Peaceful Change: A Study in International Procedures;* Council on Foreign Relations (New York), 1937.

Dupuy, R. Ernest, and Eliot, George Fielding—*If War Comes;* The Macmillan Company, 1937.

Eagleton, Clyde—*Analysis of the Problem of War;* The Ronald Press Company, 1937.

Fay, Sidney B.—*The Origins of the World War,* two volumes; The Macmillan Company, 1928.

Ferrero, Guglielmo—*Peace and War* (translated by Bertha Pritchard); The Macmillan Company, 1933.

Foreign Policy Association—publications

Gillin, John Lewis—*Social Pathology,* Chapter 25, "International Disorganization"; The Century Co., 1933.

Gooch, G. P., and Temperley, Harold, editors—*British Documents on the Origins of the War, 1898–1914,* Vols. I–X; British Library of Information (New York), 1936.

Hasluck, E. L.—*Foreign Affairs, 1919–1937;* The Macmillan Company, 1938.

Hocking, William Ernest—*The Spirit of World Politics;* The Macmillan Company, 1931.

Holland, W. L., and Mitchell, Kate L.—*Problems of the Pacific, 1936.* Proceedings of the Sixth Conference, Institute of Pacific Relations; University of Chicago Press, 1938.

Hudson, Manley O.—*International Regulation of Trade in and Manufacture of Arms and Ammunition* (report submitted to the Special Committee of the U. S. Senate); Government Printing Office, 1935.

Hudson, Manley O.—*The Permanent Court of International Justice;* The Macmillan Company, 1934.

Huxley, Aldous, editor—*An Encyclopaedia of Pacifism;* Harper & Brothers, 1937.

Ireland, Gordon—*Boundaries, Possessions, and Conflicts in South America;* Harvard University Press, 1938.

Jacks, L. P.—*Cooperation or Coercion?;* E. P. Dutton & Co., 1938.

Kellogg, Vernon—*Military Selection and Race Deterioration;* Carnegie Endowment for International Peace Publications, Oxford, The Clarendon Press, 1916.

Knapp, Dr. Ir. W. H. C.—*World Dislocation and World Recovery: Agriculture as the Touchstone of Economic World Events;* P. S. King & Son, Ltd., 1935.

Kohn, Hans—*Force or Reason?;* Harvard University Press, 1937.

League of Nations—publications.

Lefebure, Victor—*Scientific Disarmament;* The Macmillan Company, 1931.

McEntee, Girard Lindsley—*A Military History of the World War;* Charles Scribner's Sons, 1937.

Mitrany, David—*The Effect of the War in Southeastern Europe;* Yale University Press, 1936.

Moon, Parker Thomas—*Imperialism and World Politics;* The Macmillan Company, 1926.

Moulton, Harold G.—*The Reparation Plan;* The Brookings Institution, 1924.

Moulton, Harold G., and Pasvolsky, Leo—*World War Debt Settlements;* The Brookings Institution, 1926.

Myers, Denys P.—*World Disarmament: Its Problems and Prospects;* World Peace Foundation, 1932.

National Peace Conference—*Conference on World Economic Cooperation: March 24–26, 1938;* National Peace Conference, 1938.

National Peace Conference—*Peaceful Change: The Alternative to War—the Basic Handbook of the Campaign for World Economic Cooperation;* National Peace Conference, September, 1937.

Nicolai, Dr. G. F.—*The Biology of War* (translated from the original German by Constance A. Grande and Julian Grande); The Century Co., 1919.

Noel-Baker, Philip—*The Private Manufacture of Armaments;* Oxford University Press, 1937.

Page, Kirby—*Must We Go to War?;* Farrar & Rinehart, Inc., 1937.

Page, Kirby—*War, Its Causes, Consequences and Cure;* George H. Doran Company, 1923.

Patterson, Ernest Minor, editor—*The United States and World War;* entire issue of *The Annals of the American Academy of Political and Social Science,* Vol. 192, July, 1937.

Popper, David H.—*The Hull Trade Program;* Foreign Policy Foundation, Inc., 1936.

Robbins, Lionel—*Economic Planning and International Order;* The Macmillan Company, 1937.

Rose, Marc A.—*Economics and Peace: A Primer and a Program* (The Primer by Marc A. Rose. The Program by a group of Thirty-four Economists); National Peace Conference, 1937.

Salter, Sir Arthur, Thompson, Sir J. Arthur, Johnston, G. H., Zimmern, Alfred, Andrews, C. F., Libby, Frederick S., Atkinson, Henry A., Steed, Wickham, and others—*The Causes of War;* The Macmillan Company, 1932.

Shepardson, Whitney H., in collaboration with Scroggs, William O.—*The United States in World Affairs, An Account of American Foreign Relations, 1934–1935;* Harper & Brothers, 1935.

Shepardson, Whitney H., in collaboration with Scroggs, William O.—*The United States in World Affairs, An Account of American Foreign Relations, 1936;* Harper & Brothers, 1937.

Shotwell, James T.—*On the Rim of the Abyss;* The Macmillan Company, 1936.

Shotwell, James T.—*War As an Instrument of National Policy, and Its Renunciation in the Pact of Paris;* Harcourt, Brace and Company, Inc., 1929.

Sorokin, Pitirim—*Contemporary Sociological Theories,* Chapter VI, "Sociological Interpretation of the 'Struggle for Existence' and the Sociology of War"; Harper & Brothers, 1928.

Sorokin, Pitirim A.—*Social and Cultural Dynamics,* Volume Three, *Fluctuation of Social Relationships, War, and Revolution;* American Book Company, 1937.

Spaulding, Oliver Lyman—*Pen and Sword: in Greece and Rome;* Princeton University Press, 1937.

Staley, Eugene—*Raw Materials in Peace and War;* Council on Foreign Relations (New York), 1937.

Steed, Henry Wickham—*Vital Peace. A Study of Risks;* The Macmillan Company, 1936.

Stone, William T.—*The Munitions Industry, An Analysis of the Senate Investigation, September 4-21, 1934;* Foreign Policy Association, Foreign Policy Reports, Vol. X, No. 20, revised edition, January 21, 1935.

Strachey, John—*The Coming Struggle for Power;* Covici Friede, 1933.

Tansill, Charles Callan—*America Goes to War;* Little, Brown, and Company, 1938.

Taussig, F. W.—*International Trade;* The Macmillan Company, 1927.

Tippetts, Charles S.—*Autarchy: National Self-Sufficiency;* University of Chicago Press, 1933.

Tobenkin, Elias—*The Peoples Want Peace;* G. P. Putnam's Sons, 1938.

Wheeler-Bennett, John W.—*Disarmament and Security Since Locarno. 1925-1931;* The Macmillan Company, 1932.

Williams, Benjamin Harrison—*American Diplomacy: Policies and Practice;* McGraw-Hill Book Company, Inc., 1936.

Woodhead, H. G. W., editor—*The China Year Book, 1937;* University of Chicago Press, 1938.

Woods, Frederick Adams, and Baltzly, Alexander—*Is War Diminishing? A Study of the Prevalence of War in Europe from 1450 to the Present Day;* Houghton Mifflin Company, 1915.

Woolley, Mary E.—*Internationalism and Disarmament;* The Macmillan Company, 1935.

World Peace Foundation—publications.

Zimmern, Alfred—*League of Nations and the Rule of Law, 1918-1935;* The Macmillan Company, 1936.

PART V

PRINCIPLES OF SOCIAL REORGANIZATION

CHAPTER XXXII

INDIVIDUAL AND SOCIAL REORGANIZATION: SOCIAL POLICY

Interrelationships of Individual and Social Deviation.—The conditions of individual deviation and of the inadequacy of individuals to meet social expectations and requirements have been outlined already in their manifold interactions with factors of the social milieu—the industrial order, government, public and private agencies, the family and the subgroups of society, and crisis situations. At the same time the inadequacies of social agencies and institutions, and their deviations from norms of efficiency and optimum service, have been indicated. Each, in a definite sense, can be shown to be conditioned in part by the other. All aspects of individual and group life are functionally interrelated.

Evidence of such interrelationship is sufficiently apparent when the handicapped person has difficulty in securing employment, becomes a public charge, or is unable to participate in normal family life. It is apparent when an industrial or social revolution, an earthquake or war, migration to a foreign country or from village to metropolis, or even a radical change in political administration, upsets the individual routine and forces readjustments. But the precipitating factor for the pathologic situation within the complex of factors, may be no more than a random decision made by parent, boss, bank executive, or bureaucrat, or—as the psychiatrist or social worker can show from case records—a cross word, misunderstood gesture, or unintentional slight occurring at a time when its victim was unable to effect a proper adjustment.

Prevention Reëxamined.—The prevention of any pathologic condition within the individual and the group has been said to involve the discovery and elimination of its cause. But our study has shown that there is no unitary cause of any ill—in the sense of being sufficient in itself to produce that ill as an invariable result. The germs of any disease cannot cause that disease unless they can reach their victim, become ingested in a specific manner and in sufficient quantity, and find their victim receptive. He may have native immunity, artificial immunity through inoculation, or acquired resistance from wholesome living. Similarly, war may not injure the profiteer (except morally); the flood may not injure the family in its path who live on high ground; technological unemployment may not harm the man who has a subsidiary occupation. Thus the effect of each causative factor depends upon the condition of all other pertinent factors—their magnitude or force and their interrelations.

Preventive policies emerge somewhat as follows:

1. To discover what factors are indispensable to produce the pathologic result—*e.g.* the yellow fever germ or the flood, together with the unprotected individual.

2. To discover the effective mode of attack upon these and upon the associated factors—*e.g.* the elimination of the mosquito carrier to prevent the inoculation of the germ in human beings (which is to remove the "cause" by destroying the transmitting agent). Or prevent loss of life and limb in floods by building adequate retaining walls and warning people of the flood's approach (prevention by circumvention). Or prevent the poverty which technological unemployment might occasion by means of labor exchanges, public works, or subsidiary occupations (prevention by physical and functional substitution). Or prevent war by training all peoples not only to outlaw war (prevention by exclusion) but also to acquire the ideology and behavior-complex of peace (prevention by constructive ideational exclusion—the crowding out of evil by "overcoming evil with good").

Prevention Policies: Negative and Positive.—By implication a well-rounded preventive policy for any individual or social ill is seen to be fourfold. For it involves measures both negative and positive for the individual and for the social order. Though these invariably overlap, it may clarify thinking to consider them at first separately.

In its negative aspect any specific program for the individual would seek to prevent the operation of the causative factors which work upon or through that individual. Thus the negative program for the individual would cover the cure of his diseases, physical or mental, the overcoming of evil habits, of illiteracy, miseducation, or undereducation, or of vocational ineptitude by retraining adapted to the individual's needs. The chief agencies of the process are the physician, psychiatrist, teacher, and social case worker, but would of course involve for specific difficulties a wide range of other professions, as for example, the minister, lawyer, banker, judge, or probation officer.

The negative program for social groups would be that designed to bring under social control those factors which at any point thwart individual development or the optimal functioning of social institutions and agencies. The social group seeks the elimination of the thwarting factors chiefly through the state by means of regulatory legislation, including all branches of social law, whether building, housing, or sanitary codes; labor, safety, or criminal law; or highly specialized legislation such as that for slum elimination, flood prevention, or control of the private manufacture of armaments. Although the removal of the factors which produce social ills has increasingly been brought under regulatory legislation throughout recent centuries, much of the process is still left to, or assumed by, other organizations than the state. These include professional organizations, whether in the learned professions, or of manufacturers, merchants, bankers, or labor; coöperative associations for mutual protection in the fields of production, credit, warehousing, and merchandising; and philanthropic effort, whether by employers for their employees, by foundations and trust funds, or by social welfare agencies. The social structure erected to eliminate the ills from which mankind may suffer is exceedingly intricate and involved. There is much overlapping in some areas of service, while other ills are neglected. There are complex and constantly changing relations both of antagonism and of coördination of effort, and a very wide range in relative efficiency.[1]

The positive or constructive program for the individual is that in which his resistance to "outrageous fortune" is built. It consists of the measures which fortify the individual—whether physically by building resistance to disease through artificial immunization (vaccination, inoculation, prophylaxis) or by building health through personal hygiene, appropriate nutrition and exercise, or adequate sleep. But it goes much farther in so far as it can develop the

[1] Any detailed list of government services, Federal, state, or local, displays a large number of agencies of government to deal with each of our major social problems—labor, housing, health, relief—imperfect demarcations of field or jurisdiction, and occasional inconsistencies of principle. An analysis of the scope and functions of the organizations represented in the social service directory of any municipality will reveal similar overlaps and inconsistencies among private agencies.

mental traits characteristic of active morality. Its measures are those designed through education to develop initiative and resourcefulness, reasoning capacity and judgment, rational objectives, sound habits, and strength of will. It is the regimen of active adaptation as distinguished from passive.

In its positive aspect the social program is concerned with the provision of a social medium which will facilitate the active development of the individual, and of the agencies and institutions that are constructive in type. In its physical aspects it covers not only city planning but regional, state, and national planning. Improved housing developments provide not only for health and safety but also for the amenities of living—convenience, comfort, beauty, and privacy. Recreation programs comprise community centers, municipal, state, and national programs for playgrounds, parks, motor highways, and public reservations. To make possible the intellectual, civic, and moral development of its citizens the government develops its educational system, extends it to reach each person, young or old, and perfects it through changes in the curriculum and the quality of instruction to contribute to the development of each individual of the population. Beyond the schools further education is provided through museums of art, natural history, or science and industry; through the municipal theater and opera; through music centers, and symphonies; through botanical gardens and waterfront developments; and through improving the quality of civic architecture. Society supplements these through a wide variety of private enterprises, coöperative or philanthropic in nature, ranging from coöperative education and recreational groups such as neighborhood theaters or literary guilds and scientific academies, to endowed institutions of learning, foundations for human welfare, and the manifold activities of the church for moral and spiritual development.

Individual and Social Reorganization.—The first principle of improvement in social organization is to so reorganize individuals that they will be interested and equipped to serve the interests of the group. The soundness and serviceability of any social organization, institution, or agency is dependent at every point upon the qualities of the individuals who direct and compose it. Church, state, school, family, industry, shop, or neighborhood may be wrecked by headstrong, egotistical leadership or by apathetic leadership. They may be injured by factional disputes, ignorance, or laziness. Communism and dictatorships are quite as subject to error or decay from these sources as are capitalistic industrial organizations or republics. The curse of inefficiency or injustice is, however, removed from capitalism or communism, totalitarianism or democracy in just so far as wisdom and optimal standards can be made to replace ignorance and expediency.

The key to the lasting prevention of poverty, handicaps, or conflict thus rests in individual reorganization or the training of mankind, whether leaders or followers, to reason and to widen the areas of mutuality.[2] It involves, as has been seen, the building of individual ideals and habits through periodic challenge and reorganization; the development of modes of living that will build initiative, resourcefulness, and strength of will; and periodic self-analysis to crowd out narrow, selfish, or destructive interests by substitution and cultivation of those interests which are pregnant or contributory to the fulfilment of organizations of interests widely shared. Emphasis in individual reorganization must, for the advantage of the social order, be placed upon the unification of each personality and the organization of his interests and life upon the basis of as much opportunity for growth as is consistent with the equal opportunity for growth on the part of others.

With the assumption of this aim, social reorganization can take its natural course. Rational men study and reason before they act (research and interpretation); they establish tentative goals (programs) consistent with their ultimate ideals (social objectives). They incorporate their programs in specific measures (legislative acts and community organization) and allot them to appropriate agencies. These programs and measures, private and public, after adequate discussion and challenge, become incorporated in broad social policies for labor, housing, health, and so on. To keep order within such a chaos of measures, to route each according to relative importance, to prevent interference of one with another involves the final step of coördination (economic and social planning).

Measures within the Social Plan.—Most human ills are preventable. Their causes are largely known; the means to their eradication are reasonably clear. But elimination is not accomplished by *laissez faire* or by piecemeal attack: these customary methods have already demonstrated their futility. Their prevention requires organized concerted action covering each of the precipitating factors and

[2] See Part I, Chapter IV on the systematic fulfilment of organizations of interests.

chains and complexes of causative factors. Ultimate objectives can be visualized and mapped; and immediate objectives planned for sequence. Able execution would involve the use of all essential techniques and coördination of all special programs within a central policy.[3]

Aspects of Social Reorganization.—As dependency is reduced, poor relief as we now know it can be abandoned, substituting specialized forms of public guardianship. The state's major concern with childhood is in education. The few dependents among children in training may thus have their incidental economic needs attended to by the Department of Education in coöperation with the social security branch for dependent children. The ill may be looked after in the same way by coördinated action of the Department of Health and the executives of public health insurance. Thus the individual whether mentally ill, defective, alcoholic, criminal, young or old, could be supported during treatment, and the needs of his family referred to the appropriate department—usually that for aid to mothers or other guardians of dependent children. The stigma of pauperism would thus be removed and injurious social attitudes toward the unfortunate would be changed correspondingly.

In social and economic planning, as in other human programs, the speed with which the goal can be reached will be determined by the wisdom and skill with which the approach is organized. A wise policy always involves full knowledge of situations, and of the alternative techniques and institutions or agencies at its command. Able leadership is indispensable. Tasks should be distributed in such a manner that their completion in proper interrelation and sequence will be reasonably certain. Special tasks can be apportioned among existing experienced agencies—housing to those demonstrating competence in architecture, building, engineering, finance, and land

[3] For elaboration of this statement and for variety in approaches and emphasis, it is suggested that, in addition to the supplementary readings at the end of this chapter, one consult recent discussions in the periodical literature, as for example, Fuller, Richard C.—"The Problem of Teaching Social Problems"; *American Journal of Sociology*, Vol. XLIV, No. 3, November, 1938: Bain, Read— "Cultural Integration and Social Conflict," and Russell, Bertrand—"The Role of the Intellectual in the Modern World"; *American Journal of Sociology*, Vol. XLIV, No. 4, January, 1939: Ross, E. A.—"Some Contributions of Sociology to the Guidance of Society," and Sorokin, Pitirim A.—"Is Accurate Social Planning Possible?"; *American Sociological Review*, Vol. 1, No. 1, February, 1936: and Waller, Willard—"Social Problems and the Mores"; *American Sociological Review*, Vol. 1, No. 6, December, 1936.

problems; malnutrition to specialized groups representing medicine, home economics, agriculture, and education; flood control to engineers and soil conservationists; labor problems to economists, industrialists, specialists in administration and labor—each under supervision which will direct and integrate. To economize effort and resources existing agencies, powers, and machinery should be utilized for the execution of the program so far as is feasible.

Research.—Effectiveness in planning and procedure necessitates that action be based upon accurate and reasonably complete knowledge. It is better to delay action if necessary for years than to defeat the program by making the mistakes which grow out of too limited information. Intensive research is required into each phase of the plan before action is warranted. Continuing research will be necessitated to discover the precise effects of plans in operation and the means to overcome their imperfections.

Though the economic plan is conceived as national in content and operation, some of its phases require international councils and agreements. This is particularly true of many aspects of war prevention, currency control, tariff and trade reciprocities, and the elimination of pestilence. International research in the problems of labor, housing, health, drugs, and nutrition also serves to bring national problems into perspective, stimulate further needed research, and make it possible for each nation to profit by the recorded experience of others, and where advisable to coöperate in a world-wide plan.[4]

Federal versus Local Jurisdiction.—Most details of a national economic plan require state legislation and state or local administration. This is particularly true of minimum-wage and labor legisla-

[4] John Dewey has presented the moral aspect of this problem as follows: "It is science, which through technological applications has produced the potentiality of plenty, of ease and security for all, while lagging legal and political institutions, unaffected as yet by the advance of science into their domain, explain the want, insecurity and suffering that are the other term of the paradox. . . . every obligation is moral, and in its ultimate consequences social. The demands of the situation cannot be met, as some reactionaries urge, by going backward in science, by putting restrictions upon its productive activities. They cannot be met by putting a gloss of humanistic culture over the brute realities of the situation. They can be met only by human activity exercised in human directions. The wounds made by applications of science can be healed only by a further extension of applications of knowledge and intelligence; like the purpose of all modern healing the application must be preventive as well as curative. This is the supreme obligation of intellectual activity at the present time. The moral consequences of science in life impose a corresponding responsibility." Dewey, John—"The Supreme Intellectual Obligation"; *Science Education*, Vol. 18, No. 1, February, 1934.

tion but, in conjunction with Federal laws and departments, it is true of most social security, housing, taxation, and agricultural programs. Though there is a marked trend toward the federalization of welfare programs, reënforced by United States Supreme Court decisions of 1937, the police powers of the states confer upon them definite prerogatives which make it possible for any state government to rid its people of much poverty on its own initiative.

In many fields the Federal government can extend its control beyond the mere advisory function to actual direction and supervision of policies. This is likely to be done largely by means of the principle of grants-in-aid, already exemplified for example in social security and housing legislation and many branches of education. The states are, however, free to go beyond the Federal standards in the service which they render and may thus be instrumental by their example in raising the standards for service throughout the nation. If each of the forty-eight states and each of the cities and counties of America are looked upon as experimental laboratories for the discovery of the most effective means to the banishment of poverty, the central research office of a national economic plan will find it exceedingly profitable to analyze closely the methods which they use and the results obtained, and bring to the attention of all other units of government the most successful instances of local accomplishment. Thus each unit can be helped to profit greatly from the collective experience.

The peril of excessive federalization of economic and welfare policies is that local units of government and citizens may be deprived thereby both of their sense of responsibility and the educational values which inhere in participation. A program exclusively Federal would cause the public to look to Washington for all assistance, instead of engaging in constructive effort themselves. They would thereby lose many of the essential values of citizenship in a democracy. Though planning and research on a nation-wide basis must for effectiveness be national, and many types of legislation, whether in conservation of natural resources, flood control, agricultural development, regulation of transportation or distribution, and international relations, must be Federal, the cultivation of state and local responsibility and of local initiative is of paramount importance.

In general, the measures to prevent persons not now poor from becoming poor require both national planning and national execution, while measures to restore to self-support persons now dependent are primarily local. Such a demarcation of function is, however, only rough and approximate. There would be abundant exceptions.

Local Service Centers.—Take, for example, the clearing house and advisory functions so essential to extricate each family now in poverty from its present distress. These comprise employment exchanges; many types of medical clinics; centers for vocational analysis, guidance, and retraining; housing records of approved houses or tenements available, with reference to size and equipment of accommodations and rentals; lists of adult educational, cultural, and recreational opportunities; nutrition advisory centers, possibly associated with the distribution of surplus foods and with training in budget-making; social security headquarters, of which at least the unemployment insurance branch must be in close association with the public employment exchange; centers for record and advice on hereditary defects and eugenic matings, on birth control, and the venereal diseases; records of the victims of each type of handicap, whether or not hereditary, together with advisory and training centers for the specialized types of service needed by the handicapped.

Clearly the national economic plan requires centralized statistical recording and interpretation of all cases and types of treatment. But the function of advising each case properly and of putting it in touch with the needed agencies of service, public or private, is local. Conceivably each community may profitably possess ultimately a building which will house these many services under one roof, or in large cities a building or group of such buildings at its center and in each of the major subcenters. Presumably within such buildings some of the executives would have Federal appointments (as for example in the public employment exchange); others would have state appointments (as for the records of the handicapped); still others (as in the case of housing records) appointments from the local government. Some of the state and local services would enjoy Federal grants-in-aid, others would not.

The Plan Inevitably Elastic.—It would be supererogatory and valueless to attempt to outline or predict the structure, organization, and administration of a national economic plan. The abolition of poverty is but one of its many objectives. Its primary function is not negative but positive—the facilitation of business and industry for the public welfare. Its structure and organization will be determined by the interplay of factors which comprise Federal and state con-

stitutions and their contemporary interpretation, statute law, existing administrative setups and the traditions behind them, and that
unpredictable variable which is termed leadership. The research
which would precede the formulation of a national policy should
include much data not yet available, some of which would materially influence the recommendations with regard to organization,
procedures, and allocation of function.

Such preliminary research and preplanning must find its way
among the traditional dichotomies—*laissez faire* versus planned
action, government regulation versus public ownership, relief versus
social insurance, mass treatment versus individualization, hunches
versus knowledge, chaos versus order, drift versus leadership. Complexities in planning as well as in operation will be innumerable.
Years may be devoted to provisional planning and years to the
cultivation of leadership and of popular demand, since public action
always lags far behind the envisioning of a need.

Other Objectives and the Social Plan.—Social planning may be
approached with objectives other than the abolition of poverty: such
as, for example, the improvement of the racial stock, the cultivation
of personalities with exceptional gifts, or the mastery of diseases.
Each of these would require for success in a democracy the same
procedures: (1) the definition of objectives—or evaluative techniques;
(2) research, challenge, and interpretation—or the techniques of
science; (3) regulatory legislation—or legal and political techniques;
(4) enforcement—or administrative techniques; (5) application to
each individual—or pedagogical, psychological, and case work
techniques. Each such approach to social planning would be concerned with the removal of thwarting factors, and the building of the
mediums essential for growth, achievement, and service. Each would
require competent leadership for its specific policies and plans, and
coördination with the general economic and social plan.

Is Social Planning Chimerical?—Social science does not yet
make possible prediction with regard to many of the matters under
consideration here. There are too many unknowns and, at least for
proximate stretches of time, unknowables in the field of human capacities, potentialities, and relationships. Yet student and scholar
continue to look ahead and to speculate upon the future; for man's
most intimate concern is his own well-being and that of his kind.

Fundamental to the defense of economic and social planning is
the necessity of applying reason to human affairs, for the protection

of the individual and of his social institutions. Anthropology, history, and sociology reveal the inevitability of change. Man's question is —can change be guided by reason? If not, the drift would appear to be toward ultimate communism, by way of the treacherous intermediate stages of either reactionism on the one hand or totalitarianism on the other—each logically creating militant antagonism on the part of its oppressed (a putative majority) and consequently precipitating in time a revolution.

Social planning is unquestionably more difficult of establishment and administration in a democracy than under an individual or group dictatorship. It has not yet been demonstrated to be impossible, though its difficulties would be great in any democracy where systematic moral training is lacking and where correspondingly ignorance, intolerance, hates, grudges, envy, prejudice, contentiousness, apathy, cynicism, parasitism, and selfishness tend to defeat honest purpose and well-considered programs.

The answer appears to lie less in measures or institutions than in whether or not man can be taught to act upon reason. Can he learn to apply dispassionate, critical judgment to his personal behavior first and then to questions of public concern. If citizens can be taught rational morality—the recognition of mutuality of interest and self-development via service—as the way of life, planning will become a possibility within democracies, and pathologic or thwarting conditions can gradually be overcome by factors more wholesome and constructive in nature.

By facing the reality that nothing is static or final, that all organizations and all plans are experimental and to be changed as new data come to light, constructive change can (with occasional discontinuity) be effected within the present social and industrial order, so long as the will to constructive change remains potent.

SUGGESTIONS FOR SUPPLEMENTARY READINGS

American Academy of Political and Social Science—*Increasing Government Control in Economic Life;* entire issue of *The Annals,* Vol. 178, March, 1935.

American Academy of Political and Social Science—*National and World Planning;* entire issue of *The Annals,* Vol. 162, July, 1932.

Berle, Adolf A., Jr., and Means, Gardiner C.—*The Modern Corporation and Private Property;* The Macmillan Company, 1933.

Branford, Victor, and Geddes, Patrick—*The Coming Polity: A Study in Reconstruction;* Williams & Norgate, Ltd., 1917.

Branford, Victor, and Geddes, Patrick—*Our Social Inheritance;* Williams & Norgate, Ltd., 1919.

Bridgman, P. W.—*The Intelligent Individual and Society;* The Macmillan Company, 1938.

Bye, Raymond Taylor, and Blodgett, Ralph Hamilton—*Getting and Earning: A Study of Inequality;* Crofts & Co., 1937.

Case, Clarence Marsh—*Social Process and Human Progress;* Harcourt, Brace and Company, Inc., 1931.

Chapin, F. Stuart—*Cultural Change;* D. Appleton-Century Company, 1928.

Chase, Stuart—*Government in Business;* The Macmillan Company, 1935.

Cole, G. D. H.—*Economic Planning;* Alfred A. Knopf, 1935.

Davis, Jerome—*Contemporary Social Movements;* The Century Co., 1930.

Dewey, John—*The Quest for Certainty: A Study of the Relation of Knowledge and Action;* Minton, Balch & Company, 1929.

Dewey, John, and Tufts, James H.—*Ethics;* Henry Holt and Company, 1908.

Fairchild, Fred Rogers, Furniss, Edgar Stevenson, Buck, Norman Sydney, and Whelden, Chester Howard—*A Description of the New Deal;* The Macmillan Company, 1935.

Faris, Ellsworth, Laune, Ferris, and Todd, Arthur J., editors—*Intelligent Philanthropy;* University of Chicago Press, 1930.

Follett, M. P.—*The New State: Group Organization the Solution of Popular Government;* Longmans, Green and Co., 1920.

Friedrich, Carl Joachim—*Constitutional Government and Politics: Nature and Development;* Harper & Brothers, 1937.

Geddes, Patrick—*Cities in Evolution;* Williams & Norgate, Ltd., 1915.

Henriques, J. Q.—*A Citizen's Guide to Social Service;* George Allen and Unwin Ltd., 1938.

Hertzler, Joyce O.—*Social Progress;* The Century Co., 1928.

Hobhouse, L. T.—*The Elements of Social Justice;* Henry Holt and Company, 1922.

Hobson, J. A.—*Economics and Ethics: A Study in Social Values;* D. C. Heath and Company, 1929.

Holcombe, Arthur N.—*Foundations of the Modern Commonwealth;* Harper & Brothers, 1923.

Laski, Harold J.—*Liberty in the Modern State;* Harper & Brothers, 1930.

Lederer, Emil—"National Economic Planning," *Encyclopaedia of the Social Sciences,* Vol. 11; The Macmillan Company, 1933.

Lippmann, Walter—*The Good Society;* Little, Brown, and Company, 1937.

Lundberg, George A., Bain, Read, and Anderson, Nels—*Trends in American Sociology;* Harper & Brothers, 1929.

MacCunn, John—*The Making of Character: Some Educational Aspects of Ethics;* The Macmillan Company, revised and rewritten with new chapters, 1920.

MacIver, R. M.—*Society: A Textbook of Sociology;* Farrar & Rinehart, Inc., 1937.

Mackenzie, Findlay, editor—*Planned Society, Yesterday, Today, Tomorrow;* Prentice-Hall, Inc., 1937.

Macmillan, Lord—*Law and Politics;* The Macmillan Company, 1935.

McNair, Malcolm P., and Lewis, Howard T., editors—*Business and Modern Society;* Harvard University Press, 1938.

Mangold, George B.—*Organization for Social Welfare;* The Macmillan Company, 1934.

Millspaugh, Arthur C.—*Public Welfare Organization;* The Brookings Institution, 1935.

North, Cecil Clare—*Social Problems and Social Planning;* McGraw-Hill Book Company, Inc., 1932.

Ogburn, William Fielding—*Social Change;* B. W. Huebsch, Inc., 1922.

Parmelee, Maurice—*Farewell to Poverty;* John Wiley & Sons, Inc., 1935.

Petrie, W. M. F.—*The Revolutions of Civilisation;* Harper & Brothers, 1922.

P E P (Political and Economic Planning)—publications; London.

Pigors, Paul—*Leadership or Domination;* Houghton Mifflin Company, 1935.

President's Research Committee on Social Trends—*Recent Social Trends in the United States,* two volumes; McGraw-Hill Book Company, Inc., 1933.

Robbins, Lionel—*Economic Planning and International Order;* The Macmillan Company, 1937.

Salter, Sir Arthur—*The Framework of an Ordered Society;* The Macmillan Company, 1933.

Sarton, George—*The History of Science and the New Humanism;* Harvard University Press, 1937.

Sorokin, Pitirim A.—*Social and Cultural Dynamics,* three volumes; American Book Company, 1937.

Soule, George—*The Coming American Revolution;* The Macmillan Company, 1934.

Soule, George—*The Future of Liberty;* The Macmillan Company, 1936.

Soule, George—*A Planned Society;* The Macmillan Company, 1932.

Spengler, Oswald—*The Decline of the West* (authorized translation with notes by Charles Francis Atkinson), two volumes; Alfred A. Knopf, 1926–1928.

Stamp, Sir Josiah—*The Science of Social Adjustment;* The Macmillan Company, 1937.

Wagner, Donald O.—*Social Reformers: From Adam Smith to John Dewey;* The Macmillan Company, 1934.

Wallas, Graham—*The Great Society. A Psychological Analysis;* The Macmillan Company, 1914.

Wallis, Wilson D.—*Culture and Progress;* McGraw-Hill Book Company, Inc., 1930.

White, Leonard D.—*Introduction to the Study of Public Administration;* The Macmillan Company, 1926.

Whitehead, T. N.—*Leadership in a Free Society: A Study in Human Relations Based on an Analysis of Present-Day Industrial Civilization;* Harvard University Press, 1936.

Wootton, Barbara—*Plan or No Plan;* Farrar & Rinehart, Inc., 1935.

INDEX OF NAMES

GENERAL INDEX

Accident, as cause of blindness, 148–150; crippled conditions, 179; deafness, 162; physical disability, 175

Accidents, causes of, 179; fatal, 179; prevention of, 267–268; statistics of, 264–267, 361

Adequacy, principle of, 346; standard of, 289

Alabama, 256

Alcoholic psychoses, 114, 117, 124, 125

Alcoholism, 74, 114, 119, 121, 143, 188–202, 233, 280; and accident, 195; and crime, 191–192, 513; and disease, 195; and poverty, 190–191; chronic, 225; definitions, 188–189; extent, 189–190

Almsgiving, 342–343

Almshouse, 349–350

Alpha and Beta tests, 91–94

Altruism, 60–61

Amaurotic idiocy, 99

American Academy of Political and Social Science, 556, 573

American Association for Labor Legislation, 362, 381

American Association for Social Security, 381

American Association for the Study of the Feeble-minded and American Association on Mental Deficiency, 144

American Association to Promote the Teaching of Speech to the Deaf, 172

American Eugenics Society, 76

American Foundation for the Blind, 155, 157, 158

American Institute of Cooperation, 428

American Institute of Criminal Law and Criminology, 517

American Medical Association, 128, 130, 170, 185

American National Red Cross, 185, 276, 521–541

American Neurological Association (See Committee)

American Occupational Therapy Association, 185

American Orthopsychiatric Association, 130

American Otological Society, 170

"American Plan," 376

American Psychiatric Association, 116, 135

American Public Health Association, 210, 283

American Rehabilitation Committee, 185

American Society for the Hard of Hearing, 169, 172

American Standards Association, 170

Animals, experimentation upon, 193

Ann Arbor, Michigan, 128

Arizona, 115, 137, 256, 451

Arkansas, 364, 451, 522, 524, 531

Armaments, manufacture of, 547–548

Army tests, 91–94, 102

Arrests, for drunkenness, 191; Massachusetts, 501

Arteriosclerosis, 114, 117, 124, 221, 222, 223, 225, 234

Association for Improving the Condition of the Poor, 36

Astoria, Oregon, 534

Atlanta, Georgia, 231, 265, 296, 534

Attitudes, as factors in war, 549–550

Australia, 197

Austria, 546

Baltimore, Maryland, 316, 534, 535

Belgium, 21–22, 544–545

Benwood, West Virginia, 522

Berkeley, California, 534

Binet test, 88, 91, 102

Birmingham, Alabama, 296, 469

Birmingham, England, 177

Birth control, 252, 255

Blind, 30, 37, 56, 73, 74, 162, 171, 182, 226, 259, 349; children, education of, 151–153; economic condition of, 153–154; pensions for, 154; vocational training for, 152–153